Studies in Occult Philosophy

Studies in
Occult Philosophy

G. de Purucker

THEOSOPHICAL UNIVERSITY PRESS
PASADENA, CALIFORNIA

THEOSOPHICAL UNIVERSITY PRESS
PASADENA, CALIFORNIA
1973

PRINTED IN THE UNITED STATES

Compilers' Preface

SINCE Dr. de Purucker's death two collections of writings left by him have been published. *Messages to Conventions* appeared in 1943. That was a manual of inspired advice to all Fellows of the Theosophical Society interested in the policies, work and purposes of the Theosophical Movement. *Wind of the Spirit* was published in 1944. This presented the devotional and practical aspect of Theosophy, illuminating the Way for each individual as he tries to live the life. STUDIES IN OCCULT PHILOSOPHY now presents the deep philosophical and mystical reaches of theosophical doctrine. Very fittingly then, these three volumes cover the organizational, the devotional, and the scientific-philosophical — the triangle of Wisdom which gives power, understanding and vision to the aspirant, lacking any one of which he is as a disciple incomplete.

In this present volume are found no new and fanciful bypaths beaten out and attractively advertised. Its metes and bounds are always the original doctrines presented by H. P. Blavatsky and the Masters. But within these bounds the drilling and the boring sinks deep, and therefore it would be a mistake to consider it a primer in occultism or a simple introduction to Theosophy. Its appeal is to the mind already bound to Theosophy, already dedicated to a constant and determined search for truth. It needs no apologia, no special championing from those already persuaded of its inherent value to the theosophical cause. But the gauge by which it should be measured is broader than this. Acceptance or rejection must in the last analysis come from *all* students of H. P. B.'s writings, to whatever branch of the great Movement they belong. They must be willing, however, to bring to its consideration minds frankly and openly impartial. This at least is to be expected of those who claim to have placed Truth above all lesser objectives, that Truth which H. P. B. described as "high-seated upon its rock of adamant, alone eternal and supreme."

Surely the time has passed in the slow onward moving of Theosophical activity when the craze for signs and wonders holds attraction. Such are for the fainthearted, as H. P. B. says. What we look for in all Theosophical writing is an explanation of life and its multitudinous mysteries, the presentation of a "philosophy of the rational explanation of things."

A few words may be necessary about the contents of the book itself. The 'Transactions of the Headquarters Lodge,' which include *The Secret Doctrine* and *The Mahatma Letters* series, were talks given at the regular lodge study-evenings at International Headquarters. At these meetings Theosophical books were studied, the topic being presented by some speaker and followed by general discussion. Then it was G. de P.'s custom to pick up the threads of the ideas brought up and to weave them into a coherent picture, correcting misconceptions of teaching, strengthening weak points of logic, explaining seeming contradiction or paradox. It was not his effort to give an exhaustive treatise on any subject, nor do the Compilers feel that this present collation presents the complete philosophy. Its value lies in the richness of hints thrown out, and as a record of what was actually for over a dozen years studied by the group at Headquarters. It likewise shows the wide range of theosophical doctrine with which G. de P. was conversant, his grasp of fundamentals and of details, as well as his manner of teaching, which was not labored or planned, but given extemporaneously and with no attempt to parade a finished style.

In the Question-and-Answer Section the questions for the most part have been left as originally formulated by the questioner. They include inquiries from students scattered all over the world, many of which appeared currently in *The Theosophical Forum,* and many others of which have been gathered since G. de P.'s death from letters he wrote to students. The Compilers are particularly indebted to scholars at Theosophical University for material thus made available — C. J. Ryan, Judith Tyberg, Emma D. Wilcox, A. J. Stover, L. G. Plummer, Grace F. Knoche.

The longer articles are from varied sources. 'The Doctrine of Tulku' was written for the Encyclopedic Theosophical Glossary, edited by G. de P., still in manuscript; 'Buddhas and Bodhisattvas' appeared in *The English Theosophical Forum;* 'Occultism and Psychic Phenomena' and 'Immortality and Continuity' are reprints from *The Occult Review* (London); 'Is it Right to Practise Hypnotism?' is condensed from *The Occult Review;* 'Survey of the Teachings on the Planetary Chains' is from a letter to a student.

With full appreciation of their responsibility in the preparation of this material, the Compilers, as in the two preceding books, have avoided anything but the most necessary editing and therefore have refrained from even such documentation as might by some be considered helpful in a work of this recondite nature.

For invaluable help in checking certain scientific data the Compilers have had the assistance of Dr. Charles J. Ryan and Dr. Henry T. Edge.

Finally, it should be on record that there are certain articles which G. de P. never saw in transcription. These are listed at the end of this volume.

HELEN SAVAGE
W. EMMETT SMALL

Covina, California, July 11, 1945

Contents

STUDIES IN "THE SECRET DOCTRINE"

STUDIES IN "THE MAHATMA LETTERS"

LONGER ARTICLES

QUESTIONS AND ANSWERS

Transactions of the
Headquarters Lodge

ESOTERIC HINTS ON CYCLES

SOME days ago it was brought to my attention that a comment had been made by a new member of the T. S., to the effect that he could not easily understand from whom came our sacred rules of calculating cycles and time-periods, as for instance, the well-known and very difficult time-periods used by the Brâhmaṇas of India, and which are likewise ours.

So intricate is what I have to say that I hesitate, and yet will do my best. Intricate because of the manifold ramifications into which Nature herself runs or is divided; although her heart is simple, and the rules upon which these very ancient calculations are based are likewise simple.

KEY-NUMBERS OF THE SOLAR SYSTEM

These calculations upon which the Theosophical seer or prophet, as the ancients would have called him, may see the future if he is skilled and clever enough to do so, are not arbitrary. They were invented by nobody. They are based on Nature herself, and mostly on cosmical movements, specifically those of the planets. Here is the key which I will now give you, and attempt to explain in some detail. The secret numbers of these Hindû Yugas, which have puzzled the brains especially of so many mathematical Theosophists, lie in a combination of the year of Saturn and the year of Jupiter expressed in Earth-years. There is your key.

The mistake constantly has been made by Theosophists of attempting to divide these numbers of the yugas by 7, and that is not possible, because the number 7 does not go into any of these key-numbers without leaving a remainder. 7 is the key-note of our Earth; 10 of the solar system, and 12 of our Galaxy, which of course includes our solar system, and the latter includes our Earth.

The key-numbers are these: The year of Jupiter expressed in Earth-years is approximately 12, i.e., 12 of our years make one year of the planet Jupiter. The Saturn-year expressed in Earth-years, or our years, is approximately 30. There are your two key-numbers: 12 and 30. Multiply these by each other, you have 360. 30 × 12 = 360.

I want to call your attention to one important fact of Nature, suspected by the most intuitive astronomers, but none as yet has succeeded in proving his intuition. It is that our solar system is an organic entity, an organism, in other words an individual, as much an organism as is a man's body. All the planets of the solar system, with the sun and our moon and other moons, are enmeshed as it were, forming a celestial machine so that they move in rhythmical or harmonic sequences. It is obvious that if this were not so, there would be no sympathy and no symphony, no harmony, in the movements of the bodies of our solar system; but these bodies would be moving helter skelter, hither and yon; and we know perfectly well that they are not.

Our Theosophical mathematicians who have not yet been given this key have all been thrown off the track because of the fact that while the years of every one of the planets of the solar system clearly prove that all these planets move synchronously together, as if they were enmeshed, wheels in a machine, yet the orbit of every one of these planets is not a multiple of some other lower orbital revolution or year. There is always a discrepancy. The year of Jupiter, for instance, is 11.86 of our Earth-years, not quite 12. The year of Mars is not exactly two Earth-years, but 1.88.

Now here is what I want to point out: It is these fractions putting the orbital times of the planets off any exact accordance with each other, which is a proof of the theory; because this shows that while all the planets are enmeshed together as it were, working synchronously and harmonically as a machine does with wheels interlocked, yet each planet itself is an individual, and has a certain liberty of movement. Keeping in mind this essential liberty or freedom we can more clearly grasp the following points: first, that the solar system is an animate organism guided by intelligence; and yet, second, that each one of the planets, although working together with all the others in harmonic rhythms and in co-ordinate times, has just a little movement of its own, as it were edging each year a little farther on; so that as time goes on, the pattern of the planets changes; and this introduces the varied fortunes and destinies not only of mankind and of the inhabitants of the other planets, but also brings about the karmic changes and modifications of the solar system. I weigh heavily on this point, because it is most important.

I want to call your attention to a few facts to show you what I mean about the rhythms, to prove that all the planets by their annual orbital motions — in other words the lengths of the planetary years expressed in Earth-years — are organically connected together.

Let us take the Year of Jupiter: Jupiter-year $= 12$ Earth-years approximately. Now mark: the Planet Mercury in one Jupiter-year has 48 of its own years, approximately, of course. 48 is 4×12. You get your 12 coming in here again. You remember that I spoke of the key-numbers as being 12 and 30 — or 6, if you like.*

Now Venus has 20 years (approximately) to one Jupiter-year. This 20 is not divisible by 12, but if you will take a longer cycle, say the cycle of 360 (18×20) years, then 12 goes into that 30 times, doesn't it? Yes. Note that 18 equals $12 + 6$ or half of 36, which is 3×12, and 36 is 1/10 of 360. I want you to see how these key-figures keep coming back, coming back. Every calculation you make in these interlocked planetary movements is divisible by 6 or 12, or 60 or 30 as factors.

The Earth of course has 12 of its years while Jupiter has one. The year of Saturn is 30 of our years. Now 12 goes into 30 $2\frac{1}{2}$ times. But that is not a very good figure, and we therefore see on working the thing out that we must take the larger cycle which includes both the Saturn-year and the Jupiter-year. This is the famous 60-year cycle known all over China, Mongolia, Tibet, Asia — all of Asia and of ancient Europe. What is this 60-year cycle? 5 years of Jupiter expressed in Earth-years. 5×12 is 60. Saturn-year, being 30 of our years, goes into 60 twice. So we then see that Jupiter makes 5 of its years while Saturn is making 2 of its

---

* "In all the old Sanskrit works — Vedic and Tantrik — you find the number 6 mentioned more often than the 7 — this last figure, the central point being implied, for it is the germ of the six and their matrix."
— *The Mahatma Letters*, p. 345.

years. The proportion or relation is 5 to 2, i. e., both enter 60 without leaving a remainder.

THE IMPORTANT 5040 CYCLE

Now then, we come to "a very difficult point," as some of our friends are always saying! The ancients in my judgment knew of the planets Uranus and Neptune, but they did not include them in their astronomical works. We Theosophists know why. It would be extremely interesting, but it would take me a week to explain this why. I will merely add that all these astronomical ages — which is what these Hindû yugas are — all these astronomical cycles and key-figures, are based on the calculated key-numbers of Jupiter and Saturn, 12 and 30, as factors. Yet a very interesting fact comes forth. How many Jupiter-years does the planet Uranus contain? I mean, one year of Uranus comprehends or includes how many Jupiter-years? 7, practically exactly. How many Jupiter-years does the planet Neptune contain, in other words one Neptune-year? 14 Jupiter-years. If you are following these thoughts carefully, the conviction will grow upon you that the periodic times of all the planets are time-connected, connected by time-periods; and my own conviction is, although I never have had time to work this thing out, that some Theosophical mathematical 'sharp' could go ahead and even find that the planets Uranus and Neptune would be included in still larger time-cycles.

One of the most important cycles mentioned even by Plato in his Dialog called *The Laws* is 5040 years. This figure is remarkable for several features, amongst which is that it is divisible by 58 different divisors among which are the key-numbers I have been speaking of this evening, to wit 5, 6, 12, 30, 60, and of course 36, 72, and 360; but what is noteworthy about this cycle of 5040 is that it is likewise divisible by 7, giving us the quotient 720 — in which we see the key-number 72 again, $\times$ 10.

Furthermore, this figure of 5040 is arrived at by multiplying by each other the simple arithmetical series of the first seven digits taken in order, to wit: $1 \times 2 \times 3 \times 4 \times 5 \times 6 \times 7 = 5040$. This remarkable number or cycle, so specifically mentioned by Plato in another connexion, was of course known to the ancient astronomers, astrologers, and mathematicians; and by using this figure or cycle, we find that the year-period of every planet, whether the 7 sacred planets known to the ancients, or those including the others supposedly unknown to the ancients, to wit, Uranus, Neptune and Pluto, used as a divisor will divide into 5040 without remainder. In other words, 5040 is a cycle which contains the planetary years of all the planets in the solar system, and thus links them up through having as one of its factors the number 7 — a most interesting fact, and one worthy of study.

The Famous Babylonian Cycle

I wish to call your attention once more to this 60. Remember that it is 5 times the Jupiter-year, Jupiter-year being 12 of our years, and two times the Saturn-year, the Saturn-year being 30 of our years approximately. It is 1/10 of the Babylonian Neros of 600 years; and take the square of 60 and you will have the famous Chaldean or Babylonian Saros, 3,600 years. This cycle of 60 years is of course the root-figure of the famous so-called Babylonian sexagesimal method of reckoning, to wit reckoning by 60s; but as we know from Berosus, as he is called by certain Greek writers who have written about him and who have left us fragments of these Chaldean writings, the sexagesimal system of reckoning or of counting was an integral part of the same system that we know to have been common in Hindûsthân since immemorial time. Berosus in the fragments left to us likewise informs us that the famous Hindû Yuga-figures, based on 4 3 2, were likewise as well known in Babylonia as in India. The sexagesimal root-figure of 60 is of course a factor of 4320 with various ciphers added according to the length of the cycle. One of the commonest time-periods known in Chinese writings is the mention of the cycle of 60 years: so many cycles of 60 years, and so-and-so lived and taught.

In connexion with the number 5, I would also remind you that the Latin lustrum was a period of 5 years observed by the Roman State and held very sacred indeed. They also knew of the cycle of 60 years, i. e., one Jupiter year times five.

Furthermore, in India, the cycle of 60 years is constantly used in mathematical, astronomical, astrological and other computations, as they also use 6 and 12.

When you look into these matters, the facts are so numerous, so scattered all over the face of the earth, and among all races of people and in all times, that finally as you study you are brought to the conviction that what we Theosophists teach is true, that there was once a Wisdom-Religion of mankind which was universal over the earth.

THE CIRCLE OF 360°

It is from Babylonia, but originally from India, that we of the West got our manner of dividing the circle into 360° — each degree consisting of 60′, the latter of 60″. Does anyone know the reason why the Babylonians chose the number 360? Why didn't they choose some other number? I will tell you: The number 360 arises from an old Theosophical teaching of the ancient God-Wisdom of mankind, to the effect that the true number of days in a year is 360, the cycle of the seasons. But as the ages passed, and due to the fact that the Earth is an individual with a will of its own, it does things at times, not exactly disobeying the mandates of the system in which it is enmeshed, not disobeying Father-Sun as the Lord and King of his realm, but determined, as are the other planets, to move a little on its own. So that as the ages pass along — taking the mean of 360 days in a year — the daily rotation of the Earth (making the day and night) quickens a little bit for a while, and the days become 361, and then 362, in a year, and then 363, 364, and now at the present time our year consists of 365 days and a fraction, $\frac{1}{4}$. Then this libration returns to the normal 360 days in a year; and then the Earth slows down its rotational period, so that for ages — how many ages is a question that does not enter into the picture here — any one of our Earth-years is less than 360 days: 359, 358, 357, 356, until it reaches the end of that libratory cycle. Then it begins to swing back; and thus the Earth continues to follow this libration.

That is why the Babylonian initiates, getting their ancient wisdom originally from India, divided the circle into 360 points or degrees; because in their Temple-crypts and Initiation-chambers they were taught that the true Earth-year consists of 360 units or days — and it actually does. Thus the circle became adopted in mathematics as divided into 360 points, cogs, degrees — call them what you like. It is a wheel, a wheel of time, which actually applies to the Earth.

DAWNS AND TWILIGHTS

But notice how the Earth-year divided into days is enmeshed again with the other planetary cycles: Jupiter-year 12 of our years, Saturn-year 30 of our years. 30 × 12 is 360. Marvelous that the number of days in our year is exactly the same as the Saturn-year and the Jupiter-year multiplied by each other. You know in the Jewish Bible there is a passage saying: "The days of our years are

YUGAS	DIVINE YEARS	SOLAR YEARS
Dawn	400	144,000
Kṛita-Yuga	4000	1,440,000
Twilight	400	144,000
	4800	1,728,000
Dawn	300	108,000
Tretâ-Yuga	3000	1,080,000
Twilight	300	108,000
	3600	1,296,000
Dawn	200	72,000
Dwâpara-Yuga	2000	720,000
Twilight	200	72,000
	2400	864,000
Dawn	100	36,000
Kali-Yuga	1000	360,000
Twilight	100	36,000
	1200	432,000

DIVINE YEARS: 12,000; SOLAR YEARS: 4,320,000

threescore years and ten" — 70. Well, actually this is an Oriental way — Jews were Orientals — of using a round figure for 72. You know how they make 72 out of 60, which is 5 Jupiter-years and two Saturn-years? What is 1/10 of 60? 6. Put down 6 for the Dawn, another 1/10 for the Twilight: $6 + 60 + 6 = 72$. In the same way you will see in the Table that there is a Dawn and a Twilight for every cosmic period; and the dawn and the twilight are in all cases of relative equal length, and in all cases are 1/10 of the cycle period. 1/10 of 4000 is 400 — the Dawn; 1/10 of 4000 is 400 — the Twilight. In the Tretâ-Yuga there are 3000 *Divine* Years, please, not our Solar years: 1/10 of 3000 is 300 — the Dawn; 1/10 of 3000 is 300 — the Twilight. The next is Dwâpara-Yuga. It is 2000 Divine Years; 1/10 of that is 200; 1/10 of 2000 again is 200 — the Twilight. And so for the last of the yugas, the Kali-Yuga, 1000 Divine Years in length; 1/10 of it, 100 — the Dawn; another 1/10 — 100, the Twilight. A shorter way, of course, is to take 2/10 or 1/5 to find the combined length of the Dawn and Twilight.

OTHER INTERESTING FACTORS

Now a further interesting thing about this 72: a human being is a child of the Universe, and being its child, its laws are his. Its life is his. Its pulsations are his. The rhythmic periods in Nature must therefore work through man. One of the greatest rhythmic pulsations in man is the pulse-beat. Do you know what the average pulse-beat for a human being is? 72. 72 beats of the human pulse every minute, or if you like, it is 60 pulse-beats plus the increment of beginning plus the increment of lapsing into the next pulse-beat. 60 plus 12; $5 \times 12 + 12$. You see how these numbers recur? 72 is twice 36. Well, now you remember 360 there, and 36 is 6×6. You notice how the numbers thus keep coming, whatever you do. 6 goes 12 times into 72 human pulse-beats in a minute. 6×12 is 72.

Here is a very interesting factor. In enumerating the years of the different planets I intentionally did not speak of the Moon, for your minds are so enwrapped with the astronomical teachings of the West in which the Moon is not considered a true planet, that I did not want to confuse you. Yet so thoroughly does Nature work throughout, after the same laws, the same rhythms, the same principles, the same pulsing, that do you realize that what the astronomers call the minor Saros, that is the eclipse-cycles, the cycle of years in which the eclipses begin again and repeat themselves nearly as they were before, is 18 years and some 10 or 11 days? We can here drop the days. 18 years: 6 × 3, 12 plus 6, ½ of 36. I want to call your attention to these key-figures, which keep coming to the fore. Furthermore, this is not all. Do you know how many is the average number of eclipses in this minor Saros of 18 years — Solar eclipses and the eclipses of the moon? The average number is 72.

Here is a very interesting fact. The sun-spots, according to modern astronomy, come, or the maximum is reached, every 11 years and a fraction, 11 and ⅓ or something like that. But here again we must allow for librations; and taking everything together, all factors included, and the way the Solar System has all its bodies enmeshed together like the cogs of wheels, yet each having a little independent movement of its own, which in time changes the pattern — a very interesting fact is that the sunspots coincide with the perihelion of Jupiter. Now explain that if you like. In other words, Jupiter like all the other planets makes its annual tour or orbit of revolution around the sun, completing it in 12 of our years. But in doing so at one point of its orbit it is closer to the sun, closer than it is at any other point of its orbit. That is what they call perihelion, close to the sun. When the perihelion of Jupiter takes place, the sun-spots reach their maximum, roughly every 12 years, between 11 and 12 years. And it is a remarkable thing — I would wager almost anything upon it — that if we could collect the statistical data we would find that outbreaks of disease and other afflictions of mankind will coincide with these 12-year periods, sunspot maxima or minima. I saw a calculation of that kind some time ago in which it was shown that epidemics of spinal meningitis broke out at every sun-spot maximum. In other words when the planet Jupiter was closest to the sun, every 12 years or so.

Do you know in modern Western astrology it has been customary to speak of the planet Jupiter as the great benefic, and the planet Saturn as the great malefic. But I think that this is pretty

near to being nonsense. I will give you one instance showing how
this idea is a distortion of facts. I read some time ago a very interesting statistical discovery made by a French writer who showed
that whenever the planet Jupiter was in its nodes as the astronomer
phrases it, crimes of violence increased enormously. Whenever
the planet Saturn was in its nodes, crimes of violence were notice-
ably few. Now that is easily explained. Jupiter excites, urges
people to do and to move. Saturn calms, brings balance and steadi-
ness, the truth being that every planet has its good side and its
bad, every planet can be a benefic or a malefic, according to its
action. This is true astrology, and all that we have been talking
about is true archaic astrology or Theosophical astrology.

The Divine Year and the Yugas

I want to call your attention to the Table again: a Divine year
is the name given according to this system of archaic calculating of time-periods to 360 of our years or Solar years. Therefore
12,000 Divine years in Solar years are 4,320,000. Made up thus:
the Krita-Yuga of 4000 Divine years — 1,440,000 Solar years,
with the Dawn and Twilight thereof — a Krita-Yuga is 1,728,000,
(and isn't 1728 the cube of 12?). The Tretâ-Yuga is 3000 Divine
years. Multiply this by 360 to turn it into our ordinary Solar
years, and you get 1,080,000 years. Add on the 2/10, the Dawn
and Twilight, and you get 1,296,000 years.

Here in the Table you get this series of 144, (the square of
12). Isn't it in *Revelation* of the Christian New Testament that
it is said that the sealed unto the Lord, or the saved, shall be
144,000 in number? You see here again the mystical figure, 144,
that is the main point. You can add and take off ciphers according
to the time-period or cycle you are discussing. It is the head of
the series of figures that is important — 144. The square of 12,
twice 72, 4 × 36, and so forth. So we go down to the Dwâpara-
Yuga: turn it into Solar Years, with a Dawn and a Twilight, and
you have 864,000; then Kali-Yuga, the age we are in now called
the Iron Age, adding to it its 2/10 for Dawn and Twilight, you
have 432,000 years. This system, or mathematical calculation of

adding an opening and a closing of every age-period or cycle which the Hindûs call the Dawn and Twilight, is an extremely archaic method of calculating based on Nature herself, for she always introduces everything she does with a preparatory period, whether of time or phenomena, or both, or whatever you may be dealing with. All diseases come with the Dawn of preparation. Then there is the disease. Then there is the Twilight of the disease as it fades out. So to get the full time-period of the cycle you must know not only the length of the cycle itself, but its Dawn and its Twilight, its beginning and its end.

You see, Companions, there are just simply so many sides to a study like this, you could go on interminably talking just as long as your recollection will bring back to you facts which you have garnered from Nature.

THE PYTHAGOREAN TETRAKTYS

I want to point out to you what is called the Pythagorean Tetraktys. It was so holy amongst the ancient Pythagoreans that they swore oaths by it, and a Pythagorean would no more violate an oath sworn by the Holy Tetraktys than he would — it was an oath that simply could not be violated. Why did they think it so holy? They gave the answer: because it adds up to 10. It was 4 plus 3 plus 2 plus 1 = 10. What is 1/10 of 10? 1. Add 1 as a Dawn; add another 1/10 of 10 as a Twilight, and you will have 12. They sometimes figurated the Pythagorean Tetraktys as thus, one sphere, then two spheres, then three spheres, then four spheres.

```
            o
        o       o
    o       o       o
o       o       o       o
```

$1 + 2 = 3, + 3 = 6, + 4 = 10$. Don't you see the Pythagorean Tetraktys, 4, 3, 2, 1, in the Yugas in their numerical order of the cycles? The same figures, the same system of counting, the same fundamental idea. No wonder the Pythagorean philosopher swore by the Holy Tetraktys, because it was equivalent to saying, "I swear by Holy Zeus," as if he had said, "Father and Lord of Life, of whom my own life is a spark, truth of truth, and life of life, real of real," — it was an oath that no Pythagorean ever dared to violate. It was like swearing by one's own Higher Self.

OTHER CYCLES

Now, here is another thought. Have you been examining the night-sky for the last year or so? If so, you will have noticed that the planets Saturn and Jupiter have been in near conjunction for some time, and will soon begin to separate. [March, 1941] It was the conjunction of Jupiter and Saturn which the ancients taught always began notable changes and events on our earth. (Elsewhere in the solar system too, but we are more naturally interested in what is taking place on our Earth.) Just when such a happening will come again, with the other planets as now they are, i. e., as they will be on May 11th, of this year 1941, would require intricate calculations. It may be thousands and thousands of years before the planets all return to the positions they *now* hold in the sky; but the two planets, Saturn and Jupiter, because 5 years of Jupiter equal 2 years of Saturn, will be, so far as those two planets are concerned, again passing each other in conjunction, near the same place, in 60 years: 5 years of Jupiter = 2 of Saturn: think it over, do not forget these key-numbers.

There are almost innumerable cycles of varying lengths, and of greatly differing importance, which were known to the ancients as well as to the few moderns acquainted with esoteric chronology and cyclical computation. As for instance, there is the well-known astronomical cycle called the Precessional Cycle of 25,920 years, divisible by many if not all of the factors or keys already alluded to, and which in its influence on the destiny of mankind is one of the most important.

Then, there is the so-called great Orphic Cycle of 120,000 years, which of course is obviously ⅓ of the still greater and immensely important cycle, because dealing with racial periods, to wit, 360,000.

THE KEY-NUMBER 72

With reference to the key-number 72, which itself of course is a cycle of varying length depending upon the ciphers added to it, the following series contains cycles, every item of which on the list is important and well worthy of study by those interested in chronological or cyclical matters:

$$72 \times 10 = 720$$
$$720 \times 2 = 1440$$
$$720 \times 3 = 2160$$ — an extremely important cycle this because entering into the computations of the precessional cycle mentioned above, for there are 12 such cycles of 2160 in the Precessional Cycle of 25,920.

$$720 \times 4 = 2880$$
$$720 \times 5 = 3600$$ — a cycle well known to historians and chronologers as the famous Babylonian Saros, which again multiplied by 100 or 10^2 equals the racial cycle mentioned above of 360,000.

$$720 \times 6 = 4320$$ — again a most famous cyclical key-number, well known in ancient Hindûsthân and in Babylonia and in the esoteric or occult schools of virtually all Asia and ancient Europe, a cycle which with zeros added is an even more important human racial cycle than is the 360,000 above mentioned.

$$720 \times 7 = 5040$$ — another extremely useful, interesting, and important cyclical period, with or without extra ciphers to define shorter or longer periods, and mentioned even by Plato in his *Laws*, as already stated.

The ancient initiate-astrologer-astronomers rarely failed in their prophecies, for it was a relatively perfect knowledge of the inter-relations of planetary movements and of other cosmic time-periods, both great and small, which enabled them to predict with an accuracy of Nature herself events which they knew would take place because of their knowledge of what had taken place in other preceding cycles of time; and all cycles are repetitive, bringing more or less the same train of events or sequences as happened before, when these cycles begin anew. It should be noted that this is in no sense fatalism; for every cycle, although repeating itself constantly in time, due to what modern astronomy calls the irregularities in planetary and other celestial movements, is never precisely or exactly what the preceding cycle was; for every such cycle beginning anew its course always differs in less or greater degree from its former courses.

CENTRAL ASIA, CRADLELAND OF OUR RACE

COMPANIONS, I want to speak to you about something that H. P. B. has very vaguely alluded to, but as I have heard some of our speakers and writers refer to this inaccurately, I feel the need of steering our ship a little closer to the true north, in this respect. It is with regard to what science used at one time to call the center of dispersal of the peoples of the earth. Old-fashioned science used to place the origin of civilization, and of the Aryan folk especially, in Higher Asia, on what are now the great plateaus of Central Asia. And that in a sense is quite true; but the subject is not so simple as that. Before our present Fifth or Aryan Race was formed as a race *sui generis,* that is to say, a race of its own type and kind, distinct from the Fourth Root-Race, its predecessor, it had had an evolution of millions of years, while the Atlantean Root-Race was slowly going to pieces. I have often wondered if some day the science of the future will not be able to discover in a certain vast tract of land in Central Asia, now a howling wilderness of sand and stone and alternating cold and heat — I have often wondered if science will not some day discover in this vast central Asian tract remains of peoples who were more civilized than we are today, more advanced in invention, more advanced in discovery, more advanced in philosophy, science, and religion, than we are now, far more.

Where is this Central Asian tract? If you take a map of Asia, and on it find Persia, Baluchistan, Afghanistan, Bokhara, and Turkestan, the Sea of Aral, and the Caspian, and to the east the Pamir and the Hindû Kush, and the Tien Shan, the Altyn Tagh, etc. — an enormous tract of country, most of it desert waste — there you will find the seat from which we came as a racial stock. The time was when that land was covered with highly developed civilizations succeeding each other in time. Hundreds of wonderful cities flourished there. The land was green and fertile, it was an aggregate of beautiful countries. And it was out of this cradle of our race, as a race *sui generis,* please, from its northern parts, that later descended into the Indian peninsula those peoples who call themselves 'Aryans,' the 'High Caste,' who later were divided into Four Castes: Brâhmanas, Kshattriyas, Vaiśyas, and Śûdras. From the southeastern parts came later the Babylonians, the Assyrians, the Medes and the Persians; and the peoples of Europe, Greeks, Romans, especially. And on the outskirts and all surrounding these highly civilized tracts of land, immense in extent, there were outlying peoples. These last were remnants of the Atlanteans, like the Chinese, the people of Japan, the Javanese, the Siamese, and the Tibetans. They all migrated after a while and changed their seats, but at that time they were the surrounding folk in various grades of civilization. On the outskirts of the more highly civilized peoples were some of their own off-shoots, later sub- and sub-sub-races to come, then in their infancy and childhood. They became the Celtic peoples and the Teutons of Europe and the West of Europe. But at that time Europe was largely under water. The Alps were rising: only the peaks and a certain amount of the foot-hills of the Alps were as yet above the sea. The Arabs at that time were just wild savages, offspring of the mixed Atlantean and early Aryan peoples. They have not come into their own yet. Some day they will.

This vast stretch of Asiatic country which, except in spots, now is a lofty plateau swept by icy winds in winter and by what some people call the hellish winds, hot as hell, in the hot months, then was comparatively low as regards height above sea-level. There was an immense inland sea to the north of it, emptying itself into the Arctic. That sea has now almost disappeared, has shrunken to almost naught, so that all that remains of it is the little Sea of Aral, the Caspian, the Sea of Azov, yes, and the Euxine, the Black Sea. There was likewise a hid sea in what is now Mongolia. H. P. B. speaks of this one. That is now evaporated, vanished; very much as the Great Salt Lake of Utah is slowly vanishing. Why? Because slowly the land began to rise; the waters drained off; vast stretches of what is now Russia began to rise above the waters; southern Germany, coastal France, later the British Isles and Ireland appeared. The whole aspect of things changed. The geography changed entirely, the climate changed.

Yet I believe that some day archaeology, by delving into the sands of the howling wastes there, will uncover the stony remnants of vast cities. Heaven knows what else they may find in Persia, Baluchistan, Afghanistan, Bokhara, Turkestan farther north. In that previous historical epoch, when this vast tract flourished, it was a wonderful land, or aggregate of lands, a wonderful continent surrounded by sea, or almost so, with outlying islands and countries.

Millions of years before that was the period of the birth of the Aryan stock from the degenerate Atlantean tribes where now the Atlantic Ocean rolls its restless waves. Seven to eight million years ago our great Aryan race was born, and migrated in serial surges under spiritual guidance to the then rising lands of Central Asia, now the desert of Gobi: another high plateau, now windswept and barren. There was then a beautiful inland sea there. No wonder we are told that Geography considered as a science was one of the sciences of the Mysteries of ancient days.

But what was the date of all this? you may ask. When lived this wonderful group of peoples, of highly civilized folk, with their many, many inventions that we have not found out yet? When lived they in Central Asia, in these lands flowing with crystalline waters, filled with wonderful verdure, having mild and equable climate? When did all this happen? It began with the beginning of krita-yuga. Count up. We are now in the beginning of kali-yuga. Therefore add: krita-yuga, 1,728,000; tretâ-yuga, 1,296,000; dwâpara-yuga, 864,000 — a total of three million, 800 odd thousand years ago. You see how it happened. As the climate changed, as the land rose, as the seas receded, as the deserts began to encroach upon the stretches of the cultivable land, the peoples found the climate becoming impossible. They migrated in turn, in surges; they spread over the newly risen lands to the west and to the east, and Europe was born. Then was to be found also the beginning of the Assyrian, the Hindû, the Mede, the Persian, the Babylonian, the Greek, the Roman, the Celt, the Teuton, the Scandinavian: not here recited in their chronological order of appearance, but just as the names come to me.

Of course they mixed; miscegenation proceeded apace. At times these peoples were as haughty and proud of the supposed purity of their blood as some of our folk are. But gradually they mixed, producing stocks as we have today. There is no such thing as a pure race on the face of the globe. We are all mixed. We simply differ from each other because of isolation. Peoples have been isolated, some for hundreds of thousands of years until even the coloring of hair and eyes and texture of the body has somewhat changed. Thus the true Chinese, although the last remnant of the last or seventh sub-race of the Atlantean, is no true Atlantean. He is a mixed Aryan, because he belongs to our Aryan race in time and karman. Mixed, also, are the Japanese and the Javanese, and many others.

But please do not suppose, Companions, that this tract of Central Asian lands I speak of was the only habitable land on the surface of our globe. I do not mean that at all. I was speaking of the origins of our Aryan peoples, those which peopled Europe with its different stocks, those which likewise sent their migratory hordes into India, Tibet, Siam, Burma, even into China, mixing with the aborigines there. But on the other side of thè globe there were vast tracts of land which were inhabited by fairly civilized peoples in some cases, others by barbarians. For example, the great Island in the Indian Ocean later called by the Hindûs Daitya, and inhabited by what they called Râkshasas, was in existence simultaneously with these early Aryan peoples who migrated from this wonderful tract of land in Central Asia. Furthermore, modern Ceylon is the northernmost headland of what was a vast island of enormous extent, now submerged. Islands great and small there were all over the globe.

Australia existed then of course. Parts of the American continent were above the waters, parts not yet; just as in the future parts will sink and other parts arise. Egypt was there. It too was coming into its own slowly. The colony of Atlanteans from the Atlantic had come in two or three migratory waves. And later on, Egypt received a migratory wave from what the ancients call the Ethiopians, not Negroes, but people whose skin was so dark, because of the torrid climate in which they lived, that they were called Ethiopians, 'burned-skin folk' out of the East, from Southern India and original Ceylon, represented by the Tamils there today. And the latest Râkshasas of Lankâ, of Ceylon, had become Aryanized. The Egyptians received the migratory horde from Lankâ called the sons of "Shesu Hor," the sons of Horus — Aryanized peoples.

Question — What has become of those egos who made that great civilization so long ago in the Gobi region? Will they come again and make on earth another such civilization?

Answer — The whole matter is complicated and deals with long periods of even geological time. There were two different epochs. One was at the very beginnings of the Fifth Root-Race, during the heyday of Atlantis, which established a focus for itself on a land-and water-district pretty nearly where now the Gobi desert is and north-western China. But this was millions of years before the time which I specifically alluded to above, which was the beginning of the European part of the Fifth Root-Race, or Asian-European, after the former focus had already become legendary through long passage of time. In any case, I can answer the question this way. The egos which then inhabited those civilizations of western Asia and central-western Asia, which I hereinbefore especially spoke of, are we ourselves; for I was not alluding to any particular esoteric focus except incidentally, but merely to the rising, racially speaking, of the Fifth Race and its early civilization in the lands I pointed out, and how when the land rose, the climate became inhospitable, the seas receded, and arid stretches replaced the once fertile countries of that district. From that district, big as it was, as a sort of center migrated east and west and south, not all at once, but through thousands and thousands of years, the beginnings or earliest portions of those peoples who later became the Chinese, and the Tartars and the Hindûs and the Greeks and the Romans and the Celts and the Germanic and Scandinavian tribes, etc. Even this was long before Egypt had come into real being, because you must remember that Egypt is really and has been the gift of the Nile: land built out into the Mediterranean Sea by silt, sand, detritus, brought down by the Nile through ages from interior Africa, and deposited age after age at its mouth, so that its mouth gradually extended into the Mediterranean and thus built up the Egyptian delta. Thus you see Egypt, though very early, came after even the second and later period I have mentioned above. But the answer to your question is briefly: the egos who inhabited those civilizations are we ourselves, or at least some of us, because there were decaying civilizations even in those far distant past times, on other parts of the earth — decaying remnants of Atlantis; and some of these last egos are among us now too.

Question — There is a hint given in *The Esoteric Tradition* concerning the fact that the mid-point of the Atlantean Root-Race was some 8 to 9 million years ago. I believe you spoke just now of the Asian cradle-civilization as having flourished as long ago as three and a half million years.

Now the point is, what are we to make of the famous 850,000 years since the submergence of the bulk of Atlantis, to judge by *The Secret Doctrine?* Or is this a mere blind? Did the main portion of the continent of Atlantis sink *while* the Asian cradle-civilization of the Aryans was flourishing, or even after it?

There is a great deal of interest at present regarding the Gobi, as you know. Any additional light on the Gobi civilizations would be welcome. The understanding is that the Gobi, as a center of civilization, was more recently so than the highland civilization of three and a half million years ago, of which you spoke.

Answer — In what I have previously said I did not attempt, of course, to go into any detail; I simply drew attention to one, or two or three highlights in esoteric history connected with Central Asia. That was all.

Answering now this latter question: the central point of Atlantean civilization, which was the kali-yuga of the Fourth Root-Race, was some four or five million years agone. This means equivalently that our own Fifth Root-Race, which had its first beginnings of birth about that time, is likewise between four and five millions of years old. Furthermore, we are likewise beginning our own Fifth Root-Race kali-yuga, and we see the first beginnings of the birth of the Sixth Root-Race amongst us today. In other words, we are beginning to see the first beginnings of the birth of the Sixth, as the middle point of Atlantis saw the beginnings of the birth of the Fifth — of us. Is that point clear?

Yet while from our original germinal condition, so to speak, we are four or five millions of years old; yet as a race *sui generis,* which means a race which is of its own type or character, with its own distinct swabhâva, our Fifth Root-Race is one million years old more or less. H. P. B. alludes to this in *The Secret Doctrine.*

Now, as said before, it was from Central Asia that were born the beginnings of the civilizations of the European stocks. Only the last of these minor sub-races of our Root-Race is known to us, the Germanic. There are but remnants today of the preceding large

sub-races, such as the Mediterranean, Greeks and Romans prominent among them; and preceding them the Celtic; preceding them
others whose names have been lost in the night of time. Yet all
these different minor sub-races of our present Fifth Root-Race were
born in Central Asia at different times, each wave coming forth from
that motherland and cradle of our Fifth Root-Race, and spreading
over the world in different directions, mainly westward; for as the
English poet has intuitively pointed out: "Westward the course of
empire takes its way." Let us change this word 'empire,' with its
infernal political associations, to "westward the course of civilization
takes its way."

Now Central Asia comprises an immense extent of territory.
Mongolia, the desert of Shamo or Gobi, Tibet, including the northern
parts of Tibet: the immense ranges of mountains there, such as the
Tien Shan and Karakorum and others, Afghanistan, Baluchistan,
Persia, and what is now called Turkestan: most of it desert land,
desiccated and dry, some of it below the level of the sea, rising thence
into some of the highest mountains of the globe, the Himâlayas.

All this land — except portions covered by lakes and seas —
that is now inhabited by partly civilized or barbarous or even savage
tribes was, at different times during the last four or five million
years since the midpoint of Atlantis, covered with flourishing civilizations which succeeded each other in different parts of Central
Asia over this vast district to which I have pointed. At one time
one great civilization in this part of it, later on succeeded by another
civilization in some other part of it, still later in time the march of
events carrying a civilization to a third part, and so forth; yet each
one of such civilizations being in its turn a cradle out of which grew
children-colonies sent forth to carry light and initiation to what were
then barbarous and uncultivated parts of the world, such as what is
now Europe, what is now China, what is now Siberia, what is now
India.

It was from one of the later of these mid-Asian civilizations that
came the early Brâhmaṇas when they descended into the Indian
peninsula, calling themselves Aryans as they did: 'the select,' 'the
noble,' terms of pride — âryas. But such is the fashion of conquerors always. Sometimes the conquerors are conquered by the
science and wisdom of those conquered. *Graecia capta Romam vic-*

tricem subducit. Greece, the conquered, subdues Rome the conqueror. It is true.

Now there are many things to think of in connexion with a study like this. There are questions geographical, religious, ethnological, and racial. Not one people alone inhabited and built up these civilizations of Central Asia. They were recurrent waves of our present Fifth Root-Race. The earliest waves largely mingled with Atlantean immigrants, emigrants from the sinking islands of the Atlantic, the sinking remnants of the Atlantean land-continent. The later ones of these civilizations were far more aryanized, far more truly belonging to our Fifth Root-Race.

As an example: whence came the civilization of Greece and whence came the glory that was Greece? Whence came the civilization of Etruria and of the other Italian folks and of the Romans? Whence came they? In these particular instances they were some of the later emigrants of Central Asia who descended from the high plateau down towards the inland sea and settled on the land we now call Greece: Crete among them first, including the mainland of Greece. Then the advancing wave at a later date settled Italy and became the Etrurians and the earliest Romans, the Sabines, the Samnites, the Oscans, and so forth. But of course all this was not done without a struggle. There were many wars in those days, terrible wars, between the dying out remnants of the Atlantean peoples, the true Atlanteans who were in continuous warfare with the Fifth races, if I may so phrase myself. So that as Plato points out in one of his *Dialogs,* telling a story told to him by his ancestor Solon and told to Solon by the priests of Egypt: "There was a time when a horde came out of the Atlantic Ocean essaying to settle on the lands that are now Greece and Italy. You Greeks are but children, children of a day. You have forgotten your glorious past when your forefathers gathered together and repelled the invaders, holding the civilization that you had intact."

In the same way was Hindûsthân builded by the Brâhmaṇas. Thus were Greece, Rome, and Western Europe likewise populated, settled, refined and civilized by the emigrants from the different civilizations that grew and waxed and waned, and grew and waxed and waned, that had their seats in that cradle-land of our Fifth Root-Race, Central Asia.

Now all these things happened within a time-period beginning some four or five million years agone — the time of the prime of the material height of the civilizations of Atlantis — down to the present. The questioner asks whether the island which H. P. B. speaks of as sinking 850,000 years agone refers to the sinking of Atlantis. Oh no! To talk about the sinking of Atlantis would be like today talking of the sinking of the different land-massifs of today. Do you mean Europe, Asia, or the two Americas? Atlantis was a far larger land-massif than our own today, but it was divided into continents, and such continents separated by seas shallow and deep. The reference by H. P. B. to the time 850,000 years ago was to the sinking of the last great-sized island in the Pacific called Ruta. And it was followed later, a couple of hundred thousand years ago from our time, by the sinking of the still smaller island called Daitya; and then there were no more sinkings of outstanding importance until 11,000 or 12,000 years ago when Poseidonis, referred to by Plato as a relatively small island in the Atlantic, an island about the size of Ireland today, sunk beneath the waves with all its civilization, temples and gods, men and women, in one night and one day, according to the legend. One night of horror following a day of terror. The island was a nest of sorcerers, magicians of the blackest sorcery. And it was from this small island about 11,000 years agone that came that wave of emigrants trying to conquer the settled people of Greece and of Rome of which I spoke.

No, the doom of Atlantis struck four million and a half years agone; and I now mean Atlantis in general, not of any one of its continents or vast islands, but of the race. That was the time when our Fifth Root-Race began to have its beginnings, its germinal epoch.

Some day I believe that our archaeologists and other scientists, delving in the wind-swept deserts, the sandy, arid plains of Turkestan, Persia, Baluchistan, will uncover remains showing that there there was at least a civilization the equal of anything we have today, if we can judge by what may then be found there in the shape of buildings, or the foundations of buildings, of imperishable stone, perhaps even artifacts of copper and glass. Who knows?

There was a civilization, some few thousand years before the earliest history that we know about Greece and Crete and Asia

Minor, in what is now the arid lands of Persia, that would have put to shame anything that ancient Greece or Rome or Egypt or Babylon could show — a civilization gentler, greater even than ours. That was the mother-land of the Greek and Roman and Italiot peoples. Thence they came as colonists; and back of this, as I have already pointed out, in still earlier times of now utterly forgotten history, what is now arid plain and sandy desert, barren mountain and howling wastes, whereon the wind plays all the laments of Hell, could have been seen beautiful lands covered with verdure and beautified with fruit and forest trees, green grass, well paved roads lighted at night, town connected with town, city with city — well organized system on all sides. Now that is all forgotten — as we shall some day be.

Central Asia is not only the cradle of civilization of our Fifth Root-Race, but our motherland. To it, in the earliest beginnings when the Fifth Root-Race began to be itself as a stock separate from Atlantis, to it the earliest Fifth Race colonists went and settled there. It was then a land rising above the waters and from its lofty plains and plateaus — through age after age, as age succeeded age — the germinal new races tried to work off the deviltry of their own Atlantean forefathers now rushing to their doom. Protected of karman, protected by the Lodge, the early Fifth lived there. Sub-race succeeded sub-race, as they slowly climbed from innocence to knowledge and from knowledge to a modicum of wisdom — and its abuses, until we now have reached our kali-yuga and are beginning to pay. When will men learn that the only road to happiness and peace, to prosperity and increase in possessions, both spiritual and material, is obedience to the spiritual and moral law, and service. That is the only road: obedience to the divine mandate which whispers in every human heart, and service to mankind. Selfishness defeats its own ends. It grabs and grasps a heavy shadow and opens the grasping hand to find naught. It is by giving that we get, strange paradox. It is by work that the arm grows strong. It is by exercising the heart that its noblest comes forth.

SIDE-LIGHTS ON H. P. BLAVATSKY

YOUR Symposium on the origin of the Theosophical Society has been exceedingly interesting. We have all enjoyed it. It has been prepared with thought, and it aroused in us all a lively recognition of what H. P. B. did. You have pointed out to us the odd, and in some instances the unusual, means that were taken in the beginning of her work to accomplish her ends: means which at the time probably seemed ordinary, but which to us at the present time seem strange and unusual: beginning a Theosophical and spiritual and intellectual Movement by means of advertising the ideas of an Egyptological crank who professed to evoke elementals from the vasty deep; and by meeting people in a room which was most artistically decorated although in a bizarre and baroque way.

How strange! How contrary to what most people think should be the grounds upon which a spiritual Movement rightly ought to be launched. But pause a moment over these facts. They are all significant. They all show the penetration of the occultist. They all show the Master-Hand using every means, be they the simplest, in order to bring about a grand end.

This is the lesson that I, as a boy, drew from what I read of the foundation of our beloved T. S.: "Truth moves in strange and mysterious ways, its wonders to perform." In these old words of the Christians, which I have slightly changed, you have the key to the situation.

One of the speakers emphasized the fact that H. P. B. was a woman, but may I ask: What does that fact matter? The work would have been performed had H. P. B. been a man, or, were it possible, having no sex at all. Let us not bring questions of sex into this matter. Consider what the Theosophical Society was founded to achieve: To sow the seeds of the religious, and philosophic, and scientific thought of future ages. It is a matter of utter unimportance, whether the Messenger who came was a man or a woman. She came as a woman, merely because as a woman she could do things in that hard and materialistic age, which a man could by no means so successfully have done. I will also point out to you that

H. P. von Hahn was a 'psychological cripple,' and that through her there worked the directing mind and the spiritual efflux of one of Those who stand very high, and who consequently was above sex, and whose utterances and pronouncements are all marked by that impersonality which we all feel when the soul of a man or of a woman speaks — the spiritual soul.

What did it matter that Jesus was a man? Not at all. It was the fiery spirit and the divine Light working through Jesus which made him so grand in his work, and not merely the fact that he was a man, because conceivably that same work might have been done by a woman.

In our work I fear any reference to the academic question whether one sex is superior to the other. I call your attention to the importance of this.

H. P. Blavatsky sowed the seeds of the thought-life of the generations of the future, and these generations of the future, my Brothers, will, in themselves, be the seeds of the next Sub-Race. H. P. B.'s own individual Teacher was he whom she referred to as M.; but the one who used her as a vehicle was not invariably he. If you only knew the mysteries connected with a Messenger from the Lodge, you would have greater understanding, and greater pity, than even the splendid and loyal devotion that you at present have for your Teachers, has given you the vision for. There is a tragedy in the life of each one of your Leaders; and I think H. P. B.'s life was the most tragic, the most tragically tragic, of all.

What a sublime thing it is to realize that the mighty spiritual influence which she brought permeated a self-ridden and wholly materialistic world, and wrought in it a spiritual magic which changed men's minds, so that now things are talked of and believed in which in H. P. B.'s own day would have sent those who might have believed in them for trial before a lunacy-commission. Think of it, and you will see the working of a tremendous spiritual power, spiritual because it is universal, which is the test of a spiritual energy. In the silence did it work, undermining wrong things, breaking the crystallized molds of men's minds, and warming their hearts. One indomitable human will did it.

Now what may we not look forward to in the future? Look to the East, the inner East, the Mystic East, the East from which springs forth the spiritual daylight, flooding the minds and hearts of our fellows. Teach men to look eastwards, for there is the Light. "Westward the course of Empire takes its way," says the English poet; but traveling constantly westwards you finally come to the East, and out of the East comes the Light.

ON CAGLIOSTRO

I HAVE listened with intense interest to this your most unusual study on Cagliostro, and I should not have thought it at all incumbent upon me to say a word, had not the idea passed suddenly through my head that two things might indeed be said, both of a helpful and perhaps of a prudential character. The latter, therefore, I will advert to very briefly as the first thing that I have to say to you.

I think it a dangerous matter to stress the fact at any time, in anything that goes out to the public — or rather to stress the idea — that the Teachers of Wisdom and of Compassion and of Peace send forth their Messengers to meddle in the political turmoils of any age, or to be involved in directing fevered human passions of disagreement into channels even possibly leading to human bloodshed, or to the rending of ties of human affection and love, thus leading to the misery of broken hearts. The Teachers guide humanity spiritually and intellectually; they instill lessons of mercy and of pity; and, even as regards the very highest of the Teachers of Wisdom and Compassion and Peace — and these last highest because they are such utterly *impersonal* servants of the Law — I know that the Masters are not instigators of strife or of human trouble; and the greatest of these of whom I speak, should indeed they ever act as agents of karmic destiny, do so with the sole objective of ameliorating conditions in human life, and because it is their sublime duty to restore peace and harmony and brotherly love. Should such Exalted Individuals ever concern themselves with the political turmoils of any age, they do so only as Peace-makers.

Now, these are words which I have chosen carefully. I do not wish to be understood as meaning that the Teachers stand apart coldbloodedly, and indifferently see things running to ruin; that is not the idea. The inference which I ask you to draw from what I say I believe to be the fact, is this: they do not instigate human quarrels, nor stimulate human passions, nor, on the other hand, direct the affairs of the world as *dii ex machinâ* — as exterior gods pulling the wires of action of human beings, their dancing marionettes. They do not.

There is a great danger in having this mistaken idea that I allude to, because as our Society grows and increases in importance and in its influence over the hearts and minds of men, we must be able to show that our record has been clean from the beginning, so that at no time in the future can an opponent point an accusing finger at any action done or at any remark made in the past by any Theosophist, and say: "Look! Out of their own records they condemn themselves to be political meddlers!" The Society is absolutely non-political, because soaring high above the stormy arena of human political passions; as an organization we have no concern with politics and never will have, although as individuals our members hold such political opinions as seem right and proper to them as honest men.

Turning now to the second idea that occurred to me, my dear Brothers: I am very doubtful as to how much I should say on this point. I speak with extreme reserve. I ask you to use your own imagination and your own intellect, and to allow your own heart to answer, when I say that there is a mystery connected with the individual called Giuseppe Balsamo and the individual known to the world generally as Cagliostro. It is upon the document issued from the Vatican containing the story of the so-called trial and condemnation of Cagliostro that most later students and historians of the checkered and wonderful career of that remarkable man assume that Cagliostro and Giuseppe Balsamo were one individual.

I can only say that there is a strange mystery involved in the story of these two: Balsamo and Cagliostro. How strange is the statement, if true, that both had the name *Pellegrini,* which means *Pilgrims!* How strange is it that Giuseppe Balsamo is the Italian form of the name Joseph Balm, suggesting a healing influence; and that 'Balsamo,' whether rightly or wrongly, can be traced to a compound Semitic word which means 'Lord of the Sun' — 'Son of the Sun'; while the Hebrew name Joseph signifies 'increase' or 'multiplication.' How strange it is that Cagliostro's first teacher was called *Althotas,* a curious word containing the Arabic definite article 'the,' suffixed with a common Greek ending 'as,' and containing the Egyptian word *Thoth,* who was the Greek *Hermes* — the *Initiator!* How strange it is that Cagliostro was called an 'orphan,' the 'unhappy child of Nature'! Every initiate in one sense is just that; every initiate is an 'orphan' without father, without mother, because mystically speaking every initiate is *self-born*. How strange it is that other names under which Cagliostro is stated to have lived at various times have in each instance a singular esoteric signification! Study these names. They are very interesting.

Perhaps I might go one shade of thought farther: to every Cagliostro who appears there is always a Balsamo. Closely accompanying and indeed inseparable from every Messenger there is his 'Shadow.' With every Christ appears a Judas. And as regards what you, my Brothers, have so admirably set forth this evening concerning the reason, as given by our beloved H. P. Blavatsky, of Cagliostro's 'failure,' let me point this out: that Cagliostro's failure was not one of merely vulgar human passion, nor was it one of vulgar human ambition, as ordinary men understand these terms. When Julian the Apostate — called 'apostate' because he refused to be an apostate from the ancient religion of his forefathers — led his army against Shapur, King of Persia, he did so well knowing that he was acting against the esoteric Law; and yet in one sense he could not do otherwise, for his individual karman compelled him to the act. I tell you that there are at times more tragedies in the life of a Messenger than you could easily understand, for a Messenger is sworn to obedience in both directions — obedience to the general law of his karman from which he may not turn aside a single step, and obedience equally strict to the Law of those who sent him forth. There are in such cases problems to solve sometimes which break the heart, but which nevertheless must be solved.

Be, therefore, charitable in your judgment of that great and unhappy man, Cagliostro!

THE SIX GREAT SCHOOLS OF THE ANCIENTS

THERE are six 'Darśanas' or Schools recognised as being correct exponents of Hindû philosophical thought, and all these six *Darśanas* — a Sanskrit word literally meaning 'Visions' — may be divided into three pairs. The six Darśanas or Visions or Schools are, respectively, the *Nyâya* founded by Gotama; the *Vaiśeshika* founded by Kaṇâda; the *Sânkhya* founded by Kapila; the *Yoga* founded by Patañjali; and the Less and the Greater *Vedânta* founded by Vyâsa; and of the Vedânta, the most important school of the Greater, the Adwaita, was due to the teaching of the Hindû Avatâra Śankarâchârya. This, the *Adwaita-Vedânta*, is probably the most widely diffused philosophical School in India at the present time.

Now these six Darśanas, called in Sanskrit the *Shaḍ-darśanas*, to the Occultist contain, all of them, truth, and indeed esoteric truth in no small degree; but again to the Occultist each one is but a single 'Vision' or 'Branch' of the all-unifying Master-School, which whether recognised or not — is the Esoteric Philosophy, which thus is the Mother of them all and the container of the master-keys by which each and all of the other six may be correctly understood and properly elucidated.

These six 'Visions' or Schools may be divided into three pairs, each couple being paired because of similarity in systemic formulation and philosophical outlook; so that the six great systems of Hindû philosophy are thus logically reducible to three, corresponding to the Ârambha, the Pariṇâma, and the Vivarta, respectively. These pairs are as follows: (a) the Nyâśa and Vaiśeshika, which one may perhaps briefly call the Atomistic School, corresponding again with the Ârambha; (b) the Sânkhya and Yoga, which because of their characteristic philosophical principles and system may be called the school of philosophy dealing with emanational evolution combined with practice in aspiration and self-training. This second pair corresponds with the Pariṇâma; (c) the Less and the Greater Vedânta, which, especially the Greater Vedânta, may be called the Idealistic School of Hindû religio-philosophy, and correspond with the Vivarta-vâda.

From still another standpoint the above-mentioned philosophical pairs may respectively be compared with the three operations of the human spirit and mind which are known in the Occident under the names of Science, Philosophy, Religion — not of course any one sectarian religious faith, but Religion *per se*. The Ârambha is to be classified with the scientific outlook; the Pariṇâma with the philosophical vision; and the third pair, classified with Vivarta, is comparable with the religious manner of visioning truth.

All these three couples, as stated above, are, each one, considered to be more or less imperfect from the standpoint of the Esoteric Philosophy, because each is incomplete. The Esoteric Philosophy unifies all three couples (or all six Darśanas) into one grand comprehensive System — the Esoteric Philosophy itself — which contains and explains the substance of all.

To explain further: the Ârambha is that view of the Universe and of the origins of things, which, qualified as being scientific, envisions the Universe as proceeding forth as a 'new' production of already pre-existent Cosmic Intelligence and pre-existent 'points' of individuality or what the Esoteric Philosophy would term 'Monads' as being a more correct term than 'atoms.' Although such newly produced Universe, from this viewpoint, is recognised as being the karmic resultant or consequence of a preceding Universe, the former 'self' of the present, nevertheless emphasis in this line of thought is laid upon *beginnings,* upon the Universe as a 'new' production, very much as even Occidental science construes the Universe to be.

The Pariṇâma, while having many points of contact with the Ârambha point of view, nevertheless lays emphasis upon the fact of the coming forth of the Universe into being, with all it contains, as a production by powers and entities and substances 'unrolling from within,' and thus bringing the Universe into existence by a species of emanational or evolutional conversion or unfolding.

The Vivarta-system, finally, penetrates still more deeply into the womb of the Cosmic Mystery and fixes its attention upon the unending duration of the Divine Essence, which it considers as producing 'appearances' of itself through modifications of itself, or portions thereof, brought about by emanational evolution from within, these modifications or 'portions' being the Cosmic Mahâmâyâ — or Cosmic Illusion. The technical name for these 'appearances' is nâma-rûpa, नामरूप, a Sanskrit compound literally meaning: 'name-form,' otherwise understood as *nâma* equaling 'idea' or 'ideas' or 'concepts,' and *rûpa* equaling 'objectivization' or 'images' or 'forms' in which these ideas manifest themselves. Hence it is that in the Vivarta-system the entire objective Universe, visible and invisible, is considered to be illusory because merely a collective modification, or series of modifications, of the productive Divine Essence, which last always remains Itself, yet produces 'appearances' of itself, or shows forth itself by way of ideas or concepts and through objectivization by unfolding procession, i. e., emanational evolution.

The above may seem to be rather high metaphysics, but it seems needful to imbody these facts for the benefit of those whose minds ask for scientific or philosophic or religious particularizations and comparisons.

THE ROOT-RACE AND ITS SUB-DIVISIONS

I WOULD like to answer this evening a very interesting question I have received. It reads:

"This has to do with *sub-races,* and branch *sub-races.* The precessional cycle of 25,920 is the length of a whole National Race. You say that a Family Race is seven times the length of a National Race, which would be seven times 25,920. Now in *The Theosophical Forum* of November 15, 1932, pages 82-3, you say 'we are actually in the fifth sub-race of the European family-race, but on a much larger cycle we are also nearing the middle point of the Primary or Major Fourth Sub-Race of the Fifth Root-Race. In other words, of this Primary or Major Fourth Sub-Race of the Fifth Root-Race, we are a small minor branchlet, which is the fifth of its own septenary cycle. . . .' Could you please explain further?"

The reason for this statement quoted is that I called the European Race a National Race according to the scheme I gave in *Fundamentals.* But here, because I was writing quickly and not consulting my former words, I am caught by saying that the European Race formed a Family Race. The answer to that is very simple. I used the word 'Family Race' not technically, but merely to show that the entire family of the European peoples formed a racial family. If you want to speak technically, those European peoples together formed a National Race, as I will explain in a moment.

The National Race is one Precessional Cycle — 25,920 years. The average man lives 72 years. Now, these are statements of averages. Every child knows that every human being does not live for 72 years. Many live much less, and many live much more. My own opinion of the actual average life of the human being today is 15 or 20 years, when we take into consideration the unnumbered millions of human beings who die before they even reach childhood; millions who are carried away in wars; millions who die from accident, or, if they reach maturity die prematurely from accident or some horrible disease. If you take every single case of death, and all the number of the human race as two billions on the earth today, and perform a mathematical computation, I believe you will find that what we call the average life expectancy of the average human being is not much more than fifteen years, maybe twenty. It just shows the perfectly awful numbers of human beings who die early, cut off or killed in railway wrecks, in steamship wrecks, in wars, in diseases of little children.

But here we give the life of the individual man as 72 years; then comes the Tribal Generation, then the Tribal Race, then the National Race, then the Family Race; and each one, after the individual man, is seven times longer than the one preceding it.

Now then: What examples have we of a National Race, which by any calculation according to the figures here is the length of 25,920, one astronomical cycle? A National Race is well exemplified by all the races of Europe today. The word 'national' here does not mean the same thing that our ordinary word *nation* means when we say the nation of the French or the nation of the English, of the Italians or Swedes. As I use it here, what I would call a National Race comprises all our present European nations, Poles, Germans, French, Swiss, Russians, Greeks, Bulgars, Czechs, English, Irish, Welsh, Scottish, Swedes, all Scandinavians in short, Belgians, Netherlanders, Portuguese and Spanish: all of them, taken all together, that is what we call one National Race. Its life-period is about one Precessional Cycle, nearly 26,000 years. And I may add just here that its life-period is a little more than one third done. About 9000 years of it have elapsed, distinct from the preceding National Race, using the term as we are using it here.

Another example of a National Race is the peoples of the New World, of the north and south continents of the so-called redskins, the Aztecs, the Incas, and all of them: they together have points of unity, of blood, links of language, forming what I call a National Race.

In another sense, but still in the same sense to a certain degree, we might likewise exemplify a National Race by all of what are popularly called Mongolians. Many of the peoples called Mongolians are not Mongolians. But there is something in that popular idea, for these are peoples with blood kinships, and to a certain extent linguistic kinships. Therefore they, collected together, form a National Race.

Now I would call a Family Race what the old ethnography of

my father's day called the different species of mankind. A Family Race I would exemplify by speaking of the so-called Caucasians. Thus the Hindûs belong with us Europeans (because the Americas have been settled by European races), to the Caucasian branch of the human family, and therefore form what I call a Family Race; but the Hindûs do not belong in our European *National* Race.

Another example of a Family Race would be the Mongolians taken on a larger scale. In that case we would include the Chinese, the Manchus, the Japanese, the Lolos, the Tibetans, the Burmese, the Siamese, probably the Malayans: they all together form a great Family Group which is distinctly different from the Caucasian group, as I have used that term.

And still a third type of Family Race or Family stock will be the heavily colored peoples of Africa, as distinct among themselves as Europeans are; speaking different tongues many cannot understand. It is the same in Europe, in our own National Race. But here I am not referring to a National Race, but to a species of mankind, what I would call a Family Race: Caucasian, so-called Mongolian — if you like to choose that very imperfect word — Africans.

And then, again, still another example of what I mean by a Family Race, collecting several National Races together, would be the original inhabitants of the New World, of the North and South Continents; although these likewise have their National Races; just as the Hindûs and Europeans form one complete stock, yet as National Races, the Hindûs are here, the Europeans are there.

Then when we come to Tribal Races, we have to pick out of a National Race a still smaller division: I mean one of those smaller races a number of which collect together to form a National Race. Thus of the National Race in Europe, one Tribal Race will be the Slavs, that is, the Russians, and the Poles, the Czechs, the Bulgars, and others. Then again, another Tribal Race would be the Teutons. They would be the Germans, the Scandinavians, the English — and there we enter into a complication which illustrates the difficulty. Practically all the nations of Europe, using the words in a popular sense, have a foundation of Teutonic stock. The English are Teutons; the French take their name from the Franks — a German people. There were the Goths, the Visigoths, and Vandals all helping to settle Spain and Portugal, and the Goths and Visigoths overrunning Italy. So you see how tangled up the thing is. But I call a Tribal Race one of the component members of a National Race. Another Tribal Race is the Celts, such as the Irish, the Welsh, the Scots, and the people of Brittany in France. These are all tribal races. Their average length of duration is about 3,600 years, which means the time from their beginning to their end. They become important in world affairs, and then they die down over a long period of time, just as it takes time for them to rise up.

Then we come to a Tribal Generation, a still smaller division in the Tribal Race, such as the Italian, the English, the Russian, the German, etc., which each in turn holds the leadership, the hegemony, among the nations. Their time is about 500 years; and if you study European history you will see some very interesting things. It takes any one such tribal generation 200 years or more to come up out of obscurity, and perhaps out of oppression, to attain full power and independence, to make their mark as the leader of other peoples around them, and then to die. You have seen it in European history time and time again — Italy, Spain, France, and so forth. They follow each other until the whole circle has been rounded.

Thus, take the whole scale: average man, would live on the average 72 years. (As it is, many men live to be greatly over that. Millions die before they have reached twenty years.) Seven times 72 a Tribal Generation, 500 years; seven times that is 36 hundred years, a Tribal Race. Seven times that is the National Race which is almost the length of the Precessional Cycle of 25,920 years. The Family Race, which I have already described as what the old ethnology called a different species of mankind, lives to be about 180,000 years: a Secondary Sub-Race, about a million and a quarter years; and when we reach what we call a Primary Sub-Race or seven times the latter we have a period of about 8,000,000 years or so for the full life-term of a Root-Race.

And now you see how these races overlap; and that fact is one of the things that makes racial computations so intricate and hard to do and to explain.

However, our European National Race still has some 16,000 years to grow old in. Let us hope it will learn a little more wisdom before its hour strikes. Our Caucasian Family Race is destined to live about 180,000 years. It has many, many tens of thousands of years yet to run, but a good deal of its time cycle has already run.

To return to the more familiar methods of computation: I would like to point this out. We are in the Fourth Round, on this Globe, our Earth. In this Fourth Round on this Globe, we are in our Fifth Root-Race. Of this Fifth Root-Race we have almost reached the central point, or the middle of the great Secondary Sub-Race. We have not yet passed or even reached this central point. I should say this Fourth or central point is the most dangerous of all in that tremendously long cycle.

We are in our Family Race, which is the Caucasian. We are in our National Race, using the phraseology of our time, called the European; we are in the type of souls called the Teutonic; and of our own Fifth Root-Race, we are closing, at the very end of, the Fifth sub-sub-sub-racelet. We are in the Fifth Root-Race, about the middle point of the great Secondary Sub-Race; and of our own National European Race we are just closing or ending the Fifth, which is a racelet, a small race. How long it will last, I can only guess. I have not had time to figure that out. Possibly a few hundred years, and then will begin the Sixth in succession.

My final thought is this: H. P. B. in the S. D. says that the Sixth Race will be born in due course, and she also states that the seeds of the Sixth Root-Race are to be born in the Americas. She also says in another place that in about 25,000 years from now, or one Precessional Cycle, or what I have called one National Race, the people of the United States will begin to have children who will be the forerunners of the Sixth *Sub*-Race. What she meant was what we would call a National Race. Now you see it is a mistake to take that statement by H. P. B. and because she says in one place that the Americas will be the part of the earth for the appearing of the seeds of the Sixth Root-Race, to say that it is going to be born in the United States 25,000 years from now. It is confusing two different statements from lack of knowledge. It shows us that the European National Race is the Fourth in number, because in the United States will be born the seeds of the next coming race when this one is ended. In the Americas will be the Fifth National Race of our present Family Race. But that is not what we have pointed out as being the Family Race Species of mankind, as for instance the Caucasian, Mongolian, African, original American.

AFTER THE KALI-YUGA — ?

THE following question in regard to the four Yugas has been sent to me for comment and elucidation.

"We are told in the *Occult Glossary* that the four Yugas, with their respective time-periods of 4, 3, 2, 1, take up just half of the duration of a Root-Race. I have been wondering in what order the Yugas follow after Kali-Yuga, in which we now are, because by analogy it might mean that they would go in the reverse order, so that after Kali-Yuga there would be Dwâpara-Yuga, and then Tretâ-Yuga, and then Satya; but reasoning from another standpoint, it seems we merge into the Golden Age, at least that is what it seems to say in the Vedas. Then from another standpoint, when a Race is dying out, as some of the primitive Races that we now know of, some of the aboriginal Races, they might be said to be in a Golden Age in one way, because they have no responsibilities, they are childlike, and in that sense might be said to be in the Golden Age to the end. So my question is: In what order do the Yugas in a Root-Race come after the Kali-Yuga?"

I think I can best answer this very interesting question in a public gathering by pointing to the history of our own present or Fifth Root-Race. We are all at present, as you know, part of the Fifth Root-Race on this Globe D in this Fourth Round. Now then, it was a legend among the Greeks that the childhood of mankind was happy, that it was peaceful, blessed with plenty, with abundance, that there were no wars and harassing anxieties in those halcyon days of the childhood of man. They called it the Saturnian Age, the Age of Saturn, mainly, I think, because there were no real responsibilities, as the questioner has correctly stated. I question very much, however, whether I for one would like to live the life of a babe unborn, in the womb, without responsibilities, a mere human lump. No!

About the middle point of the Fourth Root-Race, our Fifth Root-Race began to take form, which merely means that certain individuals who had passed through the Fourth Root-Race incarnations up to that time on the Earth, made among themselves a society, not organized, but the mere fact of their being and having more or less arrived at similar mental and spiritual outlooks made them in the middle part of the Fourth Root-Race to be as it were a people apart. Do you catch my thought? It was not an organized Society, an organization, a brotherhood, at first. It was simply that at about the middle point of the Fourth Root-Race certain individuals were born, which means that they had reached a time when Fifth Root-Race qualities and attributes were to begin to appear in them; just as in our present Fifth Root-Race we have almost reached its middle point, we are in its fourth Sub-Race, and the forerunners of the Sixth Root-Race are just beginning to appear amongst us here and there over the world. Sporadically they appear, forming no definite body, organization, society, or brotherhood; but nevertheless beginning to imbody, to incarnate.

Now, as time went on, the Fourth Root-Race, which was then in its Kali-Yuga, began to descend the *facilis descensus averno,* the easy descent to Hell more and more; but at the same time a greater number of more advanced human monads were incarnating, thus constantly increasing the number of the then Fifth Root-Race in the throes of its birth. These individuals were for the Fourth Root-Race set apart. Nature favored them, which does not mean that they necessarily had a very easy time, but Nature favored them. They were fortune's favored pupils; they were receiving, because they had won all these benefits, special guidance, special help, special instruction, mostly unconscious except for the highest among them. Why? Because they needed it. The balance of the Fourth Root-Race was simply running down-hill, and with each thousand years going faster down. But these favored individuals, fortune's favored sons, were helped, guided, protected, sheltered — sheltered as far as it could be done — because they had merited it on account of their previous evolutionary strivings to ascend; and because they were the seeds of the Fifth Root-Race to come, our present one. They were in their Satya-Yuga, the first and the longest.

Thus the yugas begin with the longest, next the next long, third the next long, and finally comes the culmination of wickedness and evil-doing in the Kali-Yuga, which we of the Fifth Root-Race have just begun. How many among us, I ask the question right here, are to be among the 'favored' to form the seed of the Sixth Root-Race now already beginning on this continent and elsewhere, but more particularly perhaps in the Americas? We have reached our Kali-Yuga; it will last more than four hundred thousand years, and we are only some five thousand years gone in it, barely entering upon it! And as the majority in the future days of the Fifth Root-Race will be growing worse and worse, and going steadily faster and faster down the relatively steep descent, the individuals of the forthcoming Sixth Root-Race will contemporaneously grow more numerous and will be in their Satya-Yuga, their highest.

I think I have given in *Fundamentals of the Esoteric Philosophy* a diagram (p. 251) in which the birth of each Race is shown as beginning at about the middle part of the preceding one. There you have the picture. Each Race begins with its Satya-Yuga, its longest; passes from that into the next, the Tretâ; then into the third, the Dwâpara; and then into the fourth and shortest and most intensely individual, the Kali-Yuga. And just about that time the seeds of the Race to follow are in their throes of birth.

I might add this — although I hope that it won't complicate your understanding — that these wonderful figures, 4, 3, 2, followed by one or two or more zeros, are key-numbers in Nature, and they are computed by means of the six, commonly called the senary, or again the duo-decimal, system of reckoning either by six, or twelve which is twice six; and hence there are the same yugas but with more zeros added — for globes as well as for Races; for Chains as well as for globes, and so forth.

Thus it is that the hey-day of civilization and progress of a Root-Race lasts through the four yugas from beginning to end; during its Kali-Yuga and towards the beginning of it, the seeds of the new succeeding Race begin to appear, and these seeds are in the beginning of their Satya-Yuga. As the centuries and the millennia roll slowly by, the scepter of dominion and of empire, of progress and advancing intelligence and wisdom, slowly passes from the former Race to the latter Race; so that when the former Race is finishing its Kali-Yuga, the succeeding Race is already beginning the hey-day of *its* halcyon times of progress and power and civilization.

Meanwhile, even after the Kali-Yuga of the former Race is ended, the more or less degenerate remnants of the former Race continue in existence, but steadily going down-hill still, and these degenerate descendants, although slowly through the ages growing constantly fewer and fewer, nevertheless last on until the succeeding Race in its turn has run through its three yugas and is entering its fourth or Kali-Yuga.

This is what I meant when I stated that although a Race begins its career at the middle point of the previous Race, it lives on for pretty much the same length as before, although in a state of degeneracy and senile decrepitude; the old waters gradually mix with the new and fresh, because the more advanced and better egos of the previous Race begin to reincarnate in the bodies of the succeeding or newer Race.

NOTES ON THE CHARACTER OF OUR FIFTH RACE

ALL the so-called savage or barbarous peoples presently existent on the face of our globe are Fifth Root-Race branchlets, most of them degenerate. I don't mean in a moral sense; I mean evolutionally degenerate, because, although living amongst us of the Fifth Race and therefore to be accounted as Fifth Race sub-racelets, they nevertheless are degenerated remnants of the great Root-Race which preceded ours — which great Root-Race we call the Atlantean only to give it a name.

To this there are two or three or four exceptions, these exceptions being degenerated remnants of the great Third Root-Race. Such are the Eskimo and the Andaman Islanders; but even these are largely Atlanteanized also. The Blackfellows of Australia and Tasmania and the Maoris of New Zealand belong to degenerate Fourth Root-Race branchlets.

To speak of these now degenerate remnants of once great races as those races themselves, is wrong because very misleading. I have heard it stated that the Negroes are a degenerate Atlantean racelet, and that they are soon to die out. This is likewise erroneous. The Negroes form one of the very few exceptions amongst us today of baby races, imperfect in mental and physical development (but not in spiritual development) — somewhat more so than we are, because of their youth, not because of great age.

In some scores of thousands of years the Negroes will begin to take a prominent place amongst the civilized peoples of the world, but they will then no longer be Negroes as we understand the Negroes today; because an enormous amount of miscegenation or intermarriage will have taken place. So rapidly, in fact, is this intermixing of the peoples taking place that we can see it on an enormous scale around us even today wherever we may look. It has been said sarcastically and unkindly by American critics of some South American peoples that they are Black and Tan Republics. I don't think it needful to be unkind in expressions concerning other portions of the human race. A man is a man because of what is in him, not because of the color of his skin. Think of the geniuses who have appeared in all parts of the world. Homer, with his black eyes and black hair and dark skin was a genius. Are we not entitled to believe that credit should be given to worth wherever that worth is found? Do we not find the most glorious systems of philosophy amongst the dark-skinned peoples of India, not only among the Aryan races of India but among the Tamils and others?

The mixing of the races proceeds apace even today, and whether we like it or not, within twenty thousand years, I will venture to say, the only Negroes to be found on the surface of the earth, as we understand Negroes, will be in Africa itself, in remote parts of that continent; while the Negroes elsewhere in the world will have by then relatively completely mixed with other races, their vital waters will have mingled with the vital waters of the other races of the earth. As a matter of fact, there is no such thing on earth today in the human family as an absolutely pure stock, such as we find among the beasts. It simply doesn't exist anywhere in the human race. We have races in which one blood-stream predominates, other races in which other blood-streams predominate; and thus even among our so-called White humanity we have the pink-skinned Northerner, and we have the dark-skinned Southerner of Italy and Spain and Portugal whose origin is as much Caucasian as is that of the Northerner. The Northern strain is mixed, the Southern strain is mixed, and these mixtures are formed from the Germanic and Celtic chiefly; and to-day over most of Europe these two intermingle with a large proportion of what is called the Latin; so that you have, for instance, the pink-skinned Scandinavian, the olive-skinned Southern Frenchman, and the brown-skinned Italian or Spaniard. Or you will find in Russia today the fair hair and pink skin of the North intermingling with the black hair and dark eyes of the typical Slav. And all these races are mingling and have been doing so from ages immemorial. They are all Fifth Race men — to be sure in different degrees of national development, but not different degrees of racial development. These are facts of the commonest knowledge known to scientific researchers. The long-headed men and the round-headed men have been known for a long time; and you will find round heads, brachy-cephalics, and long heads, dolichocephalics, among all the branches

of the White stock.   The Celts apparently seem to be mainly brachy-
cephalic.   The Scandinavians and the Germans, peoples of the
Germanic branch, and also the Negroes, are dolichocephalic, as
a rule.   But you will find brachycephalics among them as you will
find dolichocephalic people among the Celts.

So you cannot go by any hard and fast rule.   Color of skin
is no criterion.   Neither is shape of head any criterion.   It comes to
this: that a race is known by what is in it, precisely as a man
is known by what is in him.   A tree is known by its fruits.   In one
age one tree, one human stock, produces fruits.   In a succeeding age
some other stock produces its fruit.   They may be as good.   They
may be superior.   They may be inferior to the other stocks.   Again
we come back to the vital point of this little discussion: a race is as
good as it is worthy; in other words a race is classed according to
what is in it, precisely as you would class a man.

Think of the geniuses in archaic India, and then consider modern
India where genius is now a rare phenomenon.   Consider the lost
glories of Greece and the majesty that was once Rome; yet where
today is ancient Greece and where is ancient Rome?   These countries
have been rising slowly, struggling once more to take their place
among the nations.   Races rise to a culmination of power and worth,
and sink because of innate corruption.   Shall we judge a race at its
period of degradation?   And compare it with another race at its
culmination of power?   The rule is idiotic.   Judge each at its culmination, and let the critic ask himself today: Is my race producing
the flame of genius and the fire of inspiration that have wrought the
works of civilization in the past?   There is the question.   The race
is of worth because of what is in it.

Why is it that among some of the so-called savage peoples of
the earth — and I now speak from the standpoint of linguistics —
some of these now called degenerate races, have languages which for
flexibility, capacity to express the most abstract thoughts of philosophy and religion, are scarcely equalled by any other known
languages, except perhaps Sanskrit and Homeric Greek?   Do you
know what this means?   It means that these so-called savage peoples,
fallen from a former high state, could not have developed a language

like that unless they had the thought, the thought expressing itself in the words: genius clothing itself in language.

You have there a proof from the standpoint of scientific linguistics of what a people can be, can have been, may in the future be; and yet we hear some of our scientists saying, and they have been saying it for fifty years: Such and such a race cannot count above the number five. I don't know a more inept, inadequate, in fact absurd, estimate than that implied by this little popular expression. How could a race which has a marvelous language, indicating a thinking power already highly developed, not count beyond five? And why did these particular now savage, but not then savage, peoples select five, the half of ten? Here you have the quinary system and the decimal system. The wonderful scientific thinkers of the days of our fathers, if they lived even today with these savage people, would find that these natives know very well the difference between six cocoanuts and five. If you don't believe me, go amongst them and try it out! And yet we are told they cannot count beyond five! That they have no words in their language to count beyond five! The answer is — as we have discovered — they don't need more than five digits to count with. They add the fingers of one hand, 1, 2, 3, 4, 5, once; 1, 2, 3, 4, 5, twice; and so forth.

Besides, it has been discovered since, that these people counted up to five, or it may have been six, because they had an esoteric doctrine of which five or six was the root cycle, and they counted by fives thereafter, just as we have the decimal, or the duodecimal, systems, and count by tens or twelves.

A few words more, and then I close. It is a remarkable thing that the more mixed a race is the greater its productions in civilization. It is precisely — I, an American, speak with reverence and not boast — because our own great country, the United States, has become the human vital alembic of our days, that its incomparably glorious future lies before it, genius pouring into it from all the corners of the earth; so that the American people of the future will be, as it were, the seeds possessing within themselves strains of capacity, young capacities containing strains of genius, drawn from all quarters of Mother Earth. If you wish a race to die out and become degenerate rapidly, isolate it, and you will see it weakening physically and mentally; because imbodying egos do not seek imperfect vehicles; they are seeking the richest, the fullest, the most complete that they can find.

Referring again to some of the ancient races, they who are now struggling once more to come up from their obscuration, to come up and take their place in the world again, such as Greece and Italy, Spain again one day, India and others. What has brought this fresh struggle about? The influx of new blood. The old water stagnated, and the races nearly died, and then came along fresher water mixing with the old which produced new human vehicles, fit tabernacles or habitations for greater egos, egos with a wish to spread in more than one direction of natural genius. Power wants a temple in which to dwell, a temple with many chambers. There genius is at home. A race dies out, Companions, when egos magnetically sense a disinclination to incarnation in the bodies born in such peoples. The women become sterile. The men likewise. For the egos will not imbody in them. That is why old peoples die out, peoples, mark you, which in their own day may have been the guides and leaders of the earth. Where is Babylon? Mounds and desolation. Where is Ancient Egypt whose sons confabulated with the gods and whose temples saw the grandest of the Holy Mysteries? Ruins. Where are the Persians and the Medes whose boast was that the Laws of the Medes and Persians shall never change? A memory of greatness, but where are they now?

ELEMENTAL KINGDOMS AND COSMIC ELEMENTS

THE question has been asked: Just what are the *Three Elemental Kingdoms* and have they any special relation to the *Cosmic Elements* of the Ancients?

Elemental Kingdoms, as all the others are, are aggregates or groups of evolving monads; whereas the so-called elements of the ancients, or the principles, were so phrased by them to describe more what we today would call the seven principles or elements of the universe, as a man has seven principles or elements. It is their way of describing it. The Hindûs have the same way, only in that case the Sanskrit name is tattvas: prithivî-tattva, âpas-tattva, vâyu-tattva, taijasa-tattva, âkâśa-tattva, and so forth.

Now then, these groups or aggregates of monads, each group being a kingdom, or in their Rounds what we call a Life-wave — each such group of monads, which means all groups, live in and work through these tattvas or cosmic elements, which the Greeks and Romans called Earth, Water, Air, and Fire. Some, like the Pythagoreans, said there was a fifth, Aether, but actually in the occult schools the teaching was that there were seven, of which only four were popularly known, and the Pythagoreans and some others in Europe openly declared the existence of a fifth. The Greek aether or the Pythagorean aether properly understood, was what the Hindûs meant when they said âkâśa.

Thus then, these cosmic elements are the different stuffs of the universe, the different substances out of which the universe is builded. We can call them the various prakritis of the universe, although of course each one of these different names has its own sub-line of thought connected with it. They are therefore not absolutely interchangeable. Consequently, the cosmic elements or these prakritis belong to all the kingdoms because all the kingdoms, as I have just stated, are living in and working through them.

What is the origin of these cosmic elements? They are the essence-stuffs or substances out of which grow the more developed planes of the universe. There being thus seven or twelve cosmic elements, when manvantara opens these seven cosmic elements begin from the top and unroll downwards, each one going down in its serial order, and each one giving birth to its first or essential stuff, its most spiritual aspects so to speak; and this last, its most spiritual aspect, is just what is meant by these cosmic elements. Then each such cosmic element as it unrolls on its own plane before it gives birth to the cosmic elements beneath it, unrolls from itself all its own seven sub-planes, or sub-cosmic elements, so that each such cosmic element contains in itself all the other cosmic elements, but in less degree. Thus the water cosmic element, to use Greek phrasing, has as its swabhâva the water-element, but it likewise contains within itself the fire-element, the air-element, the earth-element, etc.

The kingdoms are aggregates or families or groups of monads. The cosmic elements are the essential stuffs in which they live and move and have their being and evolve.

Now then, one final thought will connect everything up, I hope. Spirit in its sevenfold aspects is the root of all these cosmic elements, or prakritis. Just as all the prakritis unroll from mûlaprakriti which is the veil of Brahman or pure cosmic Spirit, so do all the cosmic elements unroll from the primal substantial veil around cosmic Spirit, corresponding to mûlaprakriti. Thus out of Spirit comes everything, all the cosmic elements; and out of spirit likewise proceed the classes or families or groups or aggregates of monads forming the different kingdoms, from the Dhyâni-Chohans down to the elementals. And lastly, when we examine and penetrate to the very ultimate nature or stuff of the cosmic elements, we can see that every cosmic element is really a vast aggregate or group of monads or consciousness-centers not yet aroused into activity, and which are therefore dormant. It is just like all the earth around us, which, representing the lowest of the cosmic elements on this plane, is nevertheless composed of simply innumerable multitudes of dormant monads which have not yet awakened to begin their evolutionary journeys and develop into self-conscious gods. Or again, as the flesh of a man is composed of molecules, these of atoms, and these of life-atoms, or life-points, which are the effect on this plane of monads on their own plane.

It is of course understood that a monad never leaves its own plane; so when we say that the earth-element is composed of con-creted or dormant monads, we do not mean the spiritual monads themselves; we mean the life-atoms, each life-atom being the representative of a monad on this cosmic plane.

What relation, then, have the three elemental kingdoms, kingdoms of the elementals, to the cosmic elements? Now in the first place, I will say that this phrase 'three elemental kingdoms' is an easy and graphic way of saying the seven kingdoms of the elementals, or the seven sub-kingdoms of the generalized kingdom of elementals; just as in a man we often generalize his constitution by saying spirit, soul, body, knowing all the time that the constitution is divisible into seven parts.

The three kingdoms of elementals in their first or original appearance in manifested manvantara, spring forth from the stuffs of the original cosmic elements; and therefore these baby-entities, which are as it were ensouling parts of life-atoms, are called elementals. This is the original and if you wish highest kingdom of the elementals, not highest here in the sense of evolution, but highest in schematic diagram. The so-called lower kingdoms of elementals are lower merely because they are farther from the spiritual part or nature of the cosmic elements, but being more evolved in that sense they stand higher. So that the lowest class of elementals, which is beneath the minerals, actually is the most evolved of all the elemental kingdoms. But they have not yet even reached the point where they can be classed as minerals or pass into the mineral kingdom.

Now the reason why there are really seven elemental sub-kingdoms, is because each such elemental kingdom springs from its own particular cosmic element. As there are seven cosmic elements, each cosmic element gives birth to its own elemental kingdom. Thus when all these elemental kingdoms are classed together, we say seven elemental kingdoms, each one such coming from its own different cosmic element.

As a final thought, it is to be noted that in occult or esoteric phraseology, the elementals are so called because whatever their class and whatever the cosmic elements or tattva from which each elemental class springs, it springs directly from this tattva or cosmic element without intermediary. Thus, the elementals are, as it were, the denizens or inhabitants of the cosmic elements, because they spring forth immediately and without intermediary from the latter.

To those who are not more or less adept with Theosophical

studies, it is important to point out that the elementals are not elementaries, this last term being adopted from medieval European quasi-occult or semi-occult Schools, such as the Fire-Philosophers. An elementary is a denizen of the astral light, and is, briefly speaking, the reliquiae or semi-conscious astral remnant of what was once an evil man on earth.   In other words, and more briefly, an elementary is the semi-conscious kâma-rûpa or in the worst case almost wholly conscious kâma-rûpa, of what was when he lived on earth, a gross and evil man.   These elementaries in the astral light are slowly decaying, but still filled with all the evil, gross, and often malignant impulses and proclivities, tendencies, and biases, that the said evil man showed when he was imbodied in flesh.

THE DOCTRINE OF SWABHÂVA

THE doctrine of Swabhâva is the doctrine of individuality, of the essential characteristic of every individual seed of the Spawn of Life. There are as many co-ordinated swabhâvas as there are individuals, entities in other words, in the Universe. Swabhâva means individuality, the essential characteristic of an individual, making it that individual and thereby distinguishing it from other individuals. That is swabhâva. Consequently it is not individuality which changes through the aeons as they pass. The changes come in and through the unfolding of the individuality, in its self-expressions or vehicles. The unself-conscious god-spark has its swabhâva or individuality, but not yet 'unfolded,' 'unrolled,' 'unwrapped.'

Do you see the reason why I so often repeat this phrase? Evolution means unfolding, unrolling, unwrapping, what is within, i.e., the swabhâva, the individuality. A rose, a violet, a horse, a dog, any entity anywhere, a god, a sun, a planet, a man — anything in self-expressing its individuality, manifests its swabhâva; and passes through the aeons, thus casting off vehicle after vehicle, casting off garment after garment, casting off expression of itself after expression of itself. For instance, the particular class or family of entities which is passing through the rose-stage — or the horse or the dog, or the man-stage — comprises entities all belonging to the same ray if you like, of the same solar logos, or to one of the subordinate rays of one of the solar logoi; and hence it continues as such an individuality, constantly manifesting its swabhâva. It lives for a time in the rose-stage — taking this stage as an illustration — and then outgrows it; and the rose-stage disappears or vanishes; the manifesting individuality or swabhâva meanwhile making for itself some new garment in which it lives and expresses itself for an aeon or twain or three or more, and then outlives this new stage and the new stage disappears. This process continues until finally the growing or self-expressing individuality, i.e., the monad, pressing forward on its evolutionary journey, constantly unfolding, unwrapping, developing forth what is within itself, and casting body after body behind, reaches the human stage; and then after the human stage comes the god-stage. When the god-stage is reached, then humans will be no more, they will have been outlived as vehicles. This process as you see likewise explains the problem facing geologists of the various great classes of entities which the geologic record shows as appearing, reaching a culmination in manifestation, and then disappearing to be succeeded by a new order of lives.

Do you understand better now? The swabhâva itself does not change in the lower realms, although it is evolving on its own lofty planes. The changes that human intelligence notices come from the constant self-expressions of the individuality or swabhâva. Swabhâva, remember, is the essential characteristic of an entity, that vital pressure, that dhyân-chohanic fluid, behind and within a manifesting entity, continually pressing upwards and forwards, and thus creating or rather building for itself, bodies after bodies after bodies.

It is a wonderful doctrine, this of Swabhâva. One could write a dozen bulky volumes on it, and then feel that one had merely touched the fringes of its import. Here is something more that perhaps I should add. I have spoken of the vehicles or expressions, the swabhâva-expressions, of the evolving entities as they pass from aeon to aeon in their long, long evolutionary journey: e.g., the rose, the cat, the dog, the horse, the man, the god, etc. Each such vehicle or garment or veil or sheath, after it has disappeared or vanished because outgrown, leaves behind an imprint of itself in the Astral Light as an indelible impression. Other entities in our rear, coming along behind us, will finally in good time reach the stage in their evolutionary unfolding where these indelible impressions exist in the Astral Light, and then these evolving entities behind us will mold themselves into these astral patterns. It is thus that the things that were shall be reproduced in future ages, as the spiritual seers of all time have stated, exactly as we are now reproducing today things that were in aeons of past time, now existing as records of an aeonic past. Do you catch the idea, this wonderful idea? Yet remember that each such new reproduction in manifestation of bygone astral molds or types is always a reproduction a little higher, i. e., there is always a step upwards, a step beyond, the stage last passed. I hope that these explanations have clarified the general idea.

Recollect always that swabhâva means the unfolding of the individual: the unwrapping, the unrolling, of the individuality: seeking, pressing forwards, to express itself, its innate or essential characteristics. Consequently, this is the reason why the rose always reproduces a rose; why the apple-seed always brings forth an apple; why the child of a man is always human, and so forth. This also explains why orders and genera and species and families are grouped together, because they are individuals resembling each other closely in their respective swabhâvas, and this is because they all belong to the same particular branch or part or class of one of the seven (or ten) solar logoi. Yet every entity, considered as an individual, no matter to what order or family it may belong, is an individual in the core of the core of the heart of the heart, in the innermost central point, of its essence.

You see how I have to repeat words in order to carry the idea into your minds. Each such entity therefore in its essence is an eternal individual; and therefore its swabhâva does not grow or change in the realms inferior to the individual, although the individual itself is constantly unfolding larger measures of its individuality as it advances to higher planes.

THE SEVENFOLD SEVEN PRINCIPLES

It is one of the glorious Theosophical teachings that worlds, just like men, die and vanish into the invisible. After a period of rest they come forth again and manifest in the visible spheres: appearance and disappearance, the rhythmic pendulum beats of the heart of eternity. Worlds — manvantara; rest — pralaya. Then the same worlds reappear, run through their phases, die, and enter the unknown spaces of space, just as man who is born a little child, lives his life, pursues his karmic destiny, dies, vanishes from earth, and comes back again.

So what I am now going to point out would serve equally well for a galaxy, a solar system, a planet in a solar system, or a human being, or indeed an animal or a plant: any individual entity. Let us imagine, then, this cosmic space when all the worlds, solar systems, clusters of stars and what not, have been swept away during the pralaya or death-period of our galaxy. There remains naught but what science calls empty space. Literally it is the lowest plane of spirit, but to us, to our eyes, to scientific instruments, because we cannot see any glittering orbs, we call it empty space. Mother Nature has slept for seven eternities in utter peace. Naught is, that we sense.

Now mark: the time comes when a galaxy or a solar system is to make its manifestation after this mahâ-kalpa or great world-period. Somewhere, anywhere, there appears first a focus of life; let us call it the monad. It does not appear on the physical plane. It is awakening from its long para-nirvâna; and it is coming into manifestation in the invisible deeps, the inner worlds of cosmic space. It surrounds itself with a nebula. Now this nebula is called in Sanskrit — and remember we are now talking of monads and not of celestial bodies — this nebula is called a Pradhâna, and the monad is called Brahman. In the case of a human being, the monad would be called Âtman, and the nebulous vehicle around it, which is not a nebula so much as a veil of living stuff, is called the Buddhi. But in either case, the full birth of the entity proceeds in the same way: by the unrolling of each part or element from the one next above it, until we have the complete sevenfold entity. Nature has one law. She cannot have different, contrary laws working against each other.

The following diagram represents the unfolding of the sevenfold entity from the highest, or pure spirit. In the case of either a universe or a human being the other six principles arise from the first and hang like pendant jewels from the first. In other words, out of the divine or out of spirit is born all that is, in a galaxy, in a solar system, in a planet, in a man.

Brahman	O	Âtman
Pradhâna	O	Buddhi
Mahat	O	Manas
Kosmic Kâma	O	Kâma
Kosmic Jîva	O	Prâna
Astral Light	O	Linga-śarîra
Sthûla-śarîra	O	Sthûla-śarîra

Death, speaking in general terms, and applying both in the great and in the small, is the reverse process. What was on the lowest rung or plane is drawn up into the next higher. It disappears. What was in the two lowest is drawn up into the next, and that finally disappears. What was in these three lowest is finally drawn up into the fourth, and that in its turn disappears. All the four lowest are finally drawn up into the fifth and in its turn that disappears. The same process with the sixth; until there remains but the pure monad.

The whole of a human being, then, manifesting on this earth, is ultimately from this monad. From âtman, the fundamental everlasting monad, eternally a droplet of the Infinite, so to speak, is born buddhi its vehicle; and yet buddhi, although a vehicle, is itself conscious living matter, conscious living stuff. It is spirit-stuff, just as âtman is the heart of spirit. Then is born from these two what we call manas, mind, the intellectual power, the root of mentation. From these three is born kâma, the principle which impels us to action, the urge to do things, commonly called desire; and it can have a very holy and beautiful aspect as well as a low one. Every man knows that. He has desires in his heart which can be sublime, divine, and desires in him which are sometimes grosser even than those that the beasts show. Then (note the plural) come the prânas, the vitality; that comes from the four above. From all these comes the model body of the physical, the astral body, commonly called the pattern-body on which the gross physical body is builded; and the astral body produces the physical body.

To repeat: from âtman is born its child buddhi. From âtman and buddhi are born their child manas: Father, Holy Ghost, Son. From âtman and buddhi and manas taken together and often called the reincarnating monad, springs forth, from their interaction in the manifested world, the principle of desire, the urge to be and to do, to become. And from these four again, from within them, comes the vitality. And from these again is born the astral, model body; and out of all these is the last child, the reflexion on earth of the divinity, of the âtman, i.e., the physical monad, which should be an imbodied god, and could be for he has it in him.

This is shown by the following diagram. It is useful for showing this and other aspects of man's nature. But if you have studied it for awhile, do not form a picture in your mind of what you have seen

	Âtman	Buddhi	Manas	Kâma	Prâna	Linga-śarîra	Sthûla-śarîra
Âtman	●	o	o	o	o	o	o
Buddhi	o	●	o	o	o	o	o
Manas	o	o	●	o	o	o	o
Kâma	o	o	o	●	o	o	o
Prâna	o	o	o	o	●	o	o
Linga-śarîra	o	o	o	o	o	●	o
Sthûla-śarîra	o	o	o	o	o	o	●

here, and imagine that the principles of man are on top of each other like a stair, or a pile of books. The fact is that they absolutely penetrate each other; so that sthûla-śarîra, as said in the Christian New Testament, actually is the Temple of the Living God, or it should be. The Christians have a marvelous story about the Avatâra Jesus going into the temple and driving out the money changers with a whip, because they were degrading the use of the temple. The money changers are our evil thoughts and evil emotions, our evil passions; and the presence of the Christ, the Buddhi, drives them out.

All the principles interpenetrate each other. I have tried to show that also in this diagram, as well as the descent of power and faculty decreasing from the top downward. You see then the reason why even the physical man of flesh not only is helped by having within him as it were a reflexion, a radiance from the âtman in his heart, but this physical man likewise, because his principles interpenetrate each other, can affect them by running up the scale as it were. You know you can affect your character by your thoughts, your feelings, whether you give way to them or master them; whether you determine to live a life which is grand or one which is the reverse. You affect your whole character thereby, and thus you affect your destiny. You make records running up, as it were, in an inverse direction along these pathways, running right up to the very spiritual heart.

Now there is another thing I have tried to show in this diagram: Every one of the seven principles of man is itself septenary. Why? Because it is nature's law that what she does in one place she will do everywhere. Nature is unitary, she has one soul and the action of that soul is uniform. Thus the buddhi-principle in man has seven sub-buddhis. The topmost is a reflexion from the âtman. Thus, following along the second column on the diagram, marked BUDDHI, we have first the âtman-buddhi; then comes the characteristic of this plane, the buddhi-buddhi; then there is the manas-buddhi, the kâma-buddhi, and the prâna-buddhi and the linga-śarîra-buddhi; and the very lowest of this column is the sthûla-śarîra-buddhi, yet to us practically pure spirit.

Here I want to point out a very important thing. Take the kâma, the principle commonly called the principle of desire. Now according to my statement above, there is an âtman-kâma, a buddhi-kâma, a manas-kâma, a kâma-kâma, *the* particular specialized color or quality or characteristic of that plane, and then the prâna-kâma — and so on down the scale. Now what does that mean? It means that even the principle of desire has its âtman. You may remember reading in the old Hindû scriptures in the Veda: "Desire first arose in the bosom of IT," speaking of the universal, cosmic desire to be, to manifest. What kind of desire is that? It is âtman-kâma.

And here is another point: It is because the âtman is sevenfold that it can unfold itself into the sevenfold constitution of man. The âtman, having the buddhi within it, drops a reflexion of its buddhi below, and that becomes the main buddhi. From the âtman and buddhi, the buddhi having a manas in itself drops a reflexion of its manas, overenlightened by the âtman, and that becomes manas-proper. The manas in its turn, having a kâma-manas, or rather a manas-kâma, drops a reflexion of it, overenlightened by the âtman of buddhi above itself, and you get the kâma-proper. And from the kâma in the same way comes the prâna. And prâna is sevenfold. Just as in the man's body there is the life of every cell, the cells of his brain and the cells of his bones and the cells of his blood, which all build one life which penetrates the whole body, so there is the life which penetrates man's whole constitution. There is the life in him which stimulates love. There is the life in him which stimulates devotion, the desire, the yearning to help. There is the life in him which has the kâma-principle or desire-principle for lower things, the lowest part of the kâma. All these are in man, all interpenetrating.

So you see how the âtman can unfold or unroll like a scroll and produce a world, a galaxy, a solar system, a planet or a man. This is the picture the Christians gave, taking a statement from the sanctuary, when they said that at the end of the manvantara the heavens shall be rolled up like a scroll. What does this mean? It means that the body will be the first to die and vanish; its component atoms will disappear into their electrons and protons and what not. What is carriable upward will be carried up to the linga-śarîra. (In the universe it would be the astral light.) And then this will be the next to die or disintegrate, and what was best in it, including what was best in the one below it, will be carried up to the next higher principle. The scroll is slowly rolling itself up, every principle in turn vanishing, being carried up into the next higher, until finally you have only the last three or the last two, depending upon the kind of pralaya.

When a man dies it is the four *lowest* principles which disappear, disintegrate, break up into their component life-atoms but all that was best in him is attracted up into the manas by the âtman and the buddhi. The man, from being sevenfold has become a triad, a threefold being. This is what happens when we men die. But what happens when a planet, the one in which we now live for instance, has its turn to die? Its own manvantara or period of manifestation ends, and its pralaya or rest-time comes. Then what will be left of man is merely the two highest principles; what was in the manas and all the four lower principles will be carried up into the buddhi.

Again, what happens when the solar system disappears, its turn having come to die, to go into pralaya? What will then remain either of the solar system or of any man who is in it? Just the pure monad, pure spirit; all the rest has been rolled up as a scroll and gathered into the âtman.

Now then, to come back to what I first stated: a galaxy, a solar system, a planet, a man, all follow the same pattern. Let us consider a galaxy. The brahman or the paramâtman of a solar system or of a galaxy, which has disappeared, because of having rolled up like a scroll all that was below in its preceding life, contains within itself all the karmic seeds of that past manifested period: all the seeds, the thought-deposits, the spiritual energies in their nirvâna, the bosom of the âtman. Now comes the time for manifestation again. A point appears in imbodied space — the inside worlds of 'empty' space please. What rolls out of the paramâtman in the unfolding scroll of the new manvantara is called in Sanskrit Mahâbuddhi, which contains the secret things which have been in the past and are now resting as seeds, to produce the future worlds. They begin to unroll themselves and become the mahâbhûtas or the great cosmic elements. Isn't this exactly the same that happens to a man after his devachan? After he has died and has had a period of rest in the devachan, the monad in the bosom of âtman slowly begins to unfold. It is like an unrolling scroll expressing what karman has written on that scroll, expressing what the man has within himself. He begins to reproduce *himself,* as he leaves the devachan and descends into imbodiment. He unrolls himself into a seven-numbered constitution; and when this has reached the linga-śarîra the infant's conception has taken place. When the child is born, then you have the sthûla-śarîra; and you have a seven-principled human being.

Rebirth is the coming out of latency into activity of what has been laid up in the higher principles when the last death took place. Death is the passing away of these temporary lower things, the rising of all that was best and noblest in them into dormancy or sleep or peaceful dreaming, into the triune monad. Rebirth, as stated, is the reverse process, the unrolling, the three becoming the seven. At death the seven rebecomes the three.

ORIGINS OF CHRISTIANITY

I WOULD like to speak very briefly on two small points of fact, and then refer to the origins of Christianity. The two points of fact first: It has been stated, and erroneously according to the writings of Origen that still remain, that he taught Reincarnation as we modern Theosophists understand this term. That is not the fact, because this term as we use it has a specific technical meaning which we understand. He undoubtedly did teach pre-existence of the human soul and of the souls of the stars and of the beasts and of all animate things; and there is a passage which I have quoted in my book, *The Esoteric Tradition,* also, where he teaches Reimbodiment on earth after a manner of his own, in which he even goes so far as to say that it is quite possible for an Egyptian in his next life to be born as an Israelite or a Hebrew, and after that as a Scythian or something else. There is just one feeble passage, I believe, alluding to this, however. Undoubtedly in his day he taught more than has come down to us; and it is likewise true that he taught some very interesting things, things that we Theosophists can perceive instantly and understand because we have ourselves received this wonderful teaching and have studied it. Our studies have given us keys by which, as I have often said, we can understand and penetrate beneath the surface-meanings of the great literatures of past ages; but the ordinary person who has not been trained theosophically may not understand these doctrines of yore as we may understand them through the blessed gift of Theosophy that we have received.

Now the other point of fact is this: "Dionysius of the Areopagus" is a legendary figure. It has even been doubted by many people, eminent Christian scholars themselves, that such a man ever existed. All that is known about him is a statement in the Christian New Testament to the effect that Paul of the Christians one day was addressing the citizens of Athens, and speaking on the Hill of Ares, the Hill of Mars, in Greek called the Areopagos, and a man there who was deeply intent upon the speaker's words came to him afterwards, and his name was Dionysius. And Christian legend, story, myth, has it that this man became the first Christian Bishop of

Athens. A legend! If anything has been proved, it has been proved
that this man referred to in the Christian New Testament was not
the author of those mystical writings which pass under the name of
Dionysian.

After the Origenistic controversies had died down and even some
time before, it was found that there were current in some of the
Christian sects certain writings which attributed themselves to an
author called Dionysius; and the Christians, pointing to the statement in the Christian New Testament, said: "Aha, the first Christian
Bishop of Athens wrote this." There was no reason for saying so,
but people were very credulous in those days; and the writings were
accepted as those of the first Christian Bishop of Athens, the man
who stood on Mars' Hill and listened to the Apostle Paul preaching.
Undoubtedly these writings are extremely interesting and contain a
good deal of what we would call esoteric fact garmented under Neo-
Pythagorean and Neo-Platonic guise.

Now I want to say something about the origins of Christianity.
I suppose you will agree with me that there is no controversial subject which has been so bitterly disputed, pro and con and back and
forth, and so much argued about, as the origins of Christianity. The
Christians of course hold the orthodox view which we all know. But
scholars almost innumerable have taken exception to the orthodox
Christian story. They have asked very embarrassing questions:
"What proof is there in what you call profane history that this one
individual that you call Jesus the Christ even lived? There is absolutely no proof in ancient literature of any kind except in your own
Christian scriptures, the four Gospels: origin unknown, origin disputed, full of contradictions themselves. Show us some proof that
your Jesus Christ existed." No proof is forthcoming — there is
none which is indubitable. That is an instance!

Now of course I think there is no possible doubt that the great
man, semi-divine man, whom the Greeks call a man-god or a god-
man, later known as Jesus called the Christos, the Christ, did live,
did teach, and did do his work in the world. We Theosophists accept that; but there is not any exoteric proof of it. Not a single
profane writer in Greece or Rome speaks of him until more than a
hundred or two hundred years after his alleged date of birth, when
his name had become familiar in the Graeco-Roman world through

the labors of the Christians themselves. Then naturally the Greek
and Roman historians began to talk about it. There are two passages which might seem to contradict this: one from the Jewish historian Josephus, one from the Latin historian Tacitus. But it has
been proved that the reference found in Josephus is a forgery, an
interpolation at some later date evidently by some Christian hand,
so we can strike that out. And Tacitus falls under the same suspicion!

I have just alluded to these not to take up time in interesting
historical controversy, but to point to a fact. How did Christianity
arise? What was its origin? These are very difficult subjects even
to speak of today. There are so many splendid people in the Christian Church that one hesitates to say a word that would seem to be
unsympathetic, unfriendly to the yearnings of their hearts, the aspirations of their souls. But this is no place for sympathy alone —
we are students of truth and fact; and the holiest sympathy is honor
and truthful speech. You cannot heal the woes of a man's heart
by lying to him — not for long!

Christianity arose in an effort on the part of the Initiates of the
day to stem the tide of degeneration and immorality which had become so strong, which was running so powerfully. Original Christianity was a Sanctuary-teaching, that is a teaching of the Adytum,
of the inner part of the Temple. They took the noble figure of Jesus,
Yêshûa', as his real name should be pronounced (a Hebrew name
which means 'Savior,' by the way, which is interesting), — they took
this ideal figure as a teacher and built around it as the central figure
of initiation what took place in the Adyta, and gave out these teachings, these facts, in thinly disguised allegory. Result: the Four
Gospels. That is why they differ among themselves to a large extent.
That is why they are so greatly alike. This is the reason of the contradictions which have been pointed out by scholars galore. They
were not written as a faithful *historical* record of the life and work
of a Jewish Rabbi, a Jewish teacher, but were written by four individual Initiates giving forth the fundamental mystery-teaching of
the Sanctuary, and using the figure of the noble Avatâra-Jesus as
a peg on which to hang the wondrous story.

Let me remind you that no one knows who wrote these gospels;
no one knows when they were written; the utmost labors of Christian

scholarship have not enabled anyone to answer these two simple facts: *Who wrote the gospels? When were they written?* All that such scholarship can do is to point as approximations to a time-period and say: We can trace them back thus far. Beyond that. . . Who wrote them? Simple faith says: Matthew, Mark, Luke, and John. Scholarship points out that these gospels themselves show they were written 'according to' Matthew, 'according to' Mark, 'according to' Luke, 'according to' John. Suppose *The Secret Doctrine* was a book whose authorship was unknown and that it simply bore on its title-page, not "H. P. Blavatsky," but *"The Secret Doctrine, according to H. P. Blavatsky."* Do you catch the point I am trying to state?

Now then, when these four Gospels were issued, by this time there were Christians more or less all over the Roman Empire which then included the Greek world; and these four Gospels were accepted. Why? Answer your own question. They were accepted because some people liked them. They told a beautiful story, a mystical story, a story which had a great appeal to the human heart. Some people liked them and accepted them. Other people did not like them and would not accept them; but those who did accept them handed them to their friends; and by and by the result was that the Christian Church with all its various sects, was thus formed with its four orthodox Gospels. And let me remind you that so slightly were some of the most fundamental teachings of Christianity understood even by the Christians themselves, that some centuries later the so-called controversy of the procession of the two persons of the Trinity from the Father rent the Christian Church in twain, one being the Church of Rome, the other, the so-called Greek Orthodox Church, likewise of Russia. This was the so-called *filioque* controversy: *filioque* meaning "and from the Son," the idea being that the Church of Rome, representing the Western world, said that the Holy Ghost issued or proceeded "from the Father *and from the Son*"; whereas the Greek Church claimed that it held to the teaching of the early Christian Fathers in proclaiming that the Holy Ghost proceeded from the Father, and then the Son from the Holy Ghost. In other words, the Western Church taught the procession as: Father, Son, Holy Ghost; the Greek Church taught it as: Father, Mother (Holy Ghost) originally the divine feminine parent, feminine in character;

and the spirit of love, from which proceeded the Holy Ghost's Son — its offspring, the Logos or Son.

I could talk to you for ten days and ten nights, and I would still have to come back to the one fact, I believe, which interests us. It is this: That Christianity originated in a very early and very earnest effort of men and women, whom we today would call Theosophists, quasi-initiates, who endeavored to set a teaching current in the world which would give peace to men's hearts, light to their minds, and strength to meet life's problems and difficulties, and thus stem the tide of degeneration and immorality. It failed. It did its work partially and then failed, and the result was a tremendously powerful, wholly exoteric Church which today actually is going to pieces. Why? Because the spirit of its human-divine Founder Jesus the Christ, has fled; and it had fled even within 300 years from the alleged date of the life-time of Jesus — and nobody knows when he actually lived! There was absolutely no proof that he lived when he is alleged to have lived.

In other words again, earliest primitive Christianity was a movement of very earnest Theosophists and quasi-Theosophists who knew something of the teachings of the Sanctuary, such as Origen who had himself been through the rites at Eleusis in Greece. Of course, in those days the rites at Eleusis were very degenerate; they had become only a form, but there was still something; these men had learned something there. But very soon the Christian movement got out of hand. Men lost the wish to guide and teach their fellowmen along spiritual lines only; and instead they gained the wish for power, for prominence, for position, for personal property. The result is the Christian Church as we have it today, the Christian Movement as we have it today in all its various branches. I know what I speak of, Companions. My own father was a clergyman. He destined me for the Church. But I did not enter it. I could not. I dare say that I spent the years between 12 and 18 of this body in one of the most heart-searching, industrious studies of Christian origins and Christian evidence that it has ever been the lot of a poor tortured lad to go through. When I say tortured, I mean torture of heart and mind. It cost me not a little to disappoint my father whom I worshiped. But I could not follow his wish!

But thus I found that those men who mock at Christianity are foolish. Let them mock at the hypocrisy, let them expose the insincerity. All that is perhaps proper. There have to be destroyers in the world, they are sometimes needed. But any man — and this I know from my own study — any man who looks upon Christianity merely as a system originally based upon priest-craft, deception, and imposture, is either a knave or a fool. That is my opinion. You will never find any Theosophist saying one word against the teachings of the Avatâra-Jesus. How can we, how could we? He is one of our own! But his teachings are not the degenerate Church which has departed from them and forgotten them. Yet even today there dwell the gleams of the evening sunset in the so-called Church of Christ; there still remains something of the original aroma coming from that great god-man's brain and heart — an entity at least — truly a suggestion of higher and nobler things than the merely material notions of the blind world around us!

So, to me, Christianity when understood and explained, is theosophical: I would not say that it is Theosophy, but it is theosophical; and even the Christian Church has enough in it to merit our respect and kindly thought. The mere fact that the ray streaming from its great Founder's heart even at this late day can give encouragement after a manner, and help after a manner, to the thousands, or tens of thousands — they used to be tens of millions! — who still are earnest Christians, shows that in the Christian Church yet the night is not fully fallen, the light has not absolutely failed.

THE PRINCIPLES OF A BUDDHA'S CONSTITUTION

I SHOULD first like to make a few remarks about the principles of a Buddha's constitution. I wonder whether you really understand just what condition or state the principles of a Mânushya-Buddha are in. We human beings at the present time are in the Fourth Round and in the Fifth Root-Race thereof, which means that we are actively functioning from the psychological standpoint in the kâma-mânasic parts of our constitution. When we shall have learned to function in the mânasic parts, we shall then be Fifth Rounders; or, referring to the majority of the human race, we shall enter the Fifth Round. Identically so when our self-consciousness shall begin to function in the buddhi within us: we shall then be Buddhas. This will not come till the Sixth Round. But as Gautama the Buddha, although living in this Fourth Round, had already so far evolved that he was self-conscious and living in his sixth principle, or in his buddhi, he was called a Sixth Rounder or a Mânushya, Human, Buddha. But mark you this: When an entity such as a man in his present Fourth-Round evolutionary degree, succeeds in living in the buddhi within him, he then has entered nirvâna. Nirvâna has different planes or degrees, just as the devachan has, or the kâma-loka has, or as earth-life has. But when a man has learned to function and to live in the buddhi of his constitution, he is then a Buddha, and his higher principles have entered into perfect rest and peace — nirvâna.

But what becomes of the inferior portions of his constitution? They still exist, because, *ex hypothesi*, he is still a man, they still are, they still live on, because these inferior portions of his constitution are composed of monads, just as the higher parts are. These inferior monads of the Buddha's constitution are learning, growing, evolving entities, beings. So then, in the case of a Buddha, while his highest parts have entered the nirvâna, which means attained celestial Buddhahood, the buddhi-mânasic parts, the Bodhisattva within the Buddha, still lives; and after the Buddha lays aside his physical body, or the Bodhisattva within him lays aside his physical body and physically dies, for that birth the Bodhisattva lives on as a

Nirmânakâya; and it is this Bodhisattva-part of the Buddha, whose highest principles are in the nirvâna, which furnishes the psychological apparatus needed to imbody the divine ray from the divinity and produce an Avatâra, as happened in the case of Śankarâchârya or Jesus or Lao-Tse and others.

Remember also that the Avatâras have no past karman, will have no future karman because they cannot live again. They never lived before, they are a product of magic — a self-conscious living compound produced by the confluence or congruence of three different currents of consciousness: the divine ray from above, the Buddha's psychological apparatus, and a bringing together of the lower elements which in ordinary course would have produced a physical human being — of the average type perhaps, perhaps somewhat higher.

So then, a Buddha means that the highest parts of him are in the nirvâna; that the higher intermediate or truly highest human parts of him are buddhi-mânasic, and this part lives on as a Teacher, as a Bodhisattva-Nirmânakâya, as a Savior of men. Then there is the physical body with its vital-astral apparatus which finally dies.

THE ARC OF DESCENT AND THE ARC OF ASCENT

THERE are two questions which I have been asked and which I should like to answer tonight. The first is: Coming down the Shadowy Arc we fall into matter; our glorious spiritual wings are clipped. As we rise out of matter on the Arc of Ascent, our pinions become strong again; we fly, as it were, into the aether. The Arc of Descent is condensing; the Arc of Ascent is the opposite, etherealizing. Does this mean that as we come down the Arc of Descent we do things — and are almost compelled by the forces around us to do them — which on the Ascending Arc we would call evil, wicked? In other words, is selfishness on the Downward Arc what Nature calls for, or is it not?

The other question is: What is there in man which makes him sin, which brings into being what we humans call evil-doing, selfishness?

To the first question I would answer that I think *The Voice of the Silence* sums up the whole thing beautifully: Work with Nature, that is, with the stream of evolution, in whichever direction it may be flowing, which means the will and vitality of the Gods; and Nature will make obeisance unto thee and call thee Master. As soon as we attempt to swim against the current, *in adversum flumen,* we set ourselves against the current of Nature's unfolding or infolding evolutionary progress, run counter to her 'laws,' so called, which is her will, and therefore become sorcerers. I think it is all summed up in the extract from *The Voice of the Silence:* Work with Nature; do her will, and Nature will make obeisance.

But before leaving this thought, I beg of you not to misunderstand it. When a Theosophist, and particularly an Esotericist, speaks of 'Nature,' he does not mean physical nature alone, nor astral nature. He is not thinking so much of the lower parts of the vast congeries of lives which form the Universe; he means all these, but in particular his attention is fastened upon the Cosmic Logos, the divine Cosmic Guide and impersonalized Spiritual Light of the World. Hence, even on the Downward Arc, though our bodies and lower parts in working with Nature aid in condensation and con-

cretion, nevertheless even in such case 'working with Nature' signifies equally an even more absolute following of and self-identification with the impersonal, utterly unselfish laws of Cosmic Harmony.
Thus, therefore, even on the Downward Arc, selfishness and egoism
are as wrong as they would be if practised at the present time when
we are beginning the climbing of the Ascending Arc.

And now for the second question. What is it in man that makes
him sin? What part of man is it which sins? Is it his body? Obviously not, because his body is a mere slave, a tool, to the indwelling
mind. Thus, a dead body does not sin, sticks and stones do not sin.
Is it man's spirit? Obviously not, because *ex hypothesi* it is stainless, sinless, of the essence of divinity. Likewise it is not the Linga-
śarîra, nor the mere life-forces, because the latter are mere vital
currents driven by will, guided by mind. You will then say it is the
Kâma in man which makes him sin — his desires, his passions. Is
it? I tell you, No. That which sins in man is his intelligence. Sin
lies in choice, in action. It is the right-hand path or the left. It is
the choice wherein lies the sin or evil-doing.

Take a child; a child before it has learned to discriminate between right and wrong does not sin, no matter what it does; it is
intellectually unconscious, it is ignorant. A beast does not sin, it has
not the power of human choice. The power of choice is slowly developing because the mânasic power is likewise slowly coming into
action, but the beast's power of choice compared with human choice
is insignificant. Therefore we say the beast cannot sin. Man sins
because he chooses wrongly, because he chooses to misuse the powers
within.

Now then, the beings descending the Shadowy Arc did not sin
until mind came to them. Mind brought vision, vision became choice.
When they could see, then they could choose. In a night that is
absolutely dark and you cannot see the bifurcation of the way, you
do not choose because there is naught to choose between. But once
the light comes and you see the way bifurcating to the right and to
the left, you choose. That is the idea.

Sin lies in wrong choice, sin lies in the misuse of the mind; and
this is precisely why the Fourth Root-Race fell. It was not because
it was the Fourth Root-Race when Kâma was most strongly developed or evolved that brought about the terrific consequences, nor

the tremendous power driven by evil choice. The evil lay in the wrong choice and the wrong use of mind. Man sinned in his mind, in his imaginations, in his thinking, in his choosings. There is an old Latin proverb, accepted from early times among Christians: *Ubi voluntas est, peccatum est; ubi voluntas non est, peccatum abest.* Where the will is (that is, the choice is) sin is; where there is no will (that is, no choice) sin is absent. A completely insane man does not sin no matter what he does, because the choice is not there.

So then, selfishness arises from the wrong choosing of our pathways in life, and the application to these wrong uses, of our powers in the mind. To misuse our powers, that is where sin lies.

On the Downward Arc as soon as the Sons of Mind inflamed with light the unconscious "men" of the time, then they could sin and began to sin. But as they were still comparatively ethereal and unevolved their choices were weak, vacillating, without much power behind Kâma; the driving power was not yet fully brought forth until the Fourth Root-Race was in full flower, and mind could choose and act forcibly. That is why in the Fifth Round the great Time of Choice will come when mind will be fully developed; and in that Fifth Round to come to the right-hand path will go those who will attain Buddhahood at the end of the cosmic manvantara, the chain-manvantara; and to the left will go those who cannot "make the grade."

Now is the time, begin now. You will have need, I warn you, of all your latent and stored up spiritual power. Do not think, "Oh, this one time I can get away with it, this is the last time." Take yourself in hand. It is what you choose which makes your act good or evil. Oh, I do hope you understand this, Companions. I wanted to bring out this, for in future years you will find it immensely important, important to remember in your discussion with others, important to remember its application to your own individual lives. Never fear to make your choice, if all the world is against you and you feel you are right — *stand;* but do not hesitate to change if all the world is against your change and you feel the change is right — *change,* and your action will be full of virtue, sinless. The ever-present need is to see and to make your choice according to your best vision and highest ethical instinct.

SYMBOLISM IN THE STORY OF JESUS

MAY I venture to call your attention to one fact? The difficulties that have been found in interpreting the story of Jesus, of his incarnation, of his life, and of his death, arose from the fact that the would-be explainers attempt to explain unnatural and impossible things. Modern critical research has of course shown this very clearly; but a great many human hearts, devoted to their religious beliefs, find it difficult to accept the pronouncements of modern critical research and are always rejoiced when these modern critical researchers are proved to be or to have been wrong.

As a matter of fact, the entire story of Jesus, later called the Christos, as outlined in the New Testament, is a Mystery-tale; a series of mystical legends, woven around the life of a man who did live — a great and noble man, a true Sage and Seer, an Avatâra in fact; but these mystical legends in no sense corresponded to the actual events in the physical existence of this Sage. This Mystery-tale, you will understand, please, to mean a setting forth in dramatic form of certain very important events which took place in Initiation chambers or crypts, and the parables included in this Mystery-tale also referred very definitely, if briefly, to certain of the fundamental teachings given to the neophytes at such times.

Furthermore, as the Initiatory Cycle in the case of individual men simply copied the grand term of cosmic existence, therefore likewise does the Christian New Testament in its symbolic allegory and imagery, in addition to being a covered and undisclosed tale of the Initiation-Crypt, likewise set forth the imbodiment of the Cosmic Spirit in material existence.

I will allude to one Mystery-fact here in illustration of the point. It is stated in the words of the story of Jesus that he came riding towards and into Jerusalem on an ass and the foal of an ass; and thereafter came upon him his life-work in the earthly Jerusalem — material existence; leading, as the legend sets it forth, to his arrest, his trial before the Roman Procurator, Pontius Pilate, and to his death.

I would like to tell you that in the Oriental Mystical Cycle of the Hither East, of what is now called Asia Minor, the planet Saturn was frequently mystically called an 'ass,' or rather the ass represented that planet in mystical symbology. And in equivalent mystical symbology the 'foal of the ass' was this Earth, because the ancient seers said that this physical globe Earth was under the direct formative influence of the planet Saturn.

When you recollect also, that the cyclical peregrinations of the Monad take place strictly according to law and order in the Solar System, and according to routes running from one planet to another; when you recollect also that the earthly Jerusalem according to the Jewish symbology was this Earth, as the heavenly Jerusalem according to the Christian symbology, was the existence in spiritual spheres and the goal of human evolutionary attainment, you may begin to have a clearer idea of what I am briefly and in part trying to tell you.

The spiritual soul rides into 'Jerusalem' — material existence — on an ass, meaning Saturn, and a foal of an ass, meaning this Earth; and the Monad, the Christ-spirit, descending into matter thus, is crucified on the cross of matter — that is to say is betrayed and crucified, following the Platonic imagery of the ancients.

I leave this extremely mystical thought with you, because if your minds are alert and if you have profited by the instructions that have been communicated to you, this thought will give you an instance of the intricate manner in which a part at least of the Christian Scriptures have been written. The one thing that you should be always on guard against is to read any single line of these Christian Scriptures as recounting an actual historical physical event. Every main thought or idea in the Christian Scriptures is allegorical, and refers directly to the cycle of initiation and to some of the teachings given during the initiation-ceremonies.

Jesus lived. Whatever name he may have had, the individual known as Jesus was an actual man, a great Sage. He did indeed live. He was, furthermore, an Avatâra. He died, or rather he disappeared; and around his personal individuality or individual person, there was collected, there clustered, there were gathered together, events in the Initiatory Cycle of the Hither East which were expressed under the garments of the legends that the Occidental world now has in what it calls the Christian New Testament. In other words, the personality of Jesus the Avatâra was used as the type-figure around which were. built up initiatory events expressed in mystical and allegorical form: and this literary material was finally whittled down into what are now called the Books of the Christian New Testament.   Finally, Jesus was not physically crucified, and furthermore he did not die an ordinary physical death.

OPPORTUNITY IN KALI-YUGA

WE LIVE in a very interesting age, Companions, a time when history is in the making. I do not think that in the recorded annals that are open to us at the present time there has ever been an epoch when serious-minded students of the Ancient Wisdom, which we call Theosophy, have the opportunities that now *we* have. It is precisely the stress and the strain which are opening our hearts and tearing the veils away from our minds. It is the same thought that our Masters have told us applies to kali-yuga, the Iron Age, a hard, rigid age where everything moves intensely and intensively and where everything is difficult; but precisely the age in which spiritual and intellectual advancement can be made most quickly. There actually have been ages in the past when chelas or students have longed for conditions to be more difficult than they were, to give them the chance to advance faster.

In the Golden Age, which it is beautiful to dream about, in the so-called Age of Saturn, in the age of man's innocence, everything moved smoothly and beautifully and all surrounding being co-operated to make everything beautiful and pleasant; and there is something in our hearts that yearns to return to it; but it is not what the chela longs for. He longs for opportunity; he longs to climb; he longs to test what is in him, to grow from within.

Isn't it a strange paradox that the hardest, cruelest, of all the yugas is precisely the one in which the quickest advancement can be gained? I think there is a world of wisdom in this thought; and I speak of it tonight because only a few days ago I received a most pathetic communication from one of "Ours" who wanted to know if there was not something good in the kali-yuga: if mankind had to go under without hope. Why it is the very time when the chances are the most frequent for progress! It is the opportunity-time.

THE EUCHARIST

THE sacrament of the Eucharist was originally a teaching of primitive Christianity about the way by which the human soul could achieve spiritual oneness with the Christ within — a ray, as it were, from the Cosmic Christ — thereby becoming a god-man when this union or yoga was complete.

Other religions speak about the Buddha within, and the cosmic Buddha, not meaning Gautama, the Hindû teacher, but a Cosmic Buddha of which Gautama was a ray, as Jesus the Avatâra was a ray of what the Christians call the cosmic Christ.

In a very short time, due to a number of converging causes, this beautiful and really holy Christian teaching of how to achieve this yoga or union became lost in the Christian Church, and was replaced by a ceremonial. In other words they substituted a ceremony, a ritual, a rite, to replace the occult esoteric teaching which had been forgotten except by the very few. These very few were attempting to hold back, as it were, or to restrain, the complete loss of the wonder out of the bosom of the Christian Church and from Christian thought. Many of them were originally pagans who were attracted to the new Theosophical Society — as earliest Christianity was — because they felt it had a new dispensation of spiritual power in it; and they took the Eucharist out of the ceremonies of the Mysteries of Dionysus. The Dionysiacs, the Dionysian Mysteries, had a communion in which the priests and the congregation together partook of the blood and of the flesh of their divinity Dionysus. The blood was wine, the flesh was the cereal, bread if you wish, or wheat.

Now the Christians took this over because they knew something of the inner meaning of this Dionysian symbol; and that is the origin of what the Christians even today, carrying on a tradition but forgetting the original verities, call the holiest mystery in the Christian Church — as it originally was.

Why, even today we can say that the most sacred teaching we Theosophists have, our most sacred mystery, our most occult effort, is so to live and think and study and be trained, that the individual man may become at one with the divine. We are on the upward arc, so that now we can bring about this union — some individuals more than others. When the union is complete you have what we call a Buddha or a Christ. When the union is less complete, you have a Mahâtman or one of the greatest chelas. When the union is still less complete, you have some of the great men of human history, mostly in the philosophic and religious lines: great thinkers and teachers such as Pythagoras, and Plato, and Empedocles and other sages from Egypt and Syria and in the Druidic lands of Germany and France and Britain; or again in Persia. Then on a still lower scale you have those men who have caught the gleams of the vision sublime and have been so enraptured by the picture of that glimpse that their whole life thereafter became consecrate to the glory. These are chelas and the great men of the human race. We can all become such, more or less.

Here is a final thought about this: When the Dionysiacs spoke of drinking the blood of their god in the wine and taking the flesh into themselves through the cereal, the wheat or the bread, they never intended it in the literal way in which it is now accepted in the old-fashioned orthodox Christianity. They intended it in a mystical sense which I will now proceed to explain. The blood of the god, in the ancient countries surrounding the Mediterranean Sea always meant the cosmic vitality, what we call Jîva, the life, the Divine Life. Thus the blood of Christ, the cosmic Christ, did not mean literally blood, but the word was used as is found even in the Mosaic books of the Jews: "in the blood is the life." The blood became the symbol for the life of the Christ, the Christ's life, the Christ's vitality, the divine vitality in individual man which transformed him and raised him so as to become at one with the Christ or with the Buddha. In that sense, by training, by effort, by yearning, by study, the neophyte raised his own life to aspire upward, to become universal, to become one with the universal life. And they called this union, or yoga, 'communion': the man thereafter communed with the cosmic spirit. "I and my Father are one," said Jesus.

And the bread, the cereal, wheat, in ancient times always had the symbolic meaning of intellect, intellectual power. Here is where you get a very interesting side-line for those who are technical Theosophical students. The ancients said that wheat was originally brought to this earth from the planet Venus. Now the planet Venus

in the cosmic scheme represents what we humans in the human constitution call the higher manas, in which the Christ in us, or the
Buddha in us, works. The vine, said the Ancient Greeks and Latins,
originally came from the planet Jupiter. The planet Jupiter, they
said, is that which controls our vitality, or *anima,* or Jîva, our life.
And Jîva is a direct efflux from Âtman.

These many and converging and correlated lines of ancient Mediterranean thought the earliest Christians seized hold of and put
together and welded fast into a lovely and marvelous teaching of
union; and then later when the truth became lost, they collected the
Dionysian thoughts, changed them slightly, gave them new names,
and you have the Christian communion as a ceremonial rite in the
Church, commemorating the process by which the sincere Christianos,
or one 'infilled with the Christos' becomes at one with the divine.

This very word 'Christian' originally meant one who is filled with
Christ, one who had evoked the Christ in himself by that union, that
yoga, the communion, the very thought I am trying to bring forth.
Originally Christians were not called Christians. They did not dare
call themselves by the title of their great Avatâra. It would be exactly
as if we were to call ourselves Buddhas, if Buddha were our teacher.
Christians originally called themselves Chréstoi, a Greek word which
meant 'worthy ones,' or as we would phrase it today, students,
learners, disciples of the Christ; and the Christians themselves tell
us that they were first called Christians at Antioch in Syria; and
heaven knows when that was! It may not have been until the third
or fourth century.

"THERE IS NO ETERNALLY UNCHANGING PRINCIPLE IN MAN"

I WAS impressed tonight with the suspicion that all of us, perhaps, have not fully understood the statement made not only by our Teachers, and eminently by the Lord Buddha, but likewise in different places by H. P. B. and by myself in my *Fundamentals,* to the effect that there is no 'eternally unchanging' principle in 'man.' Yet perhaps on turning the page, you will come upon a statement that the different monads in man's constitution are children of previous manvantaras, therefore implying that in man there are principles or elements which perdure for enormous time-periods. How in the name of goodness can this latter statement be true if the former statement be likewise true? I call your attention to this apparent contradiction, and real paradox, because I feel the need that many experience of having these contrasting statements explained.

The teaching of Gautama the Buddha was, when it is correctly understood, the teaching of the Lord Jesus of the Christians, and of all the Mahâtmans of our own Esoteric School of doctrine; to wit, that there is no 'eternally unchanging' principle in man which is different from the rest of the universe, which is in constant change of revolution and evolution.

According to the old idea of all the orthodox — crystallized — schools of religion or philosophy, there is in man an individuality which perdures unchanging, and this is exemplified in the Christian teaching of the personal 'soul' supposedly created by almighty God, which soul lasts for eternity *as that soul,* and never can be other than what it is, i. e., never can enter into the Cosmic Life except as an unchanging guest, or if you wish, as an unchanging observer; the usually unspoken implication being that as such unchanging entity, it is not an integral part of the Cosmic Life: not life of its life, bone of its bone, essence of its essence; because such orthodox and exoteric religions and philosophies postulate that the universe is but a temporary and evanescent creation of a supposititious God, and that the unchanging soul finds itself in the universe as a guest, an observer, a learner, only — not, as above said, as an integral and unto eternity inseparable portion of the Cosmic Essence.

From the standpoint of the Esoteric Philosophy which envisages man as an integral and inseparable spark of the Cosmic Essence and therefore for ever a part of it, there is no principle or element in man's constitution which eternally abides as such soul, its only modifications or modes of change being those of accretions of experience, or of growth.

There is no such abiding and eternally unchanging ego or soul or even spirit in man, an ego or soul or spirit which is different in essence in each man from what it is in any other man, nor is there any such abiding and unchanging individuality which is different in some god from what it is in some other god. All change; everything grows; the universe itself, as well as all within it and of it, our human souls and spiritual principles included. Out of the same vast kosmic womb of consciousness-life-substance, unitary and one, we all flow forth; and as individuals, and still more as persons, we are illusions by comparison with the Eternal, for that is everlastingly Itself. Whatever modes of change it may have, whatever phases of growth its innumerable parts may experience, whatever contrarieties, diversities, differentiations, may take place, the Eternal is nevertheless the Eternal, perduring from frontierless duration unto frontierless duration; and the essence of each one of us and of all beings and things, is THAT.

On these simple facts of teaching, reposes the doctrine of what the Buddhists call the heresy of separateness: that there is in me a 'soul' or spirit which in its essence is different from the 'soul' or the spirit in you, my brother, or in any other being or thing. This is the heresy of separateness; and it was against this intellectual bane, this deceitful phantasm of a fundamental difference in essence, that the Lord Buddha taught so powerfully in saying that there is no eternally abiding, unchanging, distinct, eternally differentiated principle or element in a man when compared with other cosmic units, such as other men, or other beings and entities. He thus voiced the doctrine so familiar to all Hindû philosophies, and so well known as existing in the Adwaita-Vedânta, of the fundamental unity or oneness of all the interblending and interwoven hierarchies and their component elements in Boundless Space. Such a conception of an eternally abiding and unchanging ego as an individuality separate in essence from the Cosmic Individuality, the Buddha-Gautama called the Great Illusion, *Mahâmâyâ*.

Yet there are in man numberless lives which compose him, as a composite constituted being, as a compound or integrated entity. Man verily is such a composite being, and this is a simple declaration containing a world of occult truth!

Now what are these portions, these elements, of his constitution — i. e., the different monads and life-atoms which make him, which build him? Each one of these monads in its essence is a spark of that central Cosmic Intelligence or Fire, the central consciousness-life-substance. We have not as yet, unfortunately, evolved forth in our vocabulary one single term that will include all these elements of the teaching, so that we have to use such an awkward term as this in order to give some adumbration of the idea: consciousness-life-substance. This is not consciousness apart from life, nor apart from substance; but a viewing of all three as in essence one: one side or aspect of it being what we men call 'consciousness'; another side or aspect of it being what we men call 'life'; and another side or aspect being what we men speak of as 'substance' — three in one and one in three; not three different gods or divine essences, but 'one godhead,' one unitary Cosmic Essence, one eternal Reality manifesting through the three masks: Consciousness, Life, Substance. This really is the proper meaning of the Christian trinity: not "three Persons in one God" as they say, but three masks or aspects or vehicles, as the human mind understands the thought, as the human mind translates the thought, of one eternal, boundless, frontierless REALITY. This is the divine root of man: of me, of you, of everything, of every god, of every sun, of every planet, of every beast, of every plant, of every atom. The root of all is THAT.

So, fundamentally and in essence we are all one, and the innumerable, utterly incomputable numbers of beings and things, i. e., of egos and selves in Boundless Space, are not eternally individualities, each different from all others and thus lasting unto eternity as unchanging, ever-enduring, separate egoities. There is a complete and utter and absolute solidarity of Essence, of which we all partake, from which we all came, into which we all shall return — albeit retaining each one of us our vastly increased individuality — when our evolutionary cosmic journey shall have been completed during any one manvantara. But while in manifestation, while in the worlds of manifestation, we are divided up as mâyâvi beings and entities,

the divine spark in each one of us expressing itself in us as individuals: as thoughts, to use a figure of human speech, of the Divine
Thinker, of the Parabrahman. 'Divine Thinker' is of course a figure
of human speech; but we have to use figures of speech when our
human intellect is too feeble to understand the incomprehensible
vastness of REALITY; we have to translate our intuition into figures
of speech so as to get some intimation or intuition of the REAL. The
'Divine Thinker' thinks divine thoughts. Each such thought is a
monadic entity. But the thought is of the essence and of the basis
of the Divine Thinker who thinks — which 'thinks.'

Now then, one thought more, taken directly out of our esoteric
cycle of studies. These various monads which go to form the constitution of any being — let us say of man in order to define, in
order to exemplify, our conception: these various monads, or each
such component monad, of man's constitution *is* not only one of
the integral parts of the constitution which ranges from the divine
to the physical, but each such monadic center is itself a spiritual
being, a living, growing, learning being, as the human monad which
we call 'man' himself is.

Now each one of these component monads, or integrals, is, as
an individual, you, I. I refer you to the diagram in my *Fundamentals of the Esoteric Philosophy,* on page 203. As human beings we
are each one of us Bhûtâtman; but the Prânâtman is likewise a
growing, learning entity, rooted in the same Cosmic Divinity that
I have just spoken of, and therefore growing, therefore destined in its
own evolutionary course to become a man; after attaining manhood
destined to become a god; after attaining godhood destined to become a super-god, and so forth, climbing the ladder of life eternally.
A marvelous picture; always climbing, always expanding in consciousness, always evolving, hence always changing in form and attributes and individuality and personality, because always bringing out
more and more of the essence of divinity within, and yet never
utterly attaining it because that Divinity is boundless. An eternal
principle, the same for every monad in the human constitution —
eternal because its essence is of the Eternal Essence; not eternal
because it has or is a 'soul,' whether it be my soul or your soul.
Hence, there is no such eternally unchanging and abiding principle
in man as an ego perduring in its unchanged or unaltered individual-

ity through eternity, for every ego is growing, which means constantly changing; and hence the notion of such an unchanging perduring
ego, or 'soul' is an illusion; it is a figment of a dream; it is wholly
illusory. Every atom in man is as much such a monad in its heart
of hearts as a man himself is; and we men, in precisely the same way,
are the composing monads of the constitution of a god. In our own
case this God is the Divinity who is the opifex of our solar system,
our solar Divinity. Think! In the diagram in *Fundamentals* to
which I have referred, we see the Âtman. It works and expresses
itself through the Jîvâtman; the latter through the Bhûtâtman; this
last through the Prâṇâtman. Only four monads have I enumerated
here; yet taking our constitution as a whole, their number in man is
legion, is incomputable, when we likewise include the armies of life-
atoms. Every life-atom helping to compose man's constitution is
at its heart a monad, therefore in essence a divinity.

My Âtman — to illustrate because we are now speaking of the
worlds of differentiation — my Âtman will some day grow to be the
divinity of a solar system; and all the various monads now forming
my constitution manifesting here as a human being will then be the
archangels and the angels, to use the Christian terms, of that future
solar system: the Dhyâni-Chohans in their various grades, to use
our own Theosophical phrasing. These various unevolved monads
which help to compose even my physical constitution live in their
various cells, and these various cells are builded up of life-atoms on
different planes; and in that far distant future of which I have just
spoken, if I make the race successfully and become the divinity of a
solar system in the spaces of Space, all these cells and life-atoms
which now compose my physical 'me' will be the component elements
of that solar system, each one having evolved to take its own particular and definite place and work therein; and I, the divinity in me,
will be the then presiding godhead of that solar system, just as we
here are component elements of former life-atoms of Father Sun
in a vastly distant epoch of the Cosmic Past.

Thus, as I have hereinbefore explained, there is no eternally
abiding and unchanging principle of individuality or 'soul' in 'man.'
Yes, an absolute truth: no abiding separate and unchanging principle in man, separate from the similar principle in you, my brother,
or in any other being. This is the heresy that the Lord Buddha

fought against and that our own Masters so powerfully teach against. There is no such immortal, unchanging, and therefore perduring and abiding 'soul'; yet the very essence of man is immortality itself. Every last atom in his constitution, in its heart of hearts is an immortal divinity because of its essence, the Essence of the Kosmic Divinity. I know no doctrine in all our School of Teaching which so cleanses our human hearts of pride, which so quickly purges the human mind of illusion, as just these beautiful thoughts that I have been attempting to speak of. You will never fully realize the glory that is within you until you become infilled with the most beautiful thought of them all. What is it? I am one with Divinity, and there is no abiding, unchanging, and hence separating personal soul in me; for I am THAT. This doctrine is the teaching of the utter solidarity, the utter oneness, of everything that is, from god to atom, with the Heart of Things.

Were men on earth today imbued with this thought, filled with this doctrine, all the troubles of earth would soon vanish. Men then, sensing their essential unity or oneness, and that what affects one affects all, would instinctively and by love act like brothers, because they would think like brothers; they would see far more of sheer human interest in the mysteries envisioned in the depths of the human eye than they would in counting the money-bags, or estimating the values in the swollen vaults of our banks. All human problems would adjust themselves easily, because men would realize that what causes you to suffer reacts on me, interiorly and exteriorly.

Carry the thought onwards. It is fundamentally the same in business as it is in philosophy. The man who tries to drive his competitor to the wall injures his own business, for that very man should be made a customer, and by Nature's laws actually is a customer unless you ruin him, drive him out of business, which means killing his purchasing power. The same rule which is thus exemplified in the pragmatic affairs in human life holds in the worlds of the spirit and of the soul. I advance far more quickly when I help my fellows, when I feel that they are component parts, so to speak, of my own being; that there is something in my fellow which is closer to me than my own hands and feet, than my own mind, than my own heart, than my own soul; for this is the Essence of Divinity in him which is identic with that Essence in me.

PLANETARY CHAINS AND PRINCIPLES

FOR years really I have felt I ought to speak about a difficult matter of doctrine, to try to correct at least a few simple errors which some of our very best students have fallen into, I fear; I am not sure, but I have the impression that this is the case. It is with regard to the planetary chains, a very technical teaching, but a beautiful teaching, and most suggestive when properly understood, a teaching having a distinct moral value on human life because of the inferences that the student draws from this doctrine of the planetary chains.

Of course there are planetary chains of which we have no physical cognisance whatsoever, because their lowest or fourth globe — following H. P. B.'s septenary enumeration — their fourth respective globes are either above or below our plane of the solar universe. Therefore being outside of the sphere which our eyes can encompass, we do not see these other globes. Nevertheless these higher or lower planetary chains exist. So much for that point.

When the planetary-chain teaching was first given out by H. P. B., shortly before and at the time of and after the printing of her great work *The Secret Doctrine,* those students who thought they understood the teaching concerning the planetary chains, imagined that the other globes of a planetary chain, such as our own Earth Planetary Chain, were but different phases of each chain's fourth-plane globe, as for instance of our Globe Earth, our Globe D for our Chain — different levels of consciousness, as it were, of our Globe D, reaching from the grossest or our physical plane up to the spiritual. So strongly did this idea sink into the minds of students of those days, and such vogue did it get, that very unwittingly and utterly wrongly, students spoke of the other globes of our Planetary Chain, or of any other planetary chain, as being the *principles* of our Globe Earth or of some other fourth-plane globe, with respect to its chain, like Venus or Saturn or Mars or Jupiter. This is all wrong. The reason for such mistake was the very striking and close analogy that exists between the globes of a planetary chain and certain aspects of the septenary human constitution little spoken of in those days, but in our day much more clearly understood, to wit, the monads in the human septenary constitution.

For many years over-emphasis has been given to this idea that
I have just spoken of, that the other globes of our planetary chain
were so to speak the principles of our Globe D, and for that reason
I have taken especial pains to change that current of thought; until
about a year ago I became suddenly conscious that the swing of
thought had gone far too much, far too far, in the other direction;
and that our members had lost sight of the very striking and close
analogy between the monads in the human constitution and the
globes of a planetary chain, and were beginning to look upon the
globes of our planetary chain, or of any planetary chain, as almost
unrelated individuals, unrelated globes, or at least held together only
by delicate and subtil karmic bonds of destiny — a thought which
is true enough, but not nearly close enough, or accurate enough.

If you can synthesize these two points of view, the older and this
latter, fuse them into a new and more comprehensive conception,
you probably will have the real facts. Let me try to illustrate: The
monads in the human constitution — and I will use the septenary
form that H. P. B. gave to us as it is somewhat easier than the
duodenary — may be reckoned thus: the divine, the spiritual, the
intellectual, the psychical, the animal, the astral-vital, and the vital-
physical; for even the vital-physical human body, temporary and
imperfect as it is, is nevertheless the expression of a monad working
on this plane, whose seat (since your western minds always want
very definite brain-mind locations), whose seat is in the human heart.
The heart is likewise the seat of the spiritual monad working through
this lower.

The globes of a planetary chain correspond almost term for
term to these monads in the human constitution; and as you know,
the human constitution being unitary, one, the principles and monads
being in coadunation but not in consubstantiality, so likewise we may
speak of the globes of a planetary chain as being in coadunation but
not in consubstantiality. Yet these other globes are not the other six
principles of our Earth. They are fellow-globes, a septenate, of which
our Earth is one. But a septenary unitary fact comes in what I
have just told you; that the globes correspond in that chain to what
the monads are in the human constitution, because each globe is
itself the expression of what we may call a globe-monad.

Furthermore, just as the principles in the human constitution are as given from the very first, âtman, buddhi, and so forth, down the scale, so the same cosmic principles, paramâtman, mahâ-buddhi, mahat, etc., are the principles of a planetary chain. Thus you see right there there is the same distinction between globes and the principles of a chain, and the monads and the principles of the human constitution, item for item. Furthermore, just as there is in man a hierarch of his constitution, just exactly so in a planetary chain there is a hierarch of the entire planetary chain, the hierarch for all the seven or twelve globes of that chain, our chain as an example. And this hierarch, who really is a kind of person or individual god for the chain, our chain, is the highest spiritual planetary of our chain, or planetary spirit.

Remember that every globe of a chain has its own minor hierarchy of planetaries. You may call them Buddhas and Bodhisattvas, if you like. I am now using the typically Theosophical term, planetaries. But these combined planetaries of the chain simply make the families of the planetaries of the chain, the highest of such planetary being the hierarch of the hierarchy, the king. Furthermore, every such planetary considered as an individual, in some past cosmic age has been a man, or a being corresponding to a man; that is, the monad now a planetary, now blossomed out, evolved forth, into being a planetary, then was passing through the stage where spirit and matter meet, conjoin, and produce man, the midway stage. We in our turn, all of us, if we make the grade, shall some day be planetaries. Furthermore, note that in the human constitution, all the monads of a man's constitution are inseparably linked, which does not mean closely linked, but inseparably (which means cannot be separated, that is torn apart from each other to become strangers unto each other), are inseparably linked for a galactic manvantara; after which evolution will have so parted them through increasing individualization that although they will still be karmically linked, they will no longer be condensed as it were into a relatively closely knit unit, as they are now in a man.

Precisely the same rule holds for a planetary chain; and remember that all that I am saying tonight is but brushing the outskirts, sketching an outline, of much deeper and important teaching that does not belong here.

All the globes of our planetary chain had a common origin, were

born together so to speak, just as the monads in a man's constitution have a common origin and were born together so to speak.
When they were thus born in past cosmic time they were much more
closely in union, united, than now they are, evolution of each globe
through the ages bringing about a stronger individualization of each
globe, and for this reason we speak of these as being in coadunation;
so that as the ages pass, they will have the tendency to separate, still
remaining connected by spiritual and magnetic and all other kinds
of bonds. The separation, as stated, comes through constantly
increasing individualization. But as each globe becomes more
strongly individualized, the constellation as it were of globes in a
chain separates farther apart. Thus a child born in a family finds
the time come some day when it leaves the family and enters the
world to carve its own way, or to follow in the footsteps of the
father, no longer as a child but as an individual, as a man 'on his
own,' to use the slang expression.

Furthermore, every globe in a planetary chain, ours for instance,
has its own septenary constitution. The Master in *The Mahatma
Letters to A. P. Sinnett*, outlines what these principles are for our
Earth-Globe, but the Master there gives only the septenate for the
physical globe. You remember, every principle in a constitution is
itself septenary, so that there is even an âtman of the physical so to
speak. Therefore, every globe not only has its own septenary principles, each principle a septenate itself; but you see this means that
every globe therefore is a fully equipped entity with divinity at its
heart and manifesting in a gross physical vehicle, veil, frame, body,
exactly as a man does. You know that even an atom in your body
is a septenary entity. Its heart is divinity. Why should not a globe
of a chain be exactly the same? It is. At the present time the
globes of a planetary chain, ours for instance, are sufficiently conjoined or coadunated so that they move through space more or less
together as a constellation, as it were; so that while they are not
inside of each other, the more ethereal inside the more material —
that is not so — while they are scattered about in space, but closely
together, nevertheless they form a constellation as it were, if you
take the twelve of them, or even the seven; and they pursue the
same orbit about the sun that the earth does, not because the
earth follows this orbit — it is only one of seven or twelve — but

it happens to be the orbit that these seven, these twelve, all follow; so that when we move about the sun, we do so, and all the other globes do so, more or less as a constellation, each globe moving and rotating. Follow your thought now: so that actually every globe from this standpoint can be called a planet. It is in itself not only a septenary entity, but if you were on Globe E for instance, or F or G or A or B or C, you would not see the other globes around you. To you it would be an earth, following its orbit around the sun, as does each of the other globes. Therefore the globes from this standpoint can truly be called planets.

What has been said with regard to our earth applies equally well to all the other planetary chains, visible or invisible, of our Solar System. And there are scores of planetary chains. Our modern science knows of only a few planets — I think the total number at present is nine, including Pluto, and about these I have not the time nor is it the place to go into here.

I am debating now in my mind, and also trying to find words in which to speak of something else. These things are not easy to speak of. The teaching is difficult indeed, because it is so utterly apart from anything that our brain-mind knows. What I have said about planetary chains applies equally well to the Solar Chain, or indeed to any stellar chain, the chain of any star. Furthermore, remember that every planetary chain is headed by its hierarch, which is the chiefest planetary spirit of that chain, the highest; and therefore that planetary spirit is for its chain what we in the West I suppose would call a 'personal god.' Now this teaching is a very ancient one, and in its popularization a very exoteric one. It has been known since immemorial time, and was the basis of what the ancients called astrolatry or star-worship. They did not worship the physical globe, they worshiped the life, the light, the intellect, the manifestation of order and beauty and harmony, for which the planet was the symbol and expression. They worshiped, in other words, the regent of the planetary chain. And furthermore, just as a chain has its own chief planetary or hierarch, so every globe has its own subordinate smaller hierarchy of planetaries with its hierarch or chief minor planetary, our Earth as an example; only these are globe-planetaries — at least those on our Earth are. Nevertheless, they are higher than we men, spiritually and intellectually.

Thus you see, "to come back to our sheep" as the French say, we must not look upon a planetary chain as an indissoluble single body or globe, of which what we call the other globes are merely finer planes. In other words, the other globes are not merely finer planes of our own Globe-Earth that we know. Our own globe that we know is only one of seven or twelve, and in some ways the least important of all, because the lowest. Nor should we again on the other hand look upon the planetary chain as composed of a number of globes, whether we reckon on the seven or twelve, which are merely held together in a kind of feeble union, unconnected in origin with each other, which is quite wrong, because they are very closely connected in origin with each other, and they shall be connected thus closely until the end of the Galactic Manvantara; and then when the new Galactic Manvantara opens, they will still be connected, but much less so than at present, obviously, because of what I pointed out a little while ago: that age, evolutionary progress, gives to each globe an increasing increment of individuality. It becomes more independent in spirit, as it were, just as we find among men. It is a very curious paradox that the lowest things are the most closely united, the least individualized, as we see in the unism of the rocks. As we follow the ladder of life upwards, we find that the component parts slowly seem to separate and become more individualized, until we reach men. And here, strangely enough, although it is among men that the sense of disunion is very strong, it is likewise among men that begins to come to birth again, in men's souls, the feeling of their oneness, the *ekatwa* or *ekatâ* in Sanskrit, their oneness with the Divine. Isn't that a marvelous paradox? Unism at the lowest, but unconscious unism as in the rocks, and in the atoms. Unity in the highest, but self-conscious unity with the Divine.

Try then to understand, to fuse these two thoughts together. The globes of a planetary chain are in coadunation, but not in consubstantiality, which means that they are karmically united as a unitary group at the present time, closely so, but are not consubstantial. That is, the stuff of which the individual globes are builded differs from one to the other.

And now, finally, do not for an instant take the metaphorical symbol used by H. P. B. of the necklace of globes as being a graph, a photograph, as it were, of the actual positions of the globes in space, for that is all wrong. The globes are scattered about the heart of the chain as it were from the central pillar of light, so to speak. And you could write a metaphorical graph of the seven globes, no longer what H. P. Blavatsky on page 92 of her *Letters to A. P. Sinnett* called a necklace of sausages and protested against it as being a wrong conception; but you could write the way the globes are located towards each other on an ascending line, 1 2 3 4 5 6 7. That would be just as accurate as the necklace of sausages; but that straight-line graph has not the advantage of suggesting the descent into matter until the bottom is reached and the rise again, which the necklace of globes does. The straight-line way of describing the positions of the globes however has one enormous advantage. It shows that every globe of the seven or twelve is on a different plane; and that no two, despite the graph in *The Secret Doctrine*, are on exactly the same sub-plane. Those are metaphors, that is, diagrams. They suggest things, and the suggestion you must try to understand; and do not take pictures, those metaphorical suggestions, as photographs of the positions of the globes.

Now it is true, and I have emphasized this point myself, that precisely because the globes are scattered about in space, although each one is on a different plane, there comes a time when they come opposite each other in their evolution. I wonder now if you catch that thought? So that it is possible, for instance, for an observer on Globe E at a certain instant in time to catch a glimpse of Globe C, the reason being that the two globes are for the instant in vibratory synchrony. That instant actually may be a million or tens of millions of years. But the globes are in movement. We are speaking now of super-geologic time; but compared with the life of a planetary chain, it is, relatively speaking, an instant.

It is in exactly the same way, or a very similar way, that H. P. B. tries to describe the outbreak of psychic disturbances in our time, foreseen and foretold by the Masters. Do you remember in some of her earlier writings she points out that the world is entering upon a period when the plane on which we live and the plane on which the kâma-rûpas of kâma-loka mostly are, come close together, the partition becomes thin, and there is an inrush of kâma-rûpic spooks into our thought-atmosphere, and into our world. It is, as it were, as if two planes came close to each other.

DEVELOPMENT OF MAN'S PRINCIPLES IN THE ROUNDS

THE matter which I am going to speak to you about tonight I approach with the utmost reluctance. It is thorny and difficult and is so entangled with other teachings that I almost despair of giving even a relatively clear picture of it. I despair, I say, of doing so without betraying the Mysteries more than I have any right to. For the full understanding of what I am this evening going to try to lay before you very simply, as far as I dare, the whole, the last word, is given only to those who have passed their Third Degree. Get that clear.

No wonder H. P. B. passed over it with scarcely more than a mere pointing of the finger. These are matters dealing with the Rounds and Races, and the globes of the planetary chain, and they may seem to you to be very simple and easy, matters which anybody has a right to know. But in fact it is all very difficult. Anybody has a right to know who has proved that right. Any human being who has made himself worthy has a right. But it is not for me, in the position I hold, to judge anybody.

So this evening I will go as far as I dare go. There is a great deal that I shall not even point to; so don't think that what I am going to say tonight covers the whole question. It does not. I will merely try to give you a brief picture, some few hints. That is the best I can do.

Now we have here a diagram which should be helpful for our discussion this evening. It is one that I imagined out myself. But remember that diagrams, though helpful, can also be very misleading. They give hints which the mind itself thereafter should pursue; but they are not *pictures* of what they represent; they are not photographs, they are not paintings. The usual diagram of the seven principles, as given by H. P. B., is merely intended to show that the most high and the most glorious is Âtman (at the top of the diagram); and that the principles then 'descend' in a decreasing scale of importance, power, and worth. It is not intended to convey the idea that the principles are one on top of another like the layers of a cake. And the only value that this present diagram has is to give the elements or principles in the order of their involved evolution from beginning to end; and to show that the fourth is the critical element or tattwa, the one at which the downward arc stops and the upward begins. That is practically the only value of this diagram, but it is very important to get that one idea clear.

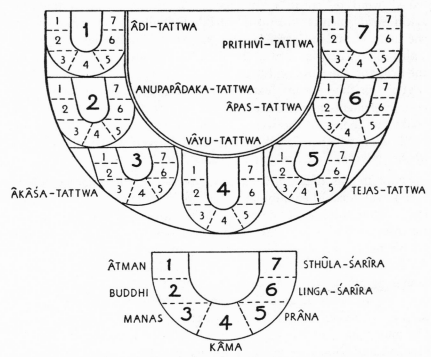

Do you know the diagram of the seven globes as H. P. B. gives them in *The Secret Doctrine?* You can consider that that diagram also represents the cosmic elements or tattwas on the four rûpa planes of the cosmos; and just as there are two globes represented on the highest rûpa plane, two globes on the next counting downwards, two on the next, and one on the lowest, so in like manner may the tattwas be arranged, as you see in the present diagram. Nature is all builded on one plan. And because this is so we can see, as this diagram shows, that any one of the planes of nature, or any one of the elements of nature, which includes the elements of man, whether it be high, as we say, or intermediate, or low, itself consists of seven subordinate or sub-planes.

Roughly the tattwas here enumerated have the following meanings: Âdi-tattwa is the primordial or first tattwa; anupapâdaka: that which is born from its own essence; âkâsa might be called 'space'; vâyu-tattwa, according to the elements of the ancients was called 'wind' or 'spirit.' You may be interested to know that the Latin word 'spiritus,' our word 'spirit,' originally meant 'wind' among the ancients, and in Greece *anemos* was 'wind,' but it originally meant 'spirit' also. Tejas-tattwa, the fifth cosmic element, means 'fire,' the brilliant, the glowing, the burning, the dazzling fire. Âpas means 'water'; prithivî means 'earth.' But mind you, these lower four cosmic elements are not the air that we breathe, nor the fire that cooks our food, nor the water that we drink and bathe in, nor the earth upon which we walk. It is the relatively spiritual elements of the universe that are given these names.

Now in this diagram I have attempted, in the enlargement of No. 4, which could equally have been an enlargement of any one of these cosmic tattwas, to correlate them with the human principles; for instance âdi-tattwa with âtman, man's essential self, the root of all his being, and the source and root of the other six principles. Anupapâdaka-tattwa corresponds with buddhi; âkâsa-tattwa with manas or mind; vâyu-tattwa with kâma; tejas-tattwa with prâna; âpas-tattwa with linga-śarîra; and prithivî-tattwa with sthûla-śarîra. Its great value is to show, both in the cosmos and in man, the importance of four as the turning-point, where the bottom is reached and things go swinging up again. As for instance here in these globes: both globes and life-waves begin at the top and gradually sink downwards, so that after Round One comes Round Two, then Round Three; and then Round Four which is the very lowest, kâma. And then the opposite process begins. When kâma has been evolved in the life-waves, you get a balance between spirit and matter. Why is it that from this globe D, during the Fourth Round where we are now, there should have begun in the Fourth Root-Race the beginning of the rise of the luminous arc? Because spirit and matter are then practically balanced, and for millions of years after that balance had been reached between spirit and matter, spirit continuously evolving forth more and more began to grow a little stronger, and there was a rise, very slow but progressive and continuous. During the Atlantean Root-Race, the Fourth, the one that preceded ours, the bottom point of evolution was reached. Spirit then balanced matter, and from that moment all things which previously had been slowly sinking into matter, stopped, the balance had been reached, equilibrium; and from then onwards things are rising; so that we in our Fifth Race, as we are, are just a little higher than were the Atlanteans, for we are 9 million years to the good, towards the spiritualizing effect. The pull of spirit is stronger and will grow constantly stronger as our Fifth Root-Race gives place to the Sixth, and that to the Seventh, and even more so when our life-wave leaves this earth, globe D, and begins to ascend the arc to globes E, F, and G.

I might add here that while human flesh is Fourth Round stuff, because we are in our Fifth Root-Race during this Fourth Round, human flesh is somewhat more spiritual than the flesh of beasts is. When we shall have reached our Sixth Root-Race on globe D, human flesh will be still tenderer, because more refined, more etherealized. When we reach the last race of this globe D during this Round, the Seventh Race, human flesh will be still finer. It will be almost translucent, but not quite. It will be cloudy. And as the life-wave rises along the ascending arc, when they reach globe G, the bodies of the inhabitants of globe G will be bodies which will be self-luminous, and by the end of that Round they will be bodies of light. From now on, all the globes and all the life-waves which up to the present have shown a tendency to sink into matter, now having reached their balance, will hereafter show a tendency to become more ethereal. The very earth we live on, as the ages pass, will show a tendency to etherealize itself, spiritualize itself; and I may point out that the discoveries in radioactivity, such as that of uranium, and certain other elements of high atomic weight, are merely examples of the steady disintegration of the grossest chemical elements known. They would naturally be the first to etherealize.

Now then, how do the human principles, as given here, come into evolutionary activity during the course of their rounds around the seven globes? This is very complicated, simply because there are so many things to think of. We are now, let us suppose for purposes of exposition, at the very beginning of the First Round.

None of these globes is yet formed.　There is just an astral nebula. But the globes are just forming, because of the work of the three elemental kingdoms.　We will call globe A the beginning of the manifestation of âtman; we will take our human life-wave as an instance of all the other nine life-waves.　But what part of âtman, which itself is sevenfold (I have tried to show it on the diagram) is manifesting during the beginning of the First Round on globe A? It is the sthûla-śarîra of âtman.　But here comes in something else. In the âtman, the âtman-âtman comes on quickly, the buddhi-âtman comes on quickly, so with all of them down till the bottom is reached, because of the pull of matter, the sinking tendency that I spoke of. So all the sub-principles of âtman are gone through, the higher six are very rapidly descended through until we reach the bottom of âtman, the body of âtman, the sthûla-śarîra; and that is the first principle of the human life-wave on globe A.

When this has been done, in other words when the seven root-races have been run through globe A, the sthûla-śarîra of âtman remains here; but the surplus of life from âtman overflows downwards into globe B, or rather the surplus of lives, because this surplus of lives is the outer life-waves.

What happens on Globe B?　On Globe B all the âtman principles are run through till it comes down here to the sthûla-śarîra of buddhi.　In other words all the seven root-races are run through there, and the sthûla-śarîra, the last and most evolved on this First Round remains; and the surplus of lives from B passes down to C. The same process takes place there, and the surplus of lives passes down to D, and so on through all the globes.　We will use seven globes.　That is the First Round.　We may call it, if you please, the âtman-round.　But âtman is not fully developed.　This is just the first round, and the lowest part of the âtman.

What happens during the Second Round?　We will call it the buddhi-round, when buddhi is evolved forth or emanated.　The life-wave on globe A specializes, and it runs through all, till it stops at the linga-śarîra; and as this is its main point during the second round in globe A, the surplus of life very quickly passes through the previously developed âtman-sthûla-śarîra, gives the buddhi touch to it, and passes down to it, through the Second Round, to the linga-śarîra of buddhi, and then goes on. Next, the surplus of life passes down to globe C, and the linga principle of the buddhi is developed in the life-wave, finishing its evolution in C; and the same thing happens, the surplus of lives passes down to D, and then upwards.

So thus far we have evolved the âtman principle during the First Round, the buddhi principle very imperfectly during the Second Round, and from below upwards. The First Round brought forth the sthûla-śarîra of âtman; the Second Round brought forth the linga-śarîra of buddhi; the Third Round will bring forth the prâna of manas in exactly the same way. The Fourth Round will bring forth the kâma of kâma. The Fifth Round, next one, will bring forth the manas of prâna. Mark you, all through the globes. The Sixth Round will bring forth the buddhi of the linga-śarîra in all the globes and the life-waves; and the Seventh Round — and isn't this remarkable? — will bring forth the âtman of the sthûla-śarîra.

This means that at the end of the seventh round, take our human life-wave as an example, all the individuals of the human life-wave will be fully developed seven-principled beings, every one of the principles fully developed for our manvantara, our chain during this Day of Brahmâ.

Why was it that during the Third Root-Race the mânasaputras at first refused to imbody and give mind to the undeveloped humans of that time? Because the vehicles were not ready. There were no proper mental vehicles to contain them, to contain the mind of the mânasaputras. I wonder if you are any the wiser!

So now the evolution begins with âtman and ends with âtman. The developmental process is from the bottom going up one stage or sub-stage with each round; so that while we begin with âtman, having no proper vehicle to work through in the First Round, we reach the Seventh Round with all the human principles fully developed, and even the body exists in its âtman state.

Round One develops the lowest part of âtman on all the globes; you have the lowest part right down the scale, what in modern science would be called the elements, the chemical part. Remember it began with âtman — spirit. The next Round we might call the buddhi-round, and that develops the next from the bottom of all of them. Then the Third Round you might call the mânasic round, just as it was in the Third Root-Race on our globe that mind came to man.

When all the Seven Rounds have been run, when every principle of man has been fully developed in him, he is a god, he has the spirit working in him, the buddhi working in him, he has the mind working in him, he has the desire — and desire in the ascending arc becomes what we call aspiration, desire upwards instead of desire downwards. He has the prâna spiritualized to become an actual individualized force in him. For instance, a Seventh Round man can then call upon his prâna if he wants to, to shoot out a bolt of electricity by his will, if he wanted to work a little magic, crush a rock or disintegrate a tree, because his prâna then is fully developed and under the power of his mind and his will. Likewise the linga-śarîra will no longer be a rather shadowy, half-developed, inchoate body of man that now it is, but it will be a marvelous instrument, attuned to the harmonies of nature, individualized, man himself. It will be like a sounding-board catching every vibration; and his body will be a body of light, actually glittering just like the light of the sun. Why is it that the sun has the body it has? What we see is the sthûla-śarîra or body, it is a body of light. A man will be that way during the Seventh Round, a shining globe, and what his inner principles will be of course are beyond description!

And now let me recapitulate the main ideas I have given you. The key-thought is this: there are two lines of evolution, the spiritual and the material, beginning respectively with the summit of the âtman and with the elementals, the lowest of the material; and as the rounds progress these two lines approach each other, the former working downward and the latter working upward; they pass each other so to speak in the Fourth Round, and at the end of the Seventh Round in a sense their positions are reversed; that is to say that at the end of the Seventh Round the âtmic part is in the highest part of the material or prithivî, having run all down the sevenfold scale; and the material part has reached up as high as it can go into the âtmic part of the material again; and this produces fully evolved *vehicles*. Here is the key-note to the whole process of evolution through the rounds: the evolving of fit vehicles to express the spiritual and intellectual faculties, monads.

Remember also, that the First Round is the outlining round, striking the pathways according to past karman for all the succeeding rounds. The very first entities that appear on the scene to build up the globes are the high entities (which I vaguely call the âtman in my explanation) from the past incarnation of the chain, commingling immediately with the elementals; and thus we have the highest beginning at the top of the âtman, and the elementals beginning at the bottom of the sthûla or prithivî, and then, as stated above, through the remaining six rounds they work towards each other, pass each other, if we want to make a picture in our minds, in the Fourth Round, and then each line continues upwards or downwards respectively as far as each can go.

This means, therefore, that the monads or spiritual entities will have incarnated, or rather imbodied, themselves fully at the end of the Seventh Round, producing god-men or equivalent beings in the other kingdoms, and the vehicles or sheaths or bodies will have through the seven rounds raised themselves up or evolved or developed as high as they can go to be fit vehicles for these now fully imbodied monads.

Another point: If we take the vehicles for a moment and consider them alone: the Fourth Round brings out the desire-principle, with both its upper and its lower aspects. Then in the Fifth Round the *vehicles* are raised to the mânasic plane on their respective positions in the scale of life; in the Sixth Round the *vehicles* evolve capacity to transmit buddhi; they become buddhic; and in the Seventh or last Round, the *vehicles* have gone upwards as far as they can in delicacy and unfolding power, and are then ready to carry the âtmic ray.

But this is only as regards the vehicles on the several planes of man's constitution. As regards the spiritual entities or rays: they lean down to meet the upward rising vehicles all through the rounds, and thus, although they are always transcendent, in other words themselves always on their own planes, because of leaning down they seem to descend, as it were, and approach their rising vehicles until the junction is made in the Fourth Round, when, taking the human kingdom, man really becomes truly man, child of spirit and child of prithivî or earth — halfway up and halfway down, so to speak.

THE MYSTICAL TEMPLE OF SOLOMON

SOLOMON was a wise man, and in my judgment a man not wise in the wisdom of this lower world so much as in the wisdom of the higher world, genuine wisdom; and if he really builded the temple which people mean when they talk about the "Temple of Solomon," one can only ask oneself: what on earth became of that particular temple-structure? Antiquity outside of the Jewish books knows nothing whatsoever about it. Traveled men and learned men, scholars, people surrounding the Mediterranean passing through Judea many hundreds of times in a year never report having seen such a gorgeous structure — gorgeous because of the description of the wealth lavished upon it supposedly, but perfectly horrible in the architectural shape and structure of it, if it ever existed — an eye-sore.

Why is it that the learned men among the Romans and Greeks and the Egyptians and other peoples who passed along one of the main highways of Asia Minor, never mentioned this wonderful temple? No traces of it exist today except a legend that the present temple of Jerusalem is builded on its emplacement. We are also told that this temple was builded by certain priest-workers, structural workers, masons and carpenters and others, and yet that there was heard no sound of tool. Isn't it evident from the very description, that this temple of Solomon was not a physical structure at all, but a mystical temple in the Heavens if you wish?

How is the universe builded by the cosmic workers, the cosmic spirits, the cosmic laborers and the cosmic architects working night and day? How is it builded? Without sound of tools, builded by cosmic wisdom, held in place and continuance by cosmic wisdom and cosmic love, and it is ineffably beautiful as a cosmic structure. How is the body of man builded, the temple, the holy throne, in its highest parts the holy of holies of the inner divinity? Builded in the silence without sound of tool, neither sound of hammer nor chisel nor mallet. Among the initiates it was a common sign that when a certain great Being founded a 'city,' he founded an esoteric school, and when he builded a 'temple' in that city, he opened a sanctuary for initiation — the temple in the city, the sanctuary, the holy of holies, within the school.

Solomon in Hebrew means peace, quiet. Do you realize that the secret Wisdom, the Theosophy of the Hebrews called the Qabbâlâh, also describes the building of the universe as a temple, not so much in the words but in the same thought? From the indescribable Primordial Point comes forth 'Âdâm Qadmôn, the Primordial Hierarch of the Universe to come: and from 'Âdâm Qadmôn streams forth the nine and ten Sephîrôth, the Angelic Hierarchies of the subordinate Architects and Builders, the contractors, the masons, the carpenters, of the universe, building the temple in the bosom of 'Êin Sûph, the Boundless. *A* Universe.

What was this mystical temple of Solomon, but the Angelic Hierarchies of the universe constructing without sound of tools the noblest work the gods have done. The holiest meaning, the most beautiful of the significances, of this temple of Solomon is of a new revealing to mankind of the ancient God-Wisdom. So we call it the Qabbâlâh of the Jews that Solomon then first gave. The tale is founded upon the then secret Qabbâlâh, the Theosophy of the Jews. How much more beautiful, how much more worthy of worship: that which makes man from man a demi-god, because unveiling, revealing, bringing forth, the god within him. Is there any religion higher than that? It is the objective, the aim, the purpose, of all the greatest spiritual intellects of antiquity: to bring out the god within man.

And you remember even what another Jew, the great Avatâra Jesus, pointed out as the noblest way by which to pray, the holiest, the most acceptable to the divinities? In substance it was this: when thou desirest to unveil thy heart in gratitude, enter into the holy of holies, thy secret chamber within thyself, wherein is peace and silence and worship. Don't do as the Pharisees do in churches, in synagogues, in temples, worshiping in public with many words. But enter into the holy of holies, within thine own heart wherein the divinity abides. There is the temple. Those who wish may worship openly, in churches, in synagogues, temples and cathedrals and in whatnot. The true followers of Jesus the Avatâra, the true followers of the great initiates of all times, may attend such places; but when their worship is highest and dearest to them, they will go within into the inner chamber, worship in secret and peace, in silence with the quiet of all the senses, for there in the silence is the still, small Voice.

The temple of Solomon is but one version of the universal allegory known all over the world and among all peoples; and probably we never would have heard of the Jewish form of the allegory if it had not been for what took place in history. If the Persians, for instance, had overthrown the Greeks when they invaded Persia, how vastly different would have been European history today, perhaps far higher; because the Persians were far more spiritual than the subtil-minded, beauty-loving and gracious, graceful Greeks: fine qualities if added to that sense of the mysticism of truth and its response within the human heart which the Greeks indeed sometimes spoke of, but the ancient Persians more often.

HOW THE HUMAN SOUL RETURNS TO EARTH

I HAVE listened with deepest sympathy to the generosity towards each other's views which you have all shown in your study this evening. All of us remember that knowledge is marked by modesty, because knowledge knows its own limitations, and therefore is never dogmatic. I have noticed also that you are patient with each other for using words in different ways. Your minds are not water-tight compartments which would not hold ideas of other people.

Now in regard to this matter of 'rays' or 'waves.' We Theosophists of many, many years' study have developed a terminology of our own which younger students do not yet fully grasp. When they do grasp it they will see that it is good. We speak of a 'ray' from the sun. The sun has been emanating countless rays through the aeons, and each such ray is a wave, an energy if you want to use the language of modern science, a language which will be changed in thirty years from now when scientists know more. This is one of the difficulties that a Theosophist has to contend with, to remember that he himself is using a highly technical series of terms which he and others like him understand, but which the non-Theosophist who has not studied Theosophy does not grasp; and therefore does not understand what the Theosophical speaker is talking about half the time. We should never forget that; and consequently when you people differ, it is not really about ideas that your minds are at variance. I would wager almost anything that ninety-nine times out of a hundred it is about words.

Now I want to say, Companions, that I desire brief speech with you upon two thoughts. The first is about these life-atoms and reproductive germs and so forth. I do not think it is good to think too much about these things and talk about them too much, and I am always amazed to see the intense concentrated attention with which an audience listens to them. They may interest doctors; it is their job; but there are so many more and vastly more interesting things to study.

Now in the first place, reimbodiment is not a haphazard thing, as of course every one of you understands. It is all done by the laws of nature, and by nature I do not mean physical nature, I mean it in the old occult way of speech. So that the imbodiment, the reimbodiment, of an ego takes place strictly according to karmic law, and karman means cause and effect, cause and consequences, the y following the x. If you do something, nature will react upon you for that act. That is karman. You may react in a billion ways. That action and reaction may take a billion years to run itself out. The reaction may come at once, or it may be thinly spread over millions of years. Who can say? It depends upon the originating cause.

So that the reimbodiment of an ego is just as much a fact of nature's laws and nature's actions and reactions as is the physical birth. Now the ego in the devachan lives in an auric sphere as it were, an ethereal rûpa. Its size may be anything. It may be co-extensive with the solar system. The probability is that it is, as far as mere physical extension goes, infinitesimal, for magnitude has nothing to do with consciousness. Magnitude is a mâyâ of our plane and of our brain-minds.

However, the ego in its devachan enjoys blissful dreams. Then there comes a time at the end of long centuries, or long periods of scores of years, when the forces which had brought about this sleep and rest to the devachanic entity begin to weaken, to work themselves out. The devachanic sleep and bliss is fading gradually. But what is taking place coincidently? There is taking place a slow awakening to a sense of consciousness of the old human earth-attractions. These enter the dream-state of the devachanî as dream-recollections of what it had been, and what it had seen and heard and thought and felt — beautiful things, however, because it is still in the devachan. Now these are the recrudescences into the consciousness of the ego of the tânhic elementals held in the ether-body of the ego. Hitherto the dreams of the devachanî have been too high or too spiritual for these rather earthly things to have any effect on the ego. But as the devachanic dreams begin to fade, die out, grow darker as it were, these tânhic, these trishnic elementals begin to grow in activity in the ether-body of the ego, as I have already said. What does this mean? It means a thickening or a coarsening of that auric body, that higher ether-body; and slowly as it were the entity drops, is attracted because of his materialized body, downwards towards this sphere. It may take centuries for this to happen, or a few score years, according to the individual karmic case.

Now then, to phrase it otherwise, there arises in the ether-body of the devachanî a growth in memory of earthly things. Its own past life comes back into its recollection, very feebly at first, stronger as time goes on. In other words there is a thickening, as I have stated, a coarsening, materializing of this vehicle. This is the beginning of the growth of what we call the linga-śarîra, the pattern-body around which our gross sthûla-śarîra, the physical, is builded atom for atom. Thus does the man reproduce himself from the last life — consequences, karman.

I have already said that magnitude has nothing to do with it. Let us suppose that the ether-body when this takes place is the size of an apple. After all, how large is a human life germ? But in this beginning of the linga-śarîra there resides a growth potency — supply your own term if you do not like that, we won't quarrel about words — a growth potency, the same kind of swabhâva, as we call it, which makes an apple seed produce an apple and not a rose or a strawberry or a banana or something else; that makes a plum seed always reproduce a plum and not some other kind of plant. In other words there is in this linga-śarîra the capacity to develop along its own karmic laws into the linga-śarîra and the physical body of the man, the child to be born.

But before this stage is reached, on account of the attractions of this ray descending from the auric body — call it a ray, call it a wave — on account of the attractions of this back to its familiar fields of life on earth, as it were a magnetic or electric contact is established in exactly the same way in which the thunderbolt will strike this tree and not that one. There is a reason for this. Everything in the universe works by law. There is no chance. The same principle of selective choice works in the case of the thunderbolt and in the case of the human ego selecting its own mother; not consciously in the way we might think it is done, but by a conscious human electricity as it were, sympathy, synchrony of âkâśic vibration. We call this a projection of the ray; and that is what I have alluded to in *The Esoteric Tradition*.

Now here comes the point: In any human being there are innumerable multitudes of life-atoms which are strictly his own atoms of life, life-atoms, jîvas, originating in his own vital font or fountain, and looking upon him as their parent. Suppose we say, just as a speculation, because no one could say how many life-atoms the human body contains — I doubt if the gods could — but suppose that we say a human body contains of these particular life-atoms a hundred billion. And after his death these become distributed among the two billion or so inhabitants of earth; so that when a reimbodying ego thus seeks its physical house or sthûla-śarîra for its next imbodiment it is sure to find sympathetic attraction to and therefore lodgment in any human body. This contact of the ray from the ego with the life-germ — germ if you please in the body of the two parents — is a contact with life-atoms that that ego used in its former body on earth. The thing seems complicate simply because it is new to most folk. And by the way, this is one of the reasons that explains what we call the fertility of races and the ability of some stocks of beings to cross, miscegenate, and others not.

Now of course it is obvious that some family milieu, some families, would give an ego a happier home and a happier physical body than other human couples would. You can understand that, and it is the automatic endeavor, run by nature's laws, of a reimbodying ego always to seek the happiest home it can find. It has the instinct to do so. It does not do it self-consciously. It is nature that does these things, for such happiest home is for the reimbodying ego the line of least resistance. Remember, it is still in the devachan, and its spirit is not in full control. This is the reason why also — and this is a delicate subject, I hope you will forgive it — this is the reason for the moral weight of the teachings given to men and women to be careful in their relations with each other, for egos are attracted to both men and women in the manner that I have endeavored to describe, and they are attracted with tenfold force when a man and a woman feel affection for each other, if that affection be real. In fact a mere flirtation you can see to be wrong, because that sets up a kind of synchrony of vibration between the couple. I wonder if you see what I am trying to drive at.

This is the way reimbodiment takes place. It is the reason, as I have endeavored to show in the *E. T.* and also this evening, why marriage is such a holy thing, and should be such a beautiful one; and why relations of any other kind are not only ethically wrong, but as you can readily see, against nature's laws of harmony. As a matter of fact, it is sufficient for a man and a woman to feel real affection for each other, especially if they have the chance to associate, for egos or these rays to be attracted to such couples. It is a very heavy responsibility that human beings hold in their hands, and they sin against nature constantly through ignorance largely. The whole thing could be so beautiful and holy, and should be. And mind you, the egos find the best bodies and the happiest homes where the marriage of the parents is a true one. That is where the entities, the beings coming to life on this earth, have the greatest chance.

It is the damnable, abominable materialistic science of the last hundred years which has wrought such mischief in the world, and has brought about the conditions that exist in the world today everywhere, teaching men that they are no better than beasts, apes, of a slightly higher kind, and that therefore it matters not what they do, that the thing to do is to get and to hold. That is a doctrine out of hell. Once the moral law is lost from the conscience of man, civilization is doomed.

THE SURPLUS OF LIFE

THE expression 'surplus of life,' when describing the building of the globes of the planetary chain, is used in a technical sense which I will try to illustrate by pointing to two growing things, bringing forth with ever greater power and in ever fuller flow reserves, surplus, to wit: the growth of a seed into a plant, and the growth of a human being from a human germ. Out of the seed flows forth the surplus, in the technical sense, of life that the seed contains. This surplus is first the green shoot, then the blade, then the stem and the branches and the leaves, and finally the fruit producing other seeds. Surplusage means that which flows forth or unfolds from what is locked up within. So the growth of a human being from a human germ is also descriptive of the technical sense of surplus. Out of the seed comes the embryo, which grows into the unborn child, which finally enters the world, becomes the child, grows to be the boy or the girl, advances to manhood or womanhood, unfolds from within the hitherto latent powers and faculties of mind and heart; then the moral and spiritual attributes begin to show, which did not show in the germ, in the embryo, in the unborn child, the youth. This is the unfolding of the surplus life.

So that the 'surplus of life' after the life-waves have formed Globe A in any one Round, does not mean merely what is left over in the ordinary sense; but means what is left over as signifying the bulk, the greater part, the immense life, attributes, and powers and faculties stored up in Globe A, impossible to manifest there because that is not their field, and passing down to Globe B and unfolding Globe B, the next stage. And when Globe B has unfolded to a certain extent, in the First Round, the same surplus of life passes down and unfolds Globe C. And so on all around the chain.

When Round the First is completed, there is no longer this rolling out or rolling forth or unpacking. It is no longer an evolution of what is within as regards *unmanifested* globes, because now they are on the scene. They are there; and the life-waves when they enter the chain anew for the Second Round and all subsequent Rounds merely follow the pathways that have been laid down, evolving of course, growing of course, unfolding the surplus life of course, in themselves; but not in the building of the chain except as improving, improving, improving. Do you catch the thought? It is exactly what the ancient Stoics meant when they spoke of Spirit unrolling from within itself, its surplus life, as a child, the next plane in the cosmos, which let us say was Aether; and when Spirit and Aether were unrolled, the surplus of life, which merely means all the as yet unrolled, unevolved, passed down to the next stage and formed the third, the spiritual Fire. And then the next, Air, Water, Earth. After that the Universe is manifested, the house is completed: Jack is in his house and Jack begins to live as a householder.

Now the śishtas imbody a very different doctrine indeed, and we can call them also the remainders left behind after the surplus of life has passed on; but not in the technical sense that is intended when describing the First Round in the building of the Globes of a chain.

I will now make a few remarks on these diagrams (see *Fundamentals of the Esoteric Philosophy,* pages 524-5). We have here the four main Monads of the human constitution — the four main ones: the Divine Monad, the Spiritual Monad, the Human Monad, the Astral-Animal Monad. It is these four especially that you will find me frequently referring to in my books. There are others; but these four are what we may call the basic ones in our constitution. These are really very wonderful diagrams. They are not pictures. They are not photographs. They are symbols, emblems. They suggest verities. For instance, it would be ridiculous if we were to say that the Divine Monad is a triangle. That is not the idea. It means that there are latent in the Divine Triad three fundamental or elemental attributes which coalesce, unite; and, rising into this divine point, a laya center, pass into a higher hierarchy. Identically so with the lower triad. Now look: here we have a point in matter unfolding itself towards spirit — what is to it spirit — growth. And the diagram shows the converse verity of an entirely different character: that if a human being loses his grip on the god within him and falls, slowly he begins to shrink, contract: attribute, faculty, power, everything: into a point in matter, after which he is caught in a current of efflux, and drops to the pit.

Another thought: The Divine Monad has a range of action and

consciousness over the entire galaxy, which includes our own solar world; the Spiritual Monad over our solar system; the Human Monad throughout our planetary chain; and the Animal-Astral on our globe, producing the mere earth-man. Thus the path downwards is technically called the lunar path, the path of the moon. The path upwards is technically called the solar path.

And a final thought: When the great cosmic manvantara approaches its end, when the prâkritika pralaya approaches, when everything in the kingdom of our sun is on the verge of passing into the invisible, then — not only for man, but the diagram will stand for any being or entity — the lower triad is folded up, drawn within, disappears into, the lower duad. This in its turn is folded up, drawn within, disappears into, the upper triad. This in its turn, when the time for the same action comes, is folded up, drawn within, and disappears into, the Divine. That is the infolding, involution; and when the period for manifestation comes again, then the Divine emanates its surplus of life, building first its garment or child or vehicle. The same thing with the upper duad: the Spiritual Monad in its turn having at its heart the Divine, emanates, unfolds, unwraps, emanates the lower duad as its 'surplus of life'; and this, having at its heart the two upper, does precisely the same thing: sends out its surplus of life, in order to make its child, its own garment, its own clothing, the earth-man.

We see here in this other diagram (*op. cit.* p. 524) the same as the second, but unfolded, unrolled — the intermediate duad coalescing and forming the intermediate square topped by the Divine triad resting on the lower triad. And now I call your attention again, Companions, to what is really a very wonderful thought: the intermediate nature cannot manifest itself unless it be born from its Father in Heaven, the Divine Monad, and coincidently find for itself imbodiments growing up from the planes beneath and expanding to receive it. A strange paradox — meeting its own child born from itself, but itself growing upwards towards the Divine. Now as I said before, and I repeat it, if the man loses connexion with the upper and is attracted downwards, then the converse of what I said takes place, and he begins to shrink to a point and vanishes.

MORE ABOUT THE SURPLUS OF LIFE

THE surplus of life: This means that during the process of the un-rolling of the manifested universe — and adopting the Christian analogy, we may speak of the unrolling of a scroll so that the writing on the scroll may be read, the writing being the manifested universe — during the process of this unrolling, whatever succeeds the first step is the surplus of life. Thus supposing the scroll unrolls seven times to bring forth the seven principles of man's constitution or in the constitution of the Universe or anything else. Each step or each unrolling is an expression of one-seventh of the entire life. Thus when the scroll of life has been unrolled once, one turn, Âtman is manifested and six-sevenths remain unrolled, to wit: Buddhi, Manas, Kâma, Prâna, Linga-śarîra and Sthûla-śarîra. When the scroll is unrolled two turns, so to speak, then Âtman and Buddhi have ap-peared, and the surplus of life is of the other five, undeveloped.

Take the analogy of the building of the planetary chain or the solar chain: When Globe A first appears, the surplus of life which begins to unfold itself from Globe A when Globe A is vanished for that *Round,* contains Globes B, C, D, E, F, G, — all the other six Globes, if we follow the septenary idea. This excess of life or sur-plus of life remaining when Globe A has received its first outline of development or appearance, is all the other six Globes. Globe B, the surplus of life, then steps down one plane and then develops Globe B. The surplus of life then remains: Globes C, D, E, F, G, — five. The surplus of life rolls down from Globe B and works on Globe C to produce it in the fashion first outlined during the First Round. The surplus of life then leaves four Globes still unmani-fested, still to be brought forth, Globes D, E, F, G. And so the process goes around until when the last Globe, Globe G, is outlined or sketched, there is no more surplus of life, the surplus of life hav-ing consisted of all the six Globes, once that Globe A had appeared.

And so it is in the human constitution. The same rule holds with regard to reincarnation. During reimbodiment the first of the seven principles to appear and act is Âtman. Then comes the surplus of life, bringing forth Buddhi. The remaining surplus of life will bring forth Manas, and so it continues until man is builded: seven steps using up all the surplus of life until you have the complete man.

The surplus of life, therefore, at any stage means that the balance of the entire constitution or vital power has not yet unrolled into manifestation. When all the steps have been taken, all the surplus of life has been evolved.

Now with regard to the matter of the monads passing through the lower kingdoms: during the First Round of the Planetary Chain, all monads must begin at the top and make the round down to Globe D, the lowest, our Earth, and up again to Globe G; and every monad during that First Round, no matter what its stage, must pass through every one of the kingdoms of nature. Why? Because every single class of the monads is needed to help in the work of building up the skeleton of the future planetary chain, each monadic class contributing its own part: the highest classes contributing their highest part, the lower classes their lower, the lowest their lowest. Thus the gods in the First Round had to pass through every kingdom in order to bring forth, to initiate, to start going, the divine points in every kingdom. Then the second class of monads started to do the same thing — the spiritual. They had to go through from the beginning, in order that this next to the highest class should initiate, start, its work, in order to give all the kingdoms that second element, principle, faculty, power, stuff. And the third class of monads did the same in passing through every kingdom of every Globe, all of them from the gods to the mere life-atoms.

But beginning with the Round Two the process changed — and you can see why. It has been stated time after time. Because then the Architects had drawn the plan, the blue prints were there; the houses, the temples, the buildings, the structures were all started. Therefore beginning with the Second Round, each monadic class thereafter, when it had to pass through the lower kingdoms, did so swiftly because there was no attraction in them for the lower kingdoms. This is exactly the same today when the human ego reimbodies: in the body of an unborn infant it passes but a few months in the uterus. There is no attraction there, but it has to do this to get its body. But once it is born then it begins to grow. But the lower kingdoms have an immense attraction for the lower parts of nature. For instance they rush down to matter, they are attracted below. We call this the law of acceleration for the lower kingdoms — rushing downwards. But when they begin to rise the attraction is so strong towards matter that the lower kingdoms are pulled back. They have a terrific struggle. It is like an auto climbing a very steep hill, and then going slower and slower and slower, until it just gets to the top. I don't know whether they make autos like that today! On the contrary, on the downward arc the attraction of spirit for the spiritual monads is so tremendous that their dropping down becomes more and more difficult the further they go into matter and the process slows up. This we call the law of retardation, because their attraction is upwards. When these spiritual entities have reached Globe D, they have so little attraction here, that once the upward arc begins, as time goes on, they begin to walk, walk fast, and finally begin to run, until finally they are rushing up. It is a matter of attraction, and what we call the law of Acceleration and Retardation covers both.

THE FOUR BEASTS OF THE CHRISTIAN APOCALYPSE

The question was asked the other evening: Just what is the meaning of the four beasts — the man, the lion, the bull, and the eagle — whether in the Christian Book of the Apocalypse or as used by early and medieval Christian artists? The question is not hard to answer. In the first place the Christian Book of Revelation was written by a Qabbalist, a student of the early, not the late, Qabbâlâh.* It was edited or touched up at a later date by a later Christian editor. No one knows what he took out, what he kept in. But it was touched up and given a more Christian coloring.

Now if you will read that chapter four of this Christian book called Revelation or the Apocalypse, you will see that it mentions these four beasts "full of eyes within," who proclaimed truths and unsealed seals, and they are stated to have encompassed the throne of the Hierarch.

Whether through this Qabbalistic book, or by early tradition now forgotten, or in some other way at present unknown to scholars,

*It is to be noted in passing, however, that the term Qabbalist as used in this connexion and similarly often used by H. P. B., refers not so much specifically to the Jewish Qabbâlâh itself as to mystical and philosophical lines of thought having kinship with the inner meaning of the Jewish Qabbâlâh, but not specifically using the technical terms of the Jewish Qabbâlâh, although of course both the Jewish Qabbâlâh and these other systems of so-called Qabbalistic thought are in greater or less degree all based on archaic Theosophy. Thus when I say that the writer of the Christian Book of Revelation, called the Apocalypse, was a Qabbalist, as H. P. B. also calls him, I do not mean that necessarily he was a follower of the strictly Jewish Qabbâlâh, but rather that he employed similar, or parallel lines of expression and thinking, which by no means necessarily had a Jewish origin. In other words the Jewish Qabbâlâh was used as a sort of standard manner of expression and terminology, yet greatly modified by these other schools who refused to accept the Jewish Qabbâlâh as such, but nevertheless followed its type and even its lead in thought in more than one particular. The reason for this of course stands out clearly: that the Jewish Qabbâlâh as well as these other later systems and indeed all ancient mystical and religious Theosophical thought, were either original offsprings from the archaic Theosophy or descendants from earlier archaic Theosophic branches or stems thereof.

possibly through neo-Platonic sources, or neo-Pythagoric, the early Christians ascribed the same meaning to these four 'beasts' of the Apocalypse, and to the writers of the four Gospels, to wit, the man, the lion, the bull, and the eagle, that the Hindûs ascribed to what they called their four Loka-pâlas, or guardians of the worlds, the four Mahârâjas if you like; albeit in simple justice be it said, the Hindû conception even today is incomparably vaster and more spiritually mystical than is the strongly anthropomorphic picture presented in the Christian book of Revelation.   These four Mahârâjas, or four Loka-pâlas, were by exoteric explanation attributed severally and respectively to the North, the East, the South, and the West; and hence by those who did not understand the inner meaning, the Loka-pâlas were called the guardians of the four quarters. The public took the husk of the explanation and left the meat, the bread of the grain of truth.

Nature being spiritually generated and spiritually governed or controlled in so far as the divine law can have its way on this earth of matter, in the lower degrees of hierarchies where the conflict of wills rises daily and nightly in a hideous shriek to heaven — in so far as the divine law can control the affairs of men, it does so in four stages: the birth or the beginning technically called the North, the divine birth; adolescence or the sun-rise, technically called the East; full maturity of spirit and power in manhood, technically called the South, and governed by the Lord of Death, Yama; and the fourth, the West, the Land of Shades, the Land of the Great Passing — so called by Egyptian, and Persian, and Babylonian, and Hindû, and Greek, and American Red Skin, in fact all over the world.

The ancients also celebrated four holy seasons in the wheeling of the year: the winter solstice and the spring equinox, and the summer solstice and the autumnal equinox. First comes the Great Birth, the winter — the birth of the sun when he first begins to reassume his powers of light, when his journey to the South is over, and he begins to retrace his journey back to the North. It is called the great birth. And then comes Adolescence at the spring equinox, when the laws of life and light begin magically to work on the earth. Trees burgeon, flowers spring forth, Nature begins to sing with the new elements of life coursing through her veins. And in the summertime comes the Great Temptation or the great trial which a man always undergoes in maturity and full power of his strength, determining whether he goes up or down; for in the summertime likewise the fruits are ready for the harvest. Grain has been cut and stored. Nature is rich and powerful, overflowing with her exuberance of vitality. And then comes the fourth sacred season, that of the autumn equinox, when the sun, as it were, seems to take leave of the northern regions and pursues his journey southward. The days shorten, the nights lengthen, chills come upon the earth, the leaves fall, the sap retreats from twig, leaf, branch, and stock, into the roots. Rest comes and peace. And this was called the season of the Great Passing.

Thus, the ancients taught that the spiritual life which governs our world has its day of birth, has its day of adolescence, has its day of full material power and strength, has its day of passing, to begin anew the same cycle, let us hope on a somewhat higher plane. Year follows year and season follows season, the manvantaras come and the manvantaras go, the pralayas come and they go. But the divine endures forever.

These four Loka-pâlas or governors of the world are the four as it were karmic divinities, actually not so much single entities but hierarchies of divinities, each Loka-pâla representing a hierarchy, one inaugurating the manvantara or the beginning of manifested life in our world. When its duty is done, then the second hierarchy takes up the task which is passed on to it. The second Loka-pâla steps into the arena of action and carries the burden for a while, like the bearer of a torch in a torch-race running swiftly to the goal, and on reaching it, handing the torch on to the next runner to carry it on to the next goal.

Thus when the second Loka-pâla has finished his work, the torch, the duty, is passed to the third; from it to the fourth, and the cycle is ended! Karman has been expended, new karman has been written in the Book of Life by the Lipikas, the divine recorders. And the next manvantara, the next period of manifestation, will see the Loka-pâla springing anew into spiritual and intellectual activity.

This is a very abstract and truly divine conception, Companions, difficult for Occidentals who are not accustomed to this way of thinking. The early Christians were fascinated by it, which showed they had their modicum of the original god-wisdom of Theosophy. But they found it difficult to explain. And by and by, the inner meaning of the four beasts, the four Loka-pâla representations, symbols of the divinities: the soaring eagle, the thinking man, the bull of strength, and the lion of courage, symbols of qualities: the symbolic concept was forgotten, and the four animals were simply painted by early medieval artists, Christian artists, as symbols of the four Evangels who wrote the Gospels; because the early Church taught that in the four Gospels was the Word of God. The Word of God is the law of the universe, and in these four Gospels are the four laws of being, the four divine laws. So therefore these beasts later came merely to symbolize these transcripts, these gospels of early Christian Theosophical teaching; and the original, almost the divine meaning was lost.

MONKEYS, APES AND EARLY MAN

WE READ in the very ancient and most interesting Hindû epic poems such as the Râmâyana that the so-called apes — and please do not confuse the monkeys and the apes, they are not the same — were almost as intelligent as men, if not so completely. They talked, they formed armies, they fought in the great epic war of India according to the story, just like the men did. They had governments of their own, they evidently had systems of law. And so we are forced to look upon the apes of the great Hindû epic as something more than the apes as we know them today. And naturally if we are of an inquisitive bent of mind, we question ourselves why this should be so. Apes today do not do things like that.

The obvious answer is that the apes of that far past time during Atlantean days before the Fifth Root-Race had as yet come into its own, were not apes as we know them today, because today apes have no governments like the governments of men. They do not form themselves into armies and fight according to standard rules of combat. They do not interchange written intelligence as men do and then did. The only conclusion we can come to is that the apes chronicled in a great epic like the Indian Râmâyana were beings just short of being men.

Now please hearken to this carefully. It is known today by biological studies that the apes are born looking more human than they do when they die — of old age of course I am now speaking of. In other words that the apes seem to grow more animal-like, more bestial, as they advance out of ape infancy into ape adulthood. And by all the laws of scientific thought well known to specialists, this would indicate, as the theory of recapitulation shows us, that there was a time in the distant past when the apes in appearance were far more human-like than now they are. And that is exactly our teaching: that when the apes first came into being or into imbodiment, they associated so closely with their human half-parent, that like children they partook very largely by imitation, imitatively and otherwise, of what their human half-parent did and felt and thought. In other words, the apes then were far more human than now they are.

This shows a degeneration in intellectual, psychical respects, quite in accordance with our theosophical teachings, that all the animals are approaching extinction as the animal beings ascend the luminous arc upwards.

Actually therefore the apes recorded in the Hindû Râmâyana were just short of being men, so far as inner faculties are concerned, and they were of different colors, as stated in *The Secret Doctrine*. Just as in those days there were blue-faced men and red-faced men, so there were blue-faced apes and red-faced apes, and a few exist even today. This is the reason, and the real reason outside of other concurrent and contributory reasons, I believe, why the ancient Hindûs, and the Hindûs even to this day, look upon the present degenerated apes not so much with reverence as with a commingling of pity and psychical wonder. A certain religious awe covers the ape in the modern Hindû's mind, and he is therefore not so much respected as protected, as exactly was the case with the apes and monkeys indeed in Egypt and other ancient lands.

If you have read the Râmâyana, or parts of it, you will remember how the apes even sat at the council-tables with the humans of that time, with Râma and his generals and prominent men, and debated points of importance. We find the apes today not doing this and not having the capacity to do such things.

The apes, including all other animals, but I refer particularly to the apes, will be practically extinct towards the end of the Sixth Root-Race in our Fourth Round. During the Seventh Root-Race they will have vanished. Their egos however will not follow the destined course of the egos of the other animal families which will likewise proceed to extinction as our Fourth Round progresses on its upward arc. Why? Because there is still enough of the psychical human traits, attributes, or characteristics, in the apes of today to allow them when their bodies become extinct towards the end of the Sixth Root-Race in this Fourth Round to imbody these egos. All the apes then will imbody in the very lowest, the least intelligent and least evolved remnants of what are now the savage and barbarous tribes of mankind. The egos of those savage and barbarous tribes will leave their present imperfect bodies to the ape-egos, and themselves will imbody in human vehicles of somewhat higher capacity.

Now with regard to the origin of the apes: we have so often

spoken of this that I know you will all forgive me if I just repeat. The apes are the product of evolution of course, as human beings are. They were egos not yet having attained the human stage in their evolutionary progress but very close to it, who lacked physical vehicles to imbody in during the Third Root-Race of this Round, and during the very end of the Second Root-Race. So what we might call cosmic karman had to provide bodies for these egos. They needed their chance just as men had it. And this was provided by the karmic webs of destiny so closely knitting together all the kingdoms of earth, and particularly the adjunct kingdoms, kingdoms just beginning to enter into each other, interpenetrating as it were. These egos finally found bodies at the very end of the Second and the beginning of the Third Root-Race by the lowest human beings lacking the proper psychical instinct and lacking mind, conjoining themselves in the unions and in the types of union of that early day with imbodied animals just beneath their own human kingdom. The result of this union was the monkeys. And later on during the Fourth Root-Race other less progressed Atlanteans repeated the 'sin of the mindless,' in the words of the ancient scripture, with the descendants of these monkeys so that the apes, as rather neatly expressed, have as it were two drops of human blood in them. The first drop of blood from that first intermingling or miscegenation, and the second drop of blood from the act of the least progressed Atlanteans mingling with these only slightly human creatures. The fruit of these unions was the apes. The first apes resulting from these unions were far closer to man as man then was, not as man now is, than the apes of today would be could they be transported as now they are to that then period. I hope I make my meaning clear. The result of this was that the offspring of these semi-human, semi-animal unions mingled familiarly with the human race. They were looked upon askance by the higher or more evolved humans of the time but tolerated, and tolerated because they had glimmerings of our active minds. They were practically thinking entities of a low type, very imitative as all apes and monkeys even today are. Of course they imitated whatever they saw their Atlantean relations do. They spoke, they had languages of their own, peculiar languages, not the hisses and calls and bellows and snarls of beasts today, but a distinct language or group of languages of their own.

Now then, what happened? The most human of these apes died out, partly because the Atlanteans, realizing the sin of their own less evolved men, made vigorous war upon them, wars of extermination; and also because the milieu, the surroundings, were not conducive to the continuance of this partly-human partly-animal race. Only the least progressed of the apes were allowed to live by the Atlanteans; and the apes today are the descendants of those who were allowed to continue to live. The forefathers of the present day apes were the least progressed apes of that far past time. The psychic bars or barriers which today so greatly render any commingling of different kingdoms so horrible to human thought, in those days did not exist, and the unions were almost invariably followed by offspring.

Now early mankind passed through many stages, rûpa-stages, stages of form — and I am now speaking specifically of human bodies, not of human egos. Thus, for instance, the first race had no form at all like our present forms. H. P. B. somewhere rather graphically calls the form of the First Root-Race that of pudding bags, globular, or egg-shaped spheres of ethereal stuff. You cannot call it flesh because flesh had not yet come into being. But astral pudding bags, astral eggs. As time passed and the First Race became the Second Race, the old waters of the first mingling with the new waters of the second, the pudding bag shape vanished, and many and curious were the karmic bodies that the human race in that extremely changing and changeful time had. For instance, towards the end of the Second Race, men had faces like dogs or as we would say like dogs today, dog-faced men. Some had faces like fish's heads, some had four arms and four feet. As you know they then had only one eye. Later on the two frontal eyes came into use, and the third eye remained functioning for a long time. Then man had three eyes. Finally the first eye, which we wrongly call the third eye, sank into the skull, was covered by bone and hair and became what is now called the pineal gland, and we now remain with two eyes. So thus man had one eye, and after a while three eyes, and now he has two eyes.

Now why did the human bodies or human rûpas during the Second and very earliest Third Root-Race assume these particular and peculiar forms? Because they were molded on models in the astral light which the human races followed because the human race or human stock or human kingdom or human life-wave (choose any word you like), had those shapes during Rounds Second and Third. It was a case once more of recapitulation, just as the embryo today in the human womb recapitulates in a short period of nine months what the human race has gone through during ages in the far distant past. So did the early races of this Round recapitulate what the human kingdom went through during the early Rounds.

What will happen to the monads or egos of the apes or animals when they shall have died out as bodies during this Fourth Round and certainly all before the end of the Seventh Root-Race? The egos in the Fifth Round will be assorted according to their karmic destiny. The apes will then take on the form of the lowest human beings in the Fifth Round as indeed they will begin to do during the Seventh Root-Race in this Fourth Round; the egos of the entire animal kingdom during the Fifth Round will during the descending arc for a while find bodies of low type, but will gradually die out before the ascending arc during the Fifth Round has advanced far along its course. The reason for this is that the animal monads, the monads of the beings of the animal kingdom, have not yet evolved the mânasic qualities which will enable them to ascend the ascending arc during the mânasic or Fifth Round.

THE CHILD MIRRORS THE RACE

THERE are literally innumerable evidences already known to scientific men of at least a large part of the past history of mankind; and as the greater part of mankind is his spirit and his mind, I include these also. But I refer now especially to the scientific evidences that man physically has passed in ages bygone through phases of his aeons-long evolutionary pilgrimage which have left their imprint upon him. And there are, as a matter of fact, a great many scientific facts which are not known.

I will refer here to one thing only, to a fact which used to have more scientific weight than it has today merely because the more modern scientific ideas are not so favorable to this fact; but I believe the scientists of the future will come back to the former ideas. It is called in embryology the theory of Recapitulation: that the human unborn child, the embryo, passes through in the small every phase of evolutionary development that the human race as a race has passed through in bygone times. Thus, is a child born today in full possession of mind, a thinking, reasoning entity? You all know the child is not. In the child's intra-uterine life we know it passes briefly through many evolutionary physical phases that the race as a whole passed through in bygone times; but it is not for years after the child is physically born that it begins to think, I mean to think self-consciously, to meditate thoughts of grandeur, to make decisions of great worth and value. These come with the growing lad advancing into manhood, for with manhood the greater powers of mind and intellect grow progressively, and also the spiritual and ethical faculties in man.

Now then, you have heard the phrase, "the descent of mind into the early Third Root-Race of mankind." It was just that. Up to that time the race had developed bodies formed by evolution to meet the needs of their as yet unintellectual state, but you must not suppose that these unintellectual early men were absolutely without consciousness. Not at all. No more so than an unthinking child is up to say five or six or seven years. Mind at that age is, in fact, already beginning to show itself; and the showing advances progressively as the child grows into boyhood, and from boyhood into manhood, and from manhood into mature years. Now the early races were just like that, like little children.

They had instinct, they had flashes of intuition, they had feeling, they had consciousness, the vague diffuse consciousness of the human child today, but they were not thinkers. The child today does not sit down at a desk and write a noble essay or plan out a campaign of thought which will help and enlighten mankind. Why? The mind has not yet fully expressed itself through the as yet infantile brain. The brain needs further hardening, forming, to carry the current from the mind within-above the man.

The early Third Root-Race were just like children in that respect. They had consciousness. They had flashes of intuition; they had instinct highly developed. But the self-conscious thinking mind had not yet come to them. Then there happened one of the most marvelous events in all evolutionary history. We call it the "descent of the Mânasaputras," the Sons of Mind, which took place not over night as it were, nor in an instant, nor through even a hundred thousand or several hundred thousand years. But it was a progressive process, exactly as on a small scale, the child does not wake up some morning and suddenly find itself in the possession of a mature mind. It is a matter of growth. Thus did the Mânasaputras gradually over-enlighten or overshadow the minds of the nascent mankind, permeating these brains, even their nervous systems, with its divine fire of thought, until finally men thought, they were awakened. The mind had come into function. This was done by these Mânasaputras, our own intellectual selves so to speak, incarnating through the ages for several hundred thousand years; and when it was ended, from the merely instinctual conscious but non-intellectual and as yet non-self-conscious early man, you have a race which thought, which could contemplate divinity; and this was possible because the link with the divine had been made. Mind was awakened.

And not only this: into a number of these prepared human beings, the most highly developed mankind of the time, there incarnated certain spiritual-intellectual entities, beings, highly evolved, who became the teachers and the guides of the then newly awakened mankind, who taught them, who showed them the ways of civilization, the mysteries, the secrets of science, the verities of philosophy. These were the days of the divine authority of our far past forefathers. It was they who founded the Mystery-Schools when they first began on this earth, and who lived and taught mankind, and were, as said, their guides, their teachers, their protectors, their instructors. And that same body, or their descendants if you wish, their successors, still remain on earth today as mankind's guides, illuminators, initiators, teachers, elder brothers, friends.

Thus does the child recapitulate in its own growth from infancy to manhood what the race has attained today. It is natural, it must be, because there is but one fundamental law in the universe, one fundamental course of action, which with its universally wide sweep touches all and everything with dynamic power. Thus we find today a key to understand those ancient and earliest thinking men: how they came to be born, how it came that the mind suddenly awaked so that they could contemplate the universe and understand it instead of being like children, or like the higher animals, instinctual, intuitionally conscious, but not self-conscious. It is a marvelous thing that happens to the little child: it grows from instinct and intuition to receive the entrance into itself, the infilling, of the inspiration from the inner god. The waiting brain, the nervous system, the body, are infilled and enlightened. Mysteries and marvels take place around us all the time!

Now, while it is very marvelous, very wonderful indeed, and fills us with great reverence for what is in the universe, to look back into the past along the annals of the race, and see the stages that our feet have trodden, yet do not forget the future. We are but at the middle point of our evolution on this earth. We must come back to earth again and again and again to repeat and to learn ever more and more perfectly what we have already known, and to gain new wisdom. What, then, does the future hold? I will tell you. As our minds were awakened in the past by the mânasaputric gods — for they are gods to men — so our minds themselves in the future shall be awakened by angels of the spirit. Even our minds which raise us from our unconsciousness to self-consciousness, and have brought us to the stage where we are now, so that we may contemplate the universe and sense divinity behind it, think grand and noble thoughts which raise our lives towards the gods — even our minds themselves need a higher inspiration, for our very minds can mislead us, lead us off the Path.

So just as in the past there took place the incarnation of the Mânasaputras, the Sons of Mind, who gave us mind — so in the future, beginning now — it began already a million years back or more, and progressing with ever enlarging measure into the future — there will imbody itself within us, in our minds and fill us with its own glory, the heavenly light from the god within each one of us. Thereafter our evolution will be safe and assured, with that celestial guidance enlightening our hearts and firing our brains. No more will our feet stumble on the path, for we shall enlighten our pathway as we march upwards and onwards, ever upwards, ever onwards, to heights at present inconceivable even to our minds. That is what lies before us. When we raise our inner eye, our inner face towards the god within us, there comes an eternal radiance, not from anything outside, but from the god within-above each one of us. Call it a Christ, the immanent Christ, call it the inner Buddha, call it by what name you will. The thing is to come to realize its holy presence. Then a man is indeed blessed.

OPENING LINES OF GENESIS

I HAVE listened with deep interest to the remarks on the Jewish Christian Bible made this evening. Let me say first that I have been astonished at the remarkable way in which much light has been thrown upon some of the meanings of the Hebrew Scripture called 'The Book of the Beginnings.'

It is true that the original word translated as 'God' in the English version, used in the opening verses of the *Book of Genesis,* is *'Elohîm.* It is a Hebrew plural meaning 'gods,' 'divine beings.' The monotheistic Hebrews, and the monotheistic Christians who took over the scriptures, in other words the Hebrew Bible, of the Jews, say that this Hebrew plural is a 'plural of majesty,' used in somewhat the same sense in which crowned heads sometimes will speak of themselves: 'We, by the Grace of God,' so-and-so — John, Peter, James, William, or what not. But there is no proof whatsoever in the writings themselves that this word *'Elohîm* is merely a 'plural of majesty.' Grammatically speaking it is a distinct, clear, Hebrew plural.

In a moment or two I shall recite to you a few verses, at least the first two verses, of the original Hebrew, and will then tell you a little something about it; but before doing so, I want to call your attention to one or two interesting facts. You speak of the Hebrew Bible as the Old Testament or Old Covenant. Do you realize that this last phrase is an original Jewish expression, simply meaning that certain writings, some of them religious, some of them quasi-historic, some of them poetic, which were the property of a small Semitic people, were supposed to evidence an ancient covenant made between this people and their tribal deity? Other peoples in the world have similar writings, similar scriptures, which are just as sacred and true to these other peoples, just as highly cherished, and considered by these other peoples of as great worth to themselves, as these particular writings were to the Hebrews. In other words, the Hebrew writings are not the only sacred scriptures of the world cherished by the people among whom they arose.

In the second place, the only scripture of the Hebrew Old Testament which, from our Theosophical standpoint, is truly occult, esoteric, is the first book, as these books now stand in their printed order — 'the Book of the Beginnings'; and indeed, only a few chapters in the beginning of this first book, are fully esoteric. This does not mean that some of the other books have no mystical meaning, such as the *Book of Job*. That exclusive idea is not what I mean. The *Psalms* of David, so called, for instance, were written by a poet-heart; and every poet-heart is a seer more or less. But the true universal wisdom of the 'Oriental Qabbâlâh' is found most fully only in the first few chapters of the *Book of Genesis*.

Now, the phrase 'Oriental Qabbâlâh' means the 'Oriental Tradition,' because this word 'Qabbâlâh' is a noun derived from the Hebrew verbal root *qâbal,* which means 'to receive,' 'to take,' 'to hand down.' Thus the 'Oriental Qabbâlâh' means the universal 'Oriental Tradition'; and the Hebrew Qabbâlâh is the Hebrew form of this body of the Oriental doctrine often called Traditionary Wisdom, handed down from generation to generation of human Seers. In other words, the Jewish Qabbâlâh is the Theosophy of the Jews; and it is one rather restricted phase, or rather one minor national representation, of the Universal Qabbâlâh or universal Tradition of the World.

Here is the Hebrew as the original Hebrew text has been in modern times divided into words, and so printed:

(1) *Berê'shîth bârâ' 'Elohîm 'êth hash-shâmayim we-'êth hâ-'ârets.*
(2) *We-hâ-'ârets hâyethâh thohû wâ-bohû we-hhoshech 'al-pnêi thehôm we-rûahh 'Elohîm merahhepheth 'al pnêi ham-mâyim.*

In the very first word you are confronted with a difficulty: How is this word to be divided? Let me explain what I mean. In writing ancient Hebrew the letters of the words followed each other without break, precisely as if you were to take a paragraph in a modern newspaper, remove all the spaces or divisions between the words, remove all the marks of punctuation, and thus have the letters run along in a solid line or file, one after the other.

Furthermore — and this is very important — there are no characters for vowels in the Hebrew alphabet, so in order to make our illustration clear and exact, all the vowels in the modern newspaper paragraph would have to be removed, and only the consonants following each other in a solid, steady file would remain. This is the picture of how ancient Hebrew was written.

Obviously then, having this series of solid lines before you, you can divide, perhaps successfully, a single such line into different and differing words; and these first two words in the Hebrew that I have quoted for you, to wit: *berê'shîthbârâ'*, can be divided differently from the manner commonly used, for instance: *Berê'sh yithbârê'*, which translated, gives an entirely different meaning.

The common division: *Berê'shîth bârâ' 'Elohîm* means: "In the beginning 'Elohîm carved (or cut or shaped)" — the two heavens and the earth. The other division of the Hebrew letters: *Berê'sh yithbârê'*, changes the meaning entirely. *Rê'sh* or *ro'sh* means head, wisdom, knowledge, the higher part, the first in a series; and the word *yithbârê'* is a reflexive form of the verb *bârâ'*, thus signifying 'making itself' or 'making themselves' — to be the two heavens and the earth. In other words, the meaning with the two first words thus divided is that the gods or cosmic spirits, through wisdom, through knowledge, through being the chief or first formative forces, made themselves to become the heavens and the material sphere.

'Heavens' — *shâmayim* — dual, plural, not one, a series; *'erets* or *'ârets* — the 'world,' translated 'earth' which Christians think is this little earth of ours, and later extended to the universe when they learned that the stars were no longer little points of light caught up there, but dazzling glorious suns, many of them larger than ours. *'Ârets* means the body-sphere, the material sphere.

You see what an utterly different interpretation can be gained by dividing the file or row of Hebrew letters in this second way.

Furthermore, the English translation called the Authorized Version, while it is dear to English people on account of the religious memories of childhood, and because also perhaps the English language of King James's day seems to Englishmen of today more virile than the current English of our own era, yet lacks entirely the proper spirit of the mystical Hebrew original; and the very fact that Englishmen love their King James's version so much distracts their attention away from the original mystical sense of the Hebrew scripture. Go then to the original tongue and ask those who really know just what the essential meaning of the Hebrew is.

When I hear some of these dear good people who talk so much about 'numerology,' as they imagine it to exist in the Hebrew scriptures, and who think that by counting the number of words in the

English translation and the number of chapters in one of the scriptures, or the number of phrases in a chapter, or the number of words
in a phrase, they can arrive at solutions of wonderful mysteries or
discover the secret of occult truths, I always feel impelled and compelled to say that they forget that they are using a translation, and
a very imperfect translation at that, of what is something quite different from their supposition in the original tongue: for there were
no chapters, and no verses, and no marks of punctuation such as
commas, periods, semi-colons, or capital letters — in the body of
the original Hebrew — naught but solid lines or files of letters cross-
ing the pages of the original books.

Now, which translation do you prefer, the usual and I may say
mistaken version of the English translation: "In the beginning God
made the heaven and the earth," or the other translation equally
authorized by the original Hebrew, and which has the further advantage of being on all fours with the Universal Tradition, to wit:
"In wisdom (or in multitude, in company, as a host) the gods carved
(or shaped, or formed)" out of already pre-existent material (for
the original Hebrew verbal root *bârâ'* means 'to cut,' 'to carve,' not
'to create') "the heavens and the material sphere"; which, when
understood, means the following: "In the beginning of the Manvantara the gods became the spiritual realms and the material."

The meaning, therefore, very briefly given, of the Hebrew account of Creation so-called is rather an account of evolving forth
from seeds, cosmic seeds, pre-existent in space, by the power of the
indwelling spiritual fires. You have a strict analogy of that in the
way a human being is born from a microscopic human seed, a cell,
and grows into a six-foot man by powers derived from within itself.

That is the way worlds came into being. I wonder why so many
have never realized what must have been before, according to their
theory, God Almighty created the universe, the world? God is not
a carpenter, or, as the Greeks put it, a Demiurge, a Builder. Divinity is the indwelling spirit of fire and love and intelligence and consciousness — the fountain of everything: atom and man, sun and
beast, flower and stone. All can be traced back to the divine source,
to their growth from within.

Thus it was that according to the Hebrew account of Creation,
the gods, the spiritual beings, the children of the divine, were em-

bryo-gods, not yet grown up, baby-gods as it were, unevolved; but the gods of our world, or our galaxy for instance, were the guiding, inspiriting fire of life and intelligence that brought our galaxy into being, our earth into being. There is the whole story, and the Hebrew does not say one word about an extra-cosmic god creating the world. This word, mistranslated 'god' in the Hebrew, let me emphasize, is plural: *'elohîm,* which means gods, divine beings, spiritual beings, creatures of love and flaming thought, children of the Incomprehensible Divine, which is the fountain of the universe out of which they come, and, after their evolutionary course is run, into the immeasurable deeps of which they again sink into unutterable peace, later to reissue again and to become through evolving aeons first men, then gods, and then super-gods, to be followed by another period of divine rest, after which a new issuing forth into cosmic activity; but ever growing endlessly.

In the two or three first chapters of 'the Book of the Beginnings,' commonly spoken of in European countries as the *Book of Genesis* which is a Greek word meaning Beginning or Becoming, you will find the Ancient Wisdom of the human race. All the rest of the Bible, all the other parts of the Hebrew Old Testament, are simply local, national, traditional, records, without much or any esoteric meaning whatsoever.

The Christian New Testament, which is the second part of the Christian Bible, read literally, with its thirty-six thousand and some odd hundreds of mistranslations from the Greek original, as existing in the King James's or Authorized Version, contains no more of the ancient and esoteric wisdom than do the books of the Old Testament. What it does contain of the Ancient Wisdom-Religion of Mankind is the story, when esoterically understood, of a cycle of initiation, with the great Syrian Initiate, Jesus, as the central type-figure.

REMNANTS OF NEOLITHIC AND PALEOLITHIC AGES

I WAS asked if I could say a few words which might perhaps, this being rather a specialized topic, help those who are studying archeology and ethnology and that sort of thing. The question was with regard to Paleolithic and Neolithic races, and why the evidences of ancient civilizations which we Theosophists claim were contemporaneous with these two groups, all degenerate men, are not found on earth. In other words, we have constantly growing evidences of the existence of earlier — science calls it late, and degenerate as we call it — races of men who, because of artifacts of theirs which we are now disinterring, are classed as Paleolithic or old stone men, and Neolithic or new stone men. And the question is: Do Theosophists say that great civilizations existed contemporaneous with these ancient and degenerate individuals? Why is it that no remains of these great civilizations exist on earth? But this is not a proper question, because it states a thing that is not true. There are almost innumerable remnants or relics of these great civilizations of the past remaining on earth. The trouble is that our modern scientists are so hag-ridden with theories which they are going to support at any cost, that everything which is truly ancient, they bring up as far as they can to the present, and make it relatively recent. There is where the difficulty is, and that is what our Theosophists have to face. It is not that the scientists mean to do anything dishonest. They think it is justifiable because they do not believe in these ancient races, and if any scientist today said there were grand civilizations a million years ago, say five million years ago, why he would be tarred and feathered, scientifically speaking; he would be run out of the country in other words. He would lose caste, his name would be a hissing and a by-word. Scientific orthodoxy. That is plain truth.

What are some of these ancient remnants of civilization? When you consider that the neolithic and paleolithic remnants are quite recent, geologically speaking — a few paltry tens of thousands of years are nothing in the history of the human race alone: When you think of that and you consider the magnificent evolutionary development that the human has attained even now, his marvelous brain, the wonder of his body, as I have shown in my *Man in Evolution*, we must place the origin of man tens of hundreds of millions of years in the past. But you see, the scientists won't acknowledge that. They cannot acknowledge it because they are hag-ridden with the ideas of civilization and the theories which they must support.

Now then, what are some of these great remnants that remain? You are not children. You have read your history books and your books on science. You have viewed the pyramids of Egypt. Take one alone, the great Pyramid of Cheops, built in such fashion that modern scientists themselves exclaim their wonder, and speculate whether with all the modern improvements and refinements of tools and machinery and genius, they could equal the work today; or imbody astronomical knowledge so perfectly that the entrance gallery, as has now been known for many years, points or would point when the circling stars around the north pole come to it, on Stella Polaris, our own North Pole Star. No need to go into that. You know all these things.

I don't know what the great geological pronouncements are about the great pyramids, but they are something ridiculous, a few thousand years; but our teaching is that the Great Pyramid was built at least seventy-five thousand years ago, and I am of opinion it was twice that long time, 150 thousand years ago. But I believe H. P. B. has stated somewhere that the Theosophical scientist who knows what he is doing could prove at least three full circlings of the precessional cycle, each one nearly 26,000 years long. You know what in astronomy the precession of the equinoxes is. A full cycle takes 25,920 years, and three full precessional cycles, says H. P. B., have passed while the pyramids have stood on the bank of the Nile or close to it; and I believe it is twice that long.

How about the pyramid of Sakhara? How about the Denderah Zodiac? How could it have been made by the Egyptians only a few thousand years ago, with the stars around our Polar star more or less as they are now, and yet show an entirely different arrangement of the Zodiac as well as of the Polar stars? I forget just what age has been assigned to it, but it was something like two or three precessional cycles. These ancient peoples were so accurate, and in the view of modern scientists so superstitiously meticulous to get the Zodiac of

the heavens where the gods abide perfect in their drawings, that
surely it is ridiculous to think they would have been deliberately
irreligious in their view and have drawn a small zodiac untrue to
nature? Answer your own question. Your answer is found on the
monuments over the face of the earth.

How about those wonderful platforms out in the Pacific built
with uncemented stone which have stood for ages, so old that they
are not merely weather-beaten but weather-worn; and in the mild
climate of the Pacific Isles you can understand that stones would
last longer than they would in the northern countries where frost
and hot sun and rain and wind and beating sand will wear down
rocks easily. How many thousands of years have those platforms
on Easter Island stood, mute witnesses of a banished knowledge of
some kind? Ask the scientists what they are. They do not know.
Probably built by some ancestors in the Pacific Islands. Why? Did
they have a grand civilization when they were younger according to
the modern evolutionary theory than they have now when they do
not build such magnificent platforms? It is like asking a child to
put up a house. Why, there are thousands of instances like that.
Look at Stonehenge in England. Look how they tried to belittle the
age of that and bring it up to our age, as close as they could. Why?
Because they have any proof? Absolutely none. They are guessing.
But according to modern scientific evolutionary theory it is impossible for there to have been civilized men more than one hundred
thousand or two or three hundred thousand years ago at the very
utmost. That is the scientific orthodoxy, and everything has to fit
in to that bed of Procrustes. Do not think I am anti-scientific. I
am not. I have spent too many years of my life in study and
reverence of true science for the spirit of research and discovery
and open-mindedness that has given us the knowledge of the science
we have today. I am not talking of science but the prejudices of
scientists, among scientific men; and it is there.

But take Stonehenge. I myself think, I have no proof, it is just
my own belief and conviction from study in my younger days when
I had more time to do these things, but I believe that Stonehenge
which is built of massive stones some not to be found in Britain —
get that fact in your heads! — has an age not less than the pyramids,
maybe a little younger, for the pyramids were built by what Plato

called the Atlanteans when the Isle of Poseidonis, a remnant of the Atlantean main continental massif, was sunk in a terrific earthquake and tidal wave between twelve and thirteen thousand years ago. It was an island about the size of Ireland today. Before Poseidonis sank, immigrants left this island in the Atlantic ocean and settled on what then was newly forming Egypt. How long ago was this? You can judge if you wish geologically by the rates of deposition of the Nile mud. Certainly tens and tens of thousands of years old.

Anyone who knows of the existence, and all of you do, of these great monuments of the past, will understand what I mean when I say that there are almost innumerable evidences for the existence of marvelous archaic civilizations antedating by thousands of years the strata in which are found the remnants and the artifacts of the neolithic and paleolithic peoples, if that is the right word. Listen to this, friends. Long before Greece and Crete were, long before Persia, Media, Babylonia, Assyria were dreamed of, in what are now the deserts of Persia, Turkestan, parts of Arabia and parts of Northern Baluchistan, all that wonderful land as it used to be — now mostly howling wastes and mounds swept by hurricanes and terrific winds, arid in the extreme hills — was green and fertile, covered with flourishing cities where civilization was reaching a peak such as we have as yet scarcely attained, where the arts and sciences and the crafts flourished. It was from this region that Babylonia and Assyria and Persia and Media and what was known of Asia Minor were born, settled by Atlanteans in the early times, or the late Asia-Atlanteans. These regions flourished at a time on the earth when geologic conditions even were different. So long ago was this fertility in the lands I have just spoken of, that what is now the Black Sea was an immense inland sea or inland ocean connecting in the north across Russia and Siberia with what is now the Arctic Ocean, and filled with islands. All this is now changed. Land has risen. Land has sunk. All is now but a memory, a legend, mounds, desolation, waste. But it gave birth to its child; it gave birth to the civilization of Assyria and Persia and part of Greece and Media and gave the populations to our own European ancestors. Thence have come the forefathers of the Scandinavians, of the Teutons, of the Goths, and covered what was then the wilderness of Europe, yes and Siberia, and these ancient civilizations that I speak of extended into what is even now Tibet, and in that high plateau where terrific gales sweep also over barren wastes, legend tells of far past times when our fathers built wonderful temples here, when the gods confabulated with men, when there were sweet lakes of fresh water and green was everywhere. Sometimes the voice of the soul of a people is more true than the speculations and guess-work of the so-called historians.

THE ORIGIN OF GOOD AND EVIL

THE orthodox Jewish Rabbis explained the origin of evil in the world as having been the creative act of Jehovah, and they pointed to their famous old Prophet, Isaiah, Chapter 45, Verse vii:

"I form the light, and create darkness: I make peace, and create evil: I the LORD do all these things."

So the Jewish Rabbis said that the origin of evil is a dispensation of God. Adonai, the Lord, created it.

Now the Theosophist knows how to interpret this in the sense in which the Prophet Isaiah, or he who wrote in the name of the Prophet Isaiah, intended it to be interpreted. But if you accept that statement with its surface meaning, do you realize what the logical impasse is that you are driven into? Evil is in the world because it was created by the Lord. Therefore evil is a divine dispensation, and right, and if evil is in my heart, it has been created by the Lord, for "I, the Lord, do all these things." If the Jewish Holy Book is divinely inspired, word for word, you see what you are led into. Furthermore, the Christians were far too wise and wary even in the early days to accept the surface meaning of this phrase in Isaiah.

Some weeks ago, in looking up this reference from Isaiah in the Hebrew Bible, looking up the original Hebrew, I found there that the authorized English version beclouds the force and strength of the old Hebrew, in which the main verb of divine action is the present participle throughout. So with these words; they read: I am forming Light and I am creating darkness, now in the present. I am making peace and I am creating evil. I, Jehovah, am doing these things now. — The idea being not that good and evil were once and forever created in some past time, but that it is a continuous process. The meaning is obvious, as being a mystical statement intended to be interpreted as the slow evolutionary flowing forth from the bosom of the Divine of the hosts of evolving creatures, entities, things, driven by past karmic impulses; so that whatever IS is in continuous production, and evolution: continuous adventures from the imperfect to the more perfect, from the worse towards the best, the best that can be achieved. It does not mean that an extra-cosmic god once and forever created good and evil, and set the world to spinning, and that human beings are but helpless entities in it, chained by an inscrutable divine Fate.

Now here is a very difficult Theosophical doctrine, and yet it helps to complete the picture, however vaguely it must be stated. It should be obvious, a deduction of the simplest kind, that the great teachings of the various religions and philosophies of the world, of the hierarchies of dhyân-chohanic or devic or angelic beings, must be based on something, these beings being partly good and partly what men call evil, in other words more perfect and less perfect; and there is no escape from that deduction. If you once get the picture of these armies of evolving beings issuing as it were from the heart of divinity after their long pralayic sleep, to begin a new evolutionary period of awakening in a new world-period, you see that there must be amongst them beings in all grades of evolution from what to us is simply divine, down to the least evolved life-center.

Furthermore, as nature divides herself into hierarchies or family groups, there must be at the head of each such hierarchy an individual divinity who is as it were the hierarch thereof, like the president of a republic, the king of his kingdom. Therefore, there must be in Universal Nature, spiritual, very spiritual, and divine beings, in all-various grades of evolutionary states. In other words we are surrounded by a "cloud of witnesses," to use the words of Paul, and these are divine, spiritual, and material and sub-material beings. So, they have been called angels or archangels or dhyân-chohans or devas, or what not. The name matters not. The main thing to remember is that they exist, and it is therefore obvious that if our minds and hearts are turned in the direction of the Sons of Light, or contrariwise towards the left-hand path, in the direction of the Children of the Dark — not demons, not devils, simply imperfectly evolved entities — we can come into touch with these former, or with the latter; from the former receiving immense inspiration and help; from the latter feeling the attraction to 'hell.' That is the reason why some of the old religions, profound as they were, worshiped angels, archangels, and what-not, as the early Christians did. And if worship means 'worthship,' not adoration which means petitionary prayer, then it is an ennobling thing to do: 'worthshiping,' revering, the Children of Light, our predecessors on the upward Path.

WHAT ARE COSMIC RAYS?

I WOULD like to say a few words on the Cosmic Rays. What are they? Where do they come from, where do they go, what is their function? Do you know, modern science today, and daily more and more so, is using the word 'radiation,' or 'radiations' with virtually the same significance and purport, with virtually the same attempt to describe facts, that the ancient theologians of pre-Christian days in Greece and Rome, Egypt, Persia and Babylon, and equivalently in other parts of the earth made in using the word 'emanation,' 'emanations.' As light radiates or flows forth from a center of energy, a sun, or an electric globe, as it radiates forth, we can replace this word 'radiates' with 'emanates.' Out of a central core flows forth light, call it radiation, call it emanation, it is the same. When you understand something of what the finest thinkers of modern science mean to say when they use the term 'radiation,' when you understand something of what they have in mind and attempt to express by that word, you will begin to understand what the ancient theologians of pre-Christian times meant when they used the word 'emanation,' flowing forth.

Thus a human being, as an instance, radiates or emanates vitality. Constantly radiating, it flows forth from him, and flowing forth from him shows that it is a thing, and this thing is a fluid. Light is a fluid, all these various kinds of rays are fluidic in character; but being fluidic in character this merely means that they are aggregates or concretions of entities, emanated entities, call them monads, call them life-atoms if you will.

Before I go on farther, let me try to illustrate what I think we should understand by the modern scientific effort to designate something which is at one and the same time a wave and a particle. If you follow in thought a bullet from a rifle you will realize that it is at once a particle so to speak, and at the same time accompanied with waves, these waves being the phenomena of its passage through the air. Now imagine a life-atom discharged from an entity. It passes with the speed of light, some atoms with a speed far exceeding that of light, and obviously their passage through substance is accompanied with intense disturbance along the track that the particle follows. Follow my thought? Thus the wave and the particle must accompany each other. The particle produces the wave; without the particle the wave would not be.

Now these Cosmic Rays we can call life-atoms if we wish. In fact, they are that, the life-atoms of the Universe but on a low, because a physical and even inferior to physical, plane in the hierarchical sense. This is shown by their intensely rapid vibration.

And again: Where do they come from — these life-atoms of space that are streaming all through interstellar space, and, in so far as our own universe is concerned, throughout our solar universe — streaming through it? Mainly from the active, superlatively active, stomachs of the various suns, pouring forth from the suns of Space in inconceivable floods, or in inconceivable numbers. They make their peregrinations hither and yon as life-atoms of a type or kind, always coming back ultimately, sometime, someway, somewhere, to their father-substance; and meanwhile passing through all other entities as they peregrinate (transmigrate was the old word), wander hither and yon, back and forth.

Indeed, it is thus that the suns feed themselves. Our own sun feeds its own store of vitality from these floods of life-atoms reaching it from outer space, drawn into its own stomach and expelled again through the sun-spots. Why, you remember that even in *The Secret Doctrine*, H. P. B. openly there speaks of the fact, quoting one of the old records, that the sun was feeding on the refuse of space. Do you remember? As a matter of fact, our own bodies do that — physical body, astral body, mental body, interior sheath of consciousness — they all do just the same thing. They emanate floods of life-atoms, radiate them away and suck in, attract in, those of others. This is just what the sun does; so that these cosmic atoms, or cosmic rays — which are merely names which the scientists have given to them because they do not understand them very well yet, and they seem to be like rays, and they seem to be like particles, but are simply the life-atoms that have flowed forth from the suns of space, and happen to reach us, passing through us — sometime they will leave us and go elsewhere. Just in the same way our globe Earth is being fed and its vitality kept up, its energy sustained, electrical, psychic, physical, and what not, from what it sucks in from outer space, and it in turn emanates forth its own light and fluids. We call them Cosmic Rays, life-atoms if you wish; and thus we see a cosmic give and take, give and take.

But these are not the only life-atoms that there are. There are many, many families of life-atoms that no physical scientific instrument will ever succeed in perceiving, or even apperceiving. They are above, outside, our plane entirely; as for instance, there are purely astral life-atoms, mental life-atoms, spiritual, and divine. But these Cosmic Rays that scientists are now just beginning to gain some knowledge of are cosmic life-atoms of a low, that is of a type even inferior to the physical in the hierarchical sense; very 'hard'; 'hard rays' they call them; and were they to strike in condensed form — as the X-rays do — they would be very dangerous.

Now when I say that our sun (as well as other suns), feeds itself on the refuse and 'sweat' of space, on these flowing streams of life-atoms, oceans of them — for space is filled, incomprehensibly full with them, it is an ocean of life — I don't mean that the sun feeds on them to the exclusion of other life-atoms. The sun attracts to itself life-atoms on all planes, some far higher than the physical.

But I want to add this. Call it an interesting theory if you like. There is an old, old, and to me very fascinating, legend which has been current in the Orient from time out of mind. It is couched in this form: the gods feed on men. Now I do not mean to frighten anyone, or to have you think that when your day of dying comes it is going to be that some god is going to make a meal of you! I do not mean anything like that. But why should human beings be the only exceptions to the universal rule? Man feeds on other things. You know, as a matter of fact, we feed on each other. Every time a group of people sits close together, as you all do, you are feeding each other, changing and exchanging life-atoms, just as we think, changing and exchanging thoughts; and thus it is that arises a phenomenon which every one of us notices, I doubt not, and it is that people who live a great deal together, like husband and wife, grow to resemble each other; and I have even seen that with pets who are with human beings. A master or mistress actually begins to look like the pet! It is the change of life-atoms, and it is not always good either. It is not good for the pet, and it is not good for the human being; and there are other reasons, though of course I know among some dear people here it would be my death-sentence to say anything against pets!! These would not understand me: "Why, that's horrid, G. de P. What a perfectly horrid man!"

NOT MY WILL BUT THINE BE DONE

HUMAN hearts that have suffered are open and waiting and receptive to the light which lighteth every man who cometh into the world. Fortunately human hearts are not made of stone, they are not adamantine in texture, yet how often we look askance upon the angels of pity who come knocking at our doors, when these angels of compassion are precisely those forces in human life which open up the channels of the heart and of the understanding. How often have we repelled the gods coming in the disguise of sorrow? How frequently do we realize that those things which most deeply stir us are our best friends?

Do you not see that no matter what our lives may be, every turn of destiny is an opening door; and the portal sublime is always for us that door which, when we see it swinging open as we approach it, seems to us to lead to the road of pain. Strange, and yet how beautiful is this paradox, that it is through suffering that we learn most quickly and drink the waters of truth most deeply.

Just pause a moment and connect up these thoughts with the Christian saying: Not my will but thine be done: not the will of the ordinary, stupid, selfish, compromising and foolish man that nearly everyone of us is, but the will, the inspiration to the lower man, of the divinity within, which guides and leads, urges and impels us constantly. I think the statement is one of the most beautiful in all human thought, and it has been taught since immemorial time and in all the great religions of the world.

The light of the spirit comes to the man who is willing, who wills, to receive it, and it is excluded from the man who wills to refuse it. Not therefore my will, but the whispering wisdom and life of the divinity, of which we are, each one of us, as individual rays or sparks. Think what this world of ours would be today if men had accepted this wonder-teaching of the Avatâra Jesus at its face value, instead of reserving it merely to be heard once a week as a thought provocative perhaps of a little religious emotion, but never, except by the few, received as a rule of conduct; and *as a rule of conduct* it was given. There is no rule more beautiful in human thought, no rule so lovely in its entrance into us, for it arouses love within us; and when a man loves he is at his best, he is manliest, for then he is self-forgetful.

Not my will but thine be done. Think what peace such a code of conduct will bring to us, and the happiness and the increase of wisdom and knowledge; because all our worst faults arise from the lower parts of us; and all our virtues and most manly expressions of character come from the highest part of us.

Do you know what I verily believe to be the simple code which men should follow — and it would be also that of the Masters and their chelas? It is that of service. There is something magical, wonderful, about self-forgetful service, because a man forgetting himself in service puts his best into it. He has no regrets, no haltings, no recoilings, no considerations of selfish profit. It is a dedication of the self for the all. It becomes thereby almost more than human, and it calls forth the best that is in a man. He becomes a power, and he moves among his fellow-men who are enchained and held back and crippled by doubts and confusions and hesitancies, as a man-god; and as this life continues, this life of service, he becomes continuously less self-considering, more self-forgetful, therefore more powerful, therefore more fully a channel for the inspirations, the intimations of the divinity working through him; and by and by, as evolution proceeds in its marvelous work, he can say truly: Not any longer my will, but thine! He becomes an imbodiment, an incarnation, of divinity.

So well are these simple truths understood all over the world that you will find in all languages a word by which those who have had some experience of all this describe it. I refer to the word which in English is *disciple*. In pre-Christian Europe, for instance, the word for a disciple was *learning servant*, the same word that the Sanskrit word *chela* is. The Anglo-Saxons, when they wanted to say 'disciple' or 'pupil,' used the compound *leorning knicht,* one who serves, and who learns in and by and through that service; and how greatly were such men clothed with dignity and power! There is majesty in such service, and I pity the human being who cannot see it.

After all, is this not a far nobler conception than that which we today call enlightened selfishness? Which would you prefer: to be strong or to be weak, to know or to be ignorant, to do or to be inactive, to achieve or to be a failure? An academic question. I know what your answer will be, and in that answer you have the key to it all. The reason we fail, that we do not achieve, that we stumble on the path, that we are weaklings, that we fear, is that, although these weaknesses are not ourselves, we consider them so and dignify them. We are our worst enemies. We do not know how to serve grandly; and no man can serve absolutely and with the largest increments of splendor within himself which will radiate from him in character and knowledge, until he has realized that service is grandeur. Yet who does not know this in his heart? We learn more by serving, and right serving of course, than in any other way.

Consider Nature around us, and you will see why H. P. Blavatsky, the main Founder of the Theosophical Movement, stated early in the days of her teaching that Theosophist is who Theosophy does; that you have no right to the name of Theosophist unless you put your principles of thought into practice, into service, for only in that way can you prove that you believe in them. Otherwise you are like the hypocrites and Pharisees — a name by the way which has been sadly misused to signify hypocrisy in European tongues.

Some years ago a clergyman made the statement that if the teachings of Jesus the Avatâra were practised, in other words put to work, civilization would not survive. Think! Is it credible that anyone would so speak of the doctrine and life of the one who was called the Son of God? Is it possible that Christianity has repudiated its own Master and Teacher, and in refusing to follow him, has built its own tomb? I ask you. The Theosophist says that the teachings of the Avatâra Jesus are meant to live by and to be practised. Show me any civilization that is going to be overthrown by the practice of right and justice and purity and honor and truth. Who wants to uphold a civilization that lacks these things? The facts of the case are that the hearts of men have been nobler than their heads; and while ecclesiastics may repudiate their Teacher and his so-called religion, the hearts of men have been far wiser, for men have always loved honor and truth and courage and purity and what we call holiness, and have practised them more or less. It is a monstrous idea to say that the following of the teachings of Christianity will overthrow civilization. It will found a civilization that will endure for aye: justice towards all, injustice towards none; malice towards none and good will towards all; pity towards all and hatred towards none. These are all noble virtues; they are the very foundation of the Christianity of Jesus and of all other religious systems whatsoever.

As usual, the average man is more decent than what is supposed to be his ecclesiastic religion, just as the average man in a nation is inwardly more decent than is the conduct of nation to nation. What does this mean if not that despite our immense follies, whispering in and through the human soul there are these continually instructive intimations from the divinity within. Even human law is based on it. Feeble and stumbling as it often is, it is based on these intimations of right and justice burning in every normal man's heart. So that we can say, even we ordinary people, with some understanding: No matter what may be the things I have done in the past, what I love when all is said is just that: Not my will but thine be done. Ask yourself if this is not true. Why then do we not live more earnestly and honestly by such a code of conduct which makes every man stronger, richer in experience, more thoughtful and kindlier to others, which fills our souls with love of justice and compassion? The gods are with us, let foolish man decry them in his thoughts if he will.

GOOD AND EVIL

In a recent meeting of this Lodge, one of the speakers made the statement that all the forces and substances, energies and attributes, of universal being are in their essence divine. Now this statement, abstractly speaking, or absolutely speaking, if we carry our thought inwards into the very heart of Parabrahman, is true. But the statement as made is not enough. If it were sufficient in statement, then there would be no evil anywhere in infinity. In other words, there could be no division of high and low, good and bad, right and left — in other words, no 'pairs of opposites' — for all would be divine. It would be a corroboration of the unphilosophic chatter of some modern absolute-idealist theorists: "All is good" — which certainly is no truly philosophical statement.

Let me tell you that while it is true enough that in the absolute sense of the statement, no particular objection probably can be taken to it — for there is the Divine, utter divinity, Parabrahman, the heart of it, and beyond and more inward still, which is the Rootless Root of all things and beings — but here we are speaking of Parabrahman, infinitude in its inaccessibly highest reaches, unattainable by any human intellect; the reference here is to infinitude, and show me a time when infinity changes itself into 'pairs of opposites' and in consequence undergoes manvantara on the one hand or pralaya on the other hand. Infinity means absolute, frontierless, beginningless and endless immutability in the sense that infinitude, as infinitude, never becomes finitude or limitation; but within infinity there are multitudes of worlds and of systems of worlds endlessly, for ever and for ever throughout eternity moving in evolutionary changes, and characterized by 'pairs of opposites.' So that there never is a time, ever and unto the utmost for ever, when everything, i. e., all infinity, vanishes into the heart of Parabrahman; because that would mean that infinity changes, and sometimes is in manvantara and sometimes is in pralaya. But these changes are predicable only of manifested things, and infinitude, as infinitude, never is subject to manifestation, for only finite things change. As long as infinity is, as long as eternity endures, which means endlessly for ever, 'good' and 'evil,' signifying 'opposites,' shall be the Universe's eternal ways; and right and left, high and low, and the endlessly differing contrasts of manifestation, and hence good and bad, shall equally endlessly offer their contrasts.

There is a warning of importance that we must draw from this. Do not be deceived in refusing to accept it. There is good, endless good, but in the manifested states of universal being; and there is likewise evil, endless evil, but in the manifested states of universal being; and these in their complex and intricate combinations are the world's eternally dual ways. What are the Mâmo-Chohans, those dread beings who preside at the pralayas, who preside in the material realms now, playing their parts in the Cosmic Drama, just as the divine gods play their opposite parts in the same Cosmic Drama? In this thought you have the truth, the two sides: darkness and light, right and left, good and bad, high and low, for ever and for ever and for ever endlessly in infinitude. Here is a secret that the Christians got partial hold of, a fragment of the occult teachings of the Sanctuary, and twisting it and distorting it, indeed caricaturing it, called one end of the contrast 'God,' and the other end of the contrast the 'Devil.' Such distortion is correct in neither of its aspects! This contrast is simply the eternal and ever-changing structure of the manifesting Universes in utter infinitude, this infinitude being the playground, the scene, the frontierless theater, of Universes appearing and disappearing, because playing their parts as the Kosmic Sons of Light; including the Mâmo-Chohans and their legions playing their own parts in constructing the material universe, and holding it together, guided nevertheless by the Sons of Light, and ascending from darkness into light throughout eternity, continually renewed by fresh influxes into the Kosmic Scenery as the gods pass onwards and upwards, and the Mâmo-Chohans trail along behind them in the rear. Do you get the picture?

The warning is: don't let your brains ever be twisted with the idea that it is at any time safe to play with evil, in any connexion, on any occasion, in any way. Such play means going backwards, degenerating, joining forces with the Mâmo-Chohans, the forces of darkness, of evil, of spiritual death. Light is light, and dark is dark — opposites. Good is good and bad is bad — opposites. Right is right and left is left, unto eternity. No wonder the Masters cry, the gods cry:

Who is on my side? Make your choice. You are all free agents.
You cannot play with the forces of Nature. Occultism is the weighing of your own soul in the balance of destiny. You will either go up,
or you will go down. There is no other choice; and I think it is high
time that these facts became better known. They are not a bit esoteric in the sense of being secret and told only to a select and chosen
few. They are openly stated in all our standard books. These facts
of Nature were the basis of the universal duality which formed the
substance of the Zoroastrian system of thought, and of others.

There is immense comfort and happiness and peace in understanding these great facts properly, because they bring intellectual
harmony and spiritual illumination into the mind; and will someone
explain to me, if only good is and there is no natural evil, how can
evil exist at all? If you say that evil is but illusory, which is true
enough when we understand what illusory means, this is not denying
that evil exists, albeit it exists as an illusion. We human beings live
in a world of mahâ-mâyâ or cosmic illusion; and merely to call it
'illusion' does not annihilate that form of mâyâ which we men call
evil. Do you catch the picture? If infinity is 'good,' it is obviously
infinitely 'good,' and then there is therein no room for evil and imperfection, and the cosmos-wide series of pairs of opposites and contrasts; and heaven knows that they exist!

Be therefore on the side of the gods, the Sons of Light, of the
Spirit. Go onwards and upwards: Excelsior, ever higher! There is
our Path. But do not play tricks with your thoughts in this connexion, for think what you will and say what you may, you are either
on one side, or on the other.

II

After speaking a fortnight ago upon the topic of Good and Evil,
I heard misconstructions of what I then said, and I thought it good
to seize the first opportunity offered to me in order to say a few words
to disabuse the minds of those who misapprehended what it was my
intention to say. When I spoke of one side of the Universe as being
evil, and of the other side being good, and of the interconnexion of
these twain, which contrast each other and thus set each other off,
as being the world's eternal ways, these were general statements,
abstract statements, and had only an indirect although real enough

application to human problems — human good and evil, and so forth. I had no intention whatsoever to give utterance to the old Christian theological idea that there is an infinite personal God who is 'good'; and an infinite something or somebody which or who is evil, and which or who, if not the Devil, is nevertheless the Devil under another coat! No, that was not my meaning at all.

Now, try to follow me in thought, not only in time but into abstract space, which means no particular portion of space like our Earth, or the planets Venus or Mars, or again the Sun, or the Polar Star; but space generally, anywhere, abstract space; and the same with regard to Time: no particular point of time like now, or tomorrow, or yesterday, or a thousand or ten billion years ago, or the same period in the future. But abstract time, any time, anywhere. *If* change, division, opposites, opposition, contrasts, light and dark, matter and spirit, good and bad, short and long, these and all other eternal contrasts, were to vanish from the infinite Boundless, then every thing, high and low, from spirit to utmost matter, would vanish likewise, because all the Universe in all its infinite manifestations — and I use the word 'Universe' here in the utterly boundless sense — is builded of these contrasts. We call that path or aspect leading upwards, the right hand, often also the side or path of light, of good, of compassion, of harmony; we speak of the other side or contrasting side, the side of imperfection, of constriction, of lack, of not yet unfolded attributes — in fact of everything that is the opposite of the right hand, as the evil side of Nature, the dark side or the left hand.

Now then, are these things which are evil on the one hand and which exist by force of contrast with the things which are good on the other hand — are these same identical things, I ask, eternally evil, eternally unchanged, for ever fixed in essence as evil? Obviously not. There is as it were a constant turning of the Wheel of Kosmic Life, of the minor Wheels of Cosmic Lives; so that the evil rising on the Wheel becomes less evil, less imperfect, for imperfection slowly passes into relative perfection. It is the imperfection that we call 'evil'; the relative perfection we call 'good.' This process has been going on from utter eternity, and it is endless. There never was a beginning; there never will be an end of it, throughout timeless Time, of *manifested* being, please understand — whether spiritually manifested or materially manifested, these twain compose the eternally

Kosmic Dual. Wipe them out, and all manifestation would vanish, because then there would be no contrasts. Is, then, imperfection infinite? Where can you show me a place where manifestation — imperfection — ends? I know no such place. It is, therefore, endless. Contrariwise, show me a place where light is not, where the other side, the other pole called the good, is not. Where does it end? I know of no such place. Thus the 'good' and the 'bad,' the perfect and imperfect, and all intermediate and relative degrees of both — but never an ending to the perfect and never an ending to the imperfect — all exist within and through and because of that utter, ineffable, unthinkable Mystery which we men with our imperfect minds can refer to only in the words of the Vedic sage — THAT.

Imperfection and perfection are relative terms, because there are degrees of both; and both are comprised in the encircling, comprehending bosom of the endless fields of the Boundless. They are all children of the Boundless. Even the imperfect is manifested by the Boundless. This does not mean that the imperfect is eternally good, for it is not. But turn in the other direction, to the right hand. Look at what we call the 'perfect.' The mere fact that there is perfect, and the more perfect, and the still more perfect, throughout infinity, shows us that even what we speak of as the right-hand — if we make distances between abstract points great enough — is a rising series of grades or stages or steps enlarging ever more to the right, and that these relative stages of increasing perfection we call 'good,' so that even that which is less to the right side we likewise call good. The same rule of thought applies to the left hand. What we call the highest imperfect, or the most perfect of the imperfect, is really divine to beings and entities so far more to the left, to the imperfect side, that by right of contrast, by right of evolutionary unfolding, of growth, of change towards the right, towards betterment, this less imperfect can be called relatively spiritual or divine. Thus there is no absolute dividing line between the right and the left.

Now comes a point which is exceedingly important. Matter is not evil *per se*. What we call concreted matter is simply incomputable armies and hosts of monads aggregated together in compact order; and, as it were, when compared with us relatively wakened human beings these armies and hosts are asleep. Each such monad in its heart is divine, yet it is manifesting as matter. These are elementary thoughts, and yet they are a sublime teaching. One cannot therefore say that matter is essentially evil. It is merely less perfectly evolved or unfolded than is what we call spirit and the spiritual ranges which the gods occupy.

The whole truth is really simple enough, but people become perplexed about it because of its simplicity. The ideas of Western minds have been distorted by the teaching that there is an infinite Mind, an Individual, infinite, without body, parts, or passions, without any qualifications whatsoever, and that it is essentially distinct, nevertheless, and separate from the things which this Mind creates — a perfect nightmare of theories illogical and unsustainable throughout.

Now then, while it is perfectly true to state that evil, even cosmic evil, as we men speak of it, is imperfection, imperfection in growth — imperfect beings living in an imperfect state because of their imperfect evolutionary unfolding, of their imperfect development — while this is so, giving constant hope to imperfect beings to grow better, nevertheless hearken: this does not mean that imperfect things or beings are essentially good. I cannot commit an evil deed, and cheat my brain into saying that the essence of the deed is divine and therefore I have done no wrong because there is no evil in the Universe. What I am trying to point out is that manifestation is the interblending of opposites; otherwise there could be no manifestation, which means limitations of all kinds of unfolding. But hearken also carefully to this: It is sheer folly for a man to accept and to believe that one side of the Universe is composed of innumerable hierarchies of bright and shining gods, who are our ancestors, the spiritual roots from which we draw our higher portions; and that all the other side of Nature, because of the law of contrast, does not balance or support the good side. In other words, I mean that there are evil powers in the Universe, evil forces: not absolutely evil, not essentially evil, not outside the womb of the Utterly Divine, but because of their relatively great imperfection they are distinctly evil to the race of men and to other beings more or less occupying our state on the Ladder of Life. Furthermore, for the same reason, there are localities in the Universe which to us are evil; they are true hells, not however in the Christian sense of the word, but globes so densely material that life or living there to us humans would be hell; and hence their influences on men are evil, and urge men to evil, for these influences are in large part the gross and heavy effluvia flowing forth from the dark side of Nature, and they are largely responsible for the temptations to which men too often succumb.

Just precisely as it is our duty to ally ourselves with our 'Father in Heaven,' with the divinities, our guardians and protectors whose strong hands hold us safe if we but follow them: in other words, just as it is our supreme duty to follow the right-hand Path; so on the other hand if we do not, and become negative and subject to the gross effluvia from the densely material spheres, then we shall as surely take the downward path — as otherwise we shall surely follow the path to the gods.

It is these thoughts, originally of the Sanctuary of the Mysteries, which were taken over into some of the exoteric religions, such as Christianity, and often grossly distorted, twisted. But there is one point on which the Occult Teaching and Christian theology agree, for a wonder! Christian theology denies that matter is essentially evil. So do we. Even in the most hellish parts of the Galaxy, in its grossest and darkest spheres, and there are some that — well, if you knew about them you would not sleep tonight — even in those places, every mathematical point of the spheres and globes of which these places are builded, is as divine *in essence* as are the spheres of light in which the gods live in their realms. Hence, do not think that matter is evil *per se*. That would mean that from eternity evil is evil and cannot ever pass from imperfection into a growing perfection, in other words that beings cannot ever from evil become good. Evil abstractly consists of transitory states or conditions — however long they may last — in which monads pass during certain phases of their endless peregrinations upwards and onwards.

Nowhere, therefore, is evil eternal because essentially unchanging; and nowhere is what we men with our imperfect intelligence call 'good,' crystallized in immobility and remaining there in such state eternally. Half of manifested infinity is imperfection, in its innumerably relative degrees; and the other half is perfection in its innumerably relative degrees; and there is no absolute dividing line between the twain. It is obvious, of course, that I speak from the standpoint of a man, and because of my humanity make my own dividing lines between good and evil. A god would make different

dividing lines. A Mâmo-Chohan again would likewise make different dividing lines; but the rule as stated would be identic for all.

III

I should like once more to say a few words about something
which I had occasion to speak of some weeks ago — twice, or it may
be thrice. It was with regard to the esoteric teachings concerning
the two Ways, the eternal Ways, of the Universe — good and evil.
Now I have at different times said a good many things on this matter; but when I ceased speaking on the last occasion, I realized that
I did not emphasize sufficiently one point, and this point was that
when we look upon the Universe as Boundless Space, without frontiers or limits, then we always find that while in some parts of Boundless Space Universes are appearing and manifestation is going on,
in other parts manifestation is disappearing — Universes are passing
out of their manvantaric existence.

As long as there is manifestation, there is imperfection, which
is what we men call evil. Consequently, as we are now dealing with
boundless infinity and eternity, it is perfectly correct to say that evil
and good are the world's eternal ways; otherwise expressed, perfection and imperfection are in Boundless Space from beginningless
duration, and will last unto endless duration, endless eternity. But
this does not mean that there are two infinities, to wit, an infinite of
perfection and an infinite of imperfection. Obviously not. If there
were an infinite of perfection, there could be no imperfection, no
manifestation which is imperfection.

Next, and now passing from the boundless spaces, let us take
an individual. Outside of and beyond and within the Kosmic infinite duality, our minds oblige us to recognise cosmic unity, and it
is out of this unity that the duality springs; the duality has its heyday of manifestation; and then into the unity it vanishes again. This
unity does not mean 'one,' because that would be the beginning of
numeration which is the beginning of manifestation, and it would
likewise be the same mistake that the Christians made, in imagining
their infinite personal God. The 'one' I here use in the sense of
the mystical zero, as H. P. B. employs it, signifying all-encompassing
infinitude, from which the one, any one of the multitudes of ones,
is born.

To illustrate: Take any one of us, a human being. We are beings in manifestation, therefore are we imperfect, and throughout
beginningless and endless time we shall in various hierarchies and in
different degrees of perfection, or of imperfection, on lower or on
higher planes, be running the eternal cyclical round of developing
and of unfolding ever more and more. But that ineffable Rootless
Root within each one of us, is the utterly Boundless. This is a very
important point of thought. It is upon this thought of non-duality
that was based all the teaching of the great Hindû Avatâra Śankarâchârya; and his form of the Vedânta — a word which means 'the
real meaning of the Vedas,' i.e., of the books of Wisdom — was
called Adwaita, which means non-dualistic, because his thought
dwelt mainly on this endlessly Divine, the Rootless Root which is
the core of the core of the core of every unit in boundless infinitude.

Thus, then, strange paradox, so easily understandable and yet
so difficult to explain: while the fields of boundless infinitude, or
boundless space, are never empty of manifested, manifesting, and
disappearing worlds, all of them are born from and return to that
ineffable, unthinkable Mystery which we call THAT. THAT is not
dual, and this is about all we can say concerning it. Hence it is not
imperfect; it cannot even be said to be perfect; because perfection
and imperfection are terms of human understanding, which means
terms of an imperfectly developed intelligence — the human. It is
beyond both perfection and imperfection. It is the ALL, the source
and fountain-head of all the hierarchies of the gods, as high as you
will; and of the lowest elements of the material worlds, put them as
low as you like. It is the ALL — we have no words with which to
describe it. The Vedic Sages simply called it THAT. It is not a
God; from it all the gods spring. It is not a World; from it all the
worlds come; and like the gods, they ultimately return to it. It is
not personal, it is not impersonal, for these again are human words
signifying attributes of human perfection or imperfection. It is beyond all of them. It does not ever manifest, because infinity does
not manifest. Only things and beings manifest. Yet from IT all
beings and things come. It includes within its all-comprehensive
bosom all that ever was in boundless time everlasting, all that now
is, and all that ever will be in endless time, or what we men call
the limitless future. It neither thinks nor does it not think, because

thinking and not-thinking are human terms or expressions, and emphatically it is not human. It is neither intelligent nor non-intelligent, because these again are human attributes — godlike attributes on the one hand, and limited attributes on the other hand.

As Lao-Tse said, imbodying the same thought: As long as ye have good men in the State ye will have evil in the State. Why? Not because of the presence of good men; but there can be good men only when we have bad men and their bad actions showing off the good men by contrast. Do you catch this profound thought? As long as there is light, obviously you will have darkness. These things, light and darkness, are limited, however vast they may be, however small; and they again are not THAT, but are all included within THAT. THAT is beginningless. The gods begin in any one manvantara, and keep cyclically repeating their beginnings. The Universes begin, they end, and they repeat the cycles of manifestation throughout eternity, albeit ever rising on loftier scales. But THAT is without because beyond cycles. It is not an Individual; it contains all individuals. Any individual is limited, otherwise it would not be an individual. An individual is a being or an entity which we know by contrast with other beings and entities against which the entity is set. You could not tell one flower from another flower unless you saw the contrast of flowers. Individuality is a sign of imperfection, of limitation; personality *a fortiori* even more so.

That is why the ancient Books of Wisdom state that THAT is neither good nor bad, neither intelligent nor non-intelligent; neither alive nor dead; neither long nor short nor high nor low. All these are attributes of limited things which we cannot predicate of the Unlimited Boundless. If it were long, however vast the length might be, it would have an ending and a beginning. Similarly with intelligence, kindliness, goodness, compassion, harmony — all these things are attributes of limitation, albeit of spirit. IT is beyond them all, encompasses them all, enwombs them all. From it they all spring; to it they all will return.

I would not weigh so frequently and so heavily on these thoughts, were I not keenly sensible of the fact that they comprise questions of high metaphysics, questions of high philosophy, questions of high religious import which some day our Theosophical exponents will have to deal with. They will have to give an account of our sublime

Wisdom to the keenest minds of the world. We shall be asked to explain our convictions, no longer to kindly audiences such as we gather in our halls and auditoriums; and we shall then need trained and polished minds, capable and capacious intellects, men and women fully acquainted with our sublime Thought-Wisdom, so that they can make statements in exposition which will have clarity, succinctness, and persuasive power to those who come to us and ask for light.

THE LIFE-PERIOD OF A PLANETARY CHAIN

THE life-period of a planetary chain — and for the sake of simplicity we will dismiss from our minds the upper five globes, although they are the most important, and consider only the seven lower ones which H. P. B. speaks of — the life-period of a planetary chain, before it dies, is called a Day of Brahmâ and consists of 4,320,000,000 years. It is followed by an equal time-period called a Night; so that Day and Night together make 8,640,000,000 years. Then the chain reimbodies itself. This time-period you already know from H. P. B.

What is the length of what H. P. B. calls a Manvantara? Here we get into trouble at once, because there are at least ten and maybe twelve different kinds of manvantaras. H. P. B. calls a minor manvantara a passage of the seven root-races on any one globe. It does not matter what globe it is. She calls that a minor manvantara. She calls a major manvantara the passing of a life-wave around the chain of twelve globes. Why? Because a Manu opens a Round on Globe A — called the Root Manu — and closes it on Globe G — called the Seed Manu. Manvantara means Manu-period, or Manu-time, the essence of Manu, that which a Manu produces or brings forth; and this essence comes forth in the evolving life-waves passing among the globes. There is likewise a Manu opening a *globe* life-period, and a Manu closing it. All these things you will find in our Theosophical books.

But now let me ask: What is the length of a manvantara when H. P. B. used the words without any descriptive epithets? You have to search for what she means. Mostly she means this: The time it takes a life-wave, any life-wave, to pass from Globe A through Globe B, through Globe C, to the middle period of Globe D. She calls this the pre-septenary manvantara; I would phrase it the prior-septenary manvantara. The post-septenary manvantara would follow through the other half of the globe-chain. You will find this described in *The Secret Doctrine,* Vol. II.

Now what is the length of such a manvantara from A to the central time-period of Globe D? 306,720,000 years; and if you add the Dawn and the Twilight each of a Dvâpara-Yuga, or 864,000 years, together forming a Satya-Yuga in length, you will get a time-period for a manvantara equalling 308,448,000 years, and that is the time-period from A to D. Here we reach the middle point. From D to the end of G is another manvantara, another half-round, 308,448,000 years. The whole round therefore is double that — something like 617 million years.

Where are we now? We are in the Fourth Round, and at the middle point of our lowest globe, Globe D. There is still half of this present Round Four to finish, and then Rounds Five, Six, and Seven, before our chain dies and goes into Nirvâna, preparing itself there for its return as a new chain.

From what has been told you, you can get certain scientific facts, facts in geology, for instance. How long has it been since sedimentation began on our earth D? Something like 320 million years; for you must count in the 308 — nearly 309 — million years for the various life-waves, ten in number, following each other in serial order, to come down from Globe A, run through its course there, then through Globe B, run through its course on Globe B, and so on through Globes C and D. 308 million would take us to the middle of the Fourth Root-Race on Globe D. Again we have the critical fourth. Half of the round is then completed. But we are now in the Fifth Root-Race, about the middle point. How many years have elapsed since the middle of the Fourth Root-Race to our present middle of the Fifth? Nearly 9 million years. So to the 309 million of the prior-septenary manvantara, you must add this 9 million more or less — a little less — to bring our time-period to where we are now. 309 plus 9, in round figures, makes 318 million years. I said 320; that is just taking a round figure. So you now know how long ago it was that the Fourth Round began.

How long has our own human life-wave been on Globe D? That is a different question. Remember what these life-waves are. You see how these things are entangled. Every moment you meet with a dozen new difficulties. The life-waves are these: First, Second and Third Kingdoms of Elementals; 4) Mineral Kingdom; 5) Vegetable Kingdom; 6) Animal Kingdom; 7) Human Kingdom; 8) Lowest Kingdom of Dhyân-Chohans; 9) Middle Kingdom of Dhyân-Chohans; 10) the Highest Kingdom of Dhyân-Chohans. Ten life-waves; and they follow each other in serial order as rounds around the globes.

How long, then, has the human life-wave, our human kingdom in other words, been on Globe D? With certain modifications, the general rule is that each root-race on Globe D, our Earth, takes nearly nine million years from its very beginning to its very ending. 9 million years back brings us to the middle of the Fourth Root-Race. We are the Fifth; the Atlantean was the Fourth. 18 million years back brings us to the middle of the Third Root-Race, then man first became, because of the entrance into him of the mânasa-putras, a thinking, reasoning entity.

But here we come upon a difficulty that throws out of line this neat calculation. You notice I carefully limit my remarks to three Races only. These are Races 3rd, 4th, and 5th. I do not allude to Root-Races 1 and 2, and 6 and 7 still to come. Root-Races 3, 4 and 5 are pretty much the same length in years — around 9 million years each. But Root-Races 6 and 7 to come will be shorter, and Root-Races 1 and 2 were much longer. Why was this? It was because Root-Race 1 was practically purely astral, the individuals were intellectually unconscious, and they passed ages in a dreaming, intellectually unawakened state like little children today.

Root-Race 2 was still astral, although verging to the physical, and almost as intellectually asleep as Root-Race 1. Root-Race 3 in its beginning was still semi-astral, but became physical at about its middle point.

Why were Root-Races 1 and 2 so much longer in time-length than the following races? And here is the crux, the difficulty. It was because Root-Race 1, in the manner in which H. P. B. speaks of it, was not only astral but, as she describes it, really represented the śishtas from the preceding Round, the Third. This Root-Race 1, beginning with śishtas, took ages before actually settling down into a root-race, that is, typically a root-race of the new round, no longer merely śishtas. The cause of the awakening and slow evolutionary processes was that the forerunners of the life-wave began coming in millions and millions of years before the First Root-Race as a race apart so to speak could be said actually to have begun.

Every life-wave, as you know, is preceded by its forerunners, sometimes millions of years ahead. Then come more forerunners in larger groups; and finally the life-wave as an aggregate body arrives. When the life-wave as an actual body arrives, then can be said to begin or to have begun the First Root-Race as an actual race *sui generis*. Previous to that time they were śishtas slowly being unfolded or affected or changed by the arriving forerunners of the life-wave. This whole process, astral in type on an almost physical globe, as I have said, took ages, before the First Root-Race came into being as a race *sui generis*. Then it lived its time — how long I would not venture to say: certainly 9 millions of years and perhaps a great deal more, when Root-Race 2 began slowly to come into being, but as yet hardly distinct from Root-Race 1. In fact, Root-Race 1 did not die out and give birth to Root-Race 2, as later root-races did; but Root-Race 1 can be said to have become swallowed up or merged into Root-Race 2, thus producing Root-Race 2. As H. P. B. phrased it, the old waters mixed with the new. A graphic explanation and very true.

There was no death in those early days of Root-Races 1 and 2. Thus Root-Race 2 is at the time I speak of on the scene distinct in notable particulars from the First Root-Race, yet still almost astral, more astral than physical. Towards the end of Root-Race 2 death began to appear but was still unusual, so that the bulk of the individuals of Root-Race 2 could be said to have shifted over gradually into Root-Race 3. With Root-Race 3 death of the individuals became the common order as we have it now. Do you see how difficult all this is to explain? To the best of scientists it would be looked upon as speculatory, and by more materialistic scientists looked upon as theosophical dreaming, although there are examples of such procedures or events in the lower kingdoms even on the earth today.

We are now at Root-Race 3 — ethereally physical but still physical and growing grosser all the time. Death has now arrived; the human shape is already common although of course there were no men and women then. The early Third Race was an androgynous race, changing over finally into the two sexes at about its middle point.

Now as to time-periods; and the relation between the Root-Races and the geological periods: It is difficult to unify our theosophical occult racial periods in their geologic eras with scientific time-periods, and it is this very difficulty which has caused these relations to be kept strictly hidden by the Teachers, as H. P. B. points out in *The Secret Doctrine;* hidden not because of any especial sacredness about them but rather passed over with just a hint or reference, because of the impossibility in her day, and even in ours, of ordinary untrained non-theosophic people understanding what it would be about.

Theosophical evolution is so utterly different from scientific conceptions of it, both as regards processes and time-periods, that the Theosophist, knowing the facts and attempting to explain, is confronted at each instance by a blank wall of non-comprehension on the part of his theosophically untrained auditors — or readers if he tries to write a book. The worst of these untrained people are the scientists themselves, because even among themselves their own views are recognised as being so uncertain and speculative. And even to trained Theosophical students the matter is not easy to elucidate.

I think it would be foolish to try to twist Theosophical doctrines into conformity with modern geologic time-periods or modern evolutionary ideas, because it simply can't be done, and one day writing of that kind will be bitterly regretted by the Theosophists who attempted it; because science is changing and growing; and it is much better to tell the truth as far as you know it in the best way you can, stating the difficulty and then going ahead. I have never believed in straddling these matters and trying to win adherents among the scientists when at every turn we could only do so (excepting among a few intuitive minds) by disloyalty to our own consciences.

The remarks, then, that I shall make are based on H. P. B.'s geological figures in Vol. II of *The Secret Doctrine,* which I believe are those of Sir Charles Lyell, the English geologist. Of course the figures of modern geology as regards time-periods have been enormously enlarged, even swollen beyond anything we Theosophists require; so that for instance what might now be called the Secondary Period would be much farther back in actual years or time than H. P. B.'s Secondary Period. Modern geology as you know, has given millions more years to nearly all the time-periods that H. P. B. adopted for illustration following Lyell. So I will use H. P. B.'s names.

The Fourth Root-Race reached its peak of development in H. P. B.'s Miocene, yes even in H. P. B.'s preceding Eocene. The Third Root-Race probably began in the Jurassic or even perhaps at the end of the Triassic and was certainly fleshing during H. P. B.'s Cretaceous, all of these belonging to H. P. B.'s Secondary Age. This places the Third Root-Race pretty well. The Second Root-Race still ran over into the Triassic, and perhaps can be said to be fleshed in the Triassic, ending in it probably, possibly itself beginning at the end of the Primary age of the Permian period. Whereas the First Root-Race was actually Pre-Secondary, therefore originating in the Primary (I personally think in the Carboniferous or Coal period) and perhaps could be said to have attained its peak and possibly its ending in the Permian period of the Primary age. This would take the First Race back many millions of years — how much, it would be guess-work to say. My own guess is that the First Root-Race probably originated in the Carboniferous or Coal period of the Primary age, and perhaps about 130 to 150 million years ago.

But in this connexion you must remember what I have said above about its astral character, the ages and ages of the śishtas which H. P. B. evidently included in the beginning of the First Root-Race; and how long the First Root-Race actually existed as a race *sui generis* I would not care to speculate upon. It would require more knowledge of geology and of zoology and of botany than I have any acquaintance with.

Thus it is clear that our Fifth Root-Race belongs to the Quaternary and originated in H. P. B.'s Tertiary; that the Fourth attained its peak of evolution in the early Tertiary and probably originated in the later Cretaceous of the Secondary; that the Third probably attained its peak of evolution in the Jurassic of the Secondary, and may have originated at the end of the Triassic of the Secondary. The Second probably attained its peak in H. P. B.'s Triassic of the Secondary, possibly originated at the beginning of the Triassic, possibly even at the very end of the Permian of the Primary Age. At any rate the Second Root-Race we can place more or less clearly somewhere in the Permian of the Primary age, and the First Root-Race in the Carboniferous or the Coal period of the Primary. H. P. B. gives some of the best hints about these matters in her *Secret Doctrine*, Vol. II, pages 711-16.

Now as regards the Root-Races 6 and 7 to come: these will be, as I said, shorter in actual length, and my own opinion is that the Sixth will be close to a Mahâ-Yuga and a half, say something over six million years; and the Seventh will be still shorter — how long, it would be just speculation to say.

Thus, you see, the life-waves evolve through the Mahâ-Yugas, but are not closely geared into the Mahâ-Yugas, for they overlap in both directions very considerably. Finally, while it is very tempting to try to collate the figures I have given about root-races and life-waves and to try to make these figures run with regularity through all the seven root-races, yet it just simply can't be done; and as said above I have carefully limited my own remarks to Root-Races 3, 4 and 5, because here *mind* had entered into humanity, things had become grossly material and therefore more or less mechanical, and Root-Races 1 and 2 were not so to speak inflexibly and mechanically geared to the yugas and Root-Races 3, 4 and 5 more or less were.

EVOLUTION INTO THE HUMAN KINGDOM — I

HERE are two questions that have been asked of me: "You have told us, G. de P., that in the human constitution there is an animal monad which in the next chain-imbodiment will become a human being. You have likewise told us that the animals on, say, our globe of this chain, on *our* globe, will be humans in the next chain-imbodiment. Question: How do you make this out? Where stand the humans-to-be who are now the animal monads in man? Where will they be when compared with the future humans on the next chain-imbodiment who are now here our beasts?"

The other question is this: "You stated some little time ago, that from the very beginning of this present chain-imbodiment, we who are now humans as monads have always been humans. How then do you account for the other teaching regarding the door into the human kingdom which closed at the middle point of the Fourth Round, in other words during the Atlantean race?"

There are the two questions. As a matter of fact, Companions, the answers to these questions, to both of them, may be found in our books and in my own books. I have spoken of them, giving answers to each one, I think a dozen times from this platform.

What I said a moment ago is true. It is our teaching that the present human monads have been human monads from the beginning of this chain-imbodiment; and please remember we are speaking of monads now. I have likewise stated that there is in man an animal monad which in the next chain-imbodiment will be human. Now I will take the first question first: The answer is this: Those animals which are now called animal monads and which are the animal parts of us men — I do not mean the physical body, that is the physical part of men, but the animal part, in other words our animal, the human animal of us, the instincts, the thoughts, the motives, the attributes, the qualities that make the human animal, and of which the body is merely an expression, the open door — these will be the humans in the human kingdom in the next chain-imbodiment; and our present animals will then be the lower and lowest units of the human kingdom in the next chain-imbodiment.

To make this more comprehensible let us reverse the process. Instead of looking ahead, we will go back to the moon, the moon-chain, the time when we were all on the moon. We then, we higher humans now in this chain-imbodiment, were on the moon the individual animal monads in the then humans of the moon-chain. Do you understand me? In other words the men on the moon-chain had, as we now have, animal monads as part of their constitution. When the moon-chain finished its manvantaric evolution and died as a chain, giving birth to this chain, the moon-humans then had become Dhyân-Chohans, had entered the dhyân-chohanic kingdom. Their animal monads had then become human, each going up a step.

Now then, what were the humans on the moon were the lowest of the Dhyân-Chohans in this imbodiment. What were the animal monads in the moon-men are now the humans in this chain-imbodiment. Is that thought clear? Again, what the animals are now, as I have already stated, on this earth or in this chain-imbodiment, will be the lower and lowest humans in the next chain-imbodiment. Reverse the process on the moon. What the moon-animals were when the moon ended its Seventh Round, then became human, not the high humans, but they entered the human kingdom. They were men, but the lower part of what we now call the human kingdom. Is that thought clear? Very good.

So we have the animals on the moon become the lower humans here. These lower humans as well as the higher humans when this earth-chain ends its Seventh Round will be Dhyân-Chohans; and our present human animal monads will be then the higher humans of the next chain-to-be, the child of this chain; and our animals now, i. e., those who make the grade, on this earth when the Seventh Round ends, will be the lower and lowest humans in the next chain-imbodiment. So you see we have thus: animals entering the human kingdom, not the bodies, the monads. That is where your constant confusion comes in. You keep thinking of bodies. I am talking of monads. What are now the monads manifesting through the animals, when the Seventh Round of this chain is ended, will have evolved, which means developed, unfolded — the *monads* will have unfolded to become human, so that in the next chain-imbodiment the animals will then be human. What kind of humans? The highest? No, we have already stated the higher will be what are now the animal monads in us men, as we were on the moon the animal monads in the moon-men. And the animals on the moon reached humanity, the human stage, at the end of the Seventh Moon-Round, i. e., those who made the grade, so that they could then become men in the human kingdom, and are amongst us now on this earth as the lower and lowest humans.

It is an old, simple teaching that every Theosophist knows, that not only are there 7, 10, 12 classes of monads, but that each such class or family (kingdom is another good word) has its own special divisions, so that our human kingdom has its special divisions; the Masters and the Buddhas at one end, the almost animal humans at the other end, like the Veddahs of Ceylon, the Andaman Islanders, and so on. Between these two classes of men there is an enormous psychological, spiritual, and intellectual range. But they are all men, they all belong to the human kingdom, because all have attained conscious self-consciousness.

Now there you have the answer to the first question and I hope you have understood it. You will realize that this matter has been explained and this question has been answered on many occasions in the past.

The other question is this, and it leads right on from this first one. I will repeat the question: "G. de P., you stated some time ago that we human monads have been human from the beginning of this chain-imbodiment. How is this reconciled with the other statement made by H. P. B. and you that the door into the human kingdom closed at the middle point of our Fourth Round, in other words during the Atlantean race? There seems a contradiction here." From what has been stated, you see clearly that there is no contradiction because the answer to the first question shows that the human monads were humans from the very beginning of our chain-imbodiment, because they attained humanity at the end of the Seventh Moon-Round.

What then is the meaning of this phrase, "door into the human kingdom closing at the middle point of the Fourth Round"? It means this: That all those entities coming from the moon-pitris, lunar pitris, which we can use now as a very general term meaning all monads coming from the moon — there are lunar human pitris, lunar animal pitris, lunar plant pitris, lunar mineral pitris, lunar dhyân-chohanic pitris — it means that all these were the fathers of everything, that is of our own chain now, the lunar fathers of all the kingdoms.

I will make a short excursus now before continuing my answer, because it may make the answer clearer. You remember that H. P. B. and others have written of families or classes of monads, in other words these are the different kingdoms of nature. H. P. B. counts them as 7, because the septenary classification is easier, and she wrote to make things easier. A more complete classification is that of 10, 10 kingdoms, 10 classes of monads. The most complete is that of 12.

Now H. P. B.'s 7 kingdoms or classes of monads were the following, counting from the highest down: 3 classes of Dhyân-Chohans, the human kingdom, the beast kingdom, the vegetable kingdom, and the mineral kingdom, seven. She merely mentioned but did not include 3 more lower than the mineral, the elemental kingdoms, three in number thus making 10 — 10 kingdoms of nature. What then are the other two kingdoms of nature to make the complete number 12, corresponding by the way to the 12 globes of the chain, to the 12 Houses of the Zodiac, or the 12 Logoi of the sun? They are these: No. 1, and the first and the lowest, if you wish, counting upwards now, is the root-manu; the 12th is the seed-manu, using the terms employed by H. P. B.; and thus you have your 12. You see therefore that the kingdom of the Manus is higher than the highest kingdom of the Dhyân-Chohans, and it is practically a divine kingdom, if we speak of the dhyân-chohanic threefold kingdom as being spiritual.

Now then, I return to my answer to the question: The door into the human kingdom means that after 3 rounds have taken place, and the Fourth Round which was the lowest and most material is over, ended, there comes a point in time and in natural functions where the descent on the downward arc stops, and from that moment begins the climb on the upward arc. The downward arc is the arc of shadows, so-called. The upward arc is the luminous arc. The reason for these names is the following: The downward arc is the evolution of matter. Matter comes forth in all its myriad multiform shapes, going with the corresponding involution or recession of spirit. The luminous arc is the reverse of this, the evolution of spirit corresponding to an involution of matter. Matter is ingathered. Spirit expands on the upward arc.

Now then, only those beings can climb the upward arc which have the germs of self-consciousness within them, because it is the arc of the opening of spirit. Do you catch that thought? Now on the downward arc, the law of acceleration came into operation for the lower kingdoms of nature. The law of retardation on the downward arc was in force where the spiritual monads were concerned, for they did not want to drop into matter, they ran down reluctantly and slowly; whereas the material entities, the lower beings expressing themselves in the lower kingdoms, had a tremendous pull down, and rushed down. So we see the lower kingdoms were under the law of acceleration on the downward arc. The spiritual kingdoms were under the law of retardation. On the upward arc that is reversed. The spiritual beings as they began to attain the luminous arc felt the attraction of spirit more and more, as their feet became freed from the mire of matter they began to feel the law of acceleration, they began to reach up.

But the creatures more heavy with matter, feeling the attraction of matter downwards, began to lag behind, the law of retardation began to work on them. They are less attracted to the spirit and they are pulled downwards by matter.

Now at this point, so far as the human kingdom is concerned, where the lowest of the downward arc is, is what we call the door into the human kingdom. All those entities whatsoever which have not reached self-consciousness, do not enter that door which will enable them to go upwards to the Seventh Round. I wonder if I have made my meaning clear. Such a simple thought and yet a subtil one. For instance, the door into the human kingdom does not concern the dhyân-chohanic kingdoms; they are above the human. It concerns the human kingdoms and the kingdoms below the humans. All the monads therefore which were human before reaching the midpoint of the Fourth Round passed as it were naturally and simply through the door into the human kingdom which was already open, and they kept right on their way; whereas the monads, like the monads of the animals, which had not achieved humanity yet during the previous three rounds, when they came to this lowest point were so to speak challenged by nature. The ancient religions such as the Egyptians expressed it by the Guardian at the Gate. Who comes here? Who art thou? as the Sanskritists had it. The Book of the Dead speaks of these challenges at the various gates. Now anyone who could give the passwords passed on through; and remember that giving the password was not any *password*, the door into the human kingdom is not any *door*. It merely means Nature's laws beginning to operate at a certain evolutionary point. This point is the middle, the lowest point of all the seven rounds — the middle of the Fourth in the middle of the Atlantean race. All the monads therefore which have been rushing onwards in the downward arc through the three rounds had now come to the Fourth. Those who could pass on passed naturally and began the upward arc: the Mânava kingdom, the 3 dhyân-chohanic kingdoms, and the human kingdom. When it came to the animals, the door closed. They could not pass. In other words they could not enter the human kingdom because they were not yet human.

Now another question! Why are the beasts still with us? As I have already explained, they have not passed the human kingdom; they are feeling strongly the attraction of matter. As each million years goes by, as each thousand years goes by, their pace becomes slower and slower, they cannot make the grade. After a while they stop, die out, and enter into the Nirvâna. This is the meaning of the statement you have heard in our books that with a very few exceptions the animal kingdom will not reach to the Seventh Round. Why? They cannot make the grade upwards. The attraction is below. They will enter into their Nirvâna and wait till the next chain-imbodiment. Then they will attain humanity. That will be their reward in a chain somewhat superior to this.

And now comes a paradox, a very strange paradox. Some of the monads which have reached in their unwrapping evolution as far as the animal kingdom, will even make it up to the Seventh Round where they will become men. In other words they will then have reached self-consciousness, and then they will be the lower humans of the next chain-round. The animal monad in us at the end of the Seventh Round will be the human monad and will be the higher humans in the next chain-imbodiment.

You may wonder about the apes. Where do they come in the scale of things? Have they entered the human kingdom? No. They are more animal than human. They still belong to the animal kingdom. But there is a touch in the apes — mind you, I am not speaking of the monkeys, I mean the apes — there is in the apes just enough human blood, through us, to enable them in the next chain to be the spiritual and intellectual leaders of the animals who will then form in the next chain-imbodiment the lower and lowest men. The beast will be the highest of this branch of the then human kingdom.

So then we really have the human kingdom, the apes an intermediate stage, the beasts; and the beasts themselves are in many sub-branches — the highest, the intermediate, and the lowest. There is an enormous difference among the beasts, between the ape and the insect, or between a horse and any other creature, a squirrel, a racoon, or what not. Such distances are enormous even among men.

And now, dear Companions, with all that I have said, I have been talking of *monads,* and in this connexion you may ask yourselves: Doesn't evolution affect bodies also? The answer is yes. But you see, scientists do not know anything about spiritual evolution except in a very small way. Their idea of evolution is a betterment of the physical body through the slow ages. True, the physical body has progressed through ages; we do not deny it, but it is the forces working from *within* upon the body, refining it, refining its organs, refining its flesh that brings about this physical evolution. But among the scientists evolution is chance, haphazard, Darwinism. To us the door into the human kingdom has nothing to do with the shape of bodies, of beings, it has solely to do with the inner parts, monadic parts, spiritual, intellectual, psychical, and astral, and when these change, the bodies change. So that I can tell you, Companions, even in a small degree the flesh of the truly good man is finer than the flesh of a man who leads a gross life. And that is why it is a true statement when the Buddhists say that the Buddha was a marvel of manly beauty, that even his body seemed to be translucent with spiritual life, something about him was not like the ordinary. It is true. There was a fire of the spirit within him working through his blood and his nerves and the very tissues of his flesh and his bones, making the vehicle more refined in every way. Actually there is a difference between the flesh of a man and the flesh of beasts. I do not say chemists can find it — they may some day. But there is; even the very smell shows it.

EVOLUTION INTO THE HUMAN KINGDOM — II

I HAVE found that some themes we have been studying are still somewhat obscure in the minds of many here, and elsewhere I doubt not. The particular themes I have in mind are evolution, the imbodying of the monads, and what we humans were on the moon-chain, what the animals were, etc. In the first place I am sure that many students of Theosophy have often asked themselves the following question: Given Nature and her laws and the different classes of the families of monads, could these monads by passing through the lower kingdoms of Nature, unaided, without help from above, gradually through learning, through experience, through evolution, rise higher from kingdom to kingdom, so that the mineral would become the vegetable, and later a beast, the beast a man, the man a god? — following the well-known statement in the Qabbâlâh.

Now without mincing words my answer is Yes. It is possible, and in fact would happen if that were the way Nature worked. But she does not work that way, and I will explain why. Furthermore, such slow, slow, slow evolution through the kingdoms of Nature of the monads upwards would take an incredibly long time. Instead of, for instance, the monad of an elemental becoming a man in six or seven imbodiments of our chain, which is something like 60 billions of years, the monads unaided would take six or seven solar manvantaras merely to pass from one kingdom to the next higher. In other words, theoretically the monads can rise without help from the kingdom above into those higher kingdoms if they take time enough for the process. But it would take a quasi-eternity to do it; but the important thing is that *Nature is not working that way.* Her law is that all lives for all, which means that every entity, wittingly or unwittingly, helps every other entity. It means that every superior kingdom is not only a guide to the kingdom next below itself, but an enormous attraction upwards to itself upon the lower kingdom.

Thus to illustrate: Take the human kingdom: It is the goal of the beast-kingdom; and mark you, in Theosophy we place humans in a kingdom separate from the animals. In the same way the vegetables aspire upwards towards the animal kingdom, and the animal kingdom draws them up. So it is with all kingdoms. But in addition to these things, there is an interchange of — how may I phrase it? — an interchange of help between every two contingent kingdoms: as for instance between the human and the animal, between the dhyân-chohanic and the human, between the second and first dhyân-chohanic, and between the third and the second. In other words what we call in our own human case the descent of the mânasaputras and their lighting of the fires of mind in the then mindless humanity, takes place *mutatis mutandis,* which means with the necessary changes of circumstances and kingdom, between every two adjacent kingdoms. So just as the lower dhyân-chohanic kingdom, the lower mânasaputras, inflamed our own minds to become awakened unto thinking for themselves — what we call the descent of the mânasaputras — so does the human kingdom inflame the very latent intelligence of the animals. And the animals in their turn are, as it were, mânasaputric beings to the kingdom below, by an interchange of life-atoms and by the conjoining bonds of the two kingdoms, where there are creatures who may at one time be called low animals or very high plants.

Now with those points established, let us examine two questions. 1. What were we humans now in this Earth-chain, what were we on the Moon-chain, the parent of this Earth-chain? Remember the moon is just a dead chain, from which all life has fled, except what we may call the life of a corpse, a chemical and quasi-physiological activity of the molecules. What were we present humans on the Moon-chain? We were the animal monads in the moon-men, in the humanity of the moon, or what, if you wish, we could call the animal moon-men, just as here on earth we speak of ourselves as thinking humans and animal humans, referring to different parts of our constitution — facts which you all know. When I say we, I mean we of the higher class of human beings.

Question 2. What were the low class of human beings on earth today, and the lowest class of human beings, the savages today — who according to the anthropologists can scarcely count to more than 10, that is can scarcely have a clear idea of what more than 10

things means, such as the Veddahs of Ceylon and the Andaman
Islanders and some peoples in the South Seas and some of the tribes
in Africa, etc., etc. — what were these lower men on the Moon-chain?
They were the moon-animals. Then you will immediately say:
"Then we are a whole kingdom higher than these others of the human
family." No. You have the explanation at the ends of your fingers.
The animals of the Moon-chain before the moon's Seventh or last
Round took place, according to the process which I have just tried
to illustrate a few moments ago, so to speak were mânasaputrized
by the moon-men, the moon-humanity. So that before those animals
reached the moon's Seventh Round, they had thus been enlightened
and raised to the human status, but a low human status.

So these lower human beings among us today, those in whom the
spark of mind now burns not too brightly, were once animals on the
moon, then were mânasaputrized into humanity before the moon's
Seventh Round ended. Thus then, when these monads at the end of
the Seventh moon-round, after the long pralaya, came to our earth,
they came already as humanized entities, as humans.

Now what on the Moon-chain were our present animals? They
were the lowest animals on the moon, the very lowest, those which
had not emanated from out of themselves the powers to allow themselves to be mânasaputrized; just as on earth we have insects and
flying things and creeping things and the lower forms of life of
various kinds; because the animal kingdom contains many classes,
from its highest representatives the apes, running through all the
grades of the quadrupeds, through the birds and fishes down to the
insects, etc.

Similarly now, instead of looking backwards let us look forwards.
We humans, that is we higher humans, in the next chain-imbodiment
will be the lowest dhyân-chohanic kingdom there. The animal
human parts of us, what we call the animal man or the animal monad,
will at the end of the Seventh Round on our present chain have
become fully humanized or man. And we, what we call ourselves
now, will then have become dhyân-chohanized or the lowest class of
Dhyân-Chohans. We shall then have Dhyân-Chohans working
through humans who themselves again have animal monads. The
lower humans on our earth today, at the end of the Seventh Round

will form the average or higher men on the next chain. And our present animal monads will then have become humanized and will form the highest type. In other words, no animal can become a man until it has been mânasaputrized.

Remember I am not talking of bodies now. I am talking of true evolution, the inner forces and powers which distinguish a thinking man from the relatively unthinking animal. That has not anything to do with bodies. I am talking of monads, of the real man, of the real beasts, of the inner being. And our highest animals at the end of our Seventh Round, provided that they make the grade upward by the last three Rounds, will be humans when this Earth-chain comes to its end and dies. Similarly for other kingdoms in nature at the end of the Seventh Round, if its representatives have succeeded in making the grade upwards, each such kingdom will have gone up a step higher. Those that make the grade among the animals will have become men. The men who make the grade amongst us will become Dhyân-Chohans.

Now then, who were the Dhyân-Chohans who mânasaputrized the moon-beings of the Third Root-Race? Our own human ancestors. They were the average or higher men of the moon, moon-men, now to become Dhyân-Chohans, called mânasaputras, sons of mind, i. e., Dhyânins, because their function is, so far as we are concerned, to awaken thought, to awaken mind in us. The beast, for instance, has as much latent mind as any man has, but it has not been mânasaputrized, awakened, stimulated, lifted, brought into self-conscious activity.

Take the case of a little child, a human child. Why doesn't it think as we do? Why doesn't it write books, why doesn't it speak on Theosophy? Why doesn't it study science? Because it is too young. Of course. But the real answer is because its mind has not yet been emanated from within itself. The parents of the child act as the mânasaputras to a certain extent. They teach it, they watch. Little by little the child begins to observe, to take note of things, begins to think, its faculties develop, and before you realize it, the child begins to say nice things, and you are proud of your offspring. What has happened? Simply that its mind has begun to open, to function. But if that child in childhood were carried to a desert island and lived there alone, provided it could live, provided it survived, it would not learn speech. Its mind moves very slowly; it would take note of what is going on around, but it would be in a worse state than a grown savage like the Andaman Islander. It would be little more than a semi-thinking human animal, because its mind would not yet have awakened, opened, developed, emanated, evolved.

For instance, when we see a child grown into a thinking man, we don't say that is a haphazard work of thinking Nature, fortuitous, chance. We say: there is law behind there, something called mind has evolved out of that entity. Something already in there has simply flowered out. In other words evolution or emanation is simply growth. Those three words are practically interchangeable: growth, emanation, evolution: because growth, as a plant from a seed, consists in the unfolding or flowing forth of what that seed contained.

Now H. P. B. in her wonderful work, *The Secret Doctrine*, divides the monads into 7, and I think even 10 classes. As a matter of fact there are 12. These 7 or 10 or 12 monadic classes in another place she divides into 3 families, 3 divisions. The first and highest are all those monads above the human. An intermediate family or division is the human and all connected with the human — and remember how many varieties of human and sub-human beings there are. The third and lowest class are all the entities below the very lowest entity which by any stretch of fact could be called human, such as the beasts and the vegetables and the minerals and the elementals. She points out that of these 3 divisions the highest are not only the forerunners in coming over from the moon who guided the elementals in the building of our new Earth-chain, but also were the instructors and guides of the next class, or division rather, which came following after. We were this next class which came following after; and they and we thereupon became the guides, the helpers, the instructors, of the lowest class which followed after us, just exactly as we see in Nature among us today.

One thing more about the mânasaputras, and it will explain what may seem like a contradiction to you if you have read *The Secret Doctrine* without care. The mânasaputras who as a body were the particular awakeners of us from non-thinking human bodies or quasi-animal bodies into thinking human beings, were the lowest class of the Dhyân-Chohans who were average or higher men on the moon, who had attained dhyân-chohanship at the end of the Seventh Round of the moon. But these, while they enlightened us, speaking now in classes, were themselves guided and helped by the two higher dhyân-chohanic classes, a few representatives of which during the early races of this Fourth Round of our globe came amongst men as gods and demi-gods, and guided them; and these are they who are referred to in the exoteric religions of antiquity under such names as Osiris, Isis, Ahura-Mazda, in other words the gods and god-men of the ancient peoples. They were the Dhyân-Chohans, some of them I should say, of the highest and second classes, who even before the mânasaputras came and awakened our mind, were already at their work of teaching. Because mark you: even in the first race of Globe A, the first globe of our chain, beginning with the Second Round, there were already men, that is to say thinking, self-conscious, cogitating, feeling, loving human beings. Those were they who have now become what we now call the Mahâtmans, the Masters, their highest chelas, lower chelas, and the leaders of men, simply because they are more highly evolved than the rest of us men. They were men. And these few men, relatively speaking, (by few I don't mean 3 or 4; perhaps a million or two, it is just guess-work) even in the first race on Globe A, were taught by the Dhyân-Chohans of the highest and second classes. The latter helped to awaken those earliest men, awaken them as a parent will awaken the mind of her child, helping to do so, teaching and guiding and instructing and lifting up and showing the path, giving ideals, sounding keynotes of truth.

For instance, we humans, looking before us into the future, shall reach the end of the Seventh Round of our chain. We humans then, those of us who shall have made the grade, will develop into Dhyân-Chohans of the third class, the lowest, the kingdom above the human kingdom — call them the angels if you like — angels of the third or lowest grade. The better name is Dhyân-Chohans, because angel in the Christian teachings is a vague term. The Masters and their highest chelas will then have become Dhyân-Chohans of the second or next to the highest dhyân-chohanic class; and every one of the dhyân-chohanic kingdoms will, each in its turn, have moved up a step, a kingdom. Our animals, those who make the grade, will become men of a low type at the end of the Seventh Round. Which animals will these be? The apes, the monkeys, possibly some of the quadrupeds. The beasts below these — I doubt if any of them will reach to the human stage even at the end of the Seventh Round. They are still too crude, too low, unprepared. But they will become men during the next chain, except the very lowest of our animals who will be the higher animals on the next chain.

Another thought in connexion with these ideas. I stated that I was not speaking of bodies when mentioning evolution, and I have not been. I have been speaking of monads, egos, souls, call them what you will, in other words the consciousness-center within an entity, that which makes him what he is as a conscious being, a thinker, a feeler, one with judgment and discrimination, one who feels love, compassion, pity, sympathy, all these lovely human qualities which are truly human as well as humane.

But now, to speak for a moment about bodies: you will find in my book *Theosophy and Modern Science* [*Man in Evolution*] how hard I tried to show that all evolution is from within outwards, that nothing can evolve or unfold into something greater unless it had not only the power and capacity inside to do so, but had already within itself what is going to come forth. If you turn the spigot, the faucet, the water won't run out of it unless there is water there to run out of it; and no man will manifest or bring forth into his life, into his actions, into his thoughts, what he has not awakened within himself. But, while all evolution is therefore from within, while all growth is from within, yet, as the ages slowly go by, even the physical bodies feel the vibration, the impetus, continually impinging upon them, and feel also the quality of those impulses as unfolding or evolution becomes constantly greater; so that even the physical bodies become more refined and slowly change. Yet there seems to be a law in Nature that no strain of physical bodies can endure after a certain period. For some reason, interesting, fascinating, Nature seems to call forth, as it were, and say to any physical body-strain — thus far and no farther. It would seem as if that type of structure could not evolve properly, efficiently. Then those bodies slowly die out, and the monads which gave them life, after their rest in the Devachan or Nirvâna come back and find new robes or bodies waiting for them of quite another kind.

There you have the process of evolution on a thumb-nail. That is why the enormous reptiles of the Mesozoic day vanished; and as modern biologists and geologists examine the records of the rocks and fossils, you will find them all expressing their amazement that these strains, these families of creatures, seem to die out suddenly. As I remember, one geologist expressed it by saying it looked as if a pestilence had fallen upon them, and in a short time, geologically speaking, they had gone. Science is utterly unable to explain why, except by guesses, some of them very silly, like the one I read some time ago, that the reason the reptiles died out was because they grew so big they could not carry themselves and died of starvation. That to me is the most grotesque theory I have ever heard. Nature doesn't build up a big body if she cannot get food to make up a big body. It was just guess-work. Far more reasonable was the suggestion I read in a geological book that the reason the reptiles died out was because they were smitten by some universal pest which wiped them out, perhaps a new kind of germ, new to these creatures. Maybe!

Isn't it a blessing that these physical bodies do in time die out!

EVOLUTION INTO THE HUMAN KINGDOM — III

I HAVE been asked to speak again on the subject of how the monads pass from the animal kingdom to the human kingdom. The question is in general: Please again state just exactly the difference between the animal monads in the animals, and the animal monads in men. Well, really, I brought this upon myself, and I am undergoing the justly earned karman, because in my great desire to give to you something of what I have studied and learned, I made the statement long ago, both in speech and in one or more of my talks, that what the animals were on the Moon-chain became the humans on this chain, and that what our animals now on earth are, will become the humans in the reimbodiment of this our Earth-chain. Well, that started a lot of things! Very rightly so. I was very glad these discussions and talks did begin. I succeeded in helping to wake up the minds of some of our students. They were taking too many things for granted too easily. They want to examine them, study them. But evidently a great many do not understand, and I do not blame them a particle. It is not an easy point of the doctrine. I meant to bring this subject out because some of the Theosophists in the world today who do not belong to our Society, have been taught or have accepted the teaching that we humans were the apes on the Moon-chain, and this is all wrong. There were apes or beings equivalent to apes on the moon, when the Moon-chain arrived at its end, before our Earth-chain came into being, but those apes, as you will see in a moment, became human.

I fully expected these discussions to take place. I foresaw them. I welcomed them. And whenever I was asked to explain, as someone told me, during nine years past I have just looked wise with a wooden face, and said, "Isn't that interesting! You keep on studying, and you will find out." Because I wanted you to get the answers yourselves, as I knew perfectly well you will never understand anything, make it a part of your intellect, a part of yourself, unless you work out the answer yourself. What you are merely told is like what a child learns in school. If it is not especially interested, it will not remember. But I have been keeping tab on how these discussions on the animal souls in the two kingdoms have been going, and I have reached a point now where I think there has been sufficient honest-to-goodness hard work to entitle those who have worked hard to an answer, and these will be the only ones who will understand the doctrine.

Now then, the difficulty in understanding this thing, which is not difficult at all, but extremely simple, has been the fact, the common human failing (I have it, we all have it), that we have persistently confused monads with rûpas, forms, bodies, so that when we speak of animals we immediately figurate sheep, elephants, horses, cats, dogs, or what not, forgetting that the real animal is the monad; and you know that I never said that the *animals* on the moon became the humans on the earth, unless I had preceded it with the explanation or statement: the animal *monads* on the moon become the humans on the earth. But which animal monads? The animal monads in the moon-men, or the animal monads of the animals on the moon?

Now for instance, we on this earth, each one of us, has an animal monad as part of his constitution. What difference is there between this human animal monad, and the animal monad of an elephant or a dog? What is the difference, the distinction, between the two? I will try to explain. In the first place, one kingdom does not turn into the next higher kingdom through evolution. When we speak of kingdoms, we mean kingdoms; and in Theosophy we have 10 kingdoms of beings, otherwise 10 classes of monads, otherwise again 10 life-waves. What are they? We count them in this manner: 3 of the Elementals, the Mineral, Vegetable, Animal, the Human — seven; and the three dhyân-chohanic kingdoms — making 10 classes of monads in all, 10 kingdoms, 10 different life-waves.

Not one of these kingdoms ever passes, through evolution or development or unfolding, into the next higher kingdom, never, because these kingdoms refer to the rûpas which shelter the monads, imbody them, enclose them, are the vehicles of the monads. For instance, the animal kingdom never becomes a human kingdom. The vegetable kingdom never becomes an animal kingdom. The mineral kingdom never becomes a plant kingdom. The human kingdom never becomes the lowest of the three dhyân-chohanic kingdoms.

What happens? It is the monads as individuals which evolve, each one in its own kingdom until it learns all that kingdom can teach it. When as an individual monad it has become animalized or humanized or dhyân-chohanized to the next higher, then at its next incarnation or imbodiment it enters into the very lowest realm of the next higher kingdom as an individual monad. Is that clear? *But the* KINGDOMS *never as kingdoms become higher kingdoms.*

You will see the point of this, or at least I will try to make it clear. Every kingdom below the human is striving to become — no, pardon me, every monad in every kingdom below the human kingdom is striving upwards towards the human kingdom. The human kingdom is its objective or goal, their objective, their goal; just as our goal as humans is to strive to become a member of the lowest of the three dhyân-chohanic kingdoms just above the human. But the human kingdom as such never *becomes* that lowest dhyân-chohanic kingdom. Why? Because Nature needs these kingdoms where she has them. They are as it were houses of life for the peregrinating, evolving monads to live in, to pass through, to graduate from and enter the next house of life or kingdom. Is that thought clear? Nature needs these through eternity. That is why long after we human monads shall have left the human kingdom and evolved up to become Dhyân-Chohans of the lowest dhyân-chohanic kingdom, the human kingdom will still remain containing monads or individuals then using the bodies kept alive by those new incoming individuals from what is now the animal kingdom. Don't you see? If the human kingdom all evolved to become Dhyân-Chohans, there would be a gap between the Dhyân-Chohans and the beast. The monads go up step by step, kingdom after kingdom.

What makes these kingdoms in nature? The records in the astral light. There is a very important contributory thought, and it explains a lot of questions I am going to discuss here. From immemorial eternity, as far as I know, there have always been, at least in our solar system and probably in our galaxy, 7 or 10 or 12 classes of monads or kingdoms or life-waves for our chain; and they have been kept going as these kingdoms because of new monads coming in from the lower kingdom, graduating into our kingdom, and human monads graduating out from our human kingdom into the dhyân-chohanic kingdom. So the kingdoms remain because the 10 classes of monads remain through eternity. It is the monads which evolve.

The question comes in — and this is incidental — don't the bodies of the monads in which the monads live when they imbody in the bodies also improve? They do but with almost excessive slowness. Why? Because the astral molds in the astral light have been improved from aeons and aeons in the past. I have no idea how far past — you might say from eternity. With each cosmic manvantara those astral molds in the astral light are slowly changing and improving. So that the kingdoms themselves, although remaining always the same kingdoms, are through the eternities themselves slowly rising, but with immense slowness; whereas the monads evolve much faster.

Now, don't confuse another thought here. There are certain rapid variations in the kingdoms themselves which are not permanent however. As for instance, take a human frame today. It is a far cry in its present relative grace and symmetry and dignified carriage to the first human beings of the Third Round or even the human beings of the Third Root-Race in this Round. If you saw them today you would say: Well, what ape-like bodies those are, they are positively ape-like. But there is not a drop of ape-blood in them. Don't get that idea. We use the term ape-like because the apes have a certain amount of human blood in them from that time; and evolving very slowly, not as fast as we humans have in shape and symmetry and beauty of form, they still contain what we call, just to give it a word, an ape-like picture of their human part-parents.

But mark you, the humans on the Moon-chain at about the same period where we are now, looked pretty much like what we now look like, and they had a time when they were rather ape-like in appearance, but with not a particle of ape-blood in them. I do hope I make this clear, because it has taken fifty years for Theosophists to understand the distinction.

Now what does this mean? It means that because the rûpa-kingdoms evolve to betterment with such exceeding slowness, they nevertheless have spurts, upshootings, of great improvement which cannot hold. They drop back, they degenerate and go back. I am talking of kingdoms now, not the monads which incarnate in those

kingdoms. I am talking of the rûpa-kingdoms. Why? I told you.
The fluid stuff forming our bodies, is compelled by nature to follow
a certain line of development partly from inherent swabhâva, but
partly because of the mold in the astral light.

Now then, what possibility is there of reconciling what I just
told you with the statement I made, and which you will find in
H. P. B., that the animals on the moon became the humans on this
chain? That our animals with us now will be the humans in the
next Earth-chain, the child of this chain? The reconciliation lies in
the fact that when you hear a statement of this kind, you should
bring to its examination all your studies of Theosophy. If you had
brought together other things that H. P. B. and I have stated, you
would not have been bothered.

I will try to explain from some other angle. The human constitution — and indeed the constitution of an entity imbodied in any
kingdom, the animal kingdom let us say, or in the dhyân-chohanic
kingdom above ours, every such entity — is sevenfold. But of the
seven principles or monads from any such constitution like our
human, some are expressed with relative fulness and others are as
yet largely unexpressed; and it is this difference which makes the
kingdoms. Intricate? Fascinating to those who have got the key.
Thus the animals have everything in them that a man has. They
have a divine monad, a spiritual monad, and a human monad and
an animal monad and an astral-vital monad and even what I have
called the physical monad; but the monads in the animal kingdom
have thus far evolved only up to the animal monad. That is why
they are in the animal kingdom; they are at home there. When in
the future the monads in the animal kingdom, the highest amongst
them, shall have begun to yearn upwards towards the human monad,
in other words begun to be humanized, the human capacities, elements, qualities, swabhâva, in the animal, will have begun slowly to
show themselves. The animals will begin to feel no longer at home
in the animal kingdom, in these lower rûpas; and as the process of
slow humanizing continues, as the animal monads rise through experience; they will leave the animal kingdom and be attracted,
psycho-magnetically, to the very lowest bodies in the human kingdom
just above on the scale of life.

What happens?   These monads formerly manifesting in the animal kingdom, in animal bodies, are now sufficiently humanized to enter into the lowest human bodies of savage barbarians, or, especially in the beginning of this Round on this Globe D, of beings who are far lower than the lowest savage we have today — but human nevertheless.   What happens?   They enter these human bodies as the animal monads there.   There is your answer, there is your key.   Similarly when a human being aspiring up to the dhyân-chohanic monad, to the spiritual monad, has reached a point where he is almost above humanity, growing out of it, when his yearnings are of spirit, higher, higher, there comes a time when incarnation among humans no longer is adequate.   He is dhyânizing himself, this monad, and the attraction to the human kingdom will some day stop.   There will be no further pull of incarnation in bodies of human beings.   The next will be in the lowest of the dhyân-chohanic kingdoms.   Is that thought clear?

So then, what is the difference or distinction between the animal monads in animals and the animal monads in men?   I have told you. When the animal monad in the animal kingdom has humanized itself through evolution sufficiently no longer to feel attracted in incarnation to the animal kingdom, it will seek imbodiment psycho-magnetically in the very lowest specimens of men, and become the animal monad in men.   Thus you see the unity of universal nature and her marvelous variety.

Now we will take the specific aspect of the moon-men and the moon-animals.   You have been told many times that all kingdoms lower than the human will show a tendency to die out as Round the 4th becomes Round the 5th; still more tendency to die out as Round the 5th becomes Round the 6th; so that by the time the 7th and highest and last Round is reached, the animals will have practically died out, the reason being that they cannot make the grade up the ascending arc.   Their monads gradually die out and go into Nirvâna, where they will wait until the next chain-imbodiment, and during Rounds 1, 2, and 3 of that next chain-imbodiment.   Thus the animals who could not make the grade up the Sixth and Seventh Rounds will have a chance again.   Then they will come in as animals again. Nature will prepare the way through the elementals and the architects.   Bodies will be there for them. They themselves will help to form the bodies in the animal kingdom. These are the animals who could not make the grade.

Now the same thing happened on the moon. Yet during the Seventh Round, whether on the moon in the past or in our own Seventh Round in the future, there will be exceptions in the animal kingdom. What are these exceptions? The apes, possibly the very highest of some of the monkeys too. The apes at the end of the Seventh Round will just have touched the human stage. The same thing happened on the moon. There the animals died out before the lunar Seventh Round was reached, except a few who just reached the human stage, just ready to enter the human kingdom when the Seventh Round was closing. There were millions of them, but compared with the billions and billions of the life-wave for the kingdom, it is a mere handful. Yes, these animals on the moon could make the grade and did. They just reached the lowest bottom of the next kingdom when the Seventh Round was reached, and became the lowest human beings on this new chain. How about the human animal monads in the Moon-chain? These were growing all the time more and more humanized and at the end of the Seventh Round on the Moon-chain they had become men; and the lunar men, the Moon-men at the end of the Seventh Round, had become Dhyân-Chohans of the lowest dhyân-chohanic kingdom. Who were these moon animal monads? We were they. And that is what I meant when I said the animal monads which reached the tip of the human kingdom on the Moon-chain became the humans on this chain. Do you see? The kingdoms do not rise. Nature keeps them there, each on its own level, for the monads coming up from below, as monads, reaching up to the spirit lunar chain as it were. Spirit yearns to help earth, earth yearns upward to spirit.

So you see, marvelous picture, although the kingdoms remain the same, as it were retain the same place on nature's Ladder of Life, the monads come down through them and then on the upward arc sweep up through the kingdoms. Thus with us. Our animal monads are the monads from the animal kingdom which had become sufficiently humanized no longer to be animal animal monads but human animal monads. So when our Seventh Round shall have come, the animal monads in us will be the humans of the next imbodiment of the chain. We humans by the end of the Seventh Round, those of us who make the grade, will have become dhyânized, chohanized if you wish, and shall have become Dhyân-Chohans at the end of the Seventh Round.

Now then, next thought. What were the mânasaputras in this our present chain-imbodiment who incarnated in us human beings in the Third Root-Race on this Globe during this Fourth Round and made us thinking men? We were in the human kingdom as bodies, but I am now talking of monads. Who were the mânasaputras who awaked us intellectually? They were those who had attained Dhyân-Chohan-ship on the moon at the end of the Seventh Round, and we were then their animal monads. They found us out again, they sought us out again, our higher selves as it were waiting for them, waiting until our bodies were ready, until the human rûpas were sufficiently subtil, flexible, to receive the intellectual fire. Then they incarnated in us. If you have read H. P. B.'s *Secret Doctrine*, you will now see why these mânasaputras could not incarnate before that time. No fit bodies for us. *They* were ready. The *bodies* were not ready. No fit rûpas, no fit bodies, for us, they said. Those bodies had to become more subtil, more delicate, refined, more proper to receive the holy intellect of the mânasaputras enlightening the latent mind of these humans, of us. Then when the time came, there came the 'descent' as we call it, the descent of the mânasaputras. Men began to think. And just let me add here, there was another class of mânasaputras far higher than anything we as individuals have been connected with, who started this wonderful work of putting the flame of mind in those early human races. They were even Dhyân-Chohans on the Moon-chain. Marvelous picture!

So when the mânasaputras gave us mind, it was merely our own Dhyân-Chohans, the moon-men become Dhyân-Chohans, and we their animal monads now become humans. It was their duty to enlighten us again, to give us back our mind, to awaken it. So shall we at the end of our Seventh Round become Dhyân-Chohans and be the mânasaputras to the humanity of the next round who are now our human animal monads. Have I made the thought clear?

And now I have almost closed. You have heard of moments or

times of choice when the great decisions must be made. One took place at the middle of the Fourth Round. Do you realize what happened then, when the moment came, when the monads were tested to see if they could pass? It was easy enough to run downhill, but could they pass that dangerous point and begin the upward arc? Millions, hundreds of millions, billions, succeeded in our human kingdom, in the animal kingdom. There was enough in them of upward aspiration to take them past the danger-point of the bottommost line and to start them going upwards. These were the animals who are we. But do you know that hundreds of millions of monads could not pass over the danger-point? They were what H. P. B. called "lost monads." They perished for the remainder of this manvantara. This merely means that they could not make the grade, had not evolved sufficiently, and went into Nirvâna. Out of it they will not reawaken until the psycho-magnetic call comes to them in the next chain to come into imbodied life. The animal kingdom will be then waiting for them, and the monads will come into this animal kingdom. The animal kingdom does not move up except with almost infinite slowness, gradually improving; but the monads are always there.

There will be another grave moment of choice at the middle of the Fifth Round, and that for us humans will be our great transition. In the middle of the Fifth Round will you and I be sufficiently dhyânized to be able to move up towards the beginning of the Sixth Round? Those who are becoming universal enough to become attracted to Dhyân-Chohanhood will make the grade. Those of us who will not have become sufficiently universalized to join the kingdom of the Dhyân-Chohans will perish for the remainder of this manvantara, in other words go into a Nirvâna and lose billions of years. That is what it means, the losing of billions of years.

Think what it means for these millions of monads who perish then. Look at the time they lose. Two billion years before our Seventh Round is ended. More than 4 or 5 billion years more before our new chain-imbodiment begins. Between 6 and 7 billion years, precious time lost. That is why the Masters are pressing all the time. Now is your opportunity to become universal in your sympathies. Do anything you can do to be more spiritually human. Aspire upwards no matter what the attractions are here below. That does not mean lose your human sympathies. You will be standing in your own way if you think that, because your human sympathies are lofty; but it means to make them less selfish, more spiritual, raised, so that when the danger-point comes, you will pass up.

THE CLOSING OF THE DOOR INTO THE
HUMAN KINGDOM

I WOULD like to say a few words about this 'door' into the human kingdom. Of course it is not a door. That is just a way of speaking. Thus the door into a profession means graduation of the student. When the animal graduates interiorly, in other words has brought forth from within, the human qualities, it has graduated into the human kingdom; that is its door.

Now, the difference between the beasts, the plants, the stones, the men, the elementals, and the Dhyân-Chohans, the difference as amongst these, or between any two of them, is one not only of potentiality, but of developing ability. Thus the human child is potentially a man or woman, but not yet so, and will not have the adult ability until he is fully grown. The potentiality is there, but the ability lacks. It is not yet brought forth from within. It will come as the child grows. Just so with the beast. The potentiality of humanhood is there, but the beast is not yet human because it has not yet brought forth from within itself human qualities, attributes, power of thought, power of feeling, self respect, all the qualities that make us men men.

Why was there a door into the human kingdom which closed at the bottom point of the present manvantara? It simply means that the animals at that point had not as yet brought forth *from within themselves* those spiritual, mental attributes, which would enable them to climb up towards the next kingdom, which happens to be the human. They could not make the grade. They did not want to; they did not know anything about it because they were not yet awakened within themselves. The humans did. Consequently there was no door for the humans. They came down the Arc of Descent, passed the critical point, and began to climb up the Arc of Ascent; and we humans shall continue to climb until the end of the Seventh Round.

Here is a very interesting thing to note: There will be a door for us humans at the mid-point of the Fifth Round, and those humans who do not pass through that door, in other words who cannot then

and there begin the grade upwards and enter into the lowest dhyân-
chohanic kingdom in the Sixth Round, will be by the fact 'failures,'
and will gradually die out, and will have to wait until the next Planetary imbodiment. But those humans who will make the grade, in
other words who will make the upwards choice — when the great
moment of upwards choice comes — they will continue to ascend
the arc.

How does this all arise? There are ten or even twelve classes of
monads. We may describe them thus: the three dhyân-chohanic
classes above the human, that is the highest dhyân-chohanic, the
intermediate, and the lowest of the dhyân-chohanic; then comes the
human, then the beast, then the plant, then the stone, then come
the three elemental kingdoms. Thus we have three elemental kingdoms on one hand, three dhyân-chohanic kingdoms on the other, and
four intermediate kingdoms, human, beast, plant and stone, making
ten distinct classes of monads; which merely means again, monads
divisible into these ten classes because the individuals of each class
have brought forth the qualities, attributes, in other words the type,
attracting such monads to aggregate together in kingdoms or classes.

When any individual, any one of these ten classes, through
evolutionary development brings out latent powers, attributes, faculties, within itself, it gradually rises and passes through the door
into the next kingdom, graduating from the lower into the higher,
and we call that a door. All the individuals congregate together
who are like each other. All the X's are attracted together, all the
Y's, all the Z's — in other words, to use the old proverb, "Birds
of a feather flock together."

As regards the beasts: they will all show a tendency to die out
in this manvantara, and it is a peculiar process which that one
statement doesn't really cover, but it gives you a key. As for
instance, all the beasts that were on earth in this Fourth Round
will reappear again on this globe earth in the Fifth Round, but
will have a shorter time here. In other words, they will come and
disappear more quickly; in the Sixth Round still more quickly;
whereas in the Seventh Round it is probable that only the very highest of the beasts, the apes and perhaps a few more, will remain.
The others will have died out. The reason is they could not "make
the grade" in any way. It is my own opinion, subject to correction

by those who know vastly more than I do, that probably the next Round, the Fifth, will see almost the last of the great majority of the beasts.

As regards the apes, there is an exceptional case. They are not human, but they are over-shadowed by humanhood. Humanhood is just beginning, as it were, to cast its rays into the ape's brain. If they can "make the grade," they will become men of a very low and degenerate type. No, the word is wrongly chosen — of a very low and *undeveloped* type during the next Round.

These classes are all monads, just as man is a monad. He makes his body to improve as he himself evolves. But when men's bodies become too gross for them, the bodies die out, the human monads won't have anything more to do with them, they are cast aside. "These are not fit rûpas for us," they will say, and the bodies will vanish in that way. We shall then bring forth bodies approaching the type of dhyân-chohanic vehicles, that is bodies fit for dhyân-chohanic entities, which we shall have become during the Sixth and Seventh Rounds; and some humans more advanced than others even during the end of the Fifth Round.

So you see, all these ten classes of monads have the same potentialities, but do not rank alike, for they are exactly like human children in different grades in a school, from the little ones up to the graduate young folk leaving the university. The potentialities are the same, but the different degrees of development vary greatly, and it is these differences of evolutionary development which actually are the ten monadic classes.

But I want to remind you once again that even we humans during the next Round shall have an opportunity to enter the, open door into the lowest of the three dhyân-chohanic kingdoms; and this open door has been hinted at by H. P. B. and the Masters under the term "the moment of choice," or the time of choice. It means this: that when we shall have reached the middle point of the Fifth Round, more explicitly, the middle point of the Fourth Root-Race on the Fourth Globe during the Fifth Round, shall we be ready? Shall we have evolved to the point where we see the beyond and desire to go onwards towards it? If we have, we shall then pass through the door of choice. We shall then begin to approach the place that the lowest dhyân-chohanic kingdom now holds, and that

kingdom will have gone a step higher. The dhyân-chohanic kingdoms are simply monads who have passed through the human stage,
and they are ascending to the god-stage. They will become gods
if they are successful. So we shall become Dhyân-Chohans if we
"make the grade."

I will just say this: There is absolutely no time to lose, life is
so rapid. We humans learn so slowly, and time is as fleeting in a
single incarnation really as it is in a manvantara. There is no time
to lose to make up your mind to succeed. And it does not require any
abnormal asceticism or martyrdom or anything of the sort. It simply
means being more human, so that by continuously becoming more
truly human, you become more dhyân-chohanic. It doesn't mean
only intellectual growth. It means moral growth, intellectual growth,
psychical growth, but above everything else moral and spiritual
growth.

Who are these Dhyân-Chohans we have been speaking of? If
you can imagine the very grandest kind of a human being that your
loftiest flights of fancy can picturate, you will come somewhere near,
perhaps. They are just like we are, thinking, feeling, evolving
beings, above us as we are above the beasts. They have their representatives on this earth called śishtas, remainders.

As a matter of fact, and turning for a moment to the subject of
Rounds, it is interesting to note that the third dhyân-chohanic kingdom will enter this earth when we as a life-wave shall have gone on
to Globe E. They are the higher class coming on the Round behind
us, not in evolution, because they are higher than we, but merely
so far as serial appearance is concerned; and these Dhyân-Chohans
are now evolving on Globe C.

Referring now to our former topic: I have often thought what
a world of warning lies in the words of the Master in the *Mahatma
Letters*, "How many millions will perish?" It does not mean that
they will be annihilated, it means that they will lose the remainder
of this manvantara because they have been malingering before the
moment of choice comes, unwilling to see, therefore too weak to go
on, too indifferent to climb, lacking in spiritual and intellectual
imagination to wish to become stronger and better and finer and
nobler. Therefore these will not "make the grade." The truth is
they just don't want to.

LUNAR AND AGNISHWÂTTA PITRIS

I HAVE been deeply interested in what I have heard here this evening, and I am sure that all present have been equally interested. There is one point which it is very important, I think, to call to your attention. I have often noticed what has seemed to me to be a confusion of ideas as regards the different classes of the Dhyân-Chohans. Some students seem to think that those Dhyân-Chohans which are spoken of as having the 'creative fire' are the highest, and they are misled, of course, by the word 'creative' in the phrase 'creative fire.'

As a matter of fact, these Dhyân-Chohans are among the lowest in the Dhyân-Chohanic Hierarchy. The reason of this is obvious. Pure Spirit *per se* cannot work in matter at all, because pure Spirit is so far above physical being. Spirit *is;* it does not directly bring forth or govern shape and form in the lower worlds. Between spirit and these lower worlds there are the other classes of the Dhyân-Chohanic Hierarchy which are the links between the two, and which transmit the spiritual energies and powers into the lower world. It is only thus that spirit can act on matter: indirectly by transmission, but not directly upon physical being. It is those entities of the lower degrees which work in the realms of matter which have and use the forces appropriate to those realms of matter; and one of these forces is the astral-physical 'creative fire.'

The Lunar Pitris, who are one class of the Dhyân-Chohans — one of the four material classes — have this 'creative fire'; and who are the Lunar Pitris? They are those entities who, when the Lunar Chain had finished its evolution, had not reached the higher Dhyân-Chohanhood, and who, consequently, entered the new chain, the child of the Moon, and who in time became the humanity of that new chain — our Earth planetary chain.

Such are the Lunar Pitris, and remember that they belong to the four lower classes of the Dhyân-Chohanic Hierarchy.

The Agnishwâtta-Pitris, on the contrary, are those Dhyân-Chohans which have not the physical 'creative fire,' because they belong to a much superior sphere of being; but they have all the fires of the spiritual-intellectual realms. The Agnishwâtta-Pitris are they who had, in preceding manvantaras, completed their evolution in the realms of physical matter, and who, when evolution of the lower had brought about the proper time, came to the rescue of those who had only the physical 'creative fire,' thus inspiring and enlightening these lower Pitris with spiritual and intellectual energies or 'fires.'

The Agnishwâttas are the spiritual-intellectual parts of us, and therefore are our inner Teachers. The Lunar Pitris, on the other hand, are the incomplete Dhyân-Chohans, incompletely evolved from the spiritual-intellectual standpoint when they left the lunar chain, and who imbodied themselves on our earth; and we as human beings are they — as *human beings*, I say, which means *human feelers, human instinctuals* — and who therefore obviously do not pertain to the higher part of our constitution.

Clearly, therefore, they do not occupy a very high rank in the Dhyân-Chohanic Hierarchy.

The Lunar Pitris, in other words, are the part of the human constitution which feels humanly, which feels instinctually, and which possesses the physical brain-mind mentality. The Agnishwâtta-Pitris are higher parts of our constitution than these, because the Agnishwâtta-Pitris are the elements in our constitution which contain spiritual-intellectual light, therefore 'fire.'

When this earth's planetary chain shall have reached the end of its Seventh Round, we, as then having completed the evolutionary course for this planetary chain, will leave this planetary chain as Dhyân-Chohans, Agnishwâttas; but the others now trailing along behind us — the present beasts — will be, if I may use the same term as before, the Lunar Pitris of the next planetary chain to come; and this term, future Lunar Pitris, is well chosen, because the present planetary earth-chain will then be the sevenfold moon of that new chain.

I hope that you have understood these remarks. I will briefly review what I have said: Those entities having the 'creative fire' belong to the four lower classes of the Dhyân-Chohanic Hierarchy; and those which have not the physical 'creative fire,' (which means the creative fire of material worlds) are they which are too high for immediate or direct work in physical matter, and therefore have no direct connexion at all with these material realms. These latter are the Agnishwâttas. They are gods, and they are our Higher Egos. They were, in their turn, Lunar Pitris in a by-gone manvantara. Now they have become Agnishwâtta-Pitris.

Thus you see how it is that every class of entities in each new manvantara goes to the next higher step on the Ladder of Evolution.

THE MONADS IN MAN

HERE is a question I would like to ask: You have spoken of the different Buddhas. You have referred to — at least you have inferred — the existence in man of different egos. We have heard on other occasions of the Divine Monad, the Spiritual Monad, the Human Monad, the Astral Monad, and the Physical Monad. Now here is my question. Just what, then, is man? How many mans — if I may so coin a plural, I won't say men, but how many mans — are there in a man? Is each one of these monads an entity by itself, united with the other entities, all together forming man's constitution; and if so, are there several mans in man, or is it just one single unitary being to which different names — I mean divided into portions to which different names — are given as we pass down the scale? Now that is a question well worth studying, and I would now like to suggest an answer.

It is not a mere figure of speech when we speak of man as having in his constitution different monads. A monad means an indivisible center of life-consciousness-substance, a spiritual ego. Therefore man, in addition to being a stream of consciousness as he is as a constitution, has within him a Divinity, a Buddha or Christ, a Mânasa-putra, a human being, an astral entity; and he is housed in the human beast — the astral-vital-physical body. All these collectively constitute man's constitution. Hence I have so often said to you: Remember in all your studies, never forget it, that man is a composite entity, which means an entity formed of other entities, other beings. Therefore did I choose the words in asking my question: How many mans — not men but mans — are there in what we call man? All through any one such constitution there is the sûtrâtman or thread-self from the inmost of the inmost, the core of the core, the heart of the Universe — through all these different monads, from the highest till it touches the physical brain of man. Thus man is both legion and unit. The Silent Watcher in him is the Dhyâni-Buddha, an actual, entitative, living ego of divine type. Man is but a copy, a microcosm, of what the solar system is, the Macrocosm. He is no different, he is the same: powers, substances, faculties, essences,

everything, only in the minute scale. What you see in the solar system, you should find in mankind. If you want to know what the
solar system consists of, study yourself. You simply copy the Great.

Now, then, the human ego which is I, which is any one of you, is
one of those particular monads as yet relatively unevolved. Above
it there is the Spiritual Monad, and above the latter there is the
Divine Monad. For karmic reasons very intricate, difficult to understand but existent, any one of us happens to be a certain stream of
consciousness, a sûtrâtman; yet you or I as human individuals are
the human monad. I am a human monad, each one of you is; so
that, as a human being you are only in the intermediate part of that
stream of consciousness which is your constitution, and the upper
part of it makes your link with infinity, and the lower part of it
enables you to learn on this plane.

Thus you are both one and legion. Thus the divinity in the
solar system is both one and an army. We are component parts
of that army. The god of the solar system has a life-consciousness-
substance, energy, being, which flows through all of us, and is the
substantial, conscious background in which we live and move and
have our being; and all that particular range of monads or egos
which forms any one of us, and forms his stream of consciousness,
is spiritually housed in this solar Divinity in whom we live and move
and have our being. It is really very simple, and it is so beautiful,
because in understanding this seemingly intricate but really very
simple thought, you have the key to so many of our deepest doctrines.

Now then, a last thought: Any one of these monads or spiritual
egos which form the constitution of a man is evolving — you are, I
am, the god within me also, the god within you also, each one on its
own plane, each one following its own pathway, and each one in
time going a plane higher, and then a plane higher still. When our
monad shall have brought out from within itself its latent powers,
its unevolved, undeveloped powers, it will become a Spiritual monad,
and we shall all be Buddhas, and we shall then work through what
is now the animal nature in us, which then will be human. Each
monad will have stepped up a degree, and be more highly evolved.
Keep this thought in your mind of your utter oneness with the
Divinity; and one of the best ways of recognising the utter unity

of everyone of us with Infinity, is remembering that we are composite, not by fastening our minds on the fact that we are just an ego different from other egos. Therein is the heresy of separateness. The differences are illusory, yet they exist. Illusory does not mean that they do not exist, it means that it is not the *real* Real, the realest Real, the fundamental Reality.

Take Father-Sun. We see only his body, and yet his vitality infills the solar system in which the planets are bathed, and all the beings on the planets, and the invisible planets. Then the innumerable armies and multitudes and hosts of life-atoms building my body, your body, the bodies of the earth, the bodies of the sun, the bodies of the gods — each one of these life-atoms is a growing, learning entity, ensouled by a monad, which is likewise a stream of consciousness.

Man is a unit when you take a particular portion of the constitution which is the human ego, which is evolving. It will become a spiritual ego, and afterwards a divine ego; and yet at the same time shot through and through with forces streaming down into him from egos superior to himself, of which he is the child. This is the esoteric basis for the old saying, that at the flame of a candle you can light all the fires of the world, and the flame of the candle is undiminished. Consciousness is just like that. You cannot exhaust it.

ON ABSOLUTE LIGHT

QUESTION — May we have more light as to the real meaning of the statement in the Stanzas of Dzyan about Darkness: "Darkness alone filled the boundless all"? Strictly these words mean that naught but Darkness was. Question: What is this Darkness, and what is Light?

E. D. W. — As I understand it, Darkness is the condition of the Universe during Pralaya or before the Dawn; and Light occurs when the Rays from Mahat or Universal Intelligence issue forth into manifestation. Just as a sunbeam shows as light on reaching the Earth-plane, so every ray of the Monadic Essence becomes light on whatever plane of manifestation it imbodies itself.

G. de P. — I do think the point is an extremely important one. I am reminded of the passage in the opening verses of *Genesis:* "Darkness is upon the surface of the deep." 'Darkness' is the parent of day. That 'Darkness' means something more subtil, as well as more essential, that goes deeper into the substance of things. 'Light' can only occur, is it not true, when there is manifestation and differentiation — for 'Light' is these. When there is differentiation it means contrast of shadows, which is a variety of light. Therefore, 'Darkness' means in this connexion absolute Spirit, which to our inept and imperfect human intellects is what we may otherwise call Absolute Light; but to our ordinary consciousness it is darkness. I am reminded again of the Pythagorean saying about the Cosmic Monad which withdraws into 'Darkness' and 'Night,' i. e. into the deep abyss of Cosmic Spirit. I bring out this point because I think it will be helpful to many younger students who may misconstrue these words by taking them at their face-value, imagining that it is something like ordinary night, a night after a day — lack of daylight; but even we know that what we call 'night' is simply shot through with radiations of many kinds, one octave of which we humans call light.

O. T. — I venture a suggestion that darkness as it is used in the Stanzas means undirected consciousness, consciousness from which intelligence is withdrawn. We must remember that consciousness is pure light. Consciousness has two aspects: spirit and matter, which are its two poles. The spiritual aspect is the space-aspect, the material aspect is the motion-aspect; but there can be no action until these two are united, and that requires intelligence — and intelligence is asleep, therefore there is darkness.

H. T. E. — I got this idea. You take the analogy of temperature. Temperature is divided into heat and cold, and when we speak of temperature we think of either heat or cold. Now what are light and darkness? They are different aspects — of what?

H. A. W. — It reminds me of the methods of physicists in splitting atoms and studying the electrons and protons and what not by the tracks made by their light in passing over a very sensitive photographic plate. These scientists theorize that matter is concreted electric charges. We are told in our Theosophical studies that light is etherealized matter; or, we may say, matter is concreted light. We find, I think in *Fundamentals,* the statement that what we see as the sun is not the sun but its photosphere, which is a higher grade of matter which we see as light. Light seems to be matter and matter seems to be light. Even if we say, adopting the modern scientific theory, that matter is electrical charges, nevertheless the corona or light sometimes present around high voltage wires, sparks, lightning, and even the Aurora Borealis or magnetic lights seems to indicate that electricity is the intermediate stage between material and light. It would seem to me then that manifestation can be looked upon as light. Pure spirit therefore can be looked upon as pure darkness. Light seems to be in everything and everywhere, and darkness is the absence of physical manifestation. I believe that this may be the idea behind the statement in the Stanzas.

G. K. — Could we think of darkness as the pralaya of light, or as that unmanifested something which, passing through the laya-center at its appointed time, becomes light?

G. L. D. — We can have no light until we get something to reflect it, and the matter side of things is the reflecting side. When spirit and matter, light and darkness, work together there is differentiation.

O. T. — I think there is a misunderstanding about the relation of light to darkness. We consider them opposites just as most people do life and death; but life and death are not opposites. Birth and death are opposites. Life is nothing but life. Life exists always. Life itself doesn't go to sleep; and darkness is the absence of that which produces light; and that which produces light is action; and when there is action there are light, heat, and sound, all three at the same time, which are three aspects of action. Light stands in the same relation to action as time does. Light, heat, and sound, physically speaking, are three characteristics appearing as magnitudes in physical nature. Light is not a thing. That is where modern science is so terribly mistaken.

E. D. W. — *The Secret Doctrine* defines time as a line of consciousness in infinite duration. Perhaps we could equally say that light is a line of consciousness in infinite darkness, because we read in this Stanza of the 'Awakening,' that vibration thrills through the darkness. Now vibration in one of its rates gives us light, in another of its rates gives us sound, which is spoken of as the Word, the Logos, and in one of our Scriptures we hear of the Word being made light; and perhaps that might give a clear idea of darkness as eternally existent just as duration is.

A. B. C. — To us as limited beings the only thing that we can comprehend is something else that is manifested, that falls within our particular range of manifestation. Anything that is beyond our range of perception, anything that is beyond the plane of manifestation on which we are, is to us unmanifested. That which is within our perception is light. That which is beyond our perception or comprehension is, to us, darkness. These words used in the Stanzas are largely figurative — used as a means of assisting us to comprehend what is beyond the limitations of our brain-mind. To our intellect that fundamental principle back of the manifested solar system is not comprehensible, hence it is called Darkness. But to our intuition, which rises above intellectual limitations, it is Absolute Light. To the 'opened eye of the Dangma,' which means fully illuminated or awakened human intuitive perception, it is Absolute Spiritual Light.

G. de P. — I always feel when I listen to your discussions as though I were learning things; but one thought struck me, Companions, a general background of thought as it were appeared in my mind after listening to this discussion, and it is this: I think there is a misunderstanding possibly amongst us all, of what we mean when we speak of Light. I would call this to your attention with some emphasis. Many people seem to think that Light is illumination, on account of the fact that whenever we turn a knob or press a switch, light springs forth and gives us illumination. Now, illumination is reflected radiation lying within such wave-lengths as our eyes have been evolved to sense. That is only one octave of light, so to speak, or possibly two or three octaves. But that is not Light truly, that is merely illumination brought about by light.

Light is invisible; light *per se* is darkness. Light is radiation, an energy, a force; and we do not see radiation until it is reflected from things and becomes illumination. Take the light, the radiation, streaming out from the Sun, that glorious sphere. As it passes through space, it illuminates only when its rays strike an object which reflects the radiation; and we call that reflexion illumination, or more popularly light. The light of the Sun is invisible, *per se.* It is darkness. Is that thought clear? It is only when the radiation is reflected from some object that we can see the light as luminosity, and only then when the reflexion is vibrational within a certain very small reach along the gamut of radiational vibrations, a very small part; and this is why H. P. B. spoke of Absolute Light, radiation *per se,* or the substance of radiation, as 'Darkness.' They are the same.

For instance, if there were no planets, or planetoids, or meteors, or moons, or comets, or any other reflecting body, in the solar system, and by some wonderful magic a celestial magician could suddenly put some reflecting object in the solar system, anywhere; then a perceiving eye would suddenly see a flash, if indeed that eye were capable of catching the radiations and transmitting them to the perceiving mind, and interpreting them.

We see the light of the sun as luminosity; we see the light of the electric current because it is transmitted to us in a certain way, and strikes objects, and is reflected back to the eye. That is illumination; we see illumination; but light *per se* is radiation, an energy, a force invisible, a vibration. And consequently illumination stands for matter, because you can only have illumination when there is radiation reflected from thing to thing, differentiation among things.

Therefore the essential meaning of 'Darkness' in the Stanzas in the S. D., is homogeneity of substance or essence. Illumination springs forth when there is heterogeneity or differentiation. Illumination dazzles, often is blinding, is deceptive. There are many kinds of light, different shades or grades of light: sunlight and moon-light and star-light, and lamp-light, and the light of the glow-worm, and the light of an electric globe, and fire-light — many kinds of light. But all these kinds are that form of light which we call lu-minosity or illumination. Radiation *per se,* which is Absolute Light, is invisible.

Homogeneity of substance, therefore, is the essential meaning of Darkness in the Stanzas; and it is the same thing as Spirit, fol-lowing the way in which these Stanzas have been written. What-ever returns to Spirit re-becomes homogeneous, absolute; and what-ever issues forth from homogeneity into heterogeneity differentiates and produces luminosity, illumination, reflected light. It is very beautiful because all being is beautiful; it is all the magic work of Spirit, and if we could see the wonderful mystery and marvel be-hind what the Christians ignorantly allude to as the Christ, we should be in continual awe; but all the same it is the evolved or un-folded spirit-side of the Universe, which is all-permeant, the hetero-geneous side, differentiated into many beings and things, which produces 'Light' as it is used in mystical writings. Essential Light, therefore, or radiation *per se,* to use a modern scientific term, is the *cause;* illumination or reflexion or again passage of energy from be-ing or thing to being or thing, is the *effects.* Consequently, we have a paradox here: Mystical Darkness is Absolute Light; differentiated light or illumination is the shadow or darkness, really, of Absolute Light.

LOKAS AND TALAS

I. D. — In *Fundamentals of the Esoteric Philosophy,* pp. 403-4, it is stated in regard to our position in the scale of Lokas and Talas that as we are in the Fourth Globe of our Chain we are in the fourth loka and fourth tala, Mahar-loka and Rasâtala. "But, again, we are in the Fourth *Round* of our Planetary Chain. Therefore we have this bi-polar principle emphasized by the Fourth Round quality, i. e., Mahar-loka and Rasâtala again. We are, furthermore, in the Fifth Root-*Race* of the Fourth Planet on the Fourth Round. Therefore our Root-Race, though evolving on that fourth Globe and in that fourth Round, is represented by the fifth of each column; Swar-loka and Talâtala." [See Column p. 399.] Now I would like to ask: If we are in the Fifth Root-Race, why is it that in the scale of the Races we should be in a lower loka and tala (i. e., Swar-loka and Talâtala) rather than the one superior to the Fourth-Round loka and tala; i. e., why are we not in Janar-loka and Sutala?

G. de P. — Lokas and Talas should always be considered as twins, that is to say, one loka should always be considered with its corresponding tala, as for instance, Satyaloka and Atala. These are inseparable and represent the positive and the negative, the high and the low, the spiritual and the material — on any plane; and so on down the scale with increasing increments of unfolding; first, pure spirituality in the arûpa-worlds. Now catch this thought: The highest twins, Satya-loka and Atala, represent as so placed a cosmic plane, that is to say each set of twins represents a cosmic plane: from spirit to physical matter. There is the answer to your question.

If you will look at the diagram of the seven globes of our planetary chain as given by H. P. B. in *The Secret Doctrine,* you will see that Globe D is represented as being in the seventh cosmic plane. That is why we are in Bhûr-loka and Pâtâla: on the lowest of the seven manifested cosmic planes. We are, however, in the Fourth Round, on the fourth globe counting by sevens; but in the Fifth Race. Now then, make your adjustments. Just as in the seven principles, so in the cosmic planes: each cosmic plane is sevenfold, tenfold, or twelvefold, according to the way you look at the matter. Satya-loka-Atala is sevenfold, which means that this cosmic plane (plane one on the diagram) has all the other lokas and talas but in the satya-loka-atala condition: they are all represented in the highest cosmic plane, held there in seed, not yet unfolded.

Satya-loka	1	Atala
Tapar-loka	2	Vitala
Janar-loka	3	Sutala
Mahar-loka	4	Rasâtala
Swar-loka	5	Talâtala
Bhuvar-loka	6	Mahâtala
Bhûr-loka	7	Pâtâla

This gives the picture of a universe unfolded, in cosmic planes; otherwise called lokas and talas, two by two — or twins.

Bhûr-loka and Pâtâla: this twin is sevenfold also; therefore Bhûr-loka-Pâtâla has *its* subordinate or sub-seven lokas and talas: it is the same all down (or up) the scale. We are in Mahar-loka-Rasâtala because we are in the Fourth Round; but in the scale of the Races we are in Swar-loka-Talâtala because we are in the Fifth Race.

I. D. — When the Seventh Round is over, by that time shall we have developed the whole possibility of evolution — shall we have unfolded all within us?

G. de P. — We shall have unfolded everything within us and in due order as far as this completed evolution permits. I hope you will get this idea: it will save a great deal of mental work. The highest loka contains its Bhûr-loka-Pâtâla because each twin is sevenfold. So this series of double-column worlds represents not only the seven cosmic planes, but the seven degrees of evolutionary unfoldment.

Man is not fully complete until he has unrolled everything within him: in other words, every quality, force, energy, substance, power, attribute that he has locked up. That is the answer to that part of your question. And it is a marvelous study. I don't blame anyone for being simply mixed up, because it is indeed 'wheels within wheels,' but yet it is such a wonderful study. The great key is analogical reasoning: hold to that firmly and it will guide you out of the maze.

I might add in conclusion that I would not fasten the attention too rigidly — with too much literalism — upon these lokas and talas as applied to the globes. Emphatically they do apply; but be careful. Now for instance, if you have the picture of the seven globes of a chain as H. P. B. gives them — Globe A, B, C, D, E, F, G — and then say Globe A is Satya-loka-Atala, Globe D — the fourth — Mahar-loka-Rasâtala, then from this we shall have to say that Bhûr-loka-Pâtâla is Globe G. That is not so; for, as a matter of fact, there are twelve globes. I would suggest to you to ponder over this thought for a while as a question to be answered by and by.

Remember first then: seven cosmic planes, in due order, each one unrolled from its preceding one and preceding ones: thus Satya-loka-Atala unrolled from themselves the next and succeeding twins — Tapar-loka-Vitala; and these two unrolled the third twins — Janar-loka-Sutala; the three unrolled the next twins — Mahar-loka-Rasâtala: and so on down the seven.

Bhûr-loka-Pâtâla has all the qualities of those that went before: it contains them all relatively unrolled, and relatively unfolded, as a flower unfolds from the seed. Thus also does a man through evolution become perfect by bringing out what is within these principles. Complete man, spiritual man, will be living in spiritual Bhûr-loka-Pâtâla or Satya-loka-Atala, but as a cosmic plane.

C. J. R. — But the difficulty is that we are in the Fifth Race, and we are more divine; and yet we seem to be farther down than up!

G. de P. — I see where the difficulty comes: you are confusing evolutionary unfoldment *per se* with cosmic planes *per se*. Consider these different cosmic planes [indicating diagrams] as the septenary degrees in world-evolution and world-building. They also figurate the septenary degrees in evolutionary unfolding of the entities peregrinating in and through these planes. Yet the two classes of ideas, while interlocked in significance, and interblending in activity, must be kept separate in the mind as distinct things.

Now, particularly with regard to your question: we as a class of peregrinating entities have reached our individual evolutionary stage of unfoldment in what we call the Fifth Root-Race on this Globe D, the fourth according to H. P. B.'s reckoning in our Planetary Chain. Thus it is that we are using this present loka and tala,

which we call this aspect of our Earth, but yet we as traveling entities are in our fifth racial stage of unfolding in this particular couple
of lokas and talas. Hence, as a racial consciousness, we have attained the fifth in the series, i. e. Swar-loka-Talâtala, although the
Globe Earth being on the lowest or seventh cosmic plane, is itself
a manifestation of Bhûr-loka-Pâtâla.

Connected with this last idea we must likewise remember that
our Earth itself is only in its fourth stage or Round of development,
and thus we have it also manifesting the qualities of the fourth in
the above series, to wit, Mahar-loka-Rasâtala.

Now all this will be easily explained if you will kindly remember
that each of these couples is itself sevenfold, so that for instance, the
Bhûr-loka-Pâtâla has all the same seven series of couples, from
Satya-loka-Atala down to Bhûr-loka-Pâtâla in itself.

Thus it is with reference to my remark concerning the stage of
the Earth, we have it manifesting Bhûr-loka-Pâtâla, because it is in
the seventh cosmic plane; yet it is manifesting likewise the Mahar-
loka-Rasâtala as subordinate planes of the Bhûr-loka-Pâtâla.

I will confess that it was with some reluctance that I allowed
these thoughts on the lokas and talas to be printed in one or more of
my books. It has let me in for a lot of trouble, and I have been explaining ever since! But it has been good, in a way, and therefore
I do not really regret it.

CONSCIENCE AND INTUITION

I DO not know — and yet I am glad to see that the fact I speak of is so — why people are so much interested in knowing what conscience is and where it is located in the human constitution and how you can make it function. We know that while man is a stream of consciousness, he is a septenary stream, and each aspect of the septenate again has its divisions, which is one reason why men differ amongst themselves so greatly and so widely; and it is a pity that this is not better understood. Men would differ more but quarrel less. Quarrels are stupid; kindly "scraps" make firm friends — if they are kindly!

Now, as I understand the matter, our conscience to which we all too infrequently pay heed, to our loss, is that friendly, warm-hearted whispering from above, which we feel as showing us the right and the wrong, and it comes from the stored up ethical wisdom in our being. It is not in the disputatious brain-mind: it is in the heart. It is the highest part of the human ego, the treasury of ethical experience, the accumulated wisdom of past lives, garnered and treasured in our higher parts; and as far as it goes its voice is infallible and powerful; but it does not go far enough to make its voice in our soul an infallible guide, because we have not had past human lives throughout eternity and we are not infinite beings, humanly speaking.

One man's conscience is strong; another man's conscience is weaker. Two reasons why: the one may be more evolved and may have learned to hearken more attentively to the inner monitor. Therefore its voice is familiar, strong, and steady, and as we say, warm and sweet. We love that, and one reason why we love it is because it is so personal to ourselves. It is the highest part of each one of us as a human being, whispering to us admonitions of right, and denying to us the ways of wrong-doing. It is the buddhi-manas part of the human being, garnering experience of past ages of births and rebirths, the echo of past sufferings and heart-aches from which we have gleaned wisdom and treasured it on the tablets of the Self. That is the conscience.

But higher than conscience is intuition: Intuition is infallible.

Its voice is immeasurably infallible, because it is the whispering within us as it were of the truths of the Cosmic Spirit. It is a ray direct from the Divine Spirit in our hearts. Our conscience won't tell us the truth about a fact of Nature, nor whisper into our minds guidance along the paths of scientific or religious or philosophical discovery, because it is the garnered ethical wisdom familiar to the soul of each one of us. But the intuition will tell us instantly, it has instant vision of truth. Its voice is neither familiar nor unfamiliar. It is utterly impersonal. Its atmosphere is neither "hot" nor "cold." It is neutral in this respect; and it is the voice of the Âtma-buddhi-manas within us, the Monad as H. P. B. called it.

Do you get the distinction? The conscience is our own treasury of spiritual-ethical wisdom. It is infallible as far as it goes, as far as we can hear its voice; and we can hear it ever more by practice, by training, by hearkening to it, by just recognising it and following it. But because it is only our own gathered treasury, it is not infinite, and therefore not in the true sense always infallible. But so far as concerns each one of you as individuals, when your conscience whispers to you, follow it, because it will whisper only when you are in danger, or when you are seeking to do aright: whereas the voice of the intuition is the voice of the Spirit within us, and it is infallible. It has no frontiers. It is, so to speak, a ray direct from the Mahâ-buddhi of the Universe; and we can allow intuition to become ever stronger within us, enlightening our minds and opening our hearts, by not being afraid of it, afraid of having hunches, by not being afraid of following our conscience, and our intuitions when they come to us. They are coming to us all the time.

Most men are ashamed to act intuitively. They don't want to make mistakes. Prudential, yes! But it is only prudence, and uncommendable, cowardly and weak, and small, if it is merely because you don't want to begin to make a fool of yourself until you have learned more. The strong man is not afraid of making a fool of himself occasionally, because he knows that that very fact will stimulate him, awaken him, make him think; and after awhile he will not make a fool of himself. He will learn to trust his inner powers. That is the way to cultivate the intuition, by cultivating it; not being afraid of what is within you. Suppose you do make mistakes — what of it? By practice in its exercise the mistakes will grow fewer and fewer.

Make a companion of your conscience.   The man or woman who has not heard the voice of conscience whispering in his soul, who has never felt its presence, is not truly human.   You know what I mean by that companionship: we call it a voice which whispers to us, it is a light which lives within you always and which tells you what is right — to follow it, and what is wrong — to abandon it.   Make a companion of your conscience, stimulate it, open your hearts and your minds to it.   Your lives will be beautified, strengthened, made happier than now they are, because you will be following the voice within which is the accumulated Wisdom of the Ages.

Furthermore, just in proportion as you learn to know your conscience which is your own self, the higher part of you, and trust it and follow it, the more will intuition brighten your lives, bringing you knowledge direct, knowledge infallible.

ROOT-RACES AND LIFE-WAVES

A. A. B. — Is there any relation or connexion between the "other humanities" [see *Fundamentals of the Esoteric Philosophy*, p. 395], that follow our Human Life-wave, and the seven human races that start contemporaneously at the commencement of our Manvantara, spoken of by H. P. B.?

A. B. C. — There is one phase of this subject, "other humanities," on which many questions have been asked and to which I should like to speak. This phrase, "other humanities" on other globes of the planetary chain, has given rise to much speculation and some confusion of thought, followed by some enlightening study and research, the result of which is as follows:

In this case the phrase "other humanities" is used as a generalizing term for the other "life-waves" below man, which are all potentially human. It does not mean that there are other hosts of monads that are exactly and specifically in the same human stage as we are, i. e., self-conscious, thinking manases, evolving on other globes of this planetary chain concurrently with our evolution on Globe D. That would be contrary to the rest of the teaching on the subject.

The phrase, I believe, is meant to remind us of the essential hierarchical unity with all the monadic hosts which primarily sprang from man and which will ultimately achieve the human state. The mineral, vegetable, and beast kingdoms are all our younger brothers, vital part of ourselves. They are differentiations of the chain hierarchy of which man is the crown on Earth. Hence they receive the impress of his character, and, in a broad way, his name, signifying that they are potentially human.

H. S. — In direct answer to the question, I do not think there is any connexion, except perhaps an analogical one, between the other life-waves, sometimes called 'humanities,' and the seven human races that started contemporaneously on our globe. This latter point has often been a subject for discussion among students. It seems reasonable to believe that the first Root-Race was different from the others, just as the first Round on our globe was different from the others;

and that it was made up of seven aspects of humanity, foreshadowing
the later development that has taken place and is still to take place
in the other Root-Races. We know that in the evolutionary scheme
each Root-Race develops one Principle — or shall we say sub-prin-
ciple; and surely the seeds of these seven types of development were
sown when man first appeared on this Earth in this Round. H. P. B.
also speaks of these seven races as evolving simultaneously on *seven
different portions of the globe* [*The Secret Doctrine*, Vol. II, p. 1],
but whether this means that the Sacred Imperishable Land which
we are taught was the home of the First Root-Race was not one
geographical locality but was seven localities known in Theosophy
under a collective name is a question we have never been able to solve.

G. de P. — Just what did H. P. B. mean in using that phrase
"different humanities"? It does not mean different bodies of human
beings, as we now understand ourselves, but was a phrase adopted
by her to hammer home the point that however unevolved the different classes of evolving monads may be, they all were on the way
to humanity, i. e., to become "men," and therefore are by courtesy,
as it were by forecast, "human beings," "humanities." That is what
the different "humanities" following each other around the globes
of the chain are: the different classes of monads of which our human
stock is one class. Our human stock again is sub-divided into subordinate classes, smaller classes, families of men.

Now with regard to the other part of the question: this is something that has plagued the thought of many, many, many students;
and it is understandable too, because it is a very ticklish point, and
yet it is easily explainable. When human evolution began on this
Globe in this Fourth Round, or in any other Round, it was a life-
wave beginning to evolve, which means a class of monads, themselves
sub-divided into seven subordinate classes; and as the life-wave
reached our Earth and struck it, of course it did so more or less as
a whole — forerunners, however, of each subordinate class reaching
the Earth and grouping themselves, not only each class to its own,
but all the subordinate classes more or less together, just as we men
do in a town: divide into families and classes, and yet we aggregate
as a town.

Consider a ray from the sun as a light-wave. We know that it is sevenfold. We can, if we wish, say that the ray of light is sub-divided into seven subordinate rays, the solar spectrum, which combine and form one compound ray. Now when a ray of light touches our globe, it touches it as a full compound ray or light-wave, i. e., life-wave; which is but another way of saying that it has seven subordinate rays. Thus, consider a life-wave to be a light-ray from the spiritual Sun making its round. When this life-wave or light-ray reaches our globe, at the beginning of human evolution on this globe, it does so as a whole. I do not mean it is *all* there, there in totality, but all its seven parts are represented; in other words all the subordinate classes have representatives in the first contact with the globe. Do you see what I mean? Each subordinate class has its forerunners forming a scouting-party, as it were. These scouting-parties touch the globe, evolution begins, the śishtas begin to awaken and to work, and afterwards there come pouring in the bulk of the egos. Just so is it when a sun-ray-tip touches the Earth: that ray-tip, so to speak, is septenary, sevenfold, it has all the spectral colors; and once the contact is made, the ray thereafter pours down and through that channel all that is in it.

There are thus two definite points of teaching here: the seven life-waves of "humanities" mentioned by me a moment agone as the life-waves making their rounds through the globes, comprise our human life-wave as *one* among them; but, referring to our human life-wave alone, it also is sevenfold, as was indicated by the forerunners of our human life-wave which reached the Earth at the beginning of the Fourth Round on this Globe: our own human life-wave reached this Globe with representatives of all its seven subordinate colors or minor classes of human monads, most of them as forerunners of the main body.

It is a very interesting thing that the seven classes of men, *of mankind,* i. e., the human life-wave, began their evolution together. What else would we expect? Pause a moment in thought. Think analogically. When a human being is born into this world, the body is not born first, and then when it is grown up there occurs the birth of the astral; and then when that has grown up the prâna comes in. Birth takes place — actually a very mysterious and wonderful process — on different planes at the same time. While the body is coming into birth, the other principles in a man's constitution are beginning to arrange themselves, and form themselves, each in its own sphere, each in its own way, making man's sevenfold constitution. Not only the birth of the human being, but the growth of a seed, a flower, what not, follows the same rule of more or less contemporaneous activity in all the principles of the entity. Thus the entire human life-wave initiated human evolution on our Globe in this Round with seven different sub-classes, most of them, however, being forerunners or representatives each of its own part of the septenary life-wave.

THE SEVEN COLORS OF THE SPECTRUM

I FEEL that all that has been said this evening on the subject of the seven colors of the spectrum has been beautifully said, informative, instructive; and personally, putting myself in the mind of each speaker, I think I can truthfully state that I agree with everyone, which means, *however*, coming to the answer that I was hunting for, I agree with none! A strange paradox! Everything that has been said has been true; but yet it was not that one answer to the question that I was seeking for. In all humbleness of spirit, with all the reserve which I feel that I should make, subject to correction by a greater mind than anyone here, than my own certainly, I would say this: that not one of the colors of the spectrum in essence is superior to any of the others. They are all divine in origin. Since the Sun is the vehicle of a Divinity, whatever flows forth from it is rooted in the Divine. That statement was made. But by comparison on the plane of material existence, and having in view the work which each of the effluvia from the Sun does on this scale of matter, of differentiated life, we are bound to make distinctions (and this was not what I had in mind), and say that Âtman is colorless, Buddhi is yellow, and so on. Kâma is red.

But now listen carefully. As one speaker pointed out — and I speak of it in especial because the same thought was running in my mind — do not get it in your heads that red is an evil color. It is no more evil than gold or than green or than yellow or than any other color. It is misuse of force which is evil, not the force itself. "Desire [Kâma is the Sanskrit term] first arose in the bosom of It" — the Boundless — the spiritual yearning, the desire to manifest its transcendent glory. Every time you have an aspiration in your heart for greater things, every time you yearn to become at one with the Spirit within you, you are in the Kâma-principle; and every time when in this beautiful aspiration you guide your steps wisely, with wisdom, then you are likewise in the color of the indigo, Buddhi-Manas, both working together.

Now, here is the answer that I was aiming for. Anyone of the seven colors of the solar spectrum is itself septenary — or denary, as you will. You can divide it into seven or ten; and these sub-divisions merely repeat in the small what the great originates. Isn't it obvious? You cannot cut a slice out of an apple and get something different from the apple. Consequently, every minutest portion of infinity contains every essential element and force that infinity contains. Consequently, every subdivision or sub-plane contains its own repetitive septenary which it derives from the surrounding universe. The microcosm simply repeats the Macrocosm.

Now, then, examine: A man whose swabhâva or swâbhâvic character let us say is in the red or kâma, if he lives in the Âtman part of it is living on a far higher plane than a man whose essential swabhâva is golden yellow, and yet who lives in the lower. Do you get my thought? It is the principle that you live in that places you on the Ladder of Life. If you live in the Âtman, the highest part, the spirit, the essential Self, the divine part of any color, of any force, of any element, you are matched only by your own feelings, and you are in the higher state of consciousness, and living far more nobly than a man who may be dwelling let us say in the indigo, but on a very low plane of it. A humble man born in a humble station of life, without education, crippled in body, everything against him — I am using this as an illustration — but nevertheless who has the mind of a Seer and the heart of a god, is planes above a man who is born with a golden spoon in his mouth, with all the education that the world can give to him, and yet who lives with a heart filled with vipers and evil.

H. P. B. once told her students that an artist— and you know what irregular and foolish lives artists often live — that an artist who in his heart sincerely yearned to be a better man, and to live a better life, even if he failed constantly, had greater chances of chelaship than a priest in a church who was wearing the skin over his knees hard by kneeling and praying to "Almighty God" every day, and who inwardly had a heart which was a den of vipers. That was the idea. It is the plane on which you live which places you where you belong. The thing is to strive to live in the highest plane where there is no color, where all is colorless glory. As soon as you descend into color, you descend into manifestation and differentiation producing a corresponding amount of mâyâ and consequent ignorance. Color shows manifestation, differentiation, the world around us, matter, in their densest and most condensed form.

Now take the spectrum: Red, orange, yellow, run through the scale to the ultra-violet. A new red begins, and if you follow it into invisible light, you will be passing upwards, till you reach a still higher red, after passing through the intermediate stages. Deduction: There is a divine kâma, there is a debased kâma; there is a divine Buddhi, there is a human Buddhi, which is the reflexion of the other. The point is that every plane is subdivided and is patterned after its grand plane. Therefore no matter in what station of life a man may be born, no matter to what "Ray," as some say, he may belong, this does not place him. What places him is where his consciousness is focussed. If it is focussed upwards, rising into the Âtman, into the colorless sphere, then he contains divinity. In the Absolute no one color is more spiritual than any other, because all are born from the heart of Divinity. When we come down into the worlds of differentiation, of existence, then we are obliged to make divisions. In the abstract — and this is not contradictory of what has been said — it is perfectly true that the more rapid the vibration, the greater the frequency of vibration a color has, the closer to matter it is; because what we call matter, physical matter, is intensity of vibration, of force. That is what produces the atom, the electrons, and all the rest of it. Modern science is now saying that they are all composed of energy-points, points of electricity, intense vibration. The greater the frequency of vibration, the more condensed the substance is. Follow out the thought, but do not jump to the conclusion that because violet is a very intense vibration, therefore it is the least spiritual of the colors. There is an Âtman to the violet, a Buddhi in the violet, and so on down the scale. It is a tangled theme of thought, and I asked the question to try to clarify our ideas. I think we have succeeded!

REQUISITES OF CHELASHIP — I

G. de P. — I would like to know, Mr. Chairman and Companions, what in your judgment is the characteristic or distinguishing mark of chelaship. I do not mean any outward sign. Those can be imitated; but what is it really which makes or distinguishes or characterizes the chela as compared with other men?

M. S. — I would like to answer this question. In my study of the present chapter, this thought came to me: That the true chela is he who in his merely human part utterly surrenders to that higher part which the Leader in this chapter so beautifully calls the Companion of Stars, the inner god; and the influence of which is stepped down to the human ego by the Reincarnating Ego. It is the human ego surrendering entirely to the spiritual law as given to it by the Reincarnating Ego.

H. T. E. — As the signs which indicate chelaship are not of an external nature, they would not be such as could be communicated to anyone except perhaps another chela; and further they would be of a kind which the chela would be reluctant to speak about.

G. de P. — What Dr. Edge says is quite true. Perhaps I had better rephrase my question. It may not have been clear, but I think Miss Madeline has got the fundamental idea. Instead of asking then, "What is the distinguishing mark or characteristic," I will phrase my question this way: What is it in or of the chela which makes him such?

C. J. R. — When H. P. B. said that the first test of true apprenticeship was devotion to the interests of others, she gave the secret password to open the door to the path. This was, of course, only the first test, but whatever comes later, such as the attainment of knowledge and power, will turn to ashes unless inseparably combined with a burning desire to help suffering humanity.

G. F. K. — I should think that what would characterize a chela as distinct from the ordinary man would be the acquiring of a vision, or, perhaps, the conquering of illusion in a fuller degree, so that through the conscious tearing away of the veils of mâyâ he would get a vision of what LIFE really meant. Then, having this Vision, he would know that the only possible way to live in accordance with Reality, consciously to live, would be a positive decision to devote himself to the service of others.

J. H. F. — One of the characteristic marks of chelaship I would say is a love for truth and a searching for it, as a drowning man struggles for air as the one thing above all most desirable. Naturally the love of truth is of varying degree, and the attainment of it, to be in any way successful, must include what Professor Ryan referred to as "the first test: Devotion to the interests of another" and ultimately of all men — in a word, impersonality. We can come to a knowledge of truth only in the degree that we seek for it impersonally — not solely for ourselves or our own satisfaction, but for the sake of all men, for the service of all.

H. T. E. — So far we have heard of several attributes which a chela might or might not possess; but as he would possess these in common with other people who are not chelas, they cannot be said to be characteristic of chelaship. What we need is a definition, not an enumeration of attributes.

S. E. — 'Chela' in a technical sense means slave, slave to the command or behest of a Guru or of Truth as the Higher Self points it out. It does not mean perfection, however — far from it. A chela can have all the wonderful qualities enumerated tonight, but also quite a few pretty bad ones not mentioned.

We must distinguish between 'chelaship' as it is understood in the Orient and the 'chelaship' of Theosophists in the West. There are strict rules governing the lives of the chelas in India and Tibet and they all have some sort of Guru or Teacher who directly or indirectly guides their lives. 'Chelaship' among Western people, or more particularly Theosophists, is something less tangible. As I see it, it means a focussing of one's thoughts, aspiration, and desires along lines of spiritual endeavor and in accordance with the teachings that we have received.

It is erroneous to imagine that chelas are necessarily altogether saintly people. In fact their efforts to forge ahead along lines of least resistance react on them in many ways and the animal nature of man rises up in protest; it is here that a chela has to win or lose. So when we see any Companion troubled by evil, let us judge not too hastily his character.

E. V. S. — I want to express my agreement with what Mr. Eek said, because I think that what constitutes a chela is *setting one's feet on the Path;* and this does not mean that suddenly one begins to manifest all the virtues. In fact, we are told that when one becomes a chela, he is immediately faced with all the difficulties and weaknesses of his nature. Therefore we ordinary beings can't judge of each other, as to who is a chela or who isn't, by the difficulties he has in his life; because one who is having the hardest times and the greatest trials to overcome may be one who has advanced far on the path. And even failure does not mean giving up one's status as a chela, as long as one continues fighting (that is, *wisely*), and keeping at least a foothold on the path.

I also agree with Dr. Edge. I don't think anyone less than a Teacher can tell who is a chela; but I think it is fairly simple to say who isn't. Anyone who advertises the fact that he is one, whether openly or by creating a mystery about himself, certainly isn't one; nor is one who is condemnatory of others and always trying to show how much more evil others are than himself. So I suppose we could arrive at it by a process of elimination.

G. K. — I think it might be called the mark of the Hierarchy of Compassion, speaking broadly and including the noble qualities that this term implies, at least aspiration and strong effort towards them. It is the mark the soul would set, in a way, upon those who are living for others and not for self, consciously and determinedly so living. It would not be a visible mark or sign, and would not be perceived by the majority, though they might see in us a certain kindliness and sympathetic understanding; but those who bear this mark, and above all the Teachers, I believe, would see it definitely as a distinguishing mark or sign.

O. T. — A chela is one who is dominated by something greater than himself, the innermost part of his being, the Master, and whose faith and devotion are so unswerving that in spite of personal shortcomings, this Master can infill his mind with a vision of universal truth and guide it to the Teacher in possession of this very truth.

A. B. C. — The characteristic which distinguishes the chela from other men is the flame of pure impersonal love burning in his heart. As the dominant characteristic of the Master of Compassion is the spirit of divine harmony and compassion, so it is by the similitude to the Master that a man becomes a chela. It is this similitude by which the disciple is recognised and drawn to the Master. It is kinship of spirit.

L. R. — A chela is one whose great hunger for Truth makes him willing to pay the price of his personal self that he may *become* the Truth. This would include all degrees of chelaship and all the virtues required for it.

O. I. C. — It seems much easier to enumerate qualities which a chela should or should not possess, than to tell what it is that constitutes one a chela. Let me offer the following: That which constitutes one a chela is a definite alliance by deliberate choice with the Order of Compassion. If there are unconscious chelas, they have made that alliance in previous incarnations. The possession of many noble qualities does not itself constitute chelaship. All the religions have had saints and heroes, who were not chelas. Chelas may have bad qualities, even very bad qualities, but being chelas they are on the best road for the rapid overcoming of those qualities. They are chelas because they are definitely and by continuing choice devoted to the work of the Order of Compassion. That devotion causes them to be accepted as chelas. If they adhere to that choice and devotion, the noble qualities which a chela should have will be developed in them more quickly than by any other means.

F. L. G. — The question can be answered in a very few words. One who has an unceasing love for humanity would through this love express all the attributes and qualities that we have been talking about: impersonality, compassion, service, etc.

G. L. D. — To my mind, any individual aspiring to chelaship has had a vision of truth conveyed to his brain-mind and intelligence from his higher spiritual essence, and henceforth his whole life is devoted to the search for truth in self-forgetful service to his Teacher and all humanity.

A. J. S. — Sooner or later, to a serious student of Theosophy comes the urge to devote everything — every faculty, all he possesses, to the service of humanity. In other words, he wishes to live the life of a chela. He sees that the farther reaches of the chela-life are greatly to be desired. He soon learns that if he live the life he shall know the doctrine — the deeper teachings — and with this desire in his heart he feels the need of a Teacher.

What are the requisites for one wishing to lead the chela-life, for one wishing to become a chela? We are told that among others there are three leading ones: Devotion, Duty, and Loyalty — Devotion to an ideal which requires the utmost of our spiritual will to follow day after day; Duty — one's own duty — rightly performed, the doing of which brings indescribable peace, as when, after wandering over and having retraced many roads, we find the right one at last; and which rightly done leaves no thing to be undone; and Loyalty, which brings trust and confidence in oneself and in others. These three requisites for chelaship have among all peoples been considered the foremost virtues. We, as Theosophists, owe the observance of these qualities to ourselves, to others, and especially to our chosen Teacher. It is expected of us.

The Teacher gives inner life and inner light. He guides the soul of the chela through its development, onwards and upwards through greater trials, greater responsibilities. For the chela meets a karmic quickening which may condense into his present incarnation the experiences of many ordinary lives. He meets trials joyfully, knowing that each trial successfully passed means the dropping of one more veil of illusion on the path to Masterhood.

I. L. H. — The question was: "What is it in or of a chela that makes him such?" May I venture a brief definition: A progressively more and more complete identification of oneself with impersonal ends for the betterment of Humanity, coupled with an ever-increasing effort to fit oneself to carry out better the duties which such service entails.

W. E. S. — In terms of the seven principles of man and nature, we might say that the Mahâtman lives in the Buddhic principle, the average man in the Kâma-Mânasic. The nearer an individual shifts his center of consciousness to the Buddhic part of his constitution and keeps it there, the closer is his approach to Mahâtmahood. The chela is one who has learned to do this with a larger degree of concentration than the average man.

S. Z. — Wouldn't a chela be one in whom the inner god has become awakened to some extent, and who has a teacher, whether he is conscious of it or not?

E. J. D. — I think that the answer by Mr. Zurek is the best yet. When we consider that man is the expression of a divinity on earth, and that any good man and a myriad Christians can feel, by aspiration, the presence of this divinity — the 'Father in secret' spoken of in the New Testament — we see that something more than sensing that divine Presence is needed in order to get direct teaching and instruction from that source. The Mahâtmans are in contact with that divinity, and we, if we understand how to constitute ourselves their pupils, have their help in learning to reach our own divinity. A chela, then, is one who is being taught by a Master of that art, the means to make his divinity vocal within him.

G. de P. — Mr. President, Mr. Chairman, and Companions: I think that my question has been beautifully answered by all who have spoken, and anything that I could say would merely be in addition. Indeed, if we analyse the answers that we have heard, I think we may divide them into two classes: those weighing heavily on what we may call the Life, and those weighing heavily on what we may call the Knowing. It is an interesting study in psychology to me, knowing you all as well as I do, to see how the individual swabhâva has come out in your answers. Some are profound and devoted students who are reaching the Light along the Path of Wisdom. Others, equally profound and devoted students, are marching steadily towards the inner glory by what we describe as living it. Now, if you will combine these two ways, unify them into one, in which both blend indistinguishably, then I think you will have not only the signs and marks and characteristics of all chelas, who you will remember are of many grades from the super-gods downwards to us, but you will likewise know how to become a chela, a greater chela, a still greater chela, yourselves.

There are many characteristics and distinguishing marks, if we analyse the chela in his life, and many of them have been pointed out. But do you know, I think if I were asked what it is in and of a man which makes him a chela, I think I should ponder quite a long time, and then I believe I should give this answer: A growing indifference to himself, and an increasing interest in all that is. There we have the path of morals, of ethics, of wisdom; and we have the Life: a man who has completely lost interest in himself, has no pleasure in evil-doing, because all evil-doing is selfish, for personal, selfish ends. It is just as simple as that. Not my will, as the great Syrian Chela and Master said, but Thine, his inner god's, a Ray of the spirit of the Universe, the law of infinite love and compassion and harmony and pity and wisdom and peace. Man, when he thus loses interest in himself, grows progressively greater. It is a strange and interesting paradox. By expanding, his interests enlarge instead of being constricted around his own core of being; he breaks the bonds and expands. His former and present self becomes uninteresting. The world, all mankind, the Universe, he loses himself in, and becomes it; and there is the secret of all initiations, from the greatest to the least. Indeed, no man can pass through an initiation until he can do this in some degree. He cannot simply because he cannot lose himself. He cannot enter into other things. He is all 'I.' The Universe is 'I' and 'thou,' I, and the world — the duality. He never can forget himself and be the other, for his whole understanding, his whole compass of thought and feeling is I. Do you catch the thought? That is all there is to it. The chela is he who is becoming uninterested in himself and accordingly more interested in others, in the world. That is why there are three grades of training. Experience of ages has shown that three are required: training, study, and a growing lack of interest in yourself. And then comes the fourth stage, when you really feel that all other men's interests are infinitely more important than your own. The greatest Buddha, the greatest teacher, the greatest man or woman, is he who is uninterested in himself and loses himself in what we call others. That is chelaship. It is a reversion of feeling, to embrace the Universe and recognise it. The 'I' is no longer 'I,' it is All. And yet how difficult it is for Occidentals to understand that we are all one, and yet for ever individuals.

There are as many chelas as there are individuals in the Universe. I sometimes think that everybody is a chela in degree. I sometimes think that even the greatest sinner, as we say, is a chela, because he is learning, poor devil!   Of course he is not a great chela, he is a very weak and humble one, a poor, stumbling, weak specimen of mankind.   A true chela hence is one who is living the Life and knows the Knowing, and combines the two into one, and thereby loses interest in himself, forgets himself. Self-forgetfulness, love of others: if men could only follow this as a life even in their ordinary inter-course, if we could only realize how uninteresting I am and how awfully interesting the other fellow is.   That is all there is to chela-ship; and the greatest man is he who can express that the most, the best.   That is why, as the Buddha said, we attain Nirvâna, we attain the stage of the "samma-sambuddha," when the dew-drop slips into the shining sea, when the little knot and point and focus of I-con-sciousness expands to be the Universe.

I will add this: I for one have no patience with those who segre-gate themselves from others and go out, away from others, and think that they are holier than others.   That is not chelaship.   You can starve till your bones stick through your skin, and you can burn yourself and torture yourself until the body, wracked with pain, dies; and you are no more chela than a snap of the fingers, because all your searching is upon yourself; you become an imbodiment of self-seeking egoism.   That is not the way to attain chelaship.   Chela-ship is an inner being, an utter self-forgetfulness in its greater reaches, it is an inner change and forgetting yourself; and in pro-portion as you do it, so much farther will you be on the chela-path, because of an ever-enlarging consciousness and wisdom and love.

G. de P. — I should like to know if chelaship is something added unto us by a way of life and a living, or is it something which pours out from ourselves as from inexhaustible fountains? Or is it both? This question seems to me to be basic.

M. F. — We have been told that there are many potentialities within each one of us, and it is only by contacts that we make that these potentialities will be awakened. I think that chelaship is a potentiality that we all have; but I believe that it needs the contact of a greater soul to bring forth that potentiality into action.

G. L. D. — I should think that chelaship is something added to us to a certain extent because it draws forth from us higher and higher feelings and stages of consciousness that induce us to work ever upward, at the same time awakening us to our responsibilities to all around us; and the consequent self-evolution and expansion of consciousness brings us so much nearer to the divine qualities that are inherent in man's constitution, and every element of his nature is worked upon and all of the lower qualities are thereby raised one stage.

F. F. W. — As a military man of many years' experience, there is an analogy brought to my mind based on the military life in its true ethical background: Groups of men are taught by drills and tests to evoke from their own minds and wills and increase their bodily strength to do the necessary co-operative acts. The chela-path seems to me to be in a similar manner the evolving of ourselves with the help of those who are instructed to develop ourselves into a higher degree so that we are more able to accomplish the greater object.

E. W. L. — It seems to me that the chela-life is prompted first by a law within oneself filtering into the mind of the man, and it assumes or becomes almost a conversational life with the Master within or a walking with that Master; but it requires a Teacher or helper to guide one even to his own Master.

A. B. C. — The question is: Is chelaship or the chela-life the drawing forth of what is within or the adding of something from without? And as I understand the answer, it is both. As man is a part of, inseparable from, and a ray, as it were, of this infinite heart of the universe, all is within waiting to be evolved; but ages and ages would be required to bring it out by the sole process of evolution alone. It is a part of the nature of this universe that this very interlinking and interlocking of things should make it the function of those who would develop the higher to help the lower. We have there the law of compassion. We have brotherhood. We have love. And so those that have developed their consciousness so that it embraces a larger love express a greater degree of this inner divine infinity. They are the Masters. It is a part of their life, an expansion of themselves, to share this wider consciousness with their chelas so that the process of the chela's evolution becomes enormously hastened.

I remember a letter by one of the Masters' chelas written in the early days of the Theosophical Society before Mme. Blavatsky had her special group of students, to the members of the Pacific Coast, stating that if you had a Master it would bridge over many incarnations of evolution, save many, many incarnations of this long pitiless struggle, because a Master having already evolved greatly shares with you; you get a portion of his consciousness, of his life, his state of divine being. In one of his letters in the book *Letters from the Masters of the Wisdom,* I think it is Letter 30, K. H. said this, which will illustrate what I mean: there was a tank filled with water, and another empty. One represents the Master, the other the chela, and they connect as it were by a pipe, and the empty one fills. That is one illustration only.

But remember this fundamental proposition of *The Secret Doctrine,* on page 17, Vol. I, that there is no state of evolution gained by any evolving being, except by effort and merit. This process of chelaship is a process of reaching nearer and nearer to the Master, a process of ever becoming more like the Master, sharing therefore in his limitless consciousness and compassion.

S. E. — Chelaship or discipleship implies the presence or the existence of a Teacher. Hence it is obvious that the disciple doesn't pour from himself the so-called benefits, if that is the proper word, but he is given them. Now the law of Karman obviously has brought the disciple in position where he has contacted the Teacher. Previous lives have brought the two together, and consequently it is only the result of previous aspirations which has placed the disciple in a position of learning more. For some reason the question of discipleship has come up frequently here during our last meetings, and I think many of us have given the question more thought on that account. It may be possible that our Human Ego will so open itself to the influences of the Higher Self that *de facto* it establishes the relationship of chela and guru within the constitution of the individual himself, this relationship corresponding to the outer relationship between an accepted chela and guru in the accepted sense of the East. The former can exist without the latter, but the latter cannot exist without the former, and it is only when the two blend that the full awareness of chelaship takes place. I believe that discipleship in its ultimate sense or meaning is a desire to live a purer and a more spiritual life. It is an intense sympathy and love of one's fellow man, a desire to see everyone happy in the best sense of the word — not a happiness that requires position, fame, etc., but the happiness that comes from a mind and soul one in the knowledge of spiritual humbleness or spiritual aspirations.

F. C. C. — I think that the life of chelaship is rather an attitude of mind — an attitude of mind which is a dedication of every act of our lives from the meanest to that which seems to us the greatest, the divinest. Consciousness expands in ever growing quality as we are able to live more and more in conscious dedication. Thus we naturally grow nearer to that heart of the Universe which is the ultimate of the chela-path. As we travel thus in dedication it will at the cyclic and karmic time bring us to that Teacher who will open to us wider views, or who will point out wider horizons, or who will point out our stumbling-blocks. This help comes from without, but that help we cannot take unless we have that inner attitude of dedication which alone enables us to accept the helping hand of a Teacher pointing the way along the Path.

G. de P. — As usual, it has struck me that all the answers have been beautiful and profound, they show advancement in study; and yet, I do not think that any of the answerers got just the drift of my question, doubtless my own fault, due to the difficulty of phrasing a question in such fashion that everybody will understand just what is meant. Most of the answers, possibly all, seem to point out the way to become aspirants for chelaship, and it is splendid that your thoughts should be running on these lines. But my question called for answers directly to this point: Is chelaship itself a giving or a receiving, a pouring out or a putting in. Do you see what I mean? I do not know that I could pick out a question harder to answer. I have pondered upon this all my life, and I am not yet completely satisfied that I have even a fair answer, but I think I have, and I am going to try to give to you what I think the proper answer is — but I assure you it is not a complete answer.

I think the reply lies in the words of the great Syrian Avatâra, which in substance are: Seek ye the Kingdom of the Divine — the Kingdom of God as it runs — and all these other things will be added unto you. And that means everything: things of matter, things of the mind, things of the spirit. Why? You have your answer in the one word Evolution. Pause a moment and follow me in thought. A beast runs past a beauteous flower. What does the beast get from seeing that flower? A man a moment afterwards passes along the same path, reaches the flower, pauses, looks at it. What does the man get? Perhaps little more than the beast. But let a man of a different type come along that road, and see that flower and look into its heart. What does he get? A revelation not only of transcendent beauty, but a sublimity of thought. He *sees* something. Why? Because he has aroused in himself something that the beast has not yet evolved forth; and that the first man had not. The first man had more than the beast, but not as much as the second man.

Do you see what I mean? You have to become before you can be. You have to pour out from yourself what is within, lying latent, before you can receive the revelation from without. If the revelation is not pouring out — marvelous paradox — you will not be able to read and interpret the Universe around you. You will pass unseeing by.

What is genius of any kind? What is even the inventive power that some men have? Ability to see! It is in them, and the outer world is a stimulus, brings forth what is within already. You cannot receive anything from without before it is already within, awakened, aroused. Teach a child in the womb if you can the wonders of the solar universe. There is no response, there is no receiving capacity. But wait till the child is born and grows to become a man, and that which is within him has come out, the understanding. Then comes comprehension.

Seek ye first the divine within yourself, cultivate it, evoke it, awake it; and just in proportion as you do this, you will be receiving from without, because you give from within. You give yourself. You cannot receive anything from without until there is something within you to receive, a receiver. You pass unseeing by. That is just why the Masters are higher than we, are greater chelas than we, because they are greater receivers, simply because they are greater givers. You have to have that within yourself calling for recognition before you can receive and recognise.

Now that is, as I understand it, a good answer to my question: Is chelaship a receiving from without, or a giving from within? It is neither alone, but both together — a paradox.

And reverence due to the Teacher? Nothing dignifies a man so greatly. It is the man of servile soul who is afraid to recognise grandeur in some other man. He is not big enough. He is afraid of giving himself grandly. The little man is afraid of being 'sat upon,' or snubbed, he won't admit that the other man is greater than he. The man who really is great inside recognises grandeur in other men, and bows to it because he himself is inwardly a great man. He recognises the security of his own manhood and can render homage and reverence and respect because he has them within himself. Reverence for a Teacher is a beautiful thing, and a sign of inner growth; and it is merely servility thinly disguised to consider that you, I, anyone is so frightfully independent and superior to others that he won't recognise greatness when he sees it. He has not it within himself.

It is precisely the same rule that teaches us to reverence the glory in the heart of a rose. We have it in us. We see it in the rose and render homage. To see beauty in the stars, their wonders, their mystery, their hid secrets, their stately movements in their orbital circuits: What is there more exquisite, more beautiful, more thought-provoking to look at than the flame of fire? What is fire? "Combustion." Isn't that an illuminating answer! What is a man? "Flesh and bones." Isn't that an illuminating answer! But to me they are not answers. They are just marks of stupidity. To me a man is a thought-producer, a lover, a giver, a genius, a creator, a power. A rose is a mystery, something from the invisible heart of Being exhaling itself in a marvelous beauty of form, perfume, color, and above everything else, something still grander, something that suggests the Beyond. You have the secret of chelaship just there.

Studies in
"The Secret Doctrine"

FAILURES OF PREVIOUS ROUNDS

We have a passage from a Master's letter which has a direct bearing upon these incarnating angels. Says the letter: "Now there are, and there must be, failures in the ethereal races of the many classes of Dhyan-Chohans, or Devas (*progressed entities of a previous* planetary period), as well as among men. But still, as the *failures* are too far progressed and spiritualized to be thrown back forcibly from Dhyan-Chohanship into the vortex of a new primordial evolution through the lower Kingdoms, this then happens. Where a new solar system has to be evolved these Dhyan-Chohans are borne in by influx 'ahead' of the Elementals (Entities . . . to be developed into humanity at a *future* time) and remain as a latent or inactive spiritual force, in the aura of a nascent world . . . until the stage of human evolution is reached. . . . Then they *become an active force* and commingle with the Elementals, to *develop little by little the full type of humanity*." That is to say, to develop in, and endow man with his Self-conscious mind, or *Manas*.　— *The Secret Doctrine*, II, 232-3 footnote

SEVERAL of our students have been greatly puzzled by a footnote written by H. P. B. in Volume II, pp. 232-33, of *The Secret Doctrine,* quoting a letter from the Master, which is published, by the way, in *The Mahatma Letters to A. P. Sinnett,* page 87. I have not *The Secret Doctrine* before me, but the Master states that in the very earliest parts of planetary and human evolution, of the evolution of the globes of a planetary chain, high spiritual entities came to this earth before or contemporaneously with the elemental kingdoms, and remained in the 'atmosphere' of the laya-center out of which the earth-chain was then forming, constituting a passive spiritual, intellectual guiding aura; according to which plan, when later the elementals came they built up the foundations of the earth, of the lower portions of it. And then again when a much later period arrived, these spiritual beings whom the Masters call 'failures' for a very good reason, when their time came and 'human' vehicles were sufficiently evolved, finding these vehicles then ready, entered into or incarnated into these human vehicles and gave them mind.

Question: Who and what are these failures that the Master speaks of? My explanation already has given the key, I believe. They are entities from the preceding chain-imbodiment, or what we now would call the moon-chain, who long before the moon-chain had reached its term or end of evolution, had themselves attained the spiritual and intellectual qualifications or status of Nirvânîs, lower Jîvanmûktas, if you understand these technical terms.

But because these human beings in the moon-chain, long before the moon-chain had reached its evolutionary term, had themselves attained the power to enter nirvâna, they were entering nirvâna when the moon-chain ended its manvantara, and remained in the nirvâna until that for them was ended; and then, precisely because they were not sufficiently strong in spirit and in intellect to attain a higher nirvâna than the one they had reached, in other words because they were not 'pukka' or perfect Jîvanmûktas, freed spiritual monads roaming the spaces, because they had not attained that highest or relatively highest state — karman obliged them to assume the rôle of world-architects. They were therefore 'failures' because they did not attain that higher plane in the nirvâna. To us they would be great spiritual geniuses. But they were failures in the other higher sense that they had not become full-blown gods. They had ended their nirvâna before the earth-chain, the child of the moon-chain, came into being; remained in the âkâśic solitudes, if you like to call it that, in the realms of the higher astral light, or rather in the anima mundi, as passive spiritual natures, before the earth-chain formed again, before the earth's monad came down to these planes and gathered about it the cosmic dust forming our chain. They remained there as a passive spiritual intellectual influence or atmosphere guiding the work of the other lower builders, so that under these 'Architects' the work by the Builders could be done and well done — the Architects guiding the Builders, engineers supervising the work of the workmen.

Who are they then? Jîvanmûktas of an inferior grade? Yes. Mânasaputras? If you wish, yes. And they remained in that passive state because the time had not come for them to work definitely on lower planes. The distance between their relatively high status and the gross ranges of physical matter was too great. The intermediary rungs had to be built up. So they remained as an overshadowing mind-group, hosts of them, of great spiritual and intellectual power, passive as far as they were concerned; but because their very nature was intellectual and spiritual knowledge, diffusing light, intellect, life around them, as the sun does on all below here.

They came first. Then almost contemporaneously came the elementals, all the kingdoms of elementals, and these last began building in the before-mentioned 'atmosphere' which guided the work of these elementals, just as the atmosphere of a clever leader of his men will be felt and will guide other men although they never feel his hand — gossamer like, and yet stronger than steel in its effects in binding together, in unifying. Call it will, spiritual will if you like. It is thus that the gods work, and the demigods. The makers or producers of this 'atmosphere' were Mânasaputras.

Then came the time when the elementals and the lower kingdoms of monads or classes had built up to the limit of their power, and the human vehicle in the middle of the Third Root-Race was in consequence then relatively ready. The nervous system, and the physical frame as then it was, although much less fine and perfected than now these are, were nevertheless just ready to become efficient carriers of the inner intellectual light. Then these waiting spiritual-intellectual entities saw their chance. Some of them incarnated in those human bodies, which there and then were endowed with mind by these incarnators. These who entered were that class of Mânasaputras who entered the bodies first and gave them light. Then thinking men began and were. These were the greatest of the human race, and have reincarnated ever since that time from age to age as the great geniuses of human history, those grand and glorious names, the Buddhas, the Christs, the marvelous geniuses who made the history of past ages.

Time passed, and others of these waiting Mânasaputras who had not incarnated, who had refused at first really because they were not strong enough — this second group of mind-giving Mânasaputras incarnated in human bodies. And later on the very last class of these Mânasaputras incarnated. The second class of such incarnating Minds became the majority of mankind, we ourselves. The third class which waited the longest before obeying the karmic law to incarnate, comprised what are now the lowest of mankind, the savages and the barbarians like the Andaman Islanders, and the Bushmen and some of the degenerate mountain-tribes in different places over the earth.

Then the door of the human kingdom closed because the bottom or nethermost evolutionary point of the Fourth Round had been reached and passed. The animals were not yet ready to receive the incarnating Monads of Mind; nor are they ready yet. They will receive mind in such manner in the next manvantara or imbodiment of our chain.

Coming back to our former thought from which we have been led into these fascinating bypaths of study, the 'failures' mentioned by the Master are what we have been describing, the various classes of the Kumâras, or rather Agnishwâttas and Mânasaputras. They, these 'failures,' in later ages became what are now the great Mahâtmans, including of course such glorious entities as the Buddhas and the geniuses of spirit and intellect who have brightened human history, whose names are household words in every civilized land. Many of the names of those who lived in pre-history have been lost, but we know the names of some of them.

And mark you, this shows how near the bottom of the Arc of Descent we still are, how much we have lost of what we have learnt and known and experienced not only in other Root-Races but in other Rounds. Here we are, we humans, with our noblest light almost obscured, truth-seekers hungry for light; and yet within us these beings are; they are we, always striving to give to us what they have, and we rebels refusing, attracted by the flesh-pots of matter or earth; and yet, albeit attracted, resenting this lower attraction, rebelling, trying. We are pulling ourselves up, turning to the light whenever the heart aches. Such is our life. And within every human being there is a demi-god, and a demi-beast, intempled together; through evolution raising this poor human of flesh up, up, up, so that some day it too may receive the light, the blessed light, the light glorious that we have received and have forgotten.

No wonder the Master speaks of these spiritual beings, who are our inner parts, as fallen angels, gods who have fallen, dropped from their azure seats — that is not mere poesy — the seats of intellectual splendor, from the old thrones, fallen from the golden glory of the Sons of Light.

When I look at my fellow human beings I no longer see the faces sometimes torn with sorrow, hungry for light. But I see the great flame within, the divinity within every human being, incarnate gods. It is a tragedy that here we live in this semi-animal part of us, wasting aeons because we will not go higher.

But one last word. Note how wonderfully Nature fashions her works. Even though we have lost our memory of what is our inmost right, of the god-man in us, wandering gods, here on earth sunken in matter and forgetting our own inner divinity, we are nevertheless aiding to raise the lower part of us just mentioned, the semi-animal part of us, some day to become no longer semi-animal but truly human, *truly human;* and we, the human part within us, then shall have rebecome the gods that within us we already are. Remember the sayings of the Christian Scripture: Know ye not that ye are gods, and that the spirit of the Most High liveth within you?

THE INCARNATION OF THE HIGHEST SEVEN

> In ancient Symbolism it was always the SUN (though the Spiritual, not the visible, Sun was meant) that was supposed to send forth the chief Saviors and Avatars. Hence the connecting link between the Buddhas, the Avatars, and so many other incarnations of the highest SEVEN.
>
> — *The Secret Doctrine,* I, 638

WHEN H. P. B. spoke of the "incarnations of the highest SEVEN" she did not mean the imbodiment of any one of the sevens, but incarnations or imbodiments of rays therefrom, and that this is back of the Buddhist teaching of the true genuine Living Buddhas of Tibet being imbodiments either of Avalokiteśvara or of Amitâbha, these being two of the highest of the Seven. It does not mean that these cosmic spirits, divinities, gods, descend in their fulness into a human being; only that a ray with this or with that swabhâva or characteristic individuality overshadows, or rather overenlightens, and finally imbodies itself in one of these Living Buddhas or Avatâras; and indeed it is just this that makes the true Avatâra.

The "highest of the Seven" refers to the highest hierarchy of our own solar system, or rather to be very technical, our own Universal Solar System — a very technical phrase. It does not mean all the solar systems in the galactic universe. It has another meaning entirely, but that is another story I cannot go into here.

Another way of describing the highest Seven would be to say that they are the seven chief Logoi of our Sun; or again, the seven chief Planetary Rectors or Governors of the seven Sacred Planets, these being actually Solar Logoi or emanations from our Sun, each such planetary chain or planet being its mansion or house or dwelling or focus — all words meaning pretty much the same thing. It is from one or from another of these seven chief divinities in our solar system that have proceeded the long line of avatâras, and indeed in another sense of all the Buddhas; and similarly every unusually great man spiritually — mark that word 'spiritually' — that the human race has produced among its children has been in a greater or less degree an imbodiment or an incarnation, a veritable incarnation, of a ray of one or of another of these seven chief Solar

Logoi. Jesus was one, and that is why he said: I and my Father [that is the Source, the Logos, or the Logos from the Sun itself] are one.

The names of these Logoi you will find given in the Hindû writings. If merely knowing names will help you at all, Sushumṇa is one; Samnatta is one more.

In regard to the Sun, the seven rays, it is clearly enough seen that it is the spiritual solar energy which is back of all these initiations and back of greatness when it appears in men. Hence the old occult saying you have heard me quote so often, that one of the titles of the adept when he has just been initiated is and was 'clothed with the Sun.' You now see the meaning. The Sun's soul, solar power, is for the time being shining through him and clothing him with solar splendor so that actually the very body shines. It is filled with glory. The man is thus glorified: 'Êlî, 'êlî, lâmâh sha-bahhtânî: O God of me, how thou dost glorify me.

In an old Hindû astronomical work, called the *Sûrya-Siddhânta,* often quoted by us, in the preliminary or beginning of this remarkably profound and interesting work, it is stated that it was dictated by the Sun to the great Atlantean astronomer Asuramaya. You now see the meaning of that: not that the Sun came from heaven into a room and dictated with an apparent human mind, but that the solar glory in this adept drove or illuminated the man's brain so that this magnificent astronomical work was one of the products of Asuramaya's genius. You will remember that often H. P. B. in *The Secret Doctrine* refers to Asuramaya as an Atlantean, and so he was; but also an Aryan, for he lived just when the Atlantean race was finishing its Kali-yuga, and the Aryan was in the beginning of its Kṛita, at the very commencing of its beginning; and this places the date of the *Sûrya-Siddhânta* as this number of years: 1,200,000 plus 864,000 plus — as we are now in the beginning of Kali-Yuga — 5000. So the *Sûrya-Siddhânta* is 2,069,000 years old. But my main point is: the *Sûrya-Siddhânta* states itself that Asuramaya, worshiping the Sun — which means raising his inner nature spiritually and intellectually to the solar ray of which he was an incarnation — was thereupon taught by the Sun, by the solar divinity within him, some of the astronomical secrets of our solar universe. The *Sûrya-Siddhânta* was the result.

THE BIRTH OF THE SONS OF WISDOM

This Third Race is sometimes called collectively "the Sons of *Passive* Yoga," *i.e.*, it was produced unconsciously by the second Race, which, as it was intellectually inactive, is supposed to have been constantly plunged in a kind of blank or abstract contemplation, as required by the conditions of the Yoga state. In the first or earlier portion of the existence of this third race, while it was yet in its state of purity, the "Sons of Wisdom," who, as will be seen, incarnated in this Third Race, produced by *Kriyasakti* a progeny called the "Sons of Ad" or "of the Fire-Mist," the "Sons of Will and Yoga," etc. They were a conscious production, as a portion of the race was already animated with the divine spark of spiritual, superior intelligence. It was not a Race, this progeny. It was at first a wondrous Being, called the "Initiator," and after him a group of semi-divine and semi-human beings. *"Set apart"* in Archaic *genesis* for certain purposes, they are those in whom are said to have incarnated the highest Dhyans, "Munis and Rishis from previous Manvantaras" — *to form the nursery for future human adepts,* on this earth and during the present cycle. These "Sons of Will and Yoga" born, so to speak, in an immaculate way, remained, it is explained, entirely apart from the rest of mankind.

The "BEING" just referred to, which has to remain nameless, is the *Tree* from which, in subsequent ages, all the great *historically* known Sages and Hierophants, such as the Rishi Kapila, Hermes, Enoch, Orpheus, etc., etc., have branched off. As objective *man*, he is the mysterious (to the profane — the ever invisible) yet ever present Personage about whom legends are rife in the East, especially among the Occultists and the students of the Sacred Science. It is he who changes form, yet remains ever the same. And it is he again who holds spiritual sway over the *initiated* Adepts throughout the whole world. He is, as said, the "Nameless One" who has so many names, and yet whose names and whose very nature are unknown. He is *the* "Initiator," called the "GREAT SACRIFICE." For, sitting at the threshold of Light, he looks into it from within the circle of Darkness, which he will not cross; nor will he quit his post till the last day of this life-cycle. Why does the solitary Watcher remain at his self-chosen post? Why does he sit by the fountain of primeval Wisdom, of which he drinks no longer, as he has naught to learn which he does not know — aye, neither on this Earth, nor in its heaven? Because the lonely, sore-footed pilgrims on their way back to their *home* are never sure to the last moment of not losing their way in this limitless desert of illusion and matter called Earth-life. Because he would fain show the way to that region of freedom and light, from which he is a voluntary exile himself, to every prisoner who has succeeded in liberating himself from the bonds of flesh and illusion. Because, in short, he has sacrificed himself for the sake of mankind, though but a few Elect may profit by the GREAT SACRIFICE.

It is under the direct, silent guidance of this MAHA — (great) — GURU that all the other less divine Teachers and instructors of mankind became, from the first awakening of human consciousness, the guides of early Humanity. It is through these "Sons of God" that infant humanity got its first notions of all the arts and sciences, as well as of spiritual knowledge; and it is they who have laid the first foundation-stone of those ancient civilizations that puzzle so sorely our modern generation of students and scholars.

— *The Secret Doctrine,* I, 207-8

THE sublime passage in Vol. I, page 207 of *The Secret Doctrine,* referring to the birth of the Sons of Wisdom, and to the Wondrous Being or Silent Watcher, has been the subject of much speculation, debate, and even misunderstanding. In this fact is involved one of the most subtil of occult conceptions: unity in multiplicity. I will try to explain.

A single semi-divine human being at the head, the Hierarch; and those beneath him being so close to him, karmically, spiritually, etc., that they are to him like his alter egos, as are the organs or limbs of a man to himself. Hence it is at times spoken of as the Silent Watcher, or again as the Supreme School or Occult body, the highest human stage on the planet; and it will remain so till the life-wave leaves this planet for Globe E. Śishtas will be left behind, of course; and it was these Śishtas of the Third Round that became this Silent Watcher, semi-divine man, and School, when our Round opened on this Globe. It is this complex of ideas to which H. P. B. alludes in the passage here referred to.

From this original Wondrous Hierarch-Hierarchy later on, in a later age during the Third Root-Race, sprang forth or were born the first regularly formed Occult schools for teaching and training, and raising ready ones to adeptship. This Wondrous Being, who as stated is at once a Hierarch of the Hierarchy, and the Hierarchy itself, and whose spiritual and intellectual union is so close between these two that they are often simply spoken of as one, as H. P. B. does in this passage of the S. D. — this Hierarch-Hierarchy actually came into being as a divine body-corporate or multifold unit in the very first Race of this Round on our Globe; and its seed was, as stated above, the śishtas of the highest humanized elements in our life-wave left on this globe when that life-wave during the Third Round passed onwards. When these śishtas felt the new incoming of the life-wave approaching Globe D during this Fourth Round, then as it were they collected or prepared themselves into a unity, and formed the Hierarchy preparatory for new increments to themselves coming with the human life-wave.

The whole matter is very complicated, very mystical, and is so utterly contrary to Western conceptions, that at first it seems difficult to understand. Yet when understood, one wonders how it could ever have been misunderstood, and one wonders how it ever could have been unnoticed.

It should not be forgotten that when we speak of beings of this type, I mean those composing this Hierarch-Hierarchy, one in others and others in and with the one, the general name as a descriptive title only for all such beings is Dhyânins, or Dhyâni-Chohans. Dhyânins is perhaps more general, and Dhyâni-Chohans should be used more for the chief among the chohans. Chohan means chief or lord, or principal. Actually this Hierarch-Hierarchy is formed of all the very highest, most evolved, most spiritual human beings belonging to our life-wave, corporated into a unity and really on the verge of continuous dhyâniship, dhyân-chohanship indeed; but who, on the principle of the Buddhas of Compassion, refuse to pass on until those trailing behind them, in other words, all the less evolved human egos, have had every help that can be given by these advanced ones. Hence the hierarchy visualized as a hierarch, in other words the hierarchy seen in this case through its hierarch as a unit, is called the Silent Watcher, the Wondrous Being, etc.

It is very much like the Cosmic Logos. Many students have been puzzled why the Cosmic Logos is spoken of at one time as an individual or a unit, and at other times as a vast body of monads collected into a unit, a hierarchy. It is the same principle. A similar point arises in the case of the Manus. Considered as units they are one, as the Logos and Wondrous Being are in such cases considered as one. Yet considered distributively, or in other words looking at the unified or collected units we ascertain it as a hierarchy in all three cases.

The idea may be perhaps made clearer by thinking of the human body. We may look upon it as a unit, and speak of it as such. But then on reflexion we see that the physical body is made up of innumerable multitudes of life-atoms, even of ordinary physical molecules and cells; and when we examine the body thus distributively, and recognise its unity and coherence as a unit, we call it a hierarchy.

THE GREAT SACRIFICE

Do you remember? In the first volume [I, 207] of H. P. B.'s *The Secret Doctrine*, there is a marvelous passage dealing with the Great Sacrifice as she calls it, the Initiator, the one who through evolution, long time since fully accomplished, has attained almost the outer limit of knowledge regarding our hierarchy, our sphere of life; but sits not only at the heart but as it were on the margin of the greater light, of greater life and greater wisdom, of a still more comprehensive hierarchy, and refuses to pass into the light beyond, but waits to serve as the inspirer and guide of all those multi-millions of pilgrims less advanced than he trailing along behind. There the Great Sacrifice sits at his self-imposed task; he no longer advances. The divine love of this wonder-being's heart will not allow him to pass onward into infinite peace until all those foot-sore pilgrims coming behind him have been led up and onward to the peace and wisdom that is his.

Who is this Initiator; who is this Great Sacrifice? Who is this Silent Watcher? Please open your ears in reverence. Ages ago when the human race on this planet during this Fourth Round was still young, mind had not yet imbodied in the then intellectually senseless early Third Root-Race, when therefore man was but slightly psychic, fully instinctual, but not yet intellectual, non-self-conscious as we understand this phrase. There were nevertheless a few in whom the lamps of mind burned bright, the most advanced of the human race who had been intellectually enlightened by Mânasaputric descents before the vast majority of the race. They were even in the early part of the Third Root-Race fully self-conscious, intellectual and spiritual human beings; and all the rest of mankind were sunken in the dreamland as it were of non-intellectual activity; very much as the mind of a little child, by and by to become intellectualized as it grows into manhood, but not yet. As a little child it is not intellectual, it is in a dreamland, full of physical activity, full of certain psychic sensitivity, fully instinctual. Mind has not yet manifested, it is just beginning. And so was the majority of mankind in the early part of the Third Root-Race. They were grown adults of

course. When I use the simile of *a* little child I do not mean little
children. They were full-grown adults; but as far as mind was concerned, they were spiritually and intellectually as little children are.
They did not yet think. For instance, the problems of science and
philosophy and religion, and even politics, literature, all the great
things, all the great thoughts that infill the minds of thinking men
today, are, for little children, not yet existing.

So it was in this early Third Root-Race; but these few in whom
the lamps of intellect had already begun to burn bright formed a
group, a band, a brotherhood, of human guides. But yet something
more was needed, something from a still higher sphere was required
for the utter safety of all mankind, for the utter safety of those few
souls, as well as of the great multitude of as yet non-intellectual
human beings. So these few took council, went into themselves and
sought the inner light. Oh how may this mystery be expressed?
Uniting their will-power and their imagination, these ethereal beings,
through Kriyâsakti, through spiritual will-power and imagination,
established contact with the waiting divinity, karmically waiting,
the destined one for this globe, and provided the physical vehicle for
the imbodiment of this waiting divinity, a true Avatâra of a peculiar
type. Through Kriyâsakti this relatively small band of men in whom
the flame and light of mind already burned brightly, united, and
created if you wish, produced by their vitality and their will and
their imagination, the vehicle. And behold, the link was made with
the waiting Dhyâni-Chohan and before their eyes it was!

At first it was a marvel-being, a very god who became their chief
and leader, their inspirer and guide; and he by teaching and inspiration and magic if you wish, prepared the way for the general mânasaputric descent into the senseless imbodied human vehicles of the
multitudes of men evolutionally behind. And after him, a relatively
short while after, this Wondrous Being who thus became the Initiator, aided by those others in whom the flame of mind burned so
bright, brought other similar descents into being, and they with their
great spiritual powers were called the Sons of Will and Yoga. Think
what that means: the Sons of Will-power and Imagination, given
bodies by Kriyâsakti in order to manifest the heavenly influx; and
this was the germ of all later revelation to men. This group became
the first mystery-school. It still exists, Companions; and this Being,

the Initiator, is the Supreme Head of all true occultists in all ages. He has been known in every land. He has been whispered about and wondered about in every country of the earth and in every age. Given numerous names, he changes form from time to time as evolution demands it. This Wondrous Being still remains our Supreme Head.

I think I have said enough, Companions. The main points are these: the Wondrous Being was brought into objectivity on this Globe D, our Earth, through Kriyâsakti by the first individuals of the Third Root-Race who were mânasaputrized because of their own good karman and more advanced evolution, in other words in whom the light of intellect and mind came first. The body or vehicle was created for this Being by Kriyâsakti. First it was this one Being; then other Sons of Will and Yoga came afterwards; and this group exists today and will continue to exist to the very end of time so far as our Earth is concerned. It will remain when the life-wave passes on to the next globe, guiding these and inspiring the sishtas, in other words the elect of mankind left behind on this globe when the general life-wave of humanity passes on to the next globe. And thus left behind and guided by this Lodge of Light, of the Sons of Light, of the Sons of Will and Yoga, it will be the nursery to produce the future humanity on this globe again when the life-wave has circled around the globes, and comes down to our globe once more. These sishtas, guided by the Sons of Will and Yoga, will provide the bodies at first; and once the river begins to flow, it will be guided and the work of magic will cease.

The whole matter is so beautiful, known to every great religious and philosophical system the world over and in every age in various guises, hinted at yet never fully explained until the Theosophical Society was founded.

Final thought: there the Great Sacrifice sits, this Sacrifice of himself unto himself, for mankind and indeed for all that lives. The whole story of the sacrifice of Jesus in the Christian New Testament is a distorted allegory copied from this one fact. The human race if it will recognise the fact, if it will pocket its petty pride of brain and recognise the facts of nature and the facts of human consciousness, will receive guidance just in proportion to the individual's receptive nature. Of course any man who in his stupid blindness

shuts his eyes and mocks and turns away, will reap what he is sow-
ing for himself.   For like the rain which is sent upon the just and
upon the unjust, or like the glorious sunlight which falls alike upon
the good and upon the evil, it is not the rain nor the sunlight which
forces itself into places where it is not wanted.   It is for those who
know what rain and sunlight mean, to receive these blessings.   And
so it is with the Mysteries.   Remember the old Christian saying:
Those of you who have ears to hear let them hear, and those of you
who have eyes to see let them see.   Those who will not hear and who
will not see have but themselves to blame.

SPHERES OF EXPECTATION

Says the Catechism (Commentaries): —

. . . *"Into the forms projected by the Lha* (Pitris) *the two letters* (the Monad, called also 'the Double Dragon') *descend from the spheres of expectation.* But they are like a roof with no walls, nor pillars to rest upon."* . . .

— *The Secret Doctrine*, II, 57

*The intermediate spheres, wherein the Monads, which have not reached Nirvana, are said to slumber in unconscious inactivity between the Manvantaras.

THESE Spheres of Expectation, at the beginning of pralaya or great period of cosmic rest when everything has resolved back into the ultimate elements are, as H. P. B. explains, those spheres wherein arise or wherein sink the evolving monads which in the just closed manvantara or period of cosmic manifestation had not yet reached the nirvâna, or condition of complete self-identification with the Cosmic Spirit. I was asked to explain just what these Spheres of Expectancy or Expectation are. It struck me that H. P. B.'s footnote is perfectly clear, and I take it that the querent wanted some elaboration of it.

Evolving entities, evolving monads, are divisible into at least ten and even twelve classes. These differences of class really mean differences of evolutionary unfoldment, of emanation. The lowest class of monads are those which have the least unfolded themselves. The highest are those which have evolved, or unfolded themselves or self-expressed themselves the most. And there are all the intermediate monads. On the ladder of life, the different rungs or the different steps or stages on an ascending scale are occupied each rung as it were by a class or group of monads which is one cosmic stage higher than the one just beneath, one cosmic scale lower than the class just above.

Of these ten or twelve families of evolving monads, some at the end of a cosmic manvantara or period of cosmic manifestation have reached the advanced stage of inner growth, or unfolding, or emanation, of what is locked up within, where they are ready for the nirvâna and enter it. All the others which have not reached that nirvânic state, which in another sense is called the dharmakâya, and do not enter the nirvâna, remain in several intermediate conditions of consciousness far lower than the nirvâna, but yet differing among themselves according to the different grades of evolving monads just spoken of; and all these latter states or stages are called Spheres of Expectation, Spheres of Expectancy, because the monads in these states of consciousness inferior to the nirvâna are as it were waiting in expectation for the next great cosmic manvantara to give them the chance to ascend where these others, higher than they, have already gone or reached. These stages are therefore the Spheres of Expectation.

Indeed the phrase may be used on a lower scale, on an inferior scale. Take the case of us human beings who have no chance, because we are not as yet sufficiently self-evolved, spiritually and intellectually, to reach the nirvâna when we die; we nevertheless enter the devachan, the state appropriate to our respective minds or conditions of consciousness; and in the devachan we are in a sphere or condition or state of expectancy, expectation. The next life we evolve a little more. Finally we shall reach the nirvâna.

So that is what the Spheres of Expectation are: conditions of consciousness. It does not matter where they are localized; they may be anywhere in the galaxy. The important point is the condition of the consciousness in such sphere. Any entity which is thus in a sphere or condition of expectation belongs to the class H. P. B. spoke of.

Again, transfer the illustration to a still lower grade than humans. The monads now working through animal-bodies are in Spheres of Expectation waiting to enter the human kingdom, expecting to enter the human kingdom. So far as we are concerned, the more evolved, more emanated, more unfolded, more self-expressed these beast-monads as we speak of them — for they are merely monads in that condition — are, the more they are in these Spheres of Expectation. The plant-world in just the same way: the different monads now passing through the plant-world are in Spheres of Expectation so far as the beasts are concerned, etc.

ASURAS AND SURAS

Two important points are involved herein: — (a) Primarily in the *Rig-Veda*, the "Asuras" are shown as *spiritual divine beings;* their etymology is derived from *asu* (breath), the "Breath of God," and they mean the same as the Supreme Spirit or the Zoroastrian *Ahura*. It is later on, for purposes of theology and dogma, that they are shown issuing from Brahmâ's thigh, and that their name began to be derived from *a*, privative, and *sura*, god (solar deities, or *not-a-god*, and that they became the enemies of the gods. . . .

— *The Secret Doctrine*, II, 59

IN H. P. B.'s *The Secret Doctrine* you will frequently find what has been to so many, many hundreds of devoted students most confusing references to the names or rather classes of certain beings, entities like the Suras, the Asuras, the Maruts, etc., and I have often been asked if some evening in speaking in the Lodge here I would not try to throw a little light on just what these beings are, these Suras, and Asuras, and Maruts.

Has it ever occurred to you — it must have, because it is demonstrated on almost every page of her greatest book, *The Secret Doctrine* — that H. P. B. brought together a wealth of illustrative material from all the different religions and philosophies of the world in order to prove the universality of our God-Wisdom? To do this she had to use the technical names employed in these different philosophies and religions. Thus from Brâhmanism were adduced Suras, Asuras, Maruts. From Buddhism, meaning precisely the same thing, she spoke of Dhyâni-Chohans; or again from Brâhmanism, Kumâras, Agnishwâttas. All these names really refer to the same entities; but what are the distinctions now between Suras and Asuras and Maruts, and between Kumâras and Agnishwâttas? This: when a monad is at the very beginning of its evolutionary course in the cosmic manvantara, the technical name given to it is Kumâra, which is a Sanskrit term meaning virgin. It is virginal in the new manvantara. It has therein incurred no sin; it is unadulterated, pure monadic essence. When such a Kumâra at the end of a cosmic manvantara, or two or three, according to its ability to evolve, has emanated forth from itself what is in it, has reached the bottom of the great sweep of evolving life and has risen on the ascending arc to the top of it, the same Kumâra then is an Agnishwâtta because it then has evolved fully forth from itself, mind, intellect, and has gained experience. Yet they are both monads, or rather it is the same thing: a monad beginning as a Kumâra, or as I have often put it, an unself-conscious god-spark, ending as an Agnishwâtta, "purified by fire," which is what Agnishwâtta means, the fire of the spirit and of experience.

A Sura is a Kumâra — a god. Because of their great purity, vir-ginality in every sense of the word, Hindû mythology called them gods. Actually they are monads in so pure, as yet unevolved, a state, so undeveloped a state, that they are swept along, as it were, in the evolutionary Rivers of Life. When this Sura or Kumâra has become an Agnishwâtta, it is then an Asura. And Hindû mythology, or rather Brâhmanical theology, with the same spirit behind it that you will find in Christian theology, says — and I will now use Christian language — "It has eaten of the Tree of Life, of the Tree of the Knowledge of Good and Evil, and it is no longer virginal and pure." That is the Christian theological way of explaining it. But leaving these dogmatic theologies of the religions aside, what actually are the facts? That from an unself-conscious god-spark, a Kumâra — the Sura, the monad, the same thing — through suffering and experience in the lower realms of matter, in the different planes, has become an Agnishwâtta. It has tasted of the fire and has become a self-conscious god, an Asura.

Asura really comes from *Asu,* the essential meaning of which in Sanskrit is 'to breathe.' You will find it in other languages. The verbal root *as,* in Sanskrit meaning 'to be,' is the same essential idea. So the Asuras are not merely unself-conscious god-sparks swept along through the ages unself-consciously on the Rivers of Life. They are those who have gained self-consciousness; or, to use a Buddhist term meaning the same thing, they have become celestial Dhyânis, celestial Bodhisattvas, celestial Buddhas.

What are the Maruts? They are one class of the Agnishwâttas, Asuras. Thus in *The Secret Doctrine,* which often quotes from Brâhmanical theology, when you read that often the Suras and the Asuras were battling together, you have a very interesting fact not only of human evolutionary history here, but of cosmical history.

It is the same thought that runs back of the early Christian legends concerning the battle fought in Heaven between the spirits of Light and the spirits of Darkness. And of course in mediaeval theology any thing that thinks for itself, an Asura, is a spirit of Darkness. Do you catch it? That is why they are called the demons or the spirits of Darkness. Here is the gist of the Christian legends of the so-called 'Fallen Angels'; a descent of all the monads which have won self-conscious freedom in intellectual and spiritual growth and have become like unto us, 'Elohîm.

You know in the Hebrew Bible: "Thou shall not eat of the Tree of the Knowledge of Good and Evil, for if thou eatest of it thou shalt become like us." But that indeed is the whole purpose of evolution! That the monads may pass from the state of unself-conscious god-sparks to that of self-conscious, fully evolved gods, knowing their divinity and taking a self-conscious part in the cosmic work. These are the Asuras, the Maruts, the Agnishwâttas. But naturally it always pleased the dogmatic priests — I do not mean the initiates but the dogmatic priests of theology — to keep the thinking faculty down; and yet it is man's saving. The thinking faculty, it is true, often leads man into error and into making grievous mistakes for which he has to pay with the very blood of his heart — As ye sow ye shall reap — but the end of it is illumination, experience, and pity, compassion. No man's heart has ever throbbed with understanding compassion over the sufferings of another which itself has never suffered. It takes suffering to make us pitiful to others who suffer — the cleansing fires of sorrow and pain; and these come through the advancing evolution of man's mind, part of which is his ethical, his moral instinct. Were it possible, as the gods can, for us humans to see a Sura, a Kumâra, we would see a starry, glorious being, spotlessly pure, radiant with the light of eternity, colorless, utter beautiful — but look in its eyes, there lacks a soul! Here lies the gist of the old European legend that the undine or the salamander, etc., must gain a soul before it can be saved. How true it is! The gaining of the soul is the story of the Kumâra passing through the experience of the lives, building up the human soul to self-understanding of what life and nature mean, and emerging from it in soul a god.

And on the other hand you would see the Agnishwâtta just as beautiful, just as glorious, shining with the glory of eternity on it;

but in its eyes the deep richness of garnered experience and infinite compassion, things which are only latent in the Kumâra. The Kumâra is the unself-conscious god-spark. The Agnishwâtta is the same, become a self-conscious god.

THE SEVEN EMBRYONIC HUMANITIES

. . . the Secret Doctrine postulates . . . the simultaneous evolution of seven human groups on seven different portions of our globe. . . .

— *The Secret Doctrine*, II, 1

I HAVE been asked to say something this evening in regard to the statement of H. P. B. in the second volume of *The Secret Doctrine*, to the effect that the 'Fathers' or Pitris in the beginning of human evolution on this Globe D in this Fourth Round began this evolution in seven different geographical zones simultaneously.

The statement refers to the fact that human evolution opened on this Globe D in this Fourth Round by the simultaneous appearance, on seven different parts of the land surrounding the North Pole, of seven embryonic 'humanities,' these seven 'humanities' being the appearance, or appearances, of the seven classes of Barhishads or Lunar Pitris. The Esoteric Doctrine, as thus becomes immediately obvious, teaches a polygenetic and not a monogenetic origin for mankind.

It is from these original seven astral embryonic humanities, forming the beginnings of the First Root-Race on this Globe in this Round, that all the later human races came. These seven primary origins of astral humanity occurred, or had their geographical zones, on what H. P. B. calls the Sacred Imperishable Land, the first continent, surrounding and including the North Pole and extending, like the leaves of a lotus, somewhat southwards from the Pole in seven different geographical extensions, or 'zones' as H. P. B. calls them.

The Secret Doctrine does not teach the descent of mankind from a single pair i.e., from an Adam and an Eve, here using the exoteric language of the Hebrew Book of Genesis. This Hebrew account itself does not really refer to one man called 'Adam' and one woman called 'Eve,' originally a 'rib' in Adam's body, but is a generalized way of speaking of early mankind; and in strictness does not refer to what we call the First Root-Race but to the middle of the Third Root-Race on this Globe in this Round. The reference to the 'rib' is a reference to the separation of the androgynous humanity of that period into sex-humanity; and the word 'rib' is an inaccurate trans-

lation of the Hebrew word, which really signifies a 'side' or a 'part.'
This Hebrew account reminds one of the mystical and quasi-historic
narrative given by Plato in his *Banquet,* where the great Greek philosopher spoke of the mankind of the date which he had in mind as
being of globular form, strong and mighty, but wicked in temperament and in ambition; so that Zeus, in order to curb their evil doing
and to diminish their strength, cut these beings of globular shape
into two, much as one would divide an egg with a hair.

Going back to the question, the student must remember that there
are, strictly speaking, ten classes of the Pitris, three arûpa or relatively formless, called the Agnishwâtta- or Kumâra-class, whom we
may call solar spirits or beings; and the other seven, the rûpa, or
having form, were really the Lunar Pitris. The three highest of
these seven classes were also relatively arûpa, and four were distinctly rûpa. It is these latter, the Lunar Pitris, who, coming to this
Globe from the preceding Globe C of our planetary chain, appeared
— when the time for human evolution on this Globe began — on the
North Pole in their seven kinds or classes, awakening the śishtas of
the humanities left on this Globe D when the preceding Round, ages
and ages previously, had ended.

I would not speak, as the questioner does, of these seven astral
humanities as seven 'races,' for this word 'races' is in this instance a
bit confusing. I would liefer speak of them as seven embryonic
astral *mankinds,* each one of these seven mankinds being the production of one of the seven classes of the Lunar Pitris. It was
especially the four lowest classes of the seven Lunar Pitris which
gave to these original mankinds their physical form.

Such then was the opening of the drama of present human evolution on this Fourth Globe D in this Fourth Round. From that time
onwards, the seven embryonic astral humanities began their evolutionary development as the First Root-Race, and continued it, each
on its own zone, until the time came for the appearance of the Second
Root-Race. When the time for the Second Root-Race appeared, the
seven original embryonic astral mankinds had mixed and had disappeared as separate individual 'humanities.' The First Root-Race
then merged itself into the Second Root-Race — *becoming* the Second
Root-Race. Even at this early date, i.e., that of the First Root-Race,
and among the seven astral embryonic 'humanities' of that very

early time, there were seven grades — or seven differences appeared
— in evolutionary development from the lowest 'mankind' upwards
to the highest or seventh 'mankind'; and this seventh or highest
even then showed the beginnings of self-conscious and thinking Man.

It must be remembered that these seven embryonic astral 'humanities' were much more ethereal when they first appeared than
was this Globe D on which they appeared, although indeed the
Globe itself was then considerably more ethereal than now it is.
Remember also that with the exception of the relatively few spoken
of above who had attained a certain degree of self-consciousness,
because belonging to the highest class of the Lunar Pitris, the great
majority of these early seven astral mankinds were unself-conscious,
and therefore what H. P. B. calls 'mindless.' They were indeed the
astral 'shadows,' i.e., the more or less concreted astral bodies projected by the Lunar Pitris: embryonic men, but 'mindless' men,
much as a child is mindless when first born, although of course the
analogy is not very close here, but is nevertheless suggestive. The
child is 'mindless'; its flesh is very tender and soft; its bones are
not well hardened; and because it is mindless it lives in a dream-
world, mentally and psychically. Just so were these seven embryonic
astral mankinds.

Finally, the seven embryonic astral mankinds were actually the
astral bodies of the seven classes of the Lunar Pitris, each class of
which appeared in, or was attracted by karman to, its own geographical zone. They were mindless, boneless, skinless, and without internal organs as we now understand this word, and were in a state of
consciousness which can be likened only to that of a heavy day-
dream; therefore likewise they had no moral sense, and in consequence there was no sin among them because no sin was committed:
there was no mind to imagine sin and to do it. Morally, they were
as irresponsible as the just born child. Remember carefully, however, that it was the lowest four classes of the Lunar Pitris which
formed and shaped, by projecting their own Astral 'Shadows' or
bodies, the then physical śarîras of these earliest humanities.

MÂNASAPUTRAS, LUNAR PITRIS, ANIMAL MONADS, ETC.

COMPANIONS, I have been asked a question which I feel will be very hearty meat for new students of Theosophy, but old students will understand. It is the question of who are the Mânasaputras, who are the Agnishwâttas, who are the Lunar Pitris or Barhishads as they are sometimes called, and just what is the difference between the animal soul in the human being and the animal soul in the animal or the beast. I thought I had been over these things two or three times, but evidently not! Then, as I was pondering how I could make my own thoughts, things that I have learned, more clear to my brothers here, someone showed me a paragraph in H. P. B.'s marvelous *Secret Doctrine,* in Volume II, and I thought to myself: Before I say what I have to say tonight to the Lodge, I will read this, preceding it with a sentence from page 79.

> The human *Ego* is neither Atman nor Buddhi, but the higher *Manas* . . .
>
> Hence, as the higher 'Pitris or Dhyanis' had no hand in his physical creation, we find primeval man, issued from the bodies of his *spiritually fireless* progenitors, described as aëriform, devoid of compactness, and MINDLESS. He had no middle principle to serve him as a medium between the *highest* and the *lowest,* the spiritual man and the physical brain, for he lacked *Manas.* The Monads which incarnated in those *empty* SHELLS, remained as unconscious as when separated from their previous incomplete forms and vehicles. There is no potentiality for creation, or self-Consciousness, in a *pure* Spirit on this our plane, unless its too homogeneous, perfect, because divine, nature is, so to say, mixed with and strengthened by, an essence already differentiated.

And then again on page 81:

> Between man and the animal — whose Monads (or Jivas) are fundamentally identical — there is the impassable abyss of Mentality and Self-consciousness. What is human mind in its higher aspect, whence comes it, if it is not a portion of the essence — and, in some rare cases of incarnation, the *very essence* — of a higher Being: one from a higher and divine plane?

The Lunar Pitris or the Barhishads, to use a Hindû name by which they are sometimes called, were those beings who on the moon, when we were all there and it was a living planet, were the animal monads of the lunar men; and the Agnishwâtta-Pitris, the Solar Pitris, because under the direct governing inspiration of the sun, yet lunar also because they came from the moon, were the thinking, intellectual men on the moon-chain. But when they had reached the culmination of their spiritual and intellectual evolution on the moon, at the end of the moon's seventh or last Round, they left it no longer as mere men but as Mânasaputras, Sons of Mind, pure intellectual Dhyânis, spirits of intellect and spirits of thought; and it was these who became or were the Mânasaputras who inspired humanity on this chain, on this earth that is, during what we call the Third Root-Race. We are now in the Fifth Root-Race.

And what were the beings that they inspired, called variously Barhishads or Lunar Pitris, pitris being a Sanskrit word which means fathers or progenitors? Who were they whom these Mânasaputras or the men who were men on the moon inspired — who were these Lunar Pitris, these mindless ones, senseless in the intellectual meaning, but who were yet purely human and not animal at all, belonging to the human kingdom? These Lunar Pitris were those animal monads of the men on the moon who had attained human status when the last Round on the moon ended. To attain human status merely means having entered the very lowest ranks of the human kingdom. The Lunar Pitris, then, as they appear on our globe, were the animal monads in the human constitution of those who were men on the moon; and those thinking intellectual men on the moon at the end of the moon's Seventh Round, the highest evolution attainable then, reached the point of the Dhyânis, the Mânasaputras, and became our Mânasaputras here on this earth.

The men on the moon had not only the divine monad and the spiritual monad, but they had an intellectual monad, the human monad, and then they had the animal nature or the animal monad; and they had physical bodies. They were fully complete men as we are septenary entities; but each portion of the constitution of the men on the moon was itself evolving, just as at present our minds are evolving just as well as our moral intuitions are evolving. There is no contradiction. It is natural, it is the way Mother Nature works. She does not evolve only a part of the constitution of her children. She evolves all her parts contemporaneously, all evolving at the same time. But, I repeat, the Lunar Pitris were what we now would call our lower quaternary, that is, the animal, the human animal nature of us. Those were the Lunar Pitris, called the Lunar

Fathers because they were the animal monads in the lunar men; and those lunar men who became Mânasaputras — that is Dhyânis — at the end of the moon evolution, were our own Mânasaputras or higher egos.

Now what are the animals — the animals on the moon and the animals here on earth? They are monads evolving in the animal kingdom, just as we humans are monads evolving in the human kingdom, and just as the three classes of the Dhyânis are monads evolving in those three classes of Dhyânis. When the monad of a beast through evolutionary unfoldment or growth passes slowly through the ages all the different steps or stages of the animal kingdom towards the top, it finally reaches the very tip-top point of the animal kingdom, and the animal monad then is on the verge of becoming humanized, which merely means that the animal monad then has unwrapped from within itself all that it needs of the animal part, and is in the process of unwrapping from within itself, not from outside, the beginning of the human characteristics; for every monad is in essence divine, and therefore contains all within itself. So when we speak of an animal monad, this is but a fashion of speaking. What we mean is a monad, in itself a divine thing, which because it has as yet not unwrapped from itself more than the animal, is evolving in the animal kingdom. That is as simple as can be. A monad of a flower is in essence a divinity, as divine as my monad is or yours, or the monad of the highest god. But the monad has as yet unwrapped only the flower part of itself. It has thrown forth from itself only the flower part, the plant part. As that same monad advances and grows and unwraps from within itself, it will leave the plant kingdom and enter the animal kingdom at the lowest range thereof, and slowly progress up through the animal kingdom towards the very highest therein; and only when it reaches the top of the animal kingdom is it on the verge of manifesting forth from within itself the human part locked up within itself. It then leaves the animal kingdom which can teach it nothing more and enters the very lowest range of the human kingdom. Evolution therefore, you see, is on invisible planes. It is from within outwards. There is no other evolution. The very word shows it, *evolvere,* a Latin word meaning to unfold, to unwrap, what is there to be unfolded and unwrapped.

The monad, then, rises up from the animal kingdom when it can

learn no more and enters into the very lowest of the human, not as
an animal, *as a monad,* and it rises up through the human kingdom,
rising imbodiment after imbodiment, a little higher, and a little
higher, until it reaches a nobler human stage; and still evolves and
rises through the human kingdom, passes out through the lower animal human into the human, and then enters a spiritual human, and
then when it has reached the topmost spiritual point in the human
kingdom, it enters the lowest rank of the lowest of the Dhyâni.

So the monad passes as a pilgrim through each of the kingdoms,
but as it comes into the human kingdom it does not displace the
animal monad of the humans. It is the monad that enters the human
kingdom, and builds its sevenfold constitution, just as we do, as we
are. There is no displacement at all.

When the time came when these Lunar Pitris — the astral beings
not yet condensed, like a wisp of light if you wish, astral stuff —
through the inherent natural forces of growth had developed a vehicle
that could sustain the fire of mind, then the egos from the moon,
the Mânasaputras, the Agnishwâttas, descended into and set on fire
with divine flame those lunar parts of our constitution, and man
became fully man. Then he was a complete entity, no longer a
divine monad unable to express itself in physical bodies.

So we humans were now composed of a divine monad, a spiritual,
a human, and an animal monad, imbodied in one. When our own
earth shall have passed through its Seventh Round, then the men
on this earth here now, those of us who make the grade, will become
the Agnishwâttas, the Mânasaputras for the child of this earth chain,
the next chain; and our animal monads, our animal parts, our lower
quaternaries at the end of the Seventh Round on earth, will have
raised themselves to the status and stature of humanity, of manhood,
the *animal* monad, mind you. And it is these animal monads thus
become men just made, or men just clothed, who in the next chain,
child of this earth-chain, will be the Lunar Pitris of that next chain,
child of this chain, and will be inflamed then and there with the
intellectual fire which we shall give to them.

Now here is one very beautiful thing, which I noticed when I
read the extract from H. P. B., and it is so beautiful I want her own
words: "Between man and the animal — whose Monads (or Jivas)
are fundamentally identical — there is the impassable abyss of Men-

tality and Self-consciousness. What is human mind in its higher aspects, whence comes it, if it is not a portion of the essence — [this is what I meant] and, in some rare cases of incarnation, the *very essence* — of a higher Being."

This refers to a wondrous marvel in human evolution. It is this: Among the Mânasaputras who came and who gave us mind — because they were we ourselves, our intellectual and spiritual selves — there were certain very superior individuals, entities who on the moon itself in the last or Seventh Lunar Round, were already Dhyâ-nis. They guided, strange paradox, the work of our own Agni-shwâttas, guided the work of our own intellectual awakening, for they, these entities — how many were there? a thousand, ten thousand, a hundred thousand, I know not — chose certain human vehicles when we had received our minds from the Mânasaputras. They entered into the selected human bodies and permanently il-luminated them their lives long. It was mutual. There was the offer of a response awaiting the imbodiment of a divinity. The divinity incarnated; and these were the great Teachers of mankind, imbodied gods, men who gave themselves to furnish, to be, the vehicles so that these unutterably grand egos could use them, these men, in order to work among mankind. Then were started the first Mystery Schools, composed of these beings gathered together. Then were struck the keynotes which have run down the ages since those far gone times, keynotes which we now call innate ideas of the human spirit, keynotes of light, keynotes of order, keynotes of intuition, keynotes of truth. They gave men light, they taught those early men the arts and sciences — humans who had just received the intellectual fire from their own egos, from the moon — taught them the arts and sciences, taught them the seasons, taught them to look at the universe around them and to consider its marvels with wonder and reverence, taught them astronomy, taught them chemistry, taught them government; and then when their work was done, may-hap it was one life of the recipient, mayhap twain or more, when this work was done, supernal, grand, they returned to their own sublime spheres. But they still wait for us compassionately and understandingly. Do you know what they were on the moon? They were the Mahâtmans on the moon become gods when the moon men became dhyânized.

THE FORCES OF THE UNIVERSE

To thoroughly comprehend the idea underlying every ancient cosmology necessitates the study, in a comparative analysis, of all the great religions of antiquity; as it is only by this method that the root idea will be made plain. Exact science — could the latter soar so high, while tracing the operations of nature to their ultimate and original sources — would call this idea the hierarchy of Forces. The original, transcendental and philosophical conception was one. But as systems began to reflect with every age more and more the idiosyncrasies of nations; and as the latter, after separating, settled into distinct groups, each evolving along its own national or tribal groove, the main idea gradually became veiled with the overgrowth of human fancy. While in some countries the FORCES, or rather the intelligent Powers of nature, received divine honours they were hardly entitled to, in others — as now in Europe and the *civilized* lands — the very thought of any such Force being endowed with intelligence seems absurd, and is proclaimed *unscientific*. . . .   — *The Secret Doctrine*, I, 424

I WONDER how many of us really know what we mean when we speak of the 'Forces of the Universe.' You will be sure to be wrong if you think that by using the term 'Forces of the Universe,' we mean to signify the so-called scientific energies of the world. We do not. Why? Because the energies of science are soulless, without life, without intelligence, working haphazard, fortuitously, which means by chance; and how on earth these big-brained men can reconcile harmony, symmetry, mathematical perfection, in the Universe, with chance, is something utterly beyond me to attempt to explain! I do not think they have thought about it.

When we speak of 'Forces of the Universe,' we mean living beings, as much alive as we humans are alive. Just as any one of you is a living being, a composite entity, with an inner life, with a spirit, a soul, and all your inner faculties working through a physical vehicle or sheath; just exactly so is there a supreme divinity, a hierarch, who is the informing principle of our Galaxy or Home-Universe. But he or it is only one of a host of others informing other similar galaxies in frontierless infinitude. The gods are infinite in number; and we are embryo-gods. If you want to understand the universe, try to understand yourself, because you copy the universe. The universe repeats itself in every one of its atoms, which means in every one of its composite elements, in every one of its building bricks.

Just as man is informed by the divinity within or above him — both; so is the universe informed by the divinity within or above it — both. And just as man is more than one, as he is a whole host of entities, all deriving their essence and being from his inmost heart of hearts, his divine monad, just exactly so are all the forces of the universe derived from the cosmic divine entity.

Take my body as an instance. It is alive, as your bodies are. It is alive because it is formed of living things, living cells. In the first place, these cells are formed of aggregates of atoms, which if they were dead would produce a dead aggregate; but the fact that they produce a living aggregate is a proof that they themselves live, are alive. The atoms, therefore, are alive, and they are alive because the building-bricks composing them are alive: the electrons and protons.

Now, that is what we mean when we speak of the forces of the universe. In the last analysis we mean gods, living gods which express themselves in the manner that we have some conception of when we look at the starry sky, or look at the sun in the day-time, or consider the world around us, and all the actions that take place there, the growing plants and beasts and rocks. They are all alive.

What is an earthquake? Something that happens fortuitously, by chance? To believe that is simply symptomatic either of intellectual laziness, or lack of intellectual penetration. I don't believe there is a single chance action in Infinity. I cannot reconcile chance with law, because chance means the negation of law, and law means order, symmetry, harmony, mathematical relations. The universe is alive because it is infilled with living things, with gods. The physical universe is the body of the god, as my body is the body of me. The idea has nothing to do whatsoever with the modern scientific theory of energies. Scientists are now even discarding the term 'forces.' It is too mysterious, too superstitious.

The way to handle these scientific thinkers is to pin them down to facts. Don't let your minds be led away by talk. Demand an explanation of why you are a living being. Don't be satisfied with talk about chemical action and reaction. It does not mean anything. Show me any chemical compound that man can make in the laboratory that moves and thinks and feels! And here we are, living and moving and thinking and feeling, demonstrating that everything we do, that every thought we think, that every feeling we have, is consciousness. This is so much so that the greater scientific thinkers today are talking about consciousness as being the fundamental essence of the universe, coming at last to admit it. What does that mean? That these so-called energies that they keep in one compartment of their brains are simply examples of what they keep in the other watertight compartments of their brains — consciousness, consciousnesses.

The very fact that the universe is formed of aggregates of individuals is a proof of polytheism, which means simply that the universe is infilled with gods; and any universe has at its head a supreme Divinity; as man, a microcosm or small universe, has at its head his own divine hierarch, his essential, fundamental Self. But any such universe is only one among an infinitude of others. That is what we mean by the forces of the universe. I call them gods, because gods they are. When the sun rises tomorrow morning, look at Father-Sun, and remember that that brilliant divinity is a living being, the source of your own being in one sense, and that you are in your essence equally great, because both are manifestations of an indwelling divinity, the spirit of boundless infinity, the essence of boundless infinity, expressing a portion of itself in that sun, in those stars, in the planets, and all the entities that infill space, high, low, intermediate.

The only reason that science has been misled from seeing the truth in the past has been the fact that men were miseducated in religion for hundreds of years, fed not on truth — although the Christian religion is founded on truth — but on men's ideas about truth, theologians' ideas as to Reality. Then when men began to think and began to investigate the universe around them, they found that those ideas could not be harmonized with what they found to be the facts of the universe. So they lost confidence in all religious thought. They did not know of any other religious philosophies or philosophical religions that they had any respect for: And instead of thinking for themselves, each man following his own intuition, the spirit of the living god within his breast, they said: "That will introduce all kinds of anarchy into scientific thought. Cling to the only things we know to be facts, the facts of the physical universe." Because they could not find a soul within living flesh (and in fact they did not know what they were looking for), they said: "Man is but an animate mechanism." But what is an animate mechanism, a living machine? Explain it. Those are mere words.

We are living in the life-sphere, the fohatic sphere, the prânic sphere, of the divinity of our solar system, which divinity is the fountain-head of all the Christs and Buddhas that the human race from time to time brings forth. All movements of the world that we see around us: the earthquakes, the meteorological phenomena, rains, lightning, moving of clouds, thunder-storms, hail-storms, sunny, bright days, and over-clouded days — all are movements of the vital essence of the planetary spirit working in and with the co-operation of the solar spirit or divinity, as that solar spirit or divinity moves within the life-sphere of an entity still greater, the galactic divinity, which in its turn moves within the life-sphere of a divinity still vaster — all precisely as the living cells which make a man's body live and move and have their being within his body, which is the vehicle of the holy presence which his spirit is, the god, the hierarch, of his constitution. It is a wonderful thought, and fills man's mind with reverence for the symmetry and harmony and majesty and beauty of the universe. It makes him reverent, it makes him respect his fellow-men; for what the human race has brought forth in the matter of great men once, it will reproduce many times.

Remember that on every occasion when you see the action of a natural force, you are seeing the automatic workings of the vitality of our own particular planetary, or it may be solar, divinity. The only reason we cannot connect it with the human emotions and human thoughts that are familiar to us, is because its action is on a cosmic scale, so far beyond our understanding that we can only see, as it were, a small portion of it. The small portion of the web or pattern of our minds cannot take in the rest, and therefore we see what we think is purely mechanical action.

I will illustrate this: An entity living on an electron, helping to form one of the atoms of my body, would have no understanding or conception of my raising my hand, or of a movement of my leg, and even less of my intent when I speak; nevertheless all the inter-related forces giving my body life affect every molecule, every atom, every electron, in my body, destroy millions of them, bring millions

of them into birth. In precisely the same way the gods, the Forces
of Nature, have a range of action so vast and an intellect so far-
reaching, and a vitality whose sweep is so all-inclusive, and a time-
period — there is the key — so immense, that our understandings
cannot take it in; and we search, as the scientists have done, looking
for *human* consciousness in the movements of the planets and the
suns, looking for *human* actions or causes, like human functions, in
earthquakes and thunder-storms and the lightning-bolt. The scale
is too vast, just as the scale of my speaking, my walking, the raising
of my hand, is too vast for an inhabitant on an electron of one of the
atoms of my body to comprehend. It perceives it, if at all vaguely,
as an affection of matter.

As the great Greek Pythagoras said of the Music of the Spheres,
the planets chiming and choiring together in celestial harmony as
they circle around the sun: the march is too great for human ear to
take it in, because the human ear has been builded by evolution to
take in only a very short range of sound; and to right and to left of
that range is virtual infinitude. The vibrations on either side, our
ears are utterly incognisant of; and the same with our organ of sight.
How small a fraction of the rays which produce vision in our optics,
how small a fraction of the entire range of vibration, are we conscious of through the eye!

To illustrate again the vast range in which the universe is
builded: There are certain stars in which matter, and therefore the
consequent play of energies and forces, is so tremendously dense,
that it is a million times denser than anything we can produce or find
in our laboratories. And in either direction also, in the fields of cosmic space, there are nebulae so tenuous and ethereal, that they are a
million times less dense, in other words a million times more tenuous,
than the most tenuous stuff that we can know or produce in our
physical laboratories. A million times a million makes a trillion —
a million millions; and we have one trillionth of this scale which we
can investigate in our chemical laboratories — physical matter, gas,
etc. Think of it, one in a trillion! Enormous density on one hand,
tremendous tenuity, ethereality on the other hand. And matter as we
know it on this earth in all its forms occupies just a tiny fraction;
and that is our entire range of investigation.

Now then, that is what I mean by a scale so vast that our human minds cannot take it in. The intellect cognises that these extremes exist. Very good. Then let your thought go out into those extremes. Remember that they are as much a portion of the universe as is this little bit which we can test in the laboratory. Remember that we know of only one portion in a trillion; and then be modest! Outside of anything else, it has always seemed an amazing thing to me that it has only recently come to be recognised that man is an integral part of the universe in which he lives and moves and has his being, and from which he derives everything that he is. Theologians and scientists and philosophers alike have always in some inexplicable way based their intellectual researches on the utterly preposterous foundation that man was something essentially different from the universe; and this false concept runs throughout all the terms of our thought: subject, object.

This is an example of the Great Heresy, because it misleads you at every turn — the disjoining of or ungearing of yourself in your thought and feeling from the universe in which you live, of which you are a component, inseparable part. Man cannot ever know an object if that object is essentially different from himself. There cannot be any union. He can only know what he himself is or becomes. True knowledge, true wisdom, comes when, to use the ridiculous phrase of Occidental philosophy (though the deduction drawn is true): "the subject becomes identified with the object," and finds itself to be not twain but one.

Studies in
"The Mahatma Letters"

PERSONALLY I think Trevor Barker did quite right in publishing these Letters. It is true that in one or even two, perhaps, of the Masters' communications, they said that these letters were not for publication. But we must use our common sense in these things and realize that these communications were written to men and women mostly between the years 1880 and 1884. Many of these men and women — all of them, perhaps — are now dead. The personal embarrassments that might have been caused by their publication when the recipients of these letters were alive now no longer exist or could exist.

I think it is quite unfair for some of Dr. Barker's critics, because they do not approve of his publishing this wonderful book, to make capital out of what common sense should show was essentially not wrong, but a very fine thing to do. There has been too much *quid pro quo* argumentation as to the early communications from the Teachers — what the Teachers said and did not say. I have even known of cases where certain individuals claimed to have these communications or to have read them and tried to use them as sledge-hammers with which to down or break the heads of some opponent. I think Dr. Barker did right in letting us have the Masters' own words, as there is not a paragraph in this book which can offend anybody, and a great deal in this book which is extremely helpful.

More than this, I for one am very happy that in these *Mahatma Letters* we have a means of checking by the Masters' own words whether this Theosophical Society is on the right path, or that one, or that one. . . . In fact I think that one of the finest things in the history of the modern Theosophical Movement has been the publication of this book, and I would like to see it in the hands of every true Theosophist for study, for study, for study.

— Extracts from remarks by G. de Purucker during a question and answer period at the Convention of the Theosophical Society at The Hague, Holland, July, 1933.

TSONG-KHA-PA AND PLANETARY SPIRITS

REFERENCE: Letter IX, pp. 43-5

PERSONALLY I am extremely glad that you have chosen to begin the study of this wonderful book. I do not think it has ever properly been studied before. It is replete, compact, not merely with the most fascinating deductions and observations, written by some of the greatest minds now imbodied on this planet, but it is likewise filled, if you have the wit to discover these, with facts which in our western civilization would respectively be classed under the heads, Philosophy, Religion, Science. It has been stated, and quite erroneously, that H. P. B.'s *The Secret Doctrine* supplanted this book since it appeared in print and was sold to all and sundry. This is utterly erroneous. The most, I think, that could be said is that *The Secret Doctrine* would help you greatly if you are an earnest and sincere student of this collection of correspondence.

I would call your attention again with great emphasis to the fact that in reading *The Mahatma Letters to A. P. Sinnett,* you will err and have difficulty in accurately understanding those Letters as they were intended to be understood when they were written, if you do not transport your thought back into the days when they were written. Understand me now. If you read the science and theology and philosophy of 1940 into these old Letters, you will be distorting them. They were written to men who had no 1940 ideas of that kind, to men who lived in the thought-atmosphere of the latter half of the nineteenth century. (These Letters were mainly written between the years 1878 and 1886, perhaps one or two later than that. There were a few more.) Now this is not an unimportant warning to give you, for these Letters were called forth in answer to questions emanating from minds which were steeped in the science of the latter half of the nineteenth century, eighty years ago say, and in the religion of that time and in the philosophy of that time. Consequently, as they were written to the merest tyros in Theosophy, men who knew incomparably less about it than we all do now, even the language chosen was the simplest that could be found. I mean the attempt was to find the simplest words, the most direct expressions. This does not mean that there were no circumlocutions and hidings of occult truth, for these Letters are simply packed with these last. It is utterly useless to talk to a savage about things for which he has no comprehension. If a man does not understand the first principles of arithmetic, you can lecture him for forty years and he won't understand what you are talking about. That is what I mean.

So remember in your future studies, when you come to phrases that puzzle you and seem contradictory to what we have now, do not think there is something contradictory, or that the Master meant something wonderful. Simply remember that these Letters were written in the language and in the thought-atmosphere of the late seventies and of the early and middle eighties of the nineteenth century.

For instance, suppose the Master had been attempting then to describe what to us is called radio, familiar and simple. But neither Sinnett or Hume nor any man living then had the remotest idea of what radio was. Suppose the Master had been attempting to describe to these or other ladies and gentlemen of that time what an automobile was. Automobiles were merely beginning to be speculated about. Not one had yet been invented. Could he then successfully have described to men who did not know the first mechanical principles of this, the principles of the internal combustion engine? To whom electricity and its marvels was but in its infancy?

This will illustrate what I mean about the Master talking to them in the scientific language of that time, and you may apply the similar situation to the religious language of that time and the philosophic language of that time.

.   .   .   .   .   .

Tsong-kha-pa was the great Tibetan reformer of a degenerate Buddhism. Buddhism was brought to Tibet it is not known exactly when, but in the early part of what we in the west call the Christian era, probably in the sixth or seventh century, by an Indian Buddhist monk called Padma Sambhava, and he labored well and long among the Tibetans and converted practically the whole country by the magic of his word, by the power of his illustrations, and by the persuasion of his fascinating mind. But it was not many centuries before the natural inertia of human understanding and its disinclination always to hold to the highest, began its leisurely work; and little by little, after Padma Sambhava died the Buddhists began to drop from the purity of Buddha's teaching with its grand ethics and wonderful occultism, dropped down to the level from which Padma Sambhava had raised them; and this level was known, or is known today, by the name of the Bhön, which is what the Tibetans themselves call it. It is a kind of naturalistic religious philosophy peculiar to Tibet, immensely ancient, archaic indeed, and probably brought over from Atlantean, late Atlantean times. It largely comprises worship of nature spirits, superstitious practices, and above everything else, the practice of magic, white and black; and there is so much akin to the Bhön in what we know as the Tantras of India, the tantric teachings, that I for one have no doubt that they have an identical origin.

Now then, in the fourteenth century appeared Tsong-kha-pa, the greatest spiritual Teacher excepting none that Tibet has ever known. He reformed the degraded or the degenerated or false Buddhism of Tibet, brought it back to its grand pristine purity; and when he died, due to his marvelous genius and ability in spreading ideas and making them more fascinating than the calls that were made upon Tibetans by the Bhön system — when he passed away or vanished or died, call it what you will, he had brought back to the Holy Path, as the Tibetans call it, practically all of Tibet proper, and raised Tibet to a higher plane of thought than it had as yet ever attained in known history; and it is today even the most powerful as well as the official form of Buddhism in Tibet. The Bhön thought and the degenerated Buddhism of Padma Sambhava, still held by people whom Tsong-kha-pa did not succeed in reaching, prevail to this day along the outskirts of Tibet, along the Indian and Chinese and Turkestan and the north frontier; and it is along this frontier that the so-called Red Caps are mainly to be found, not wholly but mainly. In the interior of Tibet you will find a vast majority of the Yellow Caps or those who have followed Tsong-kha-pa. The distinction is really, so far as dress goes, only in the cap or hat, because both the Red Caps and the Yellow Caps of Tsong-kha-pa wear pretty much the same clothing, usually red and dark orange, the old Buddhist robe of India.

Now, what was Tsong-kha-pa? He was what I would call a tulku. A tulku means what was explained at our gathering here a fortnight ago. Like Jesus, but in other ways differing from him, Tsong-kha-

pa was both Tulku and Bodhisattva. In fact, tulku means bodhisattva. He was not Buddha, or a Buddha. He had refused the Buddha-state. You may call him one of the highest of the Sambhoga-
kâyas today, or Nirmânakâya. I myself am not sure on this point.
But he is not a Dharmakâya. That would mean going into the Nirvâna, and for ages and ages and ages passing out of all possibility
of helping the millions and millions and millions trailing along behind. Going into Nirvâna, assuming Dharmakâya, simply means
cutting off all connexion with the lower planes and rising up to the
highest realms of spirit. Of course this is a consummation which is
unspeakably grand, glorious, wonderful. But the Buddhas of Compassion and the Bodhisattvas refuse it. They prefer to remain behind and help those who know less of the Law than they do.

Tsong-kha-pa became a Planetary. Now what is a Planetary?
A Planetary is a cosmic spirit. They can be of many different grades
on the ladder of life of that planet, our planet in this case. There are
high planets, high planetaries, low and intermediate. But I have no
doubt that Tsong-kha-pa could be classed among the intermediate,
for the simple reason that being a Bodhisattva, he has not cut himself off by ascending so high that re-descent is not possible in this
manvantara.

And Planetaries. Here again this is a very interesting subject, and
when time is allowed we must go into it more profoundly than we
shall have time tonight to do. As stated there are high planetaries,
intermediate, and low. This is because there are planetaries belonging to our entire planetary chain. The influence of the very highest
extends over all the seven or twelve globes of our chain. There are
intermediate planetaries whose influence is the very highest over any
one globe, such as our earth, or Globe D; and there are lower planetaries who work under these higher planetaries whom we may call
those planetary spirits closest in touch with poor mankind. Their
work is beautiful, compassionate, indeed sublimest of all the planetaries.

But yet we must remember that when we speak of planetaries,
we must not figurate to ourselves anything that even approaches
infallibility, for even the low planetaries are not infallible. Think
what infallibility means. It would mean having a mind co-extensive
with the galaxy, practically boundless infinitude. It would mean

having a will co-extensive with the immense will of nature, in other words you would have to be Mother Nature herself to be infallible, and no planetary is that. But compared with us men even the lowest planetaries have a judgment and a discrimination and a wisdom and an insight and a power which are virtually infallible. They can be trusted. This may sound like an academic discussion, but it is not so. I know there are certain people in the west today who imagine that a certain great Ecclesiastic official is infallible. They are welcome to their opinion. History does not support it.

Now the question may be asked: Can you give us an instance of a planetary as recorded in some other religious or philosophical system? Very easily. What the Hindûs call the Manus are planetaries of one kind. What they call the Prajâpatis are planetaries. You can also say, and you won't wander far from the truth, that the Manus are also Prajâpatis. They are also instances of planetaries so far as the human life-wave is concerned. Other instances of planetaries are the references in many of the old religions and religious philosophies to what the Christians, following the Greeks, called angels and archangels. And here is your key. What the solar logoi are in and to the sun, that the planetaries are for a globe of a chain or for an entire chain.

HINTS ON THE HISTORY OF THE ROOT-RACES

REFERENCE: Letter XVIII, pp. 119-22

ALL the great religions and philosophies of the past tell us of a time when death actually did not exist in the earliest human races. It entered into human existence or into human habitudes only when what the Christians called sin entered the world. This brought death with it, not only physical death, but, as we Theosophists try to point out, soul death also. But we are now speaking of death of the body.

Race One and a good part of Race Two did not live for millions of years as individuals. That would be utterly absurd. That would mean that a soul-like entity, no matter how perfectly ensouled, passed relatively unchanged through millions of years of bare existence, and that is nonsense. Nature shows us no example whatsoever of such unchanged identity. Even today in the cellular bodies there is a constant change and throwing off, a constant changing from day to day, movement.

So what happened corresponding to death during the First Race and a part of the Second Race? Individuals did not then cast aside their worn-out bodies and take unto themselves new and fresh ones. That habit of nature had not yet been brought into existence for human beings or for the beings of that time. The bodies then were like enormous pudding bags, as H. P. B. called them, or cells, and these cells lived and budded themselves largely by osmosis and end-osmosis and exosmosis. At a certain period these cells were thrown off and from one cell two came. Each of those cells thereafter lived for a certain time, the time of fission for each one, and then each of the twain divided into two, and then you had four cells, four individuals. But there was no death. Later on the method of propagating the species as you might call it changed. But we are now speaking of these early races.

The cells as individuals did not as individuals live unchanged for millions of years, which would be an absurdity. But the cells kept dividing and dividing, each cell became two, two became four, four became eight, eight became sixteen, etc., etc. But then what happened? You might think that by and by all these cells would cover the earth so thickly that none could move. But they did not. Nature does not act in that way. Even here, as biologists know, perfect order prevails. When a species seems to have reached its maximum of propagation, barrenness ensues, or fecundity seems to die out. The balance is kept, because there is always a certain number of monads or entities living in these bodies. There can be no body unless there is an entity to ensoul it so to speak.

Then the Third Root-Race, by this time the human race, had passed through the stages of propagating their spores or seeds or eggs, just as they do today as a matter of fact only in a somewhat different fashion. Nature has not dropped off all her processes. We still propagate our species through cells or eggs and so forth, only it is differently arranged. We have now reached the Third Root-Race which were androgynous. Sex had not yet appeared, and there were huge creatures. The outlines of the human form as we now see it and understand it were already pretty well limned; the human structure was there, different from what it now is, less refined than what it now is, less grand in a way; but the distinct outline of the human form was there during this androgynous time.

Then at the middle of the Third Root-Race androgyny became two sexes as we now have them, or Adam-Eve became Adam and Eve. And by the way I might say in passing that even in the Hebrew of the Book of Genesis in Chapter 3rd, I think, it states, "And their name was Adam," not *his* name, but *their* name. "And Adam and Eve were — and their name was Adam." That contains a whole lot that could be said of it.

However, at about that time, before the race became really sexed as we now understand it, there were huge creatures, I don't know how high they would stand, with huge feet about eight feet long. But mark you, they would be soft-fleshed, very tender, very soft as compared with us hard-fleshed humans. I could entertain you with a lot of wondrous tales and yet keep strictly within the boundaries of occult history, of occult archaic biology.

Then as the race went on and became sexed and became Atlanteans, even these although greatly dwindled in size from the Third Root-Race or so-called Lemurians, were themselves about twenty-four feet tall. You know, it is a tradition among all the ancient races and all the ancient religious and philosophic writings, that there were giants on the earth in those days; which does not seem so strange if you look at what modern biology and archeology are beginning to show us of the size of living beings in those early times. Well, the flesh of the Atlantean giants was even grosser than ours, terrifically gross, pebbly, ugly, yet definitely human flesh. We have become some-what refined since those days; and as time goes on and the Sixth Root-Race shall be established on this earth, say in 4,000,000 years from now more or less, the Sixth Root-Race will be individuals leaving sex behind. The embryonic organs of sex that nature still pre-serves with us, shows us what she is intending to bring forth in the future, and androgyny will again appear, but in a more refined form; and the flesh of the Sixth Root-Race men will be very tender and soft. They won't realize it; but if you could have a Sixth Root-Race man amongst us today, perhaps smaller than I am, smaller than the smallest man here, you would marvel at the luminous effect his flesh would make on our eyes, tender, soft, as if light were behind it; and mighty of intellect, and great in spirituality. And the Seventh Root-Race will begin to be having bodies of light, hardly light, yet the beginning. It is so difficult to describe things that are coming millions and millions of years hence. They sound just like dreams now. I do not know that we have anything that can be likened to these things, unless it be a jelly fish. Of course that is out of the past, but there you have a living entity whose flesh is extremely soft and tender.

Then in future *Rounds*, in those glorious far future days of hundreds of millions of years in the future, men will be like the angels as the Christians would say. They would in fact be approach-ing Dhyân-chohanship, titans in spirituality, giants in intellect, no longer men and women, but nevertheless glorious human beings.

SPIRITUAL FAILURES

REFERENCE: "Now there are — there *must be* 'failures' in the etherial races of the many classes of Dyan Chohans or Devas as well as among men. . . ."
— *et seq.*, see Supplementary Notes to Letter XIV, p. 87

IN THE address of tonight a quotation was made from *The Mahatma Letters to A. P. Sinnett* with reference to failures, spiritual failures; and as I know that this word has been greatly misunderstood, or at least apprehended wrongly, I ask your kind attention to what I have to say.

What may be failure among the gods, may be a glorious achievement for a human being or for a demi-god. The 'failures' amongst the Dhyân-Chohans, or the gods if you wish, is a phrase which refers simply to those high beings, even amongst the Dhyân-Chohans, who have essayed more than they could successfully accomplish. But you see in a way how creditable this effort is. It is one of the divinest things in the consciousness not only of human beings, but of the Dhyân-Chohans, that they aspire forever beyond themselves. Such failures are victories in the long run, for they represent a sublime effort. And it is far nobler to try to seek the companionship of the gods in this life and fail because we are ourselves not yet gods, than it is to be forever merely human and reck not whether the gods exist or not. So that these failures, all honest failures from the strictly logical meaning of not having done what was envisioned to be accomplished — these failures as beings are among the most glorious even among the Dhyân-Chohanic hosts.

Now it is just these failures who were unable to top the last celestial rise and who had to wait until the next Manvantara before they could cross that peak of achievement — it is just these failures who headed the hosts of those who returned and built our earth and taught earliest mankind, who laid down the lines of work on which the elementals and the lower Dhyân-Chohanic hosts later labored to construct our world as it is. It was these failures who caught the vision, and, guided by the karman of our past, brought that karman as it were up a little higher. Failures, but saviors of us.

So indeed there are failures amongst human beings; and if we just take that word 'failures,' and do not know the teaching, how unjust could we be. Far nobler is the man who strives for chelaship and fails because of past weaknesses, past karman — far nobler is he than the man who has no such divine hunger to be more and to be better, higher than he was before.

There are failures also in initiation; but all this type of failure is glorious, for it represents noble effort, enlarging vision, increasing strength, and beautiful yearnings. It represents accomplishment. There are failures among the chelas who cannot reach Mahâtmaship in this life. But how beautiful is their failure, for they tried and almost won. Fancy, if they had never tried. It is these rare spirits, whether amongst the gods or amongst us men, who see and try, and succeed or fail; but that failure itself is a success; and it is such failures as these that the mahâtmic writer alludes to.

And what is it that H. P. Blavatsky says in *The Voice of the Silence:*

"Remember, thou that fightest for man's liberation, each failure is success, and each sincere attempt wins its reward in time. The holy germs that sprout and grow unseen in the disciple's soul, their stalks wax strong at each new trial, they bend like reeds but never break, nor can they e'er be lost. But when the hour has struck they blossom forth."

CORRESPONDENCES IN THE ROUNDS

REFERENCE: Letter XV, pp. 89-93

THE Fourth Round is a copy of a more advanced type of everything that took place in the Third Round. Similarly, the Third Round was such of the Second. Remember that, after all, forms and shapes and bodies are all relatively unimportant.

There was a time in the Third Round correspondential to the descent of the Mânasaputras in this Fourth. There was a time in the Third Round correspondential to the arrival of sex on this earth. There was a time in the Third Round correspondential to what will happen in the future when sex will disappear in this Round. And so with all events through which we have passed and are to pass in this Fourth Round.

Indeed, during the First Round, even, there was organized intelligence on this earth, not merely mindless entities. If you think that there was no intelligence of any kind in the First Round, it shows that you keep your thoughts restricted too much to human evolution. But there are the different evolutions of the Dhyân-Chohanic Kingdoms; and even in the First Round there were human beings. Never mind what the bodies were; that is of no importance. There were beings with will-power, who thought and felt. They were few, to be sure, but they did exist; and they were the star-sons, the Sons of the Firemist spoken of by H. P. B., the first grand Adepts on this earth and indeed on the other globes of our chain. There were very few because this was the First Round. There were more in the Second; more in the Third; more in the Fourth. There will be still more in the Fifth, and so forth; because every new Round raises every Kingdom one cosmic sub-sub-plane higher on the evolutionary scale. So much for that comment.

THE ONE BECOMES THE MANY

I agree with those who just cannot see how the One could do otherwise than become the multitude. Consider the Universe around us everywhere. It represents the many. Reason tells us that being subservient to one common law, essentially formed of one common cosmic stuff, originally all the multitudes of beings and entities in this Universe must have come forth from one cosmic fountain of being and life. It is the teaching of Occultism of all the ages that back to that divinity all things are marching now: out from divinity as unself-conscious god-sparks for aeons and aeons of cosmic pilgrimage, undergoing all the various marvelous adventures that life in all its phases brings; then rising on the pathway and re-entering the bosom of the Divine, to issue forth again at the next cosmic mahâ-manvantara. It is incomprehensible to me that anything else could take place; and there are so many remarkable illustrations that can be given of this eternal process.

SEDIMENTATION ON OUR EARTH

When the Masters or H. P. B. speak of the 320 million years since sedimentation on our earth took place, they refer to the beginning of *this Round* on Globe A; and when the impulse of the three elemental kingdoms, followed by the mineral kingdom, reached our earth, then not only sedimentation but volcanic action began. That is all there is to that. If you will read what I have to say on that in my *Fundamentals of the Esoteric Philosophy* (and I labored hard in that book to make the process of evolutionary development on the different globes during a Round clear): if you will look to that book, you will have it, I hope, clear enough for comprehension.

As a matter of fact, we have so much teaching that our dear people forget most of it! That is the plain truth. Our books are just packed with information; and one of the greatest helps possible to us students is to learn to collate and build up a picture by that collation, bringing together fact after fact and never being satisfied until we have made a proper place for every fact. Then you have a picture, and you won't forget it.

MAN-BEARING GLOBES

It is true that globes in a solar system, and planetary chain too — it is the same thing really — can advance so high in their evolutionary or emanational development that they have passed the stage where human beings or the human kingdom can find place on such globes of a chain, because they have passed high above the human kingdom — the whole chain has. But that is only half the picture.

The other reason why there are non-man-bearing globes, that is chains in our solar system which are not man-bearing, is that these other, forming the other part of the picture, have not yet reached the point where their life-waves have risen to the human stage. Do you see?

So then, the idea is that every globe in a planetary chain has been, is, or will be, man-bearing some time, *some time*. Those not yet having reached the stage of man-bearing produce the lower kingdoms, or some of them. Those which have evolved beyond or higher than the possibility of bringing the human kingdom on their globes bear the races of the Dhyân-Chohans exclusively, and beings even beyond those last.

So there are man-bearing chains or globes in our solar system, and there are those which are non-man-bearing. As a matter of fact, you can say the same thing about any kingdom. There are globes in our chain which bear Dhyân-Chohans, as an example, and others which do not bear Dhyân-Chohans.

ALL THINGS CONTRIBUTE TO ALL THINGS

REFERENCE: Letters XXIIIA and XXIIIB
Question, page 146, and Answer No. 8, pages 160-2

IT IS the teaching of the God-Wisdom that every member of the solar system is a living entity, a god imbodied. Such is the sun, such is every planet, such is every comet. Furthermore, the solar system itself as a whole is an entity, precisely as our human body is an entity as a whole, a unit, yet containing within itself different organs, each such organ itself being an individual, a unit, a living entity with a consciousness of its own kind.

Do you see what this means? That just as our body, an organic entity itself, is helped in being such by the different organs, the heart, the brain, the kidneys, the liver, the stomach, and so forth, so the solar system, itself an organic entity, is aided in being such by all the organic units within it: the sun, the planets, the comets, and so forth. They all co-operate to produce a greater thing, i.e., the Solar Kingdom, with the sun as its king or chief.

What deduction must we draw from this? That, co-operating as all these units do towards a common end, nothing can be done properly in the solar system if a single one of these bodies refuses co-operative action and union in effort; and 'union' here does not mean two or three organs joining to oppose two or three other organs. It means all organic units without a single exception co-operating for the common universal good. If there is not this co-operation, if, for instance, one single organ were to die, then the whole organism dies, because the harmony and symmetry of the greater unit is interrupted, killed, stopped. It is just the same with the human body. Suppose my heart stopped working, died — my body would die. If my stomach disintegrated, my body would die; and similarly so with any other organ — even the skin or the tissues or the flesh or the bones: we need all these different things to make a complete and rightly functioning human body. So it is with the solar system.

Thus when we say that all things co-operate to produce all things, we may be referring to all things on this earth; but it may also mean that this earth in its turn co-operates with *every other* body in the solar system to produce the proper effects on every other planet and on the sun. How about rain, for instance, and the other meteorological phenomena of this earth? How about storms of any kind: snow-storms, hail-storms, rain-storms, electric storms? Shall we say that only one thing in the solar system produces these, whether it be sun-spots or the planets, or perhaps one planet, as some astrologers quite wrongly say? No. All things work together to produce all things everywhere.

Thus, when we come to answering the question: Are the sun-spots the cause of the meteorological phenomena on this earth? the answer has to be no, because that would exclude all other contributing causes and causers. The sun-spots play their appropriate part; so does every planet. But what is the most important factor, the greatest cause in the production of these things on our earth? It is the earth itself. But the earth itself could not produce them unless it had the help of all the other co-operating or consentient gods, as the Greeks and Romans phrased it; in other words of the sun, the planets, the comets.

What makes heat? What makes rain? What makes cold on this earth? Magnetism, to be sure; electricity, to be sure. But these are the forces. What makes these things fundamentally? The vitality of the earth co-operating with the vitality received from the other planets, and from the sun and the comets. *All things co-oper-ate to make all things.* A key, a master-key.

Actually, if you want the mechanical cause, the immediate cause, that is, the cause just preceding the effect — not the first cause — it is the dilatation of the earth's atmosphere and its contraction. The atmosphere of the earth is one of the most marvelous organs of our Mother-Earth. Look upon the earth as a living being, or as the Latins would say, an animal (from the Latin word *anima,* meaning life). Animal in Latin means a living being, a human or beast, for instance. Even a plant is an 'animal' in this sense, only very feebly so; because *anima* meant, more particularly, what in Theosophy is called the animal soul — the *nephesh* of the Qabbâlâh.

The earth is constantly surcharged with vital power. There are times when it is almost bursting, and the inner power must have an escape: it must be discharged, because the pressure of the whole solar system is behind it. Take the instance of earthquakes: they are my pet horror, they just turn my blood cold because I am always thinking of the damage to human beings, and the wretchedness that they can cause; yet they are one of the greatest blessings, for the earth is releasing energy which could otherwise become devastatingly explosive. Our earth would simply burst; it would blow up, if there were not these periodic discharges.

It is like the vitality that a human being is constantly throwing forth — by his walking, by his speaking, by his moving, by the circulation of his blood. Every time he lifts a finger he is throwing off energy. Suppose all the energy that the body produces could by some magic be clamped down and kept in the body, the body would explode, simply blow up; the tissues would be torn apart.

Of course there is the other side of the picture: if the expenditure of energy is too great, then you have the other extreme, and you have disease or death. But why does the human body do this? It is doing in its own small sphere, in its own small line, what the planets are doing, contributing its quota to the vitality of the earth; and this vitality comes into the human body from above, and from what passes in and out in the exchange of the life-atoms amongst us all. *All things contribute to all things;* they receive and give constantly.*

---

*So strangely does the human mind wander into vagaries of imagination, that I find it needful to append this footnote lest the words in the text above be misunderstood by thoughtless or careless people as a kind of indirect endorsement in our human life of the dissipation of vital human forces through immorality or in some other way.

Such misunderstanding of my meaning would be so utterly monstrous, so utterly contrary to every teaching of Theosophy and Occultism, that on no few occasions have I asked myself just how far I can go in stating even simple occult facts, when, as experience has shown me, one or two or more hearers might wrongly take the sense or the significance of what I was trying to say.

I state here without qualification, that any dissipation of the vital powers of the human body or mind in immorality of any form, immediately hastens the approaches of disease and old age, because wearing the body out, and because unnatural. Such dissipation of vitality would be a wilful waste of the life-forces, thus co-operating with the work of the Destroyers. Not only would such waste invite disease and premature senility, but even worse than this would be its effect on the moral stamina and ethical instinct of the human mind, and it could in an extreme case result in moral and intellectual degeneration.

Let it be stated that self-control, strict moral conduct and self-forgetfulness

Do you realize that there is more vitality in the body in old age than there is in youth? Old age is not a case of deprivation of vitality; it is a case of too much vitality. The body cannot build up fast enough. The intense life of the adult human being is slowly wrecking the body, causing it to age. The body cannot build fast enough. The life-pulsations are quicker than the building power. Consequently you get the greying hair, the failing eyesight, the failing hearing, and all the phenomena that age brings. Health is simply balance; and the longer you can keep in health the longer you live — if you want to! If it is advisable! Some people seem to think that a long life is a mark of sanctity. It is very often not just so. Sometimes the grossest people are the longest-lived. There is an old Latin proverb which says: "The gods love those who die young," meaning the gods take those they love when they are young — not when the gods are young, but when those they take are young. The gods themselves are perennially young.

Now to return to the matter of the earth's atmosphere, which is continually dilating or expanding. We know that when this expansion occurs we have the dropping of the barometer, that sensitive instrument we have learned how to build which registers the air-pressure. It is a sign of rain. And we all know the chill in the air that follows a rain-storm even in the summer-time. We say "It cooled the air." The opposite effect, heat, is produced when the atmosphere condenses or contracts, and the greater pressure on the barometer causes it to go up. "Fair weather," we say, "and heat," — relative heat according to the season, of course.

What causes these contractions and dilatations of the earth's atmosphere? Mainly the periodic, vital pulsations in the earth itself. But these pulsations are intimately connected every instant of time, without a second's interruption, with all the other bodies of the solar system. *All things contribute to all things.* The sun and all the planets are connected with the dilatations and contractions of the

---

are the path of Theosophical occultism, and this is stated without any qualifications whatsoever. Any misuse whatsoever or in any manner of vital power, even such as over-eating or gluttony, drunkenness, or anything along any line causing the body extra strain or depletion is a waste of vital power and therefore has a tendency to bring on disease, speedy old age, and as above hinted, even worse things in its train.

earth's atmosphere. Thus far the astrologers are perfectly right. But to say that it is the planets which make these things, that the planets are the sole cause, that is all wrong. All things contribute to all things: the sun and planets give me health; they give me disease. But so do I give myself both health and disease. *All things contribute to all things.* That is the master-key.

Now these contractions, or pressures as the modern scientific phraseology has it, of the atmosphere, and these dilatations of the atmosphere, are mainly caused by the actual meteoric continent surrounding our globe like a thick shell. You will say, "But how can it be such a thick shell when we can see right through it; we can see the sun and the stars and the clouds?" Suppose instead of my present eye-sight I had an electric eye. Why then I could look right along a copper wire. Such things as copper and iron would be transparent to me. But with my present eye-sight I cannot see through a copper wire or along a 5000 mile stretch of copper wire because I have not the electric eye. On the other hand, with the electric eye I could not see things I now see. The fact is that our eye-sight has been evolved by Nature, or, if you like, evolved by Karman, so that we can look right through this meteoric mass surrounding our earth like a shell; and all we see of it is what we call the blue of the sky. That is the real explanation of the blue of the sky. The scientific theory that it is very fine dust mostly from earth which intercepts the blue rays of the solar spectrum, might be called a weak, partial explanation. I dare not omit even this, because if I did my explanation would be by so much imperfect. There is some truth in it, but to say that it is the cause of the blue of the sky is not true, because that excludes everything else.

All the other planets except Mars are likewise, each one, surrounded with its own meteoric continent. Science knows this and calls them the clouds of the different planets. Call them clouds if you want to. Say that they are clouds of cosmic dust and dust from the respective planets. All right: but they are actually mostly interstellar and interplanetary meteoric dust. Every one of the planets in our solar system except Mars, as I have said, is surrounded by such a continent of meteoric dust; and even Mars has a thin gauzy veil of meteoric matter surrounding it. Mars is different from the others because it is in obscuration at present; and on Globe D of the Martian Chain the forces of attraction holding the meteoric continent together have been relaxed, as it were. These magnetic and electric forces surrounding Mars are weak because the meteoric continent around Globe D of Mars has been more or less dissipated throughout space — not quite, but almost. That is the reason we can catch just glimpses of the Martian Globe; but even those glimpses are still uncertain. Our astronomers are not sure that what some see others see. You know the interminable dispute aroused by the discovery of the so-called canals of Mars which Professor Lowell of Flagstaff, Arizona, and others have quite believed so long; and which others deny. Schiaparelli, the Italian astronomer, was the first to speak of these lines years and years ago, and as they seemed to him to resemble canals, he called them *canali,* the Italian word for canals or channels of any kind; and then people got the idea, because they took the word in the English sense of water-courses, that they must be water-courses. That is still not proved; it may be and it may not be. I do not care to say anything more about that.

Please remember this, Companions: The solar system is a living being, of which the sun is both the brain and the heart. The different planets are the organs of this organic entity. Our earth is one. They all work together to produce the solar system as an organism, or a group of organs. *All things contribute to all things.* Nothing happens on this earth, from the waving of a frond of fern in the wind to the most awful earthquake the world has ever known, except by such co-operating cosmic agency. All are produced mainly by the earth, but with the co-operation of the sun and moon, the planets and comets, for this organic entity moves in synchronous measures of destiny. *All things contribute to all things.* The birth of every baby is produced by the solar system, by the earth, especially by the mother; yet all things contribute to produce that baby. The stars do have their effect upon us, most undoubtedly so; and the sun and planets and comets, because the solar system is an organic living being, and therefore everything within it anywhere is affected by everything within it everywhere. Surely this is true; and it is a wonderful picture.

PROCESSES AFTER DEATH

REFERENCE: Letters XXIIIA and XXIIIB
Questions 15-20, page 147, Answers 15-20, pages 170-4

I WOULD like to point out one thing first. We speak of accidents. I wonder if people realize when they use that term what they are implying. If such things as accidents really are in the way the men of the West understand this word, then the universe is lawless, it is chaotic, there is no order, no sequence of events in it. If anything in the universe can happen haphazardly, by chance, without a preceding cause, the whole universe is wrong, because chance cannot be a part of it, and all the rest of it be against chance. It is like saying a part of an apple is apple and all the rest of it is not apple, which is an absurdity. The apple is all apple and the universe is all law. Accident is merely a word which in the West is used to hide ignorance. Accidents are usually unforeseen events, and because we do not see the preceding causes, we say accident. In that sense there is no such thing as accident. Everything is the fruit of a precedaneous cause, and this precedaneous cause cannot touch any individual unless that individual was the producer of that cause, originally or intimately connected with the production of that cause.

As for instance, two or more people may be working together. By that fact of working together they are karmically connected. Karman governs all things with infinite justice, for it is the establishment of the law of harmony; and we with our feeble human understanding cannot always easily see how, when a thing is past and done let us say ten million years ago, harmony can be re-established ten million years later. But I ask: Why not? We must remember that our conceptions of time are pertinent to the time-sphere in which we live. Our ideas of time would be exceedingly long to the time-ideas of an individual living on an infinitesimal part of matter, let us say an electron, where a whole cosmical universe may appear and run its course and vanish during the time-period of what we call a tick-tick of the clock. Time to such individuals is enormously speeded up. Our time to such individuals would be like eternity. Yet what is our time when we compare it with the vast cosmical chronological sequences which are counted in our human years by billions and trillions and quadrillions and even higher figures of solar years, or, as we say, human years? To an individual living in that vastly extended time-sphere, or space-time-sphere, to use the jargon of the day, our time would be very quick. Ten million years is not anything from the standpoint of a genuinely cosmic law, and it might seem only an hour ago, or, as one might say, a moment in the past. We might say with the Jewish scripture, ten billion, trillion, quadrillion years in Thy sight are but a second of super-divine time. And so it is.

So with accidents. There is such absolute justice in this universe that an act cannot be committed, a thought thought, or an emotion experienced, without its due and orderly consequences. Why, everybody knows that. Now just apply the cosmic law to all these things. When we see something happen we cannot understand, we say accident. That is merely expressing our ignorance of what the past was. But it could not have happened to that man unless that man had been in the past, either in this life or some other life, in some way entangled in causes which brought the fruiting of those causes about now. It just happens now. Either this, or we live in a crazy world without law and order, and where chance and fortuity and accidents can happen. Where do we see any signs of this?

For example, ten men are in a boat. Nine drown and one is saved. Or one drowns, nine are saved. Why? Chance? A man is run down by an automobile, or something falls from above and crushes his skull. Chance? That is easy. If we could solve life's problems by chance, or accident, nobody would ever have a headache. I want an *explanation*, not just passing the buck to the God or devil, or something you call chance. Not on your sweet life!

Mark this: That while this body knows that it has an accident, the imbodying ego knows it was the result of karmic justice; and as this body is but a vehicle, and as the consciousness and the moral sense dwell in the imbodying ego, the cognising entity is the important thing.

Now about this matter of a man's thinking at the moment of death, and the consequences that that last short period of concentrated thinking has as a cause on the next life and after lives. Our Theosophical philosophy is so strictly logical that you can readily see here that such a thing cannot take place unless the few last moments of thinking were themselves the production of preceding causes. What then do we mean by the Master's statement? The significance of it is simply this. What a man thinks during the last vegetative instants of this life are the thought-habits — there is a key-word, *habit* — the thought-habits of that life and preceding lives. The preceding lives of course have made the thought-habits of the life just closing; and what a man thinks when the egoic consciousness is temporarily stunned by the impact of death, what the brain then thinks, is the automatisms of that habit. Isn't that simple? All the habits of thinking of all the previous lives at the last moment sink into those automatic habits; habit meets habit thinking habit-thoughts. It is the man's character expressing itself in the automatic thinking of his last moments, and that will be his character which he has earned for the future. And just apply it on a larger scale to the thoughts the man has, let us say at the end of a Round or the seven Rounds. It is precisely the same rule.

Whatever your thinking habits have been during life, will be the ones that at the instant of death, not merely the loss of consciousness, but actual death, will be the ones that express themselves as automatic thought-currents governing that mental panorama which begins with the first instant of recollection from childhood, going rapidly through every single event and feeling you have ever had, right up to the moment of passing. Then there is unconsciousness, swift, quick. That is the idea.

Now there is no suffering about this, unless indeed a man now old and tender and wise may look upon that passing panorama in disgust and say: Why didn't I, when I had that chance, seize it? Why was I not strong in doing what I was doing, putting more force and power into it? Those are the reflexions of the higher mind as it sees the panorama. But essentially these thoughts are part of the automatisms of the past thinking, the thought-habits of the past. Everything is infinitely just, all your good and all your bad, and always will be.

Now another point in connexion with thoughts. Let us say that seven-principled man is composed, for the purpose of this illustration, of two parts, a higher triad and a lower quaternary. Let us call the higher triad X. This is the spiritual and the higher intellectual, higher psychical part of man. Let us call the lower quaternary Y. These are the emotions, the lower thoughts, the feelings good and bad and indifferent that form us as we are from day to day when uninspired by the higher parts. We will call that Y. And putting it in the form of an algebraic equation: X plus Y equals Z. Z is the man as we know him, as you are, as I, as we feel and think and act and do. X is the higher part of us, the upper triad. Y the lower part, the quaternary. Z is the whole man, acting through the brain and nerves, through the body.

Now then, when death ensues, the body is dropped because it is just a vehicle, a suit of clothes. Actually it is no more, although it is the vital abode of Y overshadowed by X. But it is dropped as a finger-nail paring. The nail is part of you, of your body, production of your vitality; but when the finger-nails are clipped, there still remain in conjunction X plus Y equaling Z. And when death ensues, we still have $X + Y = Z$ minus V. We will call V the physical body.

Now what happens as time goes on? X separates slowly from Y until the strain of the separation can go no farther and there is a break. X ascends. Y drops. That is the second death. Until the second death occurs, the man is the man he is on earth in the physical body practically, in form a nirmânakâya, although of course not a nirmânakâya. He is a complete man minus only the physical body. Now then, when the second death occurs, X ascends, enters the devachan. What happens to Y? Y drops; no longer held up by X, no longer inspired by X, it drops to its own level in the astral light, wherever that level may be. Every individual case has its own of course.

Now then, what kind of thoughts has Y? We now call it the kâma-rûpa, or the spook. What kind of thoughts should it have except the automatic thoughts that it had when X plus Y equaled Z in the physical body? Its thinking now is feeble and weak. It is simply repeating, automatic, just a machine. It does not know what it does. It slowly runs down, the pendulum goes slower and slower until it finally stops. When the vital pendulum of a spook stops, that is practically the time when the spook is virtually disintegrated.

So it is utterly impossible to summon X into a séance room. There is no appeal to it. X cannot be reached except by spiritual love. Even thought won't reach it, at least the thoughts most men think. The Y can be reached. Y is still chock full, just after death, of animal vitality, animal magnetism, which is one of the reasons of the break with X. X insisted upon going up, and tried to drag Y after it; but the tendency of Y is down, and finally the inevitable break came. It is just as simple as it can be, and I am trying to use simple language especially for our friends who have not studied Theosophy as we have.

So the Y, the spook, the kâma-rûpa, thinks all the thoughts that are in its nature to think. It cannot think something that it is not thinking. Surely that is obvious. If you are thinking about apples, you are not thinking about stones or solar spectra. And if apples happen to be the automatic thinking process of the spook Y, about apples it will think, apples, apples, apples. Or again, the spook might be thinking about his favorite treasures, what during life it fancied most. That part of the nature is the lower part. The automatic thinking of Y will keep on and on, only it will keep on going less and less strong, because Y is disintegrating and decaying; and finally becomes — pardon me — a filthy stinking astral corpse, which is exactly what it is. It even smells putrid, of the graveyard, of decay.

So that is happening all through the ages, and when these dear spiritists in their ignorance try to establish communication with the departed, with their beloved departed, the only thing they can possibly, in nature's law, establish communication with, if anything, is Y, the spook. And what else can Y be but itself? If its name was John Smith, it will say, "Yes, I am John Smith." If it lived at 472 West Burlington Avenue, "Yes, 472 West Burlington Avenue." It is decaying, going to pieces.

You know, there is a pathos about these things. I appear to be ridiculing it, but it is not in my heart to do so. I am trying to make very graphic the situation. Of course this spook Y, this kâma-rûpa, will remember its name. It probably will remember where it lived, and remember the names, or some of them, of its companions or family. "My wife Emma. Yes, Emma. That is Ruth, Emma. Come tomorrow. I am called now. Good-bye, dear." You get in touch with the automatic functioning of the spook, but the mental procedure is gone. A clever question by a medium who is in astral-psychic touch with a spook like that will start all its automatic processes following the question: "Are you John Smith?" "Yes, John Smith." "Where did you live?" "So and so." "Were you married?" "Yes, I was married. No I was not married. No, Yes, I was. Her name was Emma." This is not a bit of exaggeration.

So when you ask what were the thought-processes of the spook you have examples right here, the automatic thought-processes that carry over from the life just closed; and as the spook is the lower part of us, you can understand what thought-processes these are.

Now on the other hand, do not mistake the medium for a mediator. That is a very different thing. A mediator can ascend and come into actual spiritual communication with X, the higher triad, the real ego in the devachan; and if the mediator is sensitive enough, by its love it can catch as it were the vibrational synchrony of the immeasurably lovely and heavenly dreams of X; and the mediator can even bring it back. The physical mind has come in touch, and what is the devachanî thinking of? It depends upon what the automatic thought-habits of that man were. If he was a musician, the devachanî will be thinking of music, composing the most celestial harmonies. If the man on the other hand was a convinced and deeply earnest religionist, religion will color the devachan. If the man was a Baptist and a convinced and very earnest one, it will be full of Baptist thoughts. If he was a Seventh-Day Adventist, or a Mohammedan or an Episcopalian or a Buddhist — it will be the same. You see here why we call even the devachan a fool's paradise, because surely neither the Baptist nor the Mohammedan nor the Episcopalian nor the Roman Catholic nor any other type of religious belief is Truth, Absolute Reality.

There is something beyond the devachan, and this is when the higher part of X comes into direct and intimate relation, spiritual relation, communion, self-identification, with the Divine mind of which it is a child, the spark, the offspring. Then you have Reality. That is Nirvâna.

"THE TOWER OF INFINITE THOUGHT"

REFERENCE: "For countless generations hath the adept builded a fane of imperishable rocks, a giant's Tower of INFINITE THOUGHT, wherein the Titan dwelt, and will yet, if need be, dwell alone, emerging from it but at the end of every cycle, to invite the elect of mankind to co-operate with him and help in his turn enlighten superstitious man. And we will go on in that periodical work of ours; we will not allow ourselves to be baffled in our philanthropic attempts until that day when the foundations of a new continent of thought are so firmly built that no amount of opposition and ignorant malice guided by the Brethren of the Shadow will be found to prevail." — Letter IX, p. 51

THESE are the words of a Master of Wisdom, and I want you to hearken to them and try to get the inner meaning of them, for they are really godlike. A great intellect composed them.

What is this Tower of Infinite Thought? It is the general Cosmic Intelligence, here particularized as the hierarchies of the Dhyâni-Chohans, the Cosmic Spirits, the Lords of Meditation and Cosmic Wisdom. We call them the hierarchies of the Sons of Light, representing the consciousness-side of the universe. They are innumerable, extending from even below man up through countless hierarchies, stretching indeed to Infinity.

This is the Tower of Infinite Thought, in which the cosmic Titans dwell and think and live and plan. These cosmic Titans are the aggregate of the cosmic logoi, the cosmic spirits, an army of the suns of light and life. And from this inexhaustible fount of all perfect wisdom and perfect love, from time to time there issue forth great souls who take imbodiment among men, and guide and lead and help and aid and inspire, and raise not only us superstitious and fallible men, but all beings less than they, for Nature is one organic unity. What is above in the highest is shadowed in the lowest, for there is but one cosmic law, because there is but one cosmic intelligence and one cosmic life; and therefore that law, that life, that intelligence, prevails throughout. So that, as you see, what is here below, is but a shadow or a copy from a pattern of what is above; and the whole secret of life, and the whole secret of living, is to become at one in consciousness and in feeling, in spirit and in soul, with that pattern of Infinite Thought.

No grander words I should think have ever issued from human lips. No more sublime conceptions have ever been penned, than those contained in the extracts from the Master's communication that have been read to you. They are a new gospel of thought and of love, a new dispensation of human effort; and a man must be blind who fails to sense and to feel the immense import, the grand content, enwrapped in these human words.

When the times are not propitious, or the times are not right, then the adepts — never indeed abandon mankind to its hopeless fate; there remain on earth at least the Brotherhood of the Mahât-mans or Masters of Wisdom and Compassion. They inspire and instill intimations of wonder and of grandeur in sensitive and recep-tive human souls. But if the times are not right for a larger spreading of the Wisdom of the Gods, then for the time being they retire up-wards and inwards into this Tower of Infinite Thought, and await there until the time is ripening once more so that they may once again work publicly, or semi-publicly, among us.

We too, even now in our smallness and weakness, inhabit this Tower of Infinite Thought. And precisely as the Masters do when the times are not propitious or not ripe for a new installment of the God-Wisdom of Infinitude, we too, although our hand is always outstretched ready to impart what little we ourselves have taken by strength of the Kingdom of Heaven, when the times are not ripe, precisely like our own Teachers, we retire into the higher conscious-ness, and to outward appearance may seem to have retired into silence and quiet. But that is only so to the outer seeming.

The Masters of Wisdom, the Adepts, simply retire when the times are not ripe for them to do their greatest work among men. They do what they can, and what human karman or destiny will allow them to do; but to a certain extent, they ascend, vanish from the outer seeming, to become only the more active and the grander in works of beneficence on the inner planes. And when the times become ripe, when men through suffering and sorrow, pain and rack-ing care, once more find their hearts yearning for a greater light, and for the comfort which is never gained by egoisms, but given only by the spirit — when men then make the inner call, soundless yet ringing unto the very spheres of light, then Those, hitherto silent but watching and waiting in the Tower of Infinite Thought, from their azure thrones, so to speak, bend a listening ear; and if the call is strong enough, if it be pure enough, impersonal enough, they leave the portals of the inner invisible realms to enter these portals of our universe, and appear amongst us and guide and teach and comfort and solace and bring peace.

How great is the inspiration to be derived from this teaching of the God-Wisdom we today call Theosophy: that the universe is not chaotic nor insane, but is an organism guided and controlled from within outwards, not only by infinite and omniscient cosmic intelligence — intelligences rather — but by cosmic love. For love is the cement of the universe and accounts for the orderliness of the universe, and its harmony and unity that every one who has the seeing eye may discern in all around him. Scientists speak of these orderlinesses as the laws of nature, as manifested in the cosmic bodies and their inhabitants, as manifested in their times and places and regularities.

How wonderful likewise is the feeling that the man who trains himself for it may enter into touch, into communication, with these grander ones in evolution above him, above him only now, because some day he shall evolve to become like unto them, divine as they are; and they themselves shall have passed upwards and onwards to divinities still more remote to us. There is a path which is steep, which is thorny, but it leads to the very heart of the universe. Anyone, any child of nature, may climb this path. Anyone who ventures to try to find it may take the first steps upon it; and these first steps may be followed by others. What a blessing to know this! What an inspiration for the future that our destiny lies in our hands! Nought shall stay, nought can prevent, no outer god nor inner, can stem the inspiration welling up from the deepest recesses of the human spirit, because that human spirit is but a spark of the cosmic divine.

How beautiful, how inspiring, how simply pregnant with as yet undisclosed significance, is this phrase: the Tower of Infinite Thought! It is a god-like phrase, and only a semi-god-man or a god-man could have so worded his sublime conceiving. What magic vistas of inner realms of faery, true faery, do these wonderful words suggest to reverent minds. This Tower of Infinite Thought, is likewise the Tower of Infinite Love, for it is infilled with love, and its inhabitants are the exponents of love. From time to time its portals open and Teachers from these inner realms come amongst us. Such was the Lord Gautama, the Buddha; such was the Avatâra Jesus; such was Krishna; such were a multitude of others whose names are known even in the Occident to every educated man. No wonder a grateful humanity has called them Sons of God, or children of the gods — a phrase which I prefer; for such indeed they are, just as we humans likewise are offsprings of the gods, our forebears and forerunners on the evolutionary path, leading upwards and inwards forever to divinity.

These Teachers of men have themselves been worshiped as gods by men who forgot the injunctions to take the message and worship it, but not to worship the bringer. Therein lies grandeur; for it is, after all, the thought of a man which is powerful, not the mouth through which the thought pours forth. It is the love in a man's heart which makes him sublime, not the mouth which declares it. I think that one of the proofs that these Great Ones who have lived amongst us and who will come again and again and again — I think one of the proofs of their divinity is precisely the fact that they accepted nought for themselves, but called attention to their teachings only.

How beautiful to the hearts of men are they who come bringing tidings of great joy. Their faces are suffused with the dawn of a newer, a grander, a more beautiful, age. For they are its prophets and its heralds, harbingers of a new time to come, when instead of enlarging quarrel and war, men shall learn that the ways of peace are the ways of strength and of power and of wisdom and of plenty and of riches.

IS IT NECESSARY TO EXPERIENCE EVIL?

REFERENCE: These comments followed a discussion in *The Mahatma Letters* of pages 74-78 during which the question was asked whether the colorless and negative characters we sometimes meet are those who have not yet been awakened by the experiencing of evil in earth-lives.

IT IS no longer necessary for human beings to go down into the intellectual and moral mire and absorb it, for the simple reason that we are now on the upward arc. We have passed the grossest point in human evolution. Up to that point it was necessary for human monads to have every experience that consciousness, slowly evolving, could take unto itself in order to make that consciousness rounded out, full, rich with experience and marked with suffering so greatly that sympathy and pity and compassion have waked in the heart when that heart sees the suffering of others.

Hence the gray and feckless characters that we see around us are not they who lack experience in the drinking of the evil cup of filth. We are now on the upward arc. These gray, colorless characters, often weak and with attributes which arouse no admiration in any outstanding human being, are unfortunate cases, or rather cases of unfortunate human beings, who are passing through a resting time psychologically speaking, on this plane. Something in their past destiny has made this present incarnation of theirs one in which they are somnolent, resting, asleep, making no especial mark on the world, "neither hot nor cold, only lukewarm."

But mark you: in the past spiritual and intellectual and psychological history of these entities, heaven knows how many times they have shaken the gates of Heaven with their aspirations and their cries of triumph. Heaven knows how many times on earth they have been victors in well fought fights. Let us not forget that. Let us not condemn because to us of a happier destiny in this life, certain fellow human beings are less strong than we are in opposing temptation, and in refusing to be swept along in the easy currents of the world's life.

But here is my point: Let it never be said that Theosophists teach that now the human race is in need of deliberate, wilful entering into the currents of evil-doing in order to assuage passion, to experience evil and by learning it, to surmount it. All that part of our destiny has been gone through. Our destiny now is to conquer the remaining Atlantean elements of impulse and appetite, no longer to indulge them but to surmount them, and to begin our march up that ladder of life, higher and higher; for we are now on the Ascending Arc!

It was very different before the beginning of the Fourth Round, or what comes to the same thing, before the middle of the Fourth Round, or the middle of the Fourth Race. Then Monads were descending into matter, dropping, attracted by it, drawn into it; and it was necessary for them to gain experience; but they did so automatically, unconsciously, without purposive exercise of will-power, and not with purposeful self-consciousness, but somewhat as little children do through ignorance, learning that if the hand is put in the fire, burning follows, learning that if you put your finger in a closing door, it will be severely pinched or squeezed. They had to learn just as the animals; and little children are learning through experience.

But we are adults, and just so with the human monads when they attained the central point of the Fourth Round. Then the descent stopped. Everything after that, by the laws of nature, is on the Ascending Arc, and we should work with nature and be one with her, obey her laws by arising with her. Then we can become not merely the champions of right and the forerunners and heralds of justice, but we shall ourselves be exemplifications of the divinity we teach.

It is no longer necessary for any human being ever to think at any time that he must experience evil-doing for the sake of going upwards. All that we have been through in the past. We have had enough of that. Too much. Now our line is upward, *ad astra,* to the stars. Now we are on the upward path; and these colorless characters are simply they who, just as we occasionally may rise from a night's sleep to face a negative and apparently purposeless day, feeling tired and worn out because we have over-eaten or our health is not of the best, and we do not feel like facing difficulties, and we do not want to argue, we want to be left in peace — we have a *day* of intellectual colorlessness; so these egos have a *life* of it. They are resting, they are sleeping. But perhaps in the very last life they rose to occasions like heroes, or it may be two or three lives ago: and perhaps in the life to come heroism will again shine out from their hearts. No one can lay down automatic quantitative durations in things like this, for every individual case is dependent upon the individual destiny or karman of the human ego.

AVALOKITEŚVARA — THE DIVINE PRESENCE

REFERENCE: Letter LIX, pp. 343-345

MAHÂYÂNA Buddhism, which is mainly the form studied in Tibet today, as it has been for centuries past, recognises three distinct entities or hierarchical Logoi in the Buddhists' hierarchy of spirit. They are the Buddha Amitâbha or the Buddha of Boundless Light, then Alaya, then Avalokiteśvara. Alaya means the spirit-source of all, the garment or clothing of the boundless light; matter cosmic or infinitesimal in nature. Out of it spring the multitudinous rays, as rays of light leave the sun for instance; and each ray is itself a being.

Avalokiteśvara does not mean "the Lord looking down," as Rhys Davids translates it, in direct violation of the elementary rules of Sanskrit grammar. *Ava* means 'down,' *lokita* is the past participle passive of the Sanskrit verbal root *lok,* 'to see,' hence meaning 'seen.' *Îśwara* means 'Lord.' So Avalokiteśvara means, paraphrased somewhat, "the Lord who is beheld everywhere," the cosmic light, the cosmic spirit, in which we live and move and have our being, whose very essence, whose very light, thrills and burns in every human soul, the spark within every human being. It is the immanence or the constant presence of divinity around us, in everything, seen down here in all its works, pre-eminently for humans in man, the most evolved vehicle of this divine presence.

Compare this wonderful Buddhist triad of Tibet, which is likewise our own, with the Christian trinity, degenerated and grossly transmogrified as this latter is through centuries of theologic and scholastic mishandling because of misunderstanding. We find that Amitâbha, the Boundless Light, corresponds to the Father in the Christian Trinity, the Cosmic Father or Abstract Spirit, the Pythagorean monad of monads, the source — in silence to us, and darkness to us — of all the monads emanating from it, streaming from it, born from it through the second logos, Alaya, the Spirit, which in original Christian teaching was feminine, the productive and generative power in nature, in spiritual matters as well as material, the mother of all, the fosterer of all, the preserver of all. And Avalokiteśvara corresponds to the original third Person of the Christian

Trinity, the Son, the cosmic or Third Logos. In Brâhmanism the triad runs: Parabrahman or Brahman, Pradhâna or Mûlaprakriti, Mahat. When manifesting in individual monads such as a human being, the trinity is Amitâbha, Âtman; Alaya or Mahâkâśa, Buddhi; Avalokiteśvara, Manas; for Manas is a direct ray from the cosmic Alaya, and our Âtman, a direct ray from the Paramâtman, the cosmic Âtman, or Brahman or Parabrahman, or the Father.

Thus we have Father, Spirit or Holy Ghost, and Son — the original Christian trinity which the Latin Church finally succeeded in turning around into Father, Son, and Holy Ghost, making the Son or Logos precede the Mother from which it is born!

So, as the Masters pointed out in the last part of the letter we have been studying, Avalokiteśvara has its temple in the Universe around us. It is the creative Logos, the Third Logos, the one closest to us as it were, from which we all spring as rays from a cosmic sun, which is the divine presence in nature, which is the divine presence in the human mânasic part, emanating of course from Âtman or Amitâbha; for the Son, is he not the Son of his Father? Is not Manas through Buddhi the offspring of Âtman? Is not Mahat through Alaya or Mahâkâśa or Pradhâna — all names for the same thing — the offspring of Âdi-Buddha, or if you wish Paramâtman or Brahman or Parabrahman?

So Avalokiteśvara is the divine presence around us everywhere, which every sensitive human soul can feel continuously, day and night, even when we are in dreamland or when imbodied on Earth. And that same divine presence is in the human breast, because the human breast, even the human body, is a microcosmical representation on this plane of the Universe. No wonder the ancients had their Holy of Holies in every temple — originally a beautiful metaphor and a suggestive one when understood by those who came to the temple to worship the divine in purity of heart and with utmost reverence — wherein as in the universe, the divine presence dwells. It was a symbol; so that when one approached the Holy of Holies, shoes were cast from the feet, the garments were wiped, the heart was raised, the mind was elevated; for the worshipers in their reverent raising of their own spirits upwards entered into the Presence, even the Presence Divine.

That Presence is Avalokiteśvara; and its ray in us through the

Âtman is the Higher Manas, illuminated by Buddhi, Buddhi in its turn infilled with the divine light of Âtman. For the Father dwelleth in the Mother, and the Mother giveth birth to the Holy Son, and the three are one and yet three, each distinct from the other. Very simple to understand, but amazingly difficult to attain a deeper realization of that marvel! Yet it is wonderful to know and to strive upwards towards. Would that every man and woman realized that in every human breast is such a Holy of Holies; for when the man, through his own self-discipline and cultivation of the highest within him by forgetting himself in service to all others, thus sinking the unit into the all, thus becoming even then relatively divine, becomes so overpowerfully strong that nothing less than It will ever satisfy, then he yearns upward, he opens the portals of his holier being, and the light streams in and fills the Holy of Holies within his breast. Then the man is transfigured, he is a Christ, he is a Bodhisattva, for the time being.

That was the effect of successful initiation, just that. Sometimes the aura of the event remained with the man for days, it may be weeks, and his very body at the time was surrounded with light. He was spoken of as being clothed with the solar splendor, the sun being a symbol of Âtman, as he is in his kingdom; and our own inner God being the sun, the inner God of our own divinity, our Father in Heaven, that ray from the cosmic Avalokiteśvara.

I think it is just here that we find the reason why the Tibetan esoterics and mystics, Initiates, and the common people — by that I mean the mass of the people, the hard working, kindly, good-natured, loving, aspiring men of the multitude — why they all look upon the Bodhisattvas with deeper reverence and a more fervent love than they do even upon the Buddhas. For the Buddhas have achieved, they have left these spheres. Behind them remains their glory as a spiritual influence. But the Bodhisattvas are still men, not yet Buddhas, men whose life is consecrated to making Avalokiteśvara a living power in the world through themselves. This is why it is the Bodhisattvas that the multitudes love. They deeply revere the Buddhas as having gone on and shown the way, but they love with an exalted human devotion the Bodhisattvas who remain behind with arms outstretched to help in pity. No wonder they love the Bodhisattvas, for he who brings Avalokiteśvara to live in this

Holy of Holies in the human breast, becomes more than man. No wonder he is loved and revered and trusted. I think these thoughts are beautiful beyond description. Their sublimity does not blind us, for it is like divinity clothing itself in human habiliments, in human apparel, and therefore becoming understandable to us humans. It is like seeing humanity clothed with divinity. The Bodhisattvas are not so abstract, so seemingly far away, as are the Buddhas.

So true is this psychology that to it is due, to it alone I believe, all the success of early Christianity, that it taught the very ancient doctrine which had become almost forgotten in the so-called pagan world, and it was this: that a man lived who had been infilled with divinity, and that he came amongst us and taught and showed the way and loved us all so greatly that he laid down his life and all that was in him so that others seeing might follow on the path — the typical Bodhisattva, the typical Christ. I think *that* one thing alone captured for Christianity those who joined the Christian Church.

But how very old is this doctrine of beauty and inspiration! The Christians received it from the Orient. It is far older than the so-called enduring mountains, for when they were still sea-slime, not yet having been raised, these doctrines were taught among men in other continents, in other ages, in other Root-Races, these same wondrous teachings of cosmic origin.

See the difference between the Christian theological idea of Avalokiteśvara as wrongly translated by Rhys Davids and others as being the "Lord who looks down," something "up there" and apart and away, as compared with the real meaning: the Lord here amongst us, the Lord of Pity, human and yet divine, the Divine Presence surrounding us everywhere, which makes the human breast recognising this the human Holy of Holies.

ELEMENTALS AND ELEMENTARIES, etc.

REFERENCE: Letter XV, pp. 97-9

I WOULD like to make a comment upon the statement quoted from *The Mahatma Letters* concerning the Teacher's observation that there are elementals which never become men. This tells us two things: (1) that elementals become men, and (2), that there is a certain class of elementals in our manvantara which will not have the time to become men during the remainder of the course of this manvantara. They won't have the time to run up the ladder of evolution through the different kingdoms until the human kingdom is reached. They will become men in the next manvantara or perhaps in the manvantara after that. Sometime they will be men. All elementals become men. Man as a kingdom is a goal which all kingdoms below the human look up to and aspire toward; and during the course of evolution every monad beneath the human stage is aspiring to evolve, is unfolding itself finally to become a human.

In connexion with this I want to issue a word of warning; it may have struck most of you, perhaps not all. It is with regard to the word elementary and the apparent almost identity of meaning which H. P. B. or the Masters occasionally give to the two words 'elemental' and 'elementary.' The reason was this: in the early days — and remember we are going back now to the very early days of the Theosophical Society — our vocabulary had not yet been sufficiently defined nor was it sufficiently extensive. During those early days words were used which were later dropped, such as the word 'rings' in connexion with the rounds and races. The word 'rings' finally passed out of theosophical use.

Now the word 'elementary' was taken in those early days by our theosophical writers, the Masters and H. P. B. pre-eminently, from the writings of the Qabbalists and also from the imperfect writings of Éliphas Lévi, the French Abbé and Qabbalist. These Qabbalists meant by 'elementary' several things, but generally what we Theosophists now today call 'elemental.' An elemental soul they called an elementary soul, or simply elementary for short. So therefore you will sometimes find the two words used indiscriminately. Words which were then used almost synonymously we nowadays do not use in that way.

Later on, I think it was mainly due to H. P. B.'s work, 'elementary' was set aside and given a specific technical meaning of its own which we now all understand. There is a peculiar meaning which we could even yet use in the word elementary — and by the way, in H. P. B.'s *Theosophical Glossary* if you will look under this word you will see what she has to say about just this point — there is a certain deeply significant and occult meaning which we could give to 'elementary' quite apart from its technical meaning that we now give to it as a rule. We have to go back to the early Fire Philosophers who said that the elements of nature were filled with inhabitants. In other words, to phrase it as we would today, every cosmic plane has its own inhabitants fit for that cosmic plane, utterly unfit for any other cosmic plane; precisely as we men could not live under water as the fishes do or as the whale does. We are not fit for that milieu, that medium, that cosmic plane so to say.

So by going back to this original meaning of the Fire Philosophers, which is quite a true meaning, we still today could say that an elementary in this other sense means an elemental soul, thus specifically described because defining it as climbing up the rungs of the ladder of life step by step upwards. At every step upwards it is a master, relatively at least, of what it has left below it, an elementary as to what is above it. That was really the way the Qabbalists and Éliphas Lévi and the original Fire Philosophers spoke of what we now call the elementals or the beings or creatures or inhabitants of the seven fundamental cosmic elements, all of them on their way to become men, on their way as we are now to become super-men, and then gods, and then higher still. In this sense we are elementaries so far as the gods are concerned. They are elementaries so far as the super-gods are concerned.

A great deal of confusion has arisen, I think, in the minds of some readers of this wonderful book that we are studying here, from not remembering these little facts of history, and that in those days the distinctions we now give to those words, 'elementals' and 'elementaries,' had not yet been established.

KÂMA-RÛPAS — THEIR FUTURE

If you contrast the kâma-rûpa, which is our astral body after death, with our physical body, which is our physical body during this earth-life, you will realize that both are vehicles, both are enlivened by monads, or a center of consciousness, both disintegrate shortly after death. But the group of qualities which make my body, my physical me, are my physical skandhas. So my skandhas physically are my physical body as that body is. Just so with regard to the skandhas of the kâma-rûpa. The kâma-rûpa is its own skandhas. Subtract those skandhas, which means qualities, attributes, the life-atoms thereof, and what have you? You have not anything. It is the grouping together of these skandhas and the life-atoms through which they work, which form on the one hand the physical body in life or the corpse after death; and similarly the astral skandhas and others which inhere in the kâma-rûpa after death, form the kâma-rûpa.

Now then, is it not obvious that just as the life-atoms which made our physical bodies in a former life will return to us when we return to physical imbodiment, similarly and perhaps exactly is it with the kâma-rûpa. The Dweller on the Threshold is a kâma-rûpa so dense and heavy with matter that it lasts from one death over to the next rebirth of the entity coming back, and haunts the new, new-old man, the ego coming back to earth. That is an extreme case. But outside of extreme cases the life-atoms which form the kâma-rûpa are picked up by the human ego or monad as it approaches our earth, and the family into which it is to be born; and those kâma-rûpa life-atoms are gradually ingathered by the attraction of the ego over them, and them over it, until finally at some indefinite time, it may be in boyhood, it may not be until the boy becomes a man, it may not be even until quite late in life, the old kâma-rûpa life-atoms, and therefore the skandhas, have been reabsorbed by the new body, the new kâma-rûpa of the ego after it has come back after death.

If you will reflect, you must realize that even our physical body — and the same goes for the kâma-rûpa — could not hold together as a unit, in other words it could not be an entity, unless there were some holding power there. In other words there is even a monad of the physical body, and exactly so there is a monad of the kâma-rûpa. Remember, the kâma-rûpa is not a shell until it becomes a shell. Very shortly after death, the kâma-rûpa which has been built up during the life-time of the man, separates from the dead physical, and thereafter it begins its course in the astral light or in the kâma-loka. And the monad is in that kâma-rûpa until the second death. Then the kâma-rûpa begins to fall apart because the soul so to speak has withdrawn itself, as the physical body begins to decay from the moment of physical death. And as long as the monad is in the physical body the latter is not a corpse.

THE DEATH OF A SUN

The Sun, or rather the period of its life referred to by the speaker quoting from the book, refers to the end of a solar manvantara, or the opening drama of the solar pralaya or dissolution time. After premonitory symptoms of decay which the Sun and those planets still surviving will experience, symptoms which it would be easy enough to describe to a certain extent if it were worth while — after certain premonitory symptoms of decay which may last for millions of years, the time will come when the Sun has reached its last instant of life. And then, like a shadow passing over the wall, like a flick of an eye-lid, the extinction of an electric light, the Sun is dead.

In exactly the same way a man dies. He may be slowly dying for years before he actually dies, but the moment of death is instant, quick as a snap of the fingers. The man may be on a sick bed for forty years, he may be dying during the last two or three years. Premonitory symptoms are there that any capable doctor can recognise. But when death comes — gone! It is the same with the globe, or in fact anything as far as I know. It is a very wise and pitiful provision of our great Parent, because dying is a very solemn thing, and by solemn I do not mean anything arousing a sense of the lugubrious in us. It is a very important thing, so important that a weighty warning is issued by one of the Masters somewhere, I do not remember just at the moment where he tells us:* in a chamber of death to be as quiet as possible, for the mind of the dying man is collecting its consciousness, is passing inwards from all over the body, the brain and the heart and other organs, and that process should not be inter-

---

*The Mahatma Letters, p. 171.

rupted by noise. No weeping, no moving if possible, the utmost reverence and quiet. Death itself is peaceful. But of an evil person one cannot say the same; death can be hard to one whose whole affection, interest, love and yearning have been knitted into the physical life. And it is hard then simply because the snapping of the psychic bonds of attachment takes time and causes psychic and mental pain. But even then, death comes quickly when it does come.

So it is with the Sun, although the premonitory symptoms may last for millions of years. Furthermore in this same wonderful book,* the Master K. H. also answers in reply to the same question: Do the planets enter the Sun at the end of the Solar manvantara? He side-steps a bit because that is an esoteric doctrine which cannot be told openly, but says this: Yes, you may call the Sun the vertex of all the planets if you wish. The meaning is very clear.

The point is here that the Sun, being as it is not only the heart but the mind of the solar system as long as this solar system remains a coherent unity, is therefore the governor of all the life-forces in that solar system — governor and controller, as well as source and final focus. Now as long as the solar system lasts, the various planetary chains in the solar system live and die, and are disimbodied and have their nirvânic rest and then come back again for a new term, and do this several times; but their dead bodies remain for a while as moons in the solar spaces, each moon really following its former orbit, although a dead chain; but when the Sun reaches its final term in the Saurya or solar manvantara, then the Sun draws into itself all the members of the solar system, i.e., the various planetary chains, which however, before they enter the Sun, have died. The process is an analog of the manner in which a dying man for instance gathers together all the vital forces inwards and upwards before the moment of physical death supervenes and it is this ingathering of all the vital forces which brings about the phenomenon which we may call the death of our bodies.

---

*Op. cit., pp. 148, 176.

HEAT AND COLD ON JUPITER, ETC.

REFERENCE: Letter XXIIIA
Questions 11 and 12, p. 146; and the Comments on pp. 167-8

UNFORTUNATELY this question about Jupiter and the Râja-Sun is
not one that can be answered outside of esoteric teachings, and I am
being perfectly frank about it. I think it would be a shame to deceive any honest and thoughtful student by side-stepping. The
explanation of this matter is esoteric and wholly so. Therefore it
cannot be touched upon in a gathering of this kind.

Let us continue then to the subject of heat and cold on
Jupiter. If our dear people would use the vast Theosophical learning
which they have — and I am not speaking sarcastically — and apply
it to this matter of planetary heat and cold, there would be no
question or difficulty about it. They would not question, for instance,
whether Jupiter is hotter than the earth or colder. Actually it is
enormously hotter than our earth, and the modern scientific theory
of its being a thousand or several thousand miles of block ice is
simply based on the theory that, being so much farther from the
sun than the earth is, it gets a great deal less heat from the sun
and therefore *de facto* must be in a state of arctic chill. But you
see our teaching is that the planets do not get their heat from the
sun, or very little indeed.

The sun is the great beating heart and brain of our system, the
ultimate fountain and source of all the energy in the solar system
as a whole. But with regard to this particular matter of heat and
cold, it is the planets which keep themselves warm by their own
vitality just as the human body does. It is not the sun which gives
me my vital heat. The body creates its own vital heat. Of course
if I go out in the sun and I feel the sun's rays pouring on my
bare head, my head will be heated just as a plant will or a stone
or anything else that is exposed to the sun's rays. But this is not
heat coming from the sun, or very little in any case, perhaps twenty-
five percent.

What is actually taking place is that an enormous efflux of electric and magnetic power flows from the sun and sets in vibration whatever this electric power falls upon. It is just exactly as every electrician knows: if you pass an electric current through a length of wire filament you encounter a resistance, which makes the particles in the wire through which the electric current passes, and which possesses this high resisting power, to glow with heat. It is not the electricity which carries heat and deposits it there. Electricity is neither hot nor cold. It is the power of the electricity meeting this resistance, which throws the molecules and atoms of this resisting medium into intense vibration, more rapid than that of billions and quadrillions of vibrations in a human second, and therefore heats it. Electricity is not itself hot. Just so with the sun. The sun is neither hot nor cold as we understand heat and cold. It is an enormous body of force, forces, which include electricity and magnetism and consciousness and life and intelligence and other things.

No, what makes Jupiter so hot is its own vital power. What produces this vital power in a heated body? You could ask the same question about our earth. What makes the earth warm or cold? The vital power of the earth — call it magnetism if you wish — interacting and reacting with the magnetic continent above our heads: give and take, electric, electro-magnetic or magnetic action and interaction. Just so does my own vital heat make my own body warm. If we had to trust to exterior heat to keep us alive and had no interior natural native vital heat of our own, if we went twenty feet from a fire we would freeze up in half an hour or in quarter of an hour. But such things do not occur.

So it is with Jupiter. When planets are young, very young, they are enormously hotter than when they grow old. So it is even with the human being in a small degree. The hottest little dynamo that I have ever known is a baby. When boyhood is reached, your heat diminishes. When you reach manhood it grows still less: you are not then burning up in a constant fevered heat as a baby is. The teaching in the book shows us clearly. The Master says: Imagine if all our oceans were turned into ice and all our atmospheric fluids were turned into liquids; then, he says, just imagine the reverse process, and you will have some idea of what it is like on Jupiter, which means, so hot there that what would be our oceans are turned

to gases and what we call metals, stones and such things are turned
to fluids. Just the reverse process. And it is strange enough that
that was originally the idea of science.

The part played by the meteoric veils over every continent
which is not in obscuration, as Mars is in obscuration — the part
played by these meteoric continents is enormous. Some people
don't like to accept this idea, although it is true, because they think
it diminishes the dignity of our glorious Father Sun. It does not
diminish his dignity. Because I have some vital heat of my own,
that does not diminish the dignity of my teacher. Why should he
be blamed or praised because I was born with vital heat? It is
not a derogation of the dignity of the sun to say that the planets
are living bodies also, living organisms.

Now Mars is in obscuration, consequently the meteoric veil
surrounding Globe D of the Mars-chain is very thin. When the
life-waves begin to come into Mars again, as they will before many
millions of years have passed, Mars also will begin again to be
re-covered with what scientists call heavy clouds, which are really
veils of meteoric dust. Attracted psycho-vital-magnetically by
the tremendously vital power of the planets which they surround,
these meteoric continents perform somewhat the same function with
regard to the planets that the human aura does for us. The meteoric
veils are composed of dust, the effluvia rising up from the earth
partly, but mainly and more largely from interplanetary and interstellar cosmic dust: the refuse, the sweat, the detritus, of other
manvantaras, karmically drawn back, as life-atoms are drawn back
to the reincarnating man.

Then there is the matter of the sun's north and south poles
spoken of in this letter. Now there is one point here that needs
clearing. I do not remember the Master's exact words, but it is
much to the effect that the sun does not take anything from anything else, nor does it give away anything of its own. A perfectly
true statement when it is understood. But do not forget this other
perfectly true statement, infinitely more important: that nothing
exists unto itself alone. Everything helps everything else. Everything lives for everything else. No accident anywhere. And this
is a cosmic statement of what we Theosophists call our beautiful

doctrine of Universal Brotherhood. The Master means this: that the sun is not vampirized — in the sense that the word vampirize has. Nor is it a spendthrift, wasting and dissipating its vital power by pouring it out needlessly through ages, as our modern science teaches it does, to be wasted in the abysmal deeps of pluperfectly frigid spaces.

The solar system is a closed system in the sense that a human body is a closed system. Agreed that every human body is builded by life-atoms from all other human bodies; but so far as itself goes it is an entity, an individual with its own vital power, feeding itself, having naught to spare to give of vital power to other bodies unless given as a gift. And likewise not vampirizing, in the normal cases, other bodies. Vampirizing and giving of gifts happen, but these are not the normal state of things. Every atom is a closed system in that sense. Yet every atom is connected with every other atom in infinite space, feeding infinite space and infinite space feeding it.

So then, the sun does not vampirize other suns, nor has it any vitality to spare for other suns. It has all it can do to feed its own orbs, the planets and other bodies within its kingdom. Just so my heart feeds my body and its organs and its molecules. It has nothing to spare for feeding other bodies — unless giving as a gift. Nor does my body vampirize other bodies. It does not steal vitality from other bodies, although in abnormal cases any human body can become vampirized; but we are not talking of exceptions and special cases; we are talking of the norm, the rule.

Therefore, what happens is this: the sun follows the same cosmic law that every planet does. It is the heart of its kingdom and likewise the brain of its kingdom. If you look upon it as the heart for an instant, it receives the influxes of the rivers of lives, the circulations of the solar system, in its north pole. They pass through the heart of the sun, are cleansed and washed and leave at the south pole of the sun. Precisely as our earth and every other planet have each its receptor at the north pole, and its ejector or vent at the south pole.

Why, even the ancient Greeks taught this. Do you remember Eolus and the cave of the winds? The cave of the winds was the earth, and the winds were the winds of the spirit, the circulations of the universe figurated as winds: a cave of which the north gate was made of horn through which the gods descend — and through which they ascend also, but mainly descend. And the south gate of the earth, or of the cave of the winds, was made of ivory, signifying the elephants of the south, as the horn does the tusks of the animals of the north. And out of the south gate go the hordes of men. So said the ancients. Why, the occult teaching is simply expressed here without a veil.

In other words, the earth feeds itself physically, magnetically, psychically, spiritually, through the north pole. The currents sweep through the earth — every word here is worth a volume — and leave by the south pole. So it is with the sun. That is the way the sun feeds its family: just as the heart feeds the body. It sends out its blood through the south pole, as it were, and after the circulation around the body has taken place, it receives it in again at the north pole. Fascinating subject!

So be careful how you read and construe. Don't let a single statement given by the Master as an answer to a very limited and specific question cover all the horizon of your thought regarding other things. In other words use your common sense.

So now, Companions, let me close my own remarks on an expression of pleasure that I always feel after hearkening to the words of those who make really wonderful addresses from the platform and the equally wonderful contributions from the auditorium. It just warms every cockle of my heart to see the progress that you dear fellow-students have made. I think it is beautiful, and it fills me with reverence. I think you deserve to know what I feel about these things.

Remember this, and then I go: All the laws of nature, so called, are but the play of conscious and semi-conscious forces. Therefore by their utter consistency and invariability they are called by us the laws of nature. These forces of nature are fluids emanating from great cosmic hearts beating, hearts sending the life blood, each one of its own especial and particular essence, force, spirit, to the farthest reaches that it can contain. We live not only in the presence of divinities, but are in very truth their children. We are builded of them and from them. Human parents are away, far away and distant when compared with the utterly infinite, infinitely intimate because identical relations and ties that exist between these great parents and us their children. Electricity, or magnetism, its alter ego, for instance, is but the fluid efflux from a cosmic entity, a being — of our own solar system in our case, because we are in this solar system. Heat likewise; all the real forces of nature are such. What is gravity? Just the same. We call it love. Some day when science will have learned that gravity is bi-polar as electricity and magnetism are, we may perhaps see returning the wisdom of the old Greek Empedocles who taught in his day that the universe is held in its courses and in its plans of beauty and harmony because of the two great cosmic powers, love and hate as they translate it. It is not a good translation. Attraction and repulsion: better but not good. You might perhaps say love and repulsion; hate is not a good word. Marvelous thoughts!

COMETS AND METEORS

REFERENCE: Letter XXIIIB, pp. 161-2

I WOULD never state that meteorites are fragments of disintegrated comets, nor indeed that they are cometary material at all. When you reflect that comets or cometary material are but one stage or degree less ethereal than is a nebula, you will realize that the fundamental idea here is wrong. It is perfectly true, however, that comets gather unto themselves in their peregrinations through cosmic and solar space, the waste-material of the universe. They accrete these to themselves by attraction, and often lose them because when they pass by a sun, the solar attraction for such material things is heavy, much stronger than the very weak attraction that the comets exercise.

Reflect that any comet, even the largest known comets, are composed of material so exceedingly fine, so ethereal, that Halley's comet, for instance, one of the largest ever known perhaps, could be packed in a hand-bag and the hand-bag would not be filled; and yet some of these comets stretch for millions and millions and millions of miles, if you include the head and the tail.

Returning to meteorites: what then are these bodies? They are the waste-material, the ejecta, of former suns; and hereby hangs another wonderful tale which would take me several hours even to sketch if it were only to make that statement fully comprehensible. Perhaps I should remark that while a sun in its life-time is extremely ethereal, at its heart even spiritual, as it approaches its end, it becomes much more concrete, thick, heavy, dense, and as we Theosophists say, material, until, just before the last flicker of solar life passes out, and the sun dies or becomes extinct, all that remains is a relatively heavy body. Then with the last flicker of the solar life it passes like a shadow over a sunlighted wall, and the living center is dead: "The Sun is dead. Long live the Sun!" At death it leaves behind a body which immediately bursts into innumerable fragments, some atomic and some much larger; and these ejecta are scattered through solar and stellar space to be swept up in later aeons not only by the reimbodiment of the sun which has just died, but by other suns, and even other planets, as well as occasionally by comets. These meteorites contain many materials found also in our earth: iron, nickel, traces of copper, carbon, oxygen, hydrogen, and what not.

You will remember that H. P. B. has a passage not only in her beautiful *Voice of the Silence,* but in one of her wonderful articles, stating that every planet was once a glorious sun which became a planet in due course of time; and that before it dies this planet once a sun will become a sun again. You have a key here to a wonderful teaching. I wish I could say more about this, but I have neither the time nor is this the place — except indeed to add that every planetary nebula becoming a planetary comet passes through a sun-phase before becoming sufficiently materialized to be a planet or planetary chain. In other words I mean to say that every planet is for a time a small sun when, just before leaving the cometary stage, it passes through a temporary sun-phase before materialized enough or concreted or gross enough to be a planet. Again, I may add that each reimbodiment of a planet or rather of a planetary chain passes again or anew through these various phases, to wit: planetary nebula, planetary comet, planetary sun, and planet.

What we call the Milky Way is already prepared world-stuff, both the luminous nebulae as well as the dark: different phases of already prepared world-stuff. You have an analogy in the human body, but of course this is not a lecture-hall on physiology, so I cannot go into that very easily.

Now then, when the time comes for a solar system to reimbody itself in the same way as a man reincarnates, a certain portion of this world-stuff which has ended its pralaya, or rather the pralaya of the former sun, detaches itself from the Milky Way and begins to pursue at first a slow and later a rapid peregrination as a comet into many portions of the galaxy, finally to reach its own destined home in space. Always keep in mind that it does this because drawn by attractions, which is really gravitation: psychic, spiritual, intellectual attractions. This nebula moves slowly at first, but gathers speed. It picks up material as it wanders through the galaxy, traversing the different solar systems: and if it is fortunate and escapes being drawn into the stomach of one or another of the always very hungry suns (strange way to speak of imbodied divinities!)

then it finds its place in space, and its movement of translation stops. It has other movements in common with all galactic bodies; but its cometary wanderings, the cometary wanderings of the 'long-haired radical' as H. P. B. calls the comet, stop because it has found its home, its locus. It then settles and is now much more concrete, much less spiritual, much less astral, as we say, than it was as a nebula, because time has passed, ages have passed during which it was a comet: and furthermore it has been gathering material, the 'refuse of the mother,' the detritus of the cosmic dust, her breath, her refuse, which it has been feeding on and taking into itself. Strange paradox that in all the rûpa-worlds entities feed — not so in the arûpa. There their food is intellectual ambrosia or nectar, as the Greeks said of their Olympian divinities.

Now when it has thus settled in the place which is the locus of the solar system reimbodied, the solar system that was, and more or less in that same place (karman you see), the nebula or comet has become a vast lens or disk-shaped body of astral stuff — call it nebular matter, call it cometary matter if you will — with laya-centers here and there scattered through it, like organs in a body. We may call these laya-centers by the more common name in science and say that they are the nuclei. In the center is the largest such nucleus which grows or develops or evolves into becoming a sun. The smaller nuclei around it in this nebular comet or cometary nebula grow to be the beginnings of the planets, and this is the beginning of the solar system. In the commencement of its beginning, as it were, the sun is voracious and attempts to swallow his younger brothers the planets, until the laws of nature come into operation, and attraction and repulsion come into play, of which science today knows only one: attraction, and calls it gravity or gravitation, although it seems to me repulsion is just as active in the universe as gravity. To me this gravity-theory is one-sided. If you will consider the behavior of the comets which come into the solar system, and how the tail of the comet always points away from the sun, you will see repulsion at work. Scientists think the repulsion is due to the action of light on the very small particles of molecules in the cometary tail. If you like. It is repulsion. As the comet approaches the sun, the head goes first, and tail afterwards; then as it sweeps around, the tail is always heading away from the sun, and when it leaves the sun after circling it, the tail precedes and the head follows.

Now the solar system is thus brought into being and finally becomes that solar system as we see it with our eyes. That means a lot, that phrase, *with our eyes;* and soon the solar system begins its career as a now formed entity. The planets slowly become more material and less ethereal. The divine laws of the celestial mechanism we call the solar system are established as now we see them working.

Now we pass over ages and we come to the ending of the life of the sun, which means the ending of the life of the solar system, for the sun is King in his kingdom. The sun feeds on the refuse of inter-planetary and inter-solar stuffs which it sucks in with its immense force and rejects as we humans do. This is the body of the sun I am talking about. This refuse, this matter in cosmic space, is the detritus of former dead suns, as you will see in a moment. Now we are approaching the end of the life of the sun. The sun's powers begin to weaken. Actually what is happening is that his manvantara is ending, his pralaya is almost beginning. His life on inner planes is opening, and that takes vitality from this plane. Therefore we say the sun is weakening in his power. That is all it means, and that is all death is: the transference from this plane to interior planes of a large part of the vitality existing on this plane when the body is at full strength.

Finally the sun dies. But long before this all the planets have died and have disappeared. I cannot tell you where here, it would take too long. Sufficient to say that the sun knows. The sun when the moment of its death comes bursts, explodes, into simply innumerable fragments of various sizes, sun-stuff, which originally were almost as ethereal as spirit; but as the sun grew older became more and more compacted, more and more materialized, concreted, until when the sun is dying, practically dead, it is not a solid body yet but on the way to becoming solid. But it explodes; there is a tremendous — words just lack to explain this — not flash, a tremendous volume or outburst of light and power spreading throughout our solar system, and far beyond its confines. Every now and then astronomers today will discover what they call novae, a Latin word meaning "new stars." But what they see is just the opposite: a death of a star; and they will see some of these novae expand and then actually dim, some very quickly, some requiring years and years.

Now then, all these fragments which were once sun-stuff grow constantly more material. Finally they become the meteors and meteorites of interstellar spaces. Originally spirit-stuff, mûlaprakriti, they are now some of the most solid portions of prakriti, iron, nickel, carbon, and all the other things that our scientists have found in the meteorites which have reached this earth. These meteorites wander through space for ages and ages until the imbodiment of the solar system comes again. Thus the cometary nebula picks up uncounted numbers of these meteorites, thus bringing back as it were its life-atoms of the former body of the solar system into its new body, just as we humans do. But it takes ages and ages for the solar system to gather up all these meteorites; and as a matter of fact all the meteorites that traverse our solar system are not due to the explosion of our former sun. Multitudes and multitudes of them are, but multitudes are not, but are the explosions of other suns in interstellar space which have wandered far and have become caught by our sun in its former state, or by our planets in their former state.

And one final thing: We have thus seen what a sun-comet is, or a comet which becomes a sun in the solar system. But a comet may be the pre-birth state either of a sun or of a planet. During the lifetime of a solar system, every one of our planetary chains has its periods of manvantara and pralaya, in other words every planetary chain dies and is imbodied again, and dies and is imbodied again in our system before the solar system and the sun in that system reach the time of their pralaya. In other words, our planetary chains reimbody themselves many many times during the lifetime or manvantara of our solar system. How is this done? The chains die, their inner principles begin their peregrinations along the circulations of the universe, exactly as a man's ego dies and returns. Remember I am just giving the barest outline, just a touch here and a touch there, leaving out 99 percent of what should and could be said. How does each such planetary chain-ego, as it were, come back to our solar system? By detaching itself where it was resting as part of the already prepared world-stuff of the Milky Way exactly as the sun-comet or cometary sun did when the solar system was reimbodying. In this instance the comet is a planetary comet which wanders through space, comes back to our solar system, is attracted here, becomes a small sun, and dying out of this state because of materializing, becomes a full planetary chain, settles in life as what we call the planet and begins its new Day of Brahmâ.

WHAT ARE THE ŚISHTAS?

REFERENCE: Letter XV, pp. 93-7

WHAT are the śishtas? Śishta is a Sanskrit word meaning 'remainder' or 'remnant.' It is a technical term which means those most evolved beings of any life-wave — or if you like of any kingdom like the human kingdom or the beast kingdom or the plant kingdom or the stone kingdom. It means the most evolved representatives of any kingdom which remain on the globe as its representatives when the monads of the greater part of the beings of that kingdom move on to the succeeding globe, to enter into that globe and undergo their experiences there.

Take the human kingdom. When our human kingdom or life-wave shall reach its Seventh Root-Race and end it, that is the last Root-Race that we shall have on this globe during this present round. In other words when the kingdom shall have reached the end of its evolution on this Globe D, then the majority of humans will take their way like birds winging their way through space and migrating, as the ducks and geese and other birds do, over to the next globe of our chain. But those humans left behind on our earth, the remnants or śishtas of our human life-wave, will be the most evolved representatives of our human life-wave. There are two reasons for this. First: when the life-wave shall return after having made its round in the globes to this globe earth again, having gained all that intermediate vast fund of experience, it is obviously the most evolved representatives of our life-wave which are the only ones fit to receive the monads or souls of the incoming life-wave during the next round to follow us. Inferior bodies would be but inferior. It must be the finest of humans to be the Fifth Round humans on Globe D.

Now why is it that these humans to be the śishtas of the human life-wave have become so much more evolved than the majority of humans? Because through individual effort and aspiration and self-control and desire to evolve and to be more and to become more, in other words through the dominance of the upsurging spirit of beauty and holiness, this urging fire within them has made them the *avant coureurs,* the forerunners of our life-wave. They have run ahead of

the majority of the life-wave and have come back and are therefore
now what we call Fifth Rounders. There is no attraction in them
or for them to belong to the bulk of the human life-wave, to have to
go through all the globes up the ascending arc and down the descending arc until they reach our globe again, because they have already
done it as individuals. They are already Fifth Rounders. They
have been through the Fifth Round, but not completely. They have
been through the Fifth Round as far as our earth. Then they are
caught here on our earth so to speak. They have preceded the human life-wave up to the end during the Fourth Round and down the
globes during the beginning of the Fifth, until they have reached our
earth where the human life-wave still is. They have far outrun the
bulk of the life-wave; so when they reach our earth here, they stay
until during the Fifth Round the majority of the human kingdom or
life-wave, having gone through the globes, reaches our Globe D, the
earth again. Here are the human forms still living on Globe D all
these hundreds of millions of years, but as a Fifth Round race, as
śishtas. They have been evolving, but evolving very slowly. They
are here in a sense as a sacrifice, because instead of trying to keep
ahead of the human life-wave and make their Sixth Round, at least
a part of it, they resign that so that they can remain until the less progressed members of the human life-wave return to Globe D during
the Fifth Round, and thus provide the bodies, and the teachers, and
the guides. Do you remember what all the great religions of the
human race have taught? That in the very infancy of our human-
kind, we were taught by great beings, initiates, adept-kings, who
were human, who taught the early races and implanted into their
minds the fundamental ideas of truth, of law, all the sciences? It
is wonderful how uniform all these great ancient systems of thought
are; and this is what is alluded to. When the monads of the life-
wave — going back now in this our Fourth Round — reached this
earth, they found their śishtas from the Third Round, human śishtas,
the most evolved at the end of the Third Round; and it was these
human śishtas who received the incoming monads, furnished them
bodies to begin their evolution and so forth.

And one further thought. It is something I have explained before, but you seem to have forgotten it. In this chapter where the
Master gives the seven principles of our globe earth, this has always

been misread to mean the principles of our sevenfold globe, and this is wrong. The Master is giving only the seven principles of the sthûla-śarîra or physical body of our Globe D; just as I might give you what I would call, and properly, the seven principles of my physical body. The physical aspect has seven principles or sub-aspects, and that is what the Master was giving. Now mark you the contrast: Our Globe D, the *globe,* I am not speaking of a chain, our *Globe* D is septenary. It has its seven principles just as every entity in nature has, and every one of these seven principles, including the earth's physical body, is in its turn septenary. So that our Globe D has its âtman, not merely a diffuse ether around the earth which is the âtman of the sthûla-śarîra of our globe, but its own divine monad or âtman, its buddhi, its manas, its kâma, its linga-śarîra (its astral light), its prâna, which is what we call electricity, its sthûla-śarîra which is the gross physical body of the earth that we see around us. So the Master here when describing the seven principles of the earth was describing the seven phases or aspects, call them principles if you wish, of the globe's sthûla-śarîra.

DIFFERENCES IN THE SECOND ROUND

REFERENCE: Letters XXIIIA, XXIIIB, pp. 147-9, 174-8

You know that the building of a planetary chain, which means the building of every globe of a planetary chain — take any globe, take Globe D of our own chain — is exactly parallel, in the way the thing is worked, to the descent of a human ego from devachan into imbodiment among the human race. You have the logos, the planetary spirit of our globe, finding its time has come and leaving its nirvâna and descending through the lower realms, dropping into matter in order to build its body, its globe; exactly as the ego in the devachan, when the devachanic period is ended, feels the impact of the tânhic pull, feeling the impact of these old elementals of thought and desire of the last life beginning to impinge on its consciousness. The ego in the devachan is attracted to the old scenes, it descends as we say, it drops; and finally, still by attraction, enters the human womb to which karman impels it, impels it and attracts it.

In precisely identical fashion does the logos of the planetary globe descend from its nirvâna to build this globe, as the ego in the womb builds its body. First the germ, which we can call the elemental kingdoms, then solidification and hardening, which we can call the mineral kingdom. Then the growing embryo passes through the vegetable phases, which might be called the vegetable kingdom; then it passes through the animal phase and might be called the human animal, as indeed it is. And then it is born. But its recapitulation of all past evolutionary experience or karman in the womb has taken place by the ego in connexion with the tânhic elementals. They are the first to appear on the scene.

So with the building of the globe: it is the Dhyân-Chohans from the previous planetary chain-imbodiment, the moon in our case, which combine with the elementals of that globe, build the outline during the First Round, make the molds of what the globe is to be. Naturally once the molds have been made, the house built, the rooms divided off, the windows put in — after that the builder, even though he may have been the carpenter himself during the construction-period, finally enters into his home and begins his life of habit: this room my bedroom, this room my office, this room my kitchen, and so forth.

These are the things that are done during the First Round which may correspond to the womb-life of the reimbodying ego before it is born as a child. Once it is born as a child, it is a child thenceforth; it does not pass any more through the elemental, mineral, vegetable, animal, reaching the human kingdom. It simply grows, it is already human. This is what we call recapitulation in biology, embryology, and similar things; and that is exactly what the planetary spirit of our globe with the attending elementals does during the First Round — recapitulates all the past evolutionary earth-history, from aeons in the past, runs through the past history very quickly.

Keep in thought the word recapitulation. That is what the First Round is, recapitulating rapidly all the past history; and this is why it is that the ten classes of monads, of which the human family is one class, during that First Round must go through every one of the kingdoms of nature to contribute its construction-part in the building of the globe; just as the ego and elementals do in the human womb. They work together to build the body of the child, recapitulating its evolutionary history during the nine months. This should be very clear and simple enough. During the First Round, all the past history of the planetary spirit and of the attendant elementals and the beings, classes of monads, all their past history is recapitulated. Everyone of them must pass through the first elemental kingdom, building it up through the second elemental kingdom, building it up through the third elemental kingdom, then through the mineral kingdom, then through the vegetable kingdom, then through the animal kingdom, then through the human; and the three kingdoms of the Dhyân-Chohans; so that when the First Round is ended, this period of recapitulatory history has produced the globe.

All further history will be the consolidation, development, and final glorification. It is very simple. How true the statement that the master-key to understanding nature, including man, is analogy. Remember the old axiom of Hermes: What is above is as what is below. What is below mirrors what is above. If you wish to discern the secrets of the laws in the kingdoms invisible, open wide your eyes, not merely the vision of habit and of use and of education, but open wide your eyes of vision upon what is around us and read the mysteries of nature everywhere, in stone and tree, and in the plant and in the celestial bodies, even in the repertory in the human heart. Everything copies everything else, for nature has one fundamental law to which everything in the universe forms one pattern on whatever plane.

Remember then that the highest and the lowest begin the work of evolution, the highest giving the plan of the architects, the lowest being the builders, the masons under the architectural plan, impressed upon the builders as instinct, automatic reactions to stimuli; and thus nature is builded, not only globes but suns, universes, galaxies, throughout life, all on one cosmic fundamental pattern.

Now, I have never at any time said that beginning with the Second Round it is the human life-wave that precedes all the other life-waves. Whatever I may have said or written, certainly it is not that thought. Mark you: all the life-waves — which means groups of monads or living beings so much alike that they form a family, like us humans, like the beasts, like the plants, or like the gods, each of which is what we call a life-wave — all the life-waves follow each other around the seven or twelve globes in the serial order that they always retain. Therefore it would be impossible for the human life-wave to precede all the other life-waves at the beginning of the Second Round, or great period of manifestation. The Second Round opens with the elemental kingdoms coming in, followed by the mineral kingdom, followed by the vegetable kingdom, followed by the animal kingdom, followed by the human kingdom, and the human followed by the three dhyân-chohanic kingdoms.

What it means when it is said that beginning with the Second Round the procedure followed in the First Round is changed is simply this: The First Round is taken up by building the foundations of the seven or twelve globes forming our planetary chain. The superstructure comes with the later six rounds. The superstructure rises to become a temple of intelligence and life, inhabited by families of beings, of which the human hierarchy is one family. This means therefore that every one of the life-waves must contribute its quota during that First Round to make the work of the First Round complete in a sevenfold way or a twelvefold way, there being seven life-waves or classes of souls, or twelve according to the way you count them.

Therefore during the First Round every one of these classes of monads or groups of souls or life-waves must contribute its own swâbhâvic or characteristic quota to building the foundations. Once that foundation has been laid, then the architects who are the highest part of the different life-waves no longer have all to go down into the grossest of matter to build the foundation. They begin with the Second Round to build the superstructure.

THE 777 IMBODIMENTS

REFERENCE: Letter XIV, pp. 82-3

SOMETIMES a little confusion was caused in the minds of earlier readers of *The Mahatma Letters* through lack of knowing all the facts. For instance they did not know that the two Mahâtmans, M. and K. H., took, each one, a different side of the teaching of the rounds and the globes. I think it was K. H. who took care of the instruction to be conveyed in what we call the Inner Rounds; and M., as I recollect, took charge of the teaching concerning the Outer Rounds. As analogy rules throughout the universe, the greater teaching contains the smaller teaching in miniature; and the smaller teaching contains within its heart the reflexion of the greater. Thus what either Master gave could, by making appropriate changes, apply to what the other Master taught, but there are certain things you have to know about this in order to discern just where the reference is to Outer Rounds and where to Inner Rounds.

Now with regard to the matter of the 777 or the 777 imbodiments, I would like to point this out: The number 777 does not refer to the actual number of incarnations that souls have. Unfortunately in the days when *The Mahatma Letters* were written, there was no clearly defined terminology as we now have evolved it, and they used 'incarnations' in the way we all did when we were boys, say thirty or forty years ago. We talked about an incarnation of the mineral kingdom, and an incarnation of the sun; which of course is a ridiculous way of speaking, because incarnation means infleshing. The proper word would have been imbodiment.

Now here is my point. The references here are not to what we now call incarnations of the human ego, but refer to the monads; and this was hinted at by more than a few of the speakers tonight. It refers to the imbodiments, or passings if you wish, of the families of monads through the kingdoms of nature on this earth, Globe D, and during the seven root-races. Try to figure that out. You will find it as difficult as the other conception, in a way, but there is the key.

Thus, one incarnation in every root-race. You see, you have the key right there. Every root-race demonstrates a power and a substance in cosmic planes, not fully but relatively. So, so far as our own Globe is concerned — and our Master was speaking of our Globe and the monads of our Globe now — the reference is, as I have just stated, to the passings or traversings of the different families of monads through the different kingdoms of nature, or if you like, through the different cosmic planes.

Now what does this mean? It means that for every kingdom of nature, or for every cosmic plane, such a monad has to build for itself a general subtil vehicle which will be permanent for that kingdom or for that cosmic plane. Do you follow that? When that kingdom or that cosmic plane is abandoned or left, and the monad passes on through the next succeeding kingdom or cosmic plane, that particular integument or vehicle builded for that cosmic plane or world is shed or dropped because no longer adequate for the monad; and an integument is built up fitted to allow the monad to express itself in the succeeding cosmic plane or world or kingdom. So there is an assuming of such an integument for every cosmic plane, one for every root-race, one for every great sub-race, and one such integument for every sub-sub-race; and so on down, if you wish, to a single imbodiment.

Now, counting these integuments — well, I am saying too much! But there is your key; and you will find it as a teaching identical with the teaching of the medieval Fire Philosophers when they spoke of souls manifesting as salamanders, as sylphs, as undines, as gnomes; because in those days they openly or publicly spoke of only four. You can add the three more that we teach.

THE BUILDING OF THE GLOBES

REFERENCE: Letter XV, pp. 94-5

To ASK for a brief answer to the whole complex subject of the evolution of the ten classes of monads, and the development of the Planetary Chain — for this is what it amounts to — is to ask for a tremendous lot! The subject if properly treated would require one hundred books, each one devoted to one aspect.

Nevertheless, everything can be boiled down or generalized to a statement, and I will try to do it as follows: There are ten or even twelve classes of monads, which means reimbodying entities in different evolutionary grades; and evolution, remember, means growth from within outwards, not the Darwinian theory of haphazard, chancy addings upon addings.

Now then: During the First Round, all the ten or twelve kingdoms combined to build the globes of a chain, or rather rebuild them from their past imbodiments. This is the First Round; and while of course there is distinct order amongst them in their work of doing this, it is extremely complicated. But get the main idea, that all the classes of monads, ten or twelve or seven, however you choose to count them, all co-operate during the First Round. It is like the picture of a wealthy man going to build a house. He and his architects and his contractors, and his foreman, all get together and lay the plans, and then they collect the workers and all the materials, and all co-operate together to build the house. Once the house is builded, then everything falls into regular order of day-to-day life, as soon as the owner and his family — and to carry on our analogy we will have to say the architects and contractors belonging to the family — all come in together and live in this huge house.

Beginning with the Second Round the different classes of monads sort themselves out, because now the lines have been laid, the different houses or globes of the chain have been constructed in at least elementary fashion, and, sorting themselves out, the different classes of monads thereafter come in serially one after the other, each class following its own path of evolutionary karman or karmic evolution.

But it is always the more evolved which set the pace and give the plan and make the pathways for the least evolved to follow on after. Thus it is that man, not counting now the dhyân-chohanic monadic classes above the human, but counting only the human and the other six classes below the human — the human, I say, sets the pace and lays the pathways for the other monadic classes beneath the human; and thus it is that the human is really the repository or evolutionary and originating storehouse of the other classes of monads seeking imbodiment, I mean those under the human monadic class; and this is the meaning of the statement which is very true, that from the beginning of the Second Round, continuing during the Third, and even up to the Fourth Round where now we are, the human monads or the human stock were the storehouse out of which the animals sprang during the Third Round, out of which the vegetables sprang during the Second Round, and out of which the minerals sprang even during the First Round, when they all were co-operating together. There is the whole thing on your thumb-nail, if you get it.

To recapitulate: During the First Round, when everything is still in the elementary stage, all the classes of monads co-operate to lay the foundations of the globes, and build them up to the point where the classes, beginning with the Second Round can, each class, follow its own line of evolution upon this groundwork laid by all the classes during the First Round.

The First Round therefore is like the embryonic stage in human birth in the womb of nature. The Second Round so to speak begins with the birth of the child, or the birth of the animal, or the birth of the plant or the seed; and thereafter each class of monads, or family or kingdom, having been separated out, follows its own special destiny along the lines laid down by the higher classes: the human for all classes beneath the human; the dhyân-chohanic monads or classes for all beneath them, including the human of course.

The seven classes or ten may be reckoned as follows: three classes of elementals or three kingdoms of elementals; the mineral class or kingdom; the vegetable class or kingdom; the animal class or kingdom; the human class or kingdom; and then above the human, three dhyân-chohanic classes or kingdoms, of which the highest is, according to the rule just laid down, the chiefest and the main repository or originating storehouse or governing group of minds of all the lower classes.

Just as we humans follow in the footsteps of the Dhyân-Chohans who help us and from whom we sprang in a sense, so the animals and the vegetables and the minerals, each slowly follows in the footsteps of the kingdom above itself. Thus it is that the animal kingdom actually sprang mainly during the Third Round from the human stock, not according to the Darwinian sense; but the human stock threw off germs or monads — not human germs or monads, but animal germs or monads carried by the human as sleeping monads. But when these were thrown off, and no longer under the human control, then they formed a class of their own called the animal class of monads, and thereafter began to evolve each along its own line; and the specializations in evolution since the Third Round, which were repeated during this Fourth Round — these specializations have been enormous: such as the quadrupeds developing four legs, or the fishes developing fins, or the birds developing wings and legs; or again the whale, which is distinctly an animal mammal, and not a fish, taking to the water and looking like a fish; or the bat which is a mammal and not a bird, nevertheless taking to the air and looking like a bird. All these are what are called specializations, and they have greatly confused the evolutionist-scientists who cannot make head or tail out of the immensely complex problem because they have not the esoteric keys. Yet all these monads were originally thrown off as germs, life-germs, from the human kingdom; and once thrown off, no longer under human control, as stated above, they began to evolve on their own and to specialize.

Thus the highest class of dhyân-chohanic monads guides and helps the second or lower class of dhyân-chohanic monads. The second or lower class of dhyân-chohanic monads guides or helps the third or still lower class of dhyân-chohanic monads. These last guide or help the human monads. The human monads guide and help the animal monads. The animal monads unconsciously guide and help the vegetable monads. The vegetable monads unconsciously guide and help the mineral monads; and these last help the three kingdoms of elemental monads, in the same order.

DEVACHAN AND THE SEVEN PRINCIPLES

REFERENCE: Letter XVI, pp. 102-6

I REALIZE tonight, my dear Companions, while listening to the study of the evening, that more earnest study will be needed by all of you before you can come to a more uniform understanding of so simple a teaching as that of the Devachan. I will not say that any speaker has been wrong. I will say that my mind found a difficulty in weaving together the different statements from different people about different aspects of the devachanic doctrine, difficulty in weaving a coherent web of understanding. This is not always so. Very often I have inspiration from the speakers from the floor. I have not had that tonight, and I am inclined to believe that some of us are flying before we have learned to crawl. That may sound like a strange thing to us, but it actually occurs. I have known of university graduates who are perfect marvels in abstract, disputatious arguments about things that interest nobody except themselves, and yet were exceedingly feeble on things taught in the primary schools. Now we must try to avoid this. Some of the things I have heard from the floor tonight have been admirably correct, I thought, perfectly accurate.

I will try to give you a few of my own ideas which I believe to be correct. First, then, we turn to the so-called seven principles in a man. These principles are not separate entities added unto a human being to make him sevenfold. Each one is born from the principle which is higher than it; and therefore all come from the âtman. Picture to yourselves the âtman as the fount-self of every septenary entity, whether this be a universe or a sun or a planet or a god or a demi-god or a man, or some other entity less evolved than these, such as a beast or a plant or a stone.

Thus the âtman at the beginning of manifestation clothes itself in its first garment of manifestation, of emanation, of evolution. This we call the buddhi. It bears the same relation to the âtman that mûlaprakriti does to parabrahman, or that pradhâna does to brahman. In other words the Self, as its first emanational clothing, brings forth from within itself the buddhi; and the essence of the buddhi is all the higher parts of the entity, let us say a human being, such as intuition, discrimination, instant knowledge, instinctive wisdom, plus all the garnered experiences from all former lives which have been gathered up into the buddhi and treasured there since the beginning of cosmic manvantara.

Actually the monad is âtma-buddhi. When we add the manas to it, as is commonly done and correctly done, it merely means all the mânasic gleanings or harvest from former lives which I have just spoken of. All these harvests are intellectual or individualized experiences become parts of the character of the individual.

Therefore neither the âtman nor the buddhi goes into the devachan dreams, because both are infinitely almost beyond the devachan. Their proper consciousness-state or conditions are the nirvânas, the various grades of the nirvâna, which means cognisance of self-identification with utter Reality. Therefore you see that any neophyte who has raised his ego, the human ego, to become at one and indeed one with the monad, enjoys omniscience, since the âtman is universal, and its buddhi is its first veiling of divine individuality, because as just stated it is the treasure house of all the collected, reaped experiences of former lives anywhere, in this solar system or any others in other cosmic manvantaras.

Thus it is rightly said by the Orientals of the true Buddhas of Compassion that they are omniscient. This does not mean infinitely omniscient; it means omniscient for our own universe. There could be no such thing as a unit, a monad, (which already means finitized, however vast, because from the All it has already shrunken to become a one) — there could be no infinite anything for even such a lofty monad. Don't you catch these subtil distinctions? We can, if you please, ascend in the scale of monads until we finally reach what Pythagoras called the Monas Monadum, or the monad of monads, which merely means the supreme monadic hierarch of any one universe; and yet we see by this very descriptive explanation that we are speaking of one universe, and therefore of a limited entity, however vast. Once it is a universe, one universe, it is no longer frontierless, boundless infinitude and eternity.

These simple propositions of philosophy should be clear to any one of you. But such a Buddha is omniscient for all within his universe, whether that universe be our solar system or our galaxy; yet would not be omniscient, if it is a Buddha of our solar system, for the galaxy which is an aggregate of billions of solar systems. If he is a Buddha of a Galaxy, he would be omniscient for that galaxy, but not over a still vaster collection, let us say a collection of galaxies.

So all these terms are relative. The Lord Buddha Gautama, the Buddha after he attained nirvâna for instance, was omniscient for all things on our earth; and indeed in my judgment over most of the things of our own planetary chain, for he was a Chain Buddha appearing on this globe. I would not say that Gautama the Buddha, having attained Buddhahood, would be omniscient over everything even within our solar system, although his knowledge was so vast, and because he had reached as high as he had, one could say by exaggeration perhaps that his knowledge was omniscient even for the solar system. But that perhaps would be stretching the thing.

Now then, âtman emanates the buddhi. This is a word meaning the state of pure waking, spiritually and intellectually, in other words Reality, in other words still the Christ condition, or more accurately the Bodhisattva condition. Bodhisattva means the essence of wisdom and love. Obviously such an entity living in the âtma-buddhi needs no devachan. From the buddhi, from the very holiest of intellectual experiences garnered from former lives on this earth and perhaps of other earths or globes, is born or is emanated or flows forth the mânasic principle, the principle of rising cogitation, ratiocinative thinking; not direct, instant intuition which is that of the buddhi. The mânasic principle is that of reason, a most valuable principle in man, obviously. This is the center of the human ego, and it is the human ego which experiences devachan. It is not the buddhi, as already explained. The human ego, the mânasic principle, experiences this devachan, although asleep in the bosom of the monad, as already stated hundreds and hundreds of times.

For this reason and others, the manas has always been spoken of as being dual in character, higher and low. As a matter of fact all the principles are, but the human ego is really the higher manas, and it is this higher manas, the human ego, which is separated from the lower manas at what we call the second death in the kâma-loka after the man dies. That frees the higher manas which thereupon rises by magnetism if you wish, spiritual magnetism, into the bosom of its parent, its Father in Heaven, the Buddhi, and therein experiences its devachan.

In future ages this higher part of the human ego will no longer need the devachan because by then it will have evolved beyond the necessity of getting its intellectual rest in the devachan. It then will have become a bodhisattva. It will have become not merely occasionally attracted up to sleep in the bosom of its parent the buddhi principle, but will perennially thereafter abide therein. As Jesus said, I and my Father are one. All Bodhisattvas, all Christs, speak thus, for it is not a question of a single individual human being here. It is a question of archaic pneumatology and psychology, in other words that every man has a spiritual principle within him which is the parent or father of the lower part of him; and when the lower part of him has become so evolved that it raises itself into becoming at one with the higher part of himself, then the Son is raised to the Father. The Son and the Father are one. They conjoin into one entity. In the same way, the Bodhisattva becomes the Buddha still higher — but I don't want to go off into that.

From the mânasic principle is unfolded or is emanated the kâma-principle. As the principles develop one after the other like the unrolling of a scroll, each turn of the scroll unrolls it a little more, and shows some more of an unwinding picture. This is a favorite simile, the wound up scroll or the unwound scroll, in the Christian scriptures. The heavens shall roll together like a scroll, which merely means that the lower will be slowly caught up into the higher, and the higher into the still higher, and so forth until they are all for the time being sleeping in the bosom of the cosmic monad.

Now the kâma, which is now unrolled from the mânasic principle, in its turn emanates from itself the vital part of us, the prânas which in their turn emanate the linga-śarîra or astral body, which in its turn develops the physical body, so that we have the âtman in heaven, the flesh on earth. And when the âtmic ray can reach the man of flesh, the Logos or Son of God, to follow the Christian scripture, descends into body, and enlightens it. This is the old Oriental teaching expressed in the Christian way, an old Theosophical doctrine.

Now then, when death comes, the body is cast off. This does not mean that the septenary entity loses one of its seven principles. It merely means that the flesh, which is a compact or compost or compound of cosmic and other atoms, temporarily united to form a flesh body, is dropped. The entity no longer wants it. It has become a nuisance, it is in the way. There remain then six bodies. The linga-śarîra disintegrates very soon thereafter, and off with it what we call the lower prânas. That makes three principles dropped. But out of each one of these three thus dropped, all the essence and the magnetic or vital essences, the aroma as H. P. B. called it, all that was best in it and spiritual, has already been gathered up or caught up by the higher principles attracting it, and they are attracted upwards because this higher part yearns for it. By and by the kâma in the kâma-loka grows tired. Its body is no longer there to exhaust it and give it an avenue for excitements and exciting adventures, and it simply becomes somnolent and sleeping, as the kâma-rûpa; and this is the time of the second death, spoken of before.

So you see the inverse process proceeds. The spiritual parts, the aethers of every principle which can go up are caught up so that even in the entity sleeping in the devachan there are above it the monad, the âtma-buddhi in their own nirvânic planes; the human ego, the intellectual part of the ego in its devachanic sleep and dream; and all the other lower principles below: kâma, prâna, and linga-śarîra and sthûla-śarîra or body held as it were crystallized or frozen or somnolent or asleep in the bosom of the devachanî, as the devachanî is held in the bosom of the spiritual monad. H. P. B. calls these lower things thus gathered up, the tânhic elementals, which, when the ego comes back to reimbodiment after its devachan, begin their work and begin to build downwards, thus unfolding the lower quaternary; and then you have the new body, the new man in the new birth.

So man never loses any principles. All his principles beneath the buddhi take unto themselves the life-atoms of the circumambient world; just as in our own gross way we eat and drink and ingest nutriment in this way, quite forgetting that our bodies continuously are absorbing life-atoms from the circumambient atmosphere and throwing them off again. It is these temporary guests to whom we are the hosts that help to build our bodies which we cast off as we cast off a coat as it were. We no longer need them, and leave the present house or body or whatever we may choose to call it.

LIGHT FROM THE EAST

REFERENCE: Letter LIX, pp. 340-3

When the ancient founders of your philosophical schools came East, to acquire the lore of our predecessors, they filed no claims, except the single one of a sincere and *unselfish* hunger for the truth. If any now aspire to found new schools of science and philosophy the same plan will win — *if the seekers have in them the elements of success.*   — *The Mahatma Letters*, p. 342

THE reference by the Masters to Occidentals going to the Orient to get truth, to get initiation, does not refer to any one School nor to any particular School of any especial epoch exclusively. I believe this to be the real meaning behind the Master's words: When the Fifth Root-Race began to settle themselves, race on race began to settle on the then new lands that had risen above the surface of the Atlantic ocean, and which in our time we call Europe and Asia Minor and parts of Hither Asia. When these lands began to be settled, the holy land, the land of initiation and mystery, already existed; it had already been previously settled by the great Lodge even in Atlantean days. It was then, it has ever since been, and it still is and functions as, the Mother Lodge, the spiritual and intellectual and psychical center to which those who are fit and ready travel for further Light.

Ex Oriente Lux: Out of the East light, refers not only to the rising sun or to the present geographical countries of the east, but to the fact, intuitively known as it were by certain humans through all the ages, that in Śambhala, let us say in a tract of land in what is now the high plateau of Tibet, since immemorial times there has been the greatest School of the sages of all the ages, those whom we call the Mahâtmans of Wisdom and love and peace. From Atlantis journeyed those who were eager for more light to this center, and either returned as neophytes to bring light to their fellow-men who were ready for it, or continued at that center to become others of the wondrous group of superhumans living there, and living there today.

Thus, ever since the Alps arose above the seas, probably in what in H. P. B.'s time were called the Miocene or even the Eocene periods, the newly settled lands of Europe bore their immigrant populations from the sinking Atlantean countries; and these, at least their own initiated leaders, knew where the greatest occult center on earth is located. So that when any particular one in these European Schools had reached a certain point of spiritual and intellectual and psychical development authorizing him, because he was ready for it, to receive more, he journeyed east as a pilgrim, with reverence and in the atmosphere of holiness. Some returned home to their own countries to give more light to the occult centers there. Those who were the greatest remained in the East, and increased the number of the Elder Brothers of mankind.

And so it was through all the ages down to our present time. The Celtic races through their Druids, the Scandinavians through their occult school, the Greeks and Romans, the Scythians and Shamans of Russia, and the wise men of what are now the plains of Hungary and the mountains of the Carpathians, wherever in the Occidental parts of Europe there were occult centers having links with the Mother School in the East — from all these and in all ages, neophytes were sent forth. These neophytes proved they were ready so to go. They were trained in these Occidental Schools to look to this great center in the land of the sunrise to them, the land of the rising sun. *Ex oriente lux. Light from the East.* They were trained with reverence to look upon this wonder-place; and from boyhood up through youth and adult manhood, even perhaps into age, those who were the attendants or disciples of the Occidental occult schools looked forwards some day to making this wondrous pilgrimage to this Mother, this spiritual Mother of earth's children. It was a wondrous thing all through those ages. It was held before the eastern neophytes as the greatest reward that they could possibly have. They were told Yes, here we give you light to a certain point. Beyond that we have not the power to give you more. But more is to be had. It is to be taken by strength, by power within yourself. Go east. And they did.

And as I said, some returned, like Pythagoras and Apollonius and others. A few did not return; they had passed higher, too high as it were to waste their time in the smaller work in the west. Their work had become mundial, world-wide instead of nation-wide. And do you know, Friends and Brothers, this same thing exactly exists today. The same grand hope is held out to our students today. The same possibilities exist for them today. But the wonder is that none can take this pilgrimage successfully until he is ready. Happy the man who succeeds. For him there is the light supernal. There is the freedom of confabulating with the divinities, the men-gods on this earth. For him there is the boundless knowledge, and for him, greatest treasure of all, there is the inestimable privilege of service, service guided by wisdom and love for all mankind, and indeed for all that is, without distinction of race, creed, caste, sex, or color. How wonderful it is!

LAST MOMENTS BEFORE AND AFTER DEATH

REFERENCE: Letter XXc, pp. 127-31

ONE of the things people are most interested in is death: What is going to happen to me when I die? And we have to show men how so to live in the present as to fit themselves for the future, for death, and for the next life. How you live now will determine what happens to you after death, and what your next life will be. The Buddhists phrased this beautifully: every man's future is the result of his present living. A man's present life is the result of his past living. So to me really the question of how to live our present life is but another way of saying what is going to happen to us when we die, and what our next life is going to be.

You have the answer to this in the one word Karman, the doctrine of consequences, that consequences or effects follow causes inevitably, and the effect is sequential upon the precedaneous cause. If the preceding cause be good, the effect will be good. If the preceding cause be evil, the effect will be evil. Just as much as it is nature's law that if you put your hand in the fire it will be burned; it will not be frozen. That is simply what karman means: what you sow you reap, *not something else.* What your present living is determines your state of consciousness after death and what you will be in your next life and succeeding lives.

Now as regards the last moments after death, it is so simple really. A man's life is the result of his past, not of a part of it, not of portions of it, but of it all. Can you omit any part of your past? Can you cut it out of the memory of nature? Can you efface a part of your character which you builded to be your character in your past lives? The answer is obviously No. Therefore we are treasuries of the past. We are builded of thought from the past, which means the past life and the past lives, and all of them. Thus a grown man is the result of every year since he was born, and of every month and of every week and of every day and of every hour, and of every minute and of every second. You cannot wipe out a day or a year or a month of that past. It is all builded into you in your present.

Now apply this rule of nature, this law of karmic consequences. It simply means that what the major force in your past life has been, is going to be the major thought-force in your consciousness when you die. Because it is obvious that ten is greater than six or five or four, and a hundred is greater than ten, and that a strong force will prevail over a weak. Therefore what your predominating thought-current, thought-impulse, feelings, emotions, have been in your past, are going to be the ones which by force of weight, by their energy, by their predominant power, will prevail as your last consciousness flickers on this plane. Isn't that simple? The meaning is not that the vagrant thoughts that may tramp through our minds when we die are going magically to govern and shape our future existences. That is an absurdity because it is against logic and against the way nature builds. It simply means that the balance of power of all your years before your death hour comes, the prevailing energy in other words, is going to be felt just at your moment of death.

In other words, your character is going to be seen by you in the pre-dying panorama, the panoramic vision which takes place for everyone. The last thoughts of a dying man are simply like the indicator of a machine, for instance a thermometer or barometer. The indicator points to the temperature of the moment when you look at it. The barometer points to the change of pressure, meaning fair weather or foul, when you look at it. Now that indicator is not the magic agent which is going to give your bad weather or your fair weather. It merely tells you what the weather is and probably will be.

It is so with character. What your character is will give you certain thoughts just as you die. Your consciousness will have reached a certain state just as you die, and by those last moments of consciousness, of thinking, you know what your character is, therefore probably what your after-death state of consciousness will be, therefore probably what your next life will be. And as character is an exceedingly complex thing, it is naturally swayed this way and that, backwards and forwards, or upwards and downwards, whichever form of speech you may please.

It seems so simple and so logical to me. The prevailing power of thought in your life is going to be the one which will be the prevailing thought or thoughts at the moment of death, because it is the dominant, the powerful thing in your character. It won't be the weak things that will come out. They have not the strength, the energy. It will be the strong that will come to the fore. So if during your lifetime, suppose for sixty years you have led a grand and noble life, and then for four or five or ten years more you have suddenly gone crazy and lived an evil life — which is going to be the dominant force when you die, the dominant note of consciousness? The strong. If sixty years of a noble life is going to be overcome by four or five or ten of an evil life, then it will be the evil thoughts that will be predominant when you die, because it will mean you have led a terrifically evil life in ten years, overthrowing, overpowering, the sixty years of good. But that is almost impossible. The sixty years in continuous thinking and feeling will make themselves felt; though the evil life will likewise never be forgotten, but will be imprinted on your character. Some day it will produce itself. But at the moment of death, this evil is not the prevailing powerful thing. The good in you, the sixty years of high living and high thinking, will come stealing in and the evil will slink away, and the sixty years of good will make the man die in peace and happiness. Thus you see the importance of living in the present.

These are practical, hard facts that we should learn and follow. They are the primordial rule of conduct, and please do not forget it. That is the teaching of all the great sages and seers the world has ever known. What you do you yourself are responsible for and will be held accountable for. What you think likewise, what you feel likewise. Therefore let every moment be a change for the better, a seed of finer and greater and grander things, bringing finer and greater and more beautiful fruitage for the future.

So the present is very important, and I think one reason why people are so anxious about death — and I say this with all kindness and respect for my fellow-men — is that they know from what they already have been taught, they know inwardly, even if they cannot perhaps intellectually state it to others, that evil thoughts make an evil character. We are taught this by our mothers, even from the cradle, that good thoughts build up a symmetrical and beautiful and strong character, and so they think of themselves: I am no longer a child. I am an adult. Death may come to me tomorrow. I may meet it in an automobile accident, in a train accident, in an airplane. I may meet it in almost any way. My time of accounting may come to me before I draw the next ten breaths. My heart may suddenly give up. What is going to happen? Isn't there an answer to the riddle of the future? And we Theosophists say there is no riddle of the future; that is an idea that has come from the materialistic teaching of the last eighty or one hundred years in the West. No such question would ever occur to an Oriental. It is not logical. It is not sensible when you really think about it. For you have the teaching: As ye live ye make yourselves. Good thoughts make good men. Good clean thoughts make good clean conduct. Evil thoughts, hatred, make evil and hateful men and unhappiness. For can you think of anything more dreadful and horrible than a man to be locked in the sphere of his own consciousness, his only companion the hatred of his own heart, a hatred which grows apace and develops talons which tear his vitals out, his own offspring, his own brood? Sometimes we call it the pangs of remorse.

None of us has led a spotless, perfect life. We would be gods were that the case; and naturally therefore, men wonder, because they do not know the holy truth, what am I? What shall I be after death? What is going to happen? The churches can tell me nothing. They just teach me to hope and to rely on a God. But something in me tells me the Divine has placed an inextinguishable hope in my heart, an inextinguishable intuition that there is truth in this world, and it can be had by us men; *and I will have it.* Life is tawdry and not worth living without it. That is what they hope, that is what they think, that is why they are interested in death. They do not want to die. They have not learned enough yet to know that this very plane of earth to which they cling so desperately is the plane of suffering and sorrow and pain and disappointment and wretchedness and misery. Yes, and our School of Experience.

And this brings me to my next point. People talk of immortality. Do you know what they mean in the West? And this is what the Masters had in mind in the passage quoted, which was the subject of study this evening. They were answering these questions to Hume and Sinnett, and they talked to them as you or I would talk to a young untutored child. They did not overburden their minds with what we now know from our studies and our readings and the teachings we have received.

So when these men asked about immortality, the Masters knew perfectly well what Hume and Sinnett had in their minds, because they had no faint conception of immortality. They thought it meant to continue as Hume forever and continue as Sinnett forever; and can you imagine a worse immortality than that, a worse hell, never advancing, never changing, never growing, always Hume, and forever Sinnett, no matter how much he learned, no matter how much he grew, always Hume, always Sinnett? Why, to us Theosophists that would be a consciousness in hell. And show me anything in universal nature that continues unchanged for the fraction of one second: the growing plant, the changes in health, the movements of the planets, the vibrations of the atoms and the electrons and what not, and the changes in growth, the changes in everything, everything changed from what it was a million years ago or ten thousand years ago, a thousand, or a year, or a minute or a second ago, to something new; and, as we see, to something better. Always a movement in evolution and progression forwards. And the historical studies, the geological researches that our scientists have made, show in fact that in very truth there is such an evolutionary advancement if only of form, a form of life. But we say there can be no evolution unless there be evolving beings. Otherwise evolution is just an empty abstraction. The only evolution we know is that of evolving beings, who evolve, who progress, who move. Evolution therefore is merely a name we give to these processes of growth. It is not something that exists somewhere out in the absolute or in the abstract and which pushes things or punches them or moves them. Evolution means growing beings.

Now then, Immortality. Would you like to be forever and forever and forever and forever endlessly what you are? The Gods save me from such a hell! And the answer of the Masters was simply this. They said to themselves: Brother Sinnett, Brother Hume, we understand you, if you understand us not. We know you are speaking of what you think is immortality, in other words your body or at least your soul never changing, always you. Never changing your egoity, always you. Very well, we will give you an answer such as your untutored minds, uninstructed in the archaic wisdom, can comprehend. Yes, there is an immortality of the spiritual ego, and we call it panaeonic immortality, an immortality which endures, that is for all the aeons of the mahâ-manvantara. And those who have evolved or who have advanced spiritually, who have trained and disciplined themselves to ally themselves with the spirit even now, because of that alliance with the spirit can carry on pretty much as now they are, as great Mahâtmans enjoying panaeonic immortality to the end of the manvantara. But then that immortality ends, my brothers. And then they said: Don't you see, my brothers, that an immortality which has an ending is not an immortality? Because it is a death. No matter how long it lasts, if it ends sometime, it is not truly immortal.

Now we know that although the Jîvanmukta, a high adept, growing in wisdom and experience all the time, might self-consciously endure as an ego to the very end of the manvantara — when that end comes what we call the prâkritika pralaya sets in, in which the whole solar system vanishes; its end has come, and it dies. Its atoms disappear. This is brought about because what we may call the spirit or soul of the solar system goes to higher things. The body dies, the body of the solar system dies, the spirit advances to higher things, repeating in the solar system what a man does when he dies. We men, children of the solar system, die because it is also the destiny of the solar system when its time comes to die. Nature has one law — not one law for the sun, and another law for man, another law for the beast or the plant. Nature has one law throughout, and this one law is as it were a body of laws which we call the laws of nature. So that what takes place in the great, is of necessity copied in the small because the small is a part of the great; and if the small could free itself from the dominance of the great, it would no longer be less than the great, but greater than the great, which is absurd. The part follows the whole. Isn't that clear?

So then, what is immortality? The only immortal things in the Theosophical sense of the word are spirit and matter — matter I mean as mûlaprakriti, or primordial stuff, which is but the shadow of spirit. And even here there are times when I ask myself, can it be said that spirit, that even god-stuff, is eternal? In its essence, yes, everything in its essence is eternal even on this plane. But there are times when I ask myself, is not even purusha, is not even Brahmâ non-immortal in the absolute sense? And my answer to myself, the whisperings of my intuition to my own soul tell me, ay, even the gods themselves are but immortal for their own life-time as we men are on our plane. And what a blessing this is. Have we not just discussed together the hell that it would be if I was always I, and never could change to something grander than I? Oh no, no such immortality for me. I want it not. I want to advance. I want to change to better things. I want my ego to become grander and greater, and if it changes even by a fraction of consciousness, in other words if it grow and develop, it is no longer the same ego, and therefore is not immortal. Cannot you see it? Cannot you see the enormous, the wonderful promise, the beauty of it all, that we are not immortal, not changeless — always forever me?

People want to live on this plane and be immortal on this plane. It reminds me of the fevered dreamings of children who dream of finally quaffing the chalice of immortality and living in a body that never dies. They love it so. They want to eat and drink and be merry, ay, and to see diseases around them and to have earthquakes and electric storms, perhaps to be struck by lightning, blasted by it, or their bodies burned and rendered corrupt and rotten by some loathesome disease. Why, they want to be immortal as they are. Wretched life! Horrible. No such immortality for me. I want to advance to grander and greater things. A son of the sun am I, an offspring of the cosmic spirit. There is my home. I am here on this earth because my thoughts and my actions and my character in other spheres have brought evil karman upon me, and I am but a man. I want to grow out of a man to be a god, to lose my manhood, to merge into godhood; and when I become a god, I shall still have, I hope, this yearning, this unsatisfied hunger for something grander and greater still than godhood, always marching upwards and onwards, into ever larger, into ever enlarging, spheres and grander consciousness, deeper appreciation of beauty and of holiness and of peace and of justice and of love and of right — weak human terms but which yet represent a gospel of conduct which gives us hope.

No immortality for me! Let me advance through unceasing change from less to ever greater things. Let me grow greater, let me leave my low-vaulted past and come out into the sunlight, into the very air, into the freedom, into the majesty of the eternal.

MANVANTARAS, KALPAS, etc.

REFERENCE: Letter XII, pp. 66-7

IN REGARD to this question of kalpas and manvantaras and time-periods and Brahmâ's Days and Nights, etc., there is a good deal of loose thinking, and always has been amongst our Theosophists even from the time of the first debate about the difference between kalpa and manvantara; and it is a strange thing that precisely because we know the master-key of analogy, it has been this master-key that has succeeded in producing so much loose thinking.

It is perfectly true that the expression *brahmânda*, the Egg of Brahmâ, can mean almost anything in space, providing you give it the right qualifying adjective. Whether you say the kalpic Brahmâ, the solar Brahmâ, the general Brahmâ, the Globe-Brahmâ — the term Egg of Brahmâ, would refer to any one of these things. You must give the right qualifying adjective, and when you do not, I would suggest to make it the rule that you refer then to our own earth-chain. That is one point to remember.

Now the Egg of Brahmâ, our earth-chain — you notice I am using no qualifying adjective — lives through various and many imbodiments, for a very long period of time which technically should be called the mahâ-kalpa, the great kalpa; and this great kalpa is frequently called Brahmâ's life. Again, no qualifying adjective, therefore the Brahmâ referred to is our earth-chain. It is 311 trillion, 40 billion years long. I am using the Brâhmanical figures as they are practically identical with our own. When Brahmâ reaches the end of his life, or its life, the mahâ-kalpa ends, and then Brahmâ enters into the Brahmâ-pralaya or pralaya of Brahmâ, sometimes called prâkritika-pralaya, because the very prakritis out of which brahmânda or the Egg of Brahmâ, our Chain, is builded, then all dissolve.

However, ordinarily when we Theosophists speak of kalpa, we mean one imbodiment of brahmânda, that is of the Egg of Brahmâ, our earth-chain. That is the real meaning of kalpa, seven rounds; and that period is as you know, 4,320,000,000 years. There is a night which follows it of equal length; just as after the prâkritika-manvantara if you wish, or after the mahâ-kalpa of all Brahmâ's life, there is Brahmâ's pralaya or the prâkritika-pralaya.

It is a very interesting fact which I spoke of years and years ago in the private gatherings from which came my book *Fundamentals of the Esoteric Philosophy*, that the Life of Brahmâ, in other words the mahâ-kalpa, is a trifle more than one-half completed; and note that as I use no qualifying adjective like solar or galactic, I am referring to the imbodiments of our earth-chain. Actually our moon, the lunar chain, was the ending of the first half of Brahmâ's life or mahâ-kalpa; and in the Brâhmanical teachings (and we can adopt this same expressive word) this was called the pâdma-kalpa — *pâdma,* an adjective from the Sanskrit word *padma,* a lotus. The present kalpa, the present imbodiment of our earth-chain, including our globe of course, is called the Vârâha, from the Sanskrit *varâha,* meaning a 'boar.' These are just technical names as the Hindûs used them, and they are very expressive. So instead of inventing words of our own or bringing out the old Senzar words which nobody would understand or know how to pronounce, it was easier to adopt these Brâhmanical terms which the Hindûs had built into a system of occult Theosophy.

Now, how many years are there in Brahmâ's life? He lives one hundred years. Each year of Brahmâ is composed of 360 days. Each such Day of Brahmâ is a kalpa. All right then. 360 days in one year times 100 years of his life means 36,000 days, in other words in Brahmâ's life there will be 36,000 imbodiments of Brahmânda, of our earth-chain. That should be clear. 18,000 such days, or half of Brahmâ's life, as already stated, has been completed. The last imbodiment of that first half was our moon — our moon-chain of course I mean, obviously. Its principles are now our earth. This present vârâha-kalpa or present imbodiment of brahmânda, is the 18,001 kalpa or Day of Brahmâ or imbodiment of our earth-chain.

We know thus what the Life of Brahmâ is, we know how long it lasts; we know where we are in cosmic history, I mean in the history of our earth-chain from the beginning of the mahâ-kalpa. We are little more than half way through our present imbodiment. We are just beginning the upward arc, back to Brahmâ. So the point we are now in in the mahâ-kalpa would represent the ending of the Fourth Race in this Round, a little more than half way around the Fourth Round. You see how low we are in spirituality.

Now we come to figures. I have spoken of all these things time and again, but I thought I would try to weave them as quickly as I could into a consistent whole. What is a manvantara? As you know, a manvantara is the time-period between one manu and the next succeeding manu. *Manu-antara,* between manus, a peculiar phrase, but that is the meaning. Now a kalpa, as said, is a Day of Brahmâ, seven rounds of our earth-chain, and in a kalpa fourteen manus reign. You will find all this teaching in H. P. B., or most of it, and in my books too. Now a kalpa is 4,320,000,000 years long: one imbodiment of our earth-chain, like the present one, the Vârâha-kalpa imbodiment of our earth-chain. Fourteen manus come within that period of 4,320,000,000 years. Therefore just how long is a manvantara? We know that there is a root manu at the beginning of a round, and a seed manu at the end of a round. In one round there are two manus therefore. The seed manu at the end of the round is merely called the seed manu because its round ends there and it is the seed for the next forthcoming round. It does not mean it begins to be when the round is ended. Therefore in every round there are two manvantaras, one beginning when the seed manu began his manvantara at least 308 millions and some odd thousands of years, 448,000. When that manvantara or time-period is ended, immediately begins the reign of the next succeeding manu whom H. P. B. in her *Secret Doctrine* calls the seed manu. When he ends his cycle at the end of the round, then everything is gathered like the fruit of a tree, the fruit the tree produces after the flower is gathered into the fruit; the seed is there till the beginning of the next season of planting, the beginning of the next round of evolution. Therefore the seed-manu actually begins when the reign of the root-manu ends. Therefore how long is a round? Something like 616 odd million years. Multiply this by seven, and you will have almost exactly 4,320,000,000. The little difference of figures comes merely because you have not included the sandhis, the sandhyâs, the twilights and dawns.

For instance I will show you. H. P. B. has told us that our manu was Vaivasvata-manu, the root manu of the Fourth Round. He was the 7th manu and yet it is only the Fourth Round. Now how can we explain that? Thus: First Round root manu, First Round seed manu: 2 manus. Second Round, root manu, seed manu: 4 manus. The same with the Third Round, two more making six. We have begun the Fourth Round: the 7th manu, the 7th manvantara. Actually Vaivasvata-manu has ended. But as this is a little point of very private teaching, H. P. B. merely says our Progenitor was Vaivasvata, the 7th Manu. We are now beginning the next manvantara leading us up to what will be the seeds for the future round, the Fifth Round, and that seed manu's name is Sâvarṇa from the Sanskrit. So we are actually in the beginning of Sâvarṇa, the 8th manu's beginning.

You will remember in discussing geological periods in *The Secret Doctrine,* that the time since evolutionary work in this round began — or sedimentation, as H. P. B. said, because she was writing about geology — was some 320,000,000 years. Now as a round is 308,000,000, how about the difference between 308 and 320? There are some 12 or more million years to go. Just think these things out. They are all keys. When did man as man in this round first begin to be? At the middle point of the Third Race, 18 million years ago. And if you count up these rounds you will see that when the 7 rounds are ended 14 manus will have reigned within that time, because in every round there are 2 manus.

Who are the manus? A manu is the collective humanity of his own evolutionary life-cycle. Yet that collective humanity is headed by a chief individual who starts the music. A band always has a bandmaster. He is one of the band and yet he is the leader who starts the music. So manu is at once an individual and a collective mankind of his manvantara. Surely that is clear; just as the cosmic logos is the all-inclusive converging center of emanation, the one out of which everything issues, so is it with the manu.

You have seen migrating birds as the seasons change. They collect together, usually on some lake, mountain-side, or some field; and when the many hundreds of thousands are there, they all rise, and circling around as if to get their direction, finally either as an enormous batch or in detachments, make their formation and go straight to their objective; and they migrate back in the same way when their spring comes or their summer as the case may be.

Now the monads as they migrate from globe to globe, gather as it were just like migrating birds, so that not only can we speak of a class of monads or a group of monads as the manu of that monadic class, but besides that group possessing individuality as a group, there is as well a leader of that group, whom the other birds seem instinctively to follow, and that is what the manu is.

THE NATURE OF THE BUDDHIC PRINCIPLE

" . . . Once separated from the common influences of Society, *nothing* draws us to any outsider save his evolving spirituality. He may be a Bacon or an Aristotle in knowledge, and still not even make his current felt a feather's weight by us, if his power is confined to the *Manas*. The supreme energy resides in the Buddhi; latent — when wedded to *Atman* alone, active and irresistible when galvanized by the *essence* of 'Manas' and when none of the dross of the latter commingles with that pure essence to weigh it down by its finite nature. *Manas,* pure and simple, is of a lower degree, and of the earth earthly: and so your greatest men count but as nonentities in the arena where greatness is measured by the standard of spiritual development." — Letter LXI, p. 341

PASSAGES out of these wonderful communications from our beloved Teachers are so filled with not only truth but beauty, that one's mind is held in the enchantment of the thoughts aroused by reading these communications or by hearing them summarized. It is amazing — and yet why should it be so, but it is to us inferior folk — to sense how the majesty of truth and the greatness of soul accompanying such majesty affect us so deeply as to move the inmost core of our being. And I for one know no experience more exalting, no experience more penetrating than this. How vain some of the things of the world when we discern the glory of Reality. I venture to say that no man or woman living, no matter how simple-minded he or she may be, is unsusceptible, is insensible, to such feelings — dare we call them that? — at any rate to such consequences of having received the touch of supernal beauty. It is an experience which in itself is worth lifetimes of ordinary garnering of life's impressions. I think that this spiritual and intellectual consequence of having these teachings in our inmost must be indeed almighty influences not only on our own characters, but on our future destiny. I am assured from my own observation and from what I feel within myself, that a man's whole future lives can be changed, because of change occurring here and now within him.

We see the compelling power of the beauty born within us when studying these great Teachers' communications, for Truth indeed is thus compelling when its exposition is directed by Master Minds; and it is thus compelling not because it is enslaved, but because it gives us freedom, the freedom of brotherhood, the freedom of fellowship, fellowship in understanding, fellowship in fellow-feeling.

The statement has been made that buddhi is negative unless it has the manas or mind to work through, and of course this is true. But don't imagine for a moment that this means that the buddhi is negative on its own plane, quite the contrary. It is as active on its own plane as the supreme truth within us, the âtman, is forever active on its own plane. The meaning is that the buddhi is negative on this our human plane of experience and action, without the transmitting principle to step it down to us, which is the mind and the psychical elements within us. Then, if the mind be pellucid as the mountain lake, crystal clear, so that it cannot transmit the non-divine, then we have indeed a man who for the time being is like unto a god, for he speaks with power, with the voice of authority; and none who listens unto him, in his heart can say Nay. Our minds are taken captive, mightily persuaded. And why? Because the buddhi in the Teacher speaks to the buddhi within us. Voice as it were calls to voice. Thought evokes correspondential thought. Truth awakens, by its impact on our minds, the spark of truth within us; and it compels us, compels us because our own best is awakened, and we know thereafter that that is freedom, that is truth, that is reality; and no man wants aught else than freedom, truth, love, reality. That is why truth is so compatible. That is why its authority over our hearts and minds is supreme, for it awakens within us itself. Strange paradox and yet so simple.

What is this Buddhic principle? It is so difficult in our awkward European tongues to give to this almost mystical Sanskrit word a proper translation. It is discrimination. It is intuition, it is the organ of direct knowledge, it is the clothing of the divine spark within us which instantly not only knows truth but communicates it, if indeed the barriers be not too thick and heavy between it and our receptive minds. Ay, reception, that is the point. Can our minds receive? If not, it is our own fault for we have enshrouded ourselves with the veils of the lower selfhood so strongly that the light from above, or from the Master mind, cannot reach our own higher mind and descend into the physical brain and into the physical heart where truth abides for all. For mystical fact it is, that although we know it not, the truth is already within us, here in heart, and here in mind; and we are like those spoken of by the Avatâra Jesus in the Christian Bible, having ears they hear not, having eyes they see not, having minds they apprehend and comprehend not.

I want to point out one more thought, that the inner God works within its own vehicle, and this vehicle is the buddhi principle, and it is just as easy to come into sympathetic relationship, into companionship with the buddhi as it is with the kâma-manas within us. In other words, it is just as easy to yearn for the inspiration of the highest within you as it is to look for the heat and fevers of the lower part of our being.

Now whereas in the old religions and philosophies the God within has always been called a Divinity or God — masculine; the Consort, the Buddhi of the Âtman, has always been looked upon as feminine. The German poet Goethe meant more than mere poetry when he uttered that remarkably telling phrase, *Das Ewig-Weibliche zieht uns hinan. The eternal feminine draweth us ever onward and inward.* It does not mean woman, it means that part of our natures to which and in which the god within works. Our own individual Buddhi is that which gives us intuition and insight and sensitiveness and delicacy and the ability in quick response to feel the suffering, the sorrow of others. It is the god within which does this, but it is what in common language we call the feminine side of us which receives it, the sensitized part of us, and carries the thought to the place where dwelleth the Âtman. It has naught to do with physical woman or physical man. There is a great and wonderful mystery here, and I may add in closing that one more small and minor phase of this mystery is alluded to by H. P. B. in *The Key to Theosophy* where she speaks of the buddhi as being the root and the key itself of individuality. There is the remote source why on this low physical plane some of our lifetimes are passed as men and some as women. By each we learn, if we have the wit. It always vexes me when I hear people talk, as I sometimes hear, about which is greater, man or woman. Which really is greater? It is the uttermost poppycock. Where would you be without your mothers? Where would you be without your fathers? Sex of course is but a passing phase. It did not exist some 18 or 19 million years ago, and some 8 million years from now it will again vanish. Its place will be taken by kriyâśakti. But at present the most complete men are the men who have a healthy dash of the feminine in them; and the most perfect women are they who have a touch of the masculine. The most courageous man is always the man who feels the most tender towards the weak and helpless. If a man has not a touch of the mother-instinct in him, look out, you cannot trust him! If a woman has not a touch of the father-instinct in her, in my judgment she is incomplete.

Longer Articles

THE DOCTRINE OF TULKU

THE term Tulku is often applied, rightly or wrongly, to a lama of high rank, and often with the same conditions to the head-abbot of a monastery.

Specifically, however, and in one usage of the term, it refers to those lamas who have proved their ability of remembering their office and standing in a former incarnation, e.g., by selecting articles belonging previously to themselves, describing details of a former life, surroundings, etc., etc. Such lamas are called 'Living Buddhas' by European Orientalists, although this is not the title given to them by Tibetans themselves.

The two most important Tulkus in the Tibetan Buddhist Hierarchy are the Tashi and Dalai Lamas. Tulku is often rendered by Orientalists as 'an incarnation,' but it should be borne in mind that incarnation, outside of the many and distinct varieties of an incarnating or imbodying Power or Energy, is in popular usage a direct continuance of a previous imbodiment (as mentioned above). These 'Living Buddhas' of Tibet, therefore, are one kind of Tulku — i.e., the transmission of a spiritual power or energy from one Buddha-Lama of a Tibetan Monastery when he dies to a child-successor or an adult-successor. If the transmission is successful, the result is Tulku.

Tulku is of many different kinds, according to the Tibetan, and indeed the Archaic Tradition. Generally speaking, the doctrine of Tulku is in Tibetan Buddhist thought very closely parallel with what the doctrine of Avatâra is in Hindû Brâhmanism: in these cases called Avatâra in Sanskrit, Tulku in Tibetan.

Another kind of tulku is where a human Mahâtman or great Adept will send a ray from himself, or send a part of himself, to take incarnation or imbodiment, it may be only temporary, it could be almost for a lifetime, in a neophyte-messenger that this Mahâtman is sending out into the world to teach. The Messenger in this instance acts as a transmitter of the spiritual and divine powers of a Mahâtman. H. P. Blavatsky was such a tulku, imbodying frequently the very life of, and hence guided by, her own Teacher. While this incarnation of the Teacher's higher essence lasted, she was tulku. When for one reason or another the influence or the ray was withdrawn for a longer or a shorter period, tulku then and there became non-existent.

Still another aspect of the tulku-doctrine, so highly mystical and deeply revered by those who know, is again illustrated by the case of H. P. B. Where is she now? H. P. B. has not *incarnated,* not yet again taken a body of flesh as ordinary human beings have. She is not yet born, has not yet been born, as a child. But she has at certain times, and for one certain individual, with that individual's consent, organized as it were tulku for that individual. For the time being, therefore, we can say that H. P. B. has *imbodied,* or partially imbodied, in that chosen individual for the purpose of special transmission. In all cases of tulku, they are 'incarnations,' or again 'appearances.' If H. P. B., for instance, were to make tulku of a person for a month or a year, for the time being that person would be tulku, but when that particular work was done, the influence would be withdrawn, tulku would stop.

There is again another kind of avatâric incarnation or tulku, that is, a temporary physical appearance of an adept really in the mâyâvi-rûpa. Certain Tibetan Lamas are known to be able to perform this feat, and thus they too have been properly called tulkus, which is the type of tulku that certain Orientalists have referred to as an 'appearance.'

Another type of tulku of an opposite, and indeed essentially evil, character is that brought about by a hypnotist who temporarily displaces the psychological nature of his entranced subject or victim through psychologization or even hypnosis plus mesmerism. This, however, is more often than not an act of Black Magic and fraught with grave dangers, both to the hypnotist and the one entranced. Every clever hypnotist actually makes a tulku of his victim in a black magic sense. When he puts an idea into the brain of his victim, that one week from now at three o'clock in the afternoon he is going to commit murder, or again do some essentially foolish or undignified act — for the time being that hypnotist is working a black magic tulku on that victim, and every psychologist and hypnotist knows the possibility of this fact, though the scientific explanation of the term may be strange to him. Speak to him of 'tulku,' and he will laugh because he is ignorant of the word, but not of the act. A key-example of black magic tulku was what the medieval Europeans used to call werewolves, or men-wolves, and thereby hangeth a wondrous tale — nevertheless that was black magic work.

This doctrine of the tulku, however, is at heart beautiful and sublime, and hence is highly reverenced by the Tibetans. Let us take the example of Jesus the Avatâra: here was a life-long tulku, a ray from a divinity: a tulku of that divinity so far as that ray goes, a divine manifestation, and hence a true Avatâra in the Brâhmanical sense. Again, what was the Buddha himself, Śâkyamuni-Siddhârtha, often called the Buddha-Gautama? He was tulku of his own Inner Buddha, otherwise of his own Inner God. The average man, however, is merely overshadowed occasionally, if he really aspires, by a touch of the divine flame from within the higher parts of his own constitution, and yet even for these fugitive instants such man is tulku. But when Gautama, later called the Buddha, attained Buddhahood, he was relatively infilled with his own god or Inner Buddha, and therefore was that god's human tulku. That was for him, Siddhârtha the man, Nirvâna; to speak very technically he then entered Dharmakâya and this portion of him was then known of men no more: that portion of him was a man become divine.

Finally, it should be clear enough from the foregoing that the Tibetan word *tulku* is one of the most comprehensive and mystically significant in the entire range of the very many important words used in Tibetan Buddhist religious philosophy; and this fact alone sufficiently accounts for the reason that travelers in Tibet, or students of its highly mystical people and their books, so often give different and often utterly mistaken meanings to the word tulku. They fail to take a sufficiently inclusive view or grasp of the subject.

BUDDHAS AND BODHISATTVAS

IT MAY be at first very confusing to the mind of the student to hear so much in our philosophy about so many Buddhas and Bodhisattvas and Wondrous Watchers and what not. But this is merely because the student is embarking upon what is for him a new expansion of consciousness; he is entering into a new field of intellectual and spiritual activity; and it is natural enough that for the first steps upon this field he may be temporarily bewildered. But the bewilderment soon passes when he discovers that things fall into their proper places, as his studies progress, with amazing quickness and mental ease. It is all so simple if we remember the fundamental law of all study in occultism — the law of analogy. What takes place, as Hermes so nobly said, in the interior and upper spheres, likewise takes place here below in our material realm and in the world of man. The only requisite for getting a proper understanding is making the requisite changes, because of the transfer from plane to plane of consciousness and the surrounding material, and events pertaining to each. Conversely, what takes place here on earth and in our world of men, takes place on a grander and more subtil and spiritual scale in the higher and less material planes where the gods abide.

Remove the old idea out of your minds that the gods are one family of beings, and men are some other and quite distinct and different family. We are children of the gods, literally. Each man is, in his inmost being, a divinity, son of Father-Sun; and the only reason we are not manifest gods now is because we have not as yet evolved forth the god within. But this will come in the future. We are embryo-gods; and the gods who now are, were once men. What the Dhyâni-Buddhas are in their relation with the Dhyâni-Bodhisattvas, that the human Buddhas are on this plane in their relation with the human Bodhisattvas. The rule in both cases is the same, on the law of analogical reasoning. To understand it properly merely means a transfer of incidents and facts and living beings from above downwards to our plane, or conversely.

Every Dhyâni-Buddha or Buddha of Contemplation or Meditation has his 'mind-born sons,' so to speak, his spiritual offspring if you like, who are the Dhyâni-Bodhisattvas. Let me illustrate: When a Teacher arouses the soul in a man so that the man can then understand what the Teacher says, and leads that now understanding man to a greater, nobler life, so that he follows in the footsteps of his Teacher, that man or pupil is then a Bodhisattva of his Teacher; and that Teacher has transplanted into that disciple's life a portion of his own life-essence, a part of his own mind, thus awakening the Mânasaputric spiritual and intellectual fires within the disciple. This is what the Dhyâni-Buddhas do to other high entities on their own plane, thus bringing about the coming into being of the Dhyâni-Bodhisattvas, and, later, the human or Mânushya-Buddhas. These Dhyâni-Buddhas on their own plane have their pupils or disciples in whom they arouse the Bodhisattvic faculty, the Buddhic Splendor.

Similarly so on the human plane. When the Mânushya-Buddhas find proper human disciples, they inspire them, infill them with holy spiritual and intellectual fires, so that thus these men-pupils, when themselves successful in the race and relatively complete in spirituality, become Mânushya-Bodhisattvas, on their way to become Mânushya-Buddhas; and this is so because the Buddha-light is awakened within these men-pupils: each one feels the inner god within himself; and from that moment he knows neither pause nor rest until he himself attains human Buddhahood.

Take the case of Gautama-Śâkyamuni, a Mânushya-Buddha. In him as a man there were three or four different elements, and every one functioning: the ordinary human being who was a great and splendid man, but still a human being in the ordinary sense of the word; inspiring this human being was the incarnate Bodhisattva; yet the mânasaputric essence within the human being — which belonged to that human being as a monad *per se* — had not yet been fully awakened in that human being, although, as said above, he was a grand man. And thirdly, inspiring and over-enlightening this Bodhisattva within Gautama-Śâkyamuni, was the Buddha; and lastly over-inspiring and enlightening that Buddha — a spiritual flame working through the Bodhisattva in the man — was the Dhyâni-Buddha of our Round, working of course through the Dhyâni-Bodhisattva of this Globe D.

Now all this seems very complicated at first glance; but it really is not. We have, first, a spiritually evolved human being in whom the native mânasaputric essence was awakening, or partially awakened, thus providing a fit field of consciousness for its individualization as the incarnate Bodhisattva. Then the Monadic Essence working through this incarnate Bodhisattva was individualized as the Buddha, these elements just specified forming the various monadic centers mainly active in Śākyamuni. In addition to this and because the incarnate Bodhisattva allowed the ray from the inner Buddha to manifest itself, there was the reception even into the human consciousness of the still more spiritual ray from the Round Dhyâni-Buddha, in its turn traveling to the human Buddha by means of the Globe Dhyâni-Bodhisattva.

This Dhyâni-Buddha working through the Globe Dhyâni-Bodhisattva might be described as the 'outside' spiritual influence working through the human Buddha; and the Buddha, and the Bodhisattva, and the partially awakened mânasaputric essence, form the triad in the constitution of Gautama-Śākyamuni acting to produce the Mânushya-Buddha. One should always remember, in studying these recondite and difficult subjects of spiritual psychology, the basic fact that the human constitution is a composite or compound thing.

When Gautama, whose personal name was Siddhârtha, left his home, according to the beautiful story so well known, and went out in his search of light, i.e., for the attaining of human Buddhahood for the sake of the 'salvation of gods and men,' in time he brought first into relatively full activity the Bodhisattva within himself. The ordinary man of him, the vehicle, grand as that ordinary man was, was nevertheless utterly subordinated — to be a perfect human instrument thenceforth through which the Bodhisattva working within him could manifest itself and express its noble faculties, over-enlightened by the Buddhic ray. Yet this becoming at one with the Buddha himself, lofty as the state was, was still not enough for the purpose in mind, because this particular human incarnation — that of the man called Siddhârtha — was to be the vehicle of the minor Racial Buddha.

Thus it was that finally, after striving in self-imposed discipline and spiritual yearning and inner conquest, and then teaching, under the sacred Bodhi-tree, the Tree of Wisdom, the Mânushya-Bodhisattva called Gautama-Śākyamuni, as the legend runs, attained Buddhahood, which means that in its turn the incarnate Bodhisattva became the willing and perfect psycho-spiritual instrument through which the inner Buddha of him could express itself.

Thus, then, when the Buddha-state had been attained, we find (1) the Buddha, (2) working through the Bodhisattva, (3) working through the awakened Man, thus exemplifying the activity in a human constitution of the three higher monads thereof, to wit, (1) the spiritual, (2) the Bodhisattva or Mânasaputra, and (3) the evolved human; and this is exactly what each one of us humans some day will have the lofty privilege and the exquisite joy to become — always provided that we run the race successfully. Everyone of you already is a feeble incarnation of an inner Buddha — and you know it not!

Now, here is another important point of thought that I must come to. When the Buddha waxed in age, and the body which had served him so well became feeble with the passing of the years so that it was no longer so perfect an instrument as formerly — a formerly perfect instrument now becoming worn — according to the exoteric teaching the Buddha 'died' at the age of eighty years. The truth of this matter was that in his eightieth year the Buddha in Gautama-Śâkyamuni entered Nirvâna, i.e., entered into the nirvânic state or condition, nevertheless leaving the Bodhisattva still active and working through the then aged and enfeebled physical frame. The Buddha-part of him in human speech, had 'died' to, or passed out of, the world, i.e., had done its work and had passed into the Nirvâna, therein to await its next task at the end of this Fifth Root-Race, at which time that same Buddha-spirit, that same Buddha-element, would again over-enlighten a new Bodhisattva-man.

Thus much for the Buddha-element in Śâkyamuni; and it was therefore truly stated that the Buddha 'died' at the age of eighty years, simply because the Buddha-element had passed out of direct concern in human affairs. Yet for twenty years more the Bodhisattva, working through the noble man Gautama-Śâkyamuni, lived and taught his inner Group or School, as what we Theosophists could and probably would call a Master. We do so advisedly, because it is that composite constitution that still remained and worked which is precisely what the Mahâtmans or Masters are: Bodhisattva-men, men of the 'essence of Buddha,' i.e., of Wisdom and of Love — just what in the West is often intended by mystics in their usage of the word 'Christ.' Of course it should be remembered that the Masters themselves exist in differing grades of evolutionary perfection, there being stages of advancement among them just as there are among all other classes of beings.

Then finally, in his hundredth year, the Lord Gautama laid down his aged body; he cast it off, for it was finished with, since it was too old to serve any more in the manner that was still required of it. He cast it off, as Krishna says in the *Gîtâ,* as we cast aside 'a worn out garment'; and he who was known on earth first as Siddhârtha, Prince of Kapilavastu, then as Śâkyamuni, thenceforward lived as a Nirmânakâya, a complete man minus only the physical body and the accompanying linga-śarîra which goes with the physical body.

How much more could be said about even this one theme of our thought! What mysteries could one not point to that lie latent in the constitution of every human being, offspring of heaven and earth truly, child of the gods and of man. The human constitution is a mystery of mysteries, a wonder of wonders. The ancient statement of the Delphic Oracle: Man, know thyself! contains almost infinitely more than the rather trite and platitudinous significance which is usually given to this archaic Greek injunction. Every great religious philosophy or philosophical religion that the world has ever known has, through its teachings pointed directly to man's constitution as containing not only all the mysteries in the Universe, but as containing likewise the master-key unlocking those mysteries themselves. In proportion, I say, as man learns to know himself, does he become able to unlock the mysteries of the Universe around him, which in his ignorance and folly he imagines to be outside of himself.

One of the greatest objectives of the Theosophical Society, and of our teaching, both esoteric and exoteric, is to awaken man to know himself; what he is, what is in him, what his duty in the world is, and how to live his life not merely nobly and grandly, but how so to live it that he may bring out from within himself the more than human qualities, i.e., the Buddhic Splendor, meaning essential Wisdom and essential Love, humanly and feebly spoken of as 'intellect' and 'heart'; yea, more than this, to teach him to live so that his fellow-men will look upon him as a helper, as a guide, rather than as a human scourge to his fellows, which, alas, so many millions of human beings are!

OCCULTISM AND PSYCHIC PHENOMENA

[This article is reprinted from *The Occult Review,* London, April, 1933]

But the interest of our readers will probably centre on those who are invin-cibly attracted towards the 'Occult,' yet who neither realize the true nature of what they aspire towards, nor have they become passion-proof, far less truly unselfish.

How about these unfortunates, we shall be asked, who are thus rent in twain by conflicting forces? For it has been said too often to need repetition, and the fact itself is patent to any observer, that when once the desire for Occultism has really awakened in a man's heart, there remains for him no hope of peace, no place of rest and comfort in all the world. He is driven out into the wild and desolate spaces of life by an ever-gnawing unrest he cannot quell. His heart is too full of passion and selfish desire to permit him to pass the Golden Gate; he cannot find rest or peace in ordinary life. Must he then inevitably fall into Sorcery and Black Magic and through many incarnations heap up for himself a terrible Karma? Is there no other road for him?

Indeed there is, we answer. Let him aspire to no higher than he feels able to accomplish. Let him not take a burden upon himself too heavy for him to carry. Without ever becoming a 'Mahatma,' a Buddha, or a Great Saint, let him study the philosophy and the 'Science of Soul,' and he can become one of the modest benefactors of humanity, without any 'superhuman' powers. *Siddhis* (or the Arhat powers) are only for those who are able to 'lead the life,' to comply with the terrible sacrifices required for such a training, and to comply with them *to the very letter.* Let them know at once and remember always, that *true Occultism or Theosophy* is the 'Great Renunciation of SELF,' unconditionally and absolutely, in thought as in action. It is ALTRUISM, and it throws him who prac-tises it out of calculation of the ranks of the living altogether. 'Not for himself, but for the world, he lives,' as soon as he has pledged himself to the work. Much is forgiven during the first years of probation. But, no sooner is he 'accepted' than his personality must disappear, and he has to become a *mere beneficent force in Nature.* There are two poles for him after that, two paths, and no mid-ward place of rest. He has either to ascend laboriously, step by step, often through numerous incarnations and no *Devachanic* break, the golden ladder leading to Mahatmaship (the *Arhat* or *Bodhisatva* condition) or — he will let himself slide down the ladder at the first false step, and roll down into Dugpaship. . . .

— 'Occultism versus the Occult Arts,' by H. P. Blavatsky, *Lucifer,* May, 1888

To LAY before the intelligent readers of any modern review which consecrates at least a portion of its pages to studies in what is popu-larly known as Occultism and psychic phenomena, even an outline of what it is today customary to call Occultism, would involve an explication of thought filling an entire issue of such a magazine as is *The Occult Review;* and even then, in order adequately and properly to understand just what Occultism is and is not, such explication of thought would doubtless consist in a startling opposition of *Occultism* on the one hand, and merely Psychic Practices and Results on the other hand. The title of such a lengthy thesis therefore would probably be something like 'Occultism versus Psychic Practices and their Results.'

There is entirely too much confusion in the minds of people generally as regards these matters, and invariably is too faint a distinction drawn between Occultism on the one hand and psychic practices and phenomena on the other hand.

Many years ago, before the modern protagonist of Occultism, H. P. Blavatsky, began her work in the Occident with the founding of the Theosophical Society, the words 'Occultism,' 'Psychism,' and 'Psychic Phenomena,' etc., etc., were used not at all or by only a few — in fact were virtually unknown except to the bookworm or the scholar; but since the founding of the Theosophical Society at New York in 1875 by H. P. Blavatsky, Colonel H. S. Olcott, W. Q. Judge, and others, these words among many other similar terms have gained wide currency. But their very frequency of occurrence in modern literature, without adequate explanations, is the cause of the confusion that I have just spoken of.

Who indeed is the genuine Occultist of today who would be authorized by actual esoteric training and experience to give to the world a clear, full, and lucid explanation of what Occultism is; and, on the other hand, to explain the meaning of the results, mostly disastrous, alas, which follow as inevitable consequences the subjection of both mind and will to what it is today customary and popular to call 'Psychism,' 'Psychic Practices,' or the 'Psychical Arts.' There are, indeed, genuine Occultists in the world, and for the matter of that they can be found as readily in the Occident as in the Orient perchance, but they are always more or less recluse and rarely or never make themselves known to the public. The only exceptions are the profound students of genuine esoteric Theosophy whose duty obligates them and in a sense compels them to devote at least a portion of their time in unfolding and explaining the various meanings of these things.

But, setting aside these instances, the great foundress of the Theosophical Society in our modern times, H. P. Blavatsky, has left a sufficiency of literary and traditional material on hand to enable anyone who is genuinely desirous of knowing what Occultism and psychic phenomena are, to gain this knowledge by a sincere and impersonal study of her works. The extract from an essay by H. P. Blavatsky which prefaces this article is an instance in point, and I recommend it most earnestly to those would-be 'adepts' or 'yogis' who imagine and always vainly imagine that a perusal or study of the exoteric literature of Occultism of the ages is sufficient to clothe them with the responsibilities, and rights and privileges forsooth, of the genuine Occultist.

H. P. Blavatsky with her master-mind and her wonderful literary ability, has set before the world, in the literary material left by her, as for instance in the extract above named, the very heart of the whole teaching regarding genuine Occultism — what it is and especially what it is *not*. Occultism means the study of the hid and secret processes of the Universe and of the beings inhabiting it — of the Universe, which includes the worlds visible and invisible, and the beings visible and invisible inhabiting them, and therefore, of course, also our own visible world, and more particularly our earth, so far as we humans are concerned. Genuine Occultism, therefore, first and foremost, and before any other thing, means a study not only of the structure and operations, of the laws, of the origin, of the destiny, and, indeed, most important of all, of the moral purposes, of the Kosmos, but it also involves, as is obvious, a rigorous and continuous study of men, comprising in their aggregate one of the families or minor hierarchies of beings temporarily inhabiting this physical sphere of existence.

It is of the first importance to state here with all the emphasis and power at my command that the study of Occultism without equivalent study of morals, ethics — which are no mere human convention, but are based on the very fabric of the Universe itself and on its inherent laws of harmony — is a study which will lead the unfortunate followers of it only to Satanism, to diabolism, and indeed ultimately, if pursued bereft or divorced from morals, to the loss of the soul and a sinking lower and lower in the scale of manifested beings.

Who are we? Whence do we come? Why are we here? Whither are we going? What is the Universe surrounding us in which we live and move and have our being, and of which we are all of us and each one of us integral and utterly inseparable portions? In the answers to these questions lies the very heart of true and genuine archaic Occultism, the only Occultism that is worthy of the name, and the only Occultism which the followers of the Masters of Wisdom and Compassion and Peace have pledged themselves to. The genuine Occultism of the archaic ages has naught to do with merely weird and uncanny things, as it is commonly and mistakenly supposed to have to do — nothing at all to do with them, except to examine them and to reject them as being psychical superficialities at the best, and psychical and ethical monstrosities or corruptions of truth at the worst. Genuine Occultism has to do solely with the secrets of Universal Being, and the closer one approaches to the great beating heart of the Universe, the more does one become an Occultist, and the more deeply does one penetrate into the inner sense and nature of what genuine Occultism is.

The so-called 'occult arts' or 'occult practices' which the *soi-disant* magicians of all times and of all parts of the earth have followed, some with relative success in small ways and some with none, lie on the frontiers only of the great truths of universal being. These so-called psychic practices and phenomena — what indeed are they? Merely the action in and through man of certain little understood and very minor powers of his constitution, and this is all that they are. They are far, indeed, from being things or objectives that we should strive after; they are not worth the game; and, what is much worse, they distract the attention of the genuine student away from the great realities instead of expanding the mind and leading the heart to beat with the great Universal Heart in rhythmic harmony.

These psychic practices and the phenomena and consequences resulting therefrom, even when moderately successful, constrict the ethereal and psychical sheaths of consciousness clothing the imbodied ray of Spirit, and therefore limit our views, enclose us within frontiers of consciousness of small diameter, and for this reason work upon us and in us exactly in the opposite manner to what every genuine disciple of Archaic Occultism strives after, to wit, an expansion of the egoic or human self to become like unto its own native essence, its 'Father in Heaven.' Nay, the genuine occult student strives to become ever more at one with the Self of the Galactic Universe, our own Home-Universe — not only to become like unto it, but to be in consciousness at one with it. For verily, as the ancient Vedic Sages of Hindûsthân taught so nobly, *Tat twam asi:* THAT, the Boundless, and thou are one!

Such is the path of the genuine Occultist; such indeed is genuine Occultism. It is an opening out or expansion of one's inner being, of one's consciousness, and a losing or etherealizing rather of the sheaths inclosing this consciousness; it is a developing, a growing, an expanding, an enlarging, a becoming ever greater: in fact, this path is a method and a training which result in an enormously quickened spiritual, intellectual, and psychical evolution of man's constitution, to become not different from the Universe in any sense or in any wise, but to become ever more and more at one with it. Yea, verily, that is what the student of genuine Occultism strives after — a quickened spiritual and intellectual, aye, and psychical evolution; but this evolution, if it is to be a safe, sane, and real path, is along the path of greatness that I have just hinted at, along the path where true inner greatness is to be found, along the path of inner development and growth.

The running after psychic practices and phenomena, so-called, and a devotion of one's energies and faculties to them, amounts really to a deplorable waste of precious time; the concentration of one's faculties on these things simply reverses the inner machinery of one's consciousness, so to speak, and, to adopt a phrase that will be readily understood today, throws the psychical engine into reverse, and one goes backwards rather than forwards. The occult arts are easy to practise once one knows the secrets of them, and these secrets are easily discovered; and the causes of psychic phenomena are even more easily found out — such phenomena as the petty clairvoyance, the fallible and often fallacious clairaudience, the insignificant thought-readings. Things like these are psychical results belonging merely to our intermediate human sheath of consciousness — and the worst of it all is that these are just the things that seem to fascinate the minds of men today. People are running after them, often losing their direction in the chase, if not indeed losing their mental balance; and at the end of the frantic course there looms the insane asylum, or perchance, what is much worse, there yawns the suicide's grave. Count, if you will and can, the broken hearts and distracted minds on either hand along the way. There is naught that is spiritually and intellectually inspiring, there is naught that shines with the holy flame of impersonal devotion to abstract truth, in following these practices — naught. Contrast them with the simple grandeur of the teaching of the ancient Sages and Seers, the Masters of the genuine Occultism of the ages of old: O, man, know thyself, for within thee lie all the secrets of the Universe and therefore of destiny, for thou thyself art that Universe, and its destiny is thine, and thine is its.

The Self, the divine, spiritual Self within us, is the path which we must follow if we yearn to reach the 'Heart' of the Universe. Learn to know, O student, that thy fellow human beings and thou are in essence the same, nay, that thou and the entire Universe are essentially one. This is Occultism. This teaching contains the secrets of the things that are hid, the science of the things that are secret. This is the meaning of Occultism.

What is this word 'Occultism,' and what is this adjective 'occult' that belongs to it? They are not new; they belong historically to the medieval ages of European peoples. Petrus Peregrinus writes that in the twelfth and thirteenth centuries of our era Occultism meant simply the 'study of Nature,' what today would be called experimental science, the study of the things that were previously hid, unknown, secret; and the word 'occult' was then used with this meaning.

It was only later, owing to a number of converging karmic lines of destiny, that the thoughts of men in the Occident became more or less turned to strictly theological directions, and the experimental research into Nature and her manifestations and her secrets had to wait for renewed life, until about the time of the French Revolution, more or less, or until some relatively short time before that.

The scientists of today, chemists, biologists, astronomers, physicists, what not, are 'Occultists' therefore in the etymological meaning of the word; and however slightly they may pass beyond the frontiers of the known, however little they may go beyond the veil of the visible, nevertheless, etymologically speaking they are experimental 'Occultists,' i.e., researchers into the unseen, discoverers of the unknown, finders of new truth — discovering what is hid, laying bare what is secret. It is of course obvious that the mere etymological meaning of the word, while interesting enough, does not contain the sublime sense which the genuine Occultist of the archaic and even of modern times signifies when he uses the words 'Occultism' or 'Occult' — the Brahma-Vidyâ, the Divine Science.

The genuine Occultist of our Theosophical School is indeed also an experimental scientist because he, too, is a discoverer of hid things, and because he, too, plunges into the deep abysms of Nature's heart; but instead of limiting his work and his discoveries to the material sphere, he knows that Mother-Nature is a vast organic Entity of which our outward physical sphere is but the exterior carapace, the outer veil, or sheath, or garment, or body; and that the Great Worlds, the invisible worlds, are they which contain the causal elements of all Being, and of all beings, producing in our outer sphere whatever we see around us.

Therefore, pursuing our thought a little farther, we see that Occultism means an exploration of the inner and invisible worlds of Being, and a becoming cognisant of what therein lies, including the hosts of beings inhabiting these inner and invisible spheres; and one cannot be an Occultist unless he become exactly what H. P. Blavatsky points to in the extract with which I preface this article, an impersonal servitor of the world. This is for the simple reason that one cannot follow the Path, one cannot pursue the Road, one cannot go on to success in such sublime discovery, unless one is thoroughly impersonal, wholly devoted, to the last atom, to the grand service of all that is, and unless one's heart be filled with an impersonal love which knows no bounds and no qualifications of time or place. One cannot see into the inner worlds if one's thoughts are continuously dancing a mad dance of emotion or of mental disturbances, a veritable *danse macabre,* a crazy capering in the mind of little thoughts about little things, frontiered and surrounded by the limited personal human consciousness of the man whose thoughts are for self and not for the world. Forgetfulness of self, a plunging into the unknown with high courage, and with the flaming fire of the spirit lighting the path before one's feet, and complete and absolute

trust in the god within, mark the genuine Occultist. It is verily so.
Only the wholly impersonal man can understand this, and therefore
only the impersonal man can succeed in the Great Labor. A heart
washed clean of all human desires for merely personal profit and all
evil things, a soul washed clean of all selfish yearning, a mind devoted absolutely and for ever to truth, utter truth, sheer truth, at
whatever cost to oneself — such is the Occultist. Verily such he is!

The causes of the psychic phenomena that have been noted in all
ages by intelligent observers arise in the erratic functioning of the
principles of the constitution of men and women in whom these principles are more or less loosely knitted together, and which, because
of this fact, often function in an erratic and imperfect manner. In
such beings the principles of the constitution act irregularly, erratic-
ally, imperfectly, and produce strange and unusual effects on the
human brain, resulting therefore in unusual and strange conditions
and productions — 'phenomena.'

Such in brief are the psychical phenomena and their causes; and
consequently a study of the psychical practices and phenomena is a
study of the lower sheaths of man's consciousness; but one learns
no grand truths of Nature in this study, nor is it productive of any
lasting benefit either to the individual or to the human race. These
arts or practices, and the phenomena accompanying them, tell us
naught about the great truths of the universe; they unfold naught
of the origin of things, nor about the nature of the world, nor of its
character, nor of its structure, nor of its operations, nor of its laws.
Nothing! In what way can a man learn the destiny of the immortal
divinity shining within him by going into a darkened room, or into
a room which is lighted, seeking phenomena therein, or by subjecting
his individual will and brain to the utterly irresponsible and most
frequently evil denizens of the astral world? All such arts and
phenomena indeed exist. Their existence is not in dispute. But in
what lies their value? Is there in them any irrefutable proof of the
survival of consciousness after physical dissolution, to use an old
phrase of our fathers? None at all. No real proof at all, because in
the first place men do not know what real immortality means; they
think it means unchanging continuance of the human soul as now it
is — and what a hell that would be! Fancy being for ever, and for
ever, and for ever what one is now!

The teaching of Occultism is just the contrary of this. Its teaching tells us of an endless growth, endless improvement, endless development, endless evolution, therefore an endless changing of consciousness, going ever higher and higher out of the human sphere into the semi-divine, and out of the semi-divine worlds into the divine, and thereafter into the super-divine, and so on *ad infinitum*. There is no such thing as immortality as commonly understood. The only immortal thing is the Universe itself; but even this is by no means immortal as it now is, because it itself is constantly changing, and its essence is its life, which is of the very essence of change which means growth, which means evolution.

Here again one has an idea of what genuine archaic Occultism meant, and, indeed, is and means today. The more deeply we penetrate into ourselves, the more deeply do we penetrate behind the veil of outward Nature, for the inmost of us and the inmost of Nature are essentially one and not twain. As I have said above, this is the path that the genuine Occultist follows, that small, old, still Path of the ancient Sages which traverses the limitless fields of boundless SPACE, inner space and outer space, the Space-Time of Consciousness-Substance.

No man who lives an evil life, thereby enfeebling his powers, crippling his will, constricting and materializing the sheaths of consciousness so that they enfold with an ever greater constriction or inward pressure, can ever be an Occultist. Occultism demands the highest ethics, the purest morality, as I have before stated, a heart washed clean of all selfish yearnings, a life devoted to the service of all things in the universe, of all that lives, and a constantly expanding intelligence. He indeed who can follow this path and who does so, is an Occultist.

Leaving aside with bare mention the unutterable loneliness that in the first stages assails the dauntless adventurer into these wonderful realms, leaving aside the personal wrenches that take place — a loneliness and a pain which in time disappear and are replaced with a sense of one's oneness with the All and with a glorious feeling of expanding powers — leaving these aside, I say, I point to the ineffable beauty of this life, to the incomparable and indescribable peace, the infinite peace, the great rest, the expansion of understanding, and the self-conscious becoming at one with the Great Mystery.

The old Welsh bards used to sing that to the initiate's ear there comes the audible song of the growing grass, and that the circling of the orbs in the sky was likewise heard as a great musical symphony; and verily it is so. Even our modern scientists today tell us that every smallest electron is in constant movement, and that every movement of a substantial particle is accompanied with a sound, a note, a musical note indeed, so that every smallest atom sings its own characteristic enduring hymn; and hence any combination of atoms forms a harmony, a symphony. Thus it is that even our physical bodies, had we the ears to hear it, would be heard by us as a wondrous symphonic orchestration of music, a marvelous symphonic melody of musical numbers.

"Live the life and you will know the doctrine," but you will never know it if you do not live the life in its amazing and fascinating richness, and 'living the life' means a great deal more than merely following conventional ethics. Conventional ethics are indeed good and important, for they put a rein upon man's vagrant and impulsive passions, and check his wandering and erratic mind; but 'living the life' means vastly more than this. It means, first of all things, an absolute sincerity with oneself, so that a man himself becomes his severest or first critic, then a surrender of all that is unworthy, to be replaced by whatever enriches the life, makes it fuller and vaster in reach of consciousness, thereby bringing into function and play, powers and faculties and energies which in the majority of men, alas, are but little more than dreams or even entirely unknown. And finally, 'living the life' means a determination of will and a direction of the mind towards the single objective, that naught can change, because genuine Occultism means the bringing out of the loftiest that is in a man; therefore the genuine Occultist can follow no man's mere say-so, nor can he ever subject in slavish fashion his will to the mandates or dictates of another. This does not mean, however, that the Occultist has no teachers. Quite the contrary; for one of the first rules or laws of the occult doctrine points out the absolute need to the student, however advanced he may be, of the guidance and help of others farther advanced along the path of wisdom and peace and knowledge than he himself is.

The Occultist follows the mandates of the god within, his supreme Master; but precisely because he is beginning to know self-consciously his own inner Master, he is enabled to recognise masterhood and spiritual and intellectual greatness in others, and to welcome the guidance and help of those others more advanced than himself.

I often hear it said in these days of popular criticism, even among the ranks of Theosophical students, who, alas, sometimes criticize each other unfairly and unfriendly, that it is sufficient unto a man to trust wholly to the god within him, and that teachers we need not. Alas, the statement is but a half-truth. Indeed, the statement is accurate enough as far as it goes, but it does not go far enough; for indeed every genuine Occultist needs teachers, no matter how far he may have progressed along the pathway to Father-Sun. The Occultist recognises a hierarchy of sublime beings ascending from unusually noble men in direct serial line and succession to the noblest and loftiest gods of our Universe and beyond; and he becomes exquisitely sensitive as time goes on of the existence of these lofty beings, and develops a keen sensibility of the fact that the Hierarchy of Teachers or of Masters in the world and above it forms a part of the very structure and substance of the Universe itself, and that his own progress is dependent upon the utterly faithful and loyal part which he himself takes in recognising his oneness, as an individual, with this Hierarchy, and in receiving instruction from above with the same impersonal devotion to his Teachers that he himself renders to those below him.

Yes, all students need Teachers, although, indeed, the greatest Teacher of a man is his own inner god; those who have traveled upon the Mystic Path know this and are grateful, and direct their faces with gratitude to those who in compassion and in the greatness of their souls, turn around, as it were, and offer a hand, a helping hand, to those behind them on the Path.

As regards the average man, he whose progress is not yet sufficient to have awakened within him the spiritual and psychical senses and faculties which not only merit but which will indeed command the aid of a superior Teacher, there is always the wisdom of the great Sages and Seers of the ages, and in this, with the help of the sublime Theosophical philosophy used as a key, the student-researcher can delve as in a mine and thus discover treasures worth more than all the hoarded wealth of the Golcondas of earth-life.

Now, as to the word 'psychic,' or more accurately the psyche,

what is it?   It is a Greek word signifying what we Theosophists,
when referring to the constitution of man, call the intermediate part
of that constitution, i.e., the lower human soul.   James of the Christians says in his Letter, chapter iii, verse 15: "This wisdom cometh
not from above, but is earthly, sensual, devilish"; and the Greek
words are: οὐκ ἔστιν αὕτη ἡ σοφία ἄνωθεν κατερχομένη, ἀλλ' ἐπίγειος,
ψυχική, δαιμονιώδης. The word here translated 'sensual' is 'psychical'
in the Greek.   But the 'wisdom' that cometh from on high, which
man already has inherent within the spiritual core of his being, is the
wisdom of impersonal devotion, is a love for one's fellow-beings, is
a love indeed that knows no bounds, a love that takes within its encompassing reach not only all mankind but the beasts and the plants
and the rocks, yea, which reaches out to the very stars in the skies,
a wisdom that knows no hatreds, a love that is a hater of hate, and
a lover of love.   This is the 'wisdom' from above, charitable, kindly,
peaceful, pure, holy, clean, very sweet.   It leads us into the Great
Peace, the Great Peace which is the silencing of all the senses so that
the inner voice may be heard for ever more.   It is the wisdom which
acquaints one intuitively with the profoundest and largest secrets of
cosmic Nature and makes them familiar to us.   It is the wisdom of
selfless dedication of all that one is to the co-operative service of all
that lives.   This, with other things too sacred here to write of, is
Occultism.

Occultism, therefore, briefly explained, is the study and investigation of the things that are secret, that are hid; but we must follow
it aright, with clean heart and impersonal motives, otherwise there is
every chance that we may be drawn into the side-paths, into the lower wisdom, and, at the best, waste our time in psychical practices and
experimentation; and, at the worst, end in sheer sorcery.   Many men
will doubt this statement probably, and yet sorcery or diabolism is an
actuality on the earth.   Men and women are found today practising
evil magic upon each other by word, by suggestion, by example, by
precept, by misleading and misteaching others, thus degrading, and
deliberately degrading, human souls; and if there be a worse sorcery
than this, I know it not.   The Occultist must have a pure soul, an inflexible will, to succeed in attaining his sublime objective, and a heart
in which compassion, and love its alter ego, reign supreme; a soul
washed clean of all personal desires.   Then he is safe, and, what is

even more important, his fellow human beings are also safe and can *trust him*. A Theosophist, likewise, is not one who talks about Theosophy, nor one who knows our exoteric Theosophical books by heart, nor one who can converse or lecture learnedly upon Theosophical topics; but the Theosophist is he who *does it*. "Theosophist is who Theosophy does," as H. P. Blavatsky once so nobly wrote; and I think that this is the test by which we may know the genuine Theosophist, or, indeed, the genuine Occultist, for the twain are really one. He practises the doctrine that he preaches.

SURVEY OF THE TEACHINGS ON THE
PLANETARY CHAINS

THE last word concerning Rounds and Races and the reimbodiment of Planetary Chains and their component globes has never yet been given in our exoteric books; and this for several reasons, because it is too complex and difficult for exoteric students to understand without certain esoteric keys, and also because the exoteric student simply must have gained a familiarity, intellectual and spiritual, with the sensitive intuitional atmosphere before he can grasp correctly the keys.

Now I will point out a few facts and leave them to your intuition.

Fact 1. There are seven and even twelve cosmic planes; but in all this explanation I will limit my remarks to the septenaries, for these are easier and therefore chosen by H. P. B. Let us then say there are seven cosmic planes.

Fact 2. Each of these cosmic planes is in itself a septenary, because Nature is analogical and repeats in the small what she has builded in the great. If this were not so we should have part of the universe ideated after a certain type, thus presenting the fundamental law, and all the rest of the universe running anarchically different from this fundamental law or ideation, which would be absurd. This is why every cosmic plane in its roots, as in a mirror, has all that the seven cosmic planes considered as a unit themselves possess. In other words, every cosmic plane being itself divided into sub-planes repeats all the qualities, attributes, and so forth that are found in the cosmic septenary considered as a unit.

Fact 3. It is not good to name these cosmic planes after the human principles. This is a very common error which most Theosophists indulge in. The latter are rather concrete principles of Boundless Space, or of our universe as a unit of Boundless Space; but the technical names given to the seven cosmic planes, and therefore by analogy to the sub-planes of any one cosmic plane, should rather be the tattwas, as the Hindûs called them.

Fact 4. Now it is on these cosmic planes that the planetary chain of our solar system, or the chains of any solar system in the galaxy,

appear, run through their different reimbodiments and in which imbodiments each such general planetary chain, or solar chain, has its
septenary cycle of Rounds.

Fact 5. Each reimbodiment of a globe of a planetary chain takes
place on one of the sub-planes of a cosmic plane. Thus *suppose* we are
at the present time in the fourth cosmic plane. I mean our Globe
Earth is so. There are seven sub-planes in this fourth cosmic plane.
In each one of these sub-planes our globe has a reimbodiment, beginning with the highest sub-plane, and with each reimbodiment
descending or progressing or evolving to the next sub-plane in serial
order from top to bottom. Understand then on each sub-plane on
our present cosmic plane our globe has one imbodiment.

Fact 6. Consider now for a moment the matter of Rounds as I
have tried to explain them in my *Fundamentals* and elsewhere, and
I will now limit my attention to a globe of our chain, our earth-globe
being the simplest for we know it best, living on it now. Being the
fourth globe of the chain, even from the very first Round its appearance is on the fourth sub-sub-plane of the cosmic sub-plane on which
our globe is imbodied, remembering that Nature is analogical or of
similar construction throughout for the reasons above stated. This
sub-sub-plane, in its turn a septenary, in other words our own present physical plane, ranges from its highest tattwa to its lowest, or
to use simpler language, from what we may call spiritual ethereality
down to its fourth state or gross materiality which is its present
physical condition; and on the ascending arc, will slowly rise through
the other sub-planes direct ahead in serial order until it reaches
the seventh sub-sub-plane.

Fact 7. Consider for a moment how the different globes of a chain
appear. Globe A appears on its own appropriate sub-plane during
the First Round. When it has undergone a certain course of evolution its surplus of energies progresses forwards into the next plane
below and builds Globe B. When Globe B has run through its seven
phases, or seven root-races if you wish, then just like Globe A did,
Globe B will project its surplus of energies to the cosmic plane beneath itself, and Globe C will begin to appear on that plane in its
appropriate spiritual ethereality. When Globe C has run through
its appropriate seven phases or root-races, then it also, as did its
predecessors, will project its surplus energy to the fourth cosmic

plane on which will appear Globe Earth, Globe D itself, which is thus the component or aggregate of the surplus of energies from Globe C. And thus exactly — and all this is during the First Round — will Globe D give birth to Globe E on the next cosmic plane; Globe E then in time similarly giving birth to Globe F on the following cosmic plane, and so forth until Globe G is reached. All this is during the First Round. Please remember that during this process of the building of the Globes during the First Round the entire Chain as a chain does not move from the cosmic planes, and secondly from the cosmic sub-planes on which that chain then as globes karmically is imbodied; nor does it move from these just stated planes greater and smaller for the entire lifetime of a *chain*. You see how terrifically complicate the thing is; but it is complicate only because we are unaccustomed to keeping set pictures in our minds, and grow confused because we lack words to distinguish a cosmic plane from one of its own sub-planes, and words lack to distinguish a sub-cosmic plane from a sub-sub-plane. We have to repeat plane, plane, plane, and sub-plane, sub-plane, sub-plane, and sub-sub-plane, sub-sub-plane, sub-sub-plane, until the mind grows weary and we become bewildered.

Fact 8. Thus we have a picture, speaking now of a single Globe and its Rounds, of all the seven Globes of a chain builded during the First Round.

Beginning with the Second Round, the mansions or houses or globes already now having been builded or constructed in outline, the evolving life-waves making their rounds around the chain of globes continue to do so in their regular and appropriate and serial order; and the life-waves pass from globe to globe as life-waves and no longer as the surplus of energy which we call these life-waves during the First Round. In the First Round these surplusses of energy proceed from stage to stage, at each such emanating one unit from the compact surplusage. Beginning with Round Number 2, the emanations having now been separated out into distinct life-waves, the Rounds proceed until the seventh in regular serial order. In other words the life-waves are now distinct groups or classes of monads. Please remember, however, that with regard to a globe and its seven rounds, even in the very First Round our Globe Earth reaches the appropriate spot on the fourth or physical cosmic plane.

Fact 9. When all the seven Rounds of a *Globe* are completed then this Globe enters its pralaya or dissolution, which must not be confused with its obscuration or sleeping or resting period. And when the last life-wave has undergone its Seventh Root-Race during the Seventh Round on the Globe, then that globe is definitely dead and will be the moon of its child-globe.

Fact 10. This child-globe will itself imbody itself on the next cosmic sub-plane of the same cosmic plane on which it is evolving. Thus we have the new picture, but new only to the exoteric books, of the evolution of globes themselves, each new imbodiment of a globe being on the succeeding cosmic sub-plane.

Fact 11. Thus from the foregoing we see that there are seven reimbodiments of a *globe* on one cosmic plane, after which comes what H. P. B. called a solar manvantara, the reference here, paradoxically enough referring not directly to reimbodiment of the sun but to a new solar influx or logoic influence into the globe when it enters a new cosmic plane, and therefore called a solar manvantara.

Returning a moment to the Seventh Round. When the seven rounds are completed, then a globe dies, and the time that it takes for seven rounds is 4,320,000,000 years. There follows a rest in pralaya or nirvâna for the globe of the same length; and thus the seven round period is called a Day of Brahmâ, both together mounting up to 8,640,000,000 of our years, thus comprising the life evolution of a Globe on one cosmic sub-plane; and when the Globe has been reimbodied through one cosmic plane seven times, a week of Brahmâ is ended, followed by its corresponding nirvânic pralaya.

IMMORTALITY AND CONTINUITY

[This article is reprinted from *The Occult Review*, London, July, 1933]

Is MAN immortal? This question is easy to ask, but the moment when we begin to examine the implications contained in this question, we are faced with many and various kinds of difficulties: philosophic, scientific, religious, as well as sentimental; and this gives me room for pondering and for asking myself the question: "What on earth do the good people who ask this question imagine they are going to receive by way of reply?" Shall one answer that "man is immortal," and that he lives unchanging throughout eternal duration, or, mayhap, that he lives and changes continually throughout eternity? Then again, as regards man himself — what indeed is man? Obviously, the questioner does not refer to man's physical body alone, because the mere child knows that the human physical body some day will die. What, then, *does* the questioner mean? Who, indeed, is man, and what is man, that one may ask this question of him and about him? Furthermore, when using the word 'immortal,' which means 'not mortal,' what do we mean by *this* word? Do we mean the unchanging continuity of an ego, or the continuity of an unchanging ego, or do we mean something else? The most superficial reflection on the implications contained in this question, shows immediately that there are difficulties here, difficulties of a very real and positive character, philosophically speaking as well as religiously speaking; and until these difficulties are cleared away, so that querent and answerer readily understand each other's meanings, anything that might be said by way of answer is not only subject to misconstruction, but almost certainly will be misconstrued.

Let us, then, first briefly examine what we mean by the word 'man,' and then what we mean by the adjective 'immortal.' First then, as to man. Ask the scientist what 'man' is, and he will probably say: "Man? You are a man, I am a man, what need of further definition is there? Any further definition that I could give you you could find in an ordinary dictionary or in a popular encyclopedia, stating that the individual human being is a living entity of the *genus homo* — one of that particular family of animated beings which at present, at least, holds the sceptre of dominion over earth's inhabitants of various kinds." But does this quasi-answer tell us anything real and satisfying about man — something that we did not know before, and something that answers the lurking suspicion in our mind that man is, or contains, something more than the merely obvious elements and factors which we recognise in each other? Such or a similar answer is merely repeating in other language what already we know. We know that we are men, we know that we belong to the most advanced family, evolutionally speaking, of all beings on earth; but does this tell us anything new? It does not. It simply repeats in other words a fact of the most common experience.

Then, again, what do we mean when we connect the word 'man' with the adjective 'immortal'? Show me, if you please, anything that is immortal — anything, or any entity, pray! Everywhere we see change and variety, movement, progress, evolution, development; but immortality, if it means anything at all, means unchanging continuity of an entity as it is; because it should be obvious to the reflecting mind that if such entity vary, even by a hair's breadth so to say, it then changes, and becomes something else, or other than what it was before such change. Consequently, it is no longer the same that it was before such change came upon it, whether this change be in what we humans call a forward direction, or in the direction of retrogression, if this last be possible, which I disbelieve. Immortality, therefore, following the definition just given, we see immediately to be a dream, a fantasy, a futile vaporing of our brainminds. Whatever changes itself, or is changed, by the fact becomes something other than what it was an instant before the change; and we search in vain for any supposititious immortality here. The difficulty even in treating such an apparently simple thing as immortality is wrongly supposed to be, leaps to the attention at once.

When the readers of a responsible magazine, such as *The Occult Review* is, peruse the writings of a Theosophist, they have a right to know the candid and real opinions of their author; and should not merely be told empty platitudes, or things they can easily learn in popular dictionaries, and in the accepted text-books used at our seats of learning, wherever these last may be. It is so easy to say, as many devout souls have preached through the ages, that 'man is immortal'; but in what essentials does this very questionable statement differ from the ideas of the untutored savage or barbarian, who thinks that when he dies his spirit — he usually does not know what he means by this term, but he has a vague idea that some part of him will survive the dissolution of the physical body — will go to Happy Hunting Grounds, or to a very anthropomorphic and materialistic 'Paradise'; and, according to the state of spiritual and mental evolution of the savage or barbarian, he looks forward to a time when he will hunt beasts for ever and always be victorious and bring home the spoils of the chase; or that he will sit in ethereal dwellings and confabulate with angels or spirits. Other thinkers belonging to more advanced and more evolved races, firmly believe that at death, or sooner or later thereafter, their spirits will be absorbed into the Essence which all races of men have felt to be the substantial fundamental of the Universe — that essence which the wise men of the west have called 'Spirit.' These views, and others like them, however greatly they may be elaborated, tell us nothing of the essential philosophic nature of immortality so-called; although in the last instance above enumerated, the absence of elaboration is due to the veil of secrecy and perhaps, indeed, to the oath of silence that have, throughout the ages, debarred the Wise Ones from communicating the Mysteries to all and sundry without adequate preparation and training.

It tells us nothing at all of value or of worth, merely to asseverate that man is immortal when he dies; because, first, who and what is this being who lives for aye and unchanging throughout endless duration? — because, as remarked above, if there be a fraction of change in consciousness, or in individuality, from what the entity was, at any preceding instant, it is thenceforth another being, modified in direct ratio with the change that has taken place. The entity that was has vanished, and a new entity born of the change that has taken place appears, or is, or becomes; and consequently unchanging immortality is instantly seen to be a mere figment of the imagination, the vaporing of an unskilled and perhaps idle mind.

It is just here that we see that the answer to the question: "Is man immortal?" must *de facto* be an emphatic negative. No. Because, obviously the physical body, which is the least part of us, is not immortal; nor can it be that part of us which we are accustomed to call our mind, for this mind is the very creature as well as the creator of change — and change, mark you well, is evolution, which means unfolding, which means growth; and henceforth we are bound to state that wherever there are change and growth, i.e., evolution or development, the entity which is thus growing and developing does not remain for two consecutive seconds of time the same identical individual, and therefore obviously is not and cannot be 'immortal.'

The inquisitive and inquiring mind of modern man can no longer be satisfied with mere philosophical platitudes, with mere philosophical talk or asseverations. We are slowly awaking from a spiritual torpor and a mental somnolence, and have become dissatisfied with the former 'easy way' of dealing with these questions; and at the present time are examining with rigid scrutiny, not only the foundations of our beliefs, but likewise are examining with a scrutiny equally penetrating and exacting, the very structure of our minds as well as of our consciousness.

Now, what does the Ancient Wisdom of the Ages say — that Ancient Wisdom which today in both its esoteric and exoteric branches we call Theosophy? This Ancient Wisdom states that the very fundamental Essence of the Universe is consciousness, or what some of our modern scientific researchers have dubbed 'mind-stuff,' although I do not like this last phrase particularly; and consequently the fundamental thing of and in man, as a being who is an inseparable part of the Universe, is therefore consciousness also. The fundamental of the Universe is in him because he is a part of the Universe. Therefore, some part of us as entities, as beings, as individuals, is of the everlasting stuff, the undying, ever-enduring stuff, of the essential Universe. But is this fundamental what we humans call 'man'? Is it what we can really call man — man with feeble will and almost feebler mind, or, if you like, with feeble mind and still feebler will: that growing, learning, 'sinning,' aspiring, loving, hating, hoping, very changeable entity which we envisage when we speak of ourselves as humans? Hardly! We recognise this universal fundamental, or fundamental of the universe, as the very essence of our being, and likewise recognise that all the other changing parts of our constitution are likewise drawn from the universe surrounding us; and yet to no one part of our constitution can we point and say that this, to the exclusion of other parts, is man. We are immortal gods in our essences, and mortal beings in our garments or sheaths of consciousness — and the human soul is one of these sheaths of consciousness; and it is these enwrapping veils or sheaths of our consciousness, which are nevertheless palpitating, living parts of our being which hide the divine fundamental splendour within each one of us, for it forms the very core, the very essence, of our being.

I, as a human being, i.e., an evolving, learning, changing entity, would consider it an unspeakable hell to be immortal, to be forever unchanging as now I am, which is what immortality means. Even if I grew or evolved throughout eternity, thus attaining infinite growth as a 'man' — a contradiction in terms involving an impossibility — then what a hell human immortality would be!

Theosophy does not teach that 'man' is immortal; its doctrines, which are based on the nature and structure and laws of the universe, are too pitiful, too wise, too profound, to misteach and mislead earnest souls after that fashion. Theosophy, in the place of this vague illusion of the mediæval Occidental mind, tells us as much as we can understand of the wisdom of the gods, and teaches us that eternal change over infinity, and throughout eternity, is the rule of Cosmic Life; and shows to us how this eternal change is eternal growth, an advance to betterment, going from evil to the less evil, from the less evil to good — as men use these terms — and from good to better, and from better to still better, to what we humans call the best; thereafter only to begin a new cycle of development, of change, of growth, of progress, of evolution, which means unfolding what is within us, after reaching at various stages on our evolutionary pathway the specific culminations belonging to the respective stages of the growth thus followed.

Now then, let me take you, reader, into a little secret place of wisdom. Confuse not immortality, vain word, with development and continuity of consciousness which is a vastly different thing. When men speak of 'immortality,' they mean the immortality of the 'soul.' They do not know anything certain about the 'soul.' They do not stop, furthermore, to consider, to reflect, what the word 'immortality' really does mean; they are pinning their faith to shadows, figments or images of their own fantasy. But a continuity of consciousness is of the very essence of the universal scheme, because the fundamental of the universe itself is cosmic consciousness. If there is one thing that you cannot ever move away from, it is essential consciousness, for this is the very essence of your being. When a man sleeps, although his brain-mind — the mind of flesh — and the astral mind, and the psychical mind, and the human mind of his human soul, are, so to say, what we call 'unconscious,' nevertheless that very unconsciousness is a species of consciousness, so subtil, so inclusive and grand, that our brain-minds cannot take it in; and therefore when we enter it, i.e., become it temporarily, to us it is like oblivion.

Continuity of consciousness is a vastly different thing from immortality, as just said, because continuity of consciousness — which last is the very essence of us — *is* always. The 'human' state of evolution is a phase of growth; the animal state of evolution also is a phase of growth. When a man becomes a god he passes through the divine phase of his long, long, aeons-long, evolutionary pilgrimage; but consciousness *per se* endures for aye. It is the one thing you cannot move away from, for it is we ourselves, our essential selves. When a man is in a trance, or when a man is sunk in deep sleep, when a man has lost all cognizing self-consciousness of himself, he nevertheless is essentially conscious; for the very essence of his being is consciousness, the fundamental of the universe. When the question is asked: "Is man immortal?", this is equivalent to asking: "Is the human state or phase of evolution immortal?", and the obvious answer is, as set forth above, No, an emphatic negative, and the reasons are obvious; but consciousness itself is immortal, whether we be conscious of our consciousness or not. Here comes in the subtil characteristic of our constitution which we call self-consciousness.

There is no death: literally, actually, there is no death, if by 'death' we mean an absolute cessation or annihilation of the stream of conscious being. This is the one thing you cannot escape, and on this fact were based all the teachings of the ancient religions, whether exoteric or esoteric, regarding heavens and hells, involving the obviously truthful doctrine that a man shall reap what he has sown, and that man, when he sows, shall reap it and naught else, in his consciousness, in himself.

I have tried to show you the distinction between 'immortality' and continuity and development of consciousness. Immortality is a vain term; for, as commonly understood, it simply does not exist. If there is one thing which we may say is verily immortal, it is the universe itself in all its reaches, visible and invisible; but we can say this only by an extension of meaning which lifts the word out of what men usually signify when they use the adjective 'immortal.' The only immortal thing in the universe is the universe itself, for it is that which has always been, now is, and always will be, although continuously and of necessity in incessant change and development or growth during its eternally recurring periods of manifestation. Even here, after admitting the fact that the universe is immortal in the sense just used, we are bound to admit, as we reflect upon this matter, that the universe itself, precisely because it is an evolving and therefore a changing or growing organic entity, is not 'immortal' in the usual sense of the word — seemingly a strange paradox! But continuity of consciousness signifies a continuity in being of the universe from eternity to eternity in endless duration. No thing endures for aye, because no thing is immortal, i.e., unchanged; no thing, therefore, lasts for ever, because all things change, all things evolve, which means that all things unfold and manifest what is locked up within them; and therefore obviously all things or entities, because of this evolving, are expressions of the manifesting power of the indwelling and continuous consciousness which men, misunderstanding the esoteric and occult teaching regarding this truth, have miscalled 'soul,' or 'spirit.' These words are not objectionable when properly understood and properly used. In fact they are necessary.

Consider the destiny of man — and I use the word 'man' here as signifying the entire *composite* constitution of the human entity, ranging from his divine essence down through all the enshrouding veils of his consciousness to his physical body — consider his destiny, I say, beginning his evolution at the time, e.g., of the opening of the Galactic Manvantara, the Manvantara of the Milky Way, our own Home-Universe. He begins this evolutionary pilgrimage as an unself-conscious god-spark, to use familiar language, an entity of divine essence, but not yet having attained self-consciousness in our own Galactic Universe. This unself-conscious god-spark passes, as the aeons flow by and sink into the ocean of the past, through all the possible changes and phases of the stream of continuous consciousness which is its core: changing, changing, growing, growing, progressing, progressing, evolving, evolving, taking body after body unto itself, and body after body casting aside, learning in each one this lesson and that; for the stream of essential consciousness continues always. But do we find 'immortality' anywhere, i.e., do we find the endless continuity of a changeless being, which is what immortality seems to signify in the Occident? Never, for the entity is growing; if it is growing it is changing; if it is changing, i.e., growing, it is progressing; if it is progressing, i.e., developing, it is evolving. Therefore, having begun its manvantaric or cosmically cyclic course of growth as an unself-conscious god-spark, and after having passed through all the multimyriad phases and events of its cosmic pilgrimage, it ends the Cosmic or Galactic Manvantara as a full-blown or evolved god, taking its place in the council of divinities; and after a long, long rest, re-emerging into manifestation once more with its eyes fixed on goals still more sublime, the ranges of the universe where the super-divinities are, and which after aeons of evolutionary time it will join.

But shall we say that any one phase or 'event,' to use the modern philosophico-scientific term, in other words any one of the bodies through which this divine monad has to pass, or what is equivalent to the same thing, that any one of the souls which this monad may at any time enshroud itself in, is 'immortal,' i.e., unchanging in character and characteristic? Obviously not. Not one such phase is immortal, and we humans are one of the innumerable phases passed through by such evolving monads who are the respective divine cores of ourselves. If we humans *were* immortal, then never could we become gods, because we should forever be humans; and we can become gods only when we abandon our imperfect humanity, outlive it, outgrow it, cast it aside, and thereafter enter into something larger and grander. Immortality is a mere term, due to a misunderstanding of the fundamental elements of man's composite constitution, and we may thank the immortal gods that the immortality of the soul is but a fantasy; but the train or concatenation or course of consciousness from unself-conscious god-spark to full-blown divinity, or full god, is without break or solution of continuity ever.

There are profound philosophical, religious, and scientific problems involved in this matter. I am not an iconoclast by preference, and indeed only rarely so in endeavor, because I do not like to throw down people's idols, since even a mental idol can at times hold a man's mind by compass to the true spiritual north. I rather admire

the boy or young man or young woman who is a hero-worshipper;
and there are times when I have profound sympathy for the earnest
religionist who loves his god or his gods, whether they be of wood
and stone, or mental images which his own yearning and aspiring
imagination puts before his mind as ideals for worthship.

A noble god in the religious sense is a noble work of man. This,
however, does not imply that gods do not exist: quite and very much
to the contrary. The universe is filled full with divinities in all-
various grades of spiritual-divine evolution; we humans ourselves
are embryo-gods, and in the far distant aeons of the future we shall
blossom forth as full-blown divinities. But I am now talking of the
false gods created by man, the gods of the exoteric religions, the gods
of the peoples. I am, I repeat, no iconoclast, and if a man should
choose to worship his false idols, the idols of his mind, whether of
philosophical, or scientific or religious character, I like to deal very
gently with him. But if he comes to me, who have myself learned
from others far greater than I, and who have at least learned how
little I myself know, and says that he is earnestly desirous of knowing a bit more than he realizes he does know, and who thinks that I
have something to tell him that will help him, then when I get this
challenge I speak and speak openly to him, and I say: "You yearn
for 'immortality' because you do not understand *your self*. You think
that if I tell you that you are not 'immortal,' this means that you will
die when the body dies; but you err egregiously in so thinking. I
tell you just the contrary of that; I tell you that you are eternally
conscious, consciously conscious and unconsciously conscious, as a
man is when he wakes and when he sleeps. The continuity of consciousness is unbroken whether he be active in his daily avocations
or whether he arise the following morning from and after sweet and
blissful rest and *oblivion* in his bed, and yet the same man because
living the one life-time."

But 'immortal'? Is that same man who questions me the child
that once he was? Is the little child running around the room and
playing with its toys, the grown man that he will be, thinking
thoughts it may be of grandeur, solving problems which tax the
utmost limits of his intellectual powers, or one of that noble band of
men who dream dreams of betterment for their fellows, and who
yearn to help others, and who conceive schemes of magnitude of a

nobly social and genuinely philosophical character? Does the little child do all this? Of course not. The little child of the man who now is is dead, yet the man lives; the continuity of his stream of consciousness is always there; but the dead child is father to the man who now is. Do you see what I mean? We human beings are like the little child; the beasts below us are like little children growing up some day to attain in distant aeons, through evolution, to the human state and stature. They too may yearn for 'immortality' as beasts, just as we foolish humans yearn to continue in our state of human imperfection unto eternity, children as we are! But when we examine ourselves, we realize that we always are conscious, although not always self-conscious; and there comes a time — and this is a bit taken for your benefit out of our esoteric teachings — in the evolution of the Theosophical student when he learns to become continually conscious and self-consciously conscious — not merely when he sleeps but also when he is what men call dead; and it is easier to be conscious then than when a man is embodied, because when a man is what we call 'dead,' the crippling sheaths of consciousness, the veils enshrouding the inner splendor, have been largely cast aside and the Glory is relatively free, relatively untrammelled, unshackled, and living in its own nobler realms.

But when a man is embodied consciousness, i.e., lives in a body, he has to live and think and feel and work through these enshrouding veils and crippling sheaths of consciousness; and usually this is a very difficult thing to do properly. When a man sleeps, which is an imperfect death, just as death contrariwise is a perfect sleep, temporarily is he freed from this prison of the brain-mind, and from the body; and so great is the field of consciousness that then he enters upon, that he does not know he is in it or on it, because he is not accustomed to be so free and to live so largely. In other words, he has not evolved to become conscious nor self-conscious in the larger parts of his essential consciousness; and this is what I meant when I said that there is such a thing as *conscious consciousness* and *unconscious consciousness*. A man is consciously conscious when he is awake; he is unconsciously conscious when he sleeps. But there is a way to bridge the chasm of what we call unconsciousness — which is merely a larger consciousness — and this way is by training and by study. In fact, there comes a time in the chela's or disciple's life when he *must* learn to bridge the gap of what men call unconsciousness, and thereafter be conscious when his body sleeps and rests; and in fact in a more advanced stage of esoteric training, he must do the same thing when he dies.

The average man has not learned to do either of these things. The human consciousness for him enters into the state which we call devachan, the dream-world, or the heaven-world. It is a phantasmagoria of exquisite and almost unimaginable beauty, based upon the unfulfilled spiritual yearnings and hopes of the life just lived, acting and reacting almost automatically in the man's consciousness; but it is nevertheless an illusion because it is not the *realest real.* There is something far more real than the devachan, far more sublime. The devachan is the time when the human soul rests in blissful dreams and in unimaginable, indescribable peace, and afterwards returns again to earth. But this other thing that I speak of — learning to live self-consciously conscious when you die — is not only, we may say, the gift of the gods, it is something more. It is something that the man must have earned by discipline and study and many lives of rigorous self-control in every part of his being. It is something *that he has made himself to be,* one of the rewards or compensations of renouncing the low for the high, of giving up the imperfect for the relatively perfect, of subordinating the weak part of himself to the strong part, and *becoming it.*

'Is man immortal?' You see now what a foolish question it is, even from this brief exposition. If I were pressed to give an emphatic and immediate answer to this question and were at the same time forbidden to explain, I should then be driven to say, No! But when I am given a chance to explain and to elaborate, I point out that a man instead of looking forwards to an impossible immortality — i.e., an unchanging continuity of his imperfections, of his humanity which is a mere phase in his eternal pilgrimage — not only can look forward to but he must himself pass through, unending changes of growth, of evolution; for consciousness is eternally continuous, because the universe is embodied consciousnesses, and there is not a mathematical point throughout boundless infinity which is other than consciousness: the fundamental, the essence, of boundless space, visible and invisible.

Remember that the realms of space are filled full with hierarchies innumerable, consisting of or builded of evolving, growing things, i.e., of learning entities, ranging from what we men, in our blindness, call the 'highest' — for verily there is no 'highest,' yet we must give some kind of term to the loftiest that we can conceive of — down through innumerable stages, or planes, or realms, of beings in the visible and invisible worlds, and extending far below man forever. The universe is filled full with gods and with beings higher because nobler than the gods; and we humans are one family only, one small hierarchy collected together in the vital organic atmosphere or being of what we call the universe; and this universe in its turn is but one cosmic cell, so to speak, in the vital organic atmosphere or being of the boundless. Every hierarchy in space is contained within the en-circling or circumscribing limits of a greater and sublimer hierarchy; and this greater and sublimer hierarchy in its turn is contained, or encompassed, by one still loftier than it, and so forth, on a rising scale forever.

IS IT RIGHT TO PRACTISE HYPNOTISM?

I HAVE often been asked the question, "Do Theosophists ever consider it right to practise hypnotism in any manner?" In answering this very important question I must first point out that from the Theosophical standpoint so-called modern 'psychologists' are not genuine psychologists at all; because true psychology means the science of the entire intermediate and invisible constitution of man, popularly called the soul, and comprising under that head all the phenomena which both normal and abnormal men show or express. Modern psychology is really a kind of psychological physiology, and modern psychologists are simply physiologists studying human consciousness from a more or less purely physiological standpoint, and therefore cutting off ninety percent or more of the entire range of human consciousness.

The word 'hypnotism' means *sleep*. It is, however, not actually human sleep, but it is a quasi-trance state; and in this entranced or hypnotized state an individual can move, can open the eyes, can go about, usually with a vapid, empty, and often silly expression on the face like a dreaming person, but with eyes that see not, and yet see awry, and with ears which hear not and yet in a sense do hear. Hypnotism, strictly speaking, is a form of trance. The individual when hypnotized is ninety percent or more unconscious intellectually of what goes on around him. He is entranced physically, and to a certain degree mentally unconscious on this plane. Furthermore, an individual can throw himself into this state. No good whatsoever comes of it, and the results are often distinctly injurious to physical and mental health and stability, but it can be done.

This, then, is mere hypnotism. However, under the one popular word 'hypnotism' are mistakenly grouped other things which should be separated if we wish carefully to distinguish among them and to study them scientifically: fascination, suggestion, including auto-suggestion, mental magnetism, the various forms of psychic attraction and repulsion, etc. Hypnotism *per se,* including self-hypnotism, properly should be called in the English tongue by the word Braidism, because first investigated and studied by an English doctor called Braid.

From another viewpoint hypnotism *per se* is a sleeping or stupefied condition of the nerves in the body; the nerves and the nervous ganglia are practically dead for the time being. The condition occurs because the upper triad of the normal human individual, which upper triad comprises all the best and finest and noblest in a man, has been expelled out of and from the lower quaternary; and you here see what a human being becomes when he is no longer ensouled by the higher triad. A hypnotized person, therefore, is an unensouled person, using the word 'soul' in the common or ordinary meaning of the word. The upper part of the man is temporarily absent, expelled from the lower; and therefore all that one sees in the man are the functions of the lower quaternary or lower parts of the human sevenfold constitution.

Now I come to the question whether it is ethical or unethical to hypnotize others — and I here use the word 'hypnotism' in its popular sense as comprising — and I may add altogether wrongly comprising — the various branches of psychological power to which I have already directed attention. Let us first take the fact of suggestion or autosuggestion. Suggestion is the implanting in the mind of some other person or persons of an idea, with the intent to make that idea control the thought and the life of that other, or of those others; and this is qualifiedly evil even where the motive is good, although, of course, the evil is a matter of degree. Some suggestions when implanted with a wicked or thoroughly selfish intent are corrupt and evil throughout. Other suggestions when implanted in the mind of a second person, or of other persons, with an intent to help that other person, or those other persons, are evil because of their effects, but are largely relieved of the onus or stigma of moral depravity. No one has a right, nor is wise enough in our age of materialistic ideals and ideas, to practise suggestion with a deliberate intention of controlling the thought or life of another.

Suggestion is the attempt, very often successful, to put your own will and your own mind into the place of the will and the mind of the weaker one, the subject. Hence it is evil, because, most important of all, it corrodes the structure of the individual's own moral power, and poisons that source of inner guidance, thus weakening his own saving will. Autosuggestion, which means suggestion practised upon yourself, can be evil if it is suggestion to yourself to be evil or to do evil deeds, to be beastly, to be cruel, to be dishonest, etc.; in other words, to follow the left-hand path. Autosuggestion, however, is always right, and we should practise it continually, if it means merely suggesting to oneself night and day and all the time pictures of spiritual and moral and intellectual strength, self-control, and improvement — things of beauty, of glory, of holiness, of purity, of charity, of kindliness; in short, all the great and noble virtues. These we should suggest to ourselves as paths of thought and conduct to follow. Autosuggestion in this sense is right because it is simply teaching ourselves, it is self-teaching of a kind. We should suggest to ourselves that we follow the path of ethics; for this is simply teaching ourselves to become accustomed to ethical thinking, to love it and to appreciate its simple grandeur. Autosuggestion of this kind, as said above, is but another form of self-teaching.

If suggestion be practised on some other person, it is right and proper if the suggestion means merely the laying before the other's mind of the picture of a path of conduct or of a thing to be done, the path and the thing being intrinsically ethical and wise, and then saying to him, "Here is an idea. What do you think about it?" This is right because this is teaching; and the suggestion does not contain the element of mastery, nor the quality of subordination of the subject's mind and will to your own. But when the suggestion becomes subtle and tricky, and is cleverly insinuated into the mind of the hearer, stealing upon him unawares with an evil motive behind it of gain for the operator, then indeed it is devil's work, devilish work, diabolic.

Indeed, every time one teaches a child, the teaching is done by suggestion, direct or indirect. Every time you make a suggestion to a fellow human being, you are practising, working, suggestion upon him. If the suggestion be good and given with a noble motive and with the intent to help the other, and not for your sake but for his solely, even if you are wrong in your vision of the situation or the fact, the motive at least is good; but the one to whom the suggestion is made should always be watchful and careful to accept it if he find it good, and to abhor it and reject it if he find it to be evil. In this way that sublime voice within us which men call the conscience is awakened and stimulated and its power increased.

Now then, do we Theosophists think that it is right, that it is ethical, to practise hypnotism, and do we approve of physicians practising hypnotism on their patients? Mind you, I speak of hypnotism at present as I have explained it above. I have already explained what suggestion is and what it should not be. One can put a person into a physically insensible state by entrancing the body, and this is hypnotism; and it actually can be brought about on very weak subjects who have already been under the control of the operator by even a simple suggestion. I have seen subjects in the hypnotic trance; and in one case the subject was so utterly unconscious of pain that three long hatpins such as women used to wear were driven into the upper part of the arm; and I saw this unfortunate subject hold the arm up with these daggers or pins sticking in it and traversing the muscle. She had no more apparent consciousness of pain than a piece of cloth would have shown, nor was there visible a drop of blood. To me it was revolting. There was absolutely naught in this exhibition of hypnotic power over an unfortunate subject which was elevating or good or kindly, or in any manner to be encouraged. I simply saw a wretched human being made the laughing-stock of the curious and morbid minds who were present.

Now the question arises: is it useful to do this or things like this? I doubt it very, very much; and in fact I have no hesitation in saying that I think it neither useful nor proper nor decent. I doubt if there be any physicians in the world today who have the wisdom of the ancients in this matter, to know when it is wise to put a person into a sleeping trance, even with the alleged motive of preventing or alleviating pain. The motive may be good, but the wisdom lacks. Such men are experimenting with something they don't understand. I had much liefer see the sick person come under the influence of an anaesthetic drug carefully and wisely administered by a moral and kindly surgeon; much liefer see that; and although this is dangerous too, it has, at least, not the moral danger hovering around in the atmosphere that any kind of hypnotic trance-production has. Who knows what temptation the doctors who practise therapeutic hypnotism or suggestion may undergo some day — temptations of many and various kinds, even the temptation "for the sake of science" to make further experiments? The same arguments in objection may be made with regard to the use of drugs; but here, at least, all know that drugging is much more easily detected and traceable than any kind of trance or hypnotic or psychologic condition is; and therefore the bars against evil-doing are obviously much stronger, because the consequences of drug-taking are more easily traceable, and usually more immediately dangerous in case of misuse.

But this is not all. No matter what form the influencing of the mind of another human being may take, whether it be hypnotism, whether it be suggestion, whether it be psychologization, it all comes to the same evil result in the last analysis, unless indeed the motive be thoroughly good, and the appeal of the suggester — and I speak now of suggestion or psychologization — be made on the sole and unique ground of endeavoring to arouse the individual's own *combative* intellectuality and individual will. In all cases where the effort is to subordinate or enslave the mind and the will for whatever purpose, scientific or what not, it is to be classed under the general heading of diabolism; and therefore I call it diabolic, infernal.

To allege a good motive is a feeble excuse and is far from enough. It is an old saying that "The road to Hell is paved with good intentions," or good motives. Good motives unwisely applied are vastly more dangerous than evil motives evilly applied; because everybody is more or less awake to the latter and resents them and repels them. A man with a good motive often deceives himself profoundly, and frequently succeeds in deceiving others.

Do Theosophists approve of the practice of hypnotism in medicine? My own reaction is an emphatic negative. I will try to illustrate what I mean when I say I would answer no. Disease, suffering or pain, human misery, moral weakness, moral turpitude or ignominy followed by suffering and pain, mental or otherwise — all of this arises originally in the mind. It can all be traced back ultimately to evil thinking, evil thoughts making people feel evilly, to desire evil things and to carry them into action, thereby weakening the body and infecting it with disease germs, to use the modern phraseology. All disease thus originates in the mind; but it is quite wrong to say that, once a disease is in the body, it is therefore not in the body, but in the mind alone. This last is preposterous nonsense.

It is right and in every way proper to try to heal disease. It is right and in every way proper to try to alleviate pain and suffering. But mark you, if that alleviation of a temporary pain, which, in itself, teaches a lesson to the sufferer, is gained at the cost of a distortion of the sufferer's soul, then it becomes intrinsically wrong and the greater is sacrificed for the less. It may seem like a 'dark saying' and a hard one to offer the suggestion that one of the psychological elements needed in Occidental life is a better understanding of the mental attitude towards suffering and pain which the old and wise Orient understands so well and practises so successfully. The results that accrue in benefit to those who understand this are very great. This, however, does not mean in any slightest sense of the word that we should be callous to, or regardless of, the sufferings of others. Just the contrary is the fact. The lessons that we learn by suffering and pain and the mellowing and enriching of character that come from these, teach us the noble lessons of compassion and pity for others. It is the one who has suffered long who is the least inclined to fall under the seductive and very fallacious viewpoint of self-pity. Instead he becomes pitiful of others. It is the old ideal to have the *"diamond-heart"* — hard and unyielding as diamond towards one's own weaknesses, suffering, wishes and desires; but, like the diamond, reflecting in flashes of light every phase of the suffering or pain or sorrow of others.

To continue my argument: Let us take the case of some trouble or weakness which is both physical and ethical-mental, e. g. drunkenness, or the drug habit, or some other form of physical or mental sensuality, multifarious and myriad as these forms are. The Occidental psychologists and speculative physicians have, for years past, been talking of 'hypnotizing,' as they call it, or suggesting, people who are addicts of one or other of these types out of their physical and mental-ethical difficulty, whatever the particular form of sensuality that is corroding the fibre of the sufferer.

Now I ask the plain question: Even if such attempts in hypnotic or suggestive practice succeed, what are the permanent results attained? First, it is doubtful if any result is permanent; second, even if permanent, in what way has the sufferer actually been aided in recovering his own will-power to react against his weakness and to conquer it? In no manner whatsoever. He has been weakened and his own will has been sent into a deeper sleep than before. His moral sense is blunted, and he has become a leaner and a craven. He is now a man artificially affected by outside influences, and is temporarily living on the thought-vitality of the hypnotic or suggesting operator. He has not learned to control himself; he has not learned to conquer his weakness nor his habit nor his impulses; and in the next birth on earth, possibly even in this same life, he not only will have the same weakness in his character, and probably will begin the same thing again, but will begin it earlier in life than was the case in the present existence.

Whatever the motive of the operator may have been, good, bad, or indifferent, the sufferer has been deliberately deprived of the saving and instructive suffering and pain — Nature's natural teachers for those who violate her laws — which would have taught the man, through suffering, to turn from his evil thought and evil courses, and take himself in hand with a will. I mean every word of this. I mean it literally. It is somewhat like the case of the dear mother who is so terribly afraid of hurting her little child's feelings that she will allow it to go wrong because she cannot bear to see it weep or hear it cry under proper control and even loving chastisement.

I am not blind to the obvious fact that all such cases are genuine problems partaking not only of a physical character, but also very strongly of a psychological character in every instance; the Theosophical physician who may be faced with problems such as these, certainly will have difficulties and objections to face in the world; among other reasons he has the strong current of ordinary human psychology running against him. People who are sometimes frenzied with foolish fear, harrowed with real or imaginary pain and anxiety, ask — and naturally ask — for relief "at any cost"; and just here is where the clever, but ethical physician, finds his problem — a problem of an ethical as well as of a physical and psychological character. Now what is he going to do? It is his duty to bring help to the sufferer and to relieve pain if humanly and morally right to do this last; and no Theosophical physician could ever turn a deaf ear to a cry of pain, because if he does he violates one of the first principles of Theosophic conduct applicable to both doctor and layman, i. e., our common duty to help each other in every way that is right and proper and possible.

Suppose that the doctor weakens under the stress and his own anxiety in the circumstances, and seeks a way of psychologizing, of suggesting, of hypnotizing, in order to give the sufferer temporary relief. He thereby gives the patient a mental injection, which is as actual a thing as is the deadly drug given by a surgeon, who, shrinking from the pain of the man he is operating on, shoots into him an almost deadly measure of a drug, till the patient is so stupefied that he is as a mere unconscious log on the operating table.

Of course, I am now speaking of a physician who really can psychologize, or hypnotize, to use the popular word. The result after a number of such injections of the mental drug, the psychic poison, is that the man goes around as in a dream. Careless on-lookers and those who do not analyse, think and say that the man is now quite changed. He no longer cares for his alcoholic poison. He no longer takes his favorite drug. He seems to have dropped his particular form of sensuality; and people say, "Behold, a cure." This is quite wrong. The man is not cured, for the simple reason that what you now see before you is no longer a normal man. He is a man in an abnormal or drugged state, or in a condition which from the mental and ethical standpoint is one of stupefaction. His intermediate or soul-nature has been hurt, i. e., dislocated from its normal functioning, because the reform has not originated within the sufferer's own being; no permanent good has been done to him; and he is living in an artificial and abnormal state, and is simply deadened to ethics and psychically stupefied, exactly as a man may be under the influence of a physical drug. It is even possible that this abnormal psychological condition may wear off in time; or the doctor who has been the 'suggester' or hypnotizer may die; and then the man's condition is worse than it was in the beginning. The old devil, i. e. the old temptation, comes back, but now accompanied by seven others worse than itself; and so far as the sufferer is concerned, in the next life he returns to incarnation worse because weaker than when he died. The man has not been permanently helped in any wise.

The proper way in which to handle these cases, or cases similar to them, is in some manner to seek a reform or inner moral and mental reconstruction in the nature of the sufferer himself; and this can be done by arousing the sufferer's interest, by restoring his self-respect, by awakening a desire in the man to take himself in hand. Teach him the truths about the Universe, about himself, about life, about the way to live properly and grandly. Restore his self-respect and self-command; and when you have shown him the way thus to live, then the man finds his own inner strength, and throws off the temptation of the drug or of the sensual attraction, or of the evil which had been tormenting him. Thus he will build up a strength of character which will guarantee him against becoming diseased anew — whether it be morally diseased or mentally diseased or physically diseased.

It is obvious, of course, that all diseases, once the seeds of them have been implanted, must work themselves out; and the sufferer in such case can be helped to bear his trouble even with equanimity and increasing hope. It is against all Nature's law that anything which has come under Nature's correcting and merciful hand can be escaped from. Effect follows cause infallibly, and it is foolish to think that 'miracles' can be worked. One cannot escape Nature's laws; and this fact to the reflective mind is the source of immense, of colossal, comfort and hope; because it means that if Nature's laws operate to cause us to suffer and thereby to gain self-control, likewise do Nature's laws help us to grow and to become greater when we do right; and give us full meed of compensation for every harmonious thought or feeling or act that we have.

Psychologization and suggestion and hypnotism and any other of these efforts are really mental-psychological drugs; they are not even palliatives; they are stupefactions. Their use stupefies and deadens for a time; but nothing is permanently cured, nothing is permanently healed; for the reason that moral disease, such as drunkenness, bestiality, sensuality, drug-taking, whatever it may be — all these things that it has been proposed to hypnotize or psychologize people for or against — all these things, I say, originate and always will originate, in weakness, in desires, in thoughts, in feelings, leading one and all to corresponding acts.

Therefore, hard as the saying may sound at first hearing, I repeat that my own feeling is that it would be unethical for a Theosophical physician ever to resort to the practice of hypnotism or psychologization or suggestion in the senses popularly understood and so often accepted as proper. A physician should be a physician of the soul or of the heart, as well as of the body, i. e. an ethical as well as a physical practitioner; and the more successful a physician is in being such, the larger and more lucrative will become his practice. Sufferers will turn instinctively to the high-minded doctor who can help them in their minds and in their hearts, as well as in their bodies. Nor is this ethical help that I speak of a matter of mere irritating preachments. Such preachments would be fatal to the physician's objective, and would simply make him become known as an unconscionable bore and nuisance.

In conclusion, remember that hypnotism is brought about by an expelling of the higher part, the nobler part, of the man out of the lower quaternary of his constitution; so that the man thereafter goes around in a state which we can call a waking sleep, i. e. in a trance; and therefore he is stupid, temporarily unensouled. Psychologization or suggestion, again, when done with an evil motive, means the planting of seeds of thought with power behind them into the mind of the sufferer so that they stick like burrs in the psychological apparatus of him who receives them. And thus the sufferer under the control of the thought not his own, of the idea not his own, is no longer fully self-conscious, no longer in control of his own life, no longer growing in strength of character and in power of moral decision; but becomes with each repetitive occurrence of the suggestion more largely enslaved to the exterior will. Hence it is that such psychologization or suggestion also finally results in expelling the man's own soul or perhaps a better term is dislocating a man's own soul; so that no longer does it function either normally or with power. Here, too, is a case where the sufferer, by means of the deliberate act of the psychologizer or suggester, becomes unensouled, for the time being at least 'soulless'; and by every canon of ethics or justice can henceforth no longer be considered to be morally or mentally fully responsible for what he thinks or does. He is a mere psychologic machine to the extent that the external power controls him.

Doubtless no two cases are identic; each case has to be judged in accordance with the respective factors involved. But in any case, to the Occidental world, the fields of human consciousness are virtually a *terra incognita* — and for this reason western experimenters are wandering in Cimmerian darkness.

I have touched only indirectly upon another immensely important feature involved in each and in every case of hypnotic or suggestive control. I mean what we Theosophists call the karman of the matter. The Universe throughout all its parts is an organic whole, and all its parts in consequence are mutually held and bound by the laws which prevail throughout. In other words, no part can act unto itself alone, or escape responsibility for what it does, particularly so when acting with choice and with will. The disturber of Nature's harmonies, indeed an actor in any wise or after any manner whatsoever, becomes, and is held by Nature's own automatic operations, immediately responsible for what the disturber has done, ay, or even thought or felt. Consequently, he who changes the thought, feeling, will, or displaces the thought, feeling, will, of another, *de facto* becomes subject to the law which he himself consciously or unconsciously invokes by his action, and will feel the reflex current thereof at an early or at a later day. Listen to the words of the LAW which prevails throughout the Universe and which none can set aside nor ever stay: "As ye mete, it shall be meted unto you"; and "What ye sow ye shall reap." Motive affects the result even greatly, but motive is no excuse nor can it stay the unerring and terrible hand of Nature's karmic justice.

Questions

and Answers

The Three Fundamental Propositions of "The Secret Doctrine"

H. P. B. mentions in the Proem of The Secret Doctrine *that it is necessary to gain understanding of the three fundamental principles. Could you tell us what these three fundamental principles are and what they mean? I find it extremely difficult to comprehend them.*

The three fundamental principles as H. P. B. outlines them in *The Secret Doctrine* are the very basis, the three foundation-stones, on which the entire structure of the modern presentation of the Ancient Wisdom rests. If you get these three ideas in your mind, you will have thereafter an outline, a skeleton-frame, of ideas.

H. P. B. writes as follows on page 14 of the first volume of *The Secret Doctrine:* "The Secret Doctrine establishes three fundamental propositions: (a) An Omnipresent, Eternal, Boundless, and Immutable PRINCIPLE [This does not mean immutable in action, but does mean immutable in its own essence.] on which all speculation is impossible, since it transcends the power of human conception and could only be dwarfed by any human expression or similitude."

H. P. B. writes practically three pages on this first fundamental proposition or principle; and it is one which I have devoted much space to in my *Fundamentals of the Esoteric Philosophy,* because it is the least understood by most students. Some of our students have imagined that this principle is a god of a kind, or a spirit of a kind, and it is neither — at least not in any usual conception of these terms. Some people have imagined, contrariwise, that it is a mere abstraction, a usage of words only in order to cover or to conceal or to disguise a hiatus in the Ancient Wisdom or the mystical thought of the Masters; and this idea is simply preposterous. It is called a 'principle,' simply because there is no word in the English language which accurately describes it.

To illustrate: What is the 'principle' of a triangle? A triangle is a geometrical figure which has three straight sides joined at their ends and enclosing space. A 'principle' of a thing describes its *esse,* its essence, its characteristic; and consequently there is otherwise no limiting description here. H. P. B. says herself that this principle in its *esse* is beyond the reach of human thought. Obviously true, because it is Boundless Infinitude; it is *That, Tat* to use the words of the Hindû Veda. Consequently it is everywhere, it is all that is, all that ever was, all that ever will be, the fountain of everything, the great source, the inexpressible source, the in-

effable source, from which everything flows forth, and into which everything finally returns, atoms and gods, worlds and everything on and in
them. It is boundless life, boundless space, boundless duration, frontierless and beginningless, and without limiting extensional dimensions of any
kind, because it contains them all. How can you describe this indescribable
THAT?   This, then, is the first principle that H. P. B. postulates as one of
the three fundamental propositions.

There is not a word about 'God' here. It is not personal nor is it impersonal — this 'principle' as H. P. B. calls it — because it includes both
personalities and impersonalities and is beyond both. It is not spirit, and
it is not non-spirit, because it includes and is beyond both. It is not time
and it is not non-time, because it includes and is beyond both. These statements are correct because all these ideas are human ideas connected with
what modern scientific philosophers would call 'space-time' and 'events.'
Yet the very core of the core of the heart of the heart of each one of us,
and indeed of every entity and thing in boundless infinitude, is this principle. It is what we essentially are as individuals and collectively. Call
it the kosmic life and you won't err; only in this case for the adjective
'kosmic' you must extend your conception to include boundless infinitude.
Call it the kosmic intelligence and you won't err, but in this case it is not
only the intelligence of a Solar System nor of a Galaxy nor of a thousand
billion Galaxies, but all these and infinitely more; nothing manifested,
however vast, even approaches the ends of it, because it has no end.

This idea cuts directly at the root of all sectarian religious thought; it
does away with all human religious postulates regarding divinity and all
human man-made gods, no matter how great. If properly understood it
washes our minds clean of all egoisms; all things sink into utter insigni-
ficance beside the adumbrations of a conception that we may have of this
— and yet it is the essence of ourselves! It is the selves of the gods; it is
the selves of the Universes; it is the selves of the Galaxies, the selves of the
great Spaces, of the great fields of the spaces of frontierless Space; it is all
the inner worlds and all the outer worlds and that mysterious, that awful,
indescribable 'something' which surrounds and permeates and enfolds and
encloses and which flashes through all. It is all energy that is, it is all substance that is, it is all destiny that is, it is everything at all times and in all
places and everywhere. How can you give the name of 'god' to THAT?
This, then, is an outline of the first fundamental proposition.

H. P. B.'s second fundamental proposition she describes as follows on
page 16 of the first volume of *The Secret Doctrine*, to wit: "(b) The Eternity of the Universe *in toto*," [not any one Universe, but what I have often
spoken of as boundless and frontierless infinitude, inner infinitude as well

as outer, the 'Universe' in the sense of a kosmic organism, but an organism which has no beginning and no ending, or rather it is organisms within organisms, kosmic cause within and beyond kosmic cause.] "The Eternity of the Universe *in toto* as a boundless plane; [here H. P. B. is describing only the astral-vital-physical] periodically 'the playground of numberless Universes . . .' [mark you this] The Eternity of the Universe . . . periodically 'the playground of numberless Universes incessantly manifesting and disappearing,' called 'the manifesting stars,' and the 'sparks of Eternity.' 'The Eternity of the Pilgrim' is like a wink of the Eye of Self-Existence (Book of Dzyan)."

By the way, I might add here that this term *Dzyan* is but the Senzar term of what in Sanskrit meant spiritual meditation; the same word is used in the phrase Dhyâni-Buddhas, the Buddhas immersed in Dhyâna. *Dhyâna* therefore is the Sanskrit form of the Senzar *Dzyan*. " 'The appearance and disappearance of Worlds is like a regular tidal ebb and flux and reflux.'

"This second assertion of the Secret Doctrine is the absolute universality of that law of periodicity, of flux and reflux, ebb and flow, which physical science has observed and recorded in all departments of nature. An alternation such as that of Day and Night, Life and Death, Sleeping and Waking, is a fact so common, so perfectly universal and without exception, that it is easy to comprehend that in it we see one of the absolutely fundamental laws of the universe." — in the boundless, in the infinite, frontierless, spaces of Space.

The second proposition sets forth that there appear from time to time in regular and periodic successions, like an ebb and flow, worlds and beings continuous throughout eternity, Manvantara and Pralaya: the appearance and disappearance of incalculable numbers of Universes in all grades, in all degrees and stages, of spiritual evolution and of vital-astral-physical evolution. I have often marvelled that here, in explaining what the second fundamental proposition is, H. P. B. should have limited it — at least in appearance — to the astral-physical side only, because actually this is an insufficient exposition of this amazing proposition which is equivalent to an intellectual revelation; but I dare say, and in fact I know, that our beloved H. P. B. thought that to give all the truth concerning this proposition in *The Secret Doctrine,* which was the first instalment of the esoteric teaching, would be too much to deliver at one time and in an era when men had no real idea of inner worlds, of spiritual and ethereal worlds, except as taught vaguely by the Christians and unfortunately and inaccurately by the spiritists. In fact, one can only commend her for her reserve in this respect.

This ebb and flow, this flux and reflux, this appearance and disappearance, of Solar Systems, of Galaxies, and of individual suns or planets, is as evident in the interior planes and spheres, in the invisible realms, as it is on and in our own astral-vital-physical plane. Periodicity or universal cyclical action is the key-note, the key-thought, therefore, of the second great fundamental principle.

First, then, we have as the primordial 'principle,' the vast and frontierless Boundless in which appear from time to time in periodical successions worlds and galaxies of worlds, galaxies and hierarchies of galaxies, coming and going throughout eternity; and man's various reimbodiments, not only on this plane on this globe but throughout the Planetary Chain and indeed also in the Outer Rounds — and you know what these are, some of you at least, if you have studied *Fundamentals* — man's reimbodiments, I repeat, are an instance in the small of the same universal law which rules everything within the mighty Whole.

Isn't it obvious that a part of a whole cannot contain something that the whole has not? Isn't this clear? Therefore, whatever the part contains the whole must have, otherwise it could not appear in a part of the whole. Conversely, whatever the whole has, the part has — unmanifest it may be, but latent there and some day to appear.

All is within each one of us. Ah! your destiny is sublime beyond all human imagining; for I tell you, Companions, that you and the Boundless are fundamentally, essentially, one. You are not merely separable parts of a whole, not merely one with it as separable parts, distinct parts, as in a loose union, but are essentially the same with the Boundless. There is no fundamental or essential difference whatsoever. The infinite, the Boundless, and you, are the same in essence, are identic in essence; and therefore you merely manifest, as manifesting atoms as it were, some of the energies and powers and forces that the Boundless contains and which therefore you contain manifest or unmanifest.

Now comes the third fundamental proposition — and this is in some respects and perhaps to some students the most wonderful of all three, to which the observations that I have just made naturally lead us in thought. This proposition appears on pages 17 and 18 of the first volume of *The Secret Doctrine.* "The fundamental identity of all Souls with the Universal Over-Soul, [which is what I have just told you] the latter being itself an aspect of the Unknown Root [the Boundless, therefore you are the Boundless]; and the obligatory pilgrimage for every Soul — a spark of the former — through the Cycle of Incarnation (or 'Necessity') in accordance with Cyclic and Karmic law, [which is the second fundamental proposition] during the whole term." Then H. P. B. continues to define.

It seems to us now greatly to be regretted that at this point in the writing of *The Secret Doctrine,* although it is done elsewhere, H. P. B. did not point out that 'Soul' is used here in the sense of fundamental Self, although the *S* is printed with a capital letter, meaning here not the lower self, not the human self, not the beast-self — the animal self — but the god-self, the super-god self, in other words the Paramâtman, that fundamental essential selfhood which is the heart of being and therefore which is your heart of being. This is what is meant by 'Soul' here, the fundamental identity not of your weak, vacillating, poor human soul or mind, which is but a shadow of the reality, but the fundamental identity of the god within you, and of the super-god within you, and of the super, super, super, super-god within you, which is the core of the core of the core of you — with this indescribable sublimity called the 'Boundless,' when manifesting in its form of 'Universal Over-Soul.' Note here the very important and profoundly interesting distinction drawn by our great H. P. B., and so rightly drawn, between the 'Boundless' without qualifying adjective which is sheer frontierless infinity and eternity, and that aspect of the Boundless in its form of manifestation which in ordinary human language can be described as the ensouled Universe, or as H. P. B. puts it 'the Universal Over-Soul.' This distinction is of the first importance for a proper understanding of what perhaps we may call kosmic pneumatology and psychology.

These three fundamental propositions are the very heart of the Ancient Wisdom, and therefore of Occultism, no matter in what words or after what human fashion we learn these propositions and take them into our consciousness. In order to make progress in occult studies, that is in the studies of esoteric philosophy, we must have these ideas thoroughly familiar to us, as parts of our consciousness, so that our mind instinctively reverts to them as invaluable touchstones in our studies and hours of quiet reflexion. The first is the Boundless; then second the periodical appearance of the Universes and of the gods; then third the fundamental identity of every entity, of every thing, with the Boundless. Here are the three propositions in brief.

FINGERPRINTS AND REINCARNATION

Is there any basis of truth in the idea that an ego might be traced through several successive incarnations by means of the fingerprints or other such marks in the successive physical bodies?

I am quite sure that fundamentally your idea is not only sound but absolutely correct. The great difficulty would be to find the thumb-print or finger-prints from former lives of an individual. It is perfectly true that for Theosophical or occult reasons the markings of the thumb and fingers of each body taken up by a reincarnating ego would very closely parallel and perhaps are almost identic with the dactylographic markings on the thumb and fingers of the preceding body of the same ego. Any changes that would be found, if we could compare two such markings, would be those brought about by evolutional changes in the soul producing modifications in the body, and also the hereditary influences from the ancestry which would tend to modify markings of such character.

MAHÂ-YUGAS IN A MANVANTARA

How can we reconcile the 27 or 28 Mahâ-yugas with the 71 or 72 Mahâ-yugas spoken of by H. P. B.?

The 27 or 28 Mahâ-yugas refers to the Vaivasvata Manu in so far as it concerns our Globe D only. Now in regard to the figure 71: In one manvantara of 306,720,000 years there are just 71 Mahâ-yugas. This manvantara of Vaivasvata began on Globe A in this Round, then finished there and passed to Globe B; finished there and passed on to Globe C; and reached its end at the middle point of the Fourth Root-Race on our Globe D, making therefore 71 Mahâ-yugas. There are about 2 Mahâ-yugas more which have run since the middle of the Fourth Root-Race when that manvantara reached its chronological end, which means that 72 Mahâ-yugas have elapsed since the beginning of this manvantara, and we are now in the 73rd Mahâ-yuga.

Another point in corroboration of this is H. P. B.'s figure of 320,000,000 years. She points out that 320,000,000 years have elapsed since the beginning of sedimentation on our earth in this Round. Thus, if you add to the 71 Mahâ-yugas of the Vaivasvata Manu, totalling 306,720,000 years, another 2 Mahâ-yugas, or about 9,000,000 years, you come very close to the 319,000,000 or 320,000,000 years as estimated by H. P. B.

LIFE-ENERGIES FROM MOON TO EARTH

Could you explain how the life-energies of the Moon-chain are transmitted to its child, the Earth-chain, at the death of the former?

When the Moon-chain died, each of its globes sent out its life-forces to make the respective laya-centers of the earth-series; as for instance: Moon Globe A sent out its life-forces to laya-center A, later to be the Globe A of the Earth.

Now after nirvâna when the time came for the building of the different globes of the Earth-chain the first of these laya-centers to awaken into manifestation was laya-A of the Earth-chain, to become Globe A of the

Earth-chain. And this received all the impulses of all the waves coming from the nirvâna, and it passed through its seven cycles during the First Round and then projected its surplus to laya-center B of the Earth-chain which in similar manner received all the remaining impulses and built itself, ran through its seven cycles during the First Round and projected its surplus of life, which means all the remaining impulses to laya-C of the Earth-chain which went through the same procedures. And thus all the laya-centers of the Earth-chain finally became the preparatory globes of the First Round.

Briefly, remember that the globes of the Earth-chain are not actually in building until the different classes or life-waves come out of their nirvâna, and coming down into the lower realms begin to build the globes. Up to that time they were just sleeping centers, laya-centers. These laya-centers were inaugurated when the Moon died and were, so to say, crystallized or placed in position in space by the lowest parts of the life-waves which came over from the Moon. This lowest part is not the physical part, which latter slowly disintegrated as a corpse. Then when the life-waves came out of the nirvâna — seven or ten or twelve classes according to the way you reckon — they naturally entered the most ethereal of the laya-centers and these built up Globe A and then the matter proceeds as I have tried to explain.

Thus it is that the Moon projects its essences, and the different globes of the Earth help in building each other.

The laya-centers are formed or rather effected by the dying Moon, but do not become active until the hierarchies come out of their long nirvâna and begin to build the Earth-chain. This does not mean that there is no activity or motion there, because the physical life-atoms of the Moon are constantly peregrinating just as the physical atoms of a man's body when he dies continue peregrinating through all the kingdoms until the reincarnating ego returns to earth-life.

THE SCIENTIFIC REASON FOR NOT JUDGING OTHERS

Could you give us, so that we shall never forget it, the really Theosophical scientific reason why we should not judge others? It is not the sentimental reason I am asking for, but the real scientific, technical reason.

There are many reasons — more than one. There is the ethical reason. It is wrong to judge others, because what right have I to judge my brother? I am not wise enough. I think I see that he is doing right and I judge him, and I say he is a good man. Well, that is all right because I do him no harm. But I see my brother, I think he is doing wrong, and I judge him, and I say that he is a bad man. Now that is not right.   I am not wise enough.   If I see him doing an act which I know is wrong, it is right to judge the act, but not to judge the man, because we do not know what the motive was. We have no right to sit in judgment on our brothers.

The scientific reason is that the man who judges others warps, shrivels, distorts, twists, his own mind; because usually when we judge our brothers, adversely that is, unkindly, we imprint on our own souls a mark of unkindness, and distort the fabric of our consciousness equivalently. We are playing with fire which burns us. Do not judge others, for by your own judgment you will be judged, because you are imprinting on your soul memories of your judgments, and distorting your character which thereafter will act in a distorted way; and the same thing you will become. If, for instance, I judge my brother as being a dishonest man — I will use this as an example — then on my own soul I leave a print of dishonesty because I had this thought so strongly in my mind it prints itself in my own mind, in my own soul; and my own mind becomes dishonest because I think so much about it, and because it automatically follows the psychic twist that I have given to it. I warp, distort, twist, my own soul. And if you do this repeatedly and continuously and do not do other noble acts, kindly acts, that at least will balance or neutralize, Nature's own judgment-balance will lean down and you will thus be weighed in your own scales of judgment, and found wanting.

By your own acts you will be judged. Karman will find in the mind which has misjudged others continuously, a distorted, warped, twisted, weakened character. Thoughts of love make us beautiful. Thoughts of hatred make us ugly. Consequently, when we judge others unkindly, because these are thoughts of evil and hatred, we become ugly inside. Therefore the rule is: judge not others. Be very severe with yourself, but forgive others their trespasses against yourself as you hope others will forgive you. Learn to love and learn to forgive. This brings about a beautiful, symmetrically shaped character.

"THE FATHER, THE SON, AND THE HOLY GHOST"

How would you explain the Christian idea of the Father, the Son, and the Holy Ghost, in the light of Theosophy?

The 'Father,' the 'Son,' and the 'Holy Ghost,' are three aspects or ways of looking at the spiritual world, and the spiritual nature of the human being. The very highest part, the Christians call the 'Father.' The 'Holy Ghost,' or 'Holy Spirit,' as the Christians sometimes call it, is the spirit of love and beauty and order that just naturally flows through and from the

'Father,' which is the highest, the spiritual aspect or part, either of the Universe or of man; while the 'Son' is the portion or part of the Father whose work is more particularly taken up with filling the Universe on the one hand, and the human soul on the other hand, with the divine Light. So thus you see that Father, Son, and Holy Ghost are really one thing at bottom, and yet, in another point of view, are three things in the way they work.

I may illustrate this by taking the spiritual nature of a human being for an instance. The higher spiritual part of man is the 'Father.' The 'Son' is the reflexion or manifestation of this Father, called the spiritual soul; while the Holy Spirit or Holy Ghost is the spiritual influence or energy streaming through the Father and the Son, and giving to the human being all the loveliest and noblest qualities of a spiritual type, such as impersonal love and inspiration and illumination, and all other sublime things like these.

The Christians, in the very first days when Jesus still lived, were Theosophists, and Jesus was a Theosophical Teacher of his time; but when Jesus died, and the first Christians died, a great deal of confusion and misunderstanding arose about Jesus' beautiful teachings, and these confused ideas became the dogmas and very set teachings of the later churches.

I have tried to put this explanation in simple language, because my own father was a Christian clergyman, and I used to have many interesting talks with him, and he agreed with me that the Theosophical viewpoint was a very reasonable and beautiful explanation.

RATIONALE OF CRYSTAL-GAZING

Can you tell me what is the rationale of crystal-gazing? Why should a CRYSTAL *be necessary in order to see into the Astral Light?*

The only reason that the globe is crystal and has any effect is on account of the light that it can gather and flash to the eye. If the globe were made of wood or stone and dull, it would have no effect. But it is well-known in modern medical studies, and has been known since immemorial time all over the world, that if you want to throw yourself into a passive state, quiet the vagrant, rampant, restless everyday thoughts of your mind and still the emotions, look at light even if it is only a spot of light on the wall or the reflexion from a finger ring or a crystal globe or a brightly burning candle. Any spot of light, especially with so-called sensitives, will if stared at long enough bring about a loss of individuality and of the starer's egoity, and will induce a negative 'half-there' dreaminess eventuating in sleep, waking-sleep, auto-hypnosis, self-hypnosis. Why? Because the eyes staring at a spot of light and continuing to stare, will transmit the message to the brain of that steady vibrational continuity, unceasing, never changing. And the brain becomes still because it is deadened; it has become insensitised and dull. Then if the glass starer or light starer is a real psychic, a sensitive, with the brain thus stilled and the eyes taking on the vibration of the light, certain faculties belonging to the psychic part of a man are freed and the voice will speak, sometimes telling truth, often not, depending upon the condition of utter or partial receptivity.

All these things are well-known by modern doctors and psychologists. But it is an awfully bad thing to follow. You are less than you were before. And you are not attaining true intuition, true vision, true clairvoyance which comes from above and can function at any time and as soon as you raise your mind upward. That is the thing to strive for. That makes you ten times the one you were or are in ordinary life.

There you have the whole reason for the effect of the crystal or of the candle flame or of the spot of light from a ring — anything that will make a spot of light. It is simply to induce a somnolent deadened insensitised condition of the brain and the nerves. And if continued too often it will make the practitioner go down instead of rise. It was well explained by a man I knew once who had made a life-long study of these things. He said the fact is these crystal gazers and others simply reduce the vibration of their own brain-mind with its individuality and fire and genius and all the other qualities that the man ought to have — they simply reduce the vibrations of the brain-mind to the unchanging vibrations of the crystal through which the light goes. It does insensitise the brain and that is why it works sometimes. It is very much the same way that a snake will hypnotize a bird or rabbit; or the man a son of man. The will of the victim, whether crystal gazer or not — a self-victim — looses its hold on the man's brain and nervous system. The brain and the nervous system become synchronously sympathetic or in synchronous vibration with the hypnotizer, with the light, with the snake's eye, with the light in the other man's eye. The will is abandoned, withdrawn or ejected.

REAL BIRTH-DATE OF JESUS

It has been said that Jesus lived about one hundred years before what we call the Christian Era. Is this statement made on astronomical calculation, or on what? [Question asked in 1934]

The statement is made from our esoteric records; but these esoteric records also are largely based on astronomical and genuinely astrological wisdom. The Wise Ones do not come irregularly, that is to say fortuitously. They come at stated periods, because everything in the Universe moves according to order and law. Consequently those who know how to calculate need not even consult the stars. They know that at a certain period after a great soul has appeared among men some other great soul will come.

Besides this, there is no record, historically speaking, of the appearance of the great Syrian Sage called Jesus in the accepted Year 1 of the Christian Era, or in the Year 4 B. C. This is one of the reasons why Occidental scholars of a critical turn of mind have said that no such personality as Jesus ever lived, because there is no historical record of his existence outside of the Christian Scriptures. But he did live — a little more than one hundred years before the Year 1 of the Christian Era.

The date of the present Christian Era was first set arbitrarily by a Christian monk called Dionysius Exiguus, Dionysius the Small, who lived in the Sixth Century of the Christian Era, under the Emperors Justin and Justinian. He did not know when the Master Jesus was born, but he made calculations according to the literary material under his hand, not much of it, but such as he had. And he set the birth of the Christian Master at about 600 years before his own time. Soon after, this hypothetical date became accepted as the Year 1 of the Christian Era, the year of the birth of the great Sage called Jesus.

We have in our esoteric calculations what *we* call the Messianic Cycle, a cycle 2160 solar years long. This is just one half of the 4320 — 4-3-2-, the key-figures of our esoteric reckoning. Every 2160 years the sun enters a new sign of the zodiac. Twelve times 2160 completes the grand year, the *annus magnus,* of some 25,920 years long. And — and this is very interesting — we are now let us say within a few years of 2040 years since the Master Jesus was born; and the Messiah of the present Messianic Cycle was the power, the influence, working through H. P. B. You may judge from her and her work somewhat of the nature of the Master Jesus. The Master Jesus as known in Christian story and legend is a mere idealization of the great Sage, an ideal figure. The great Sage actually lived, had his disciples, did his work; and when he died, as the years passed his disciples wove a web of story and legend about him; and this web became the Christian New Testament, the four books of *Matthew, Mark, Luke,* and *John.* And the story and the legend that was woven about the central figure of the Master was taken from the Initiation-schools of Asia Minor. The important thing about these great Sages is not their persons, but the power flowing through them and the Message that they bring to their fellow-men.

At the beginning of the last quarter of every hundred years our great Teachers make a special effort in the world towards a new spiritual and intellectual awakening. Now then, some Theosophists think that the world must wait until 1975 before any new spiritual teaching can be given to men through the Theosophical Movement. This is wrong. It is not only illogical but it is contrary to fact. These Theosophists seem to look forward to the one who will come in the last quarter of this century as a sort of modern Buddha, as a sort of modern Christ. This is wrong, because the Messianic Cycle was opened by H. P. B., and she was the beginner of the new Messianic Cycle — the power working through her I mean, the Master's influence. She was the 'Messiah'-person, to use the old Jewish-Christian word, of our present cycle of 2160 years (but not at all like the supposititious Christ-person of legend and story, because that type-figure is almost wholly ideal). But a special effort will be made by a chela at the end of every hundred years until the 2100 odd years of the Messianic Cycle initiated by H. P. B. shall have run its course. Then a new Messianic Cycle will open.

I think that the chela, the Teacher, the Messenger, who will come in the last quarter of this century will be rejected by many Theosophists who now think they are very faithful to him who has not yet come, (unless indeed their minds change greatly between now and then, if they live so long) because they will not understand him; they will look for a creature of their own imaginations, instead of accepting the one who is to come as he is; and because this noble-hearted chela, this noble-hearted man, will appear quietly and simply and give his teachings more or less as the other Messengers of every hundred-year period have done, many will reject him; but I hope that in our Society at least, due to the teachings that you have had and will have, the one who comes in 1975 will find a home amongst us; that he will not be rejected because he came simply and nobly as H. P. B. came, with no blowing of trumpets, with no great advertising. Many of us will have passed on by 1975, and will not see this, but the children amongst us, and the youngest ones amongst us, I hope will be helpers.

CONCENTRATION AND MEDITATION

In meditation and concentration if the body feels any physical reaction such as becoming hot, what does it indicate, and should one continue meditating, or should one stop when this occurs?

I take it that you are attempting to pursue one of the methods of Indian Yoga, which in the technical language of that country is called *Hatha-Yoga*. The methods of *Hatha-Yoga* are always dangerous to the health of the body, and in many cases to the stability and clarity of the mind, and I feel it incumbent upon me, as a sheer duty towards fellow human beings, to warn you most earnestly of the dangers that lie along this path.

Of course, the answer to your question is exceedingly clear and very brief, and it is the following: Stop immediately, and discontinue the practice. The warmth that you speak of under the adjective 'hot,' is doubtless a physiological nervous reaction, and, I am convinced, is simply Nature's warning to cease the cause producing this effect.

I beg you to forgive me if what I herein state seems a bit abrupt, or if the suggestion that I give to you is unwelcome. But I know how exceedingly dangerous to both mental and physical health these practices are, and, as said before, I feel it incumbent upon me to warn any human being against them.

Concentration and meditation themselves and alone, apart from physical practices, are valuable spiritual and mental exercises; and if properly pursued they bring about clarity of the mind, quiet and peace of both mind and body, and are productive of a strengthening of the mental apparatus. But I here speak of genuine concentration and meditation, which have nothing to do in themselves with physical postures or practices. Meditation is simply holding steadily a thought in the mind, and dwelling upon it continuously and in peace until the idea or problem that the mind holds is clearly understood or solved; and concentration is simply a centering of the mental attention upon the thought thus held in the mind.

As a matter of fact, meditation and concentration are two sides of the same thing, and, if properly conducted, no dangerous physiological reactions at all follow. Anyone who pays close attention to what he is doing, and who concentrates upon what he is doing, is simply exercising mental faculties which bring about success in the duty taken in hand. But if there is a physiological reaction, such as you speak of, it is a sign that the practice as pursued is a dangerous one, both to physical and mental health; and, since you ask my opinion, I will answer that the practice should be stopped immediately.

THE NATURE OF THE TIBETANS

Is it known why the Dalai Lama drove the Tashi Lama out into India? He has had to fly to Mongolia and live there in seclusion and hide there. It seems a mystery. [Question asked in 1932]

It *is* a mystery. I can tell you this: if the truth were known, there was no 'driving out' at all. Tibet has been doing its best in desperation to keep its frontiers inviolate against the hammering tactics of Western European powers trying to penetrate into the country; and they have resorted to the age-old Asiatic ways of diplomacy — letting things appear which are not so, if you understand me.

It is true that Tibet in the past has had abominable intestine struggles and wars; but that was mostly before the reformation of Tsong-kha-pa. After his time, which was the fourteenth century of our era, things have been quieter; and century after century has seen a happy people, light-hearted, loving learning, cultivating the things of the spirit and of the mind.

There is a great future before the Tibetans. They are a 'young race,' evolutionally speaking. They are going to come forth in the future. But they won't be Tibetans then as the Tibetans now are.

TIBETANS OF TODAY

Will you tell us something about the educated, cultured Tibetan class, which I suppose must exist? At present we know nothing about the Tibetans except the uncultivated, unwashed class; and then we have heard of the Masters as living in a part of Tibet. [Question asked in 1932]

In the first place, don't think that the Mahâtmans are all Tibetans, because they are not. Among them there are Hindûs, Chinese, Tibetans, and some Europeans. For instance, there is an Englishman; there is a German; there is a Hungarian; and there is also a Greek. These four I happen to know of. The Mahâtmans may belong to any race of men. Some of them have been highly born, socially speaking; some of them have been born in humble homes; but that fact has nothing to do with their spiritual standing in evolution and in their great Brotherhood.

The home of the Great Lodge is in Tibet. I don't mean to say that it is near Lhassa or Shigatse, but nevertheless in Tibet. There are also subordinate places, of which one is near the Desert of Gobi, and another around the region or district called Amdo.

The Tibetans themselves are of course an Asiatic people, belonging to the same stock, I believe, as the Burmese, the Siamese, and perhaps some of the minor Chinese groups — I mean the peoples inhabiting China near the Indo-Chinese Peninsula and the eastern Tibetan frontier. They are a people who are not far advanced in the graces of ordinary western civilization, as Europeans understand it — not more so than the Burmese and the Chinese are. In spite of the rigors of the Tibetan climate and conditions brought about by the high tableland on which they live, the arts of Society have nevertheless been highly cultivated after the Tibetan fashion, but by no means in the Occidental way or idea of these things.

The Tibetans, like every other people, can be divided into three general classes of beings: the majority, who are humble laborers — if we can call them that; then there is a smaller middle-class, mostly merchants, *literati*, and what you might call the nobility of the country; then, third, there is the hierarchy of priests drawn from all classes, called *lamas;* and there are many grades of lamas. There are the *Red Caps,* mostly found around the frontiers, especially in the East and South along the Indian and Chinese borders; and they, most of them, profess what actually is a degenerate form of Buddhism, very largely mixed with the older indigenous Bhön practices; Bhön is the name given to this before the reformation of Buddhism under Tsong-kha-pa in the fourteenth century of our era.

The two heads of the country, men possessing both spiritual and temporal authority, are the Dalai Lama and the Tashi Lama. The Dalai Lama is the official head of the country, the man who attends to most of the official business of the country. He is a lama, i.e., he is a priest; but he is also what you might call the 'president' or 'king' of the country — therefore a priest-king. The other chief lama usually living at Shigatse is the Tashi Lama, who, in theory at least, is the spiritual head of the Yellow-Cap Buddhism in Tibet. These two rank on a parity, probably, so far as mere rank goes; yet ancient tradition, that is, ever since the reformation of Buddhism by Tsong-kha-pa, has always asserted that the Tashi Lama, living in Shigatse in retirement, or who did live in Shigatse until recently, in retirement, holds a spiritual status superior to that of the official head of the country called the Dalai Lama, the 'Ocean'-Lama. One of the titles of the Shigatse Lama or Tashi Lama means the 'Ocean of Wisdom' or the 'Great Jewel of Wisdom.'

Tibetan Initiates or Adepts may be drawn from any class. The humblest laborer, born as a common cultivator of the soil — I mean in a family of cultivators of the soil — may indeed be born in that condition and yet may rise to a high rank in the spiritual hierarchy to which our own Mahâtmans belong.

Within recent years there has been an infiltration of Occidental ideas into Tibet. The Tibetans are now a people who, it is stated, are beginning to have police-courts somewhat after the Western idea; it is also said that quite recently they are beginning to introduce Occidental inventions such as electric lights and a postal system; but these things after all are very doubtful blessings, if human happiness is the standard to go by; for the reason that the Tibetans — I mean the majority of them from the peasants to the two great lamas — have hitherto been a race of simple-minded, indeed spiritually-minded, people, which fact means a great deal. For ages they have not been spoiled. Their spiritual instincts are still alive. They may live — many of them indeed do live — in what to Occidental ideas is in unhygienic and dirty places. It is said that in many places a man may have several wives, or more commonly that a woman may have several husbands.

These are some of the unpleasant attributes of conditions in Tibet. But I am not speaking of these conditions; I am speaking rather of individuals. Many of the Tibetan lamas, especially those inhabiting the frontier districts, are a disgrace to Buddhism — sensuous, sensual, self-seeking men and women; but there are — especially among the *Yellow Caps,* as H. P. B. calls them, who are practically in control of the country and who reside more in the central and northern parts — thousands and thousands of lofty-minded, spiritually-minded men, really great men, who pass their lives in the study of spiritual things; and mainly from this class have been drawn the Adepts, who, if they succeed in their spiritual objectives, aspire to join the Great Brotherhood.

The Tibetans are a backward people from our Western standpoint. They eat with their fingers and blow their noses with their fingers and have many other unpleasant habits, at least most of them have; but there are likewise Tibetan gentlemen and Tibetan gentlewomen. Education in many parts is held as a pass to official rank, as it used to be in China. Wealth won't always put a man in official position, unless, indeed, there be a corrupt official somewhere.

The Seven Original Human Groups

In THE SECRET DOCTRINE *(Vol. II, p. 1) H. P. B. speaks of "the simultaneous evolution of seven human groups on seven portions of our globe." Are we to accept this literally, or is she referring to some occult aspect of the teaching which is not generally given?*

This passage and other passages appertaining to the same point of the occult teaching, mean just what they say, and are not to be construed metaphorically. These passages do not refer to inner and outer Rounds, nor to the other globes of the earth-chain, nor to the seven different human principles, as astral, physical, etc., except indirectly; as is shown very clearly by H. P. B.'s own words, "seven human groups on seven different portions of our globe." Here it is our Globe D or Earth, our planet Terra, which is meant.

Thus it is a fact that original mankind, which does not mean any branch of humanity but the very beginnings of what we popularly call the First Root-Race on Globe D in this Fourth Round, refers to the matter of the śishtas from the preceding Round. In other words, it means that our human life-wave as a whole or totality, when it again reached our Earth during this Fourth Round on this Globe D, awakened the seven classes of the then living śishtas on this our Globe D, because the forerunners of our life-wave were themselves composed of the seven different kinds of human monads.

In other words they were composed of what, in other connexions, H. P. B. has called the different classes of the Pitris. This is a little intricate but very simple when other teachings about the incoming life-waves on a globe are properly understood, and must not be confused with other life-waves; and I may add of course that the last word of this teaching is highly esoteric and belongs to higher Degrees.

However, mark the following points: the śishtas waiting the incoming septenary human life-wave were themselves sevenfold, i.e., seven different groups of śishtas, each group being composed of individuals who through evolution were more or less alike. The life-wave when it reaches our Globe, is thus composed of the bulk of what we call the First Sub-Race of the First Root-Race, intermixed with forerunners, i.e., more advanced monads of six other kinds, representing the other six classes of human monads.

Hence it was that all the seven classes of śishtas were more or less contemporaneously awakened, as it were, which means that they became vehicles for the different classes of the incoming monads, and began to increase; and thus it was that in this Round, on this Globe, as H. P. B. says, there was a "simultaneous evolution of seven human groups on seven different portions of our globe." These seven different classes of monads of the incoming life-wave, including the majority and the forerunners of the other six, started the seeds of the different Root-Races, which in time were to develop in this Round on this Globe, and of which Root-Races 1, 2, 3, and 4 have come and gone, and we are now in the Fifth, although there are representatives amongst us even today, forerunners, of the Sixth and Seventh Root-Races to come before our life-wave passes on to Globe E.

It is thus clear that *The Secret Doctrine* teaches not a monogenetic origin of humanity, i.e., the birth of the human race from a single individual, or from a single couple like the Jewish biblical story; but teaches a polygenetic origin, that is to say an origin of the human race from seven different living foci, which I have hereinbefore called the seven different types or kinds or sub-classes of the śishtas, each one such type or sub-class being awakened by the similar incoming portion of the human life-wave. Of course the portion of the incoming life-wave which was to become specifically the First Root-Race was the most numerous at that earliest period in our humanity, and became the First Root-Race. Then when it died out, it was followed by the growth in numbers of the class of the monads which was to become the Second Root-Race, etc.

In this connexion, it must not be forgotten that all these seven types or classes of monads in the incoming life-waves are not separated in water-tight compartments, any more than the different types of men today, advanced and less advanced, are all separated off from each other. But they more or less mingled as time went on, yet the members of each class as it were gravitated to its own particular group and part of the globe.

From this teaching we likewise see that there may be, and indeed are, groups of humanity which inhabit portions of a globe and remain almost quiescent for ages, until their time comes to begin to increase and to become the dominant Race or Sub-Race.

Thus H. P. B.'s words are to be taken literally. Of course, what is here briefly said took scores of millions of years to come about, up to the time of our own Fifth Root-Race.

CYCLIC PROGRESSION NOT REPETITION

Will all things now existing exist again after pralaya in more or less the same form as hitherto? Will the cycle just repeat itself in a kind of predestined way, all entities repeating their previous work and accomplishments? As just one instance, will the great world scriptures such as the Hindû Râmâyana come into being once more with the same individuals composing its history?

The idea of repetitive cycles imbodied in this question is nothing new in the history of Oriental philosophy, nor indeed in that of ancient Greek philosophy; for it was one of the foremost and favorite teachings of the old Stoic school: that the Universes, or our universe rather, and all in it, repeated itself cyclically through immense intervals of time, so that what now is, took place in the previous cosmic cycle, and what now is, will again repeat itself in due serial order when this present cosmic cycle is ended, the rest-period is completed, and the new cosmic cycle begins. It is the principle of the turning wheel, the favorite symbol of these repetitive cycles with their undoubted mechanical aspects.

Now there is great truth in all this. But what most of these statements ignore, either deliberately or through ignorance, is that while these repetitive imbodiments of the Universe certainly take place, this being one of the fundamental teachings of Theosophy, yet each imbodiment for any particular or any one universe is always on a higher plane than the one on which it was last imbodied. Thus it is not a perfect identity, and therefore there is no dead mechanism about it and no merely frightfully useless running the round on the wheel of change with no hope of progress. This last would be the worst kind of fatalistic horror.

The universe repeats itself, reimbodies itself, and each repetition governed by the karman of the preceding produces a universe closely alike to the one which preceded it — just as a man in one life is very much like the man of the last life; yet in both cases the imbodying entity, whether universe or man, is always a little higher, a little more forwards in its evolutionary course, than before.

Thus it follows naturally enough that the Râmâyana will again be written in the next cosmic manvantara, and will probably doubtless contain the same more or less accurately reproduced figures of that grand epic. But they will not be the mere identical reproductions of identical entities, not one of which has advanced, because those of one manvantara graduate into a higher plane: the karmic molds of destiny they have left behind them in the cosmic astral light, bring things about so that the multitudes of monads trailing along behind us will naturally walk in our footsteps. And yet because these entities are different individuals, and because the universe itself is somewhat advanced, while there will be a reproduction of the Râmâyana with all its incidents, etc., everything will be a little better, because on a higher plane.

IS THE SUN HOT OR COLD?

When the Teachers say that the Sun is not hot does that mean that it is really cold, or is there some deeper meaning behind that statement? Dr. D. H. Menzel of Harvard Observatory gives reasons to believe that the part of the Sun's Corona very near the surface of the sun is intensely heated, far more so than the surface itself. Does this explain the apparent heat of the surface?

The sun is a body of power, a ball of energy, or rather of energies, and is no more hot as such than is a block of ice, although of course even a block of ice has some heat as compared with something still colder.

Thus, electricity is neither hot nor cold, although it can chill things and heat things, with proper mechanical apparatus. Sunlight is neither hot nor cold, although because it is energy, it can set up movement in the molecules and atoms of the bodies on which it falls, like our skin, or a rock, or the side of a house, and thus give us the impression that the sunlight is hot. It is like electricity, which, because of the response of the metal through which it passes, heats the metal red hot, which therefore gives heat. But the electricity is not hot, no more than the energies coming from the sun are hot.

Most of the heat on our earth actually arises from magnetic and electric interplay between the earth itself and that marvelous continent above our heads, as the Master says.

The earth gets very little heat direct from the sun, as compared, I mean with the heat generated in the manner above explained between the earth and the meteoric continent above our heads.

Now, turning to the sun, the sun as a body of forces is cold, and yet I hate to use this word, as it does not give the meaning. As a body of forces it is neither hot nor cold. Temperature does not enter into the picture. Temperature arises out of the play of forces on resisting media. *But* — and here is the important point — what you might call the sun's outer garment, not near the sun but around the surface of the sun, what science means when it speaks of the corona, can be heated by chemical and alchemical action to great heat, or to less heat, or to no heat at all, in spots, according to circumstances.

Thus we might say that the sun itself is neither hot nor cold, being just a body of forces. But these forces in their interplay with the garments of the sun, call them gases if you like, or ethers, can produce actual heat, as we understand heat. This means that the sun's forces playing and interplaying on the atoms and molecules of these garments of the sun, can at times, and usually do in spots or in areas, vast areas too, make heat, even great heat. But this heat has very little to do with heating the earth. It is simply radiated into space, or sucked in again towards the body of the sun, and is dissipated.

Thus the sun is neither hot nor cold. It is neutral to these two adjectives, so to speak; but the sun's outer garments can be and usually are, sometimes more, sometimes less, very hot, sometimes not hot at all, according to the way the forces play and interplay at this time or some future time, or did in some past time.

WAS THE FOUNDING OF THE T. S. PREMATURE?

In THE MAHATMA LETTERS TO A. P. SINNETT *there is a suggestion that the effort made by two of the Masters in helping with the founding of the T. S. was deemed by other and higher Masters in some sense as premature. Someone said to me that thus it became in a certain sense a failure, and this made necessary 'the new effort in 1909 which was accomplished by Max Heindel.' Can you say if there is something in this or not?*

My answer is an emphatic no; and there is not an atom of proof that this is so.

I will begin to answer this question at the end and move towards the beginning at my end. I believe that Mr. Max Heindel was an earnest man who had mystical and astrological and what he called Rosicrucian ideas of his own. I will speak quite frankly: like all these others — every one of them — the other mystical and semi-mystical societies which have been born in the West since H. P. Blavatsky came in 1875 and gave the world Theosophy, all of them have drawn upon our Theosophical teachings for the good that they contain. They take without acknowledgment from our treasury! This I would not object to, because I am anxious that all in our treasury that the world can accept shall be given to the world; and if unauthorized takers crash the barriers, even then I am happy. I ask only that the takers be honest and acknowledge the source of their inspiration, saying: "I have taken from your treasury because I found the door unlocked!"

To come to the next point: there is not a word of truth in the statement that the Theosophical Movement has failed — not one word of truth. I will admit that the Theosophical Movement has made some serious mistakes, grievous errors, in the past; but they have been mistakes not due to the heart but to the difficulties involved in introducing a very strange (as it seemed to the West) Religion-Philosophy-Science into the Occident.

The Theosophical Society today is an organization which covers the earth — sparsely, it is true, but which has branches everywhere — and I should perhaps say the Theosophical Movement, including all the Theosophical Societies. Some of them in my judgment are more true to the original purposes of our Great Teachers than others; but I do not condemn. My wish is to be brotherly and to help.

But to state that the Theosophical Movement failed, when it was founded by the Masters to help mankind — failed within thirty-four years of its founding — is not only to utter a falsehood but to traduce their holy names; for they knew what they were about, or they didn't.

Coming now to the first part of the question, which is the last part of my answer: It is true that, as regards the founding of the Theosophical Movement in 1875, there was a difference of opinion among some of our Great Teachers. Some thought that it would be wiser to wait a few more years; and among these, I may say, was the Great Soul whom we Theosophists revere and call the Mahâ-Chohan, the Teacher of those two noble-hearted gentlemen, the Mahâtmans M. and K. H. He, too, thought the time was as yet not quite ripe. But he said to his two Chelas, our two Teachers: "Try!" And they tried. They tried because their hearts were filled with sorrow for the world.

Look back, you older Brothers, if you have lived that long, to the year 1875, and consider in what a state men then were. Religion in the Occident was mostly dogmatism and forms: the spirit had largely fled from the churches. Science was introducing a scientific materialism into men's minds and hearts, so that men had lost all faith in their spiritual intuitions and their feeling that there is an interior and invisible Universe. They had lost all faith that there is a moral law in the world; had lost all faith that men would ineluctably reap what they themselves sowed.

The result was that in those days the human race as a whole, especially in the Occident, having lost the guiding light of the spiritual Star which guides mankind through the ages, thinking themselves to be but beasts of a better kind than the apes, were rushing for the maelstrom of material sensuality — the sensualities of an utterly material existence. This would have involved the loss of hundreds of thousands if not millions of souls, and heaven knows what untold spiritual and intellectual misery and harm to men and women, whose intuitions were still alive but blighted, and who knew not where to look for light.

The churches gave it not for they had it not. The scientists never had it. They were just researching, hunting, and had not yet found. And these two Great Men, men of Buddha-like souls, took the karmic responsibility upon their shoulders (and only the esotericist knows what this means) of making themselves karmically responsible for the sending out of a New Message to men, which, by the force of its innate vigor and the persuasive power of the teachings which it contained, would induce men to think despite themselves.

H. P. B. came. Laughed at and derided, scorned and persecuted, she worked alone until she found a few helpers — Colonel Olcott and Mr. Judge being the first among them; and by means of her indomitable, her inflexible, will and her magnificent intellect and her amazing spiritual intuition, she taught and wrote and built up a society which cried "Halt!" — and it succeeded. A new impetus was given to the thoughts of mankind. Science from that time began to have strange stirrings of new thoughts. New impulses were sent forth into the thought-atmosphere of the world through the newspapers, through books, through traveling lecturers. Men were taught that there was a sane universe, that men are responsible for what they do; that there is truth in the universe and that it may be had by him who yearns for it and who will have it.

And then the magic was wrought. New thoughts began to percolate into the consciousness of men. Suddenly the world was startled by the work of Crookes, Becquerel, and Roentgen with the so-called 'X-rays' — a marvelous revelation to the materialism of the time, proving an interior world which was invisible to the sense-apparatus which we have. Following this came the work of the Curies, Rutherford, Soddy, and others. Radium was discovered. Men's thoughts took a new turn. They began to think along new lines, or rather, along the old lines which the church had forgotten and modern science had not yet discovered.

And today, what is it that our greatest modern scientific thinkers tell us as the result of the deductions of their discoveries? That the fundamental thing in the Universe is consciousness; and this is why I repeat this in every public lecture that I give, if I can find the chance to do it; for it is so important: Modern science is now telling us that the material world is illusory, an illusion, that the only reality is behind the visible, behind the veil of what we can see and touch and feel and taste and smell and hear: old thoughts, thoughts which we Theosophists have been teaching for innumerable ages, thoughts which H. P. B. gave in her books in outline, almost in detail, from 1875. She it was who awakened the world to the new realities — the old realities, the real things in the Universe and in human existence. Oh, if I could tell you the true story of her life! Some day if I have the time and the strength I will write it or tell it.

It is the duty of the Theosophical Society to continue to be the leader in the thoughts of men, to carry on the work which H. P. B. did, to keep the link with the Lodge unbroken; and if we slide backwards, if we become mere followers, then indeed the Theosophical Movement will have become a failure and the strictures of our critics will be justified.

FOSSILS FROM THIRD ROUND

H. P. B. says the fossils found in very early geological rocks are relics of the Third Round. Are we to interpret this to mean that FOSSILS *have been carried over from the Third Round and persisted through the early ethereal state of the Fourth Round?*

When H. P. B. correctly points out that at the opening of the Fourth Round on our Globe D certain Third Round forms still existed which now are occasionally discovered by us as fossils, this must not be construed as meaning that these now fossil forms have existed as such since the end of the Third Round. The meaning is that these fossil forms continued as *living entities* during the opening drama of the Fourth Round of our Globe D, coincidentally and contemporaneously with the different śishtas of the life-waves. But when these life-waves began coming in to our Globe D, thus opening the drama of our Fourth Round on Globe D, the śishtas mainly were affected, and these living Third Round forms more or less quickly or belatedly died out, and became fossils. That is why we occasionally find their fossils. They were replaced by the evolving or developing life-waves working through and multiplying through the śishtas. This resulted in the changing of the śishtas into more evolved forms which took the place of the Third Round śishtas of the different kingdoms still alive from the Third Round.

Tremendous geologic and volcanic convulsions open the drama of a Round on each globe, ours included. But the śishtas, being the product (because the seeds) for the future, survive more or less successfully;

whereas the *original* śishta-forms brought over from the Third Round, gradually died out or were swept away by these convulsions, because in cosmic ideation they were no longer useful to the monads, the monads having already evolved new forms and finer and more developed vehicles through the śishtas that were saved. Herein lies the essential meaning of the Hebrew Noah's Ark and of Vaivasvata's story in the Hindû Purânas.

HEART AND INTELLECT NEEDED IN THEOSOPHY

Is there not a greater need for stressing the ethical side of our work? It is so easy to lose the heart-touch in our intellectual studies, and we will never catch the multitude with mere intellect.

The need of ethics and the need of more heart in our work is perennially true. It will always be so. But there is an equal, and an equally perennial, need for an emphasis of the intellectual side. The two must unite and become one; and it is foolish to say: No intellect and only ethics; or, No ethics and only intellect. The first makes a man a gentle fool. The second makes of man an ungentle demon. Combined they make the real man.

I am always intensely irritated at the idea that some of our people have, that Theosophy must rake in people by the tens of thousands, and have them flock in droves. It would be lovely if the droves were composed of sincere people. But I have never looked upon the work of Theosophy as a popular, emotional movement. Its duty is to be in the van, to lead, to show the way, always to be several steps ahead of the multitude, in other words a guide; and such a program, right from the jump means the alienation of the sympathies of millions who cannot understand anything beyond their noses.

I am well content with the fact that we are growing, albeit slowly; although I am human and therefore ambitious for more rapid growth. But in my calmer moments I know perfectly well that it is better to grow slowly and be firm, as we are doing, than to grow rapidly and then go to pieces because of lack of sufficient spirit within to build a material basis which would endure.

NATURE OF COSMIC ETHER

Not long ago scientists generally accepted the existence of some kind of substance, called Ether, which fills all space. Much discussion and disagreement has arisen about this in recent times. What is the Theosophical interpretation of the Cosmic Ether?

I think this can be safely said, that whatever the new discovery about Ether may be, or be supposed to be: (a) some discovery has been made which proves that an Ether of some kind exists, probably not the old scientific idea of Cosmic Ether, about which I will have something to say in an instant; and (b) that the tendency of science today is away from Einstein's former idea that an Ether according to the general theory of relativity really is not needed. In this Einstein is quite wrong. It arose from the fact that the mathematical chopper gives you back just what you put into it. It is correct reasoning upon premises laid down, and if these premises are wrong or partly wrong, the deductions will be logical and correct in logic, but wrong or partly wrong in fact. Mathematics never proves anything if the premises are imaginary or uncertain.

Now here is the main point of all I want to say to you or any other Theosophist. When these scientists talk about an Ether, our Theosophists constantly confuse our theosophical idea of a Cosmic Ether, or many Cosmic Ethers, with what the scientists mean. And the scientific view of an Ether has ranged all the way from a kind of gas very dense and elastic perhaps, but still physical matter in a gaseous form, to something slightly more subtil but still quite physical stuff; and naturally the scientists wonder why such a Cosmic Ether if it exists does not affect the movement of planets, suns, comets, and other bodies, through it. But this is not our idea of a Cosmic Ether. Our idea of a Cosmic Ether is physical prakriti or matter in its first or second or even third or possibly fourth states, counting downwards from the highest. When we Theosophists speak of an Ether we never mean physical stuff, however tenuous, and emphatically never mean a gas, such as the laboratory understands the term. Therefore scientists have been quite right in refusing to admit the existence of a mere Ether of gas, however tenuous. But they have been quite wrong in refusing to admit an immaterial Ether, immaterial here meaning something which is not matter in the physical sense, but nevertheless distinctly substance in our theosophical and philosophical sense; and yet not spirit, for spirit is infinitely more tenuous and etherealized so to speak.

Einstein's relativity is a theory and a helpful one. His fundamental idea of the relativity of nature in its various functionings and departments is sound archaic philosophy; but some of his premises in his mathematical reasonings are utterly unacceptable to us, and therefore, as I have said, we cannot accept most of his mathematical reasonings, not because his mathematics are wrong, but because his premises are only partly right or wrong. I hope this is clear. Nevertheless, when I speak of our theosophical Cosmic Ether, I do not mean a mere unsubstantiality, something which has no substance, which is not stuff. I mean just the contrary. It is at once, physically speaking, almost spiritually tenuous, and yet it is a prakriti on our own Cosmic Plane, but in physical prakriti's highest forms there, and it is certainly far too gross to be called spirit. Therefore it is matter in our theosophical sense. But it is not matter as the scientists understand it. For when they say matter, they mean things which are solid, liquid, or gaseous, in other words what we call the grossest, even sub-astral matter of physical space. And the Ether of space, or the Ethers of space, are far more tenuous and ethereal than such scientific conception has it. The Cosmic Ether does not affect the motion of bodies through it, because the bodies are grossly physical and the Cosmic Ether, while matter of the lowest prakritic cosmic plane, is immensely more tenuous than physical matter.

You might as well say that heat or light will prevent the bodies moving through cosmic space, because of pressure. It is true that they will, but in an exceedingly slight degree, practically too slight to be observed. Already scientists know about the pressure of sunlight, for instance.

The Ancient Language of Senzar

Many Theosophists seem to think that H. P. B. wrote The Secret Doctrine *and* The Voice of the Silence *from two Senzar books, one called the Book of Dzyan and the other the Book of the Golden Precepts. Is this correct?*

No, it is a mistake. Senzar is not only a language, consisting of words, and once spoken as the tongue of the ancients all over the Oriental and archaic American world, but it is likewise a language of symbols or a language greatly addicted to the use of symbols.

To illustrate, as H. P. B. tried to in the opening part of *The Secret Doctrine:* In using Senzar, Initiate X, let us say, in China, writing to Initiate Z, let us say, in Peru, or anywhere else, about a certain cosmogonic problem, would start off with words, and then introduce a symbol, an empty circle or a circle with a dot in it, or a circle containing a cross, which would mean pages of explanation to the receiving Initiate Z. And the Initiate X would go on again in Senzar words, and perhaps in a moment use another symbol, and what he had to say would be ended, partly in symbol understood everywhere, and partly in words.

In a small way we have the same practice with us. When we sometimes use the Arabic numerals instead of writing out the numbers in spelling, we would write 6 in the Arabic numeral, instead of writing six. Or again, we would use the symbol for *and* &, instead of writing out the word *and*. Or we would use *etc.*, instead of writing out *et cetera*. We are following just the same principle, using symbols, but we do it in a very small degree. And yet if we remember how one of us, writing to a friend, might make a funny remark, and then put "etc." or the symbol for *and*, we would immediately sense a whole humorous line of thinking back of that symbol, and we would know what the writer intended to convey.

Now, just carry this idea into the profoundest philosophical conceptions, and you will have an idea of the Senzar language. It is not Sanskrit, although Sanskrit, I believe, is the closest extant living or dead language to the archaic Senzar. I believe also that the ancient Zend of Persia comes from the same root we find in Senz- ar.

I do not think myself that even the archaic Senzar, or Zenzar — there are different or modified ways of spelling it — was ever an occult racial language in the same way that Russian is or English is or German is or Italian is. It was more like the original Sanskrita compared with Prâkrita. I do not think actual Sanskrita, as we now have it, was ever a language spoken by a race of people. I think its very name, Sanskrita, meaning composed or constructed or builded up, means that it was a priestly or initiate tongue, perfected by initiates as a means of communication among themselves, but founded more or less upon some great popular and widely diffused tongue. In other words, I think that Sanskrit in a smaller way in the beginning was much like Senzar was, although Senzar always seemed to have been kept very secret, and Sanskrit for some unknown reason finally became practically public property. Anybody, especially the Brâhmanas, could learn it. Books were written in it for public reading, etc., and I think this is the reason why H. P. B. once spoke of Sanskrit as the language of the gods, meaning, according to the occult way of speaking, that it was the original composed language of some of the highest initiates of the early Fifth or so-called Aryan Root-Race, who, because of their great wisdom and knowledge and intellect, and divine life, were commonly called gods, though they were men of course, semi-divine men.

ORIGIN OF THE RED INDIAN

What is the origin of the native Americans?

The origin of the native Americans, popularly called Indians, is one of the most difficult questions that could be asked, for the reason that while all are of late Atlantean extraction, the American continents, North and South, were populated by different migrations from different parts of Atlantis, both from the Atlantic and the Pacific. The Pacific immigrations into the Americas were perhaps somewhat higher in type, and from these Pacific immigrations came most of the more civilized peoples of South and Central America and the Mayas.

But also there were civilized immigrations from the Orient, and this is what the ancient Mexicans of the Spaniards' day meant when they said that their forefathers came from the east, which really means from different Atlantic islands.

I have never had much faith in the Bering Strait immigration idea, although I have no doubt that a certain trickling back and forth between Siberia and North America has taken place through many ages in the past, and not only from Siberia to America, but from America to Siberia.

It is evident to me, and always has been, that *different* Atlantis races populated the Americas, by different waves of immigration, some very small, some larger; for while there are close parallels and likenesses between the Red Indians of the United States, for instance, and the so-called Indians of South and Central America, and even of Mexico, there are equally great distinctions in physiological type. The profile, for instance, of the Iroquois or of the Sioux or of the Cherokee, resembles somewhat the profile of the South American and Central American Indians, and yet there are distinct differences. All this points to different waves from different peoples, although all these peoples were of Atlantis origin in the far distant past.

Microsomes and Centrosomes

(a) Is the action of the microsomes caused by the "inner soul of the physical cell" (H. P. B.) awakening the centrosome? (b) Does the nucleolus when it disappears pass to another plane of consciousness?

Answering your first question: In each cell there is a central prânic nucleus which is the life-germ of a life-atom, and all the rest of the cell is merely the carpentry of the cell builded around it by the forces flowing forth from the heart of this life-atom. The modern cytologists see only the house, and do not discern the mystical dweller within, but the occultist looks to the mystical dweller within, or the life-atom. From your description, I would say off-hand that the life-atom works through the two tiny dots or sparks in the centrosome which fall apart at the beginning of cell-division and its energies stream out from these two tiny dots, and each tiny dot, as it were, is already the beginning of a new cell; or, to put it in other words, one remains the central part of the mother-cell, while the other tiny dot becomes the central part of the daughter-cell, etc.

All these phenomena of mitosis or cell-division are simply the works of the inner soul of the physical cell awakening the nucleolus and thereafter the nucleus. There is the strongest connexion between these two tiny dots and the nucleolus of every cell, although this may not be immediately apparent. Remember that it is the nucleolus which is the closest physical garment of the life-atom.

For the second question: The sudden apparent disappearance of the nucleolus, followed by the sudden re-appearance of the nucleolus in each one of the two cells resulting from the division of a cell, is simply the breaking into twain of the original nucleolus for the purposes of cellular growth. But the original life-atom remains intact, and now works through the two new nucleoli, and thus the cell-division continues until the body is finally builded. You may say that the nucleolus when it disappears passes to another plane of substance but this is a mere manner of expression. It would be better to say that the creative life-atom disintegrates the original nucleolus and then re-integrates it into two new ones, and there again into four and so on. No, it does not vanish in a laya center. It is a case of disintegrating and reintegrating on the physical plane. The whole gist of the matter is this: The heart of an original nucleolus in a cell is the life-atom, and the two tiny dots or spots in the centrosome are, as it were, extensions or fingers of its energy. The energy of the original life-atom, which is the heart of a cell, works throughout the entire cellular framework or structure in general, but more particularly through the nucleolus and also through the two tiny dots.

Arctic Origin of Plant and Animal

In my studies I came across the following rather startling statement which I should like to ask you some Theosophical questions about. It is from Edward Wilber Berry's Tree Ancestors: A Glimpse into the Past.

The great frozen north of today had not yet been hinted at [referring to the Cretaceous Period], a warm climate prevailed even in the far north, and Greenland was the garden spot that its name implies. On its western coast many plant-beds have been discovered, containing the remains of tree-ferns, cycads, incense cedars, figs, camphor trees, magnolias, and other natives of warmer climes. This northern region with numerous land connections to lower latitudes was probably the original home of our modern floras and faunas, which spread southward in successive waves of migration. We know that that Mid-Cretaceous witnessed the apparently sudden appearance of a host of new and higher types, and the basal Eocene witnessed a like sudden appearance of mammalian types and a second and more profound modernization of the floras. It is in the frozen North or the unexplored heart of Asia that we look today, hopeful that in one or the other of those strategic regions we will find the fossils that will shed their light on our problems of descent and distribution.

With this quotation in mind would you answer the following questions:
1. Did the plant stocks coming in during the Cretaceous Period and the Eocene Period, and which are the dominant types of today, originate

in the Arctic, sweeping southward in successive waves, as we are told is the case with civilizations? This seems to be a fact, and yet there is evidence that at one time Antarctica furnished types of vegetation which passed northward into South America, the South Pacific Islands, and the East Indies.

2. Was Antarctica in the north at that time, due to the inversion or inclination of the poles?

3. Do both poles originate life forms which progress towards the equator?

4. Do some of the Tertiary deposits of the southern lands belong to another cycle than the Tertiary deposits of the north?

The quotation from Professor Berry's book is extremely interesting, and generally what he says is true. It is in the north that things originate and beings too, including humans. But this is a very *general* statement, and should not be ridden to death. There are always backwashes of both botanical and geological units.

So the picture is this: a big wave beginning in the north, sweeping through the ages southwards; but in all this big wave there are often smaller waves that temporarily turn back northwards for a way, last for a while, and then are swept southward again because of the greater force of the big wave. In other words, there are smaller currents within the larger currents.

Thus, in answer to your question (1) the answer is Yes. The plant-stocks, generally speaking, follow the southward march through long ages that the animal and human stocks follow. But the little backwashes I have mentioned will account for any alleged plant-types that may have seemed to come out of Antarctica up northwards for a certain way.

In answer to your question (2) No, because there it is not so much a question of which way the poles point, due to inversion or inclination of the poles, as it is the geographical or rather climatological states of the poles, whether they are covered with ice or enjoy a mild climate. Antarctica, so far as our earth is concerned, is always the south, has always been and as far as I know always will be; and the North Pole in the same way — both during *this* manvantara. But north does not necessarily mean ice and snow, for there have been times when the North Pole enjoyed almost a mild climate; and the South Pole similarly.

Question (3) has already been covered in my previous remarks. The North Pole and its regions are the originators of new life-forms which, through long ages, sweep south; and from the South Pole there are small backwashes. Therefore there are no life-forms which regularly progress from Antarctica to the equator and still farther northwards.

Your question (4) is not very clear, but I think I understand it. The so-called Tertiary deposits are geological deposits, depending upon the climate which in its turn depends upon many factors; but both the North and the South Hemispheres of the earth are pretty much the same, with minor differences as regards climatological matters. Hence the Tertiary in both North and South Hemispheres belonged to the same cycle.

HEART, THE MOST EVOLVED ORGAN

As a physician of long practice I have come to the conclusion that the heart is the most evolved organ of the human body. Does this agree with occult teaching?

Yes the heart is the chief organ of the human body, the hyparxis, physically speaking. That is because the heart is the physical organ in the body of the spiritual ray. And in exactly the same way, and just after the heart, the pineal gland is to be classed in identic fashion. First the heart, then its organ of spiritual-intellectual activity in the head, the pineal gland. Both these working together stimulate and throw into vibration the organ of the intellectual will, which is called the pituitary body. Thus we trace the line of spiritual descent, touching the heart and inflaming it with invisible light, communicated in a manner I cannot here speak of, to the pineal gland, which in its turn thus thrown into rapid vibration, touches with its vital energy the pituitary. This, being aroused, communicates the transmitted influence to the brain and nervous system, and the entire body thereafter feels the effects.

The Hindû doctrine of the chakras is closely connected with this process, but so much nonsense and indeed false knowledge has been said and written about the chakras that I do not care to bring them in except otherwise than by mention here. Actually the chakras are esoteric and indeed physical points in the entire body; most of them working from power received through the spinal column from the heart and brain, and are thus the distributors to the body as a whole.

TEACHINGS ON CHAKRAS ESOTERIC

Why do we not find more about the chakras of the human body in our Theosophical books? I had always understood that they were an important aspect of occult study.

In our School we follow the ancient esoteric tradition, that the teachings of the Esoteric Wisdom dealing with the chakras and the very dangerous forces locked up in the human constitution form a topic of study highly improper for the uninitiated to have anything to do with. As you will find

in your study of H. P. B.'s books, she tells us that such study for the uninitiated or those untrained will lead definitely to the precipice of Black
Magic and possibly to the loss of the soul. No genuine occultist has ever
given the real teachings about chakras and their development.

IS DOWNWARD ARC NECESSARILY EVIL?

*It is evident that on the Downward Arc of evolution, egoism evolves
and the entity descends into the material world. But this is so much a rule
of nature that it seems to me it would be wrong to call this descent, or
practice of egoistic thought and activities, necessarily evil.*

The Book of the Golden Precepts offers the best and most direct answer. Work with Nature; do her will, and Nature will make obeisance.
In whatever direction Nature may be flowing, which means the direction
of the will and vitality of the Gods, work with her. As soon as we attempt,
however, to swim against the current, *in adversum flumen,* we set ourselves
against Nature's evolutionary progress, whether unfolding or infolding. We
run counter to her laws, so called, which is her will, and therefore we become sorcerers.

RECORDED LIFE OF KRISHNA AN ALLEGORY

*From my theosophical study I have come to realize that the so-called
historical lives of the world's great avatâras are in the main pure allegory.
Is this not likewise true of the life of the Hindû Teacher Krishna and the
rather peculiar, even revolting, incidents which legend has woven around
him?*

Yes, practically all the tales told about Krishna, or indeed any other
great man, excepting those rather pragmatic facts which commonsense can
pick out, are allegory or even fiction. If it is allegory, it was probably written by someone who knew the ropes, as it were, and was giving the religious public something for their religious thoughts to center upon, knowing
that initiates would understand. But there is generally also a lot of fiction,
and today both allegory and fiction have become so entangled as to be in-
extricable.

A few actual facts are known about Krishna; as for instance that he
was born in India, in a certain district there, that he had his friends and
his enemies, and that from early life he showed marvelous abilities, although of course not anything like the perfectly exaggerated metaphors
of the allegories. He lived and taught and did his work, and his death
was the beginning or introduction of the Kali-Yuga. He was, in other

words, the spiritual power which closed the Dwâpara-Yuga, and opened the Kali.

All the other allegories about the sixteen and odd thousand wives, and his living with the Gopîs or Cow-Girls, and many acts of apparent cruelty — these and a hundred other things can all be ascribed to allegory, with that fertility and richness of imagination for which the Hindû mind is so noted.

For instance, in one particular but very restricted sense, Krishna's dancing with the Gopîs, as H. P. B. said, symbolizes the Sun with the planets dancing around him or moving in their orbits around him; or it could likewise be applied to the spiritual Sun of the zodiacal constellations encircling the central Sun of our system. But this interpretation is rather a restricted one. Generally, the feminine friends of a great Teacher are allegorical representations of his spiritual powers.

Take even the case of the Buddha, who actually lived and had a wife and even a son Râhula. Yet legend has so cleverly worked even here, that his mother's name, for instance, was Mâyâdevî, or roughly, the Goddess Mâyâ: the Buddha born from mâyâ into Light. Actually her real physical name may have been Mâyâdevî too. I admit that as a possibility.

AUTONOMY OF A THEOSOPHICAL LODGE

If our lodge wishes to study psychology, astrology, or kindred subjects not strictly Theosophical is it permitted to do so?

This is a matter for the lodge itself to decide. If a T. S. lodge or a number of members in it or a single member in it has a strong leaning towards psychology, or modern astrology, or what not, and wants to study one of these, put it up to the lodge to be voted upon by the members of the lodge, and have the motion carried or lost, according to the rules, or by-laws; that is, let the majority vote rule. I imagine only a few, if any, of our lodges would devote their time to these subjects above mentioned, or if they did the time given would be only a portion of the whole time that the lodge would give to genuine Theosophical studies. In any case if the matter is put to an honest vote by the lodge, then there can be no complaint one way or the other.

Let me emphasize that it is in line with the constitutional prerogatives of any one of our lodges to conduct its studies as it pleases and to undertake such kinds or classes of study as it pleases; and I feel there is very little or any danger in this policy, but real benefit in it, because it becomes obvious on thought that if any lodge is not Theosophical at heart it will soon go to pieces anyway, whereas by giving them their rein and realizing that they are autonomous under the provisions of the Constitution and are authorized to conduct their own affairs as they please within the Constitution, sooner or later hopefully if they have any real Theosophy in their hearts they will grow tired of wasting time in frilly studies and will naturally be attracted to the more genuine Theosophical studies. Putting the matter to the vote of the lodge is undoubtedly the fairest way to decide lodge problems, and as it is the democratic way or policy in modern history few people would object, and if they do they will automatically drop out with the minimum of heart-burnings or hard feelings.

RADIOACTIVITY AND THE ROUNDS

In a recent scientific magazine Dr. A. Knopf of Yale discusses the minute spherical stones of radioactive origin called "pleochroic halos" which, he says, confirm the testimony given by the transformation of radioactive elements into helium and lead that a constant rate of transformation has been kept up throughout the ages. By means of these evidences geologists believe that a reasonably accurate estimate has been attained of the ages of the principal strata of the earth's surface. How does this harmonize with the idea that etherealization of the earth did not begin till the middle of the Fourth Round? These halos occur at a far earlier period.

One explanation that might be offered is that these halos are due to a radioactivity which took place at the end of the preceding or Third Round on this Globe, and which, despite the tremendous seismic and volcanic upset or overturn when the Fourth Round opened, might nevertheless have escaped destruction and remained to our day. It is quite a possible explanation, even if hardly probable; which means that it can be the case but is unlikely.

There are two or three other explanations of the facts, if they are indeed facts and not mistakes of the geologists: (a) even on the Descending Arc, before radioactivity (which means disintegration or etherealizing of the grossest elements) could have begun on a grand scale over the earth, due to the cyclical or spiral character of evolution, even on the Descending Arc, certain parts of the Globe could have been on a temporary uprise towards etherealization, sinking later again into a deeper trough to accord with the general downwards current of the Descending Arc.

Now, such temporary uprise would almost certainly have brought about a temporary etherealizing of the grossest elements, but thereafter, when the wheel within the wheel rushed downwards again, such radioactivity would stop automatically, and condensation or materialization continue. And (b), even if the rocks found by geologists were actually of pre-Cambrian or at any rate primordial origin, it is no proof — because radioactive halos may be found spotted here and there — that these halos actually signify radioactivity which took place when these pre-Cambrian rocks were first laid down, or perhaps for long ages afterwards. In other words, I mean that even in Cambrian and pre-Cambrian rock-strata, there may have been localized nodules or particles of chemical compounds or elements still grosser than the rocks themselves, still heavier, and consequently after the middle point of this Round it would be these nodules or local bits of such grosser compounds or elements, which, feeling the general etherealization over the earth, would begin to disintegrate, which means to become more or less radioactive. Such halos might well have been produced in actual pre-Cambrian rocks, but long after Atlantean days.

Thus, then, there are three perfectly good and probable explanations; and it would be impossible for me to give you any more light on the subject until and unless I could have all the data and feel perfectly assured that they are facts and not mere theories.

As an example: Are these particular rocks actually pre-Cambrian in fact and not in theory? Are the halos of supposedly radioactive character found in these rocks of much later date, or co-eval with the pre-Cambrian era? Or, is it just a relic or remnant, a happy survival from the end of the Third Round on this Globe D? Until an exact answer to these questions can be given, it is more or less guess-work, because of lack of accurate information.

Four Classes of Mânasaputras

It is evident that the majority of those entities in whom the Mânasaputras incarnated millions of years ago now comprise what we call our average humanity. What about the degenerate races? Did they also receive the mânasaputric spark?

When the Mânasaputras, or Sons of Mind, incarnated in the relatively mindless stocks of the Third Root-Race in this Round, they divided naturally, that is by karmic decree, so to speak, into four general classes, which I will call, for mere purposes of distinction, those whose light burned brilliantly, the highest class; those whose light burned less brilliantly, the second class; those whose light burned low, the third class; those whose light burned lowest, who put off reincarnation till a later day. All this was of course due to Karman.

The first class, those whose light burned brilliantly, had immediate and full incarnation then, and became the guides, leaders, and teachers of the then stocks of humanity, and are they whom today we would call the advanced Fifth Rounders, and the occasional, very, very rare, Sixth Rounders. These today are the most evolved and the greatest lights of the human race, the Buddhas, the Mahâtmans, etc.

Those whose lights burned less brilliantly are they whom today we would call the noblest and highest men of our usual mankind; but, nevertheless, beneath the first class. They are the early Fifth Rounders, or very advanced Fourth Rounders. These comprise the great philosophers, poets, scientists, statesmen, religious reformers, etc., etc.

Those whose lights burned low are they whom today we would call the great average of mankind, the great bulk of humanity.

Those whose lights burned lowest are they whom today we would call the inferior or less evolved men and women of our present human stocks, the rather inferior types; and among these last would be classed the so-called savage and degenerate races, although these savage and degenerate races do not comprise all of the individuals of this last and fourth class of monads. This is why these especial monads find their natural and karmic and sympathetic bodies in the present degenerate races.

There is still one more class of monads whom we might call a fifth, and these were the monads who, in the Third Root-Race, refused to incarnate at all, but simply let the aeons slip by until the next, or Fourth Root-Race, when they began to sink into imbodiment; and this last, or fifth class, rather small in number, are found among the present anthropoid apes, and the very highest class of simians or monkeys. They were so backward in evolution that these terribly inferior bodies just suit them today.

So in this answer you have the reason why certain monads are drawn to the bodies of the present degenerate races. Their lights still burn so low that they cannot carry, or inform, or handle, bodies of more advanced type. It is the old rule of water seeking its various levels according to circumstances.

THE BOOK OF DZYAN

Can you tell me something about the antiquity of the Book of Dzyan, upon which H. P. Blavatsky based her Commentaries in THE SECRET DOCTRINE? *Does it date back to Atlantean times?*

The Book of Dzyan, as a physical roll or book or manuscript, or Tibetan type-print, call it what you like, as a physical thing, is, as H. P. B. says, not very old, probably about a thousand years, and is part of a well-known, more or less common Tibetan series of works, well-known even exoterically, called Kiu-ti as a general title for all these volumes; just as *The Secret Doctrine* is in two volumes, etc.

The substance, however, of the Book of Dzyan, which is simply the Tibetan or Mongolian way of pronouncing the Sanskrit Dhyâna, is very ancient, even highly archaic, goes right back into Atlantean times, and even beyond as regards the doctrine taught.

This original doctrine, the original Theosophy of the spiritual beings or Mânasaputras of higher type who brought it to ancient mankind in this Round, has percolated all over the earth, and is found, or could have been found, in many languages. Some of these have vanished, been destroyed. A few have been preserved. The Masters of course have records of all, samples that is, in their secret libraries or cave-temples, call them what you like.

The Book of Dzyan was especially selected by H. P. B. to write from because it contains the original archaic teaching, admittedly covered up in the Kiu-ti scriptures with a lot of extraneous material, legendary stuff, marvels and miracles which the Tibetan populace delights in, etc. But she had been taught to read underneath these things to find the thread of pure gold among all the exoteric and devotional trash.

The Book of Dzyan, one of the first of the Kiu-ti series, deals with the cosmogonic building of the worlds and of our planetary chain, especially, and to a certain extent deals with the first appearances of man or of the Root-Races, just about as H. P. B. has dealt with the matter, generalizing it all, in her two volumes of *The Secret Doctrine*.

There was another famous Commentary, famous throughout all Tibet, written by Tsong-kha-pa, a great Tibetan Buddhist reformer and the founder of the so-called Yellow-Caps or Gelugpas, as the Tibetans call them, the reformed Buddhist Tibetan Church, and today the most powerful in the country and the purest. This Commentary is called Lam Rim, sometimes written Lam Rin.

This is a remarkable Commentary, partly exoteric, partly esoteric, on various matters, written under the guise of the reformed Buddhism which Tsong-kha-pa brought about, but actually containing a lot of genuinely esoteric or actual teachings. Very few people have ever seen a copy of the Lam Rim; I do not know why, but it seems to be the case. I have never seen a copy, which does not mean anything because I do not live in Tibet. I have never heard of a traveler who got hold of a copy, though I have heard of several claims. For some reason, up to the present, Lam Rim has been guarded carefully. Perhaps in the future it won't be so.

Thus, to summarize: The Book of Dzyan is written in Tibetan, at least part of it or most of it, is interspersed with a lot of exoteric stuff, but the real occult part of the Book of Dzyan is one of the first of the

Kiu-ti volumes and deals mainly with cosmogony, and later on to a less extent, I believe, with anthropogony or the beginnings of mankind.

THE DELPHIC ORACLE

Could a deeper light be shed on the real significance of the Delphic Oracle?

The Delphic Oracle was one of several in Greece. They were all cases of human beings in an abnormal state, usually consisting in a quasi-paralysis of the lower quaternary partly brought about by artificial means, such as vapors, sulphureous or otherwise, or possibly relatively harmless drugs. Then the Oracle found herself, for the Oracle was usually a woman, in a state which is recognised today, and commonly spoken of, as a highly sensitive psychic state in which the mind can receive truth, but quite as often merely distorted psychic vision.

Now the Delphic Oracle was one of the best in Greece, because one of the most carefully guarded. In these cases when the Delphic Oracle delivered its dicta, or statements, they usually came from the inspiration of the priestess's own inner divinity impressing the sensitive psychic nature, which in turn spoke through the human mouth. The fact that the Oracles were usually delivered either in metaphor, or in ambiguous terms, is one of the phenomena of the working on this plane of the higher psychical apparatus of man. It is only the lower brain-mind that pays any attention to points of accuracy like number of steps, or the correct page of a book, or the exact length of a skirt, or how many times a man lifted his arms in an hour, or whether when a priest returned home he would have curds and barley for supper or boiled mutton and thin wine. All these are matters of the lower brain-mind.

THE DOOR INTO THE HUMAN KINGDOM

What is the so-called "door" into the human kingdom?

This door into the human kingdom has been stated by H. P. B. as closing at the middle point of the Fourth Round, as it did during the Fourth Sub-Race of the Atlantean Race. Contrary to the wording of this statement, many students have construed that closing of the door as an opening of a door, and have there made unnecessary confusion. The door does not then open into the human kingdom. It shuts, and the meaning is this: Let us speak of our own Fourth Round only, though the same events took place, *mutatis mutandis,* that is making the necessary changes, during the Second and the Third Round, and will also take place in the future during the Fifth, Sixth, and the last. The meaning is this: that from the beginning of our present Fourth Round, the different families of monads of all classes, of all the kingdoms of nature, were in the very beginning as it were more or less confused. In a sense they were much closer; just as the human germ is very much closer to other kingdoms of nature as long as it is a germ, than when these germs have separated themselves out and become grownup men, grownup humans.

The meaning of the phrase, the door into the human kingdom *closes* at the middle point of the Fourth Round, is simply this: that during Root-Race One, Root-Race Two, Root-Race Three, and half of Root-Race Four, these various classes of monads were separating themselves out into families more distinctly than they were before, so that when all the classes of monads on the downward arc reached the central point of the Fourth Round, those which were already then human could pass onwards and begin the ascent, which they did. Those who had not attained humanity would pass on but were not the humans. Those above the classes of men when they reached that point, would pass on but would not pass through the human door. They would pass through other so-called doors, which is but a figure of speech, through the dhyân-chohanic door; or those below the humans through the beast-doors, or the plant-doors, etc. It simply means that the various families of monads on the downward arc during Root-Races One, Two, and Three, and half of Four, separated themselves out distinctly into families, and after that time those entities which were not human could never become human for the remainder of this planetary imbodiment. The door into the human kingdom closed against all monads below the human for the rest of the three and a half rounds. This means the lowest point had then been reached, and from then onwards there is a steady rise.

PARTHENOGENETIC REPRODUCTION OF RABBITS

Scientific experiment claims that by certain mechanical or chemical means and reactions an animal, say a rabbit, can give birth to apparently normal young without the usual mating process. Is this possible from the Theosophical viewpoint? That is, with our knowledge of Nature's processes of reproduction during earlier Races, could this scientific method be a forced throw-back to such times, or again a forced push-forward to future times? I quote the following report given in the Los Angeles Times *of November 23, 1941, to make my question clearer, and would much appreciate your comment.*

Philadelphia, Nov. 22 (AP) A small bag of ice cubes from the refrigerator, placed on the side of a rabbit for an hour and a half, sometimes causes conception, the American Philosophical Society was told today by Dr. Herbert Shapiro of Hahnemann Medical College, Philadelphia.

After Dr. Shapiro had finished, the chairman of the meeting, Dr. Edwin G. Conklin, Princeton University biologist, said:

"We have just listened to what really may be the beginning of a most important result. I am sure it would greatly interest theologians. Possibly we are on the way to see the explanation of a miracle."

The ice treatment, Dr. Shapiro said, has caused virgin conception in a number of rabbits. The seeming miracle is only occasional. None of these first rabbits in which conception took place was allowed to live. But Dr. Shapiro said some later will be allowed to go on to the point of giving birth to the young, if they do. All the scientific evidence points to success when this is tried, he explained. There is now living one rabbit, born in January this year, whose daddy was a tube of ice water, inserted by surgical operation into the abdomen to chill the mother's unfertilized ova, or eggs, for a few minutes. This ice water rabbit is a female, perfectly normal, and already has had two litters of young by normal reproduction. Those ice water experiments were made by Drs. Shapiro and Gregory Pincus.

In addition there are also today, in this country, three living rabbits whose fathers were merely concentrated salt. This salt technique was the first scientifically recorded virgin birth of mammals, and the ova were fertilized by a surgical operation which exposed them to the salt.

Work done by other scientists and not mentioned today raises the question of the possibility of human conception under similar circumstances. Surgeons in Philadelphia have found that human ova, obtained during operations, take the first steps of conception when exposed to chemical solutions.

The question is of course intricate, and not the kind of thing that can be answered in a short sentence, as the entire history and generation of the human race in this Round is really involved in or bears upon the alleged reproduction processes of non-impregnated females among the animals.

Abstractly, I see nothing impossible in such reproduction, which only by courtesy ever could be called Virgin Conception, for Virgin Conception in Christian theology means only one thing, the unique instance in eternity(!) of the Jewish maiden Mary becoming a mother through the incarnation of the Third Person of the Trinity. I doubt if Christian theologians would like to apply this theological conception to the parthenogenetic reproduction of rabbits! It is of course not virgin birth, though it is or abstractly could be a form of biologic parthenogenesis.

Abstractly, I say, parthenogenesis is not impossible. In fact, unless I have forgotten all the biology I once knew, it is occasionally still found in the animal kingdom, females reproducing young from within themselves. This was once a common mode of reproduction of the human kingdom during the First Race, during the Second Race, and during about half of the Third Root-Race, although the methods employed in these two and a half Races changed with evolution's procedures and work.

I have often said that the present sex condition in mankind, and even in animals, is but a passing phase, and will be succeeded in due course of time by another method, in my own opinion a partial return to hermaphroditism or androgyny, to be followed again by something still less suggestive of sex; and it is obvious that these methods will be preceded in the human kingdom's evolutionary history by facts casting their shadows before, which will be looked upon at first as playthings of nature, *lusus naturae,* and then become universal; and the present system will be looked upon as a rapidly dying out reproduction-method of degenerates, until it disappears. The animals, although dying out as a kingdom, will reflect likewise and copy more or less what the human kingdom goes through, passes through, evolves into.

Now then, our teaching regarding reproduction is the teaching of the norm, the rule, the regular thing, but with many hints or allusions to coming changes, and with a finger pointing into the historic or pre-historic past. The cases of these rabbits, non-impregnated females, producing fertile young because of cold applied locally to the female's reproductive organs, or salt applied by a surgical operation to the same organ, can be explained in various ways, and until I were thoroughly acquainted with all the details, it would be partly guess-work on my part to try to state what actually did occur, although I have a clear enough suspicion of what could happen, which I think actually did happen, if this newspaper report can be accepted as authentic, and not just some newspaper reporter's yarn about something which indeed took place, but which the reporter, being no biologist, either did not properly understand, or embroidered.

I have a notion, therefore, that what took place was something like this: the means employed by these experimenters temporarily paralysed or perhaps dislocated what we might call the female or feminine current of kâma, and threw the generative organ of the female, or rather the ova, back to a condition resembling, if not identical with, the hermaphroditism of the early Third Race. Then the ova would follow the line of least resistance, and there being always in every human or animal of our day a double sex in each, in women the male being recessive and the female dominant, and in the male the male element dominant and the female current recessive, the ova in such cases, or an ovum in such case, would develop from the double current innate in the mother rabbit, and thus produce offspring pretty much as the hermaphrodites did towards the middle of the

Third Root-Race. Or indeed the process might more nearly have resembled that of the Second Root-Race.

But of course I can only assume and search here, as I do not know all the facts. But I know what must have taken place in a general way. Such a female mother, if left alone and not further interfered with or meddled with, like those creatures who meddled with the human eggs in the early Third, would probably not reproduce again except in the usual way, or by again being interfered with by human experimenters.

Thus I discern nothing impossible in this report, but having only end results and not the full story, I can only know what must have taken place; but just which aspect I cannot say. But I think the experiment reported in the clipping reduced the female rabbit's ova to about the condition of the human ova towards the early or middle Third Root-Race.

Could such meddling or interfering or experimenting produce the same results on human females?

I don't see why not. But the subject to me is repulsive, and I think rather dangerous. It is infinitely better to leave these things to the laws of nature as we find them. It is evident that the dhyân-chohanic 'fluid,' which merely means the fluid emanating from the reincarnating ego, is as present in a human or animal female, as it is present in a human male. But nature today follows present procedures automatically, and will only change them and revert to pre-history when her courses are stopped or interfered with. If the stoppage is heavy, nothing will result. If the stoppage is a mere diversion, something will happen. Reversion will take place in such instances. Heaven knows what such offspring will be or would become! Personally I think it would be greatly disadvantaged, because produced abnormally, and out of nature's present rule. I think such experiments are little short of black magic, but what do scientists know of magic, either white or black? Unable themselves to explain, they think it is enough just to experiment like the schoolboy in the chemical laboratory.

Therefore do not confuse the norm as nature now has it, and which our Theosophical teaching has tried to illustrate, with the abnormal experimentations which, because abnormal reversions but outlived, are now dead evolutionary stages.

THEOSOPHY AND OCCULTISM

Are Theosophy and Occultism the same thing, or different things?

Theosophy and Occultism are in one sense the same thing. In another sense they are different things. Let me try to illustrate that point. Do not the Christians for instance say that the teachings of Christ and the Christian theology are the same, yet different? They claim that the theological doctrines originated in the teachings of Jesus Christ, but that the actual teachings which Jesus Christ gave in his day were not — and it is true — the theological doctrines of later times.

So Theosophy is the ancient Wisdom-Religion in an all-inclusive sense. These wonderful and sublime doctrines were originally given to mankind on this planet by spiritual beings from other spheres, gods among men, and have descended in the care of this great Association of the Masters of Wisdom down to us even unto this day, and are given out from time to time, from age to age, when the world needs a spiritual rejuvenation. That body of teachings, of doctrine, is Theosophy, the wisdom of the gods, the key, the master-key, to all the great religions and sciences and philosophies of the past.

But Occultism is that part of Theosophy which treats of the deeper, hid, mystic, esoteric, side of nature and of man. It is Theosophy indeed, but that part of Theosophy which the average man cannot 'eat' — to use the figure of the New Testament, the metaphor of the Christian Scripture — because he is still a little child. He needs must be fed the milk — to use again the figure of the New Testament — that is to say, to begin with the simpler teachings.

Discipline, as we Theosophists say, precedes the Mysteries. Occultism, therefore, is that branch of the general Theosophical philosophy which treats of these operations of Nature and the secret laws of Nature and of man. These two are one and the same fundamentally, and yet that same thing, as it were, is made up of two branches: one for Esoterics, and the other the all-inclusive source from which streams the current of the teachings for the exoterics. But these two divisions are not arbitrary. It all depends upon the applicant. You cannot keep a good man down, is an old saying; and the man who comes to our doors and knocks and gives the right knock — we know what the right knock is — enters.

SUFFERING IN ANIMAL KINGDOM

Is it true that animals killed by other animals or through the agency of man really do not suffer, and in fact, as stated by certain well-known authors, actually feel a kind of joy in their last moments?

No. This is all poppycock. What actually happens is, both in humans and animals, that the fright and the nervous shock are so tremendous on a beast's sensitive nature, as well as on a man, that there is a temporary stunning, almost a hypnosis. But how about the moments or times preceding the stunning, which is Nature's compassionate way of dulling and stupefying? It is preposterous to allege this shock, which is in fact a proof that animals do suffer greatly or are horribly frightened, as an excuse for saying that animals do not feel pain when the crisis comes. The fact is that there is a terrific amount of bestiality and horror and murderous impulse and suffering and pain in Nature; and Nature in her compassion at the last moment makes the suffering so exquisite as to produce a nervous shock bringing about a sort of sleepy feeling with temporary indifference. People confound two things here: (1) the suffering undergone; and, on the other hand (2), the fact that the horrors exist in our physical sphere. These are two quite different things, and they should not be confused.

VEGETARIANISM

Do you consider that a Theosophist must be a vegetarian to be a good Theosophist, and does THE SECRET DOCTRINE *teach this?*

I take it that the words *The Secret Doctrine* refer to our wonderful H. P. B.'s book, or indeed they may refer to the secret doctrine, the Ancient Wisdom. I have never found any passage in H. P. B.'s *The Secret Doctrine* forbidding the eating of flesh-food. There are many passages in different parts of our esoteric works which state in unmistakable terms that the eating of flesh-food is not good for two reasons. You know them, but there is no forbidding of it; and I can tell you plainly that I have known strict vegetarians, strict fruitarians, who had the heart of a tiger, and the unforgiving nature of an ape. It is not what goes into a man's mouth which purifies him. It is man's own will set to purify the Augean stables of his brain-mind. No, the eating of meat is no bar to chelaship in the beginning. Of course when you become an accepted chela, and are strictly following the rules of development required for higher degrees, when you become a disciple in training, meat-eating is impossible.

But the main argument against the eating of flesh-food is our doctrine of compassion, of pity. Nevertheless, there are times and there are reasons when and for which even the lower chelas do eat meat in small quantity. But don't think for a moment that what a man eats or does not eat is the cause of his going to the Masters. As I have told you, I have known some people who were strict vegetarians and even fruitarians whose hearts were filled with iniquity and all the poison of unkindness; and how they ever supposed that by living on vegetable food, or on beautiful fruits of the earth, by doing this alone with a corrupt nature, they could tread the path to the gods, I do not know; but they thought it! Mind you, I do not condemn, I simply state the fact as I have found it.

But remember also that the sweet vegetarian products of the earth, and the delicious fruits of our common Mother, are a far sweeter, more succulent, and purer food, than is the flesh of the unfortunate beasts who must die to provide the flesh that some use regularly and unthinkingly and in quantity far too large as their daily food. Every Theosophist if he can do so will probably have better health by following a wise and judiciously selected vegetarian diet, avoiding overeating, which is the usual cause why attempts at following the vegetarian diet sometimes fail. In such case the would-be vegetarian overeats from a false fear that his body needs more nourishment than it does; and the consequence sometimes is a badly impaired digestion, possibly auto-intoxication, and even disease. Common sense, and as above said a vegetarian diet selected with judicious care, comprising a well-balanced ration, and with due care not to overeat, will probably result in better health, more vigorous activity, and a clearer brain, than the eating of meat could ever bring.

Masters not Infallible

I have been told that not only the Masters are infallible but also H. P. B. and succeeding Leaders of the Theosophical Society. My commonsense rebels against this and I must protest.

No, no. The Masters are not infallible, and they themselves have pointedly disclaimed it; nor was H. P. B. infallible, nor those who succeeded her. H. P. B. brought rather heavy batteries directed against this same stupid idea that infallibility can be claimed by any human being. To be infallible one would need to be above all manifested life whatsoever, and in this sense of the meaning of the word, we might almost say that it is only the First Logos who could be called 'infallible' in the strict meaning of the word; and all beneath that first stage of manifestation, and increasingly so as the light recedes from the divine fountainhead, or sinks deeper into matter, all, I say, grows increasingly more fallible.

Now it is perfectly obvious that the word 'infallible' is sometimes used with some fair degree of logic to signify mere certainty or surety or what is absolutely known. Obviously this is not real infallibility; but what I am trying to say does point out the fact that there are in all manifested lives or life such things as certainties, sureties, positive cognitions of the Real, and this occurs when any individual, super-god, god, demi-god, or human, comes into relatively perfect union or communion with the divine Monad within; for these divine Monads are in their essence of the very stuff and substance of Cosmic Reality itself. But how many individuals are in such perfect and complete union with the Divine?

Many beings can achieve a nirvânic state which approximates temporarily at least such union with divinity within the heart of the individuals; for such short time they speak with the certainty of the spirit, or their knowledge is of the surety of Reality. But these cases are almost as rare as blue moons, and are virtually limited to the Buddhas or the super-Buddhas.

As a further development of this thought, it becomes perfectly clear that proportionately as even a fallible human being can come into touch with the god within himself, he becomes proportionately thereby more and more certain of the utter reality in things; and this is why there is such a thing in the cosmos as evolution, or development of the spirit from within outwards, why there are on the evolutionary ladder of life beings of an ascending and increasing stature of developed faculties. Thus it is that the gods are more certain and more sure than men are, and therefore can speak with authority, relatively so of course. On a still smaller and somewhat pragmatic scale we have what men call the trained expert, as the expert chemist or the expert engineer or mathematician or musician, or the expert in any line, who has by work and striving evolved forth a relative faculty of surety in what he knows and what he does. This is why men have confidence in each other, and have confidence in teachers, and have confidence in the greater and grand things of life, brought to us by those higher than the average, when they are closer to the Center of Reality than is the average.

Thus the word 'infallible' I myself have often heard used in this latter sense, and unquestionably wrongly used, in my judgment, by people who merely mean to say that the trained expert can speak with the voice of knowledge of things that to ignorant men are but an untrodden field.

But 'infallibility' in the Papal or Romish sense of real infallibility in doctrine has never been claimed by any Theosophist who knows his 'stuff,' and certainly never by the Masters nor H. P. B. nor anyone who has followed H. P. B., certainly not Judge nor K. T. nor I, for any such claim would be a mere lie. If the Masters repudiate it, i.e., 'infallibility,' any man claiming it would be a downright fraud, an impostor of the worst type, and the claim would disprove him as a Leader or Teacher of any kind.

Yet we receive the teachings of the Masters with reverence, for we realize that they know incomparably more than we do about the things that our god-wisdom contains. That is why we likewise reverence and look up to H. P. B., for the knowledge that she obtained, strived for and achieved, which was why she became the Masters' representative; and our reverence is based on the facts lying in the teachings she gave us, for they prove themselves — to us. Truth is its own proof, for nothing in the universe will ever overthrow it; and this is why it is really grand, beautiful, and in my judgment almost majestic in the manliness of it, when a man has sufficient awakened grandeur within himself that he can recognise another human being as his Leader and Teacher, as all true Theosophists have learned with H. P. B., and as she learned with her Masters. 'Infallibility'? No, of course not, but relative certainty and surety based on actual knowledge, emphatically yes.

THE ABSOLUTE

Will Dr. de Purucker kindly state whether in his judgment his idea of the Absolute, which has caused some discussion among Theosophists, is the same as H. P. B.'s idea, as explained in her THE SECRET DOCTRINE, *etc.*

My answer to this interesting question is an emphatic affirmative, given without qualification; except that perhaps H. P. B. is at times more familiar in her usage of the word 'Absolute.' But her real meaning, leaving words or terms aside, is absolutely identic with my own — a meaning which I have expressed with sufficient clearness, I believe, a number of times, and which may be found briefly explained in my *Occult Glossary* under the term 'Absolute.'

It is true, of course, that (a) H. P. B. *at times* used the word 'Absolute' in what has long been a common European philosophical sense; and (b) that I use the word in a more limited and strictly etymological sense, fully agreeing as I do with Sir William Hamilton, that it is wrong to employ this word otherwise, whatever careless thinkers or writers may say.

But leaving this aside as a matter of unimportance, I can state that the discussion concerning my use of the word 'Absolute,' which discussion at times, unfortunately, has verged upon acrimony on the part of my critics, has been on the whole informative and useful; for, if nothing else, it has made people think, and it is beginning to uncover one of the profoundest and most fascinating aspects of the Theosophical esoteric philosophy.

H. P. B. with her wonderful literary power and her amazing lucidity in expression, occasionally used the words 'Unconscious,' and 'Unknowable,' as being virtually synonymous with the word 'Absolute,' and this appears in her *The Secret Doctrine,* Volume I, pages 14 and 15; and I would call the attention of the questioner to the instructive and illuminating passage on page 106 of her *The Secret Doctrine,* Volume I, which I will briefly quote as follows:

> The Doctrine teaches that, in order to become a divine, fully conscious god, — aye, even the highest — the Spiritual primeval INTELLIGENCES must pass through the human stage. And when we say human, this does not apply

merely to our terrestrial humanity, but to the mortals that inhabit any world. . . . Hegel, the great German thinker, must have known or sensed intuitionally this truth when saying, as he did, that the Unconscious evolved the Universe only 'in the hope of attaining clear self-consciousness,' of becoming, in other words, MAN. . . .

This passage is often overlooked; and although the word MAN here is employed in a collective sense, MAN or mankind is obviously composed of men; and all mankind is limited indeed when compared with the 'Absolute' or the 'Unconscious.' The inference to be drawn, and the deduction to be made, are obvious, and in this one passage, as well as elsewhere, H. P. B. with her graphic power states our common case far better than I can.

I might add in conclusion that the Unconscious or Unknowable of European Pantheistic philosophy is not exactly the same as the frontierless, illimitable Infinitude or Duration of the Esoteric Doctrine, which Infinitude obviously is pure ETERNAL SPACE in the most abstract and absolute use of the term. But this abstraction again cannot be limited by the human concepts 'conscious' or 'unconscious,' 'knowable' or 'unknowable,' and therefore is not the 'Absolute.' ETERNAL SPACE is beyond all limitations of extension or time, as even the noblest human intuition perceives these.

DAYS AND NIGHTS OF BRAHMÂ

We are taught of a Day of Brahmâ, and also of a Night of Brahmâ. When the Night of Brahmâ comes on, all the entities in the Universe return whence they came, is it not so?

Generally speaking, Yes, but the question is not quite adequate. A 'Day of Brahmâ' refers to two things: First, the Seven Rounds of a Planetary Chain, which event has to do with one planet of our Solar System only. When Seven Rounds have been completed or lived through, that is one Day of Brahmâ. The term is also used for a single Round, but more infrequently. But this refers only to one planet of our Solar System. We can likewise speak of the *saurya* manvantara, a Sanskrit adjective derived from *sûrya* or the sun, when the Solar System and all that is in it, sinks into its Solar Pralaya. That is expressed by some three hundreds of trillions of human years; yet this refers only to our Solar System. Then there are figures, which it would be perfectly futile to talk about because we could not understand them, by which we could express the Manvantara of our entire Galaxy, our Home-Universe. And then beyond that we can speak of the Manvantara of our Kosmos, and of all the Galaxies that belong to something still greater, and so we could go on step by step. But the 'Day of Brahmâ' refers either to one Round, or much more frequently to all the Seven Rounds of our Earth's Planetary Chain; and that is expressed in some 4,320,000,000 human years — quite a long time! And yet you know, even in the Solar System that is a very short time. It is but like a day, and then there are the cosmic weeks, and the cosmic months, and the cosmic years, and then the lifetime of Brahmâ, hundreds of those years, and then we must think of Brahmâ's passing out of imbodiment and going into 'his' Nirvâna corresponding to the human Devachan, and returning again. And so we can continue in thought until our very brains become bewildered, reeling with the magnitude of the numbers involved.

But there is rule, there is law, there is order, in everything, and if we understand what happens in the case of the small things of our Earth, for instance, we can, *mutatis mutandis,* by making the necessary adjustments of figures and of places that we strike off, come to very clear conclusions as to the time-periods of the Solar System and of the Galaxy and of what not. The Day of Brahmâ includes all the Seven Rounds of our Earth's Planetary Chain.

Each Root-Race Has its Kali-Yuga

As I recollect, we are now on the Luminous Arc, having passed the bottommost part, the lowest part, of our racial evolution; and yet we have lived through some five thousand years only of the Kali-Yuga.

The reason is that each Race has its own Kali-Yuga, each great Race that is, each Root-Race; and our own Fifth Root-Race in this Fourth Round in this Fourth Globe has advanced only to the point where we have not even yet reached the lowest part of the Fifth Root-Race. In other words, we have not yet had our racial catastrophe, that catastrophe which cuts every Root-Race in twain at its midmost point, its lowest or most material point. We have passed only five thousand years of the Kali-Yuga cycle of our Race, and we shall not have reached the lowest or bottom point of our Fifth Root-Race until the racial cataclysm comes. That will come during the Kali-Yuga; and as a matter of fact the Kali-Yuga takes place at just that time, because the two kinds of events converge: the lowest evolutionary point, and the most material point, which likewise is the Kali-Yuga.

I understood we had passed the middle point of the cycle, even in the Fifth Race.

No, we have passed the middle point of the Fourth Round. That took place during the Fourth great Sub-Race of the Atlantean, that was the bottommost point of all the Seven Rounds, and you might call it the Kali-

Yuga of the Seven Rounds. Kali-Yuga means the most material part of any cycle of growth, of evolution. We have Kali-Yugas in each Round, which is the middle point of development on the Fourth or lowest globe. Then there is the Kali-Yuga of each great Root-Race; and furthermore there are small Kali-Yugas in the Sub-races. As a matter of fact, Kali-Yuga like all the other Yugas, is more or less a generalizing term. Kali-Yuga means the 'Black Age,' the age of material expansion, and the age of spiritual obscuration; and as everything runs in cycles and there are cycles within cycles, if you follow the idea it becomes obvious that the middle point of everything in its evolution is its most material point.

PARADOX OF THE MÂNASAPUTRAS

I would like to ask for a little further light on the Mânasaputras. We read that the Mânasaputras awakened the minds of men, yet in other places we read that the Mânasaputras are really ourselves. It sounds as if we are awakening our own selves.

Yes, we are told in one place in Theosophical literature that the Mânasaputras enlighten us; and we are told in another place that we, being enlightened, are nevertheless in our higher parts the Mânasaputras. Does it mean that we light ourselves? Do candles light themselves? Strangely enough, in spiritual things they do! You have given your own answer to the question.

The fact is this: 'Mânasaputra' is a compound Sanskrit word, *mânasa* an adjective from *Manas*, of which the nearest translation that I can give at the moment is 'mind.' But it means something different from mind, it means more and in a sense less. *Manas* pertains only to the human constitution. The same energy when manifesting in the Universe is called *Mahat*. When it manifests in particular entities it is called *Manas*. *Mânasa* as said is the adjective from this, signifying creatures, or beings, or angels, or devas, or whatever name we may call them by, who are endowed with the fire of self-consciousness, the ability to think self-consciously, to carry on trains of self-conscious thought and meditation. *Putra* means 'child,' or 'son,' or 'offspring.' Therefore *Mânasaputra* means 'child of mind,' and the plural — 'children of mind.'

We are all children of the Cosmic Mind — not exactly in this sense of the Anima Mundi however. The Universe is as much an organic being — and when I say the Universe I mean the Galaxy in this instance — as a human being is such an organism. It is ensouled. It is as infilled with monadic essences as we humans are, because we humans simply copy in the small, as microcosms, what the Galaxy or the Universe as the Macrocosm originally contains. All we have and are we derive from the surrounding Universe in which we move and live and have our being, as Paul of the Christians said. The Universe is rooted in infinitude and in eternity. We as parts of this cosmic whole are likewise not only rooted in it, but are also ourselves in our inmost and in our uppermost, in our highest, eternal and infinite. And the whole purpose of evolution is a larger and in ever increasing measure bringing out or evolving, bringing forth or unrolling, unwrapping, what is already within.

A little child is born. It is mindless. It has no mind. But the mind is latent there. And as the months pass by and the years drop into the past slowly and slowly, as it were step by step we see the little child beginning to think, to think self-consciously, to become a manifestation of, or to be endowed with and in progressing measure, the flame of thought, of self-consciousness. It begins to think, to cogitate, to excogitate, to think thoughts to a definite conclusion, to make plans. It begins to take an individual and a lively interest in life, because it is thenceforth a thinker.

This exemplifies what the descent, so called, of the Mânasaputras was into the mindless man or mankind of the early Third Root-Race. Shall we say that the Mânasaputra descended from above, or from outside, into an entity which did not already have the same mânasaputric faculty or organ latent or inherent within it? We cannot do that. The child can bring forth only what is within it, which is obvious enough. And yet the case is an actual descent, it is an actual incarnation of a flame, of the flame of thought and self-consciousness from the Monad hovering, as it were, over the brain, and permeating the brain and entire being of the growing child.

The Mânasaputra, therefore, is both ourselves and a descent into us of our higher Selves. And the descent of the Mânasaputra before the middle of the Third Root-Race was not a complete descent. It was only a partial descent; and I tell you that the Mânasaputras have not yet fully incarnated in us; or, in better language perhaps, have not yet fully manifested their splendor within us. Our minds are not yet fully evolved. We work even yet with imperfect minds. The thing is still in progress, it is still in the doing. And the Mânasaputras will not fully have incarnated within us, and thus be able to show forth to the full their god-like powers, until the very end of the Fifth Round, the Round next to come after we have finished this Fourth and undergone the interplanetary Nirvâna between Globe G and Globe A.

When a man dies, an adult in full possession of all his intellectual or mental or psychical powers, can anyone say, would anyone presume to say — I would not — that the divine flame of intellect had expressed all of its fulness within the man before he died? Why, the titan-intellects of the

human race have not yet fully expressed the powers of the Mânasaputra
above and within them. The Mânasaputras are incarnating all the time,
and incarnating ever more and more, just as in the growing babe, the growing child, the adult youth, or man or woman, as each year passes there is
a larger development of mental power.

So then, you see, the descent of the Mânasaputras is the descent into
our ordinary brain minds, into the human soul, of our spiritual soul, the
Mânasaputra, the spiritual side of us. But yet they are our Selves. The
Mânasaputras, in other words, are our Selves because they are our higher
Selves, from our higher Selves. Just as in the growing child — it is both a
descent and the child himself in his highest. That is the Mânasaputra.

And now, in addition to this — and I touch upon esoteric matters and
therefore I speak with some hesitation — in addition to this, there was still
another class of Mânasaputras who, as it were, started the whole thing
going by inflaming with their own intelligence, with their own fire of intelligent thought and self-consciousness those of the human race who, at that
time, in the early part of the Third Root-Race in this Round, were ready,
who caught the flame; and then their own mental apparatus, their own
mânasic powers, burst as it were into bloom as a rose unfolds rapidly its
petals when the season comes for it to do so. And these Mânasaputras,
this class of Mânasaputras, were the highly evolved entities from previous
cosmic manvantaras, who deliberately, belonging as they do to the hierarchy of the Buddhas of Compassion, as it were left their own sublime
spheres and descended among men and taught them — and then withdrew.
But that is another story.

Answering your question generally, the Mânasaputras are both we and
yet not we: we because the highest parts of us; not we because above our
ordinary humanity; and it is in our ordinary humanity that most men live
and think and feel. We are human monads, we human beings. But we
are overshadowed — what a strange English expression — over-enlightened
by the higher triad, the highest part of our constitution.

GENUINE MEDITATION

*What is meditation? I ask that question because there are many dif-
ferent theories as to what meditation really is.*

"What is meditation?" I would say in view of the many and very different opinions that are held about what men call meditation in the Occident, that meditation is the choosing of a subject of thought and allowing
the spirit to brood upon it in quiet and peace, holding it steadily before the
inner eye, and studying it without any effort of the brain-mind (for that

tires); brooding upon the idea in peace and quiet. It is a wonderful spiritual exercise.

But there is something even higher than meditation: the entering into the very heart and essence of the thing which you wish to understand. Don't you see that you cannot really understand a thing, which means making it a part of your consciousness, until you become it? You must actually vibrate synchronously, actually become a thing, before you can understand it through and through and through. Love is an instance of this. Any man who has not loved cannot understand what love is, but one who has loved needs no words to explain it to him; he knows. He has become love for the time being. And exactly the same with the exercise of the intellectual powers. No one, unless he has used his intellectual faculty and has penetrated deep into things, can understand what real intellectual thinking is; but to the man who has done it words become futile, he understands, he has intellectually become for the time being the thing he is investigating. And there is a faculty in the human being, a faculty which alas in most men is utterly unused, the power to penetrate into the very heart and essence of things and for the time being to be them. Thus you *know*. You return from this wonderful pilgrimage or journey of exploration a nobler and better man. You have enlarged your consciousness, you have learned something; and this is the real meaning of genuine meditation when this exercise is practised in less important things than the one just mentioned above.

TWELVE GLOBES IN A CHAIN

In FUNDAMENTALS OF THE ESOTERIC PHILOSOPHY *you give twelve globes. In one of the Letters in* THE MAHATMA LETTERS *the Master says there are fourteen in all, that the number has been given out correctly for the first time. Would that mean two, or rather* FOUR, *connecting the lower and higher hierarchies, instead of two? It puzzles me rather. . . . Looking up Letter XIV I now understand that the number fourteen relates to the seven lokas and the seven talas. Is that right?*

There is no need for being confused about this, although I readily see how confusion might arise. The number of globes is twelve, but the Master, in the Letter that you speak of, refers to the *seven manifest* globes of which H. P. B. herself almost invariably writes, and also to the World of Effects which are not Lokas or actual spheres, but inner parts of the constitution of each globe, much as a man's astral body is one of the principles of his constitution and yet not different from him.

Where you say that "I now understand that the number fourteen relates to the seven talas and the seven lokas. Is that right?" is quite correct, because the seven Lokas and the seven Talas include the principles both of any globe and of any man. But I must point out that the Master, in the quotation which you make from him, is more particularly referring to the "Worlds of Effects" or astral worlds, commonly grouped under the name Astral Light, than he is to the Lokas and Talas specifically. Nevertheless the Lokas and Talas are almost the same thing.

The matter is very involved, so it is small wonder that you should be puzzled. If you will look in *The Mahatma Letters,* on page 71, at the bottom of the page, you will see that the Master M. states specifically: "The worlds of effects are not lokas or localities." Remember, then, that there are actually twelve globes, seven of them manifest, and five unmanifest, at least to us human beings; but that the quotation from the Master's Letter refers rather to the particular Lokas and Talas conjoined which are to every globe its own specific "worlds of effects," the astral world and its connexions with the other parts of a globe's constitution of seven principles.

ARE THEOSOPHISTS NON-SOCIAL?

It has been said that there is likelihood that the Theosophist may become a-social (non-social). This statement was ascribed to the fact that the Theosophical teachings give an idea to the student of the eternity and boundlessness of life, and that in the course of time the student becomes conscious of this. Consequently he would see the relativity of everything, or of many things, and this might lead to a tendency to hold non-social feelings. My question is: Could it do harm or be deleterious to the real man, the inner man — with a view to his evolution on this earth — if he keep away from the society of this world, in which there is no doubt much evil?

There is not the slightest chance or possibility of a genuine Theosophist becoming a-social either in outlook or in feeling, if he follows the lines of teaching of the ancient Wisdom-Religion of the gods as given to us by the Masters of Wisdom and Compassion first in recent times through their Messenger, H. P. Blavatsky. All religions, all religious philosophies, and all philosophies with a religious tendency, are bound to arouse in a certain cast of human intelligence a desire to separate themselves off from the rest of mankind, and, as it were, to feel the need of a personal advancement on the road of spiritual and intellectual progress quite apart from one's duty to one's fellow-men. When this mistaken view prevails, then we have the phenomenon of monasticism and the conventual existence, such as grew to be so important at one time in the early medieval history of Christianity.

Of course it is true that by thus separating oneself from the world, one can free oneself to a certain extent from temptation, and make a kind of spiritual progress; but after all, it is a purely selfish progress and therefore in the end defeats the very object which this kind of life hopes to attain. True Theosophy does not approve of this kind of thing, for it shows us that we are all brothers, members of the human family, that we have intimate karmic responsibilities, one to all and all to one, and that the proper way to lead the Theosophical life is to live in the world but not to be of the world, i.e., to do one's whole duty by family and country and by one's fellow-men throughout the world, but yet in so doing to make of this very fact the means of inner spiritual growth. The Theosophist does not and should not flee from temptation. It is his duty to overcome and to conquer and not to run away. The very fact that the Theosophist by his study and life gains a keen understanding of the relativity of all things is the very reason why he feels his duty so strongly, and realizes that the quickest way in spiritual progress is by using every faculty that he has in accordance with the highest ethical principles, and with a feeling of deep and intense interest in the welfare of his fellow-men, and of compassion for the sufferings and troubles of our fellow human beings.

Therefore I think that the questioner is correct in saying that it could be bad for the inner real man to remain outside human society. The reason is that every man is an individual unit in human society, and he has a duty to human society; and therefore he should fulfil this human duty.

Of course there comes a time for every human individual when he may feel the urge to follow the lonely path of chelaship, of discipleship; but every true disciple or chela realizes that this path of seclusion is followed only up to the point where the disciple becomes a Master of life; and thereafter more than ever before does he become a servant of the law of Compassion and a servant of the world in the sense of devoting his whole life and all that is in him to awakening the spiritual and intellectual consciousness of his fellow-men.

I speak of the life of training that a disciple must pass through as a 'lonely' path; but this is a mere manner of speech. It is somewhat like a student in a University who has a difficult examination to pass; and in order to get the freedom from anxiety and distractions that otherwise would be upon him, he secludes himself in his rooms for a while until he has mastered the tests before him. Then when he has taken his degree, he comes into the world again and does his duty by his fellow-men — or at least he should do so.

I hope this answer is clear; and from it it will be readily seen that it is utterly wrong to say that Theosophists have a tendency to become a-social, i.e., non-social in the proper sense of the word 'social.' Also please note carefully that this has nothing whatsoever to do with politics of any kind. It is a question of morals, ethics, and of intellectual and spiritual growth and improvement.

EXPLANATION OF HEAVEN AND HELL

If you are asked by a Christian what you have to give in place of their Heaven, what would you reply, please?

May I answer this question by phrasing my answer not so much as an answer but as an explanation, inversely as it were. The Christian Heaven, a place of peace and bliss where the righteous shall dwell through eternity with a recognition of the glory of God Almighty upon their souls, and bathing in the spiritual elevation that they are one with Him and in His holy favor! How narrow! Would not the very angels, according to the Christian system, turn in horror from such spiritual selfishness? Think of the millions and millions and millions of uncounted hosts and multitudes of suffering creatures who have not attained such or any Heaven and who, according to the Christian theory, the orthodox theory, are undergoing the pangs of inextinguishable fire, burning in unspeakable torture to time without an ending! How can there be a Heaven when such hellish conditions prevail? Forgive me if I offend, I do not mean to. I am no believer in such a Heaven. I reject it because my whole soul rises in revolt. I want no Heaven unless every entity everywhere, unless every thinking and sentient soul, shares it with me. The self-isolated saint in his holy Heaven lives in a paradise of fools — and of very selfish fools!

Give me rather our own grand, sublime teaching of the gods: that there is eternal progress, that there is eternal evolution, eternal advancement, eternal growth, eternal unfolding of faculty after faculty, of power after power, of constantly increasing expansion of the human consciousness into the divine consciousness, and of the divine into the super-divine, and so on unto endless time. Give me our sublime teaching that as we grow and expand and our consciousness takes unto itself Kosmic reaches, we become co-laborers in the Kosmic Labor, in the Kosmic Work. Ah, there is a vision to enchant the soul; there is a vision to rest the heart; there is a vision which stimulates the intellect: the recognition of one's oneness with the Universe. Endless progress, endless advancement for all, excluding none, the tiniest atom, the mightiest god, two different stages of growing entities. The atom becomes a man, the man becomes a god, the god becomes a super-god, and so on *ad infinitum.*

There is no place for a static 'Heaven' in my philosophy, and on the same grounds as there is no place for a static hell in my belief. There are of course the intermediate spheres and stages of bliss and felicity where we rest, for instance in the devachan after death, or in the nirvâna; but all these are transitory as compared with beginningless and endless Duration. Of course there are temporary heavens, and there are likewise temporary hells. If a man follows through many ages a path which takes him constantly downward, a path in following which there is constant increase in pain and suffering because a constant constriction of every faculty and energy, becoming more and more tightened into oneself — there are indeed these things; but even they are temporary. And the same reflexion applies to the ascending path, towards the Heavens innumerable. But as compared with eternity they are, to follow a favorite metaphor of mine, but like dissolving wisps of cloud upon a mountain-side. They come, they endure a moment, and they pass. Far greater than any such heaven, than any such sphere or loka of bliss and felicity, is the grandiose vision of endless growth in faculty and power, and endless opportunity to work for the world. There is no joy like that!

MAN A HOST OF MONADS

How may we reach to an understanding of the essence of us, of each one of us, which is beyond what we call the Monad? Or can we reach beyond the Monad?

This is a question which has bothered some of our most intellectual students. Yet the answer is very simple. You have the answer in *Fundamentals of the Esoteric Philosophy* and of course in all of H. P. B.'s philosophical works. Have I not often said that man's real nature or composition is legion: that he is a composite entity, and that within every human constitution there is not merely one Monad but many — one essential Monad, the root of the individual's being, giving birth to hosts of children-Monads, and that these children-Monads build up the vehicles in which the primal or primordial essential Monad lives and works? Have I not often pointed out that man is a composite of an actual army of entities, of a host, of a multitude, extending from the heart of the Universe down to his physical brain and body? To illustrate: There is the astral Monad which the beast has or is conscious of in itself. There is the human Monad which we humans have and are conscious in. There is the spiritual Monad which the great Masters, the higher ones at least, are because they are conscious in it. There is the divine Monad, in the consciousness of which the inner god of each one of us lives. There is the super-divine Monad in which some entity, still a part of us, still more sublime, is conscious and lives;

and so on for ever. The difficult thing in this study is to get it through our dull human intelligences so miseducated through hundreds of years, that man is a composite or compounded entity, a microcosm: that we are not merely animated bodies built in a certain way by natural forces, but that we actually are rays — I cannot think of a better term — flowing forth from the heart of Infinity; and that for each one of us such a ray is our essential Self; and along this ray, so to say, at certain intervals there are knots of consciousness. Each one of these knots along the ray is a child-Monad; and the farther one goes inwards or, in other words, the higher one goes, along this ray of consciousness, the diviner the Monads are found to be as we reach knot after knot of consciousness ascending upwards or inwards.

Now then, as the human being yearning for more light and truth spiritualizes his consciousness, in other words rises to higher planes of consciousness, he ascends along this essential ray and becomes cognisant, first, that he is more than a merely beast-Monad, or later in time that he is more than a merely human Monad. There is in him the consciousness of the Monad of the Masters, the spiritual Monad; and when he becomes a Master he realizes that there is something within him still higher than this, to wit, the god-Monad; and as he continues to ascend along this ray of consciousness, this 'pathway' about which I wrote so much in *Fundamentals* and elsewhere, as he goes still higher, with each ascent, with each step upwards, with each reaching to a higher Monad, he attains an added expansion of essential consciousness. Thus this expansion grows from humanity into spirituality or into Masterhood; from spirituality his consciousness becomes divine in its reach, including even the Galaxy or Milky Way. He then ascends still higher along this essential selfhood, along this ray within him, until his consciousness becomes kosmic and takes in a reach still more vast; and so on for ever.

The teaching is an amazing paradox and an amazing verity. Remember that of course a paradox is not a contradiction. A paradox means a statement which contains at least two elements contradictory apparently, but only apparently so because we don't understand the two elements. When we understand it, the paradox disappears and we see their coherence in the unity of conception.

If I rightly understand it, it comes to this: When we use the word Monad, it represents the relatively highest state of consciousness which the being in question has reached at the time, but of course as an evolving being, yet it always represents the highest attained at the time.

Exactly so. There is always a Monad superior to our stage of evolution, whatever that stage may be: there is always one still higher just ahead of us. In other words, it is the principle of veil after veil, each veil hiding a nobler vision, a grander expansion of consciousness; and all evolution is simply an unveiling of consciousness, an unfolding of potentialities, of potencies hitherto lying infolded, involved. This, then, is what evolution means: unfolding, unwrapping from within of what hitherto has lain latent there, or rather unmanifest.

OVERLAPPING IN GEOLOGICAL PERIODS

Would you say that there is any overlapping in the great geological periods, or is each one entirely distinct from the one which follows it?

It can perhaps be said that the geological periods overlap, but such overlapping is minor in manifestation. The main point to remember is that the different great stocks of mineral, vegetable, and animal and human lives follow each other with coincident or co-ordinate great changes of land and sea, and therefore also of climates. In other words, the stocks of beings, or monads, co-operate or co-ordinate, and thus produce the different and serial and successive patterns of what we today call geological eras, or what the biologist or zoölogist and botanist would call the successive waves of plant and animal and human life.

Thus there are successive geologic eras, each one accompanied by its own monadic families in all the kingdoms; but there are survivals in any one geologic epoch for long periods, of the preceding epoch and even preceding epochs. For instance the elephant today and the rhinoceros, while still alive, as beings really belong to a preceding time. They are slowly dying out. The reason of their survival is that the monads inhabiting these bodies were able to conform to the new mammalian era. Certain other types of living beings have died out, or almost died out, like the dodo or the platypus and kangaroos in instances, although the kangaroos still hang on.

SÛFÎISM AND THEOSOPHY

What can I say to a friend who is very desirous of having me share her deep interest in Sûfîism?

It is amazing that so many people move into these exotic Oriental beliefs without really knowing what they are. Sûfîism is one of the best of them all; but it is really naught, as it now stands, but a species of exoterically esoteric Mohammedanism. So far as it goes, it is quite a beautiful belief, teaching love and brotherhood, kindliness; and the existence of a personal god of a rather impersonal character — a curious mixture. There is much that is very fine about it and that is what catches our Occidentals. But, as I have often said, why prefer a chapter out of a book, to the whole blessed volume, which Theosophy is?

I really think that you can interest your friend in Theosophy. Tell her beautiful things. Talk of love and harmony and mercy and beauty, and of the great Seers and Sages of the world, of the Hierarchies and of Universal Nature, of the Path to Wisdom which lies in the Great Self of every human being, one's inner god. Talk of a spiritual Brotherhood, utterly impersonal, non-political, non-sectarian; in other words, show her how much more beautiful the Theosophical conception is, and how much more all-comprehensive. She does not realize what she has moved into: she sees only the beauty of the modern Sûfî mystical thought, but does not realize its philosophical and scientific incompleteness.

But say nothing against Sûfîism itself, for indeed there is much that is admirable about it, just as there is in Christianity or Brâhmanism or Buddhism, or any other kind of mystical thought. It is the Oriental novelty which attracts Occidental women to these exotic beliefs, but we Theosophists must appeal not only to their hearts but also to their intellects.

No Communication with the Dead

Do you think one is ever justified in consulting mediums in order to, rather, in the effort to, communicate with the deceased?

I can answer this by saying that it is the teaching of the Wisdom-Religion of mankind, today called Theosophy, that any attempt to communicate with those who have passed on, by mediums or sensitives, or in any other wise, is a cruel injustice, perpetrated, alas, usually in ignorance, upon souls which are struggling to wing their way into brighter and grander spheres; and any such effort, even if only moderately successful, holds the departing spiritual essence back.

Furthermore, it is utterly impossible, by Nature's grand and compassionate laws, physically to communicate with the *spiritual* essence of any human being, for when such spiritual essence has broken its links with the material world at the death of the physical body, which is cast aside as a worn-out garment, the spiritual essence cannot ever be materially reached at all. The utmost that could be done would be a psycho-magnetic communication with the astral reliquiae, or what the consensus of mankind has called the 'spook' or the 'bhûta.'

Please understand that this answer to your question is in no wise intended to be a slur upon the many splendid and kindly people who belong to the so-called spiritualistic ranks. I would not hurt their feelings for anything, and yet I am in duty bound, as a Theosophical Teacher, when a question is asked of me, to tell honestly and without reserve what the teachings of the Wisdom-Religion of mankind are.

I may add this as a comment to what I have just written, that there is, nevertheless, a sublime way of coming into heart-touch with those whom we have loved and who have passed on, and that is through our own spiritual nature — in other words by raising our hearts in impersonal love towards the memory, the blessed memory, of those whom we have loved, and who are no longer physically with us.

There is a real spiritual companionship, an actual one, if those left behind in the physical body can be so impersonal and loving of heart that they can do this. The spirit is universal in its reaches, and love overleaps all boundaries either of space or time, and thus even the living on earth can come into loving spiritual touch with the ones who are freed.

But any attempt to do this through mediums or through psychics or sensitives, etc., I feel in duty bound to tell you is not only unfortunate misjudgment but deleterious to the spiritual health of both the medium and the one who so tries. Alas that there should be such ignorance of Nature's great laws among people who are otherwise in so many cases devoted, kindly, splendid people.

DIVINITY, SPIRIT AND SOUL

What is the difference between the divine and spiritual on the one hand, and the spirit and the soul on the other hand?

The words 'divine' and 'spiritual' of course are adjectives. Whatever is of the spirit is spiritual. The divine is a very different thing from the soul. 'Soul' is one of the most difficult words in the English language to explain, simply because it means a thousand and one things. Say 'soul,' and fifty thousand men will have fifty thousand different opinions about it.

However, we may speak of soul as the center or habitat of an ego which is the soul's inspiring flame. The encircling veil or garment is 'soul' and as each man has within his constitution a divine ego and a spiritual ego and a human ego and even a sort of beast-ego, there are corresponding souls for all these. Soul, we may say, therefore, means 'garment,' 'vehicle,' 'body.'

The divine, I may perhaps say, is the loftiest part either of the Universe or of man. Whatever is of the gods, is of divine character. Whatever is of the nature of divinity, is divine. The highest in any hierarchy is the divine; then comes the spiritual through which it works. Underneath that, let us say in our own case, comes the human, through which the spiritual works; then the beast-element in us, the kâma-astral-vital part, through which the human must work in order to express itself on this physical plane. Then comes our physical body. I hope the answer is somewhat responsive, at least.

ARGUMENTS FOR REINCARNATION

I was talking today to a clergyman on the subject of Reincarnation, which he did not believe in, of course. How could I convince him that I am right?

I don't know! In my own work, many people ask me questions and I have found that the best way to convince them that I am right is to make the questioner himself or herself think that he has given me a very difficult question. Then you can lead him on, at least I do so, to explain just what he means by that question. As, for instance, lead him on to explain what he means by his terms; and in a very little while he is tangled up in definitions and diffuseness or incoherent details; he then hardly knows what he himself means, and is less convinced than before and is more ready to listen to what you have to say. If you have truth to give, there is your opportunity to point out — that is, if you understand it yourself — that the questioner, in thus exposing his ignorance of the idea has not only helped himself to clarify his mind through analysis of his thoughts, but has also shown to himself that he has not understood the logical elements of his own question.

As a matter of fact, most people do not think clearly, and some don't seem to think at all. It is obvious that a Christian questioner you would have to treat in one way, and an agnostic in another way, and a Hindû yogî in a third way, etc. Success in answering all questions, I believe, arises from first making the questioner think for himself, and secondly and coincidently giving him new points of view to think about.

What are some good clinching arguments for Reincarnation?

Many, to my mind. Each argument should be according to the questioner. What might not convince a Roman Catholic or a Methodist, might appeal to some one who is an Atheist. When that question is put to me, realizing the difficulty of giving a brief and lucid answer, I in my turn begin to ask questions after the Socratic method, and I say: What do you understand Reincarnation to be?, and then my questioner begins to define what he understands or misunderstands by the term. There is my chance to correct and to instruct. In other words, instead of answering directly,

I often take a round-about way, a psychological method of treating the different minds that come to me with questions; and by questioning my questioner, I make my questioner think for himself, clarify his own ideas, until, little by little, after talking with him, he realizes that Reincarnation is at least interesting to think about, and that is the first step.

I do not think that there is any definite, brief, conclusive answer to the question: What is an absolute proof of Reincarnation? There are many perfectly true answers that might be given. For instance: Why are we here? By chance? Then rigidly pursue that line of thought. There is no chance. We are here because it is Nature's working which has put us here, Nature working always according to law and order. This means a chain of causation stretching far back into the past. If we are men now, we are so merely as the present end of a chain of causes and of effects; and the causes producing consequences, 'Karman' in other words — the Doctrine of Consequences — can produce only what is innate in that chain itself. I mean, if there be a chain of consequences which, if led to its successful conclusion, will culminate in an electric light, it is obvious that this identic chain of consequences if led to its successful conclusion will not culminate in anything else than an electric light. Follow along this line, and make your questioner think for himself. Then go on, as Socrates did, step by step; and in a little while he will begin to argue with you, and possibly will even show you, of his own instance, some excellently good proofs of reimbodiment or rebirth.

FUNDAMENTAL REMEDY FOR SUFFERING

It is often said that Theosophy has the remedy for the distress and suffering existing in the world. I believe it, but how are we to make this understood by those who may not be members of the Theosophical Society, and by those who are suffering in their material circumstances?

I don't think that any sane man can deny that the world is in a state of consciousness which proves that men lack a genuine philosophy of life. It is commonly believed that men are merely physical bodies, animals, animated machines. This is the root of the whole world-trouble today, causing wide-spread immorality, blatant, flagrant, parading itself — and when I say immorality I do not refer to sexual immorality alone, but I refer also to political immorality, social immorality, ethical immorality in general. It is always thus when men have no standard of right and wrong which they can prove to be based on natural law. In such case men have no guide in life, and the consequence will be corruption, deceit, self-seeking, war, and all the other evil things that follow in the train. The teachings of materialistic science during the last hundred years have brought mankind to the pass where they have actually lost hope. Men today don't really believe anything; or, if they believe in something vague, they have no proof of it. Fortunately, our great scientific researchers are beginning to teach a new doctrine.

The deduction immediately follows from what has been said that according to natural law what one man does affects all others. Realization of this induces a feeling of moral responsibility, in other words a recognition of ethics; and it is our duty to teach our Theosophical doctrines, which show men a philosophy of life: that what they sow they reap, that they are now what they have made themselves to be in the past, and that in the future they will be what now they are making themselves in the future to become. Our Theosophical doctrines give to man not only a great and sublime hope, but they also give to him ethical principles by which he will live, and a grand philosophy which adequately explains those principles. Hence, wars will automatically cease when the world is finally Theosophized; corruption in high places and in low will become an awful memory of the past. This regeneration, among other things, is what we are working for. This question also has brought out one of the fundamental reasons for the founding of the Theosophical Society.

INTELLECTUAL INTEREST IN THEOSOPHY

Should one ask a person to become a member of the Theosophical Society, even if he knows it is only an intellectual interest that causes the person to read our literature?

Emphatically yes. Immortal gods, think what we have to give! We are fishers for the souls of men. Let us hook those souls with the bait of truth. If some one comes to me and says: "I am interested in so-and-so. What can I do to learn more?" shall I shrug my shoulders in an indifferent sort of way and let him wander and stumble on the path? No. I would say: Come in, learn more, here is where you can find it.

By all means invite him to join us — help him to make his way smoother. Think of what the Masters have done for you. Did not they make the way smoother in giving to us the immortal Theosophical verities by sending out their Messenger H. P. B. in our day, a part of whose work was also to found the Theosophical Society? Remember there is always a standing invitation to enter into the Temple of Truth. Yes, Brothers: invite, do more even, do everything that is honest and clean and true to help outsiders to join the Theosophical Society.

I have absolutely no sympathy with the opinion that some people seem to have that it is a wrong thing to suggest to another to take the Theosophical path. Indeed, it is our duty, it is our human duty, to warn a man walking towards an open trap-door, towards a pit-fall — it is our duty to tell him of it; it is our duty to tell him that in a certain direction lies the path of safety, the path of light. If you find a man wandering in a dark field surrounded by noisome gases, it is your duty to show him the way, to show him towards the light.

PRAYER AND PETITIONING

Why do Theosophists not believe in prayer, and that prayer will be answered by our Father in Heaven?

Just exactly what do you mean by prayer? Does it mean petitioning "the Father of men and the Creator of the universe" to send us rain or to give us success in our material enterprises, or to send us a baby boy instead of a baby girl, or to make the crops grow green or to give us comfort and solace when perhaps death has taken a loved one from us? What kind of prayer is this? It is wholly selfish. It is a confession that we are seeking to get something for ourselves; it is a confession also that our view of and opinions about and convictions concerning that unnameable Mystery, whose very heart is compassion and wisdom, are purely human. It also signifies that we believe that the Divine does not know as well as we do what is good for the world and for us. Petitionary prayer, to us Theosophists, is not only wrong, but, if we may use ordinary human terms, is a spiritual impertinence.

On the other hand, those who suffer, whose hearts grieve, who are in doubt about some deep ethical problem, who are uncertain after which manner a certain act should be done — should remember the words of all the great Teachers: Go into thine own inner chamber and there commune with the god within thyself; for, as Jesus is reported to have said, "I and my Father are one" — that is, each man is one with his own inner god, the essential divinity within him, his link with the Boundless Infinitude. There is a fountain of wisdom within us all, a fountain of love inexhaustible; and the pity of it is that men do not realize this — one of the sublimest truths of human life. They do not know what they have within, and all the teaching of the Sages and Seers of the ages has been: Look within, search within, find truth within, become one with thine own inner god, and be at peace! *There* is the source of wisdom and love and peace and happiness; and the way to reach this source is beginning with a boundless sympathy for the souls of men.

The one true and only genuine prayer is loving; give love boundless to

everything both great and small; feel your essential unity with the stars
in their courses; feel at home in the Universe; have a kindly thought and
a compassionate feeling for everything that suffers or is in pain or that
grieves or that yearns for light and truth. This is the path of discipleship;
this is the ideal of the chela-life. Theosophy makes an appeal to the spirit
within man himself, and if this idea is understood and developed within
one, then in a little while light comes, peace comes, happiness comes, and
great quiet. No longer do pain and sorrow exist in such a man or woman.

The key is self-forgetfulness! Remember that the very heart of Nature
is harmony, which means love; for love and harmony are one, being two
sides of the same thing. Wisdom is but another name for the same thing,
for love is wise: it is wisdom and clairvoyance; and wisdom is always harmonious. Actually, love and wisdom and peace and harmony are really
words for the same inexpressible Mystery which men in their ignorance
call God. When we begin to delineate it and define it, we endow the Divine
with our merely human figments of thought, imperfect, limited, because
we are imperfect; and therefore it is that we Theosophists always speak of
this wondrous, ineffable Mystery by the one word THAT. This is infinitely
more reverential than to begin to label the Divine or to ticket it or to
qualify it with the imperfect attributes of our human existence.

All petitionary prayer is, in the last analysis, selfish. Take two armies
on a battle-field, for instance. Each one prays that it may be victorious
and the enemy be vanquished. Whose prayer is your God going to grant?
I repeat again: all petitionary prayer is selfish. A man may ask for guidance; but even this is for himself alone. It is a nobler prayer, I admit,
than if he were to ask for an increase in his wealth, or something of that
sort; but nevertheless he is asking for something which in his imperfect
judgment he thinks to be the best thing for him. But you can yourselves
change the course of your own lives, because you are a part of Nature, you
are an integral part of the Universe, and therefore a part of that very heart
of compassion, although as yet very imperfect and feeble expressions of It.

Even if you pray for another's good fortune — how about the moral
aspect of this? Don't you realize that you have no right deliberately to
influence, or to try to influence, the evolutionary growth or development of
a brother or of an entity inferior to you, unless it be strictly in accordance
with Nature's inner laws, which are non-interference with others, except
in loving and in compassion and in impersonal helping? Do you think you
could have a right to influence a rose, for instance, to change its color from
red to blue? If so, then, following along the same line, you would have a
right to influence some human being's destiny, and to try to change him
from a bad man to a good man or from a good man to a bad man. No, we

Theosophists say No, because, suppose that you were successful in changing a bad man into a good one, and did so by your own power, you would leave him still weak and imperfect and you would thus deprive him of the opportunity of gaining strength for himself, which is the only genuine strength and the only way by which he can grow. It is in Nature's law for him to learn his own lessons, to evolve himself, to strive himself for strength, for light, for growth. Interference in the affairs of another is unwarrantable, and the very gods in their majestic courses cannot and will not interfere with the evolutionary growth of men by listening to their feeble petitionary prayer.

ETHICS AS WELL AS INTELLECT

While we know intellectually the truth of the Theosophical teachings, we are not self-conscious of these great truths. How can we bridge the gap in order that we may better help others?

That is a nobly beautiful question. If you are intellectually conscious of the truth, this alone is a great step forwards — having intellectual recognition that certain teachings are true. This is a 'revelation' in a way, it is like an open door; and if you will just follow that intellectual recognition faithfully, and try to live in accordance with it, and at peace with yourselves and with all other men, looking upon this intellectual recognition as a guiding light, your intellectual conception will finally come into sympathetic vibration with the higher portions of your constitution, and you will gain as much of the inner wisdom and love and peace as your personal nature can contain at the time.

I am astonished that this questioner has put his question as he does, because it is usually the intellectual conception which comes last. We often feel truths which we are unable intellectually ever to state or perhaps even to understand fully with the brain-mind. We cannot as easily express the thoughts we have, as we can feel things. There is always the danger that the intellect may finally gain an undue preponderance in the character, and that has to be avoided because it may easily lead to the Left-Hand path. We must above everything else cultivate the ethical or moral sense equally with the intellectual, otherwise we are apt to become one-sided creatures, and such development is unwise.

"How can we bridge the gap in order that we may better help others?" My answer is, by opening your heart and your mind to the calming and soothing influences of your spiritual nature guided by the light that Theosophy will give to you; and then devote your life in unremitting service to all that lives. This is extremely beautiful and brings with it as its natural guerdon not only wisdom and the Great Peace, but an opening out of the inner being of the aspirant, so that finally he becomes wholly at one with his god within, which means becoming a Master of Life consecrated forever to the service of the world and to helping all beings.

The whole nature of man must grow, must be awakened; we must not grow merely in one part of us. It is symmetrical growth which brings the inner harmony, the inner peace. Do not be discouraged in thinking that though you understand the Theosophic teachings, you cannot easily get the feeling of the truth of them. Simply follow the light that is in you, and if you have the intellect to understand, as you say you have, this itself is an enormous step ahead. Try to cultivate the ethical instinct at the same time and all the time, and strive always to find the ethical values of truth — I mean the moral value of the intellectual teaching. Get the inner consciousness that a thing is right, as well as the intellectual sense that it is right. A person may have an intellectual perception of a truth, but be cold-hearted, with no urge to help others, no urge to pass on the light to others. Such a one does not sense his inseparable unity with others and his inescapable responsibility to them.

Sub-Races of the Fifth Root-Race

I have been a reader of Theosophical literature for a number of years and have understood from the teachings that we are now in the fifth Sub-Race of the Fifth Root-Race. But I read in Dr. de Purucker's illuminating book, Fundamentals of the Esoteric Philosophy, *that this is a mistake; that we have not even reached the middle of the fourth Sub-Race; and that earlier teaching has been an intentional blind on this point.*

The present condition of the world certainly suggests that we are not a whole sub-race beyond the "acme of materiality." But if such is the case, why was it necessary to withhold this teaching until today? And why are we more ready to receive it now than fifty years ago? Can anything further be said on this subject?

The questioner, on the whole, has correctly understood my various references to the matter of the Races. It is, however, erroneous to suppose that the teaching concerning this matter has been 'withheld' until today; and, consequently, the above statement suggesting that we are now more ready to receive the teachings than others were fifty years ago is likewise a mistake. I would also like to point out that the earlier teaching on this matter was not "an intentional blind"; but H. P. B.'s teachings regarding the Races as given in *The Secret Doctrine,* have not been in all respects properly understood.

In *Fundamentals of the Esoteric Philosophy,* on page 239, I have treated of this matter at sufficient length, it seems to me, although briefly; and I suggest that the questioner and others who may be interested in the facts, turn to H. P. B.'s *The Secret Doctrine* and especially to its Volume One, page 610, and ponder over the very clear and definite statements therein made.

"The acme of materiality in each" Race is always the fourth stage or sub-race "or central point," e.g., the fourth Sub-Race of any Root-Race. Further, H. P. B. on this page of *The Secret Doctrine* says very clearly that "we are in the mid-point of our *Sub-Race* of the Fifth Root-Race — the acme of materiality in each — therefore the animal propensities, though more refined," etc. Now, these words, "the acme of materiality in each" solve the problem instantly, because two things are here referred to: the Fifth Root-Race and its "acme of materiality" which is the fourth Sub-Race; and, again, "the mid-point of our *Sub-Race.*" It should be clear enough to anybody that being at the point where the "acme of materiality" *in each* is found, this places us therefore at, or nearing the middle point of, the fourth Sub-Race of the Fifth Root-Race. However, as there are always cycles within cycles, and smaller cycles again within these, even a fourth sub-race has its upward rises towards a relative intellectual development or a relative spiritual development, and also its descents thereafter.

Since the discovery of America, we have been on the upward rise of a small minor cycle within the fourth Sub-Race; and this accounts for the great development in brain-mind intellectuality and for the flowering of material energies which the most myopic of modern individuals can see the signs of around us everywhere.

To speak more accurately, we are at the present time actually passing through a small fifth *subordinate* race, forming part of a Family-Race, which in its turn is part of the fourth Sub-Race, which is the lowest great sub-race of the Fifth Root-Race.

Again, as every industrious student of the archaic Wisdom knows who has pondered over the statements in H. P. B.'s *The Secret Doctrine,* every Root-Race, when its time comes, is cut in two in its middle part, i.e., at about the middle point of its fourth Sub-Race, as Atlantis was, and as Lemuria was. Such racial catastrophe obviously has not yet befallen us of the Fifth Root-Race; and the deduction is of course immediate and obvious: we have not yet reached the middle point of the fourth Sub-Race of the Fifth Root-Race — although we are not far from this middle point.

H. P. B. in *The Secret Doctrine* furthermore shows that the karmic geologic destiny of Europe — when the final closing of many racial accounts will take place — requires some sixteen thousand or more years before that event, a geologic racial catastrophe, reaches its maximum. But meanwhile, "coming events cast their shadows before"; and very serious seismic, tidal, and other catastrophic events will happen to certain European countries between now and the sixteen thousand years period of grace that Europe still has. H. P. B. has alluded to these events on several occasions in her writings, as in *The Theosophist* in an article later republished in *Five Years of Theosophy*, and also in articles in her *Lucifer*, in which places she calls attention to tidal waves and disastrous earthquakes that are already occurring, and clearly pointing to what will come in the future.

Were we now in the fifth Sub-Race, as some have mistakenly supposed, we should have passed the cutting in two of our Fifth Root-Race; but this last has not occurred. The conclusion is therefore obvious.

I hope that these observations, which it seems to me any earnest student could himself have gathered from H. P. B.'s *The Secret Doctrine*, will throw some light upon an intricate and confessedly obscure teaching.

METAPHYSICS OF CONSCIOUSNESS AND THE NATURE OF SUFFERING

(a) How is it that the divine spark — which in its evolutionary journey from non-self-consciousness is to rise to self-consciousness — can be imperfect in its core at the moment when it is sent forth from the womb of being? (For non-self-consciousness is not perfection, is it?, since perfection, however relative a conception, would seem to include self-consciousness.)

(b) How is it that this evolutionary pilgrimage can involve such untold suffering for human beings, while according to Theosophy, the core of a human being is not affected?

Answer to (a): I think the answer to this question should contain, first of all, the statement that there is rather a misunderstanding of terms used in this teaching than any fault in the teaching itself. It would be quite wrong to speak of the divine spark before it begins its evolutionary journey at the beginning of the cosmic manvantara as being 'imperfect.' It all depends upon what we mean by the two terms 'perfection' and 'imperfection.' It is admitted that perfection is relative; therefore imperfection must likewise be so.

And if we remember that the entire purpose of the evolutionary journey is twofold — first to enable the divine spark to gain self-consciousness on lower planes than its own and also to aid the evolution of the life-atoms which form its various vehicles on the different *planes* of evolution, we shall see that this term 'self-consciousness' itself is a relative term. The divine spark is continuously perfect, so far as all lower planes are concerned; and 'perfect' here is a relative term, not an absolute one. But as the entire galactic universe, of which it is a member, is itself evolving just as much as are the untold hosts of divine sparks within it, each new manvantara or manifestation-period of a galactic universe presents new phases of growth or new possibilities of self-consciousness, which the divine spark will be obliged to evolve into, or make a part of itself, before it can become a Master again in the new manvantara which the galactic universe is undertaking.

The question therefore shows that the questioner has probably not grasped the enormous complexity of the situation. Not only is the divine spark itself evolving — that is, bringing out from within its own womb of being continuously new aspects of itself, and recognising them and becoming conscious of them, but the universe or galactic universe, in which it is native and with which it evolves, is also evolving: i.e., growing; i.e., changing; i.e., having constantly new aspects.

Remember, also, that any one divine spark is but an individual or single unit in really incomprehensible multitudes of others like unto itself; and these multitudes, in order to be fully self-conscious in their own home-universe must become self-conscious of each other and of the various phases or sheaths of consciousness in which each and every one, and therefore all, are individually and collectively inwrapped.

The self-consciousness spoken of in the teachings means self-consciousness in our solar system — a mere point of the Galaxy. But the Divine Monad must attain similarly another self-consciousness in each one of other Solar Systems in the Galaxy; and each such Solar System must begin its evolutionary course therein at the beginning and pursue it to its end.

The question, therefore, is properly answered by pointing out, as said above, the enormous complexity of the teaching; and that the words 'perfection' and 'self-consciousness,' and even the phrase 'womb of being,' and many others, are all terms *relative* to the Divine Monad in any one, and therefore in all, phases of its pilgrimage — a pilgrimage which lasts from Eternity to Eternity.

Trying to answer more briefly this question, it should be pointed out, therefore, that the Divine Monad is 'imperfect' at the moment when it is sent forth from the womb of being, only because it has not yet become self-consciously cognisant of the universe in which it is then evolving. When it has so become it is a Master in that universe and passes to higher spheres, where it repeats the process of becoming self-conscious in these higher spheres, and so forth, and so forth.

Remember that ultimate perfection as an infinitely completed and ended process is non-existent; i.e., the Divine Monad is evolving for ever. There is no such thing as an absolute finality in evolution — that is, in growth.

Answer to (b): This question is asked from the standpoint of the human soul, which very naturally rebels at what it calls its 'untold suffering.' The human soul forgets that suffering and pain, as men call these events in evolution, are merely the growing pains always coincident with expanding consciousness. To this must be added the other part of the teaching, that suffering, when properly seen to be the great friend and helper that it is, loses nearly all of its distressing and perplexing aspects. It is like the growing pains of a child: these growing pains are at times extremely disagreeable and in some cases even nerve-racking; but yet how may the child grow or change its childhood into youth and advance into manhood without passing through these changes?

Here, then, we have the answer to the question: change — i.e., evolution — i.e., growth — always has a painful aspect. But it likewise has an aspect of great joy, when realization comes that change means improvement — a growing or rising into better and nobler things. It is true that "the core of a human being is not affected" by suffering, except, perhaps, in the sense that the suffering brings out the latent powers — the sleeping or dormant faculties and abilities lying in the core of the evolving entity.

Then, as a final thought, I should perhaps add this: that we human beings live at the present time in a very grossly material sphere of existence, which in fact in Tibet is called *Myalba* and frequently is referred to as a *hell*, which in very truth it is, when we contrast it with the spiritual or more ethereal realms. In these more ethereal or spiritual realms growth, instead of having an aspect of suffering and pain, is a continuous process involving joy and a self-conscious recognition of felicity; just exactly as a man's mental growth can hardly be called painful always, because already being of a more ethereal character than physical growth, there are few pleasures or joys so keen and sweet to the one who is evolving mentally as the realization of the expanding intellectual consciousness.

This becomes still more clear when we realize that spiritual growth involves no suffering or pain at all, but is a process involving such exquisite, sheer joy, that in this fact itself there lurks a danger to the unwary.

I conclude by saying that evolution has no suffering or pain about it at all for those who merely drift along with the current of the advancing evolutionary tide; i.e., the slowly advancing river of lives. But for those whose eyes are set upon the distant peaks and who desire to advance more rapidly than others, there must be always the breasting and buffeting of the wind and waves; or, to change the figure of speech, the climbing of the steep ascents, the still small path, rather than following the broad and easy one winding round and round the mountain.

Be not afraid of suffering; for it is a good sign. It means that you are growing more rapidly than the majority. Suffering is always an opportunity as well.

————————

Answers to a series of questions asked at the European Convention in October, 1932, at London, England

No Conflict in Duties

E. W. — Could you tell us if the duties of the members of the Theosophical Society differ from those of other people?

G. de P. — I cannot conceive that such a thing could be. The Theosophical duties are human duties. I think we make a great mistake in setting the Theosophical duties, as it were, on the right hand, and our own home-duties on the left hand, and drawing a distinction between these twain. Why, they are one! You cannot do properly as Theosophists your home-duties and your duties to your fellow-beings unless you do them in the Theosophical way, as Theosophists. I see no distinction between one's home-duties, the duties we owe to others — fellow-comrades or other human beings — and the duties we owe to the Theosophical Society. The more we follow out our Theosophical duties the better men and women we are, believe me. Do right because you think right; and you think right because you feel right. Do wrong, it is because you think wrong; and you think wrong because you feel wrong. There is the whole thing.

A Great Teacher once said: 'Render unto Caesar the things that are Caesar's,' with the implication that you should render to the spirit the things that belong to the spirit, whereas I tell you that the things that are truly Caesar's are the things that are truly of the spirit. Inversely, if you understand me aright, Caesar has no rights that are not spiritual rights. Do you get it? But Caesar *has* rights, because Caesar is a spiritual being; and therefore we should render willingly to Caesar the duties and rights that are due to Caesar. Doing so, we do our own duty first to the god within each one of us; and when we do that, then we do our full duty by our fellow-men. A man cannot err, he cannot do a wrong thing, without offending first himself, then his fellows. A man cannot work for himself alone without committing an evil deed. Everything that a man does that is right, is good for his fellows. I don't see any distinction between the one and the other. I see many artificial distinctions, but I won't recognise them, because I think that is just where the world, in the Occident especially, has failed in the past.

Don't you think, dear Brothers, Comrades, Friends, that we of the Theosophical Movement should attempt to introduce into the thought-milieu of our Occident, precisely those Theosophical principles of conduct and of action, therefore, which we love, because they will remodel the mental atmosphere, change it from the bottom up? The atmosphere, the mental, the psycho-spiritual atmosphere of the Occidental world sadly needs modification. Men today are losing trust and hope in the fine old standards of our fathers. It was not the standards of our fathers that were wrong: it was in many cases the wrong application of our duty to those standards. I don't see any distinction between the Theosophical duties and the duties to our fellow human beings. I cannot conceive that a Theosophical duty, properly understood, can conflict with a family duty. If you neglect a family-duty you are acting untheosophically. That is clear. On the other hand, if you do your Theosophical duties well you will fulfil all your family duties well; because the first duty of a Theosophist is to live to benefit mankind, one's own family included.

THE NATURE OF DEITY

H. P. L. — We are told in THE MAHATMA LETTERS *that God is unconscious and unintelligent; and it is rather difficult to put that to an ordinary audience and not rather shock them. It seems rather vague and unsatisfactory. They want somebody to be thankful to, and they miss that.*

G. de P. — Wasn't the great American agnostic, Colonel Ingersoll, the one who first uttered the thought that God is man's noblest creation? — with the implication, therefore, that all human ideas or conceptions of divinity are born in the mind of man — man-made ideas. It is true. Is it not obvious that no human intelligence can encompass infinity, eternity? Therefore whatever ideas or conceptions or ideals the greatest human intellect can comprehend are ideals, ideas, conceptions, ideations, born of his own spirit. If these ideas or ideals or conceptions or ideations be in the nature of questionings as to what divinity is — where and when and how and why is it — is it not obvious that these spring from the mind of the thinker himself? Men of the Occident forget that the only divinity a human being can comprehend is the God within, our link with the Unutterable, the inmost of the inmost in us, not only inseparable from the Heart of the Universe, but that very Heart itself. Each one of us is an inseparable part or portion of the Cosmic Spirit, of the Heart of Being.

Therefore, the way to understand Divinity, Deity — God, to use the old Anglo-Saxon word — is not by looking without, for that is but painting mental pictures on the horizon which your mental eye envisages before you, but by going within, into the silence, into the Great Peace, into the quiet, into yourself, your spiritual self, the divine self, the divine flame within you; and thus you come into immediate touch with the Cosmic Consciousness, which is yours. Therefore all human gods are man-made: they are idols; and worshipers of gods are idolaters, because they worship what man's imagination has pictured. They are image-worshipers — idolaters. That is iconolatry.

Now, I agree with the Master that these are ideas which it is our bounden duty to disseminate among our fellow-men, so that they may find peace, so that the harrowing anxieties, the cankers of thought which so many human beings have when they search for it over humanity and find it not, may no longer become the haunting ghosts that are found among the religionists, such as the Christians. It is peace and happiness that it is our duty to bring to the world, in giving men a new thought, a new idea, a new vision, the Vision Sublime, in teaching them of their oneness with Infinity and of their identity with Eternity.

I am an 'Atheist': Oh! how terrible! But what does this mean? It means that I refuse to accept any man-made god; for it is beneath my dignity as a man to worship an image, the child of my own creation. Shall the father worship his child? On the contrary, teach man to look within to the divinity, to the divine flame within his own being. There, there is divinity; there is Infinity; there is Eternity; and the Self, the Divine Self within you, what the Hindûs call the Âtman, is the pathway to God, the Deity, to the Cosmic Spirit.

I verily believe that one of the reasons for the Master's using the language that he used in the letter in *The Mahatma Letters* that the questioner speaks of, was the forevision that he had of the introduction, even into the Theosophical Movement, of a new spirit of religious sectarianism, introducing new gods, or the worship of old gods; and in this sense it is my feeling that we must be iconoclasts, breakers of images, destroyers of temples of iniquity, so that the cleansing sunlight, the light of Father Sun, may stream in and purify.

I know it is difficult for people to understand these thoughts; but I think that if we have them clear in our mind, if we know just what our philosophy teaches, we shall ourselves become so well acquainted with these doctrines, with these teachings, that we shall find it much easier to answer these difficult questions; because they *are* difficult to answer sometimes and not because we don't know what to say, but solely on account of the dormant and obscured minds of those whom we try to help.

Let us worship no god which can be enshrined in any temple, whether of material substance or of the fabric of human thought. If we do, we shall then belong to the lower class of religionists, worshiping mental images, and only a little higher than the idolaters, who worship graven stone or graven wood. It is the divine spirit within us, the living fire of truth, which is nameless, which is deathless, which is ever unstained, which is pure always, which is infinitely compassionate, which is always helpful, which is inspiriting, which is inspiring, which is elevating, which is ennobling, which brings us peace — peace beyond the understanding of men; for it is Truth. That is the Deity that we worship — the Spirit of Truth enshrined in no temple, unless indeed we may use the noble language of the Roman poet and speak of Boundless Space as the *templum* in which dwells All-Father Living Spirit.

It is a very difficult question to answer, because the problem is to meet the minds of people who ask these questions — hungry hearts of people who are wrongly educated.

O. S. — Could you couple your answer more directly with the idea of the hierarchical system, because the hierarchical system, after all, offers us a symbol of, the explanation of, what is called the worship of God. Of course, God is a symbol, a word and a symbol, but people use words very differently and they are misunderstood because different people imply different things by the same words. But after all, the Theosophical system presupposes so on and so forth; and while it is only a stage in this system where we may introduce the word GOD after we have left the word MAN, and so on, we may go on and use a still bigger word at a later stage, I suppose; because we have to express it somehow.

G. de P. — The idea of the hierarchical system lies very near to my heart; because it exemplifies Nature's structure; and the whole attempt of the Masters in founding the Society was to inaugurate among men a structure, mental and spiritual as well as physical, which would represent among us, as far as could be done in human concerns, the structure and fabric, the carpentry so to speak, of Nature herself. Now the questioner has put his finger right on the link that is needed. Consciousness has no frontiers. It is our own wills and lack of vision which delimit, circumscribe, put a frontier to, the working of our consciousness.

All evolution consists in pushing back these barriers of consciousness; in other words and changing the figure of speech, rending the veils, the sheaths of consciousness which we have built around us, and which form the imperfect parts of our constitution. Therefore man's conception of divinity enlarges, as it grows steadily grander and greater, as his consciousness enlarges. He overpasses, oversteps, soars beyond, the enshrouding sheaths of the lower consciousness, which less evolved men than we Theosophists should be, live in; and this process of overpassing these veils or barriers or limitations goes on throughout Eternity.

Now then, here comes in the question of Deity. Where is Deity? What is Deity? Who is Deity? And the answer is seen to be: immediately behind every veil there is a great vision; but behind every vision there is a veil. Behind the second veil there is a still greater vision surrounded by a still greater veil; and so on forever. Consequently, our idea of Deity or of Divinity enlarges or expands, grows greater and more sublime, as our consciousness grows greater and grander and more sublime; until, finally, even the small compass of a human skull can contain conceptions which are truly divine. We can have some conception of the Deity, the Cosmic Guardian of the Galaxy, our own Home-Universe. This we may call God, Deity, Divinity.

But shall we stop there? All the thirty or forty billion suns with their attendant planets, which make up what modern astronomers call the Milky Way, the Galaxy, are collectively but a mathematical point, an imperceptible point or speck, when we contrast it with utter Infinitude. Why make to yourself graven images — images graven by your own mind upon your own consciousness?

Think of the hierarchical structure of the Universe — something small surrounded by something greater from which the smaller receives a delegation of authority; the greater surrounded by something still greater, and so on *ad infinitum;* so that, as our consciousness expands, as we grow ever greater and larger, stronger and nobler, purer and higher in conception and in reach of consciousness, our ideas of divinity enlarge steadily, until after a while we cast behind us the things that we once thought grand, as indeed being but the conceptions of little children; and we step into man's estate; and then these things which are of man's estate become, as we grow and expand, like the conceptions of children again, and we go to something nobler and better.

Where is Deity? Echo answers 'Where?' There is none. The world is filled full with gods, all occupied in the work of the Universe and actually forming the Universe; but nowhere is there one Supreme Ultimate, beyond which naught. Always is there something grander; always is there something greater to grow unto and to become; for growing is becoming, and becoming is being. You will never worry about God again if you get the thought; for you children of Infinity, offsprings of Eternity, have Infinity and Eternity before you. You yourself, each one of you, is an incarnate god; and if I have spoken of consciousness as expanding, it is but a metaphor, a trope, a figure of speech. I myself love to phrase the matter differently and I say: going within, becoming more and more myself, my divine self, that self which is boundless, for it is the Universe. *Tat twam asi:* 'That thou art, O chela.' I will recognise no god inferior to me; but I bow my spirit in reverence before all that is nobler than I. That is the hierarchical spirit. We find God, as we ascend along the hierarchical ladder of life, receding constantly, constantly receding, growing ever greater and greater, grander and more sublime, until finally we reach the knowledge that God is but a name for the vast, unutterable mystery which the Vedic Sages of India called *Tat:* 'THAT.'

VIOLENT METHODS UNWISE

Question — Referring to the warning which you gave us concerning the sudden changes in our personal conceptions of theogony and cosmogony, and references recently to the Jñâna-Yoga, would you give us an explanation of that? I think it would help us to be on guard in regard to those practices?

G. de P. — What is your question, my Brother?

Question — A little explanation of that to enable us to be on guard in concepts on the theogonies and cosmogonies.

G. de P. — Certainly I will try, if I understand your question.

Another Questioner — I think I remember seeing what the brother is talking about. It was suddenly trying to arrange a new conception in the mind violently, that upset the atoms which are lying in the brain according to the method that one has been trained or brought up to think in. It is the effect of thought, the changing of thought suddenly, doing violent injury, perhaps, to the brain.

G. de P. — I think I understand, and it is simple. It involves a question of the advisability or non-advisability of violent revulsions of thought, violent changes of thought. All violence is unwise. I never would think of suggesting to a very devout and orthodox Christian, that within the space of twenty-four hours or a fortnight or a month, if he could do so, he reverse all his psychological conceptions, all his religious views, and try to enter into something entirely new. It would be very unwise. Such violent methods can work a permanent injury to the brain, for the reason that the brain-particles are set in a certain way. I am not a machine-man; I am not acquainted with machines; but I think there is such a thing as wrenching the works of an automobile in such fashion as to disorganize the gears. Is that right? That is the principle, I suppose. *Festina lente:* hasten, but hasten slowly; in other words, 'More haste, less speed,' the old English proverb meaning exactly the same thing.

All great things require time for growth. Mushroom-growths are usually useless, and they are not permanent. This matter is especially important in questions of esoteric training. It takes a chela sometimes several lifetimes before he can so readjust the parts of his constitution as to become a fit and ready and an adequate instrument under the Master's hand. And mark you, it must be his own inner Master first. No outside Master would ever use a chela's body or brain-apparatus, unless it had previously been prepared by the inner Master, the man's own inner being.

No, violence in any wise is not good; and the danger lies especially in these methods of Yoga-training. Now, I speak with hesitation, as you see; because my whole policy is to try to bring these searchers for truth into our ranks in a kindly way; and you know, Comrades and Brothers and Friends, that you cannot ask a man to come to your meetings and then, as soon as he enters the temple or the door, slap his cheek because he does not accept what you say. That is not the way to gain recruits to the T. S. We must be all things to all men in a wise and kindly and honorable sense of that policy. I don't want to say anything unkind about these yoga-practices; but they are not necessary. They are *not* necessary. The Yoga-practice that *is* necessary is that which is taught in Theosophy, and it is the only real Yoga. Yoga means union — union with the god within; and this kind of Yoga has been called Râja-Yoga, or you can call it Jñâna-Yoga, either 'Kingly Union' or 'Knowledge-Union.' Yoga means getting union with one's god within; it means following the ethical practices which Theosophy teaches us; it means being kindly, generous, truthful in speech at all times — not telling the *whole* truth always, but when you speak, tell the truth and only the truth. Do you see what I mean? Sometimes it is unwise to speak; and a man must have discrimination and judgment to understand this and to do this. It means acting always as a Theosophist should act — kindly in action, gentle in thought, firm in self-control, always having command of a situation. Take command! It is your duty. Whenever you rise on a platform, whenever you approach a fellow-human being, take command of the situation. If your motive be pure and good, you are practising the proper yoga. Don't be negative. Take command. It is a duty. Be leaders — leaders of your fellow-men. This is the yoga that we can follow, the yoga of truth, the yoga of right as against wrong, the yoga of compassion, the yoga of pity, the yoga of inner aspiration, the yoga of looking within, of union with the divine; and all these other different kinds of yoga — Karma-Yoga, and Bhakti-Yoga, and Jñâna-Yoga, and Râja-Yoga, and Hatha-Yoga, and all the rest of them — don't amount to a snap of the fingers as contrasted with the actual spiritual and intellectual training under our Masters. All these things are but crutches for men who do not know anything better. Do you understand? Is the answer responsive?

WHY WERE "THE MAHATMA LETTERS" PRINTED?

D. A. — Would you tell us why THE MAHATMA LETTERS *were printed, when the Masters said they were not to be published?*

G. de P. — Why don't you ask Brother Barker?* I can only say that I am profoundly glad that *The Mahatma Letters* were published as a book. I think they have done more good in helping along our own work, the work of our own beloved T. S., than any other single incident in the entire history of the Theosophical Movement. They contain the very heart of Esotericism; and that was the reason why the Masters did not want them published at that time: the times were not ripe; men were unready. Times have now changed. The Theosophical teachings have more or less permeated the thought-atmosphere of the Occident, and we can now talk about things in public, and write about things, which if talked about or written when *The Mahatma Letters* were written to the recipients, would have been simply not understood; and I don't think there is anything more dangerous than a religious teaching which is misunderstood. It leads to dogmatism, hatred, wars, all kinds of uncharity. That was the reason. And then in addition portions of some of *The Mahatma Letters* deal with rather personal affairs and teachings. You know that the men or women who received these letters are now dead, have passed on. There were motives of kindliness and courtesy. Our Masters are men, you know — just men, but very noble ones, great ones, gentlemen in the true meaning of that good old English word. I think Brother Barker did a splendid work.

O. S. — There must be masses of such letters existing, because this volume contains only a selection of letters written to a certain man or to a few men; and there must be many more documents of the same character. I was wondering: aren't we going to have a few more of them gradually?

G. de P. — I think it would be simply a wonderful work if we could. If all the letters that the Great Teachers wrote could be gathered together and collated, printed, I think it would be fine; but I don't think there are so many, after all. Probably there are a few scattered around. Mrs. Laura

*[Editor and compiler of *The Mahatma Letters to A. P. Sinnett* and present as Chairman of the meeting when this question was asked.]

C. Holloway probably received a few, and one or two other people. The Masters did not write so many letters, you know.

O. S. — But they have been working for ages.

G. de P. — If we could go back and read in the astral records, would not that be great! But not all, in fact very few, of the Masters' letters were written with their own hand or hands. Almost all of them came through chelas; and I believe that H. P. B. speaks of this herself somewhere. In fact, the Masters do. Now you see that this fact, which we have no reason to hide — it is the truth — would throw any letter purporting to be a Mahâtma-letter into the field of doubt — doubtful authenticity as regarded by Occidental minds, because the Master himself did not write it with his own hand or with his own pen and mail it in the usual way, but precipitated it or wrote it mentally through the mind of a trained instrument, a chela: who but a Theosophist would accept such a letter as authentic? Would such a letter be received in a court of law today as genuine? It might, if judge and jury were Theosophists, but otherwise I think not. And yet, they were the Masters' letters, the Masters' own words, even the handwriting more or less the same. For what does the chela do? The chela throws himself into a negative attitude of receptivity. It is not negativity in the bad sense, but he merely casts out of his own mind every thought and becomes, as it were, a blank page, a mental page, on which the living fire of the Master's mind traces words, and the chela writes down these words which his consciousness receives. He knows what is going on. If the receptivity is perfect, the reproduction is perfect. If the chela is interrupted or ill or tired, the receptivity is correspondingly poor, and the production will be correspondingly poor. But it is the Master's own mind writing the letter, just as much so as if I were to dictate to my secretary there and she were to write the letter in her own hand, and I would say: 'Just sign that for me and have it go on.'

Theosophy and Mahâyâna Buddhism

W. Y. E.-W. — Would you go so far as to say that the writers of these MAHATMA LETTERS *would ally themselves with the better aspects of the Mahâyâna School, such as Nâgârjuna or Âryasangha?*

G. de P. — Yes, certainly; providing that in giving that answer we understand the real meaning of the teachings of Nâgârjuna and Âryasangha. Now, the teachings that these great teachers have left behind them have not been properly understood in the Occident. The sectarian spirit is rather stronger than that of the occult vision — which indeed has no such sect-

arian spirit. But I would say in answer to the question that what Nâgârjuna and Âryasangha, as representatives of the Mahâyâna School of Buddhism, the 'Great School,' taught, is identic in essence with the teachings
of esoteric Theosophy.

I have often stated in public lectures and otherwise in writings that the
great religion which is the nearest to our own Theosophy is Buddhism.
Even exoteric Buddhism is the least degenerated of all the world-religions;
and I always look with sympathy on those of our people who study Buddhism. I only wish that they would in some cases help us a little more in
the Theosophical aspects. I believe that the heart of Buddhism is the same
as the heart of Theosophy. I believe that the crusts, the veils, enshrouding
that heart in Buddhism are less thick than are the veils enshrouding the
core or real meaning of the teachings of the Christian Jesus, the Christian
Master. We are not Buddhists; but we can truly be called Esoteric Bud-
hists, with one *d;* that is, followers of the Esoteric Wisdom; and Esoteric
Budhism, with one *d,* is identic with Esoteric Buddhism, with two *d's.*

THE ABSOLUTE, A RELATIVE TERM

*Question — Will you formulate a question on the permanency of the
Absolute? Is there one or are there many?*

G. de P. — Is the Absolute one or plural? In most people's opinion
there can be but one Absolute, because they use the word (a war of words!)
in the ordinary Occidental way as meaning Infinitude, the Infinite.

Now 'Absolute' does not mean that. The word 'Absolute' is the past
participle of the Latin verb *absolvere,* 'to set free.' *Absolute,* therefore,
means *freed,* freed from all conditions beneath it — any entity which is
'absolute' is freed. The Absolute, therefore, is an exact translation or an
exact rendering of the Sanskrit Mukti or Moksha, which means 'freedom,'
'set free.' A Nirvânî, one in Nirvâna, has attained Mukti or Moksha, has
attained Absoluteness. Consequently, in the proper usage of this word
'Absolute,' it simply means one who has risen above, or who has become
freed from, all the limitations, all the shackles, that fetter average man.
The Nirvânî is 'absolute' in his Nirvâna. *Absolute* is a relative term:
you can be free from small things; you can be free from greater things.
Each one in its own sphere is 'absolute' there — freed.

Now then, it is quite customary in English and in most Occidental
schools of philosophy to misuse this word *Absolute* to signify Infinitude;
but it is a misuse which I have always protested against and always will;
and there are certain philosophers who are with me — Sir William Hamilton, for one, who speaks of this very fact. Now, in *Fundamentals of the*

Esoteric Philosophy, I use this word in its exact, primary, and etymological sense, as signifying an entity that is so far evolved that it has become freed from all inferior things, free, a free spirit, a Jîvan-mukta, a spiritual-divine Monad.

Every Monad which attains Jîvan-mukti or freedom of the spiritual jîva, of the âtman, is an 'Absolute,' is in a state of absoluteness, true freedom from everything beneath it — for instance, in our own Galaxy, our own Home-Universe. Everything in the Universe is relative. Einsteinism if you like; but everything in the Universe is relative; all the Absolutes are relative, each one to its own Universe; and there may be a limited Absolute, a greater Absolute, a still greater Absolute, remembering that *Absolute* means *freed.* Therefore there are as many Absolutes as there are Jîvan-muktas — as many Absolutes as there are Guardians of the Universe. Do you understand? There are no permanent Absolutes. If there were, that would simply mean that an entity, a spiritual entity, having reached divinity, or quasi-divinity, becomes crystallized or permanent in that state and cannot go farther on, cannot evolve to greater and sublimer heights.

Now, that is impossible, because everything that is, every living entity everywhere in Boundless Space, is continuously and forever growing, evolving, expanding. What a doctrine of hope! There are no permanent Absolutes; and the Absolutes are as numerous as are the Jîvan-muktas, the freed spirits.

Is the Spiritual Ego Immortal?

W. Y. E.-W. — I think that in correlation with what you have been saying, we might perhaps have some information from you in respect to the statement in one of the letters about the 'spiritual ego.' The point I should like to make here is: How far are we to follow the Buddhist thought in the matter of the ego or non-ego, or the matter of Âtmâ or non-Âtmâ? There are a good many differences between the two schools of Buddhism; but one thing they agree in is the non-existence of a permanent ego. If you go back into the idealistic movement of the Northern Buddhist school in the first century, you will find that they all agree on this. What, then, is meant by 'Spiritual Ego'?

G. de P. — Thank you. That is an awfully good opportunity you have given me. This question is a very pertinent one, because it goes to the very root of the question, so-called, of the continuance of individual, or rather personal, consciousness. Is personal consciousness immortal? In other words, is the ego immortal? Are we Theosophists, like all schools of Buddhism, followers of the doctrine of the Anâtman — are we Anâtman

Buddhists, or Âtman Buddhists? Do we say that the ego is immortal, or do we say that it is mortal?

It has been a common theory in some Theosophical circles outside of our own, that the Ego is immortal; and I have fought that doctrine tooth and nail, whenever I have had a chance. I cannot conceive of a more horrible destiny than for me to remain permanently as I am in my Ego and never be able to change and go higher. To me that doctrine is horrible. It has brought about more misery in the world, more selfishness, more suffering and pain, than even the doctrine of so-called 'God' has. Men have fought about questions of God until the gutters have run with blood. Religious wars have always been the most bitter and sanguinary in history; and we have to stop that kind of thing.

But concerning this question of Ego and non-Ego, as a matter of fact both the teachings are true. The Ego is mortal; but, just like the human body, being mortal, it re-forms itself at the next incarnation or reincarnation. The Ego re-forms itself of and from the life-atoms which now compose it; so that the same man returns after the devachanic interlude. But to speak of the Ego as immortal, which means enduring for aye, perpetually, as it is, no! That is not the teaching of Theosophy; that is not the teaching of the Ancient Wisdom-Religion; it is not the teaching of the gods.

Everything changes. Nothing that is composite is immortal. *Immortality* means continuity, unchanging continuity, of a being or thing as it is; and that means that such an entity could never evolve, never grow: it would have to be for ever and for ever just exactly as it is. If it changed an iota in thought, in feeling, in consciousness, in any wise, it would no longer be the same; it would have changed: the old Ego would have passed. Deduction: everything grows; everything changes; everything moves — the Âtman as much as anything else, or the Paramâtman, or Parabrahman, which is merely a name to describe all that is beyond the Over-Guardian of our Galaxy: even *that* changes. Everything is growing; everything is moving; everything is alive. Change is of the very essence of evolution itself, of the very essence of growth.

But then, does this teaching mean that the Ego never returns — that our present Ego is ended utterly, completely annihilated, absolutely wiped out? That teaching is as idiotic as the other. How can a thing which exists utterly vanish? It is an entity; it is a composite entity; it is a union, nay, a unity, a unity of life-atoms which make the entity which now exists. It will exist again, because the attractions which brought those life-atoms into coherency in this life and made me an ego and made you an ego — the same attraction, the same laws, will work in future incarnations and reproduce me and reproduce you — more evolved, changed, therefore no longer the same ego, but practically the same.

Why, our very bodies change from the time when we are infants, when we are little children, as we grow to mature manhood or womanhood, and then descend the slope to old age. 'Change and decay in all around I see.' Thank the immortal gods that it is so! Think of the horror of everything remaining for ever as it is! Think of it! Is there any difference (and this is one of the great lessons that we Theosophists must learn clearly and give to the world) — Is there any difference between the truths of this world and the truths of the spiritual worlds? No; because truth is truth; and this world is but a reflexion of the worlds of the spirit, but a reflexion, a copy.

Relatively speaking, the Âtman within us is immortal — relatively speaking; but from the standpoint of Infinitude, which is frontierless, beginningless, endless Duration, even the Âtman changes and grows to something sublimer. Do you get the thought? Personal immortality would be a worse gift than the robe of Nessus to Hercules. Growth, change, progress, evolution, bringing out in ever larger measure the stored-up fountains of life, of intelligence, of being, lying within us: That, *That*, THAT — is the future, not static immortality.

Therefore we Theosophists say that both these doctrines are true, when properly understood; but coming down to exact analysis of each, we discern that they are two sides of the same truth. The Ego is relatively mortal, relatively immortal. It is conditionally mortal, conditionally immortal. Then again, which Ego do you mean: the Human Ego, the Spiritual Ego, the Divine Ego? Man's name is legion.

Our Lord Buddha said in his last words: 'Brothers, all things that are, are composite, are component, built up of elements. Find your way to truth,' or, as it has been mistranslated by scholars brought up in Christian thought: 'Seek out your own salvation.' The way to peace and happiness is in recognising truth and feeling that here within is the Cosmic Life, the Cosmic Intelligence, which is neither Ego nor non-Ego — something which is deathless; for it is Infinity; it is Eternity; it is *That*. I am It. Thou, Brother, art It. It has no name. It is indescriptible. It is neither spirit nor non-spirit; for it is both. It is neither Ego nor non-Ego; for it is both. It is *That*.

Speaking in simpler and more imperfect terms, we might say it is the Cosmic Life. But I use such words under protest, because they are so miscolored and misused in the Occident. You use the words 'Cosmic Life' to ten men brought up in Occidental schools of philosophy, and you will have ten different interpretations of what these words mean.

Question — Could one ask the question thus: Is the Swabhâva of the Spiritual Ego continuous? People want to feel that the individuality itself is continuous — not that it stops growing, but that the germ of the individuality is to go on for ever.

G. de P. — Yes, and they tangle themselves up in philosophical words and phrases, and don't know what they are talking about. You have schools of philosophy in the Occident trying to study the philosophy of the Orient, and Orientals who study the philosophy of the Occident and do not try to understand their own. The very question is a proof that there is Something — call it what you like — within every entity and being who collectively builds Boundless Infinitude. That Something is deathless. 'It is the Self,' said the Sages of Vedic Âryâvarta. They did not mean a human ego; they did not mean an angel or a deva, or a god: they meant an Essence — the Essence of the Universe — THAT!

There is just one thing an entity cannot avoid, and that is continuous existence. That is just the one thing that cannot be wiped out. If it were possible to extract, to take away, to eliminate, one single atom, one mathematical point, or Monad, from Boundless Infinitude, Boundless Infinitude would crash into cosmic nonentity. Every point is as important as every other point.

But what Occidentals find so difficult to understand is this noble doctrine of the non-immortality of the personal Ego. They don't stop to think that it would be a hell to any of us to continue for ever and for ever as now we are. Yet there is in the heart of every entity, which means every being anywhere in Boundless Space, evolved or unevolved — spiritual, ethereal, physical, or sub-physical — there is at the heart of the heart and forming the heart of the heart of such entity or being — THAT — which is deathless, the god within — call it by any name you like, or call it the SELF. It is such a simple idea that it often amazes me that Occidentals find it so difficult to understand it. Just get the one thought, that if there is anything in Boundless Infinitude that cannot be annihilated or wiped out, it is continuous, unending existence, continuous unending life.

From THAT we all come, and to THAT we all return. It is the great Fountain of Life, the *fons et origo*, the great Fountain and Origin of all things. Life is like a great cycling wheel; and this is the figure of speech that our Lord has given to us. (I say, 'Our Lord': I speak esoterically, of course, for we are not Buddhists; yet we follow the esoteric doctrine of the Lord Buddha. I don't care *that* for the opinions of Occidental scholars that the Buddha had no esoteric school, or that there is no such thing as esoteric Buddhism. It is nonsense.)

Here is the figure of the wheel, the circling wheel of life, slowly turning through interminable, endless ages; and we are like spots or specks on the rim of the wheel; and we go constantly up and down; and each such wheel is a galaxy, a cosmos. Now, it is the peculiar nature of this wheel that, as the ages pass, it grows constantly more and more ethereal; the wheel itself changes; the wheel itself is mortal — grows, that is evolves, to something higher and better. A very mystical figure, but very true.

Masters do not Interfere

The Chairman — Here is a written question. It refers in the beginning to two so-called 'controls' of a medium at the present time practising in London. Question — I have been very much interested in the teachings given out by —— and by ——, ——'s control. They seem to me very splendid and helpful; and I know some old Theosophists who think very highly of them. Yet I am told that these teachings, though they resemble Theosophy, are unsound and misleading. I am confused and troubled. If the mediums in these cases are honest and genuine, why is it that deceiving spirits are ALLOWED *to use them? Could not the Masters intervene and speak themselves through the mouths of the mediums and state the truth? It seems wrong to allow those who are trying to be true Theosophists to be deceived.*

G. de P. — In a way I am sorry to have to answer this question; but of course it is only right to try to do so. Now, in the first place: how often has not this question been asked before: 'If the Masters are all that they are said to be, why don't they step into the arena of human affairs and right all the wrongs of the world?' That is the idea and it is an unfair idea. The Masters never interfere with the karman of anyone. They cannot; they dare not; it is contrary, not only to the hierarchical system of government under which our society is run — and when I say that I include the Masters' own lodge, of which we are the outermost extension — but it is contrary to the first teachings of Theosophy, that anyone shall interfere with the soul-destiny of anyone else. He must learn his lessons. Help we should, whenever we can rightly do so. Compassion speaks all the time; and you may be sure, my dear Brothers, that the Masters are watching things like this, not only in London but all over the world, and render what help they can; but miracles they cannot work, nor will they try to work them.

Each instance of a medium is a psychological case that only karman can explain, and which only karman must solve as a problem. That is all the answer that can be given. I have no right, although a Theosophist and a Theosophical Leader, to go into the family of a brother-Theosophist, because he happens to be having quarrels with his wife, for instance, and interfere in his private affairs. It may be very regrettable, and my heart may be wrung with pity for both; but I have no right to 'butt in,' as some folk say. My duty is to observe and to help, when help I can, and when help I may; but that is all; and the situation is exactly the same with the Masters.

It was just this fact of the inrushing tide of psychic influences, which were going to flow into our Occident during the coming hundred years, that was the main cause of the sending forth by the Masters of their Envoy, H. P. Blavatsky, to try to attract men's minds into saner and less psychical channels — upwards instead of downwards.

Now, it is our duty to oppose all kinds of errors; but to do so by Theosophical ways, by kindliness, by teaching the truth, by instilling thoughts of reality, explanations of these things, into men's minds. But it is quite wrong to suppose that the Masters have any right to go in and forcibly to put an astral restraining hand on another. They cannot do it, simply cannot do it.

I was asked the following the other day — it was not so long ago, a couple of months ago — by a person to whom I had given a similar explanation to a question somewhat similar to this: 'Why, G. de P., if you were passing along the street and saw a man murdering some other man, would you just say: "That is the murdered man's karman. Let it go on."' I should say no! I should not. It would be my bounden duty to rush to the rescue. 'But then,' he asked, 'is it not the Masters' bounden duty to rush to the rescue of these people who are deceived?' 'Ah,' I replied, 'in rushing to stop the murder, would you want me to murder the murderer? The Masters are wiser than we. It would be my duty to stop the murder if possible, even to cripple the murderer so that he could not continue his his evil work when I had left; but to murder the murderer? No.'

INSPIRED DANTE

J. G. — Was Dante an Initiate?

G. de P. — I would not say that the Italian poet, Dante, was an Initiate; but I will tell you my own private conviction about him: I think, like the case of Dr. Einstein, that there was sufficient spiritual life in the man to allow the entrance into his consciousness, if you understand me, of a divine ray, which touched his brain, so that when he wrote his immortal poem he mentally set forth, although in Christian phrasing and terms, a great deal of the teaching of the ancient doctrine. There are the nine stages, or the nine or ten hells; there is purgatory and the terrestrial paradise; there are the nine or ten heavens — a typical medieval example of the Oriental teaching of the lokas and talas. Of course it is all told in Christian terms. But it is a magnificent poem. And mark you, Dante made his guide, his mystic guide through the infernal regions and the purgatory, the so-called 'Pagan' poet Vergil; but when he came to describe the heavens — probably in order to satisfy his Christian critics — he chose his Beatrice, a Christian maid, to conduct him through the heavens!

The Many and the One in Man

F. A. L. — We have had many interesting talks about different questions; and it seems to me that it would be very fine if you could tell us something that could demonstrate that, though we are composite beings, and not only we men, but all living entities, perhaps, composite of thousands of entities, after all we are not many but still one? I have experienced that when we break up man into so many pieces, some of them angels, others devils, and so on and so forth, most people do not feel very comfortable; and I like always to close our lectures with some suggestion that, after all, we are not separate, even if we are separated in the outer world; but that Reality is one and not many.

G. de P. — Yours is not an easy question, dear Brother. It amounts to what is known in Esotericism as the great mystery of the One becoming the many; and at the end of things, the many rebecoming the One. It is one of the most profound of the mysteries of the Esoteric Philosophy. It is one which requires literally years and years of the most hard, searching study, adequately and completely to answer. It is a question which arises doubtless in the minds of all inquirers, even of those who are honest in their study of the Ancient Wisdom. It is, therefore, a question which must come before all lodge-presidents, before every individual Theosophical propagandist, for answer. It is a remarkable fact that this very question is one which never has received full treatment by the great Sages and Seers. I mean a treatment given out in public exposition. The reason is that it simply cannot be done. It is not a question which can be fully answered before the public and to the public. It is wholly an esoteric line of thought. But the mere fact, dear Brother, that you have phrased your question as you have phrased it, shows that you have already meditated upon it, and in meditating upon it have found at least some answer or some answers, which will satisfy, to a certain degree at least, those who put the question to you.

I would suggest the following: Just as man is a copy in the small of the cosmic *Vast;* in other words, just as man is a microcosm, a little world, a reflexion or copy of the macrocosm or great world; and just as these twain are one fundamentally and in essence, in origin, and in future destiny, in present being and past being; likewise, on similar grounds of thought, the One — which is the core of the core of the heart of the heart of the Universe — is the core of the core of the heart of the heart of you. This entire matter is referred to by the Lord Buddha in one of his teachings. It is technically known in oriental literature as the doctrine of the Âtma-vâda, the teaching of the enduring self, or 'ego,' as occidental scholars usually translate this word — and wrongly.

It must become obvious from what I have just said that the Cosmic Self, although your inmost self, is not the self of you or of me as a man. You are a human self, a human ego; I am a human self, a human ego; nevertheless each one of us as individuals or human egos exists and has its being, and all our life we live and move and have our being in the cosmic profundity which we can only describe in the language of the Vedic Sage as THAT. It is the illusion of personality, even of individuality if you wish, which induces human beings as thinking entities, to imagine that the lower ego-ship, the lower ego-self itself, endures forever, forgetting, or perhaps not seeing, that it is precisely in this doctrine, false and erroneous, of the continuous and unchanging perpetuity of the human ego-self, that lies the fruitful source, the fountain, of all human woe, of all human sorrow, and of all human sin, because of all human selfishness.

When a man knows, and in knowing feels with every atom of his being, that what he is is but a cosmic atom, so to say, in the fabric and substance of the absolute Vast of our Galaxy; and that he is as important as that Galaxy in his essence and relatively unimportant as a microcosm, as a human egoity — when this conviction burns itself into his consciousness, he becomes truly impersonal; he becomes a Man — with a capital *M*, a Superman, a Demigod; because the very essence of the consciousness of divinity is then trying to penetrate into his human consciousness.

We as human beings exist; but in the very essence of things we — as humans — are not. There is the key. It is a matter of Mâyâ, or rather of Mahâmâyâ, Cosmic Illusion; and Freedom, Moksha or Mukti, *Absoluteness* in the way I use the word in *Fundamentals of the Esoteric Philosophy*, consists in shaking off this illusion, that, for instance, the musician is different from the music he gives us, or that the poet is other than the poesy he brings to us, or that the seer is different from the vision which he sees. The twain are one. Is a man different from the love which fills his heart? There is the key — a key given rather by suggestion than by entangling the reason with brain-mind words.

We do exist as human beings, as individuals; and we shall exist throughout the entire duration of the cosmic or solar Manvantara, as individuals constantly growing greater and vaster, ever more sublime, until finally we shall reach the grand *consummatum est,* the final consummation of all things at the end of the solar Manvantara, and blossom out as full-blown gods. And when the cosmic Pralaya sets in, which many men, even Theosophists, in their ignorance and blindness, look upon with dread, then even the divinity of our being will fade away into the fulness, into the indescribable, unspeakable, ineffable fulness of quasi-infinity. The dewdrop has returned into the shining sea. The little consciousness of the human god has become once again the untrammeled and cosmic consciousness of the Universal Divinity. The many have rebecome the one. There's the picture.

Hadn't I better leave it there? I fear that if I say more, by using more words, we shall entangle our understandings in words and lose the thought.

THE MÂNASAPUTRIC LIGHT

Question — In our Theosophical reading, we learn that the human race was mindless until the Mânasaputras incarnated in the Third Root-Race and endowed it with mind. Elsewhere in our literature it is said that during the time of the Third Root-Race, humanity evolved mind with the help of the Mânasaputras, who lighted the fires of mind in it. Question: Did the Mânasaputras, coming from other realms, bring mind with them, or did they merely light up the dormant mind that was already latent in the Third Root-Race? How are we to reconcile the two doctrines?

G. de P. — This is one of the most interesting and nevertheless one of the most difficult questions of the entire teaching; and if I may venture to develop the thought just a bit, Mr. Chairman, I would point out that both sides are absolutely right: Mind was given, but there was already mind — but unevoked, latent mind; and it required the coming of the superior developed mind, a part of its own flame, like the approach of the flame to the wick of the unlighted candle to set the unlighted candle aflame in its turn. But it could not be set aflame unless mind were already there.

The incarnation of the Mânasaputras may be likened to the case of a little child receiving from its own inner being the divine gift of intelligence. A child is born. It is mindless. After a year, or two, or three, or four, or five, depending upon the infant, its state is exactly like that of the Third Root-Race of mankind in this Fourth Round on this Globe D. Now, as the child grows by the natural process of evolution, the mind within it begins to function, begins to appear. But mark you, this process of evolution would be much slower in its work, if the child were, let us say, alone on a desert-island. It would take years and years to bring out the latent intellectual and spiritual faculties of the growing boy or girl. But the child has its over-watching parents, its loving guides and helpers, 'the Sons of

Mind,' the father and the mother, who guide its vacillating footsteps, who teach it, who teach it to think, who by example and precept evoke what is already within the child. Otherwise it could not be evoked.

Manas is not an entity: it is a faculty, an organ, a principle, in the human being; and there is Manas in the wood of this table, but it is unevoked. It manifests itself in the atoms of that table in their cohesion in the form which wood is, which wood takes; but it is all unevoked; it is latent; it is dormant. Manas is the offspring of Mahat. (I do hope you will get the pronunciation of these Sanskrit words right.) Mahat is the cosmic principle; Manas is the cosmic principle manifesting in the human constitution. To speak of Manas as 'the thinker' is inaccurate, if we desire strict accuracy; because the thinker is the egoic principle acting on the mânasic plane; it has evolved to function on the mânasic plane, the mânasic entity, the Mânasaputra, the sons of Mahat. But Manas or Mahat is in everything, in every entity, is always there. But in entities inferior to the human, it is unevoked, unevolved, not brought forth.

In the Third Root-Race, the Mânasaputras or 'Sons of Mind' descended into the most evolved rûpas of the then child-like and intellectually dormant human race; and by their own divine, intellectual fire and-flame quickened the latent or dormant fires in the infant humanity, brought them to think, made them think, as the parents make a little child think, bring out its mind, teach it to think, by its books, by precept, by example, by words. It is the most simple thing in the world and yet one of the most glorious. It shows how inferior creatures are protected by the Dhyân-Chohans; because the Mânasaputras are a race of Dhyân-Chohans, particularly and especially evolved along the lines of the mânasic principle.

'Did the Mânasaputras leave mankind when they had quickened its dormant intellectual faculties?' Some did, but in all human beings our own highest intellectual parts are still for each one of us that particular Mânasaputra, which, to use H. P. B.'s word, incarnated and set aflame our own dormant mânasic organ. Each one has his own Mânasaputra still working within him; and this Mânasaputra is the Christ, the Christ immanent, in each man.

How to Meet Despair and Depression

Question — This is a rather more practical question. I believe that in LETTERS THAT HAVE HELPED ME, *Mr. Judge, speaking about Theosophists in their study having periods of being very down, says, if such a period comes, just to sit still and wait and it will soon pass over and everything will come out all right. One of the other Leaders — I believe it was our pre-*

sent Leader — somewhere says, if such a period comes, to hold on like grim death — I think that was the expression — and peace will return. Now, in a recent issue of THE FORUM, *I believe, I also read something about it; and there was more or less an explanation given of such a period. So, as several of the Leaders have spoken about it, it is of course an experience that not only I myself have, but many people must have also had it. Now, I wanted to ask this: Can we, besides waiting, do something else to make it pass over quickly? During such a period you try to work, but you really can't even work; your thoughts seem to freeze before they become clear, and your words seem to freeze before you can utter them. It is really a time of great misery for the one who experiences it, because deep down in his heart there is the desire to go on, yet there is something which prevents it. Now, I would like to ask whether there is any way just to help a person over such a period?*

G. de P. — I think I understand. If that question were asked of me in the privacy of my study, I would give exactly the same answer that I will now try to give; and it is very brief. It is this: If you are strong enough, rise and go out in service to others. Forget yourself, your sorrows and your pains, in alleviating the sorrows and pains of others, lightening them — the first duty that comes to hand; because all our pain and sorrow, all our wretchedness and misery, when it comes and as it comes and whatever it may be, arises from a reaction on our own human mentality and feelings, of conditions that we ourselves have brought about but grieve to face.

Brother Judge gave a very good rule: wait until the storm-clouds roll by. I suggested the same with the phrasing that the questioner has also quoted: 'Hold on like grim death'; never despair; that is failing. But I would like to say now, in addition to holding on, seek out others who are suffering more than you are and extend the hand of helpfulness, and your own sorrows will vanish away like wisps of mist in the morning before the sun — always. It will never fail, because you forget yourself; we forget ourselves. It is an infallible rule. Most people don't like it, because (this may astonish you) many, many, many people — most human beings, perhaps — like to suffer! There is an extraordinary psychology about this. They love to torment themselves. There are even certain human beings of such distorted psychological mentality, that they torture themselves deliberately and find a pleasure in doing so. There are men and women who deliberately, for the pleasure of the thing, make themselves miserable and other people around them too. Technically, in modern psychology, this is called Sadism, a word taken from a French nobleman who was notorious, famous — or rather infamous — for his cruelties and for the pleasure which he took in inflicting cruelty; and whether this hideous psychology existing in a man's or woman's mind is practised upon his or her self, or upon others, it is the same.

The way to forget one's own pains and sorrows is to help others, help the ones nearest to you; and you will be amazed how many you will find whose faces you can gladden with a smile, whose hearts you can lighten with a kindly word. Try it! Forget your troubles! Forget your suffering! Forget your sorrows! Forget your misery! It does no good to linger upon them. It just increases them. If you are normal you know that life is full of sorrow and pain. We have to accept these things. We are in a very low state of evolution; but how great, how grand, is the man or woman who can rise above these things and be helpful to others! There is where the real chela-spirit, the Master-spirit, comes in.

> Laugh and the world laughs with you,
> Weep and you weep alone;
> For the sad old earth must borrow its mirth,
> But has trouble enough of its own.

You know the old verses.

It is our duty to throw off our own sorrows and sufferings and pains and to work to help others. We Theosophists especially find it incumbent upon us to do this; and the great-minded Theosophist is he who can do this; and the more he can do it, the greater he is. There is the remedy. Try it; and you will go to sleep that night with a light heart, at peace with yourself and the world. If you practise it, it becomes continuously easier, ever more easy, every day a little easier; and finally you will attain peace, a place of peace and inner rest, where you will be actually above the reach of pain and sorrow.

Seeds are wonderful things. Keep the seeds of these thoughts in your minds; and even though you forget them at times, they will some day come back, because they will strike roots in your mind. The egoity of these thoughts will be reborn in your mind.

This reminds me of something I would like to add to my answer to the former question. It is along exactly the same line of thoughts: cyclic recurrences of things that happen. These gods and demigods, who at the Pralaya rebecome the One, 'the shining dewdrops rebecoming the shining sea' — do you imagine that those dewdrops are annihilated? Why, that is impossible. They could not have become the many from the One unless there was some reason for these many individuals. Each one is a seed, an entity, an individual, a monad; and when the great Pralaya reaches its end, the shining sea gives up again its dewdrops; and the dewdrops reappear as monads, enter upon a new cycle of cosmic manifestation, but on a plane loftier and grander than the one previously ended.

And so it is with thoughts and feelings of suffering and pain: they will come back; but we must be above them; and we can be above them; and we should practise the yoga, the union, of forgetting ourselves in service for mankind. Oh, the peace, the happiness, the indescribable feeling of blessedness! Old thoughts, but very, very, very true ones!

H. A. P. — Mr. Chairman, may I ask a question on the same subject? I would ask: How can we help persons who are in such circumstances as described in the last question? Those who are unhappy, how can we help them?

G. de P. — By setting them first an example of what we can do with ourselves. The force of example is more powerful and more telling than a hundred thousand words. When you see a man bearing a misfortune with manly fortitude, standing with unflinching face to the wintry blasts that beat upon him, when you see him with unbowed head facing destiny, and facing fate, and yet advancing to it, it stirs every spark of heroism in those who watch, and we say: 'Ah! a Man!' It is thus we give courage, we stimulate courage in others. We are like the Mânasaputras. We bring the flame of something holy and beautiful into others' lives. Just the same when others are in pain or sorrow, are suffering: set them an example of all that we know would help us if we were like them. Often without words is best. I think it is fatal to preach at a person. It makes people so tired when you preach at them! Sometimes the voiceless example is a thousand times more powerful than anything else. Occasionally a gentle word, a kindly expression, will work wonders. Sometimes human hearts in pain are just longing for a kindly touch, a friendly word — just that, no more than that; and then set the example of cheerfulness; but not overdone. Do anything that occurs to you, according to the person who needs the help, setting the example, showing what your feeling is. I think that is the best way. The circumstances are practically infinite. I would have to talk all the afternoon and give a quasi-infinitude of examples to cover every case. But it is so simple: set the example of what you would do if you were in the person's place, what you would do to go away from the condition.

LEAVE THOSE IN KÂMA-LOKA ALONE

Question — In connexion with what has been said about the sufferings in Kâma-loka, can we on Earth do anything to relieve the sufferings of those who are in Kâma-loka, especially the relatives whom we have lost and whom we suppose to be suffering there?

G. de P. — That is a question which has been asked by many kindly human hearts in the past, and in what are called the Pagan times asked more insistently and more often than in Christian times — in fact, asked so frequently and an answer so insistently demanded that the Christian Church, in the Roman Communion at least, instituted what it has called the Masses for the souls in Purgatory. If you will kindly understand that you need not worry about those whom you love, when they go through the Kâma-loka! Their Kâma-loka is painless. They are, in most cases, utterly unconscious of the passage. It is really only the evil-minded men, the grossly minded human beings, who have the unpleasant kâma-lokic experience. It is infinitely better not to think about it, infinitely better. But there is one method of direct action we can do; and it is very important in these days: Whatever you do, don't try to enter into communication with them. That is the worst and most cruel thing you could do. Here again it is my duty to speak the truth. Our Spiritistic brothers, through ignorance and often being men and women of kindly hearts and noble aspirations, have rushed in where even angels would fear to tread. They simply don't understand. Nature's methods are always kindly, always just. A prayer of the Romans was a noble one: *resquiescat in pace:* 'let him rest in peace.'

(Conclusion of the series of Convention Questions and Answers)

THE KÂMA PRINCIPLE IN MEDIUMSHIP

In your lecture last Sunday, you said that a medium was a person in whom the principles were loosely knitted together. Could you explain that a little? How can our principles be loosely knit and how can we avoid that unfortunate condition?

To say that the principles are loosely knitted together is of course a figure of speech. These are H. P. B.'s words. Perhaps I would phrase it in this way — I am sure I could not improve on H. P. B., but I have been asked this question so many times that it shows H. P. B.'s words have been ill understood — I would change the figure of speech, and say that the principles in the case of the medium are functioning badly, as in a machine. Now I am no mechanician at all, but I have noticed in riding in an automobile sometimes there are jerks and jars, and it is hard to start the thing going. The medium is something like that. The principles of the constitution are not under the control of the higher will. They do not function smoothly and easily, but there are jerks and jolts and jars. This is because the principles being more or less freed from the dominating control of the central spiritual will, are affected by outside influences. They do not function easily and are not closely welded together, compactly, so to speak.

Remember that all the principles of man are but phases of consciousness. We see it around us all the time. We see it in children; we see it in adults; we see people who do not seem to be able always to live in their highest and to do their best. They strive and yearn to do what is best but they do not always succeed. The principles lack sufficient coherence, or rather subserviency to the dominating spirit within. The Kâma-principle, for instance, wants to run a bit on its own, wants to be a little independent, you know. How familiar that sounds! Or perhaps the Linga-śarîra has a notion it wants to run a bit on its own apart from the other principles, and it does. And when this happens a door, as it were, is opened, there is a crack — how can I express it? — an entrance is made for the incoming into the constitution of outside influences, astral influences in this case, and the man is more or less swayed by foolish or evil thoughts; they come tramping into his brain like a lot of vagrants, and he becomes *pro tempore* subject to them and follows them — foolish or evil influences, wicked suggestions, vile thoughts, or it may be trivialities.

Whereas the man whose principles are under the control of the spiritual will, takes command and he is a man in every sense of the word. What he wills he does, and the principles function as smoothly and as easily as possible. That is the idea.

Now the mediums I do not mean to suggest are all foolish and evil people. On the contrary. But they are unfortunate people in whom self-control is even less manifest than in ordinary or average people. They are people in whom the spiritual will lacks full or relatively full control of the whole being.

THOUGHTS ARE ELEMENTAL BEINGS

What are thoughts?

All thoughts, *in esse, per se,* are elemental beings, learning entities. A thought is surrounded by a thought-form, i.e., is imbodied in a thought-form, but the thought itself is an elemental energy. We ourselves at one time, in the far distant aeonic past, were thoughts of other self-conscious entities. "Guard well thy mind, O Chela, against the thoughts which impinge upon it and seek entrance therein" is one of the rules of the Esoteric School. Some of the unfortunate criminals you often hear say, in extenuation, or in attempted extenuation, of a crime: "Judge, I just couldn't help it. I don't know what was the matter with me, but something seized me and I couldn't stop!" Such cases are weak men, lacking moral self-control, lacking the protection, the âkâśic barrier, which automatically keeps out evil thoughts. Of course evil and good are relative, you understand that. There are evil things in the world, that is, imperfect things; but there are also good things. Here is the gist then of my answer: Every elemental is, at the core of the core of the heart of its being a divinity, a divine spark; and all evolution, all growth, is simply an unwrapping, an unfolding, of latent capacities locked up in the loftier parts of each evolving entity or thing. This applies not only to men but to the super-gods, the gods, the demi-gods, men, beasts, plants, minerals, elementals, what not!

SOULS AND MONADS

May I receive a little more light on two passages from your FUNDAMEN-TALS OF THE ESOTERIC PHILOSOPHY? *Page 154 states that our human souls in a future manvantara will become Monads. Well, I was under the impression that our souls were already Monads.*

This is a very interesting and intricate point of doctrine. As a matter of fact, a soul is a vehicle which in time will bring out from itself its own swabhâvic key-note; and when that is done it becomes a monad, but it is not a monad until it becomes monadic. Do you get the idea? We have the divine monad enshrining itself in its divine soul; we have our spiritual monad enshrining itself in our spiritual soul; we have the human monad enshrining itself in the human soul. We have the animal monad enshrining itself in the animal body, because our own physical bodies are animals when considered alone and apart from the higher part. A soul is a vehicle, but a living entity. And it must become monadic, in other words a god. That is just what we are in process of becoming — slowly, but we are on the way. At the present time we self-consciously live in our human souls. It is our future destiny through evolving, that is bringing out what is wrapped up, enclosed, within us, to become from the present human souls human gods. The human soul will have recoalesced with its human monad, a divine being.

THE DUAL ASPECT OF MANAS

The Manas or the Thinker is the reincarnating being. Its nature be-comes dual as soon as it is attached to a body. My question is: What is the meaning of its being attached to a body and what is the meaning of 'as soon as'?

This is an interesting question because the teaching concerning the Manas as a function or organ of thought or consciousness, is a very deep and mysterious one. It has been said by some Theosophical teachers that Manas is, as it were, the mind. But strictly speaking in technical Theo-sophy it is erroneous so to speak of it. Manas is an organ of thought, as well as the faculty of thinking the thoughts of the kosmic consciousness which we perceive through this mânasic organ. Now it must be obvious from this brief description, that an organ can be undeveloped, partially developed, or fully developed; and in the human race at the present time it is about half-way developed to what we may call relative perfection.

The question which the questioner has asked refers to the time, as I understand it, when Manas became active in the human race. Its nature becomes dual as soon as it is attached to a body. It begins to function at a certain period in the history of the human races. To speak of it as being attached to a body is but an easy, a graphic, manner of speech. Strictly speaking, the mânasic faculty is no more attached to a body than the spirit is; but the former works through the body by the intermediary of a subordinate organ which we call the brain-mind. One cannot say that consciousness plays with its delicate fingers directly upon the substance of the brain because consciousness is one of the finest of energies, and the brain-substance is exceedingly coarse by comparison therewith. But between consciousness, the mânasic consciousness, and the physical substance of the brain, there are stages or degrees of decreasing ethereal substance, forming, as it were, a small hierarchy or ladder of differing ethereal substances; and it is through this ladder, through these various planes or grades of substance, from the pure Manas-principle to the physical brain, that the mânasic ray works. Is the answer thus far responsive?

Questioner — Brain then is body?

Well, brain of course refers to the body, because I cannot conceive that Manas acts through my toe; but the mânasic principle permeates the body by means of the brain. Just as the brain is the guiding mental organ of the physical body, so is the mânasic part of the constitution the guiding thought-principle of that constitution. The brain is a part of the body. I think your question had some reference to time. You emphasized the word 'time.'

Questioner — The brain in the infant is there before man becomes dual —

Now I think I see your point. All things are dual. Even electricity is dual in its action. The scientists speak of the positive pole and the negative pole. There is a positive side of consciousness and the opposite side of consciousness. Electricity is merely repeating in electrical spheres of action what happens everywhere.

Thought is bi-polar; therefore the mânasic action is bi-polar, but it becomes bi-polar only when it reaches this plane of bi-polar action; and this took place in what we call the Third Root-Race of the present Fourth

Round of this Globe D. Do you understand? If you do not understand and are not fully convinced by the answer, try again.

Questioner — When does the Manas become dual in entering into the brain?

Just as soon as it begins to manifest as thought. We all know that a little child does not think as a grown man. No little child can write one of the wonderful plays of Shakespeare. That comes with time. But just as soon as the mental faculty begins to function through the child's brain it becomes dual, because duality belongs to this plane. There is the higher and the lower. Just as soon as the child begins to think, it begins to perceive right and wrong, high and low, the secret or hid and the open or obvious. The Manas functions dually just as soon as the child begins to think, and this is because in our time-periods in this Fourth Round in this Globe D Manas functions in a dual action, in a dual way.

Questioner — Then at what point does it cease to be dual after it is disattached from the body?

Ah, that is a different question. We cease to be dual in action, in thought, we cease to be torn by the passions of our weak and vacillating human character, when we have risen above division and duality and reached the divine flame within. That will come fully at the end of the Fifth Round and in perfection at the end of the Seventh Round on this Earth, which of course as you know belongs to one of the Planetary Chains. Is the answer responsive or is it too abstruse?

Questioner — Does the brain after a while become an impediment to one instead of a help?

Not only after a time, but even at the present time. Do you know, there is a way of living in thought rather than in thoughts. It is thoughts with which the brain deals. But there is an organ of the brain which we cannot call the brain even though it is a part of it, but it is a center through which pours thought rather than the mere thoughts which harass and distract us all. Now when we can rise out of the region of these limiting little personal distracting and harassing thoughts into the regions of pure thought, live in the mânasic principle voluntarily, that is with a will, then we shall have risen above mere thoughts, and the brain becomes non-operative then, and yet we think.

Just pause a moment. We must all of us have experienced times when, under the governance of some great idea or ideal, or under the holy guidance of an impersonal love, we realize we live in a region or in a sphere which is entirely outside the brain; and as soon as we descend into the brain-atmosphere again, or allow the brain to control our feelings or emotions, it is like a fall. This illustrates the dual action of the mânasic faculty, the lower and the higher Manas.

THE ABSOLUTE AND THE INFINITE

(The following is a stenographic report of an informal gathering at Point Loma, in which a discussion arose regarding the use of the term, 'Absolute,' in *Fundamentals of the Esoteric Philosophy* by G. de Purucker.)

G. de P. — It is the philosophic *One*, the originant, which is the Absolute: from the *One* comes the *two;* from the *two* the *triad;* from the *triad* the *tetrad*, etc. The point is this: the philosophic *One* or the cosmic *One* is the cosmic Absolute; but it is not the *zero*, representing Infinitude; consequently the *zero*, Infinitude, holds an infinite number of such *Ones* or Monads, whether cosmic or not.

O. L. — *I understand the way you use the word 'Absolute' in* FUNDA-MENTALS OF THE ESOTERIC PHILOSOPHY: *you there define it, so that it is quite clear; but what is the real reason for your emphasizing that meaning of it, which is of course in the etymological derivation of the word? It is different from the usual meaning carried by the word 'Absolute' in philosophy here in the West.*

G. de P. — That is true. I so use it, first for purposes of accuracy; second, because it is a wonderful philosophical key: every Absolute being the Hierarch of its Hierarchy, the One from which all series thereafter outflow — one, two, three, etc. — to the end of the Hierarchy; and each such *One* is an Absolute or *Mukta, Jîvan-Mukta, absolutus*, signifying 'free,' 'set free,' — free from servitude to all the lower planes and master thereof.

O. L. — *I have understood that; but still, could not that fact be said and explained without using the word* ABSOLUTE *for it?*

G. de P. — It could, but it seemed inadvisable. You see that the word 'Absolute,' derived from the Latin, is an exact equivalent of the Sanskrit word *Moksha* or *Mukti* of Brâhmanism; and I deliberately chose that word and tried to point out the inaccuracy of the use of this phrase 'The Absolute' in the West in order to signify 'Boundless Infinite.' This is not only an etymological, but a logical, fault, and I desired to point this out. The word as I used it is a true key to great things.

O. L. — *It will arouse criticism; and people will say: "Of course, your etymology is true; but what is the use of it? The word 'Absolute' has acquired this specific meaning in our Western languages, in all philoso-*

*phies: what therefore is the use of your change? Why make use of it with
a different meaning?" It only mixes things up for ordinary people studying
philosophy, and therefore arouses criticism.*

G. de P. — Many people will doubtless say just that; but I do not object to criticism. It arouses comment and thought. My use, outside of
anything else, has the virtue of being accurate, of being philosophically
exact, of employing a word in its proper, original, exact, etymological sense;
and best of all, it is a wonderful key to greater things. It is perfectly
indifferent to me if the entire Occident uses a word wrongly, because I am
going to use it aright, if by that use I can strike a new keynote of thought,
point out a pathway of consciousness, and give a key to a wonderful doctrine. Do you now see? If it arouse comment and criticism, as in fact I
knew it would, all the better!

O. T. — I think that the way you use the term in FUNDAMENTALS OF
THE ESOTERIC PHILOSOPHY *is one of the most wonderful parts of the whole
book.*

G. de P. — Once that you miscall Infinity by the word 'the Absolute,'
it becomes *a* being, therefore limited, therefore finite. It is impossible in
true philosophy to predicate absoluteness of Infinity. It is neither absolute
nor non-absolute; *absolute* is a definite adjective, having certain logical
attributes. *Infinitude* has no such attributes; Infinitude is neither conscious
nor unconscious; it is neither alive nor dead; because consciousness and
unconsciousness and life and death belong to manifested and therefore
limited and therefore to non-infinite beings and things.

*O. L. — All those things Occidental philosophers say about the Abso-
lute; they give that meaning to 'Absolute.'*

G. de P. — That is just what they should not do; and that is just what
I am challenging; my use therefore is a challenge.

*O. L. — It is a challenge; but even apart from what the word itself
means etymologically, if we investigate that, there are many such words.
They have acquired a different meaning in the language; and they are
used with this meaning different from the words in the language, apart
from how the words themselves originated.*

G. de P. — That is perfectly true, my Friend, but remember that a
mere fact, however common, is no proper plea in extenuation of a fault.

O. L. — One cannot say that such a word is wrongly used in this way.

G. de P. — True, in a way; but the word nevertheless is wrongly used;

and it has obtained currency. Let me illustrate my meaning: In English there is a most extraordinary grammatical, or rather ungrammatical, expression, which has obtained universal currency in the English tongue, and it is wrong. This expression is, "I am mistaken." The current meaning is, "I am wrong: I have expressed an erroneous view." But the real meaning of the words is, "I am *misunderstood*," and this was the original meaning of the phrase, "I am mistaken."

I have heard your argument time and time again. People say: "Why do you bother your head about it? Everybody knows what you mean by the common usage. Why not employ it because it is a common usage?" Yes, I answer, but it is a wrong usage and foolish logically, historically, and grammatically. Among my many other faults, as some people say, I try to make people think. Why not correct an obvious error? "I am mistaken" means literally, "I am taken amiss: I am misunderstood." But when a modern Englishman says, "I am mistaken," he means, "I have misunderstood." He uses an entirely wrong grammatical form.

O. L. — You will never succeed in changing that usage; because it is universally common, and everybody understands it.

G. de P. — Assuredly so, my Friend, nor am I trying to change this particular phrase. But as regards the Absolute, here is a case of a specific philosophical doctrine of the first importance; and I desire to challenge thought by challenging a crystallized and hoary error — so far as Europeans are concerned. This misuse arose out of the psychology in all European philosophers' minds of the Christian theological scheme, which they could not shake off: the personal god, the infinite person, the Absolute. They pursued a logical train of thinking arising in a proper conception; but the term used to express this fundamental conception is absolutely wrong; for this term 'Absolute' does not mean infinity. A *person* cannot be *infinite:* this is a contradiction in terms. But there can be an absolute person, a Hierarch, the summit of a Hierarchy; and this Hierarch is only one of an infinite number of other Hierarchs, of other Hierarchies — an infinite number of such Ones; but the Infinite, without number, attribute, qualification, or form, is therefore non-absolute. *'Absolutus'* means 'freed,' and can apply only to a limited entity, however grand and sublime. I want to make people think! I am furthermore striking at the roots of old theological superstitions, and old philosophical superstitions. If my use arouses argument, if it arouses attack, and if this makes people think, it does not much matter to me personally. They can charge me with trying to introduce new things, or with any other foolish motive. The charges being untrue, I don't care particularly about them.

O. L. — In that way of thinking your use might be well worth something.

E. L. — It is breaking the molds of mind.

G. de P. — If Occidental people had only studied, or studied a little more carefully, even the elements of some of the greater Oriental philosophical systems, they would see the difference between the *Jivan-Mukta,* which is an Absolute, a Freed One — and *Tat:* THAT.

H. P. B. does use the word 'Absolute' apparently in the usual Occidental way; but if you examine carefully every instance where this occurs, you will find that actually she is referring to some great or super-great cosmos — in every instance. 'Absolute' is a relative term. There are no 'Absolutes' in the sense of 'Infinitudes.' Everything that is, no matter how great, how vast, is relative — related to something else and to all else.

The critics seem to think that I mean by 'Absolute' an 'Infinite Being,' because they have such a vague, nebulous, undefined, and cloudy idea in their own minds. They are tangled in a web of words. This very word 'Infinity' is but a human word, and it acknowledges that human imbecility of intellect, as compared with frontierless time and space, can find no better word to describe it than 'Infinitude,' which means 'Non-finitude.'

I would like to tell you something more. You know that Sanskrit is probably the most perfect language for the expression of philosophical human thoughts that is known. It is, nevertheless, an offspring of human consciousness; and even the great Sages and Seers at times find themselves hard put to it to express the children of their consciousness in human words, i.e., to express their thoughts adequately.

Now, as an illustration of what I mean, there is absolutely no such sphere of *esse* or consciousness as what the Occidental calls the 'Infinite' — really a word with which he cheats his mind, an abstract term. The Occidental, when he says 'Infinitude' and 'Eternity,' means by these terms endless extension and duration, which is as far as he can go intellectually — which is merely another way of saying: 'Things as they are now, more or less changing continuously, but lasting endlessly'; and as regards the former word especially, 'Infinitude,' the average Occidental's mind becomes a blank when he uses it. He sees, or thinks he mentally sees, non-understandable, frontierless Space. That to him is Infinity. But really it is a cheating of his consciousness.

In the Sanskrit, Infinity is not commonly expressed by a negation, such as 'Non-finity,' but by the words *Parabrahman* and *Mûlaprakriti* — two sides or elements to the one fundamental conception. What does *Parabrahman* mean? *Brahman* stands for the Absolute, the Hierarch of a Universe, a Cosmos. *Para* means 'beyond.' Do you now begin to get the thought? Infinitude thus is simply that which is beyond the loftiest reach of human consciousness. Human consciousness does not pretend to limit it by saying anything about it; it does not qualify it with any adjective; no operation of human consciousness can reach it. *Parabrahman* is confessedly a mere term: 'Beyond Brahman,' and Brahman is the Absolute.

Mûlaprakriti: Prakriti means 'Nature'; *Mûla* means 'root'; therefore *Mûlaprakriti* signifies 'elemental,' or 'originant' Nature. *Parabrahman* therefore is but a word: 'Beyond Brahman'; 'Originant Nature,' *Mûlaprakriti;* and thus you get a different conception from the vague, Occidental mental abstraction signified by a negation — 'Non-finite.' The Oriental conception accepts the manifested universe and points to endlessness beyond it, and says 'Parabrahman' or 'Mûlaprakriti.' The Occidental also accepts the manifested universe, but does not point beyond it, and simply uses a term signifying 'something different from the manifested universe'; and this latter conception is philosophically and fundamentally erroneous, for it makes a distinction in *esse* between the This and the Beyond.

The Orientals, and likewise the Ancient Wisdom, never use the word 'Eternity.' This is a conception which is rejected, because it is merely like a mental cloud in any human mind to speak of 'Eternity.' The best way in which Occidentals can express this conception is by saying 'Endless Duration' — not 'Endless Time,' because 'time' is a human limited conception but 'endless enduring' — that which endures for aye.

All that the human consciousness is authorized to postulate is that Parabrahman, 'Beyond Brahman' or the Absolute, is exactly what we see around us, as far as our human physical sense-apparatus can translate it to us, but limitlessly so. Parabrahman, therefore, is not an entity; it is not a being; as a term it is a descriptive adjective turned into a noun, and means simply 'Beyond Brahman.' "As above, so below" — and there is no fundamental essential difference between the 'above' and the 'below.' Every atom has its home in a molecule; every molecule has its home in a cell; every cell has its home in a body; every body has its home in a greater body; the greater body, in this case our Earth, has its habitat or dwelling or home in the solar ether; the solar system has its home in the Galaxy; the Galaxy has its home in what we humans call the Universe — our telescopes carry us no farther; the Universe has its home in one still more vast; and so on, as Occidentals say, *ad infinitum;* and that *ad infinitum* is exactly the Occidental's way of saying what the Oriental means when he says *Parabrahman* — 'Beyond Brahman,' with this profound and radical difference, however, that the root-idea in the mind of the Oriental is the inner, invisible, spiritual worlds, which the modern Occidental almost universally ignores.

Everything exists in something else greater than itself, and contains hosts of beings inferior to itself; and *Parabrahman* simply means 'beyond our Absolute,' 'beyond our *Brahman.*' *Brahman* is the Absolute; and *Parabrahman* H. P. Blavatsky has called 'SPACE' — not meaning 'emptiness,' but using here just a descriptive word, a descriptive noun, just as when she says 'Duration.' Duration is filled with time, moments, time-instants. Space, similarly, is filled with manifested Monads, and Absolutes which are Monads of a far advanced type; and these Absolutes contain armies and hosts of evolving inferior Monads.

This, then, is all that *Parabrahman* means, and *Mûlaprakriti* is but its other side — the side of expansion and change, so to speak. You can say that *Parabrahman* is the consciousness-side of it, and that *Mûlaprakriti* is the space-side of it. It hurts me sometimes to hear Theosophists talk about *Parabrahman* as if it were a kind of god. It is simply Space. It does not mean anything in particular, however, because it is a purely generalizing term. The word *Parabrahman* simply means 'Beyond Brahman.' It too is a confession that here the human consciousness stops: it cannot go any farther.

O. T. — I would like to ask you a question. We Western minds think more analytically; and when you spoke, a little while ago, about the Infinite as being the only thing that was not relative, it also occurred to me that the center of consciousness which each one of us is, in the, from the, middle point of that consciousness, reaches out in opposite directions; that is, inwards and outwards — inwards towards the infinite, and outwards towards the finite; and the two are equal at all times.

G. de P. — Yes, but I did not speak of the Infinite as "being the only thing that was not relative." Even this word 'Infinite,' if you analyse it, simply means 'not finite.' It does not mean anything in particular. It is man's confession of ignorance and of inability to penetrate deeper. It is a word exactly like *Parabrahman;* it simply means 'not finite,' meaning by that, that the human consciousness can no longer reach into what we call the frontiers of the finite, and seize, grasp, comprehend, what is there; and being unable to do so, it simply says, "Ah! that, that is beyond all we know; it is *in*-finite, not finite, the All." The very word 'Boundless' so often used in Theosophy, is simply a counter, a verbal counter. This very 'Boundless' is filled full of, made up of, composed of, finite, bounded things — individuals, beings.

J. H. F. — Would you not say the same of 'Infinite'?

G. de P. — Absolutely the same, therefore just so. People use these terms which are pure abstractions as if they were concrete realities, and create thoughts about them, and thereby they cheat themselves. I repeat that these words are mere abstractions.

S. E. — *With your definition of* PARABRAHMAN *we can no longer say that* PARABRAHMAN *on the one hand and* MÛLAPRAKRITI *on the other, are two aspects of the same thing, which have produced the first Logos; because* MÛLAPRAKRITI *then is a definite noun, while* PARABRAHMAN *is merely a descriptive adjective.*

G. de P. — No, that is not the idea. *Parabrahman* and *Mûlaprakriti*, simply meaning 'Boundless Space' with all its indwelling hosts of beings, at any one particular point of itself finds a Logos springing into manifestation from its pralaya. That may happen here, there, or anywhere: millions of these Logoi may contemporaneously be bursting forth into new manvantaras; but millions of them contemporaneously may be passing into their respective pralayas.

Now then, in order to describe cosmic evolution and its beginning, the Teacher — whoever it may be, any great Sage — says: "In the beginning was THAT"; and this beginning is not merely an absolute commencement of all infinitude, which is absurd, but one of any beginnings of a system in Boundless Duration. At its commencement of time the Logos springs forth, the Logos merely meaning one of these innumerable monadic points in THAT; and from this Logos — one such Logos — is evolved forth a Hierarchy — whether it be a Cosmic Hierarchy, or a solar system, or a planetary chain, or a human being, or an atom. Do you understand the general idea?

S. E. — *I understand you; it is a wonderful conception.*

G. de P. — And these logoic points are numberless. Every mathematical point in Space is a potential Logos. Also there are many kinds of Logoi; some are much higher in evolution than others; but the doctrine as I have stated it is given in generalizing terms applicable to all.

S. E. — *I understand that perfectly well; it is a wonderful explanation. But when you said that* PARABRAHMAN *really was not an entity, but merely everything beyond what the human mind can reach to, then* MÛLAPRAKRITI *must be an aspect of something else.*

G. de P. — No, the other side or *alter ego* of *Parabrahman*, but more particularly the root-matter of any and therefore of every hierarchical system or cosmos.

S. E. — *The other side of something — yes, but they must be the abstractions, nevertheless, of something else which is above them.*

G. de P. — That is included in the conception of *Parabrahman.*

S. E. — *Yes, I understand; because being qualities, they have to qualify something.*

G. de P. — I think I see your point. A universe is both; it is *Mûlaprakriti* in its essence; it is also in its essence *Parabrahman;* because it is formed of hosts of individual monads. The heart of a monad is boundless space; and boundless space has two aspects, life or energy, and substance or form. You cannot separate the one from the other. Life or energy is what we may call *Parabrahman;* the substance-side or vehicular side is the *Mûlaprakriti*-side. Wipe out *Mûlaprakriti,* if it were possible, which it is not, and you would have pure consciousness, pure energy; and that is not possible, because energy and matter are two sides of the same thing; force and substance are two sides of the same thing; electricity, for example, is both energic and substantial; consciousness is both energy (or force) and substance.

S. E. — *What you have just said there has cleared away a few of the greatest difficulties in my mind.*

G. de P. — Your body, my body, any body, is fundamentally *Mûlaprakriti,* Root-substance, fundamental Essence, manifesting in form. So is everything else — a star, a bit of wood, a stone, a beast, a bit of thistledown floating in the air. Its essence is *Mûlaprakriti;* and out in the abysmal spaces, in the deepest deeps of Space, is *Mûlaprakriti,* but also *Parabrahman.*

S. E. — *But even so, having said that in the deepest deeps there are Mûlaprakriti and Parabrahman, and as far as our imagination can penetrate, they are nevertheless mere words; because beyond 'That' there is again something.*

G. de P. — Absolutely; but only because everything — even what we call THAT — is contained in something greater. But the word THAT is nevertheless sufficient to include the entire range of this conception. The entire Galaxy is a Cosmic Cell; and what the modern astronomers call the Island-Universes, are other Cosmic Cells; and these Cosmic Cells are bathed in the inter-galactic ether — using human words — and these Cosmic Cells are united into some ultra-cosmic, incomprehensible BEING, just as the cells of a man's body, viewed only under the microscope and under the microscope apparently separate from each other, are united in a man's physical body; and a man's physical body lives in a world. Our Galaxy is therefore like a Cell in a Cosmic Body surrounded by the abstraction we call Infinitude.

S. E. — May I ask you another question, following the other direction in thought: Let us take the atom or the very smallest possible form of an atom or molecule that we can think of — an electron: is there no end, as it were, on the downward scale of smallness?

G. de P. — None. There cannot be an end; otherwise you would have an ending, after which, what? Let me tell you that your difficulty is reasoning in forms familiar to our human conceptions. It is much easier to reason along the lines of energy: an electron, for instance, is but a bit of compacted electricity, and electricity is particular, that is, formed of particles; hence the electron is particular, formed of particles. Consequently the electron is divisible and these divisions or sub-particles cannot be considered to be indivisible, because then we should reach an ending, which is absurd, because we should immediately have to ask ourselves what lies beyond or beneath.

S. E. — Is it correct to think that on one of such electrons there are White and Black Masters, Śambhalas, and other things such as we know them in our world?

G. de P. — Think for yourself, my Friend: consciousness is not limited by space, because consciousness is an energy, one of the highest forms of energy, perhaps the highest, if indeed there be a 'highest.'

O. L. — The 'small' or the 'great' depend only upon what measure one begins with.

G. de P. — Just so. We measure things by the human yardsticks of ideas which we in our consciousness are accustomed to.

S. E. — You did answer one question in the Temple recently, to the effect that greatness of form does indeed represent a higher evolutionary development.

G. de P. — It does in a certain sense; but not necessarily so, and not so much from the standpoint of consciousness as from the standpoint of *Prakriti* — evolving Nature. You have often heard me speak of the expansion of consciousness as one evolves to greater things. Consequently, the consciousness co-extensive with our Galaxy is more highly evolved than the consciousness co-extensive with an electron, for instance. But contrariwise, it is quite possible that an electron of a certain kind might contain a more evolved consciousness, individually speaking, than that which functions in our Galaxy. We must free our minds absolutely from the limitations imposed by our conceptions of 'space' and 'time.'

It is the same thought here that I have elsewhere often tried to explain

as the 'reach of consciousness' — an idea deliberately chosen and suggesting a continuously increasing enlargement of the consciousness. Do you
now understand me? A man can constrict, can shrink, his consciousness
to the point of being suited for inhabiting an electron, and yet in still
deeper profundities of his being be as free as the wild winds or the free bird,
because consciousness is not and cannot ever be bounded by material space
or extension. Space is *Mûlaprakriti;* therefore in a sense limited, however
vast; but sheer or pure consciousness is free, whether it be expanded to
cosmic dimensions, or whether it be, as we humans say, shrunken to electronic magnitude.

On certain ones of the electrons composing even our physical matter,
there actually are entities as conscious as we are, thinking divine thoughts,
thinking about the Universe, just as we humans do. We humans are still
very imperfect in our evolutionary growth. There are beings on other
planets of our solar system — you would not call them humans, and yet
they are actually more evolutionally advanced than we human beings are
— who think diviner thoughts than we do. There are also entities inhabiting the Sun, and consequently the Sun has inhabitants thinking godlike
thoughts, having a godlike or solar consciousness. All these questions are
relative, please remember, and not absolute, for there are no absolute absolutes in the grotesque Occidental sense of the word that I am opposing and
arguing against.

*O. T. — Is there any reason why we may not consider ourselves as be-
ing on one such cosmic electron?*

G. de P. — Certainly there is no reason against that idea. Quite to the
contrary. We are on such a cosmic electron, but on one of cosmic magnitude; nevertheless it is an electron, relatively speaking; and compared with
one of the super-Galactic Entities that I have just spoken of, we on our tiny
little Earth, whirling about our protonic aggregate, which we call the Sun,
are inhabitants of such an electron, which is our Earth. Now, such a vast
Cosmic Entity of super-Galactic magnitude, might look upon us in his
thought, and wonder and think: "Can such infinitesimals have thoughts as
I have them? Is their consciousness free like mine? Can it reach into the
abysmal bosom of things?" My answer is, of course, Yes, because consciousness is the very heart of things, the essence of things; and when you
ally yourself with pure or sheer consciousness, you then enter the Heart of
the Universe, the Heart which is nowhere in particular because it is everywhere; and the more you reach out in consciousness, the more you expand,
following (as I said a little while ago) the mûlaprakritic idea, the greater
you become.

For instance, our human consciousness, limited to this Earth and possessing vague concepts and dreams of a solar life, enables us to look outwards through our telescopes into the Galaxy and towards the Island-Universes beyond the Galaxy, and have thoughts about them; but they are *thoughts;* they are not the actual becoming of our consciousness *into* those things — i.e., actually becoming those things. But as our consciousness expands through evolution, it expands self-consciously to take in the solar system, and then still later in aeonic time to comprehend the Galaxy.

O. L. — Can it not happen that an entity on an electron, say on one in our body, may evolve to such divine power that it gives to the whole human entity a saving divine impulse, because it is so spiritually mighty?

G. de P. — Yes; but do you know what that electron is? That electron is our individual spiritual Monad — the very one you speak of. My answer to your question is Yes. Our spiritual consciousness is the entity on the spiritual Monad that you speak of, for the Monad is itself, both the entity and its habitat.

You will remember how the Hindû *Upanishads* nobly express this thought: "Smaller than the smallest atom; vaster than the Universe." It is verily so; for *this* is consciousness. The *Upanishads* speak of Brahman, as you know, as being more minute than an atom, and yet comprehending the Universe. Oh how lofty is this conception to think about! Why our Theosophists do not ponder over it more, is amazing to me. Try to enter into the cosmic atom within you, the cosmic electron which is your own Monad. It is the very heart of you, and you are the inhabitant of it, and it is your habitat.

THE SEVEN PRINCIPLES

Why is it necessary to have seven principles? Cannot Divinity work through one good vehicle?

Between divinity and the manifested universe there must be intermediate links, because any thinking person can see that Divine Perfection cannot engage in efforts of imperfection. And consequently the Sun itself, for example, consists of a fundamental Divine Being breaking up or radiating into the seven solar logoi. Each of these in its turn copies the example of its divine prototype. We see in this example, understandable by children, the reason for the vast and almost incomprehensible range of entities in the manifested universe and accounting for the progressively greater increase of imperfection as our thought ranges from Divinity on the one hand down to the lowest degrees of the manifested world. Now we break up this infinite variety into seven principles or logoi streaming from the Divine ONE, not only as a symbol of numeration because that springs from the zero, philosophically speaking the All, but ONE merely in the sense that it is incomprehensible Infinitude which our feeble human minds cannot easily expand to the point of grasping. From the Divine Unity springs forth the manifested world, the physical world of manifestation. And it is for these foregoing reasons that the Masters and H. P. B. insisted so strongly that for the proper comprehension of the Theosophical teachings we know the seven principles of the universe and man.

Perfection does not produce imperfection. Therefore between the perfection of the Divine Unity and the imperfection of the manifested universe, that dark and somber place, there must be a virtually infinite range of intermediary stages running from Divinity to the utmost dregs of materiality. Thus we call these the seven principles in man from the Âtman, corresponding to the Divine in the universe, to the physical body, corresponding to the lowest manifested plane. Man obviously is not divine, neither in devotion nor in thought, nor in any characteristic, for if it were so men would be gods. But men are imperfect and it is this range from the perfect to the imperfect in the universe that corresponds to the seven principles of man.

THE ANCIENT EGYPTIANS

I have always considered Egyptians as a very religious people, but at the same time have countered a tendency among my theosophical friends to look upon all Egyptians as perfect and everything Egyptian as marvelous.

The Egyptians were good, bad, and between, just like us, and Egypt was a land like all other lands. It bore a reputation among the ancients of being a land 'shadowing with wings' — a direct allusion to her reputation for producing magicians and sorcerers, and it is true that perhaps in recorded history no land and no people west of Suez (or Aden) has ever been so religious. Their religion was of two kinds: sacramental and ceremonial worship which they believed in and governed their outer or exoteric lives by, and the religion of the sanctuary, which was the religion of the heart and intuition, including the higher intellect, for it was the religion of the initiation chamber. And in Egypt these two kinds of religion combined into one, so that everything an Egyptian did was religiously done in the sense of their being guided by the teachings found and heard in the temples and given out by the temple priests. And the lives of the Egyptians were very successful while they lived by the teachings which were received from behind the veil, from the sanctuary. So religious were they that they rose, bathed and ate and clothed themselves, worked and ate again, and worked again and studied and wrote and ate again, and lay themselves down to sleep at night, and did every action governed by the teachings they had received — a procedure which to the Occident is incomprehensible and would be looked upon as slavery, the West quite forgetting that slavery never is what each man longs and yearns to do but only what is imposed upon a man against his will.

We are not religious enough, being unable to do as the Egyptians did and find happiness in it. I don't mean Theosophists. I mean the Occident generally. It has lost faith in its religion, and that religion has great beauty in it as well as outstanding faults in its history. Today if a man gives himself, as the Egyptian did, to his religion, which he has been taught presumably from his childhood, he is looked upon as weak-minded or as a fanatic, both criticisms equally unjust.

Yes, Egypt gained the reputation of being religious partly because of her high white magic taught in the sanctuary and partly because of her sorcery. Study the facts and you will see. Why, the common name in Rome about the beginning of the Christian era for magicians was Aegyptii or Chaldaei. But don't think of the Egyptians as demi-gods or archangels come to earth, and that we poor human wrecks ought to become Egyptians again! Not at all, though it is undoubtedly quite true that a number of men and women, perhaps a very large number of us, lived in ancient Egypt once, twice, thrice; but some of us also came from other countries of ancient times. I recognise distinctly Roman traits in some of my friends, Hindû traits in others, Greek in others, et cetera.

FUTURE OF CHRISTIANITY

Has Christianity as a world religion run its race? Is it about to die?

I believe — I may be wrong, but it is my innermost conviction, that there is the possibility for a renascence of primitive Christianity in the West. It will be when among the ranks of the clergy there shall be found some courageous and high-minded enough to trace back the origins of their grand teaching, their theology, to Pagan antiquity, finding brotherhood in the fellow-thoughts of the ancient races, of Egypt especially, of Greece, yes, even of Rome. For then the religion of the West will have fresh blood flowing through its veins, a new revelation will have come, arising from the spirit, and a new illumination thrown upon the secrets of the past. Then Christianity will be properly understood, and will be seen to be grand; for primitive Christianity was grand because it was the same as Theosophy, the original wisdom of the Gods.

BEING TRULY HUMAN

Should not the chela try to eliminate from his life all personal friendships? Have not all the leaders of the Theosophical Society done so?

Leader and teacher as I am, I believe I have a right to cherish in my heart warm friendships, and I do not think I am losing in my spirituality, or losing my ability to help others, by allowing the heart-impulse to have free play just as long as I am just, just as long as I am true and sincere. I do not believe that any of the great Teachers of the world ever wanted one of his chelas to be — well, a mossback, a fossil. I believe that every part of a man's being should receive its due meed of cultural work. I do not believe that the human heart, the human hearts in the world, can be best reached by a man who has no heart himself. I do not believe that a man who does not understand the problems of his fellow human beings can help them. I believe that it is only when we are fully and truly human, and rise above our humanhood occasionally into the deeps of divinity welling up within us, that we do our best work, for that means that we understand the human hearts around us. Our heart then beats in sympathetic rhythm with the pain in others' hearts. We understand it. But believe me, we can rise above the pain into the peace and quiet, and thereby become efficient in help.

SEEKING A TEACHER

What is the ethical attitude toward looking for a Teacher? Should we look for a Teacher?

Should we look for Teachers? I would most emphatically urge upon every normal human being not merely to look for Teachers, but to accept them. Make the call and that call will be answered. Look upon Teachers as one of the commonest phenomena of human history. The call is strongest when despair is harshest, when discouragement threatens to overwhelm non-thinking but sensitive humans. When the call for help is most urgently torn from the human heart, that call evokes an answer. It has throughout human history, and it will do it today. It is a magnificent spiritual and intellectual exercise, not merely to expect help but to demand it; and you have no right to demand help until you prove yourself worthy of it. Then the combination is irresistible, and the Master comes, comes to you as an individual, or comes to a people, to a race. The man who is worthy makes

a call that is not merely for himself but for all, so that he may amongst
the others feel the blessed warmth of the divine sunlight of the spirit shed
upon all. He who makes his call by the token universal, is a magician,
strong, and his call is powerful, and he has a right to make that call. But
I would advise before making a call for an exterior teacher, make the call
to the greatest Teacher for every man that any man can ever know, the
Spirit within man, the god within himself. This very appeal transforms the
man's life, and makes him more worthy and makes his call for the outer
Teacher incomparably stronger. Cleanse your own Temple before you call
upon a god to enter in and abide there.

THE MEANING OF OSIRIS AND ISIS

*What were some of the deeper meanings of the Egyptian symbology
concerning Osiris and Isis?*

How many people, I wonder, who have not studied Egyptology, know
that there was an older Osiris and a younger, an older Isis and a younger,
an older Horus and a younger?

Osiris according to Egyptian theology, was what is known since ancient
Egyptian times in the west as the Spirit of Intelligence in the Universe, or
the solar system; and Isis, the Divine Consort; just as in Hindûsthân we
have similar thoughts with Brahmâ and Prakriti, Brahman and Pradhâna,
Parabrahman and Mûlaprakriti. All the ancient divinities, in whatever
land, were considered to be two-sided, a masculine aspect and a feminine,
so that there was the divine Father and the divine Mother of the Universe.
The divine Father, the old Osiris, was the Cosmic Intelligence ruling all,
governing all, giving birth to all, stimulating all; and the older Isis was his
holy, divine Consort, the spirit of love, productiveness, and compassion
showing itself throughout the Universe. According to earliest Christian
theology it was the Father and the Holy Spirit — which latter was feminine, in original Christianity please remember, not as a later Christianity
turned it into a masculine principle.

Horus was the son of the divine parent, what the Greeks and Christians called the Logos, the logos of life, the so-called Creator, the Demiurge.

Then there was the younger Osiris and Isis who were considered in
ancient Egyptian theology to pertain especially to this our Globe or Planetary Chain. In this case Osiris was that one of the seven (or ten or
twelve) solar Logoi or solar Forces emanating from the spiritual Sun, and
especially infilling our own Globe as its spirit of Intelligence, the mind,
the highest planetary spirit; and Isis was the spiritual counterpart of this

younger Osiris, that which works itself out on our Globe — and especially in the hearts of us human beings who in this imbodiment are children of our Globe — as sympathy, love, pity, productiveness or creativeness, the bringing forth power whether of our minds or of our hearts.

Horus is their son, the product of the best in man, which we could call in this case enlightened mind in man. This is a bit of ancient Egyptian theology, and so greatly did this one time Egyptian concept steal into the hearts of early Christians that they adopted it practically wholesale — in some cases took over the names substantially exactly the same. For instance, Isis with the divine child Horus in her arms, became the original of all the later Madonnas, as the Italians called them, with the moon under her feet.

The Symbol of the Winged Globe

Can you give me some information on the symbolism of the Winged Globe of the Egyptians?

The symbol of the winged globe, the globe carried through time and space on the wings of spiritual force or of the spirit, is one of the most beautiful of ancient Egyptian symbols, because it combines both religion and philosophy. The globe is just one form of representing the golden germ, Hiranyagarbha in the Sanskrit, which in its movements through time and space is carried by the wings of the spirit on its evolutionary journey. This is the keynote of one of the thoughts of the winged globe.

Another thought about it, or aspect of it, is that the winged globe is the monad, which is in a sense practically the same as the cosmic germ or hiranyagarbha, and the wings there signify the same thing, conscious mind moving through space and time in the form of the monad and expressing its power in the movement of the wings, consciousness moving in the evolutionary journey upwards and upwards forever.

Still another way of interpreting it — all the same at bottom because of the law of analogy — is that the globe would represent a celestial orb, a sun or a planet, in its turn carried on the wings of its spirit along the evolutionary journey into the distant future, and out of the past.

With reference to its standing for the human soul or the reincarnating ego of a human being, it has its application there in just the same way, the monad, the golden germ, the ego, or if you wish the soul, represented by the sphere or globe, or the primordial point again from another standpoint.

There are really a thousand ways of interpreting it, or rather applying the interpretation to different aspects of our cosmic philosophy. Yet the interpretation is the same for all these different aspects, making only the adjustment according to whatever entity it is that is thus adventuring through the cosmic planes and through cosmic life and through cosmic time.

It is thus also a symbol, as it were a declaration, of spiritual individual hope for the future, a proclamation and symbol of the immortality of the spirit or of the monad, or of whatever entity it is that the symbol is applied to.

Then when we add the serpents, as is often done, one on each side of the globe with raised heads, yet with bodies or tails intertwined, this is but another graphic way of speaking of the dual serpents of Wisdom and Love, the two great dominant powers in the constitution of any entity, both shielding and protecting and inspiring, and yet carried along by the monad, of which both these faculties, wisdom and love, of the winged globe, are the symbols.

These are the general keys, and anyone can elaborate them, if he thinks carefully, almost indefinitely. It is a wonderful symbol.

THEOPHANY, THEOPNEUSTY, THEOPATHY

Did the fifth degree of the Mysteries as described by Theon of Smyrna include the three interior revelations called by the Greeks Theophany, Theopneusty, and Theopathy?

By Theophany, Theopneusty, and Theopathy, the Greeks meant as follows: Theophany, vision of the divine; Theopneusty, the next higher, means the divine breathing through one in addition to the vision; but Theopathy means the complete incarnation of the Divine for a greater or less period of time, and therefore includes both the Theophany and Theopneusty. Hence, Theopathy I would say belongs to the sixth or rather the seventh stage.

Theon of Smyrna speaks of this fifth degree as "friendship and interior communion with God, and the enjoyment of that felicity which arises from intimate converse with divine beings," — signifying by this enjoyment, the spiritual and intellectual enjoyment of the realization of one's own inner communion with the God within, of having the Divine within oneself constantly present in one's life, not so much as merely being the vehicle for the Divine, as in the case of Theopathy, but more like Theopneusty, the Divine Breathing through one, at least occasionally. I would therefore say that what Theon is referring to is what otherwise is called Theopneusty; or perhaps taken all together we can say it was the Divine Vision or Theophany with a more or less occasional Theopneusty, or the Divine Breath blessing one with its presence, at least on occasions.

Theophany, Theopneusty, and Theopathy, are illustrations of what takes place in the three highest, the fifth, sixth and seventh degrees. The

Eleusinian Mysteries were ninety percent ritual and ceremony, but when occasionally a neophyte was discovered who was fully prepared, at least before the Mysteries were degenerate, then he was taken in hand privately, as it were, by the hierophants.

REJECTION OF A TEACHER'S MESSAGE

You once spoke of the failure or partial failure of the message that Jesus brought. Is the progress, the evolution, of the true teacher or the messenger from the gods, retarded or sped, according to the degree of the acceptance of his message by humanity?

I would not say so, if I understand your question correctly. The question runs to this: If the Teacher come from the gods or if the Envoy come from the Lodge of the Masters of Wisdom and Compassion and Peace, and his message is rejected, does this rejection retard the evolution of the Envoy?

I think not. In fact, I rather believe the contrary may be the case, because there comes a sorrow, a deep grief, when the bearer of truth is repulsed. It is like a man who comes in aid to a fellow human being who is in danger, who is in peril, and by whom the offer of help is rejected. If the helper is a good man, the incident does not imply that the next time a chance to help comes, he will then say: "Well no; I am not going to try to help again. I have made a fool of myself once, and I am not going to do it twice." No. The man of heart will understand; the man of heart and vision will help even despite the rejection. If you see a little child in danger of burning or of drowning and you rush to its aid, and the child pushes you away, are you going to be a little child yourself, and turn around haughtily and walk away? No, indeed; you help the little child despite itself. Do you realize what Jesus, the great Teacher you speak of, said in substance to his disciples: Children, in the vision of a true Teacher, ordinary men and women are like little children, to a certain extent to be humored, to be loved, to be cared for, to be understood, to be educated, to be helped.

There is the mother-heart in every good man as well as the father-heart; and every decent man never forgets his instinct of protection and brotherly kindness. I tell you that the man who would refuse to go in aid when a cry of help comes, no matter what the danger is, is unhuman, to a certain extent at least unhuman, is not a full and complete man. Do you think that the great Teachers would be less than a good man, than an ordinary and average good man should be? Their evolution is not retarded by the rejection of their Message, except in the sense perhaps that they will try

again later, and this keeps them longer in the same sphere of life. Their
evolution is perhaps helped, because it gives them an added opportunity
for the pouring out of the inner Buddha, of the spiritual Christ.

IMAGINATION AND FANCY

*What is the essential and guiding fact that separates idle fancy from
constructive imaging? I think these are very much mixed.*

The great Plato used these two words when he spoke of fantasy and the
faculty and power of the *nous*. The noetic power, i.e., of the *nous,* is that
which originates ideas, ideals, which visions truth, which therefore is coherent with the structure and operations of the Universe. Whereas fantasy
is the reflected moonlight of this in our little human minds. I can imagine,
for instance, a street-railway from Earth to Moon, but I cannot build one.
This is fantasy. I can use mere words, and speak of a triangle which is a
square, but that is impossible, because a triangle has only three sides; if
it had four it would not be a triangle. This is fantasy. But were I great
enough, I could envisage wondrous truths of the Universe, I could see them,
I could feel them. This is the proper working of the true image-making
faculty in man, seeing truth; it is intuition.

*What is going to guide the person so that he avoid the one and function
properly in the other?*

That is a more difficult question to answer. It is the old, old problem.
I yearn to live the Life Beautiful, but my feet constantly stumble on the
Path. How may I walk so that my pathway shall be safe? How difficult
it is to answer this question for everybody! I would therefore answer that
the guide is an aspiration that weakens never; a yearning to know the
truth which will be satisfied with naught less than it, a heart which is filled
with love and beats in sympathy with all beings. In other words, become
harmonious. Try to attune yourself to the Cosmic Life. That is the pathway, and it is difficult. But it can be done; and the great Masters of life,
whom we Theosophists call the Mahâtmans, are just they who are succeeding in doing this. The gods have succeeded more than men have, and there
are gods who are but one stage higher than men. The Christians call them
angels. There are gods still higher than these that I have just spoken of,
and they are closer still to the Heart of Being, and the Christians call these
archangels, and so on up the Ladder of Life. This is at first a weary
journey, it is true, and bestrewn with perils, but it leadeth to the heart of
the Universe, and is accompanied with a splendor which brightens into
glory unspeakable. An open mind, an eager, searching intellect, the striv-

ing to have an unveiled spiritual vision: these are some of the keys which will lead you safely on the path, so that your feet stumble not thereon.

PANTHEISM AND UNIVERSAL CONSCIOUSNESS

What is the difference between Pantheism and the Theosophical idea of the Universal Consciousness?

That is a good question. It would be very easy to explain if everybody had studied philosophy. But I will try for the benefit of those to whom philosophical thought is relatively unknown or obscure, to give an answer which I think all may understand. The average idea of Pantheism, as it is understood in the Occident, is confused, is vague. It is a generalized idea that the Universe has back of it — mark you that — has back of it a Kosmic Spirit, therefore considered to be impersonal, but working through all things as an all-permeant life or energy, and that even these 'all things' are portions of the Kosmic Spirit itself. This is about as far as Occidental Pantheism goes, I believe.

Now then, the Theosophical conception of the universal Consciousness-Life-Substance says not only that back of the sevenfold or tenfold Universe is this universal Consciousness-Life-Substance, but that the Universe itself is a partial manifestation of it by means of an almost infinite number of hierarchies. This obviously does not mean that every stone, every bit of wood, or every flower, etc., is god or a god, but that the essential substance, the world-stuff, the mind-stuff, the consciousness-energy-substance, is the same in it and in me and in you and indeed everywhere, thus manifesting in innumerable individual forms.

Occidental Pantheism is a great step forwards towards the Theosophical idea, but it is an imperfect step. It does not go far enough. It is one thing to say that there is a Kosmic Spirit which permeates all things, and that the Universe is this Kosmic Spirit imbodied — all of which is true. It is another thing to go all the length of the thought, as Theosophy does, and point out that this Kosmic Life is, as it were, like the sunlight broken up into innumerable rays, countless hosts, of evolving entities which in their aggregate make the Kosmic Spirit; although the Kosmic Spirit continuously soars above them and is not wholly included even in the kosmic aggregate of innumerable individual manifestations; and each one such ray or manifestation is nevertheless in its essence and in its root that Kosmic Spirit in its totality. "Thou and the Universe are one." This is a most wonderful thought and requires deep reflexion for grasping it in its amazingly suggestive reaches.

Next: The Theosophical philosophy teaches that there are invisible worlds and realms and spheres of which our physical world or realm or sphere is but the outer garment and therefore does not contain the fulness of the Kosmic Spirit. Occidental Pantheism has little or no idea of this last. It seems to have the idea that there is a Kosmic Spirit which in some way — I don't think I have ever heard an attempt to explain it — but which in some way is allied to the gross physical universe, and that this gross physical universe in some other inexplicable way is a portion of the Kosmic Spirit; which of course is true as far as it goes.

Now, that is not the Theosophical teaching because it is incomplete and imperfect as an idea. This physical universe is merely the garment, the outer physical garment, alive, nevertheless, of a conscious Ladder of Life, extending inwards, inwards, ever more inwards, and indeed ever outwards too, for SPACE *per se* has no directions. Thus we can range in thought, from the physical to the astral, from the astral to realms and spheres still more ethereal, from these last to others more ethereal again, and then to realms spiritual, then to realms and spheres divine, and so on *ad infinitum,* and never reach an end, although at intervals the Ladder of Life is seen to be divided into separate parts or portions which we call hierarchies.

Occidental Pantheism has no conception at all of this grandiose idea in its fulness; but nevertheless it is a step towards the wonder-teaching of the Ancient Wisdom today called Theosophy. We are therefore truly Pantheists, but in a vastly greater and nobler sense than the Occidental ideas imply. We are Pantheists. To us everything that is, is essentially alive. But all things exist in all-various grades of evolution. The tiny atom, the lichen on the stone, the sea-weed, the plant, the flower, the sponge, the beginnings of the so-called animal kingdom, ascending through all their various orders and families up to man; and, as our teaching says, beyond man there are other beings ascending in an endless Ladder of Life, both inwards into the spiritual realms and outwards into the spiritual realms.

So, then, I would answer more briefly, that Occidental Pantheism is but one small facet, one small step, towards what our teaching is. It is nevertheless exceedingly good that the step has been taken.

MEANING OF THE TERM CHALDEAN

Did the ancient Greek and Latin writers refer actually to the Chaldeans as natives of Chaldea, or was there some more general meaning to the term?

The so-called Sumerians and Akkadians were really the beginnings of the immigrants from India, who became the Chaldeans and Babylonians and later the Assyrians.

Chaldeans were called Initiates by the classic Greek and Latin writers. This arose out of the fact that during Latin times, and to a less extent in later Greek times, the Latins and Greeks looked to the Mesopotamian countries, or the countries surrounding the Euphrates and Tigris valley, as the homeland of sages, very much as modern Theosophists rightly or wrongly, usually wrongly, look upon the Tibetans as a kind of spiritual race, or as being more or less developed sages, all of which is utterly untrue.

This attitude of the Greeks and Latins was so marked that in the later days of Rome and Greece, when they used the word Chaldaios, or Chaldean, they meant an astrologer, or one erudite, or supposedly learned in occult philosophy. So great, however, became the abuse of this custom, because of imposition and cheating in Rome, that the later Roman emperors passed extremely severe measures against what were then popularly called Chaldeans.

But there were, before these later classic times, schools of Occultism in Chaldea and in Babylonia which had no small hand in helping to teach the Greeks and the Romans the Occult Philosophy, and it was to those periods in time that the term Chaldean as a learned man originally referred.

When Greece and Rome were 'young,' i.e., before they had reached the apex of material life and influence, there were actually in Chaldea and in Babylonia, as in Egypt, occult schools from whom missionaries were sent to the West, and it was in this way that the Greeks and the Romans constantly looked to the East for light. This accounted also for the fact that later on, basing their attitude on this original true fact, every impostor in Greece and Rome called himself a Chaldaios.

ANCIENT AMERICA, EGYPT AND INDIA

In a preface written to Dr. Alexander Wilder's series of articles on the Egyptian Dynasties, published in the old UNIVERSAL BROTHERHOOD PATH, *occurs the statement that "Egypt is older than India, and America older than either." This preface is signed by Katherine Tingley.*

This statement cannot be reconciled, it would seem, with the many statements made by H. P. B., both in THE SECRET DOCTRINE *and in* ISIS UNVEILED, *to the effect that India is older than Egypt and that Egypt owed her civilization to India. For example the following:*

. . . Egypt herself had, in those unknown ages when Menes reigned, received her laws, her social institutions, her arts, and her sciences from pre-Vedic India.
— *Isis Unveiled*, I, 589

. . . Egypt owes her civilization, her civil institutions, and her arts, to India.
— *Op. cit.*, II, 431

Egypt owes her civilization, commonwealth, and arts — especially the art of building, to pre-Vedic India. — *Op. cit.,* II, 435

Isis Unveiled *has several other statements, and* The Secret Doctrine, II, 417, *reads:*

India and Egypt were two kindred nations, and the Eastern Ethiopians (Egyptians) have come from India, as is now pretty well proved, it is hoped, in *Isis Unveiled,* II, 569-70.

I have heard a statement that certain Atlantean stocks, foreseeing the coming catastrophe, when Atlantis began to sink, migrated to new lands, and these lands became the Americas, became Africa, became parts of Asia, and that in time they lost all memory of their homeland and became the stocks of the ancient Americans, the Mayas, the Incas of Peru, and ALSO THE ARCHAIC EGYPTIANS, AND THE VERY EARLIEST ARYANS.

Question: Can you throw some light upon the contradictions? Is it possible that Dr. Wilder wrote that preface himself, as he wrote the preface to Isis Unveiled, *which preface admittedly contains errors?*

No, no. The statement therein is from Katherine Tingley and is quite true. America was, strictly speaking, the fifth continent to appear about the time of the sinking of the mainland of the Atlantic continental system. But for ages and ages after the first part of the original Americas had risen above the waters of the ocean, semi-continents, quasi-continents, great islands, of the Atlantean system still endured. And not so very long, geologically speaking, after the Americas had arisen above the waters — not then having their exact present configuration — the first roots of what later became Egypt, 'the Gift of the River Nile,' appeared; a little later than that, the larger part of what is now called upper Asia.

There is no contradiction at all between the statements, and I have often wondered why a contradiction should apparently be sought for where none exists. Is it not possible to understand that two statements can mean the same thing, but are made because viewing the same thing from two different angles? It is perfectly true that America is older than Egypt, and that Egypt is older than what is *now* called India.

What is now India was first colonized from the north, but almost contemporaneously from the south: from what was in ancient times, aeons agone, called Lankâ, of which now vanished land, what was the northernmost highland is today called Ceylon. Lankâ was one of the quasi-continents that I have just spoken of — I mean the ancient Lankâ of the wide-flowing Atlantean system. The peoples inhabiting the ancient Lankâ, of which Ceylon is the northernmost tip or prolongation, were mythologically spoken of by the Greeks as the 'eastern Aethiopians' — not meaning negroes, but Easterners, who were called 'Aethiopians' on account of the dark color of their skin — as if the skin had been greatly sunburned.

Thus then, the original part of India had likewise received settlers from the south, coming from the remnant of the ancient Atlantean Lankâ, inhabited, if you will remember, by Râvana, the foe of Râma, and by Râvana's armies of 'monkeys' and 'half-men.' The common Sanskrit name for the inhabitants of ancient Lankâ was Râkshasas.

Now, preceding the time when the Asiatic Atlantean Lankâ was in the heyday of its prosperity, there existed in what is now called the region of the Atlantic Ocean, a great and extensive and highly civilized range of land which was the continental backbone throughout the ages of Atlantis. When this Atlantic Atlantean continent finally broke up and disappeared, leaving behind it large and small islands — which last condition existed after the original Asiatic Lankâ had also broken up and disappeared — emigrants from these remaining islands of the Atlantic traveled eastward and settled on new land which had been rising out of the ocean to the eastward of these remnants of the Atlantean continent, and these new lands later consolidated — these new islands — and became what is now the district of the Abyssinian highlands and lands somewhat to the north of these.

As time passed, these Atlantean emigrants who had settled upon these new lands to the eastward, followed northwards the continual northward rising of new land — the extension of their shores northwards into the Atlantic Ocean; and this was the earliest Atlantean root-stock of what in later ages became the archaic or primitive Egyptians. Remember that the Egypt of history is the 'Gift of the River Nile.' The Nile flows northwards, and through the ages it has brought down enormous accumulations of sediment in its waters and has deposited these continually on the shore of the Atlantic Ocean into which the Nile flowed, so that little by little through the ages this shore-deposit of the Nile extended ever more into the waters of the Atlantic, as the river kept bringing down, through the passing millennia, ever more and more detritus and earthy material, carried northwards in its waters and derived from the mountains of the hinterland, the back country, Abyssinia, and what is now Nubia and the other countries there. Thus the entire Nile Delta, as the Greeks called it: in other words the Egypt of history, and as it is today, is literally the Gift of the River Nile.

This original Delta was settled anew by further colonists of a later age from the last remnant of Atlantis, which Plato called 'Poseidonis,' which existed some eleven or twelve thousand years before his time; for Poseidonis then still existed in the Atlantic Ocean beyond the Pillars of Hercules; and this Poseidonis at about that time was a large island more or less of the size of Ireland today. These Poseidonians were they who settled anew on the Egypt of the Delta and built the Pyramid some seventy or eighty thousand years ago. You see, therefore, that these Egyptians of the second important immigration were a much later Atlantean immigration than were the first that I have told you about. Furthermore, the Poseidonians had already become more or less mixed in blood with the Aryans — the new race which had already for several ages been coming down from the plateau of Asia, where, as Atlantean stocks, they had found refuge from the continental agony of Atlantis.

Remember, therefore, that these Aryans coming down from the plateau of Asia belonged to the original Atlantean emigration which I have told you of, which went eastwards to the new lands arising out of the waters of the then Far East.

Once more, still later than the time when Poseidonis sank, which was some twelve thousand or more years ago, Egypt was again invaded and settled by emigrants from what is now southern India who came into Egypt by two routes. The first route was over the Indian Ocean to Abyssinia and the countries around that range of land; and thence down the River Nile into Egypt, the immigrants conquering and settling the country as they went. The other route was a land-route over what is now the Isthmus of Suez. These last immigrants into Egypt from southern India, the Egyptian records refer to as the 'Sons of Horus,' the Sun-God, coming out of the East.

Thus you see that Egypt had first a primal or primitive immigration of Atlantean stock before the Egypt of history had as yet been made by the River Nile. Then came a second and much later emigration of a mixed Atlantean stock from Poseidonis into Egypt, which mixed stock settled on the Egypt of history, some eighty, ninety, or one hundred thousand or more years ago. Still later again there came the third immigration into Egypt of history, it may have been eight or nine thousand years ago or more, these immigrants coming from southern India; and it is this last immigration of Indian stocks from southern India — who were the 'eastern Aethiopians' who mixed with the Atlantean Egyptians and thus produced the composite racial stock which known history, recorded history, knows as having produced the dynasties of Egypt.

Thus America was the oldest continent; Egypt in its beginnings was much earlier than India; then came India; but also southern India at a later time sent her civilization, her arts, her mysteries, the teaching of her great mystical schools, to Egypt. These last south Indian immigrants into Egypt were themselves a mixed people partly of early Aryan stock but of a still stronger infusion of the ancient Atlantean inhabitants of the then already sunken and almost forgotten Atlantean Lankâ.

CIVILIZATIONS OF PRE-HISTORY

Archaeologists have found no remains of developed civilizations earlier than about 7,000 years ago — not long before the beginnings of Kali-Yuga.

There is positive evidence from tens of thousands of years before that, of a 'primitive' mode of living — stone implements, etc., — and negative evidence of the same — the absence of pottery, metals, buildings, etc.

H. P. Blavatsky says the lack of progress during the immense period of the Stone-Ages was due to the heavy Atlantean karman.

Was humanity really brutal and savage as a whole during the Stone-Ages, or are the appearances deceptive, and did a higher civilization exist during the 900,000 years since the destruction of the continent of Atlantis, though lacking the appurtenances we now consider essential to 'civilization'?

Brutality and brutishness walk the streets of our cities; and you will see among us many examples of the so-called Stone-Age man of the archaeologists. There are Stone-Age men today, savage and barbarian tribes, using stones; and there are so-called civilized men also today. Consequently, my answer is, that higher civilizations have existed during the last 900,000 years, most emphatically so, certainly so. During the 900,000 years that this querent speaks of, which is by no means all the time since the downfall of the Atlantean civilization, but even within this smaller period of 900,000 years, there have been great civilizations in various parts of the globe, which were born, which flourished, which brought forth the best that they could achieve in the plenitude of their power, and then decayed; and not a wrack of them remains as a witness today. Our fate will be exactly the same; but while these brilliant civilizations flourished in various parts of the world, there were Stone-Age men then, just as there are today.

There are different kinds of waves of civilization which sweep over the earth, such as that which existed during the times of the Greek and the Roman Empires, when all over the world civilization was fairly low when looked at from a standpoint of merely mechanical achievements, and not so high in that respect as our civilization is at the present time; but from a nobler standpoint, higher than civilization is at present. The essence of civilization is the bringing forth into manifestation in human life of the spiritual and intellectual faculties and powers of men, whether men have automobiles and flying machines, or not.

When a man thinks and produces the fruits of his thought in noble works, in literature, in the mysteries, in religion, in philosophy, in human kindness, there we find a true civilization. It is a civilization of a higher type than one like our own. Yes, there have been many civilizations in the past more brilliant even than our own at present. We have not reached the fullest expression, the highest point, of our present cycle of growth. But that highest point is not far off, and then our turn will come to decay — unless the Theosophical Movement can arouse generally in the hearts of mankind some greater longing for spiritual things; unless our spiritual movement arouse in the hearts and minds of men — so that it will carry them over the difficulties of the future — a vision, a vision of Truth, and of Reality; and above everything else, unless it can evoke brotherly kindness, brotherly love.

You will find brutes walking the streets of our great cities today, types and examples of those purely imaginary figures which the imaginative archaeologists portray as the 'dawn-man,' or the 'paleolithic man' or the 'neolithic man,' or the 'Stone-Age man.'

Not so many thousands of years before Greece attained the remarkable brilliance which characterized its civilization during the Periclean Age: not so many thousands of years before that, there flourished a civilization which would put ours to shame, actually a series of civilizations, and they had their habitat and stage in what is now Persia and Western Afghanistan, and in the lands to the north and east of these, lands which are now barren and desert countries. Brilliant civilizations flourished there. There were also civilizations which once covered with a perfect web of cities and towns what are now the Gobi plains — a howling waste of sands and desolation, but which were then dotted with prosperous cities and towns and villages. The land was highly cultivated. Astronomical observatories and chemical laboratories were as common as they are with us. What remains of them? Naught but legends, dreams of the past, a few scattered archaeological remnants, which are supposed by the degenerate inhabitants of the Shamo desert today to be the dwelling-place of spirits or genii. Many parts of the earth were the seats of once brilliant civilizations of which not even a memory remains today.

AGE OF THE GREAT PYRAMIDS

What is the true age of the Great Pyramids of ancient Egypt?

I would say that the Great Pyramids are at least three Zodiacal years, or 75,000 years old, and perhaps more, a good deal more. Any attempt to fix even an approximate age would depend upon the geology of the Nile delta and other similar things, which would act as time-checks. The Great Pyramid of Cheops was builded at the time of the second Atlantean immigration-period. After the first great pyramids were builded, many other

pyramids were constructed in later ages; but between these two periods —
the original Atlantean immigration and the later ages — there took place
the heavy immigration from the Orient, from what is now Southern India,
Ceylon, and the other part of the big island of which Ceylon is the sole
remaining remnant.

The pyramid is a typical Atlantean structure; and that is why they are
found in the New World also, in Yucatan and Mexico, the principles of
pyramidal construction having been carried there by Atlantean immigrants
from the sinking Atlantean islands.

SWABHÂVA AND THE MONAD

*In regard to Swabhâva, is the idea correct that different classes of mo-
nads pass each through certain different types of self-expression in all the
kingdoms — one class through certain genera and species in each kingdom,
another class of monads through different ones? And if every monad must
pass through all the types from monad to god, how is the actual difference
in its own swabhâva developed?*

The swabhâva is the characteristic individuality of a being or entity,
one having swabhâva X, another swabhâva Y, another swabhâva Z, a fourth
swabhâva Q, a fifth swabhâva P, etc., etc., these swabhâvas being the
stored-up treasury of experiences from preceding cosmic manvantaras. Just
so with human beings: each man has his own swabhâva, and yet all men
are linked each through his highest with the Cosmic Monad from which all
originated in the dawn of manvantaric manifestation, and to which Cosmic
Monad all will at the end of the manvantara be ingathered again. When
these individual monads reissue forth at the dawn of a new cosmic manvantara for a new life-period, each will do so with his own treasury of ingar-
nered or ingathered experiences from the present cosmic manvantara, and
each thus will have his own improved or evolved swabhâva or individual
characteristics — or individuality. These armies of monads issuing forth
from the Cosmic Monad, i.e., from its bosom, will thus break out into the
welter, into the incomprehensibly vast multitudes, of beings in differentiation and in manifestation, which will produce the amazing and fascinating
variety and differences of the future cosmic manvantara; just as the varieties around us now were born in the manner above explained from the
experiences gathered in during the previous cosmic manvantara.

Thus slowly through the revolving ages of endless time, the Monads
gradually change or rather evolve their swabhâva or 'character' or individuality, ever towards higher and nobler and loftier types, because the swabhâva or individuality of each grows from the less to the greater, from the

more imperfect to the more perfect, but always bringing out from within, and not growing by adding increments from outside.

Summarizing, then, in our thought, this wonderful picture, we see that karman obliges every individual Sparklet or Droplet of the ocean of the Cosmic Monad to pass, in the whirling of the Wheel of Life throughout endless time, through all possible phases of experience in the cosmic manvantara as these succeed each other.

To particularize: it is quite wrong to imagine an individual monad *being* in one of its evolutionary stages a tiny particle in the mineral kingdom, such as of hornblende or quartz or granite or whatever it may be, and slowly becoming through time perhaps an atom in the flesh of some beast, and finally becoming as a separate entity the monad of a Humboldt or of a Newton or of a Dante or of a Vergil. Here the attention is wrongly centered upon the monad as being an entity disjunct and 'separate' from the Cosmic Monad, in the materialistic fashion of the science of fifty years ago when H. P. B. wrote; and this is very misleading. The truth is that the Individual Monad passes through and helps to form each and every one of the kingdoms of Nature, becoming more and more individualized because of the ever greater expression of its own inner swabhâva flowing from within itself, the stage finally being reached in this development from within upwards when the Monad can express a sufficiency of its inner and hitherto latent spiritual and intellectual and psychical powers, so that it then brings forth in the human kingdom a Humboldt or a Newton or a Dante, etc.

Thus, then, the correct way of phrasing the teaching is: The Monad expressing itself with others in every kingdom of Nature, or passing through these various phases of its long evolutionary pilgrimage, at each stage unfolding from within in continuously larger measure the powers and faculties and attributes latent in its swabhâva.

Reincarnation and Early Christianity

The Doctrine of Reincarnation was generally taught and accepted in the pre-Christian times, but was discarded during the early days of Christianity. Could you tell me why this was done, and when?

It dropped out of belief and acceptance because Christian theology, during its first three or four or five centuries of development, discovered that the doctrine of Reimbodiment, with its collateral doctrine of intrinsic retributive justice and compensation, did not harmonize with its own ideas of salvation by 'the blood of the Lamb,' plus repentance no matter how black one's sins might be. The doctrine thus gradually fell into oblivion, and

people thereafter began to imagine that they could be 'saved' by believing
on Jesus as the "only Son of God, who was sent into the world by God
Almighty to die for our sins, and if we believe on Him and repent we shall
be saved unto life everlasting, because we shall be washed in His blood" —
that is, our souls will be, I suppose!

The doctrine, in the form of Pre-existence as taught by the great
Church-Father, Origen, was formally anathematized and condemned at the
'Home-Synod' — which is another term for a minor council — held under
the Primate Mennas in Constantinople at a date which modern scholars fix
between 538 and 543 (they are not certain of the exact year), as a consequence of the theological and other disputes over the teachings of Origen,
the great Alexandrian Church-Father, which had racked the Christian
Church for nearly two hundred years or more previously. These particular
disputes are called the 'Origenistic Controversies.' Among Origen's teachings was the implicit statement that all the Universe is alive, even the stars
being living creatures and having souls, and therefore involving themselves
in moral responsibilities; and that, furthermore, imbodied souls must have
pre-existences as well as post-existences, before and after death, and hence
souls are responsible for their feelings, thoughts, and acts.

As just said, at the Home-Synod under the Primate Mennas, this was
one of Origen's doctrines formally condemned and anathematized and pronounced heretical; and when this anathema and condemnation were repeated and confirmed at the Fifth General Council also held at Constantinople in 553 under the Emperor Justinian and with the strong arm of the
Church enforcing the anathema, backed by the equally strong arm of the
State, the doctrine of Pre-existence and of Reimbodiment fell first into
heretical disrepute, and finally, within a short time, into oblivion.

The full Theosophical doctrine of Reincarnation, that is to say the
technical doctrine as we now teach it, cannot be said to have been condemned and anathematized at these two Constantinopolitan councils: it
was Origen's particular form of the teaching expressed in his doctrine of
Pre-existence and of moral responsibility arising out of it, which was thus
banned and declared heretical. His doctrine in many respects is very
much the same as our complete doctrine of Reincarnation; but it is not
exactly our Theosophical doctrine, because Origen's form is incomplete and
therefore imperfect. Don't make the mistake of ignoring this subtil distinction, because if you do you may be caught some day by some clever casuist,
and become confused over what after all is mere words. Origen undoubtedly taught the doctrine under his own form of Pre-existence involving the
soul's having lived before birth, and the fact that it will live again and
again, and will take imbodiment in different nations of the world, at one

time being, as he put it, an Egyptian, at another time a Jew, etc. Yet Origen taught the doctrine from his own particular or rather individual viewpoint, attempting to link it with half-formed theological teachings. Hence, he did not teach the full and complete doctrine of Reincarnation as we give it today.

Thus, to state baldly and without further qualification that the two Councils held at Constantinople, in 538-543, and again in 553, condemned and anathematized and declared heretical our Theosophical doctrine of Reincarnation, is a dangerous thing to say, because, first, it is inaccurate because incomplete, and second, inaccurate because it was only Origen's form thereof that was condemned. This form is partly true, three-fourths true let us say, but yet not accurately stated.

There is little doubt that the full Theosophical teaching of Reimbodiment would have been condemned and anathematized with even more vigor and detestation than was Origen's white-washed form. I might add in conclusion as showing how the spiritual powers in the world are continually at work, that just about the time when these two Councils condemned Origen's doctrine of Pre-existence and Reimbodiment, a new and much more spiritual current of theological teaching based on Neo-Platonic and Neo-Pythagorean doctrines began to have large currency in the then Christian Church. This new current took its crystallized and literary form in the writings of the Pseudo-Dionysius, the Areopagite, and affected all later Christian theology tremendously, profoundly modifying and spiritualizing it.

Is there anything on record showing that Jesus himself taught the doctrine of Reincarnation?

I don't think there is any record except in the Gospels themselves, in vague allusions of a purely mystical character, such as the question of Nicodemus; and again the statement: "This is Elias which was for to come"; and we must always remember the more general fact of history that the teaching of Reincarnation in one or in another form was a doctrine well known and accepted by the Pharisees of Judaea of the period in which Jesus was said to have appeared. It was as commonly known and as commonly accepted — indeed much more largely then — as it is in the world today. I think people would be surprised to find out how commonly the teaching is taken for granted in our own times. It is no longer considered to be a funny or a peculiar doctrine. It is 'in the air.' Tens of thousands of people accept it openly, and multitudes of others accept it tacitly but do not talk about it, because they do not understand it; and just so it was among the Pharisees and others.

What about the question asked of Jesus: "Who did sin, this man, or his parents, that he was born blind?"

Yes, there are four or five such allusions, but no direct and specific declarations. But if the question is: "Did Jesus Christ teach Reincarnation?" the proper answer is: I am perfectly persuaded that he did, because it was such a common doctrine and so universally accepted in his time by the best minds, that if he did not at least accept it, he would have been considered to be a man of small insight and perhaps of small education. But there is absolutely no authentic record that he taught it. The Gospels themselves were written by men who lived anywhere from fifty to two hundred and fifty years after Jesus died.

Reincarnation was also one of the commonest beliefs in the Roman Empire, which included practically all the civilized European world then, outside of Parthia and the Orient. The Roman Empire included practically all of Asia Minor and Egypt, Italy, Greece, Gaul, Spain, part of Germany, most of Britain and spots in Ireland. All the Germanic peoples believed in it; all the Celtic peoples accepted it as a matter of course. It was one of the Druidic teachings. It was one of the intellectual 'stock in trade' beliefs of the time.

THE THREE LOGOI

I am often confused in Theosophical literature over the use of the term Logos or Logoi which seems to be used in different ways in different places. Can you clear up this matter?

Logos is a Greek word which originally means 'Reason,' and finally also came to mean 'Word.' Why? Because when a man addresses a man, he utters an idea of reason; reason or thought is conveyed by words between man and man; and taking this simple thought, certain Schools of the philosophy of Greece transferred it as a figure of speech, as a picture, to Cosmic processes and said: First there was the divine Reason, the divine Thought, which in order to communicate the life and intelligence within itself needed a vehicle, needed a Word, to pass itself on. And the Word or vehicle was produced by the functioning of the Reason, just as human speech is produced by the function of human reason, human thought.

There are of course many Logoi. Every different plane has its own three Logoi: the unmanifest, the partially manifest or quasi-manifest, the manifest, otherwise called First, Second, and Third Logoi. Why is this? Because Nature's operations and functions and structure are repetitive on all planes — what is in the highest is in the lowest, and *vice versa;* or, to put the thought differently, because the entire Universe is constructed of and in hierarchies which repeat each other on the different planes. Therefore each hierarchy, each plane in other words, has its First Logos, its Second Logos, and its Third.

You see how simple this thought is; and there is no reason to be confused when you see in *The Secret Doctrine* or in other writings, different statements about the Logoi or about the Third Logos or the Second or the First. First examine and find out which hierarchy or which plane is spoken of. This is why in *Fundamentals* I put the First and Second and Third Logoi in places relative to others, which are perfectly correct, but would be inaccurate if you transferred these relative positions to the Cosmos Universal, because in the Cosmos Universal Mahat is the Third Logos as it is indeed in man; Âtman the First Logos, Buddhi the Second Logos, Manas the Word, Reason, the expressed reason, the reason delivering the life of its progenitor to others — the Third Logos or Manas.

The teaching is very simple indeed. Do not boggle over words and think there are mysteries where there are none. There are mysteries enow, I tell you, without trying to find new ones, and that is what we all do! Find out first which Logos is spoken of, to which plane it is properly referred; then ascertain other facts about it; and you will find your way as clear as you could wish it. You will have no difficulty whatsoever. Every hierarchy, which means every plane, has its own three Logoi: the First or highest, the unmanifest for that hierarchy or plane, the Hyparxis, if you wish; its clothing or offspring or expression, the Second Logos; its child or offspring or clothing, the Third Logos.

AGAINST MEDICAL INOCULATION

What is the Theosophical point of view regarding medical inoculations of human beings as preventive measures against contagious diseases? Does it approve or is it opposed to them, and if so, why?

While there is no doubt that the injection of virus or so-called anti-toxin-substances from human and animal bodies into the veins of some other human being may, indeed certainly will, have its effect, nevertheless it is all too often overlooked that the injection of foreign poisons, often of a disgusting origin, into the human blood-stream, is bound to have one other and inevitable result, and this is, weakening the body's normally active powers of resistance, as well as the body's own inherent and instinctual production of substances which in the normal case will be produced in order to protect the body against invasion from outside, whether by germs or in any other manner; and even should invasion occur, to neutralize their poison.

People are all too often swept off their feet — and with due apologies to the profession, medical men in particular — by the realization that a new antitoxin has been discovered which, when human bodies are inoculated with it, will prevent, it is hoped, the spread of a disease; and in consequence frequently human beings showing no sign of the disease are inoculated simply as a preventive measure.

I have no desire whatsoever to touch upon occult or esoteric reasons in connexion with this question, for these reasons would have no appeal whatsoever to the ordinary man in the street, and might even prejudice him, because of his blindness and lack of thought, against Theosophy, and Theosophists themselves as being in his view simple 'cranks' or 'mild lunatics.' The situation must be met on its own grounds. The annals of medicine present us with too many cases where this fad or that fad has been followed and at first acclaimed as a heaven-sent blessing, but later discovered to be a hell-sent curse! It is the short-sighted view that usually prevails, unfortunately.

I might as well point out that nobody will contract any disease whatsoever unless the germs of that disease are already in the system, their being there because of a proclivity towards that disease, this proclivity itself being due to karmic causes. Thus inoculating an otherwise healthy man of this type with the antitoxin-virus of some loathsome disease not only weakens the body of this otherwise healthy man, but because of this weakness predisposes his system towards reception of the latent disease, despite the efforts of the body to react protectively against it; and, furthermore, because of weakening the body it predisposes it likewise, on account of this ensuing weakness, to other possible invasions of still other diseases.

I am convinced that, by means of stricter hygienic and preventive measures, a wiser future medical science will bend most of its efforts towards stamping out the diseases which afflict both man and beast. In itself there is something unspeakably revolting in injecting virus from unfortunate and diseased animals, or from the bodies of human beings suffering from loathsome disease, into the blood-stream of apparently healthy people, in the hope thereby to render them immune against contracting of such diseases. Vegetable poisons are incomparably less dangerous to the human system when properly used in a prophylactic or preventive manner, although of course it is true that some vegetable poisons are as fatal as any known.

Summarizing, therefore, I for one may say that I am absolutely opposed to poisoning the blood-stream of human beings with antitoxin-virus of any kind taken from the diseased bodies of man or beast. The mere fact that this is running counter to so strong a stream of current medical opinion, is a matter to me of utter unimportance. Medical science, like all other sciences, changes so rapidly that the opinions of one day, however widely and loudly proclaimed, become the discarded theories of a succeeding age. The proper way to do, therefore, it seems to me, is to take all natural, cleanly, sane, and normal preventive measures, both in the individual and in the collective fields, especially sanitary and hygienic measures, paying due and proper attention to exercise, diet, and personal cleanliness of all kinds. Then, if one contracts a disease, it becomes a duty to try to recover health in every cleanly and sane manner possible, and it is perfectly right so to do. It is extremely doubtful in my opinion if it is either right or wise in any case whatsoever to inoculate human beings with the disgusting virus drawn from the diseased bodies of either man or beast for this purpose. I am convinced such inoculation brings along with it ten devils worse than the disease itself.

THE NATURE OF EVIL AND FREE WILL IN MAN

In what way did the Stoic teaching differ from that of Theosophy as regards (1) the nature of evil, (2) Free will in man?

We must remember that the Stoic Philosophy, a really grand system of cosmic thought, has been badly understood by moderns trained in Christian ways of theological thought. The Stoics had virtually the same fundamental or esoteric teaching that the Platonists had, and consequently 'the nature of evil' is just about what I have explained in my answers to former questions. Evil is imperfection, i.e., insufficient evolution, and is therefore relative; because what men might call 'good,' the gods who are above us might actually call 'evil' by comparison with their own supergoodness.

It may be illustrated by the example of light: There is weak light, light of moderate strength, and dazzling brilliance. The beings who live in the intermediate light, would say that the weak light is evil. On the other hand, the beings who live in the dazzling brilliance, would say that the intermediate light is evil. Therefore, the nature of evil, as taught in the Stoic Philosophy, or, indeed, as taught in Platonism, or, indeed, as taught in modern Theosophy, is simply imperfection. Any being who or which is insufficiently evolved to have brought out divinity from within itself, at least to some degree, can be called 'evil' by comparison with beings much more evolved, who are therefore much more perfect.

Next, as regards the Stoic doctrine of 'Free will in man,' this Stoic doctrine is exactly the same as part of the Theosophical teaching on the same topic; and please remember that the heart of Platonism or Stoicism is identic with the heart of Theosophy. But alas, this esoteric heart moderns have never understood because of their Christian prejudices and biases. Free will in man arises out of the fact that man is a child of the Universe, divinely, spiritually, intellectually, psychically, astrally and physically, as well as morally. Consequently, free will in man arises out of the heart of his being, which is as much as saying the heart of the Universe, of which he is a child, because the Universe is the Great Whole; therefore the part must have whatsoever it may be that the Great Whole has. You see how beautifully this thought works: Man has free will because he is of the same essence or substance as the spiritual Universe, which is or has free will. Conversely, we can prove that there is free will in the Universe because man himself has it, man being a part of the Whole — it being inconceivable that a part can possess something which the Whole has not.

PLATO ON TWO WORLD-SOULS

Would you be good enough to explain what Plato meant by the much disputed passage in the LAWS, *in which he refers to two world-souls, one the author of good, the other of evil. The passage is as follows:*

Athenian: And as the soul orders and inhabits all things that move, however moving, must we not say that she orders also the heavens?

Clenias: Of course.

Athenian: One soul or more? More than one — I will answer for you; at any rate we must not suppose that there are less than two, one the author of good, the other of evil. — *Laws*, x, 896

Taken in conjunction with the remainder of the Platonic philosophy and its constant reference to divine beings in the Universe, the explanation of this passage becomes immediately clear enough: i.e., that there is a spiritual Universe as well as what we moderns call a material universe, the two of course working together and under the general governance or superiority of the World-Spirit which moves to and works for 'good,' while the other is that part of the world or universe composed of inferior or less evolved beings, which therefore by comparison with the superior World-Soul can be called collectively the author of imperfection, or what men today call 'evil.'

I will repeat the answer in other words now. The Universe is a vast aggregate Hierarchy or Cosmic Family composed of beings in all grades or stages of evolution, from the Hierarch or topmost point of divinity of the Hierarchy, down to the most material beings composing the Hierarchy; and these latter are of course the least evolved of all the entities in the Hierarchy and therefore form the material world. The Hierarch or spiritual entity of the Hierarchy is therefore the source of all law, order, love, peace, harmony, beauty, compassion, pity, and active intelligence in the Hierarchy; and all the inferior beings in this Hierarchy derive what they have of harmony and beauty and peace, etc., from their supreme Chief, the Hierarch.

Thus you see there are what Plato, in order to save words, very briefly calls two 'souls' — one the author of good, and one the author of evil; i.e., one the source of law and beauty and harmony, and the other the great material aspect of life, which, because it is material is imperfectly evolved, and therefore can abstractly be called the 'author of evil.'

But now, mark you, any such Hierarchy is but one of countless multitudes of other similar Hierarchies alike unto it, scattered through the infinite fields of Boundless Being; so that, therefore, 'World-Souls' are literally infinite in number. I point this fact out with some particularity so that my answer will not seem to contain the 'Supreme Personal God' idea.

This, therefore, is the real meaning of Plato in the passage which you quote, and which Christians find it extremely difficult to understand, because of their education and mental bias along Christian lines. Plato of course was a Polytheist, or a believer in a Universe filled full with divinities and beings less than divinity, forming a Cosmic Family, just as we Theosophists teach. In fact, Plato was a Theosophist.

THE MYSTERY OF THE PRATYEKA-BUDDHA

In regard to the statement, as quoted in 'The Mystery of the Pratyeka-Buddha' (LUCIFER, August, 1934), that the path of the Pratyeka-Buddha is "a noble path in a way . . . nevertheless essentially a selfish path, etc.," a correspondent asks if the path of the Pratyeka-Buddha, being both noble and selfish, thus makes really a third or middle path — so to speak a 'gray path,' lying in between the utterly selfish path of the Black Magician and the utterly selfless white path of a Buddha of Compassion.

In answer to this question, it may be observed that it is possible for the sake of mere categorical convenience to speak of the path of the Pratyeka-Buddhas as being a third path, or what the questioner calls a 'gray path,' lying between the black path of the Black Magician and the white path of the Buddha of Compassion; but such a distinction is rather an arbitrarily convenient one than true to Nature. The very fact that the Pratyeka-Buddhas are Buddhas of a kind, shows that theirs is a 'white path,' to follow the metaphor that the questioner used. But it is a white path which is nevertheless a negative or passive path, instead of being an actively compassionate and beneficent white path, which is what the Buddhas of Compassion follow.

We have thus the path of matter followed by the Brothers of the Shadow or the Black Magicians, which goes downwards; we have also the white
path which goes upwards. In the middle, so to speak, of this white path we
find the Buddhas of Compassion steadily pressing forwards, but nevertheless deliberately and compassionately keeping in touch with and helping
all beings trailing along behind that it is possible to help: the Buddhas of
Compassion thus acting as world-leaders and world-guides, and doing so
with deliberately compassionate intent; whereas, on the sides, so to speak,
of the same white path we find individuals who, their eyes fixed on the
glory of the vision before them, are blinded by it and, as it were, forget the
suffering thousands of millions of beings trailing along behind.

Thus, then, these Pratyeka-Buddhas press forwards along the white
path, doing indeed no harm to anyone, but completely absorbed in their
own 'salvation' as the Christians phrase it. They will finally reach their
destination where they will rest for aeons. Meanwhile, the general course
of evolution, led by the Buddhas of Compassion, will in time pass them by,
so that when the Pratyeka-Buddhas finally awaken to their new period of
evolution, they will then discover themselves in the rear, although still on
the white path. Remember that the Pratyeka-Buddhas are not actively
evil, quite the contrary. They are even a negative or passive kind of
spiritual influence in the world; but yet their course is what one can truly
and faithfully describe as a sort of spiritual selfishness, yet not an evil kind
of selfishness as is the path of the Black Brothers. The Pratyekas must
lead pure lives and keep their minds constantly on the celestial vision ahead
and do no harm to anyone; but their whole attention is centered on their
own 'salvation,' and they progress oblivious of the sufferings and stumbling
steps of the uncounted millions behind them.

This is so beautifully and succinctly stated by H. P. B. in *The Voice
of the Silence:*

The rugged Path of four-fold Dhyâna winds on uphill. Thrice great is he who
climbs the lofty top.
The Pâramitâ heights are crossed by a still steeper path.

These Pâramitâ heights are the heights upon which the Buddhas of
Compassion fix their gaze, for theirs is a still steeper path leading to heights
far greater than those attained by the Pratyeka-Buddhas.

Thus these latter are vegetatively or passively good, instead of actively
good as are the Compassionate Buddhas. The difference is somewhat like
that which we so often find as between two men, both of them fairly good
men, both of them on the whole desirous of doing good; but one man
of the twain longs to do good because his heart is mightily moved by pity,

and he thus goes out of his way in order to do good to others; whereas the other man of the twain merely dreams of doing good, but is still more interested in his own progress forwards and in the matters that pertain to his own advancement. The former man opens his ears to every cry for help, and obeys the instincts and dictates of pity; the latter man likewise may or may not hear the cries as the case may be, but is so involved in his own purposes for self-progress and self-advancement that he forgets, and finally by force of habit becomes selfishly oblivious of, Nature's first mandate — helping where help is needed.

The North Polar Continent

In Volume II of The Secret Doctrine, *page 401, is the following statement:*

If, then, the teaching is understood correctly, the first continent which came into existence capped over the whole North Pole like one unbroken crust, and remains so to this day, beyond that inland sea which seemed like an unreachable *mirage to the few* arctic travelers who perceived it.

Also on page 400, Note No. 857, the same statement is made, followed by the following:

All the central continents and lands will emerge from the sea bottom many times in turn, but this land will never change.

These statements seem to be a direct contradiction of the discoveries made in recent years by Admiral Byrd and others. In a recent article by the Admiral he states that there is a polar sea over the North Pole about 10,000 *feet deep and a continental plateau over the South Pole about* 10,000 *feet above sea level.*

How are these two statements reconciled?

We must never forget that H. P. Blavatsky was not permitted in many cases fully to give out all she knew, but could only make statements which sufficed to arouse the intuition of her students and to start them on new lines of inquiry. Notice that she begins the statement first quoted by the questioner with the word *if*. "If, then, the teaching is understood correctly . . . ." As Shakespeare says, there is much virtue in an *if!*

We must remember that the discoveries of Peary and Byrd (the latter to a large extent based upon Peary's findings, at least as regards conclusions) while seemingly accurate enough, need further confirmation. Next, that according to the teachings of the Esoteric Philosophy, the physical land-mass around the North Pole is mystically called the sacred imperishable land, which does not fundamentally change from the beginning of a manvantara — a Round — until its end. This by no means signifies that this land-mass remains untouched by and immune from the natural secular forces which prevail over the entire globe. On the contrary, the Polar Regions, just as much as other regions, are subject to changes of various kinds, minor subsidences, minor elevations. In this manner, just as occur in other regions, constant variations in the topography, so to speak, take place in the oceanic land-massif which surrounds the North Pole and its vicinity in all directions.

The meaning of this should be sufficiently clear. The North Polar continental massif is never, from the beginning of the Round to its end, subject to the complete and continental elevations and submersions that all the other land-massifs undergo during the long ages comprehended in a Round. The Second or Hyperborean continent, and Lemuria, Atlantis, and our own Fifth continent, have either already disappeared or will in the future. The ocean's turbulent waters are now rolling, or will roll, where once those archaic land-masses existed, or still exist in the case of our present continental system. Here is the difference between all those continental regions, past or future — each one the continental system of a Root-Race, past or to come — and the sacred 'imperishable' land-system surrounding the North Pole.

The North Polar land, as said above, is subject to the same secular variations of topographical outline as those of other portions of the Earth, but these are of minor character: small portions sink, other small portions arise. The geographic center of the Earth at the North Pole may or may not be at any one time under water, but surrounding it there is still the same slightly shifting, slightly changing continental system which in one age presents more water than land, and in another more land than water, but which, as a continental system, never undergoes those major and universal subsidences to which all other portions of the Earth's surface are subject in the course of the cycling ages — excepting the two "ends of the Earth." The same general observations apply to the South Pole.

Here, then, we have the explanation of what is mistakenly called a riddle only because certain statements have been too literally construed, and the matter has not been sufficiently studied. Consider a hypothetical case nearer the equator. Such a case could never actually occur, but it will illustrate my point. Take the Australian massif, including Australia, Tasmania, New Zealand, and the surrounding archipelagoes. Imagine that this vast continental system is never completely submerged, but is nevertheless subject to minor or partial cataclysms which entirely change the topographical outlines of the massif. Never does it vanish as a whole, but its outline is constantly changing because of the inroads of the sea in certain parts, and the elevations above the sea of hitherto sunken portions of this vast continental tract. This, as said, cannot happen except at the Poles, but it is precisely what *has* happened there, and will continue to do so to the very end of the present Round-manvantara. Though at first a continuous system or massif, the northern continent changes throughout the ages but never completely vanishes. It is subject to continuous secular variations in its topography due to sinkings and risings of portions thereof. The actual geographical center at the Pole may be either above or below the water, but the surrounding system of islands, large and small, peninsulas, etc., will remain, despite all minor changes, from the Round-manvantara's beginning to its end. It never finds as a whole a watery grave in the abysmal deeps of the ocean's floor.

The Writing of the Four Gospels

What is KNOWN *in regard to the time when the Gospels of the New Testament were written?*

Nothing at all is definitely known as to the *exact* time when the four Gospels of the New Testament were originally written. The first three are called by Christians the 'Synoptic Gospels' from a Greek word meaning 'seeing together,' the idea being that they give a general view of the alleged incidents in the life of Jesus in pretty much the same way — which they don't! Nobody knows, not even the ablest Christian or skeptical scholars, when a single one of the four Gospels was written, although Christian apologists have tried to set tentative dates. Skeptical scholars, on the other hand, who are not under the Christian sway of thought or bias, are pretty well of the common conclusion, or of the one idea, that all these Gospels were written in Alexandria probably between the first and third centuries of the Christian Era. These same scholars are likewise pretty well of the common opinion that not a single one of the Gospels was written by the Apostle whose name it bears: Matthew did not write *Matthew,* Luke did not write *Luke,* Mark did not write *Mark,* nor John, *The Gospel according to St. John;* and they say that this is shown by the fact that the very titles of these four Greek Gospels are 'The Gospel *according to*' — the Greek word being *kata,* which means 'according to' or 'after the views of.'

It is commonly supposed, or at least supposed by a great many scholars of independent thinking, that the oldest of the four Gospels is *The Gospel according to St. Matthew* — but some say that of *Mark.* Most scholars think that, as there are strong similarities but yet strong differences even amounting to contradictions, as among the four Gospels, they were written by different people at different times during the first three centuries of the

Christian Era, and possibly the first two; i.e., *The Gospels according to St. Matthew* and *St. Mark* were written after the pattern of an original and quasi-mythical earlier scripture, called 'The Gospel according to the Hebrews,' of which, however, no traces remain at the present time.

One might add that the Fourth Gospel, *The Gospel according to St. John,* bears, especially in its opening paragraphs, strong evidence of having been written by a Christian of Platonic leanings.

How (i.e., by what method) were the present books of the New Testament selected from a great number of others and proclaimed as being 'the Word of God'?

This, too, is a very difficult question to answer, because opinions differ so greatly. Older orthodox Christians, especially the clergy among them, stated that each Gospel was written by the Apostle whose name it bears; but modern scholarship has utterly rejected and disproved this. The four 'Canonical,' or Gospels presently accepted as being orthodox, are the four which most successfully survived the times of extremely critical and embittered controversy among the Christian sects during the first centuries of the Christian Era — in the time of what is called the primitive Church. Nobody knows why these particular four happened to survive — but guesses have been many.

There are many other 'Gospels' which have still survived, and they are now called 'Apocryphal,' which in modern meaning signifies gospels of doubtful or rejected authenticity, which some branches of the Christian Church allow to be read for interest or for edification but not for doctrine. These Apocryphal Gospels — a score or more of them, I believe — have most of them been translated into English by an Englishman called Hone. The Apocryphal Gospels, it should be stated, are all of them much less sober in content, much less reserved in narrative, much more full of wonder and miracle, than are the present so-called four Canonical Gospels.

There is a story of old date, probably reaching back fifteen hundred years or more to the early ages of the Christian Church, and recorded by a writer of small value, named Pappus, who tells a curious and interesting yarn about many Gospels having been gathered together in a Church at one of the Councils; and as the Christian theologians — bishops and others — then and there assembled, could not decide which ones were 'the Word of God,' all the Gospels were placed over night in the Chancel or Holy of Holies of the said church — the doors were then locked and everybody left. In the morning, so the yarn runs, all the Gospels except the four now accepted, were found on the floor, and these four were found on the altar, and in consequence they were then and there considered to have been placed there by God's angels, and hence were to be accepted as the Canonical Scriptures. This yarn, of course, is quite without substantiated authority, and is universally rejected by Christians. Probably the present books of the New Testament, which include *Acts, Epistles*, etc., were finally selected or recognised to be orthodox as the result of much dispute and argument during the early centuries of the Christian Church. This is the only possible answer to give, because history is silent on the subject.

SUGGESTION AND AUTOSUGGESTION

That hypnotism is dangerous, I know full well; is autosuggestion dangerous as well? I have understood that it is so — but then Christian Science must be a very dangerous creed indeed!

Autosuggestion can be used for very noble purposes, and it can be used for beastly purposes, as is perfectly obvious. Autosuggestion simply means suggesting thoughts and therefore actions to oneself; and isn't it obvious that you can dream about evil-doing or beastliness in the same way in which one can dream about noble doings and holiness? It depends upon what the suggestion is, whether it be holy or unholy.

As regards Christian Science, this is merely the belief of a modern society of 'deniers,' whose philosophy, if we can call it by that name, although containing many elements of good, as is only to be expected, is nevertheless in my judgment neither really Christian nor really scientific. It is a species of idealistic doctrine to the effect that matter does not exist, and that only the lower consciousness, which they call 'mortal mind,' produces the evil in the world — a proposition which, put baldly like that, no one would probably deny; with the single exception that Theosophists claim that matter and evil do 'exist,' otherwise they would not need to be denied. Neither matter nor evil have absolute being, but they exist. In other words, this is what we Theosophists call mâyâ, or the illusory nature of the existing material universe. Both Theosophists and Christian Scientists, however, agree in the obvious proposition that good is harmony and evil is disharmony, and that it is our bounden duty to try to ally ourselves with the spiritual elements within us and to refuse to place ourselves under the sway of the ignoble elements of our being.

Answering the first part of the question, I would point out that hypnotism can be exceedingly dangerous, and that psychologization especially in its form of suggestion is not only extremely perilous for ignorant minds to dabble with, but even for those who have studied the matter, to undertake to practise; for one would need the wisdom of a Buddha or of a Jesus, and the heart of a Buddha or of a Jesus, in order to know just how far to go and when to stop.

Suggestion, on the whole, is one of the most subtil and ill-understood powers of the human mind, although it is none the less practised daily and constantly and often ignorantly in all ranks of human society. In this connexion we must not forget the doctrine of Karman with its rigid action which makes a man responsible for whatever he does, responsible for his thoughts and for his feelings, and therefore for his acts, and that Nature will hold him to the strictest kind of accounting, "to the last farthing" as the saying goes, for whatever he makes himself responsible for by his thoughts and by his feelings, and therefore by his acts.

Man Made in His Own Image

Page 268, The Secret Doctrine, Vol. I, bottom, says:

. . . the *Pilgrim*, having struggled through and suffered in every form of life and being, is only at the bottom of the valley of matter, and half through his cycle, when he has identified himself with collective Humanity. This, *he has made in his own image.*

What does this last sentence mean? How "in his own image"?

A man reproduces himself on earth from his own inner self, from the elements of his own inner being. A man cannot be anything other than what he himself is, obviously; and as his inner nature evolves, so will he reproduce in his physical and astral and vital parts ever-improved and more perfect instruments and fitter vehicles for expressing the spiritual and intellectual and psychical nature within him. A man thus is his own father or progenitor, and a man in future lives will be his own child — or children; I mean that a man makes himself in this life to be what he will be in the next life and in future lives. A man is a composite entity formed of a divine, of a spiritual, of an intellectual, of a psychical, and of a vital-astral-physical part. The lower parts of him flow forth from the higher parts of himself, much as the oak-tree flows forth from the life and matter-elements within the acorn.

There, then, is the keynote of the explanation, which is very mystical, but very beautiful and very profound; and thus it is that the 'pilgrim,' which here in H. P. B.'s language represents the collective army of evolving monads, reproduces, when it reaches the human stage, humanity, and in its own image. Man is thus brought about through evolution as an imperfect image of the indwelling or inner god; and the god meant here is the inner spiritual divinity, the immanent Christ, the inner god, or the inner Buddha. At the heart of every being is a fountain of energy which reproduces 'shadows' or 'images' of itself in the material worlds. These 'shadows' or 'images' of itself are its various bodies, and being shadows of itself are obviously images of itself. Therefore the 'pilgrim' — a name used by H. P. B. in this passage for the collective army of monads — reproduces Humanity — which is the name for the collective host of men — in its own image or images.

Soul the Intermediate Principle

Why, if the soul as I have understood it, is omnipotent, should it need to manifest in the material worlds?

The soul is not omnipotent, the Spirit is but not the soul. Man is composed of a divine part, a spiritual part, an intellectual part, a passional part, and a vital-astral-physical part, coming downwards. Man is composed of all the essences in the universe, from the highest to the lowest. The highest part in man is omnipotent, at least we can say omnipotent in this universe, but not the soul. The soul is the intermediate part, the part between the Spirit and the body; and it is the soul which is learning, evolving. It is the soul which says: 'I am I'; but it is the Spirit which says: 'I am.' Do you see the difference? 'I am,' is the same all over the universe. Every creature everywhere feels 'I am.' But the soul with its reflected consciousness — as the moon reflects the sun — does not realize that it is the same in essence as the universe, and makes a distinction or a separation between other souls and itself, and says 'I am I,' and 'you are you.' Now that is not very high. It is like a man who says: I am a Swede, I am an Englishman, I am a German. It is good as far as it goes, but it is not the highest. The noblest part of us says: I am a son of the Divine, my home is the Universe, I am at home everywhere. All are my brothers because all come from the same source whence I come. The Universe is my home.

It is the Spirit which is universal, which is relatively omnipotent; but the soul, the human soul, is a learning creature; it has not yet fully evolved.

The Doctrine of the Trinity

From where did the early Christians derive their doctrine of the Trinity: Father, Son, and Holy Ghost?

The early Christians derived the *essentials* — I do not mean all the later theological squabblings about the Trinity, but the essentials of the teaching — from the early Pagans, especially from the great nations of the Hither East, such as Egypt, Babylonia, Persia, Syria, etc. Many or all of these ancient nations had a wonderful mystical Theology which taught the existence of a Cosmic Life-Intelligence, which for purposes of easy description they often called the 'Father.' And because the Universe evolved or came into manifestation, the first and most spiritual period of this manifestation was called the 'Son' of the Cosmic Father, or Cosmic Intelligence-Life, and in ancient Greece was often mystically spoken of as the Logos, or Reason or Word of the Father, which was exactly the term that the Christians adopted for their Divine 'Son,' whom they most curiously tangled up in a web of contradictions with the otherwise beautiful and noble character called Jesus Christ. The Holy Ghost, said these ancient mystical theologians, was the spirit of love and harmony and peace pervading or permeating the Universe; and we must remember that the phrase 'Holy Ghost' is but another form of the phrase 'Holy Spirit.'

We see, then, that this triad can be considered as a trinity, and was adopted by the Christians, at least in its essentials, to wit, the Cosmic fundamental Essence often spoken of as Life-Intelligence-Substance, permeated with the spirit of love and order and law and harmony, called the 'Holy Ghost'; and there was always the 'Son' or Logos, who was the actual intelligent creative power.

LEARNING THROUGH SUFFERING

Would you suggest that Theosophy teaches that pain and suffering were part of the original program?

This question is not so easy to answer as might appear at first sight, because, can I say off-hand without qualification that it is necessary for human beings to pass through sorrow and pain and suffering and wretchedness — must I add sin and evil-doing? — and thereby preach a doctrine of evil? Therefore I will phrase my answer in this wise, and I will use the well-known phrase: It must needs be that evil be upon the Earth, but woe unto the evil-doer! Do you catch the thought? It is a very profound one. Imperfect beings actually do learn through suffering and pain because they do evil things. They learn by it. See how beautiful and kindly Mother Nature is. She lets us learn even when we break her commandments or laws. But when we do so, we reap pain, we reap sorrow, our hearts are broken by the misery that we ourselves have sown. Strange but true paradox! We learn through the evil we do. But, merciful heaven, how we suffer from it, and it need not be. So merciful is Nature that we can learn even from the evil that we do do, from the evil things that we commit. But we can learn without doing evil, and then we suffer not, nor do we undergo pain.

I would say in brief then: Yes, we learn through suffering and pain, but we need not so. There are other ways of learning. There are other ways, for instance, for a child to learn that fire burns besides the risky one and painful one of putting a finger into the flame. We have our mind, our intellect, our intuition, the keen percipient consciousness.

SYMBOLISM OF THE SERPENT

Why did the ancients consider the serpent a symbol of wisdom, while today it is often associated with deceit and evil?

Why should the serpent, or the snake, have been called a 'liar,' 'deceiver,' and that pathetic figure of mediaeval theology, the Devil, be called the "Father of Lies"? Why should it have been thought that the serpent in the Garden of Eden which tempted the first human pair to evil-doing, was an imbodiment of or the symbol of Satan? Why should the serpent have become the symbol of insinuating evil, of evil doing, of deceit? Or on the other hand, why should the silent, creeping serpent with its slow sinuous progress have been taken as the symbol of Wisdom or of the Initiate, as in the expression attributed to a very lofty source in the Christian New Testament: "Be ye wise as serpents and harmless as doves"?

The answer is simple enough. Just as the forces of Nature are neutral in themselves, and become what humans call 'good' or 'bad' because of their use or misuse by individuals, just exactly so a natural entity when employed as a symbol becomes usable in either a good or a bad sense. Such use as a symbol depends upon certain characteristics or qualities which the human mind by force of association of ideas, chooses or separates off from other characteristics or qualities, and employs in a symbolic or metaphorical sense in order to depict either abstract or concrete ideas. This fact is shown for instance in the Sanskrit language, where Initiates of both kinds, i.e., of both the Right-Hand Path and the Left-Hand Path, are referred to in words conveying serpentine ideas or characteristics. The former kind, otherwise called the Brothers of Light, are more properly designated as Nâgas; whereas the Brothers of Darkness or of the Shadows are more properly designated as Sarpas, this latter word from the Sanskrit verbal root *sṛip*, meaning 'to crawl,' 'to creep' in sly and stealthy manner, and hence metaphorically 'to deceive.'

We see here the main reason why the serpent or snake has in probably all countries, and certainly in all times, been used as a symbol or emblem on the one hand of the Brothers of Light and their servants, and on the other hand of the Brothers of Darkness and their slaves. The reason is obvious, because both the Brothers of Light and the Sons of the Dark are focuses of power, of subtil thought and action, of wisdom and energy in the former case righteously and lawfully applied, and therefore belonging to the 'right hand'; and in the other case, wrongly or evilly applied to the uses of the 'left hand.' But, mark you, both uses apply to the cases of initiates, because both the initiates of the right-hand and of the left-hand are alike in one thing: they employ subtilty, the forces of Nature, secret wisdom, or rather secret knowledge. The same powers of Nature were employed by both — one class used these powers for impersonal and holy ends; the other class used these same powers and energies for unholy and evil ends. One class, as just said, are the Nâgas, the spiritual 'serpents' of Light, who are subtil, benevolent, very wise, and endowed with the spiritual power to cast off the garment, i.e. the skin or body, when the initiate has grown old, and to assume another fresher, younger, and stronger, at will. This class are all kindly, always inoffensive, perpetually engaged in works of human beneficence, and are still and secret in their operations, partly in order to avoid the plaudits of foolish men.

The other class are insinuating, worldly-wise, worldly-shrewd, deceitful, venomous in motive and action, therefore very dangerous, and yet using the same powers as the former class, but used for evil ends. Thus it is that on the one hand you will find in all the greater of the old scriptures, 'serpents' spoken of as symbols of wisdom, of the Sons of Light, possessing power, knowledge, love, and glory, as being Sons of the Sun; and, on the other hand, why other 'serpents,' 'snakes,' are spoken of as being symbols of the dark, often called the Black Brothers, who are essentially from Nature's own standpoint wrongdoers, engaged in their unholy work of deceivers of human hearts and minds, and all too often succeeding in their diabolic work by means of lies and misrepresentations.

SIGNIFICANCE OF THE SWASTIKA

In using the symbol of the swastika, in which direction should the arms be bent, to the right or to the left? Please explain its significance when one finds it with the arms bent either one way or the other. Is one aspect good and the other malevolent?

There is really no significance whatsoever — at least for present-day purposes — in which of the two directions the arms of the swastika may be bent over. H. P. B. in the beginning used them one way, and in her later work she used them with the arms bent in the other direction; and I do not think that either form was deliberately chosen. It just happened to be drawn in the one or the other way each time. The value of the swastika is in its larger structural significance; and the way in which the arms are bent is of very little present-day significance.

However, answering the question more particularly: Suppose that we have the arms of the swastika bent towards the right, signifying that the swastika runs or turns to the left. Now this could possibly mean that the swastika is moving on the left-hand path; but it could also mean that the user is moving from the right-hand in order to help unfortunates on the left. Or, take it moving in the other way, from left to right. Someone here might say that this form signifies that the swastika is on the left-hand path and that it is trying to move towards, in order to injure, someone on the right-hand path; or one could say equally well that the user is on the left-hand path and is moving out of it into the right-hand path.

So, you see, as there are a number of different interpretations, that either way may be considered right, the matter reducing itself to a merely personal preference. Most of us prefer it in the form which we use when printed on most of our books and pamphlets, and usually in our seal.

The points of mysticism involved with regard to triangles are quite different, because here there is a very ancient and quite definite significance attached to the way in which the apex of the triangle points. If the apex of a triangle points downwards it signifies a falling or descent from spirit into matter, i.e., an attraction to the matter world; contrariwise, if the apex points upwards, it means a rising towards the sun or into the spirit, just as the flame of fire rises upwards and vanishes in a peak or point. The interlaced triangles do not signify the desire of anyone to move in either direction, however, but this figure merely pictures Nature's two perpetually opposing energies: the spiritual energy rising upwards, and represented by the triangle with its apex upwards; and the material or descending energy or energies going downwards, represented by the triangle with its apex pointed downwards. When these two triangles are thus conjoined, they are called Vishnu's, or sometimes Śiva's, seal or symbol, or what the Westerners sometimes call Solomon's seal.

Of course I do not deny that with regard to the swastika, it is possible that careful and accurate archaeological research might prove that one of the two forms in the distant past was preferred by our own School; but this, I fancy, would not be very easy to prove, and it is only as a possibility that I point it out. At the present day I would not criticize anyone for having the bent ends of the swastika pointing in either direction, because one can find a good significance in either way, and an evil significance in either way. The real meaning of the bent arms of the swastika is motion, i.e., motion forwards, which means progress, evolution, combined of course with the other symbolism of the crossed lines, the vertical and the horizontal.

The three joined running legs which form the coat of arms of the Isle of Man are the same mystical idea of progress in one direction or another under another form, and a very graphic form, too. This interesting and curious symbol consists of three legs all running in the same direction at high speed and connected at the hip parts; and the distances between the three legs are equal around the circle, which means that each leg is separated from the other leg by an angle of 120 degrees, although the circle itself is not shown in this coat of arms or emblem — unless indeed the circle may be taken as being the periphery of the seal on which the symbol is engraved.

The Seven Jewels of Wisdom

What is the significance of the Seven Jewels of Wisdom as discussed in your book Fundamentals of the Esoteric Philosophy?

Collectively they comprise the full treasury of human possible wisdom and knowledge. All initiations in the Secret School are but enlargements of understanding of these seven fundamental principles of knowledge which point with emphatic finger to the structure and carpentry of the Universe around us — a structure and carpentry existent not merely on this lowest of cosmic planes which we call the physical Universe; but existent likewise in and on, because actually building, all the planes, realms, spheres, of the Invisible Universe.

All of H. P. B.'s *Secret Doctrine* was written around, so to speak, as central pivots of esoteric thought, these Seven Treasuries of Wisdom, these seven mystery-keys, 'Jewels' as they have been very properly called. Furthermore, all the religious and philosophic books of the ancients, especially those dealing with the Mysteries, have been written around them. These Seven Jewels, again, are always given for study to chelas who are just putting their feet upon the Pathway. They are likewise given to chelas who stand higher than the former, higher because stronger, knowing more, feeling more, realizing more, seeing more. They are also given for study to the Mahâtmans themselves by the still greater Teachers of these last named Great Ones; and I daresay that it would be no exaggeration to state that the very gods in their azure thrones study these Seven Jewels of Wisdom, as we humans do, but study them with their own godlike and penetrating understanding. Verily, these Jewels are filled full of meaning, and the more you study them the more do you finally come to realize that they are esoteric keys opening up to you all the portals of comprehension of your own inner and indeed Inmost Self.

You cannot understand these Seven Jewels, even imperfectly, until you have begun at least to be them yourself. The only true way of understanding anything is by being it. No man can understand love who is not a lover; and here I do not mean anything merely sentimental, although this indeed is included in the general rule. No man can understand reason until he begins himself to be a reasoner. No man can understand or feel feeling, unless he begins himself to be a feeler.

Hence I say that the Seven Jewels are put into the hands of neophytes, of chelas, of advanced chelas, of Masters, yea even of the Nirmânakâyas, because they are cosmic keys, wonder-keys. You will find these seven Jewels in all the ancient sacred scriptures, scattered about it is true, but you will find them if you look for them. It is only in our own Theosophical books that you will find them in listed or categorical form. Nevertheless, as stated, in all the ancient sacred scriptures of the world you will find them: perhaps not all together in a single scripture, perhaps only two or three in a single scripture, perhaps one here and one there and another one elsewhere, and with hints at the existence of the others in the list; but if you study them and thus learn to know them when you encounter them in your reading, you will find them in these ancient works. They may be named by other names, and explained in manners other than those familiar to us in our Theosophical reading; but all this last is but the garments in which these wonder-keys are clothed. The point is that the wonder-keys can be found where I have told you.

And finally, I venture to say that there is no interesting problem that our study of Theosophy can give to us which cannot be answered by a sufficiently adequate study of these *sapta-ratnâni* or Seven Jewels of Wisdom.

The Question of Creation

Looking back at the beginning of all things, of the origin of life — how is it possible that something could exist, something could be created, out of a mere nothing? Who is the power that created this?

That is an old-fashioned question. I think that in the Christian religion only this false idea exists, that the Kosmic Spirit is a creator who, out of nothing at all: vacuity, utter emptiness: creates the Universe. This teaching is not found in any other part of the human race, at least not so baldly stated, except perhaps among a few tribes of savages. It is found in no other great religion; and furthermore it is not found in the original teachings of Christianity. It is found only in the theological works of certain Fathers of the Church and those who followed them. All the more ancient religions of mankind, the greatest philosophies that human genius has brought forth, teach that our Universe and all in it come forth out of the bosom of the Kosmic Spaces, as reimbodiments of what had existed before;

precisely as the ego of man, the soul of man, comes forth from the spiritual worlds into the physical world, and after death passes again into the spiritual worlds for a rest, only to re-appear in the next reincarnation in the physical world, again to die, again to rest, to re-appear anew.

Just as the human soul thus reincarnates, coming out of the bosom of the worlds invisible, so do the Universes in boundless space appear periodically out of the womb of the Infinite, run their majestic courses as we see them in the midnight skies: stars, nebulae, interstellar spaces: run their long, age-long periods of evolution, and then pass away to appear again but on a higher plane; for evolution or development rules in all the Universe as it does here on Earth.

How do you know that man and the Universe were 'created'? We have no proof of this. That is a theory. It is imaginary. All we do know is that things appear and live and vanish, and that other things appear and live and vanish; and all the greatest philosophers and religionists of ancient times, and the greatest scientists of today, are inclined to look for a Universe which appears out of the womb of Space, runs through its evolutionary course, and dies as man dies. All the Hindû schools of philosophy teach this same truth; and they point to the analogy with man. Man appears from a microcosmic germ of life. He is born as a baby, he grows to maturity, he does his work, he dies. But whence came those forces which we call a man? It is not chance. Chance is an old-fashioned word that modern scientific thinkers have abandoned. Remember that man himself, a child of the Universe, has everything in him that the Universe has: the divine, the spiritual, the intellectual, the psychical, the astral, the vital-physical; and therefore man is the rule by which we may judge the Universe, because what is in the whole is in the part. Man himself has a spirit, has a faculty, by which he can penetrate into the spirit of the Universe because the two are one.

THE EVOLUTIONARY URGE

What is the cause and the aim of the evolutionary urge which influences all entities?

The urge behind evolution and the objective which this urge is impelling us towards, is simply the divine hunger in the Universe to grow greater, to advance, to grow: Excelsior! It is innate in the Universe. Why this is so, no one can say. Perhaps the gods do not know. All we men can say is that it is so. Everything grows and yearns to grow greater, to become grander, to rise, to advance, to evolve; and the objective is to become one self-consciously with the Boundless — something which never can be reached! Therein is infinite beauty, for there is no final ending for growth, which means progress or evolution, in beauty and splendor and wisdom and love and power. The Boundless Universe is our home.

What we may call a blind striving or struggle for betterment in the atoms, becomes in man a self-conscious yearning to grow, a recognition that man is a growing thing, a son of the gods; and this same urge becomes in the gods a divine knowledge that they are parts of the Universe and are growing to take a vaster self-conscious part in the Universal Labor.

EXPLANATION OF 'GROUP-SOUL'

Some Theosophists often speak about what they call a 'group-soul,' referring to the monads of plants and animals evidently. What are the teachings about such a conception of a 'group-soul'?

The term 'group-soul' is used in an attempt to find a word which would describe, however imperfectly, the peculiar aggregates of entities more or less on the same plane or grade of evolution and who, because of that fact, find themselves more or less reimbodying in groups or aggregates. In one respect the term 'group-soul' is unfortunate, because it gives the idea that there is but one soul in the same plane which manifests through all the individual members of such aggregate groups; and this is inaccurate.

If the questioner will remember that individuality as an achieved factor in cyclic, organic evolution, is definitely won, although as yet imperfectly won, when an evolving monad reaches the point of the attainment of self-consciousness, as in human beings, he will readily understand the idea behind the term 'group-soul.' Minerals, for instance, are enormously alike; i.e., minerals in a particular group or aggregate are all like each other, although, of course, there are different groups or aggregates within the grander group of the monads manifesting or expressing their force in the mineral kingdom. Similarly so with plants. There is the aggregate group of the oaks, for instance, or of the plum-trees, or of the rose-bushes, or of the strawberries, or of the pampas-grass, or of the date-palm, etc., etc. But all of the plants together may again be considered to form a still larger and more general group called the vegetable kingdom.

Going higher in the scale of organic beings, we come to the animal kingdom, where individuality is still more perceptible; and yet even the beasts can hardly be said to have attained self-conscious individual existence. They are conscious; they have the faint consciousness of self-consciousness and show it; but they don't act as willing and discriminating individuals in the full extent that human beings do.

Reaching the human kingdom, we enter again a new kingdom, because it is the kingdom of self-consciousness, of individualized monadic activity. But even here the same general rule prevails; and the entire human kingdom in one sense may be called an aggregate group, as is sufficiently obvious, with smaller racial groups composing it or forming its component parts.

The reader has but to carry the thought herein briefly outlined in both directions, forwards and backwards, and he will readily understand somewhat of the nature of the elementary kingdoms in the beginning and of the dhyân-chohanic kingdoms ahead of the human kingdom.

I repeat that the term 'group-soul,' when properly understood is expressive enough; but it is unfortunate for the reason already mentioned.

WHERE AM 'I'?

Where on earth am 'I' in this wilderness of swabhâvas and individualities and I's and inner gods? Who am I and where am I? I am sevenfold, I have seven âtmans or divinities co-operating to make me what I am, as chemical elements co-operate to make an entity; but which parts of this compound are that part of me which co-operate to say 'I', that little unimportant part of me which is so aggressive? What part of me is I, and what part is not?

Man is all his sevenfold being, from the divine downwards through all intermediate stages, even to the body. All is the individual, so to speak. We may express it perhaps to our minds as a pillar of glory, a column of light extending from divinity to the physical man. Now, where our center of consciousness at any one time may be, I take it that is the part we for that time speak of as our I. The beast has it down here; we humans have it a bit higher; the Masters have it somewhat higher still; the Buddhas and Christs still higher, the divinities on a still higher stage of the scale. All the sevenfold being is himself, so to speak, and his I is that point upon which he dwells in conscious selfhood at the time.

Of course this does not change the other fact that just because there are several monads in man, so there are several actual monadic I's or egos. But this is another story.

LOST SOULS, LAGGARD EGOS, AND THE DESCENT OF MATTER

In THE MAHATMA LETTERS TO A. P. SINNETT *on page 47 there is the following:*

Matter found entirely divorced from spirit is thrown over into the still lower worlds — into the *sixth* 'GATE' or 'way of rebirth' of the vegetable and mineral worlds, and of the primitive animal forms. From thence, matter ground over in the workshop of nature proceeds *soulless* back to its Mother Fount; while the *Egos* purified of their dross are enabled to resume their progress once more onward. It is here, then, that the laggard *Egos* perish by the millions.

Does this refer to the doctrine of the lost souls, or is there some other doctrine involved?

It is not at all astonishing that this passage should confuse you because it is very condensed, extremely recondite, and refers to two things at least. First, the Master here writes of material substance which is unable, because of a tendency to go downwards, to rise along the Ascending Arc. It continues downwards and is finally dissipated into its component elements. This is done in the 'Planet of Death,' if you understand me. This refers to matter which is "entirely divorced from spirit," in other words matter in its lowest hierarchical or gross form. Then the Master goes on to say that matter which is thus divorced from spirit, or in other words which has become *soulless,* i.e., which has wrenched itself away from the guiding influence of the imbodied souls, proceeds back to its primitive nature or element; whereas the egos or 'souls' that have been thus liberated from their too grossly material attachment resume their progress onwards, but have to do so by evolving new intermediate vehicles or sheaths of consciousness between themselves and the gross matter which after this breaking of the tie between them they no longer have.

Matter which thus is on the way to divorce itself from the guiding energy of spirit or 'soul' falls, as it were, in its peregrinations or cyclings into lower kingdoms: For instance, leaving the human, the matter thus divorcing itself from spirit is attracted to the animal, vegetable, and mineral worlds, and the monads which compose this matter thus divorced, monads which are in their primal or elementary stages of evolution, return to the Mother Fount, as said above, where they begin their own peregrinations upwards again.

When reference is made to the matter-side as just above described, this concerns the life-atoms or monads in the life-atom stage that cannot rise or retain their contact with spirit. Their further evolutionary tendency is downwards; and in this connexion remember that all material substance is composed essentially of life-atoms. The wood of the table before me is made of life-atoms passing through this particular phase of their evolutionary path. The gold in my seal-ring is likewise life-atoms in a mineral phase; the life-atoms which compose the substance of my clothing, likewise the life-atoms of my flesh, or of my bones — and yours too — are life-atoms passing through that particular phase of their myriad peregrinations.

However, there are hosts of life-atoms which have been sufficiently spiritualized or evolved in previous manvantaric manifestations so that when they reach the lowest point of evolution in this manvantara, they can pass it safely and can continue upwards — *ensouled*. But many millions, billions, trillions, decillions — indeed, an uncountable number of life-atoms — have not yet reached that point of safety in their evolution where they can continue to evolve in connexion with spirit in *this* manvantara; and it is *these* life-atoms — or monads in these states — which form the material substances that go down into the lower realms, and are there ground over in Nature's workshop and proceed *soulless* "back to the Mother Fount." Nevertheless the egos or 'souls' which have been evolving and using *these* life-atoms as vehicles or as bodies in their aggregate, had long since reached the point of safety in their evolution, and no longer feel the attraction matterwards as do these descending monads or life-atoms; consequently those egos, because they are quasi-spiritual, pass the turning-point or point of danger in perfect safety, and continue their evolution, although deprived of, or freed from, their unworthy atomic vehicles.

The Master then says: "It is here that the laggard *Egos* perish by the millions." This particular sentence has reference to certain hosts of retarded or unevolved life-atoms or monads or 'egos' which, because they are not sufficiently spiritualized to pass the danger-point, fall into the maelstrom and are attracted downwards, and there they perish for that manvantara. These last egos are not the former egos which were spoken of as those which were "purified of their dross," and which pursue their progress once more onwards. These egos who perish by the millions are the highest class of the material monads, but are not yet sufficiently spiritualized, as said before, to pass the danger-point and ascend along the upward arc.

Turning now to human egos, we have also a third class which are the least progressed of the first class above spoken of. I now refer to that relatively small number of retarded or unevolved human egos which at a certain point on the Ascending Arc begin to lag and to tire in the climb, so to speak; and little by little they are left behind until finally they can go no further and gradually slip backwards towards matter again. These are those instances of what we Theosophists call 'lost souls.' These are the egos which are so sunken in matter, so drunken with the fumes, as it were, of the lowest kingdoms of earth, that when in their evolution down the descending arc they finally reach our Planet D, this Earth, they cannot go far or rise far with the rest of the army of advancing egos who are more spiritualized; and this is because they are too heavy still with matter, and consequently their attraction is not upwards, but is downwards; and these are what we call 'lost souls.' They are very rare instances, almost as rare in their occurrence in the human race as are the Masters rare at the other pole of being in the human kingdom. But nevertheless, through the ages and speaking in the aggregate the number of lost souls is relatively large.

This question, therefore, as you may easily see, is a very abstruse and difficult one to answer, because it contains so many similar but different points of teaching. I will try to give you two illustrations which, perhaps, will clarify the matter in your mind. Every systemic universe, although an organic entity *per se*, i.e., a unity or an individuality, is nevertheless composite, that is, composed of different parts or portions, and indeed of different elements reckoning from the highest of such a universe to the lowest. Now every universe is a kosmic hierarchy enclosing a vast number of subordinate hierarchies; but above such a universe or kosmic hierarchy there are other kosmic hierarchies rising upwards, and below such a kosmic hierarchy there are other kosmic hierarchies which are inferior. All these kosmic hierarchies, small or great, are filled with hosts or multitudes of evolving, living entities, from gods in the highest realms to evolving monads or life-atoms in the lowest realms. Consequently, these hosts of living beings are in many different states of evolutionary development.

Now then: these hierarchies feed each other. I mean by this that if, for instance, we take Hierarchy A, this Hierarchy feeds Hierarchy B beneath it by the failures in Hierarchy A above it. The failures of Hierarchy A which cannot proceed in evolution when they reach the danger-point or turning-point upwards, then drop into the lower Sphere, i.e., into Hierarchy B, and there they form certain ones of the evolving hosts of Hierarchy B. Similarly the Hierarchy above what we have called Hierarchy A feeds with the failures of this Hierarchy, Hierarchy A. Thus there is a constant flow of Lives from the one Hierarchy into another Hierarchy.

The second illustration will clarify the former, and also I hope will clarify my general answer: We men are in one very true sense 'failures' of the hierarchy above us, and took the downward path at the lowest point of our evolution in the hierarchy above us when we had reached that lowest point; and this was because we were then insufficiently spiritualized to ascend along the rising arc. The meaning obviously therefore is that we have found our level in the Kosmic Life, and continue our evolution in and upon our new level or plane. Here in this hierarchy we are now evolving, rising upwards, and of course forming an aggregate part of this our present hierarchy; and in it we are growing, learning, progressing, evolving; and the time will come in the distant future when we shall have so well learned all the lessons that the matter, i.e., the substance, and the energies of this hierarchy can teach us, that this matter and these energies no longer will attract us downwards, for we shall have outgrown such attraction, progressed beyond it, i.e., we shall have become sufficiently spiritualized so that our attractions or tendencies are upwards; and then we shall return to our superior home, the hierarchy above us.

It is for this reason, among others, that in some of the ancient mystical scriptures men have been called 'fallen angels,' fallen gods, for that verily is what we are! We are spiritual monads fallen or sunken in the realms and whirlpools of the material worlds. Do not however confuse this teaching of fallen gods or fallen monadic life-atoms with the other fact or teaching dealing with the so-called 'lost souls.' The lost souls pertain to our present state of evolution, and are the 'failures' amongst us now: they are those unfortunate beings who have lost, or who have broken, the link with the god within. A 'lost soul' is one whose inner constitution is dissolving, going to pieces; and in the case of a 'lost soul,' the Monad or the inner god which had ensouled such a 'lost soul' must begin anew in its own realms to build up a 'new' human soul in which it can work and evolve in human spheres in the far distant future.

DOUBTFUL VALUE OF CERTAIN VISIONS

Often I have wonderful experiences on inner planes, and inner visions come to me. Sometimes I feel frightened or disturbed. Does this show that I am progressing spiritually?

These 'inner visions,' so-called, are not uncommon in the case of devotional characters, and usually signify that the soul and mind are experiencing changes in the inner life, and therefore are contacting planes between our ordinary earth-plane and the spiritual plane, and therefore usually in the psychical realms; but one must exercise great care in these matters.

In fact, it will be much better if you can try to turn away from these things, because they are so distracting to the quiet and the peace of the spiritual life. Try to bring calm — beautiful, sweet calm — and the spiritual vision of life and godlike splendor, into your thoughts; and then when these 'visions' come, resolutely turn your eyes away, and with all calm and peace refuse to see them, and try always to expand the heart and the mind with thoughts and feelings of love for all that is, both great and small, far and near, high and low. Then the blessed Light will come stealing into the heart, a little at first and very gently, but as you practise this 'yoga of the spirit,' the Light will steadily grow stronger.

The secret is to cultivate this inner calm belonging to the spirit, this inner peace of the soul, and then the vibrations become calm and quiet and rhythmical, and no outside forces can touch us. We then *know* that we are in the care of the Great Law whose "protecting arms," as Katherine Tingley used to say, are constantly around us. Then also the very gods and our inner warrior will be with us, and we shall feel their presence.

THREE KINDS OF DEATH

Generally speaking, there are three kinds of death: First, the natural death resulting from illness or old age. Second, that by accident. Third, that by self. I have heard that Theosophists say that these three kinds of people have different experiences after death, but I never had any satisfactory explanation why it should be so, or any authority for such teaching.

I would suggest that this questioner study our Theosophical doctrines. There are indeed three kinds of death, generally speaking: death by disease or natural causes when the body is worn out like a machine — because it is a machine in one sense which wears out; death by violence or accident; and death by suicide. These are three different ways of dying. The first is when Nature herself quietly withdraws the soul from the worn out body, and then the usual processes take place. This is the general rule. Then comes death by violence or accident, and this is different from death by suicide; because although suicide is by violence also, it contains a tremendous factor in the suicide himself, an ethical factor which death by accident does not contain. Therefore logically, obviously, death by suicide, which introduces the ethical factor, is different from death by violence or accident. The soldier who is killed on the battle-field, or a man who is killed by some lunatic or brigand, has not the same death as the man who kills himself through cowardice — for all suicides are cowards, say what you will.

Let us try to illustrate by the case of sleep, the brother of death, the other side of death. When a man is very tired he falls asleep by Nature's own working, simply drops off and sleeps. Again, a man may be given a drug which makes him sleep, although the body is not tired. This is like death by violence. A drug is a violent way of bringing about sleep. It may even produce death if the drug is given too largely. Then there is the case of the man who himself takes drugs continuously, not once, but continuously. You see these three are quite different ways of bringing about sleep: Nature's way let us say, the doctor's way in order to give a sick man a little sleep which he needs, and the drug-addict. Nature obviously here acts in three different ways, but they all produce sleep.

So it is with death. The man who dies by Nature's way, passes through all the changes of the kâma-loka until he reaches the devachan, quietly, simply, without pain, without consciousness, just like a tired man falling asleep. The man who is killed, like the soldier on the battle-field, dies of course because he is killed; but he is not yet ready to die. His time to die has not yet come by Nature's own laws. So he remains unconscious it may be for years in the astral world until the time in years comes which would have brought his death in the usual way. And then he too dies in the inner worlds and enters the devachan; the reason being that every man has a certain quantity of vitality so to say, and until this quantity of vitality is exhausted, burnt out, until the machine is tired out, the man cannot die, I mean die completely. The man who is killed on the battle-field remains in perfect peace but unconscious in the inner worlds until the time when he would have died if he had not been killed on the battle-field. Then he too enters the devachan.

But the man who commits suicide does so because he is afraid. He is terrified at something. It may be that he is afraid of disgrace; it may be that he is afraid to meet life and its problems like a man, and he kills himself. His consciousness is full of these thoughts, full of these day-dreams, fear, fear, fear, until he can stand it no longer. And as man is fundamentally consciousness, when he kills himself there is a short period of unconsciousness; and then the unfortunate suicide awakens in the astral world and lives, as it were, in an evil dream, going over in his consciousness again and again and again, all the time for years it may be, the horrible thoughts, the cowardly thoughts, the terrors, the fears that made him kill himself, and the act of self-killing, just like the drug-addict; for the drug-addict has most horrible dreams, the drug-addict goes crazy over his dreams.

Remember that man is fundamentally consciousness; and therefore the processes that follow the death of the physical body are changed by the one or the other of these three kinds of dying.

THE DEAD AND OUR PRAYERS

Is it right to pray for the dead ones?

I hope I will not offend anyone's feelings if I tell you I do not think it is wrong, but I do not think it will do any good! Nature in her wonderful compassion, in her harmony, in the great music which is at the heart of things, knows far better than we humans do what is good for our dear ones who die. They are well cared for.

It is not wicked to pray for the dead, but to whom will you pray? Do you wish to tell the great Spirit of the Universe what you, poor man or woman, think is good for your dear dead? Nature knows infinitely better than we do. If you pray for the dead and you get happiness in it and consolation in it then you may pray. But there is no solid good in it *per se*.

Remember this: That the dead are infinitely well cared for. What is important is to live the life beautiful while we live; then we need not fear death. Death is beautiful, very beautiful.

Love, pure holy love, can reach even beyond the frontiers of death, and reach our loved ones; but it must not be a selfish love, because this hinders Nature's work in the invisible worlds. Let our love for our dear dead be impersonal; and our best prayer for the dead is this love. It is helpful, and ourselves are benefited and made better by it.

LIFE LIKENED TO A PACK OF CARDS

The other day I was told by a Theosophist that just before birth we have a choice as to the life about to start on earth; but I have always understood that, since we are the sum-total of all that we have done in past lives, we have no choice, but that our lives are already determined before birth, like a pack of cards in a dealer's hand?

Both these statements are correct: first, that our destiny in life can be likened to a pack of cards, if one cares to use this figure of speech; second, that we have free will. Is it a contradiction to say that a man must undo the wrongs that he did? He does so because he has free will.

We have, then, not one life only preceding this present one in which there would be but a single path of action to follow, following the figure of speech of a pack of "stacked cards"; but we have lived lives innumerable before the present one; and in no one single past life has any human being been able to exhaust all the causes set in motion therein — bring to fruition all the seeds that were then sown; and it is just because of this stored-up karmic treasure that we have to live life after life after life after life in order to work these causes out.

In each life we play a new game, but in playing that game we use the pack of cards that we select from former use of it, and take that pack as we formerly shuffled it. The pack of cards is the life; and before the soul reimbodies itself, guided by the divinity within it, that wonderful faculty of free will, the power of choice, it has in consequence the power of selecting those particular and confluent, congruent causes which in that life then opening it can best work out; in other words it plays the pack of cards which it takes up again in a new game in accordance with its intelligence. This is simply the employment at the beginning of a new birth on earth of what every normal man does his whole life long. He selects from moment to moment the pathway which seems to him best; and there are possibly a thousand million by-roads or pathways that he might have selected at each such moment of choice; just exactly as he plays from the cards in his hand according to his best judgment. Do you catch the idea? The cards are stacked, but they are played, when dealt to the player by life, according to the player's intelligent choice.

We have an infinitude of experiences behind us; and when each new life opens, when we appear on the stage to play our new rôle, a new game, we do so according to the rôle that we have chosen from the book — in this case the book of memory and vision.

Those causes not selected by us we shall have to imbody in a subsequent selection, when in some future new life we shall begin again. But in any one life there are certain conditions, a certain path of action, before us, certain civilizations, certain families — and the waiting Higher Self sees this field of choice, this path, and this path, and that path, just exactly as a man does in driving his motor-car. When he comes to bifurcating roads he knows not the pathway, but he says: "I will take this path in preference to the other two or three or four branching out from this point." He might have taken another; but in either case he makes his choice.

Proof of After-Death States

There are many philosophical teachings concerning the condition of men after death, but they all seem to me quite arbitrary as they cannot be supported by intellectual evidence. Do you really believe that we can know anything about the conditions after the passing?

This question is not a very well considered one, and is built on a false basis. The theory in this question is that what our senses do not tell us about is non-existent; and where would our modern scientists be if all they knew about the Universe was only what we could see, touch, taste, hear, or smell! No scientist has ever seen an atom, nor an electron, nor a proton. No scientist has ever seen the center of the sun. No scientist can explain human feeling. As Kant, the great German philosopher said in substance, no man has ever successfully reduced to naught the ethical sense which dwells in the human heart. There is a way to go behind the veil of the outward seeming; and if a man trains himself and lives the life, he will know the doctrine, not merely think about it but know it.

The question is like this: A blind man says: There are no museums in which great and wonderful works of art or archaeology are exhibited, because he does not see. But other men who are less blind know that such museums exist. And there are other men, clear-eyed, who build the museums and paint the pictures, and create the works of art. Live the life and you will know the doctrine!

This question is not a very thoughtful one, nor a very sensible one, for it can be reduced to this: What I cannot experience by physical senses has no existence; and we all know this is a lie, for the most beautiful things in human life are unseen, unheard, untouched. Man's intuitions, man's sense of beauty, his sense of right and wrong and justice and harmony and purity: these are the great mainsprings of human civilizations, and these are the things which move men's minds and hearts. It is ideas which make men great, and it is ideas which make civilizations, which build them up. And it is ideas which tear them down. Plato was right: Ideas rule the world. And the greatest of our modern scientists have given up the idea of our recent forefathers, that physical substance was the sole reality in the Universe. Now, with Theosophy, they say that physical substance is an illusion, and that the essence of the Universe is mind-stuff, consciousness. The whole Theosophical position is admitted by this. We are builded of mind-stuff, of consciousness. The atoms which build the mountain are essentially atoms of mind-stuff, of consciousness. It seems to me that the asker of this question has not kept up to date with modern scientific discovery. His mind, or her mind, lies in the past of fifty or a hundred years ago.

The mysteries after death! We live in the midst of death all the time. It is the most familiar thing to us. It is as familiar as life because it is a phase of life. There could be no death if there were no life. Death is an event, as the ultra-modern scientist puts it, an event in life, in consciousness. When a man sleeps he dies partially. Sleep is an imperfect death, death as we men call it is a perfect sleep. Death and sleep are brothers, said the ancient Greeks; but I tell you that they are more: sleep and death are one. And if men only knew it, every time men sleep, every time we lie down in our beds at night for rest and recuperation of mind and of body, we die partially; and that is why we rest. And when we have dreams, beautiful dreams or evil dreams, holy dreams or nightmares, it is because during our lives we have lived beautifully, grandly, or we have lived basely. So it is with death!

REINCARNATION AND THE EARTH'S POPULATION

How do you explain the increase of population on the Earth in connexion with the doctrine of Reincarnation? For instance, in Holland at the present time there is a great increase in population.

Examine the world. You will find one people increasing in numbers, but another people is decreasing in numbers. Look at the Roman Empire, the empires of Babylon and Persia, Egypt and the Far East. There, millions upon millions at one time filled their countries. Now Egypt is but a historic recollection; Babylon is mounds, hillocks of the dead; but our Occident contains nations swelling with every hundred years in population. The explanation is obvious. As one people or nation dies or decreases in number, the reincarnating egos go elsewhere to ever newer and fresher stocks which grow and increase and populate the portions of the Earth where they have their habitat.

Look at the Mexican Empire, and the Empire of the Incas in the times of Cortez and Pizarro — memories! Look at the population of Europe during the Middle Ages. As pointed out, the population of Holland among other countries is increasing rapidly; but this shows that a few hundred years ago its population was less — just what I have said. Consider Europe during the Middle Ages. A man could travel for days and scarcely come upon a village. Where were the human egos now so numerous there? In other parts of the world. There is a constant turning of the Wheel of Life. In one period one group of peoples hold the scepter of power and civilization, and their numbers swell with the incoming armies of reincarnating egos. Then their time comes to descend the Wheel of Life; the populations decrease and become smaller and smaller; but nations on the up-rise increase in population.

The truth of the matter is that it is our teaching that the population of the globe is limited. The present incarnated population is about two thousand million human beings, including everybody, savages and barbarians and civilized beings. Two thousand millions! But there are many more than these two thousand millions who are in the interior worlds waiting their time to take human bodies. I do not venture to say how many reincarnating egos there are to come to Earth. I would not even try to estimate. Possibly ten thousand millions, I do not know, but what I do know is that the populations of the Earth shift geographically. Sometimes it is Asia, sometimes it is America. At present it is the European peninsula and the Americas which show the upward rise. Asia is temporarily static but from appearances it would seem as if the coming great populous centers of the Occident will be the New World. But not yet; a thousand years from now perhaps.

The Nightmare of War

Is a great war necessary to make all people better and to make them see the errors which they have experienced?

My answer is No, and that this is a damnable doctrine. This is a doctrine from hell. Certainly not. When men are wise enough and use their hearts as well as their brains, war will be looked upon as a nightmare of the past. Ask the doctors if a man needs to have a high fever in order to get health. A high fever weakens him, depletes his store of vitality, and the body is weaker for ever afterwards as long as it lives.

On the other hand, out of evil will come good. Suffering and sorrow are our best friends. This is the other side. But when I am asked if suffering and sorrow in the form of war, which is insanity, are required in order that men may evolve, my answer is No, and this is an infernal doctrine.

THOUGHT AND FANTASY

What is the difference between thought and fantasy?

Thought is the activity of that part of our inner constitution which we men call the intellectual, the mânasic, to use the Sanskrit term. Fantasy is the product or result of the activity of that part of our constitution which we call the lower human soul. We are dealing in fantasies when we dream — dream at night or day-dream when we wake. This is fantastic, this is fantasy. We are using thought when we employ our intellect in reasoning, in intuitive visioning, and in the functions of the higher human consciousness.

THE SPIRITUAL STATE OF NIRVÂNA

We are taught that to reach spiritual development we must free ourselves from 'personality.' If we become truly impersonal and conquer 'the sense of separateness,' shall we lose every quality that distinguishes one person from another and become as alike as two peas in a pod? Is the Theosophical teaching of Nirvâna the obliteration of individuality? I hope not.

No, indeed! No one can be more irritated than I am concerning the misunderstandings about nirvâna current in the Occident, which is full of such misunderstandings about recondite teachings of a philosophic or esoteric character. The misunderstanding about nirvâna is simply the idea that after all beings have evolved through a mahâ-manvantara and have individually attained nirvâna, *ex hypothesi*, thereafter all Nature, as beings, sinks back into a dead uniform identity of consciousness. This is absolutely and wholly wrong.

One might as well ask oneself: What is the use of all the evolutionary effort of the Universe, and of its enormous multitudes of individuals, if they merely issue from homogeneity finally to fall back into it again? Nirvâna is not one uniform thing or state for every monad. Nirvâna means a state in which all the lower is washed out, or rather risen above, by the evolving armies of monads. But each monad, because it has gained individuality, reaches the nirvânic condition of cosmic freedom as a god-entity; and every monad, from the standpoint of individuality, is therefore more strongly individualized spiritually speaking than it was at the beginning of its cosmic evolution as an unself-conscious god-spark, although of course nirvâna as a generalizing term means the attainment of such spiritual condition by all.

Take Devachan as an illustration on a much lower plane. Devachan does not mean that every excarnate monad has the identical, the absolutely identic, visions and dreams. Not at all! And just so it is with nirvâna. Nirvâna means the rising above all the differentiated and therefore crippling elements of the lower spheres. The *process* is the same for all, but the nirvâna is unique for each Jîvan-mukta or freed monad.

Think it out for yourself, and do not misjudge Theosophy — nor the real teachings in this respect of the Buddha — because certain people you may happen to meet do not understand these deeper teachings, so suggestive and illuminating in their profundity and subtilty.

MIND, THE SLAYER OF THE REAL

I am continually asked the question why H. P. B. in THE VOICE OF THE SILENCE *states that "the mind is the slayer of the real." I would ask you to give me a little light on this so that I may deal with those who make a god of the materially intellectual in this age of admiration of the mind.*

Isn't it true! What is it that brings about diversity of feeling or of opinion among men? The mind, the brain-mind. What is it that prevents our receiving a greater truth than that which we now have? Preconceptions, prejudices, feelings against this or against that, the mind, the brain-mind. What is it that prevents intuition from flowing to our human consciousness in a steady stream? The mind through which it must pass. The mind is but an intermediate organ or faculty, and does things either from below or from above; and alas, most of us humans live in the lower mind.

Cannot you see why the mind is the slayer of the real? Of course the word 'slayer' is but a figure of speech. You might phrase it otherwise and say the mind filled with its tramping, useless, fugitive, silly thoughts keeps out all higher intuitions, all higher thoughts, all higher things. In other words, there is no room for them. You know what Bernard of Clairvaux, a Frenchman, once wrote in substance: Empty the mind of all that it has and is, and the spirit of Truth will enter in. This is the gist of his meaning. Just cleanse the mind of all the little lower passional small things, and the spirit of Truth will enter in.

In this fashion I think one can easily explain the statement in *The*

Voice of the Silence, that the mind, meaning the brain-mind, is the slayer of all that is real; and yet the brain-mind should be the instrument of the Real, it should be the organ through which the Real works within us, the receiving organ passing down even into our ordinary lives all the noblest that is in us.

LUNAR PITRIS BEFORE FOURTH ROUND

The first race of this (Fourth) Round was created by beings known as the Lunar Pitris or Fathers — the most progressed entities from the Moon Chain. What did and where were the Lunar Pitris before the Fourth Round?

The Lunar Pitris before the Fourth Round began were in their inter-global Nirvâna between Globe G or last of the preceding Third Round, and Globe A or first of the Fourth Round to follow. This explains 'where they were' and 'what they did.' If the question, however, rather asks: "What did and where were the Lunar Pitris before their entrance into this Fourth Globe D during this Fourth Round?" — then the answer is as follows: They were on and evolving in Globe C of this Planetary Chain; in other words, in Globe C of the Fourth Round. When they finished with Globe C on this Fourth Round, they passed to this Globe D or Fourth Globe of this Fourth Round.

MÂNASAPUTRAS BEFORE FOURTH ROUND

During the latter part of the third race that wonderful mystic event took place — the incarnation of the Mânasaputras — the Sons of Mind — into the hitherto mindless entities. What did and where were the Mânasaputras before the Fourth Round, also during the First, Second and Third?

The answer is precisely identic with the answer to the former question, only here we are dealing with the mânasaputras instead of the lunar pitris. In other words, the mânasaputras also were in their inter-global nirvâna after leaving Globe G at the end of the Third Round and before beginning their evolution on Globe A of the Fourth Round. If, however, the question rather means: "What did and where were the mânasaputras before the Fourth Round began on this Globe D, then the answer is the same as regarding the lunar pitris of the preceding question: they were evolving on Globes B and C or the globes which preceded Globe D or our Earth.

This question also deals with 'First, Second, and Third,' presumably meaning Rounds; and this latter part of the question is different in answer. During the First, Second, and Third Rounds, the mânasaputras were evolving on higher spiritual planes on and in realms of consciousness above

the seven globes of our planetary chain. They were waiting until the seven
globes of the planetary chain and the lunar pitris evolving on these seven
globes during the First, Second, and Third Rounds, had prepared fit, appropriate bodies in which the mânasaputras could incarnate, and in which
bodies they could work. These bodies finally became ready during the
Fourth Round, as is shown in H. P. Blavatsky's *The Secret Doctrine.*

Remember that both the mânasaputras and the lunar pitris evolve on all
the globes of the planetary chain, remembering also that the lunar pitris
begin this evolution from the very beginning, and build up the globes and
build up the bodies on those globes in preparation for the incarnation of
the mânasaputras, who, during the same long period of time are also evolving, but on planes superior to those on which the lunar pitris are evolving.

Even during the First Round on Globe A at the very end of its Globe-
Manvantara, there were certain ones of the mânasaputras who then appeared and formed the then humanity of Globe A. These were mânasaputric forerunners. The entire question of the Rounds and Races is exceedingly involved, although the general principles are simple and clear.

MEANING OF FOHAT

Can you tell us something of the deeper meaning of Fohat?

I wonder if, in your Theosophical study, you have ever thought of the
deep and illuminating information that so often can be garnered from a
study of the origins and etymology of words or names. Fohat may be considered to be an instance in point, for really it is a term of Mongolian
origin. The main verbal root is *fo,* or more properly *foh.* It is the Mongolian term used for the word Buddha or even Buddhi, or again often enough
for Buddha-Wisdom. It is so called for the following reason: Fohat, which
is essentially cosmic vitality, works and operates and performs its manifold
wonders, in weaving the web of universal being, because riding, or working
through it, or directing it, is the cosmic Buddhi — called Mahâ-Buddhi.
Fohat is the steed, the Thought is the rider. To this cosmic vitality, which
is the prâna, so to speak, of the universe, and representing in the universe
what the prânas are in our own bodies, did the Mongolians and the Tibetans
give the term or word, Fohat, which as said above, we may perhaps para-
phrase by rendering it as Buddha-life, Buddha-vitality.

Please note that here I am endeavoring to give to you the reason why
the Mongolians speak of the cosmic vitality in connexion with thoughts
properly ascribable to the terms Buddhi, Buddha, Bodha, Bodhi. Their
vision refused to see in the wonderful, symmetrical, mathematical, and harmonic structure of the universe, that purely imaginary play of blind and

soulless forces on dead matter which has been the bane of Occidental scientific thinking for the past hundred years or more. To these early Orientals the universe was an expression of cosmic Wisdom, of the cosmic Buddhi, of Mahâ-Buddhi; which guided, i.e., which rode, the elements or matters of the universe much as a rider rides, guides, and directs his living steed. Hence they called this cosmic vitality, connected invariably in their minds with the indwelling intelligence, by the term Fohat, to be paraphrased as I have above stated. To them, Fohat was not as cosmic energies are to most Occidentals, merely forces of Nature empty of all occult, mystical, and therefore real significance; but they gave to it the name we are discussing, because their consciousness conceived of the cosmic vitality ever active in universal being under its proper meaning — Buddha-life, the intelligent foundation of the manifested universe; the cosmic life, ridden by universal consciousness, universal wisdom, and therefore correctly understood to be universal life, imbodying and directed by universal intelligence. Fohat is the steed; Cosmic Thought is the rider.

RACIAL BUDDHAS

Will Gautama the Buddha be the only Buddha to appear among men during this Root-Race?

There are two Buddhas appearing in every Root-Race, one towards the beginning, one towards the middle or the end depending upon circumstances; but one of these two is especially devoted to the Root-Race as a Race. The same Buddhic influence, however, working through the especial Race-Buddha, manifests itself in quite a large number of Bodhisattvas, all belonging to the same Race, who may be called minor Buddhas; and these appear at periodic intervals during the Race. Gautama the Buddha was such a Bodhisattva in and through whom the Race-Buddha manifested its transcendent power.

There is a real esoteric mystery in all this which requires much more explanation than these few lines; but what has been said is quite correct as far as it goes and at least briefly answers the question.

To repeat: one Buddha or Buddhic Spirit for and devoted to every Root-Race. Yet every Root-Race sees the appearance of two Buddhas, one towards its beginning and one at about its middle or towards its end, depending upon circumstances. In every Root-Race, in addition to the above, there are quite a number of Bodhisattvas, very spiritual and highly evolved intellectual men, who are on their way to become in time Buddhas themselves, and who incarnate or manifest the influence of the Race-Buddha in the Race in which they themselves appear. These Bodhisattvas usually also are the individuals who appear at the beginning of every so-called 'Messianic cycle,' which is ordinarily of 2160 years.

The Buddha who appears about the middle or towards the end of a Race, mentioned above, is the particular Buddha of the following or succeeding Root-Race, who thus appears a little ahead of his own time, so to speak, in order to guide, in collaboration with the racial Buddha himself, the end of the Race towards coalescing with and connecting with the succeeding or following Root-Race.

A PLANET AND ITS SATELLITES

In THE OCEAN OF THEOSOPHY, *Judge says that the life-waves on this earth came from the moon-chain. This, then, explains the relation somewhat of the moon to our earth. How are we to understand, then, the relation of Jupiter and its so many satellites?*

If this questioner will study the various places in which I have referred to this matter, I admit in more or less veiled terms, he will, I think, understand. Each planet of the solar system has but one lunar parent, which lunar parent, considered as a fully entitized being is a planetary chain. The parent of the earth-chain was the lunar chain; and the parent of Globe D, our earth, was Globe D of the moon, of which we see the dead remnant or kâma-rûpic shell in the skies.

When a planet has more than one satellite, these satellites exist by reason of different causes; but I could name two. One only I will speak of, and it is the most usual case. Excepting the moon which is the actual parent of such a planet, Jupiter, for instance, the others may be called 'captures.'

THE PENALTY OF SEPARATENESS

If we are all inseparable parts of the Universe, what is the penalty for running counter to the Universe's fundamental law, and for trying to break ourselves away from an inseparable union?

The penalty for trying to cut yourself off from the Universe, which is utterly impossible of accomplishment, is that thereby you shrink to smaller compass than that which you had before. Your consciousness becomes shrunken, smaller, less wide, less expanded; and consequently you lose in both faculty and power. The whole aim of development, whether of atom or of man or of god, is an unfolding of latent powers and faculties within each one; and progress in evolution is marked by an expansion or increase of sympathy in ever enlarging spheres. If you turn your face backwards, instead of following Nature's fundamental law of progress which means an ever-expanding consciousness and ever more fully evolving power, you swim *in adversum flumen,* against the current, and you lose proportionately. You go backwards instead of forwards. Your consciousness shrinks; and instead of advancing forwards to become familiar with the gods our forefathers, which is the ultimate destiny of man, you go backwards, towards the beasts, towards the plants, towards the as yet unevolved infinitesimal entities that dwell in the rocks and make them.

There is the penalty for running counter to the Universe's fundamental law. You lose everything, and progressively.

SIGNIFICANCE OF DREAMS

Has every dream a spiritual significance, or are dreams simply the result of interchanging thought during the condition of sleep?

It would be impossible, I think, to say that all dreams have a spiritual significance, because then we would have to say that some of the frightful nightmares that men undergo have a spiritual significance. There are many kinds of dreams: good dreams, bad dreams, and indifferent dreams, holy dreams and unholy dreams, dreams of a spiritual character and dreams of a very material type. Some dreams can be called spiritual because in these cases of spiritual dreams they are the actual resultant of the spiritual part of man's constitution, the root of his being, the finest energy in him, working upon the physical brain, reaching out and touching it, feebly because the distance, so to say, is enormous between the Spirit and the physical body. But when the divine flame of the Spirit even touches by a ray the physical brain, then the dream is beautiful, very peaceful, full of majesty and prophetic.

On the other hand, there are dreams which are merely the reflex action of the workaday brain-mind, partly awake and partly asleep, and as it were making crazy runs, because the inner man, the real ego, is no longer dominating that physical brain with its steady current of will-power, and fixed habit. These last dreams that I now speak of are simply automatic repetitions, usually however distorted, of what the day brought forth. I will try to explain. A man passes his life long every day working in a manufactory and putting heads on pins, week after week he puts heads on pins. Suppose that man has a dream some night that he is standing at his bench putting heads on pins. Obviously it is but a reflex action of what the brain had in it during his working day. There is no spiritual thing in that at all. Take some other kind of dream. A man dreams of doing some evil thing, it does not matter what, something that is shameful. This too is the result of some hid part of that man's constitution trying to force its way into the brain, the result of some past thought or action. Because the thought or action was stamped upon the brain, the man on this night dreams it, repeats it, perfectly or imperfectly.

So you see there are many kinds of dreams. Dreams are simply the working of consciousness on the physical brain; and when the man is not fully asleep, when the brain is still a little awake, then he dreams: good dreams, or bad dreams, or indifferent dreams; and if these dreams are beautiful and holy, then they are spiritual, because it is the higher part of the man's being reaching this brain half-asleep, and touching it as it were. But when the dreams are evil, ignoble, impure, what you will, it is the result of the human being's daily life — perhaps not of the previous day, it may be the result of a thought or an action that the man had or did a month before or a year before. But whatever a man thinks or does is indelibly stamped on the brain.

Theosophical Attitude Towards Spiritism

What is the attitude of Theosophy towards Spiritism?

We Theosophists have no creeds and no dogmas. Consequently, anyone who believes in Universal Brotherhood is invited to join the Theosophical Society. We have in our ranks, I believe, Buddhists, Brâhmanists, Taoists, Christians, Spiritualists, materialists, agnostics, and even atheists! So a man can be a Spiritist and yet be a member of the Theosophical Society. If you ask me what *I* think about Spiritism, then I will answer what I think. I do not venture to say what other Theosophists think; because if I said what other Theosophists thought, it would be equivalent to proclaiming a dogma in the Theosophical Society; and this I cannot and will not do.

But I will tell you what I think. I believe that the spiritists in general are a body of very earnest, honest, good people, who are convinced that they can commune with the spirits of their loved ones who have passed beyond. Now I believe that this is absolutely wrong. I think it is an entire misunderstanding. It is perfectly true that there are mediums who are good, who are of a psychical constitution which is more or less unbalanced, not in equilibrium like the average man's is. And consequently they can do things or produce things which are unusual. But to say that these unusual things are the working of spirits from the other side has never been proved.

I do not want to hurt the feelings of any spiritist. But I would like to ask the spiritist this question: Have the spiritists ever given to the world since the first manifestations at Hydeville, in the State of New York, in 1848 I think it was — have they ever given anything of religious or philosophical or scientific value to the world? Any great natural truth explained? Not one! Any great religious truth elucidated? Not one! Any great scientific advance predicted or even explained? Not one!

I will go a little farther — and I ask forgiveness of my brothers, the spiritists, if my words hurt their feelings; I would not willingly hurt the feelings of anyone; but since I have been asked the question it is my duty to answer. I have studied this question, and I have found that the communications so-called, coming as they come through mediums from what they call 'spirits,' are as a rule really twaddle. It is what I have found to be the case. These communications often contain ordinary ethics, but ethics that everybody knows, and even then very badly expressed. The communications are often so paltry as to be merely trivial and often nonsense; and I for one refuse to believe that my dead father, for instance, could be guilty of some of the nonsensical twaddle that comes, as our dear brothers the spiritists say, through the mediums from the other side!

Now what really happens is this — and this is the teaching of all the Sages of the past ages who have warned men against these practices which we call necromancy or prophesying by means of the dead. They say this: that in the astral world, which is the world immediately beyond the physical world, consisting of matter less physical than ours, less material, a little more ethereal, there live the shades, the simulacra, the relics, of the astral bodies of dead men, astral corpses. Just as the physical body when the soul has left it is a physical corpse, just so in the astral world: when the soul has left the astral world it leaves behind these astral corpses. We call them shells; just as the physical body is a shell when the soul has left it. Now it is these astral corpses or shells which are attracted to séance-rooms, and they fasten themselves on sensitives who frequent such gatherings; and they can affect the mind, the brain, of the medium; and thus it is that sometimes communications are received through mediums which give the name of some dead person or tell of some little unimportant, usually foolish, incidents that happened to the dead person when he or she was alive.

But these astral remnants are not the glorious spirits of human beings. The spirit of a man when death comes has flown to its parent-star like a flash of lightning, quicker than lightning. All that remains in the physical world is the cadaver, the corpse. All that remains in the astral world is the linga-śarîra or astral body, an astral corpse. Do you begin to understand now? I do not care to say more because I do not want to hurt the feelings of anybody, and I suggest that if any are interested in what Theosophy says about spiritism they study our books, especially the books of H. P. Blavatsky who made a special point of dealing with this matter.

In conclusion, I should also say that many of the so-called true communications received in séance-rooms are actual psychical pickings of the brain, unconsciously done of course by the medium, of those who attend, and who may themselves have utterly forgotten that they had ever known or experienced or heard of the incidents thus picked out from what it is now popular to miscall the 'sub-conscious.'

MAGNETIC HEALING AT A DISTANCE

Doubtless you have received a great many psychic letters, which leads me to the following question. Is there, in your opinion, any possibility of magnetic healing at a distance?

I can only answer, Yes, of course. But I do so with a good deal of reluctance, and I will tell you why. I think it a very dangerous thing for a man, even with the best of motives, to attempt to use his magnetism upon another human being. I know that good can be done. But I also know that evil can be worked. I know that there are noble-minded men who do heal; but I think it extremely dangerous. I would not allow it on me. And if I loved a friend, I would never suggest that my beloved friend be submitted to the magnetism of any other human being. Do you need to ask me why? Just ask yourselves. No man is wise enough to be able to touch the mind or even the body of another human being magnetically. It is playing with fire.

I know that this answer may be a little unpopular; but it is not my duty to search for popularity, but to tell you what I know or believe, as the case may be, to be true. Magnetic healing really is but another form of hypnotism or psychologization, call it what you like; and this can be, and often is, made a devil's work; so much so that there are laws today in most civilized countries against the indiscriminate practice of hypnotism, particularly in the medical schools.

LESSER PATHWAYS TO TRUTH

The question has been asked, whether we Theosophists claim to be the only pathway along which truth can be found. Could you enlighten us about that?

I will answer this question by using the words of the great Frenchman, Victor Hugo: "In the night I accept the authority of the torches, although I know there is a sun." If Theosophy, in explanation, is the formulation in human language of Nature's operations and laws, then it is truth and utter truth; and the more we know of this truth the more we shall know our Theosophy. But there are certain human minds and certain human hearts for whom the glorious sun is too bright. They like the authority of the torches. They like the smaller lights because the smaller lights are more easy to follow, more indulgent, easier to understand. But some day they will walk out of the shadows where their only lights are the torches, out of the cave which Plato spoke of, where men saw only the dancing shadows on the wall. They will walk out into the sunlight. Then the torches will be laid aside.

About Group-Souls

Do animals after they die merge into a general 'soul reservoir' and lose their individuality in what may be called a 'group-soul,' or does each animal have its own separate monad, individualized?

While 'group-souls' is an unfortunate term and not quite correct, it nevertheless contains a germ of truth. If we remember that individualization proceeds steadily from the elementals up to the Dhyân-Chohans, and that all monads belong to or are affiliated with, one or other of the seven or ten or twelve Solar Logoi, or what are called 'Rays' by some, we at once see the real teaching behind this group-soul idea. Nevertheless any animal at any time is an expression of the indwelling monad just as much so as man is, just as much so as a plant is, just as much as a chemical atom is. But the farther back we go towards the chemical elements, the more closely are such monads bound together in families. We see this instanced, for example, in the minerals, which are much more alike, although divided into different kinds of minerals, than are the plants, which again are much more alike each other, although divided into different orders, genera, families, species, etc., than are the beasts. And again the beasts, although divided into various races, are more alike each other than are human beings. Perhaps a better word than group-souls, or block-souls, which was a term used in H. P. Blavatsky's time, would be kingdoms.

The monads in the lower kingdoms are much more closely interlocked and more alike each other than are the more individualized monads in the higher kingdoms. But it is entirely wrong, wholly erroneous to say that the monad of a beast, for instance, sinks back into an ocean of soul, or into a group-soul, and never again issues forth, but that merely new differentiations of the ocean issue forth, new droplets. Keep the monad traveling through time and space constantly in your mind, struggling ever to express itself more fully as its vehicles become more greatly individualized, and you will have the correct teaching. But the monad is an individual from its earliest appearance in any manvantara as an unself-conscious god-spark, from our standpoint. The monad actually never is an elemental transforming into a mineral, transforming into a plant, transforming into a beast, and then transforming into a man. This is wrong. But the monad manifests first in the mineral kingdom, and produces its own atomic vehicle. Then, when it has run through its seven rings in the mineral kingdom, it passes the borderline and enters the vegetable kingdom. Running through its seven rings there, it then emerges and manifests as one of the lowest types of beasts, or rather animals, like a sponge for instance, or one of the similar half-animal, half-plant creatures. And then, finally, it enters the animal kingdom, and so onwards.

Remember always the statement that you will find in the *Gîtâ*, attributed to Krishna, where he says in substance: "I established all this Universe with a part of myself, and remain separate." Just so is it with the individual monads in all their incomputable numbers. Each one, from the time of its first appearance in a manvantara, establishes its own changing vehicle with portions of itself, and yet remains continually 'separate' from those vehicles through the ages, simply manifesting or working through them, until, finally, after even advanced Dhyân-Chohanship, the evolving soul rebecomes the monad again: the Buddha or Christ becomes once more its 'Father in Heaven,' which is the monad.

THE MISTAKEN IDEA OF TWIN SOULS

Please tell us something about the doctrine of twin souls.

This doctrine has caused mischief in the Theosophical Society in past times. Many people have misunderstood it, and there have actually been cases of immorality, due to a misunderstanding of this doctrine. I do not like this term 'twin souls,' because, as a matter of fact, not only are all human beings sons of Father-Sun, but just as the human race is divided into families, so certain portions of mankind belong as it were to certain respective spiritual energies or forces, which in their aggregate make the Spiritual Sun.

Some Theosophists call these energies, Rays. This is not a very good word because it reminds one of the physical rays of the sun, and that is putting the idea on a material plane; but nevertheless 'Rays' we can use if you wish. I prefer the word 'Energies' or 'Forces.' Now certain races of mankind, or certain bodies of men, belong to the same Energy, to the same Ray; other bodies of men belong to other Forces or Rays. There are ten principal Forces or Rays, and we can thus divide mankind into ten principal Families. These are the same as the ten classes of the Monads that

H. P. B. speaks of. And on this wonderful mystical idea, a fact of Nature, is based this mistaken idea of the twin souls.

How did this idea of the twin souls arise? Simply from this fact: That between two human beings who belong to the same Energy of the Sun, the same particular Solar Force, there is a quick and instant sympathy, a feeling as if they had always known each other. And taking the affairs of our ordinary human life, the cases of genuine, real love between a good man and a good woman are based on this fact.

Now that is all there is of truth in the doctrine of the twin souls. It is a very dangerous doctrine as commonly understood, because it can be so easily misused. But when understood, as you see, it is a doctrine which is full of profound truth.

No Historical Record of Jesus

What is known through historic channels of the person Jesus?

Absolutely nothing is known through historic channels of the person Jesus — if we omit the Christian Gospels themselves. Even the reference in Josephus, the Jewish historian, to the fact that a certain man called Christus lived in Jerusalem shortly preceding his own date, is now almost universally believed by scholars outside of the Christian Church, and by many Christian scholars also, to have been interpolated in Josephus' works, perhaps by Eusebius. There is absolutely no historical record whatsoever in any 'Pagan' historian of his real existence, beyond the vague statement in Tacitus and one or two other writers; and these statements are obviously founded on mere hearsay, doubtless emanating from early Christians. So much so, that dozens of scholars have concluded that the whole story about Jesus was simply an early 'solar myth' — which is not what the Theosophist accepts. Undoubtedly there did live at a time, which we call the beginning of the Christian Era, or in the century preceding the commonly accepted date of the Christian Era, a Sage, a Seer, who lived and worked in Palestine, who probably was called Yêshûa', which is the Hebrew word meaning 'Savior.' This is the original form of the name which became Iesous in Greek, Jesus in Latin. He is the one whom Theosophists refer to as the Avatâra.

I don't think people know how utterly unfounded many of the accepted stories of Christianity are. There is absolutely no proof, according to the usual standards of proof, that Jesus ever lived. The Christians have been frequently challenged to bring forward some exact proof, and they have not succeeded. But they do argue, with good show of reason, that there must have been some original figure around whom clustered the myths, stories, legends, which later were imbodied in the various scriptures, as in the four Gospels presently called canonical, and in the score or more of presently called apocryphal Gospels.

When one considers the bitter conflicts, theological and otherwise, the centuries of battling that the early Christians had among themselves, constantly fighting for the first five hundred years or more, one will realize that scarcely anything originally true could have survived. What did survive was the result: Christian theology; and this again was broken up into different Schools; as, for instance, the Greek Orthodox Church, the Roman so-called Catholic Church, the Armenian Church, the Nestorian Church, the Coptic Church, the Syrian Church, and other smaller sects. And then added to these there were the great Christian theological parties, like the so-called Orthodox party and the Arian party.

Present-day Christian theology is simply the result of a hodge-podge of theological squabbling for the first five hundred years, and the fourteen hundred that succeeded!

Obscure Origin of the Gospels

What is known in regard to the tampering with original texts so as to make them the better to fit in with the ideas of the Church-Fathers? I remember reading in The Theosophical Path *of one Lactantius, who spilled the beans as to how he juggled the texts, but I cannot now locate this article.*

The reference to Lactantius I believe is erroneous in this connexion. Lactantius was one of the later Christian Apologists who lived in the early part of the fourth century of the Christian Era, when the Four Gospels already had probably been accepted as more or less canonical. Nobody really *knows* who were the ones who tampered with the Gospels, if, indeed, they were tampered with, as they probably were — some more, some less. It is a sheer fact that all that scholars really *know* — outside of opinion and hypothesis — about the Gospels is that these four, now called canonical, finally prevailed over many others; and about the fourth century of the Christian Era had become the accepted four canonical Gospels or Scriptures of the Christian Churches. This is all that one can state with certainty. All the rest is obscurity, opinion, and guesswork.

It is evident to anyone who reads the four Gospels that they must be works written after, i.e., according to, others which were originals and which have disappeared: because the present Gospels contain sufficient likeness and sufficient identity of content to suggest this conclusion. They likewise contain a sufficient number of mutual contradictions to prove that different hands had been at work upon them or wrote them. The Christian Fathers were some later and some earlier than the Gospels.

WARNINGS IN DREAMS

Where do warnings in dreams and visions come from? Are they from excarnate spirits?

No, not from any excarnate human 'spirits.' It is the inner ego, the spiritual ego of the man who has the vision or who hears the voice or who gets the inspiration. In much rarer cases such warnings come from the Guardians of mankind, who, for karmic merit to the individual having earned it in some other life, will give a warning or send a vision or send a dream.

PRAJÂPATIS, AMSHASPENDS, KABIRI, ETC.

Are the Prajâpatis the same as the Amshaspends? H. P. B. seems to use both terms and I don't see much difference between them.

Prajâpatis is a Sanskrit compound which means 'parents of progeny,' 'beginners of races,' usually reckoned as 7 or 10 in number; actually 12. What in India are called Prajâpatis, among the Persians were called the Amshaspends. In Jewish Theosophy, the Qabbâlâh, they were called the Sephîrôth. In the Orphic occult teaching of ancient Greece and Asia Minor they were called Kabiri, who were especially revered in the Mystery-Schools of Samothrace. Or again, all these are practically identical with what in Christianity were called the Archangels; and if you understood the original Christian teaching about the Archangels, you would understand the functions of Prajâpatis, Sephîrôth, and Kabiri. Another name for the Prajâpatis, when the human race alone is alluded to, is *Manus;* and these are practically identical with the Rishis.

So then, the Prajâpatis, the Sephîrôth, the Kabiri, the Archangels, the Amshaspends, and similar beings or entities in other ancient systems, are the beginners of races; and on a smaller scale the beginners of civilizations, the Manus and the Śishtas when we are talking especially of our human race or life-wave. Each Prajâpati corresponds, in one very interesting way of viewing the thing, to one cosmic plane; or to put it in another way; there being 7 or 10 or 12 classes of monads, according to the way you count, each prajâpati is the head of one class of monads.

It is good to remember these correspondences or equivalents, because you will be able to read H. P. B.'s *Secret Doctrine* with a much clearer understanding of what she wrote. She had a habit, a wonderful habit in a way for one who was a true scholar, but she had a habit of bringing illustrative material from everywhere she could find it, and lumping it all together without always explaining that these things are equivalent. Thus some students of *The Secret Doctrine* when they saw Prajâpatis and Sephîrôth and Kabiri and Amshaspends and Archangels all together thought they were all entirely different things. They were the same great beings, but with different names, as reckoned in different parts of the earth or among different races.

THE LOGOS AS INDIVIDUAL AND HIERARCHY

Is the Cosmic Logos an individual from which radiate all the minor monadic individualities composing it? Or is the Logos on the other hand merely the collected totality of all monads?

Let me in response phrase the question by means of a picture: Is a tree merely an assemblage of atoms grouping themselves into roots, trunk, bark, branches, twigs, leaves, flowers, and fruit, without an entitative individuality in itself? Or is it an entitative individuality built up of these minor lives, as the life-atoms build up the body? It would seem easy to answer offhand, and say a tree is an entity builded up of minor lives, and this answer would be quite correct. But yet it is not fully satisfactory, because it is clear that no root of the tree nor the bark nor the trunk, nor a branch nor a leaf nor a flower thereof is the whole tree.

Another illustration: Is the table before which I sit an entitative individuality in invisible planes which through abstruse karmic powers has been cut from different trees, shaped by different human hands, polished by them, and formed into the aggregate of woods now before me, these different woods themselves composed of molecules and atoms? My answer again is: Both. The table before me could not exist unless it had preexisted in the astral light, which means unless it has an entitative existence of its own, difficult for us humans to comprehend but nevertheless real; and yet when you consider the table in detail, just as when we consider the tree in detail, or when we look at the details of a logos which are the various hierarchies making it, we are inclined to think there is no entitative reality to the table or tree or logos, but that each is a mere aggregate of its component parts; and this would be partly right and partly wrong.

The Logos, the tree, the table, and in fact any other entity which appears in the universe, be its existence long or short, is a karmic reproduction in imbodiment, of an entitative individuality in the invisible worlds, call them the spiritual worlds if you trace it back far enough.

Yes the Logos is an entity, an individuality, of high spiritual character, comprising numerous minor hierarchies which are radial groups from itself, or groups from its rays. So that if we look at the matter from above, we must say that the logos is an individual composed of its hierarchical monads or life-atoms; and if we look at the matter from below, we are apt to see the logos as a mere collection or the complete aggregate of the innumerable individuals composing the universe.

In conclusion, I sometimes question myself whether these very interesting queries are of value except to philosophers, and yet I am inclined to think that they are because they take men's minds away from the gross and material aspects of life, and give to them ideas and intuitions of greater things. The loss of soul usually is caused in its beginnings by a loss of ideals; and for a similar reason I have always highly approved of the study of the cosmic structure and therefore of planetary chains and rounds and races, and similar fundamental teachings, for they elevate the mind out of matter, induce feelings of a common unity or of universal brotherhood, and are therefore seen to have immense and powerful ethical or moral value, with its consequent effect on us.

NATIONS AND RACES AS ENTITIES

Is it correct to consider Nations and Races as actual entities?

This question is not so easy to answer. In a sense Yes, because every unit, great or small, racial, national, regional, or on a smaller scale like cities and towns and villages, and even a family, represents a swabhâva which is the imbodiment therefore of a kind of unit in the spiritual realms. Indeed the Greeks and Romans even carried this entification of abstractions to the extent that they actually said there was a goddess Virtue, and a goddess Patience, and so forth, and a goddess of Strife and equivalent gods, etc., all of which has some abstract reality, because Patience and Strife and Love and Sympathy and Virtue are all qualities flowing forth from the cosmic hierarchy, and therefore in a sense can be entified and made into individuals. But this must not be carried so far as to make them identical with, although much larger than, an incarnating and reincarnating human ego.

Thus again, is a hive of bees the expression of an inner monad or entity? Or is a hive of bees merely an aggregate of small bee-monads? Answer: It is both. The bee-monads are certainly there, and each is an individualized reimbodying entity. But the hive as a collection of such monads is the representation of the collectivity of the monads united in a common swabhâva or minor logos, which is an entity in its highest, but a merely collective and quantitative expression through radiation as a hive.

The Americans as a nation, for instance, are a group of human monads. Their destiny or karman is drawing them together, and as time passes they will grow more powerful and their native qualities will grow more pronounced when the assimilation of so many immigrant people in the United States has been completed. Now what is, or what then will be the American people? What is it now, what will it then be? Can we say that there is a spiritual being or entity or monad existent in the spiritual spheres which expresses itself for a time through its radiated qualities on this earth as the American people, formed of the monads that come and go through reimbodiment in this spiritual-astral mold of radiation? The answer is Yes. But this must not be looked upon as a reimbodying entity taking material imbodiment again and again, because that would make it merely — I mean here the nation — a reimbodying monad.

On the other hand, it is quite true that over vast periods of manvantaric time, what has been is cyclically reproduced, but cyclically somewhat higher than its last appearance. This is an old Stoic doctrine; so that all that now exists, in some far past manvantaric time then existed also on a somewhat less evolved plane than now, because the astral molds were shaping then, and will again appear in the far distant future, but on a somewhat higher plane. But we as individual monads now taking part here will have moved onwards into higher spheres. Thus we can see that this abstract spiritual entity will again manifest itself as a nation, but this will be manvantaric ages hence, and with new monads forming its life-atoms, so to speak.

Thus then we can say that every nation is the expression of a national Genius, signifying here a national spirit, and similarly so every people, every race, every globe's general population; and on the decreasing scale, similarly so every abstract of a nation, and again every city or town or village or even family. The whole thing is a very subtil and difficult thing to explain, but it becomes clear enough if (a) we remember that each such unit karmically expresses itself on earth because it is a manifestation of inner invisible spiritual causes, inner spiritual qualities radiating from a spiritual focus; and if we also remember (b) that this is analogical with, but not identical with, a reimbodying ego like a human ego. Further, we must never forget that every local or national unit is the sister or brother of all other local or national units, just as human beings are brothers, for all are born from one common source; and when we remember this last most important fact of all, then we lose our fanatic nationalisms, our tendencies to consider our own nation or people superior to all others on earth, and we realize that we as human individuals in our next life may be born in the very nation which today we may happen to dislike, provided of course our rebirth is not too long delayed, because then the nation may have temporarily passed into disappearance.

THE TOWER OF BABEL

Is there any inner meaning to the story of the Tower of Babel?

There is no historical basis for the story of the Tower of Babel as an actual Tower. The Tower of Babel as related in the Hebrew Bible is an allegory told after the Jewish manner of the late Atlantean magicians aspiring to conquer even 'heaven' by their human magic. So in the allegory the Atlantean magicians built a 'Tower of Thought,' but as this was earthly and not spiritual, typically Atlantean in character, after it had reached a certain level in construction, according to the allegory, evolution, the ordinary human evolution, or evolution of mankind, spread confusion into this attempt to 'scale heaven' by human magic. The confusion of tongues meant that the Atlantean races split up into various different human families, and confusion and separateness resulted from this.

The Initiates of the Right-hand path likewise built a "Tower of Infinite Thought," as Master points out in *The Mahatma Letters,* but their tower is based on spirit instead of matter, and therefore is united throughout itself, therefore making confusion impossible. No confusion and misunderstanding is there possible, such as is the case brought about by merely human efforts, by human magic, to scale the 'ramparts of heaven.'

PYTHAGOREAN INJUNCTIONS

Why were the Pythagoreans told not to eat beans?

I wonder if Pythagoras would have been very welcome in a certain town in New England — baked beans and brown bread! Is there anything wicked or criminal in eating beans, or brown bread and beans even though they are somewhat indigestible? But that is not the real meaning. Do you know, a certain small early Christian sect thought that the fig was the fruit of that especial tree in the Garden of Eden which Mother Eve tempted Father Adam to eat? And why did they pick upon the poor fig to make it so holy that they forbade those who believed with them to eat figs? Another case of 'beans,' you see, because they reasoned that the little seeds in the fig were symbolic of the seeds of life, and they made a symbol of that fig; and they made it a holy thing, tabu as they say in the South. So — do not eat figs: they are too holy to eat! And doubtless they pointed to those particular phrases in the Hebrew book of Genesis where, because

Eve and Adam ate of the forbidden fruit, the angel with the flaming sword chased them out.

So the Pythagoreans had a teaching along exactly the same line, and they looked upon beans — they might have chosen peas, or apple seeds, or anything else that has seeds, but they happened to choose beans — as symbolic of life, as monads, productive of a whole future, a plant producing other seeds, beans, peas, what not. And later Pythagoreans, when the School had dropped from its earlier high understanding, took the prohibition as meaning that it is wicked to eat beans because they are foul, which is the reverse of the meaning.

I don't think even Pythagoras would have said that any one of his pupils could not eat a mess of beans. Can't you see how utterly ridiculous the thing is when you bring it right down to brass tacks? Beans with them were like a pass word, alluding to a wonderful secret occult doctrine which was not edible, that is to say partakable of by any except those who were strong enough to stomach it, to understand, to digest. Consequently, beans became prohibited.

Any doctrine which is not productive of a better life is horrible. It is not worth anything. If a doctrine does not improve your life in every way, I would say, to use the old English word, eschew it, abhor it.

Now why is it that the Pythagorean doctrines so radically changed the characters of those who studied them? On account of the effect of conversion, the old Christian word, changing the mind, of changing the mind from things here below to higher things; and this is exactly what ails the world today. It has almost forgotten the need of thinking and thinking aright in order that men may live aright. And in order to think aright you must have rules, rules which men believe in, are convinced of the truth of, and this truth is brought by spiritual and intellectual persuasion through study. That is why the study of religion, of philosophy, of science, can ennoble a man's life, take him out of the range where life as he sees it is but a struggle against other men, bringing out all the animal within him, the fighting qualities exercised against his fellows. Thinking aright ennobles a man's character because it enriches, it enlarges, his views, gives him other views of his fellows.

Why did Pythagoras enjoin five years of silence on his disciples?

I don't believe there was any such rule! I think the meaning was that no pupil, outer or inner, was allowed to teach, to speak, until he had been adequately trained; and five years was considered the time within which he might, as we say today, graduate, have his diploma and practise. And it was a very wise provision indeed, because today just look at the mushy clap-trap, folderol, all kinds of perfectly indescribable stuff that you pay for merely in order to read — without instruction, without learning, often without decency. Anyone who wants to can get up on his legs and talk and say almost anything, and if his legs are long enough and his inventive genius is strong enough he can get away with it. The rule of Pythagoras prevented that kind of thing.

EVOLUTION AND THE CONTROL OF THE LIFE-ATOMS

How is it possible that we, who were rulers of a solar system, i.e., in the time when the atoms were our dwelling houses, cannot rule the composing beings of our body today? We are developed from the atoms and we will rule a solar system in the macro-cosmos in the future. Is our state of consciousness lower now than in the time of our atom-life?

The reason that we human beings find it difficult in this stage of our evolutionary pilgrimage to control the lower elements, including the atoms, electrons, etc., of our bodies, is that we are at the mid-point in our evolutionary journey, because we are sunken in the material worlds, although we are now beginning to rise towards Spirit again. This situation means that the matter-parts of our being, including the atoms, etc., of course, are more in their own sphere, and therefore have greater individual power than they have in the higher spheres; and consequently they act more strongly in their own individual ways than they do when they are again in Spirit, or in the spiritual worlds, and more under the divine influence of being in the spiritual worlds. Thus the sun, the divinity in and behind the sun, can control the lower elements and lower atoms much better than we can, because this divinity, being so much ahead of us, attracts more spiritual types of atoms than we do, because we are naturally much less spiritually evolved than is the solar divinity.

Thus it is that in the future we shall be able to control perfectly not only our own matter-elements, but the very atoms, etc., which compose these matter-elements of us, because we shall in time gain in spiritual power; and even these matter-elements of us will have risen more towards Spirit, and we and our component lower elements and atoms then will have become more alike, both more spiritual, than now we are. Hence there will be more harmony, greater ease, in what we may call brotherly co-operation, in our journey back to Spirit.

You have given the main idea correctly when you say that the Mahâtmans much more easily can control their lower elements and atoms than we can, and this is because of the two main reasons I have just stated: In evolution the Mahâtmans are beyond us, and therefore stronger than we are; and they attract to themselves for their bodies, etc., more spiritualized atoms than we do. Hence there is greater harmony there between the higher and the lower than there is with us.

THE PRACTICAL VALUE OF PHILOSOPHICAL THINKING

Is it advantageous or practical for men today to put their minds on thoughts of abstract beauty such as are taught in technical Theosophy? Do we gain anything from studying about grand figures of history such as the Buddha, or, let us say, what is known in Theosophy as The Silent Watcher?

In the name of holy Truth, what can be more practical in human life than inducing men to think, than giving them thoughts and ideals of beauty, of law and order, and in instilling into the hypercritical and irreverent mind so common today ideals of human grandeur and sublimity, as examples for all men to follow? The value of it all lies in the fact that in so doing we are awakening the souls and hearts of men, replacing aridity of thought and barrenness of ideas and ideals with mental seeds and suggestions which, in their flower, ennoble human life and inspire courage and hope to face life's manifold problems. This is just what the teaching of Theosophy does: it makes men more truly men: it gives to them inspiration, even to do the daily task, inspiration to face the so-called problems of life with a vision into the future, thus enabling men to surmount these problems grandly. It teaches men nobly to live and nobly to die.

Is there anything 'practical' about this? The man who has been a mere money-grubber all his life, and who, when he dies, dies with an empty soul, leaving behind him all that he has gained in life — for this 'all' is merely material things — is one who has left no permanent record of himself in the sphere in which he moved; certainly no record proving that he has influenced his fellow-men for better; and I would indeed love to ask whether such a man is one who truly can be called a 'practical' man? In my judgment he is far otherwise. He may have been a hard worker: he may have sacrificed comfort and peace and human happiness to increase his material possessions; but it seems to me that in all the qualities that make a man truly a man, he has accomplished really nothing at all, and dies a human failure. I think such a man is a most impractical man, for he has abandoned everything that is really worth while in life, and has exchanged it all for what the Bible of the Jews and the Christians calls a 'mess of pottage.' He cannot take his money, his land, his stocks and bonds, nor his material possessions in any form with him; he leaves them all behind, to be squandered usually by those into whose hands they come.

Now this does not in anywise mean that I think that a man should not do his duty in life along these so-called 'practical' lines. Quite the contrary. A man should do his duty in the sphere of life in which he finds himself, and should do it in as upright and human, as well as humane, a way as it is possible for him to do. My point is that a concentration of all his energies, intellectual, psychic, and physical, in merely so-called 'practical' works, starves the soul within him. The vast ranges of his inner consciousness have never had a chance to have their play in action in his life. Therefore I call him a failure.

Contrariwise, the man who "lays up for himself," as the Christian New Testament has it, "treasures in heaven," which means within the realm and sphere of his own inner being: who has inbuilt into his soul the treasury of mighty and grand thoughts, thoughts of sublimity and universal benevolence which not only sway his own life and make it grand, but sway the lives of those who touch his sphere and who thereby are affected by his example — such a man, I say, is no failure; and I look upon him as having lived a most practical life in the proper sense of the word, because he has made his life affect others powerfully, even in the material sphere, for good. He has been an example, an ideal, for others to look up to and to follow — to copy in short; and this is because he has lived his life roundly: every part or function of his complex constitution has been brought into play, into activity. His life thus has been lived universally so to speak; and he has not confined, cabined, restricted, his whole existence into the small corner or small field of merely one phase of human intercourse. During his life he has grown on all the planes of his being, because he has been a lover of, a student of, and therefore follower of, ideals and ideas. Indeed, it is ideas that move and that rule the world; it is not at all the mere hunt for material possessions. Who are the men who have made and unmade civilizations? They are the thinkers! These are the men also who affect other men, and Theosophy above everything else teaches a man to think as well as to *be* more by giving play to the various capacities for action which lie latent in the constitution of all men.

Now, coming to still more recondite thoughts: the training in subtilty in thinking, the training in thinking impersonal thoughts so that one's own inner cogitations become ever more impersonal in character; and the constant seeking to elevate one's feelings and emotions to ever higher planes, are spiritual exercises of the first importance; and this, among other very practical results, is what the study of our Theosophical teachings does for us. Teachings concerning the Rounds and Races, and the relation of the different Buddhas and Bodhisattvas to each other — taking these two instances merely as examples — impractical as they may sound to the ordinary man who can see no farther in life than the tip of his nose, not only take us out of the ordinary humdrum, commonplace affairs of human life and refresh our souls with courage founded upon hope, but also awaken within us a perennial spiritual fount from which flow inspiration and intuition.

TIME-PERIOD IN THE KÂMA-LOKA

What would be the difference in the period of time to be spent in the kâma-loka state between a strong young man who had died of pneumonia; a physically wasted young man who had died of tuberculosis; and an average old man?

While in the case of the strong young man dying, his physical desires would probably still be strong, on the other hand it might be argued that if it were his karmic destiny to die then, that would be the "natural" end of his life.

The question runs to the point of ascertaining the periods of time spent in the kâma-lokic state by different individuals who on earth were strong, or physically wasted by disease, or one passing out averagely old. The answer is simple: every human being whatsoever after death remains in the kâma-loka precisely as long as the as yet unexpended store of vitality needs for its exhaustion — the vitality here of course being what one might call ordinary astral-physical-vital energy.

Let me try to illustrate: let a man's store or stock of vitality or vital energy at birth be called X, for every human being is born with a certain vital power, precisely in the same way as an ordinary physical machine constructed to do a work will last for as long or as short a time as it has been built to endure, a strong machine obviously lasting longer than a delicate machine subjected to the same usage. Thus, then, the vital store of energy at birth we will call X. When the man dies, he will have expended of this vital store an amount which we can call, if you please, Y. Now, the difference between X and Y, let us say is Z, which means the balance or unexpended portion of his vital energy. Thus, X minus Y equals Z. Thus, Z is the unexpended vital energy which has to be exhausted in the kâma-loka.

Now, old people usually have expended most of their vitality, and practically wholly so when they die of sheer old age, so that in their cases the Y is usually nearly as large as the X, or quite as large; and in these cases the kâma-lokic residence, if they are average men and not desperately wicked, is very short — perhaps a mere unconscious passing through the kâma-loka. A strong young man or woman who dies from an accident, or some quick or sudden disease, like pneumonia, let us say, has not yet expended much of his vital energy or X, so that in these cases the Y factor is small; and hence when we come to the same equation as before, X minus Y equals Z, we see that the Z factor is fairly large, so that in these cases there is a good deal of unexpended energy which has to be exhausted in the kâma-loka, or in the Astral Light, or World, before the Devachan can begin.

On the other hand, take the cases of men and women who perhaps in early manhood or womanhood, or even in youth, have been long afflicted with some wasting disease which utterly exhausts them, and carries them away prematurely. In these cases the Y factor becomes large; and when we make our equation, X minus Y equals Z, we see that the Z or remaining balance is relatively small, and perhaps is almost nil, so that then we can write our equation, X equals Y, or X minus Y equals zero.

Hence we see that all cases whatsoever depend upon the amount of vitality or vital energy expended or used up while the human being is alive on earth; if this expenditure has been great, then Z becomes very small, perhaps zero; if this energy or Y is very small, then the unexpended energy or Z remains large, perhaps nearly equalling X, as in the case of still-born infants, or infants dying young. Consequently, except by stating some such general rule with regard to the original store of vital energy with which a human being is born, one cannot answer the question otherwise than by saying that in all cases whatsoever it depends on the individual.

Furthermore, we must remember that appearances are often deceptive, so that an apparently hale and hearty young person may actually be expending his original store of vitality at a great rate, without realizing it, so that as the years pass, becoming weaker and weaker in this store, he becomes more and more subject to attack by disease, etc., and perhaps the disease may take him or her even in youth or early middle age. The above is what is meant by our Theosophical writers when they speak of "what would be the natural life on earth," if the man had not died prematurely for one reason or another, as in the case of accidents or suicides or disease, etc. Karman in all cases brings about death, just as it brings about birth, and just as it brings about the kâma-lokic period.

As regards *consciousness* in the kâma-loka, this is not imbodied in the question, but perhaps the questioner has it in mind; and if so, there is unnecessary confusion, and I have written about this matter and explained it in many places. Consciousness in the kâma-loka depends upon the materiality or the material tendencies of the man or woman while living on earth. If the material tendencies were strong while alive in the body, and if the death occur before the vitality has been exhausted, as above described, there is a certain vague and fleeting consciousness in the kâma-loka. If the man or woman was very spiritual while on earth, then after death from whatever cause, accident or what-not, or wasting disease, the consciousness in the kâma-loka is extremely faint, scarcely that of a vague dream, and perhaps there may be no consciousness whatsoever, for the more spiritual a being is while alive on earth, the less is the tendency to awaken to the dreamy kâma-lokic existence.

FORMATION OF THE KÂMA-RÛPA

Please explain what Mr. Judge means by the statement in the OCEAN *p. 47 orig. ed., that the astral body, (i.e. linga-śarîra) coalesces with the Kâma-principle of the departed entity, and that it is this astral body which gives the kâma its rûpa, so to speak, and forms the kâma-rûpa? How is this statement to be understood in the light of the other statement in various places, but notably by you on page 97 of your* OCCULT GLOSSARY, *that the linga-śarîra fades out pari passu with the physical corpse?*

Here I believe there is a confusion in the questioner's mind. Mr. Judge on the page of his *Ocean of Theosophy* referred to, is using the term "astral body" in a rather loose way, and quite in the fashion or style of these earlier days, when a great deal of effort was made to explain our technical Sanskrit words, and when the simplest possible manner of speech was always sought for. But it is clear, I believe, that what Mr. Judge means by the phrase "astral body" is the linga-śarîra, although of course "astral body" could refer to any number of permanent or temporary vehicles which the ego could use in the astral realms, such as the mâyâvi-rûpa for instance, formed of the higher astral substance and therefore in a certain sense an "astral body," which can be made visible on the physical plane by the adept.

Now I have often stated, following strictly in the line of H. P. B., that the linga-śarîra disintegrates *pari passu* and almost molecule for molecule with the disintegration of the physical body or *sthûla-śarîra;* and this statement is a fact. But the kâma-rûpa is formed of astral substance emanating mainly from the auric egg of the individual, originally during its life-time on earth and when freed from the physical corpse forming the kâma-rûpa after death; and as a large part of the lower or grosser portions of the kâma-rûpa is formed of astral life-atoms drawn from the decaying or decayed linga-śarîra, we thus see that Mr. Judge is quite correct in stating in the general and rather vague way he does, that the dead man's "astral body" and the principle of passion and desire "leave the physical in company and coalesce." Of course it is so; but very soon the kâma-rûpa frees itself from the disintegrating linga-śarîra, although taking some of the life-atoms of the linga-śarîra with it, because these life-atoms are still strongly attracted to the desire principle in the kâma-rûpa.

Mr. Judge's words are strictly correct and accurate. It is, however, inaccurate to say that it is the "astral body which gives the *kâma* its *rûpa*, and thus forms the *kâma-rûpa*." It is the unexpended vital energy of the man which, attracting astral atoms and life-atoms from the decaying linga-śarîra and elsewhere, form a shape or rûpa around the center of desire, and thus make the kâma-rûpa as it appears as a shape after death. When the ego finally casts off the kâma-rûpa at the time of the Second Death, then the kâma-rûpa becomes just an empty shell — as much so as the linga-śarîra and the sthûla-śarîra were at death and very shortly after death of the man on this plane.

To recapitulate: (*a*) The linga-śarîra fades out *pari passu* with the physical corpse; (*b*) certain atoms or life-atoms are attracted from the linga-śarîra by the desire-principle in addition to other astral atoms drawn from the astral light, and thus coalescing produce the shape or rûpa of the kâma-rûpa; (*c*) at the Second Death, when the ego begins to enter the devachanic state, the kâma-rûpa is cast off and thereafter in the case of normal human individuals begins to disintegrate, to go to pieces, molecule for molecule and atom by atom, just as the physical corpse does when buried, or as the linga-śarîra does. (*d*) Of course there are the instances of sorcerers, dugpas, whose gross passions and material desires keep them in the Astral Light and lead them to an immediate or a very quick reimbodiment in a physical body; and other sporadic cases like infants dying young, congenital idiots, and a few more.

THE SEVENFOLD KÂMA-RÛPIC MOON

The moon, which is a kâma-rûpa, has seven globes. Hence it is a seven-fold entity. Reasoning analogically, is the kâma-rûpa of a man a seven-fold entity?

Yes, the kâma-rûpa of a man is sevenfold; so also is every principle, cosmic, or human. The moon-chain as a whole is a kâma-rûpic entity, and every globe of the moon-chain is a kâma-rûpic entity. In other words each moon — each globe of the earth-chain having its corresponding moon of the moon-chain — each moon is a kâma-rûpa to its corresponding earth-chain globe. The seven kâma-rûpic globes of the moon-chain are on the four Cosmic Planes on which our earth-chain is. These planes are named by H. P. B. in *The Secret Doctrine*, (I, 200) counting from the highest of the four to the lowest, as: (1) Archetypal, (2) Intellectual, (3) Astral forma-tive, (4) Physical material. The reason why we see the kâma-rûpa of

Globe D of the moon-chain is that our Globe D of our earth-chain is on a *sub*-plane higher than Globe D of the moon-chain, and similarly all the globes of the earth-chain are each one on a sub-plane of their respective Cosmic Planes higher than the corresponding globes of the moon-chain. Each one of the principles, as said, whether of a man or a globe, is seven-fold.

NOT ALL PLANETS HAVE KÂMA-RÛPAS

Do all the planets have kâma-rûpas or Dwellers of the Threshold during their earlier Rounds?

No. Some planets have kâma-rûpic Dwellers just like some men; but these in actual fact are not very numerous.

SOME PROBLEMS OF THE DEVACHAN

I think I recall reading in THE MAHATMA LETTERS *that K. H. speaks somewhere of the periodic devachan that the adept can enter into, even during imbodied existence.*

Yes, but that is not the case of the high adepts, but of the high chelas who have not fully passed beyond the need of the devachan. Now there is an occult law well known to the adept, by which a man can shorten his devachan, by taking certain resting-periods, devachanic resting-periods if you wish, in a single imbodiment, set aside a certain number of weeks or months or even years in any one imbodiment for the purpose of going into a temporary but intensive devachan then and there.

That may be a very good way to do for a high chela. For instance, if he is given a work to do, he does his work it may be for several years, and he needs his devachanic rest before he will be called upon again. He profits by that time, let us say by going into the devachan more or less so, right then and there, and rests himself for a while. Then when he comes out of it, he is in the same body, and strong and inwardly recuperated and ready to go on again. But that of course is the case of chelas or adepts who still need the rest, or some devachanic rest.

This matter of the devachan is a very peculiar thing. I have met people, men and women, going about their ordinary vocations, who were actually living in a devachanic state. They were dreaming, they were lackadaisical. Perhaps you have all heard of that kind of folk, people who do not seem to care. They just go about in a sort of half-asleep state. They are not really living. They are still in the devachan to a certain extent. They want to lie abed so long, so to speak, like children do sometimes. They have hardly come out of the devachanic state. They have come out of it enough to take a body, but their minds are still partly in the devachanic dream.

And I have met Theosophists too, whom I deeply revere, who have left the devachan to come into our Work before their devachan was really ended. They are like people who have waked from sleep before the body has had enough of it to rest it. They are high-strung, nervous, active, quick, that kind of people. These are two extremes which one meets in human life: those who are still in the devachan more or less, although still imbodied — I do not mean completely in the devachan, but in a devachanic dreamy state and hence not fully at work, or awake to life's calls; and those who have not been in the devachan long enough; and I will say that some of this last class comprise a few of our very best workers, and they are having a hard time of it, because they have to fight an inner psychological state of inner weariness which is almost impossible to describe unless you have been through it. They are usually not strong in body, high-strung, nervous individuals, but they are doing a grand work. They have given up a portion of their rest, semi-consciously as it were, in order quickly to take their part again in humanity's destiny.

Shortening the Devachan

Would it be possible for any of us to shorten our devachanic period?

Quite possible, if you have the will to do so. Any human being who is willing to renounce his rest, the utter peace and calm which is the thing most longed for by the tired human soul, and who trains himself to this renunciation, can shorten his devachan automatically. But it is only high chelas who can actually do without the devachan, because they have risen above the plane where the human ego requires and longs for rest.

In the far distant future, not only will all human egos on earth have passed beyond the need of the devachan after death, but they will have passed beyond the need for the present type of sleep for the body. What are now our gross physical bodies, in those days will have become practically bodies of condensed light, wonderful bodies, radiant, luminous. They won't need rest as our gross physical bodies now do.

But I would advise any devoted student to think carefully before trying to shorten the devachanic rest, because you may bring upon yourself complicate and possibly disastrous karmic consequences. It is something like a man who, because he has some very important work to do in view, deliberately goes without his sleep, or cuts it short, night after night after night. He can do it, but he can ruin his health that way too; and so in the end he really doesn't get what he is after.

The best way is to think to yourself: I hope that my devachan will be only so long as absolutely needed for rest. I hope it won't be like sleeping in bed longer than one has to, merely because one likes to sleep and rest in bed. That attitude of mind is quite right and safe.

WORSHIP OF THE INNER DIVINITY

What is the idea behind the portrayal in Egyptian hieroglyphs of the King worshiping or adoring himself?

We have here no self-adoration, as our Occidental Egyptologists wrongly state — no adoration of a person, no kingly individual worshiping himself as the figure-head of a civilized community. That would be tawdry, paltry. But we have the case of a man who looked upon himself as representing the divinity within him and as the vicegerent of his inner god on earth, and thereby clothed with spiritual dignity and power, with heavy responsibility in his hands — the guide and shepherd of his people.

The adoration and worship was paid symbolically to that divinity, as it were, like a species of prayer: "Not my will" — that of this feeble man, the King of Egypt — "be done, but thy will be done" — your Father in Heaven. "Make me a full vessel of thy kingly majesty and power, that I in turn may do my duty to my people, my sheep, my brothers, my children." This at least was the original idea, however much it later may have degenerated. It was a right royal and kingly thing, sublime in its priesthood — the king-priest, the priest-king, as they existed in the far-distant ages of the past before Atlantis fell.

For during the Third Root-Race when self-consciousness came to men, they worshiped each one his own individual divinity, worshiped it as a bright and starry god to which he aspired: my Self, my god in heaven, my link with the Infinite; just as Jesus the Christ did in reference to his "Father in Heaven." And as time passed and the realization, the keen realization, of man's oneness with the god within vanished, fell, disappeared, men began to worship themselves in the lower sense, the selfish self instead of the divine Self, even worshiped images of the human body which they put in their temples. Not that they abandoned the old worship, they degraded it, turning the temple of the divine into places where hellions found their home. The same thought must have been in the mind of the writer of the Christian New Testament where he represents the Avatâra as going into the temple and cleaning out the money-changers and the gatherers of taxes.

Let me tell you that every Initiate, every Adept, knows his "Father in Heaven," recognises him and calls him "Father-Sun," or "Father-Flame," or "Father-Fire," or "Father-Star," and looks upon himself, the man himself, not only as an efflux flowing from this inner divinity, but as its child, its representative here on earth, laboring to imbody the mandates and the dictates of the god within. And the ancient Initiates — and the Kings of Egypt in the days of Egypt's glory were all such, were all Sons of the Sun — knew it even in those already degenerate days.

When I speak from a public platform and see my audience sitting before me and realize that behind those faces of flesh and those brightly shining eyes there are living gods, I put myself in that frame of mind and address myself — or try to — to that within them which I know will understand with a word. Oh! if we could only realize, we men and women, the living reality of the god within each one of us, each one with his own "Father-Flame," "Father-Fire," "Father-Sun," "Father-Star"! This is the Silent Watcher of each of us. When a man addresses it or aspires to it, he addresses, or aspires to, his own Silent Watcher — that bright and luminous divinity living with patience infinite through the entire solar manvantara, waiting, waiting, waiting, refusing to go on, waiting each one for his child — me, you: the Christ and the Christ-Child: Âdi-Buddha, Mânushya-Buddha; primeval, primordial wisdom, love, compassion — the human representation thereof, the human Buddha.

That is the real meaning of the Egyptian King worshiping himself; and of course degeneration of such things could only take place when a man had fallen from his pristine estate of understanding, in which pristine state intuition was not beclouded by reason because reason had not yet grown up to be pure intellect. It will in time, but it has not yet so grown. Any one of you who has once felt the touch of the god within never is the same again. Never can you be the same again. Your life is changed; and you can have this awakening at any moment, any moment that you will take it.

The Lamaic Succession in Tibet

Is there any truth to the current idea that the Tashi Lama in Tibet is always a reincarnation of the Buddha? Is this a real succession, or is it merely a tradition without meaning?

The Succession of the Tibetan Lamaic hierarchy since the time of Tsong-kha-pa in the Fourteenth Century is a real one and takes place through different individual men. We must remember that the principle regarding this matter is comprised in that deeper Buddhism which really is Esoteric Buddhism — let our Western scholars say what they like.

Neither the Tashi Lama nor the Dalai Lama is a reincarnation or reimbodiment of the Bodhisattva Śâkyamuni; but the Succession beginning with

Tsong-kha-pa *is* a transmission of a 'Ray' in each individual case of the line of Tashi Lamas derivative from the spiritual Mahâ-Guru whom H. P. B. calls the Silent Watcher of this Globe.

There is an important distinction to be drawn between successive reincarnations of Gautama and the successive imbodiments of rays from an identic source in the Hierarchy of Compassion which I have just called the Mahâ-Guru. It is just here that all Theosophists as well as all esotericists stumble and wander from the facts.

It is indeed a transmission in serial line of a ray from the 'Buddha'; but the 'Buddha' in this case is not the Bodhisattva Gautama, even though he attained Buddhahood, which is a state, but the Dhyâni-Buddha of whom the Bodhisattva Gautama himself was an incarnated ray and the noblest and most complete and the fullest since the beginning of our Fifth Root-Race. This is why the Exalted One, Gautama, later attained Buddhahood.

Even the Tibetans of nearly all classes, with the possible exception of the Tashi and Dalai Lamas themselves, look upon this transmission in Succession or serial line through repetitive imbodiments of the 'Buddha' as being repeated incarnations of Gautama the Buddha in the two Head Lamas of the Tibetan Hierarchy. But this is erroneous; and it is just the point where the stumbling hereinbefore referred to occurs.

The higher members of the Tibetan Hierarchy, including the Khutuktus, and, I sincerely believe, the Tashi Lama himself and in all probability the Dalai Lama, are as perfectly acquainted with the esoteric facts in this case as H. P. B. was; and they know perfectly well that these reincarnations of 'Living Buddhas,' as Westerners call them, are not, as said above, repetitive reimbodiments of Śâkyamuni, but repeated reimbodiments of identic rays or of an identic ray inspiriting and enlightening one Tashi Lama after the other; and a similar ray in repeated imbodiments inspirits and enlightens one Dalai Lama after the other. This has been the case since Tsong-kha-pa's time. It has been so up to the present and there seems no reasonable doubt that the Succession, as above described, will continue unless and until human vehicles are found which are too imperfect to continue this esoteric line of Succession.

If people only understood the true meaning of the teachings of Tibetan Buddhism regarding the Dhyâni-Buddhas and their human representatives on earth, then they would have the key to this continuous mystery of the Succession of living Buddhic rays in the higher members of the Tibetan Hierarchy; and it is just this that H. P. B. spoke of when she wrote as openly as she dared then to do.

To put the matter in other words which will be consistent with facts and accordant with common-sense: Every Tashi Lama from Tsong-kha-pa's time to the present has been the reimbodiment of an identic Buddhic ray, emanated from the Dhyâni-Buddha of this Globe, in other words, the mysterious Individual or Personage, whom Esoteric Tradition states as living in Śambhala, concerning which mysterious land every Tibetan, high or low, has heard somewhat; yet these different Tashi Lamas have been men, seven-principled men, and therefore all have been distinct individuals, each different from his Predecessor and from his Successor, yet each has been the vehicle or channel of transmission of an identic Buddha-Force, which I have hereinbefore called the Ray from the Mahâ-Guru.

We have then the Succession of an identic spiritual Buddha-Individuality through a long serial line since Tsong-kha-pa's time of different men who thus become recognised for what they are and who are appointed or raised to the position of Successors in the Hierarchy of the Tashi Lamas.

While this wondrous fact continues in Tibet even to this day, in former ages an identic Succession of true Teachers existed in other parts of the world and has formed the basis for the mysterious stories commonly current in the ancient literatures of Hierarchies of Initiates continued through the ages because of being linked with the Master-Adept whom H. P. B. in *Isis Unveiled* and elsewhere at times refers to as 'Mahâ' or 'Mahâ-Guru.'

No Remission of Sins

What is the meaning of the following quotation from St. John, *xx 23?*

Whose soever sins ye remit, they are remitted unto them; and whose soever sins ye retain, they are retained.

These words are an ecclesiastical addition to the original theme of the gospel, made by heaven knows whom and heaven knows when. They have no actual meaning whatever, but simply satisfy the priesthood that they have special God-given powers, and are therefore obviously inserted or originally written by someone with that point of view. In their open construction they are utterly against the doctrine of Karman — that a man is responsible for his own good deeds and misdeeds. Sins cannot be remitted by either God, demon, or human. It is like saying that a man's character can be remitted. If you did so you would annihilate the man.

If they have any moral value at all, it is simply the injunction to forgive injury against one, and not to make them worse and carry them on by hatred and revenge.

We should understand that a great many things in the Christian gospels are not holy truth, or the laws of Nature, but the Christian gospels were written by no great initiates, and even after the first writers finished their work, interpolations occurred later on which are now recognised as such even by Christian scholars. Therefore, one will find many things in the Christian gospels that do not need even pausing over, because they are often half-meaningless interpolations, even sometimes put in the manuscripts by fanatics who happened to have the upper hand: but there is a substratum of actual truth in all the gospels.

HIERARCHIES WITHIN HIERARCHIES

Not only has every individual his own Inner God, but these Inner Gods collectively form the body corporate through which a superior divinity works. The superior divinity again in its turn is but one of a still more sublime army or host collected together under a godhead still more sublime; and so on ad infinitum. Is this a correct conception?

Every individual entity is an expression of a Divine Monad, which is but another phrase for 'an Inner God.' Every Monad in its heart of hearts is an individualized divinity; therefore every human being, as well as every other entity, however high or low, is an expression of a Divine Seed which is an Inner God.

This vast cosmic aggregate of Inner Gods or Divine Monads forms the body corporate of a hierarchy, the hierarchy of the Cosmos; and for this hierarchy there is the supreme Hierarch in which all these hosts of Inner Gods are included, much as the body contains all the life-atoms which compose itself. Such hierarchies being infinite in number in Boundless Space, there are, therefore, logically, an infinite number of cosmic hierarchies.

A further deduction from these premises is, therefore, that not only is every being, such as a human being, an expression of an individualized divinity called his or its 'Inner God,' but all these 'Inner Gods' are under the sway of, and living in and forming part of, some superior divinity, which in its turn is but a divinity forming a part of a superior host collectively aggregated within the life-sphere of some divinity still more sublime; and so on *ad infinitum*. So that at every step we may use the language of Paul of the Christians in saying that "In It, we live, and move and have our being."

THE TAKING OF HUMAN LIFE

Can it ever be justified to take a human life, as for instance when defending the native country or to defend one's child against assault?

Unfortunately, yes. In this present stage of evolution and in the conditions of the world in which we live, it may be at times in the line of duty and for the reason that we find ourselves at times confronted with two courses of action, two lines of duty. Ideally, the answer to the question must be No. It is wrong to take life whether human or animal. But equally is it right and our bounden duty to defend one's country, and to defend one's home and one's family. Thus in time of war, seeing that each citizen of a country is an integral part of the nation to which he belongs, it is his duty to obey the laws of the government of the country to which he belongs.

I have answered this from my own standpoint and as I conceive would be my duty to act in either of the events mentioned in the question. What I have said above, however, has no reference to capital punishment which is utterly wrong and unnecessary, and is not a deterrent of crime in the long run. Capital punishment is to be condemned absolutely.

SELF-CONSCIOUSNESS IN THE THIRD ROUND

Were we self-conscious human beings at any time during the Third ROUND *on this Earth-chain?*

Yes, towards the end of the globe manvantara when the mânasic faculty began to manifest as best it could in Third Round conditions. This faculty, however, was not then as fully manifested as now.

A CASE OF QUICK REINCARNATION OR CLAIRVOYANCE

May we ask you to give us your opinion about the following matter: In several periodicals and papers people read about a so-called 'definite proof' of reincarnation. It concerns the case of a young Hindû girl whose extraordinary statements about her 'previous incarnation' are described and investigated; and we get questions about it. You will, no doubt, also have read about it. According to the teachings of Theosophy such a quick return to the next rebirth of a human being and such strange 'recollections' would be impossible. Can this be a case of self-delusion, or something of the kind?

I think you are wrong when you say that according to the teachings of Theosophy, "such a quick return to the next rebirth of a human being . . . would be impossible." You are almost right, but not quite. Such quick reincarnations are very, very, rare when compared with the hundreds of millions of normal human beings; but they do take place; and in the aggregate these very, very rare exceptions, if one could collect them together in a group, would *seem* to be fairly numerous.

As far as I have been able to gather from the reports in the papers about this Hindû girl, who is little more than a child, it would seem to me that her case is to be explained on either one of two possibilities; and as I myself do not know all the facts in the case, and also as I have not been really particularly interested, I put the two possibilities before you, and if *you* are interested, you can make your own selection from the two.

(a) It is probably one of those very rare cases of almost immediate reincarnation of a human ego, which, despite their great rarity when compared with the hundreds of millions of normal human beings, nevertheless, taking those rare exceptions as a body, are not so awfully uncommon. In this matter is involved the whole teaching regarding reincarnation, and the stay in the Kâma-loka and the Devachan, the details of which teaching every studious Theosophist knows; and these teachings can be briefly summarized by saying that the more spiritual a man or woman is, in life, the longer the Devachan and hence the interval between two successive incarnations. Contrariwise, the more material or the greater the love for the physical world that exists in a man or woman, the shorter the Devachan, and therefore the shorter the interval between two incarnations.

There are also the cases of congenital idiots, of children dying young, and of lost souls — three very different kinds of human beings, it is true — who, because of having had no chance to evolve spiritually, that is in a fairly long life, reincarnate almost immediately. (See H. P. B. on the matter of immediate reincarnation in *Isis Unveiled*, Vol. I, p. 351, and her article 'Theories about Reincarnation and Spirits,' where she throws added light on the subject.)

Now, it is quite possible that this Hindû girl belongs to this last *general* class, which does *not* mean that she is a lost soul, or that she died as an infant in her last life, or that she is an imbecile; but merely that she is not one of the more spiritual types of human beings, but is probably one who loves, or did love, in her last life the physical spheres, one in whom the higher intellectual and spiritual powers were not yet awakened. It is these powers which make the Devachan long or short, in proportion to the strength of these powers in a man's or a woman's life. Consequently she had built up a slight devachanic potentiality; and also probably being quite a good young woman in her last life — for she says she died very young — there was no long stay in the Kâma-loka for purification purposes.

(b) The other possibility is one which I myself would not select as the true explanation, and I mention it here only because it is a possibility — and it may be true. There are some people who are born at times with unusual clairvoyant power, and with a very strong and vivid imagination; so that this combination of clairvoyance and immensely vivid imagination, makes these individuals actually 'see' things that exist in other places on earth while they are alive; and when they 'see' these things, their vivid imagination and faculty of constructing mental and imaginary pictures, makes them imagine all kinds of possibilities. Thus, then, if this girl is such a natural clairvoyant, at least at times and along a certain line of clairvoyance, she might have had actual visions of this other town where this man and his present wife live in India, and her imaginative mind, with her romantic feelings, may have woven about this picture, or these clair-voyant pictures coming to her, all kinds of feminine imaginary emotional visions about how the man was her husband in a former life, etc., etc., etc.

This last class of people is quite common, especially among girls. This class is so well known that doctors in their practice frequently come across such cases, and very many of these doctors call them cases of peculiar hysteria. Such individuals are always abnormal; they are excessively imaginative; they are always building 'dreams' and 'visions,' and if they happen to possess a clairvoyant power, whether strong or weak, at the same time, this combination of clairvoyant faculty and power of imagination work together and make these subjects think that they are the heroes or the heroines in all kinds of romantic dreams.

It is just these psychic matters, on account of their apparent mystery and the difficulty of explaining them, which fascinate men and women 'in the street' as the slang expression goes in this country, and generally speak-ing they should not be stressed.

The Suicide After-Death State

What is the exact state after death of a person who commits suicide to avoid present conditions? Does he remain in a temporary state before entering the rest due to one who has died a natural death?

Yes, a temporary state, and it depends upon the suicide's character as to just what kind of state this temporary state is. As ye sow, ye shall reap. All suicide is wrong, ethically and in every other way, for it is cowardice, it is shirking; and you know what happens to shirkers in life. As I have often said before, every human being is born with a certain magazine and reservoir of vitality; and the composite entity which is man holds together until that reservoir of vitality is exhausted. Then the composition breaks up. The spirit goes to Father-Sun; the reincarnating ego goes into its devachan or heaven-world of unspeakable peace and bliss; and the lower parts break up and dissolve into their component atoms.

But in the case of a suicide, here is one, a human unfortunate, who, it may be harassed and wrung by sorrow and pain, in folly takes his life, thinking, blind man, that he can thwart Nature's purposes. He simply destroys the body, and all the man remains in the astral world in conditions which are at the very best the reverse of pleasant; and in the cases of evil suicides — men who suicide and who have also been extremely evil men —

in their cases they are in a condition which is awful, for their whole consciousness is burning with all the unholy passions, hates, loves, fears, terrors, dreads, which caused them to commit suicide. They have no escape; in taking their own life they made the condition a thousandfold worse.

But there are suicides and suicides, and the individual case depends upon the individual suicide. That is all there is to it. The mental state in which the suicide was before he committed the act, continues in the astral world, but intensified tremendously. Of course the time will come when the reservoir of vitality will be exhausted; and then whatever of beauty and grandeur and spiritual light there was in the soul of the suicide receives its recompense in the devachan then. But suicide is cowardice, and this should not be forgotten.

MAN'S RELATION TO THE TWELVEFOLD SOLAR SYSTEM

As we are truly children of the whole solar system could it not be said that we are no more Earth entities than we are Venus entities or Mercury entities, or of the other planets?

True. It is only for the present manvantara that we are attached to the Earth-chain, and this is the secret of the Outer Rounds.

Are we then solar entities evolving through different vehicles on all the twelve planets of the solar family?

To speak of twelve planets of our solar system has reference only to ourselves. There are only twelve sacred planets for us in the solar system. The sun is our common Chief. This is why — and here you get an inkling as to the thirteen — this is the secret why Jesus had twelve disciples while he himself was the thirteenth or teacher.

CONSOLATION REGARDING DEATH

I have studied the technical Theosophical literature and understand that man is a composite being. Also, I have read about what happens to the sevenfold hierarchy 'Man' when he dies, but has not Theosophy also an ethical side in regard to death, with love and compassion?

My question is: What consolation for the heart, what inspiring hope and courage, does Theosophy give to those who fear death, to the dying, to those who have lost their loved ones?

Theosophy teaches that death *per se* is not to be feared. It is a change to a better state, but only when death comes naturally. This questioner evidently has not read much of our Theosophical literature, wherein he

would have been told that ethics are of the very essence of every doctrine
that Theosophy has. Ethics are of the very structure of the Universe, for
they mean harmony: that right is right, and that wrong is wrong, and that
the correct thing is the correct thing, no matter when and where it is; also
that the straight thing is the straight thing no matter where and when it is.

The ethics of our teaching regarding death are what I have so often
stated: That it is naught to fear; it is inexpressibly sweet, for it means
ineffable rest, peace, bliss. When a man dies, he enters into the great
Silence, just as happens when a man falls asleep and later awakens. These
few words tell you the whole story, although none of the details of the
story.

Do you remember what Robert Louis Stevenson wrote in his *Requiem?*
He wrote this for his own grave, they say:

> Under the wide and starry sky
> Dig the grave and let me lie;
> Glad did I live and gladly die,
> And I lay me down with a will.

> This be the verse you grave for me
> "Here he lies where he longed to be.
> Home is the sailor, home from the sea,
> And the hunter home from the hill."

Ay, very beautiful, for in it the spirit of Robert Louis Stevenson spoke;
but why did he say: "Dig the grave and let me lie." Don't you see here
the old horrible thought that the man is his physical body? I would have
written: "Dig the grave and let me go free." I, an incarnate energy of
the Universe — can you keep me within a grave? I, a flaming intelligence,
an imbodied spirit, can you enchain me within a coffin? Ay, the very
bonds of the world are too small for me. My soul is native with the stars,
and whether it be Canopus or Sirius, or Stella Polaris, there I dwell on
familiar terms. There I belong. Free me! "Glad did I live, and gladly
I die, and I lay me down with a will. This be the verse you grave for me.
Hence he has gone, where he longed to be."

*Take the case of one who dearly loved someone else on earth, and the
one who loves, dies: Does the dead one who loved, continue to love?*

A very natural question indeed. The very meaning, the very essence,
of the heaven-world state, or devachan, is bliss and love, because bliss and
spiritual yearnings have as their main motive-power that abstract impersonal function or energy of the human spirit which we men call love. The
devachan signifies all that is beautiful and good and sweet and holy and
true and clean and pure. Love is immortal; it continues always; and,

mark you, the more one loves, of course impersonally, the nobler he becomes. I don't here mean the ordinary gross, passional love, for that can be even of the fires of hell. But I mean that inexpressibly sweet, divine flame which fills life with beauty, which instills thoughts of self-sacrifice for others. Love of that kind, impersonal love, is the very heart of the Universe. Therefore, I say, the one who loved and who died, loves still, for it is of the fabric of his soul.

DEATH IN BATTLE OR ACCIDENT

What happens to those who are slain in battle?

I daresay that the questioner thinks there must be some identity in what happens to those who are slain in battle and suicides, merely because death in each case is quick; but it is not so. It is the motive, in every instance of violent death, whether wilful suicide or murder, or death in battle or accident, which governs the post-mortem state. Those slain in battle sink into utter unconsciousness, for in them there is no stain of cowardice seeking to shirk the duty, as in the case of the suicide, and therefore no harrowing anxiety, no harrowing and corroding fears of life itself. Those slain in battle simply lapse into blissful unconsciousness and so remain until the reservòir of astral-physical vitality is exhausted. Then they enter the devachan, the heaven-world. Nature is rigidly just in all her rules and actions, because she is rigidly compassionate. Compassion, remember, means law, harmony, regular procedures of cause and effect. The very heart of Nature's being is compassion. The man who dies in battle, and the man who gives his life to save the life of a brother, are very much the same. Unconsciousness, dreamless and inexpressibly sweet, that is what they receive until the reservoir of vitality is exhausted; then they enter the devachan, or heaven-world, and therein remain in inexpressibly beautiful and blissful rest until the next reimbodiment on earth.

HOW OLD ARE THE HINDÛ SCHOOLS OF PHILOSOPHY?

Can you give me any hint as to age or time of origin of the six Darśanas or Hindû schools of philosophy? When did Kapila and Patañjali actually live? There is so much argument on these two personages and the time of their birth.

You ask first about the origin, and second about the various ages, of the Six Great Darśanas or Philosophic Visions, otherwise Schools of Philosophy in India; and collaterally with these you ask about the ages of their various Founders, such as Kanâda, Kapila, Gotama (not the Buddha of course here), Patañjali, etc.

First, as regards the ages of the founders: The truth is that all the ages, or dates rather, given by European Orientalists are little more than speculations; they have never been proved, even though they may be generally accepted. Consequently we Theosophists refuse to accept them. They are almost invariably too late in time, too close to us. That is what I would say.

On the other hand, I would accept with much more respect a date that might be worked out as given by some eminent Hindû of old times himself. Of course I know this would be a vast work, sifting the material, and I merely mention it to show that I would prefer the Hindû tradition, as to when so-and-so lived, to the theorizings of modern Occidentalists who are all psychologized with scientific ideas of the recent development of thinking man, etc., etc.

In the old days it used to be held that the world was created only six thousand odd years ago, and this was a then Christian view; and consequently every date had to be brought down as close to ours as they could push it. So much for the dates of the founders of these Schools. Every one of these founders was not actually a founder in the sense of starting a new School, but merely carried on, perhaps rejuvenated, perhaps modified, what already had been known for heaven knows how many ages before he lived: somewhat in the same way that H. P. B. brought the archaic Theosophy to our age and presented it in its modern form, although it is ageless as time.

This leads me to the origin of these Six Darśanas. Occidental Orientalists, as I have already pointed out, in trying to keep within the limits of their new facts, say that each such School was probably started by the philosopher named. But I have just pointed out why in actual fact this need not be so.

It is my opinion, in fact my conviction, that every one of these Six Darśanas is of enormous age. The fact that they are such natural productions of the human intellect shows that they must have occurred ages and ages and ages ago to other philosophic minds. Personally I think they run back in their reaches even to Atlantean times, not in their present presentations or forms, but I mean the philosophic ground-thoughts that these Schools respectively represent. The various so-called founders were merely more or less recent; and by that I mean long after Atlantis, but not in our time — Hindû philosophers who themselves were attracted by one or other of the Schools; and each one was so successful in interpreting and propagandizing his own particular choice or philosophic preference, that in time he became the founder of this School or that School.

For instance, take the Yoga School of Patañjali. I think that it flourished ages beyond the age of Patañjali, whenever he lived, because Yoga has been active in the thought of man's mind since immemorial time. Patañjali did not discover it. He merely acted as I have above stated. The same with the Nyâya School of Logical Philosophy of Gotama, or the Vaiśeshika, the Atomic School of Kanâda. Thoughts like these must have been in the minds of men since Atlantean times. Similarly with the Vedânta, especially the Adwaita. The Adwaita form of it was magnificently presented and formulated by the great Śankarâchârya, and this is just an instance in point. Some occidental scholars now call him the Founder of the Adwaita-Vedânta, as if men never had the thoughts in the Adwaita-Vedânta before Śankarâchârya. He merely took this aspect of the Vedânta, and re-formed it according to the ideas of his time, and did so wonderfully that he became known as its great Teacher. But Adwaita-Vedânta is so native to the human spirit, it must have existed for ages and ages before ever Śankarâchârya was dreamed of, by the Gods that be.

As we Theosophists say, the Six Darśanas contain the six various types or methods in which human philosophy through the ages has been cast, and we unite them all in the highest or seventh, which is our own Wisdom-Religion or Theosophy — or to put it more correctly, it is from this God-Wisdom or Wisdom-Religion that all these six various Darśanas have come forth as six special presentations or six specializations of philosophy, each one along its own line, the scientific, the mystical, the logical, the scientific-mystic, the objectively idealistic, call them by what names you like.

HEALING METHODS AND KARMAN

What is your opinion in regard to the various kinds of healing by vital or so-called 'magnetic' processes, whether the 'laying-on of hands' or magnetic passes, or what some semi-ignorant schools call 'absent treatment' etc., etc.?   In my estimation this whole matter has grown to have real importance because of the way it has spread, even clergymen taking hold of it, trying to follow in the footsteps of their Master Jesus, who healed as they say 'by faith' and spiritual power.

All these various forms of healing, apart from regular medical or surgical practice, depend upon the innate, i.e., inborn or inherent, ability of the 'healer' or practitioner to convey healthy life-force from himself to the diseased person. This is the key to success, or the lack of success, in all cases, and in all kinds of healing, of whatsoever so-called 'school.'

If a person is a natural born 'magnetiser' as Colonel Olcott was in a small way, or as Mesmer in a fairly large way, then such a person can cure by magnetic or so-called 'mesmeric' passes by stroking the afflicted organ or part of the body, sometimes without any motion, but an intense mental concentration to that end.

If the 'healer' or practitioner is not such a born or innately endowed 'magnetiser,' his success is either nil or poor. The whole explanation lies in the successful conveying of prâna or vitality from his own healthy body to the diseased body or diseased organ or part, which healthy vitality or life-force 'expels' or changes the inharmonious vibrations from the afflicted part, and restores harmony therein, thus bringing about health. Such cures *can be* permanent; usually they are temporary, lasting a few days, a few weeks, months, possibly a year or two or three. All these methods and processes were well known to the ancients. To the modern Occidental they are generally classed, because of ignorance, under headings such as 'healing by hypnotism,' 'healing by mesmerism,' 'healing by magnetism'; sometimes when passes and strokings are not used, then 'healing by faith,' as practised by the Christian Scientists and the faith-healers.

Here you have the key to all the processes, all the successes and all the failures.

What about karman in this connexion? Is it wrong to heal in these ways, or is it right? And does it 'dam back karman,' making it rush forth in the future with accumulated force, thus bringing about a disease worse than that which was temporarily stayed or stopped?

If — and this is important — if the magnetiser is physically healthy, mentally well-balanced, and most important of all, morally and intellectually clean, there is no harm whatsoever in these healings by mesmeric magnetism, but not by hypnotism, please; if the practitioner is unclean morally, intellectually unsound, even in his view of right and wrong, or again if the practitioner himself is not properly physically healthy, diseases can even be transplanted, or transferred, in germ, and even death can be brought about, by evil magic thus worked, which last case is plain murder, and very difficult to trace. But there is nothing wrong in healing sick and ailing people, whether by regular surgical and medical practice, or by a highminded, healthy, and compassionate 'vital healer,' even if the latter acts in ignorance of the philosophical rationale. This last case is not 'damming back karman,' because karman already is exhausting itself in the diseased person, and the healing is merely helping nature to bring restoration of health, to re-establish normal conditions in the sufferer.

But karman is dammed back, and therefore the healing of any kind becomes positively pernicious and wrong, in cases where the healer attempts to act upon the will, the conscience, or the moral integrity, of the sick person, the patient, the sufferer, by hypnotizing the mind and will power and conscience of the sufferer into the belief that sickness does not exist, or that the sufferer is a victim of fate, instead of being the sufferer from his own evil past. I wonder if I make my meaning clear. If the mind, especially the will power, or moral integrity, of the patient is touched by the practitioner, this at once becomes black magic, tends to reproduce wrong ideas in the patient, thus damming back the disease, although this practice likewise can temporarily heal because of the hypnotic condition of the will power and mind induced in the patient under an illusory, quasi-philosophical, wrong teaching. Thus in this last case karman working itself out is dammed at its source, the disease is forced back into the con-stitution, the body may be benefitted; but the disease lies latent, for ultimately all disease originates in wrong thoughts bringing about wrong feelings and wrong actions; and this is what is meant by damming back karman. But the merely vital magnetiser does not do this. He treats the suffering body alone, as the ordinary physician and surgeon does, helps to restore harmony in the prânic currents of the sufferer's body, but does not touch the will power or moral nature of the sufferer; and consequently his work is not evil — I mean in the case of an upright good man who practises or heals, as above stated.

And finally, the best way of all these drugless healing methods or pro-cesses, commonly called 'vital healing' or by some similar term, or healing by passes, etc., is the case where the sufferer himself is brought into a state of mind of hope, self-confidence, the higher kind of resignation bringing peace and inner quiet in its train, all of which helps the body back to a condition of harmony, thus aiding the natural healing processes in the sufferer's body itself. This is why some kinds of faith-healing are the best because they do not touch the will or the mind except to bring about inner peace, resignation to the inevitable, and the instilling into the sufferer's mind of a condition of hope, of vital energy, and a happier outlook, all of which tends to help the sufferer's body. The best attitude of mind for the sick person is that of hope, the growth of inner peace, and self-confi-dence; and these are best brought about by a sound philosophy, which is what is alluded to in the Christian New Testament where the references are to the various healings by Jesus on the basis of re-establishing the suf-ferer's 'faith,' as the New Testament word is found, and the injunction: 'Go and sin no more,' the 'sin' here meaning bad thoughts, evil feelings, and their consequent actions in daily life, such as vice in all forms.

The whole situation is extremely complicated. No greater mistake could be made than to think it is all simple and can be answered in a single paragraph. Even a Black Magician can heal a body if it is to the Black Magician's profit to do so; but in this case the body is healed at the ex-pense of the soul, so to speak, and possibly even new diseases are planted in the sufferer's body in seed or in germ, because the mind and will are distorted, bringing about mental currents from within the sufferer poisoning the sufferer's own prânas.

Thus the secret lies, as you see, in arousing the sufferer's own innate powers of resistance, of vitality, etc., and thus making these dominant, thus making the body heal itself; and *not* in overpowering the sufferer's will, or imagination, or moral instincts, resulting in making these recessive, numb, or asleep. The former is good and white, the latter is bad and black.

This is but a hasty outline of an exceedingly tangled situation, the tangling arising in the utter ignorance of most people about the complicated structure of the human constitution. Some healings are good, some healings are bad, some healers are good, some are bad, some are frauds.

OCTAVES OF RADIATION IN THE COSMIC SCALE

Do light and radio act through different media of transmission and if so, which are these media?

The questioner thinks that all energy, being One Force, can be transformed from one form of manifestation into another, and he seems to believe that light and radio cannot be combined in healing work on account of the fact that they work through different media.

I think there is a confusion of thought here. Light-waves, radio-waves, heat-waves, and those other wave-radiations which are called x-ray, cosmic ray, etc. — all these are different parts of, or different octaves in, the great scale of nature, and hence although all of them radiations or wave-forms (using modern scientific terminology here), they are as distinctly separate, because of their different energies or frequencies, as are for instance a mile and an inch or a centimeter.

For instance, the radio-waves are very long waves. Then come the heat-waves which are shorter. Then come the light — visible light that is — waves which are still shorter. Then come the ultra-violet waves, still shorter; then after an interval come the x-rays which are very short. And then after another interval come other waves extending into the shortest known radiations among which are the gamma-rays and cosmic rays. Thus very high frequency waves, like x-rays and cosmic ray radiations, are called 'hard' waves, simply because they are of frequency so high, that is, of vibration so tremendously high, that they are like tremendous bumps or thumps. Whereas the long waves like radio-waves, the frequency being so small, that is, the vibration or wave-length so long, we might call 'soft' waves.

Here then is the answer to the question, an answer by the way which is known to all scientists. It is true that all the forces in the universe are

reducible to one Cosmic Force, but this one Cosmic Force during manifestation in cosmic manvantara, in its lower forms is broken up into these
multitudinous different radiations or wave-lengths, each wave-length having
its specific individuality.

For instance, we can, if we wish, in order to give an example, say that
the waves of health are of a certain length, a certain frequency; the waves
of disease are of another frequency. Yet they are both waves, and the
only difference between them is in the different frequencies or vibratory
rates. Thus then it is theoretically possible, quite possible, to change the
hard, short diseased waves into the longer, softer, gentler waves of health-
radiation. Naturally it is extremely difficult to do this, but thought can
do it, mind can do it, because thought and mind are superior to these waves
and can therefore control them, thought- and mind-power being relatively
spiritual and healthy, and disease-waves being relatively physical. Thus
it is that while One Force is at the bottom of all, being the Cosmic Force,
the great spiritual Force of the Universe; yet these different other subordinate forces: light, radio, heat, electricity, etc., etc.: are all different
octaves of the one cosmic radiation scale. Thus it is quite possible in
theory to transform one into the other, but in actual point of fact, to transform a long radio wave into an x-ray, let us say, would be tremendously
difficult, because it would be changing a wave-radiation of a mile or two,
or several miles long, into a wave-radiation, that is the x-ray, which is an
infinitesimal part of an inch long. Hence for practical purposes, it is of
almost cosmic difficulty to transform one such force into another force.

The way to heal disease by radiation would be to apply to the disease-
frequency another frequency or vibratory energy of a softer, gentler, but
stronger because more harmonic type. To change the figure of speech, let
us say that the health of a human body is a certain key-note or key-tone.
If a certain part of that body, let us say the heart or the liver or the brain,
is in disease, it means that that particular organ rebels against the keynote
of the body, and is establishing a little keynote of its own; and this produces a discord in the body which is what we mean when we say disease.
The way to heal that disease is in some way to change that harder vibration or frequency of the diseased organ, into the keynote of the whole body,
thus re-establishing the keynote of the body and bringing back health.
Scientists of the future will learn how to do this without injuring the body;
but it is quite possible that the body could be seriously injured if not killed
by ignorant experimentation, for the diseased organ might actually be rup-
tured or shattered if the proper radiation or frequency be not applied to it.

Thus then the answer to your question is to remember the following:
All these different forces above named: radio, heat, light, x-ray, cosmic

ray, and all the intermediate frequencies: all belong to the cosmic scale, and each one such is but a small octave of that great Cosmic Scale. This is even ordinary science today. All these forces or forms of radiation are just that: different forms of radiation. Just as in an octave in a piano, the do re mi fa sol la si do, are different sound-frequencies belonging to the one piano-octave. If one changes such a note on a piano-octave into some other note, or tries to rather, it is a very, very difficult thing to do, because you destroy one note by increasing its frequency, or decrease its frequency in order to make some other note.

Thus, to change light into radiant heat, you would 'soften' or diminish the frequency. Or, in the other direction, to change visible light into ultra-violet light, one would have to increase or 'harden' the frequency of vibration. And to do either of these would be real magic. Nevertheless, as said, it is perfectly true that fundamentally all these different frequencies are radiations belonging to the cosmic scale, and while theoretically it is possible to transform one into another, it would require a magician to do this. Hence the healer attempting to do this with radio or light or electricity or sound, would have to know how to apply the healing frequency to the diseased frequency of a diseased organ.

THEOSOPHIC CONCEPTION OF DENSITY

What is Dr. de Purucker's conception of density? Is it dependent on and measurable by the frequency of the vibrations of the intra-atomic constituents or of the atoms themselves or a combination of both?

Is density as Dr. de Purucker uses the word dependent in any sense on the number of electrons or other constituents within the atom?

The querent seems to suppose, or rather perhaps to suggest, that I have used or do use the word 'density' with a meaning somewhat different from that commonly employed. I doubt if this is the fact. As far as I can recollect, I always use the word 'density' in the manner in which it is commonly used by most educated people, realizing that the word has a general significance as well as many particular applications to different cases; and I find that this somewhat vague manner of employing the term 'dense' or 'density' is that followed by almost everybody. Density is the closeness of constituent parts, generally speaking, whether we be referring to electrons or atoms or molecular groups.

Density has been defined as "the mass or amount of matter per unit of bulk." So I understand the term; and, generally speaking, I suppose that we can measure density by the weight of a unit of bulk or by the specific gravity. In other words, density, therefore, is the amount of matter in or the mass of a material unit. Other somewhat looser definitions of density are compactness, or the state or quality of being close in constitution.

I think some confusion has arisen in the minds of those who have followed my various statements with regard to density, etc., because of the common wide prevalence of the idea in the western world for ages that the greater the activity of the units in a system, the more spiritual it is; whereas the exact contrary is in fact the case; and this is just what I have tried on many occasions to show, realizing full well that I was in conflict with common opinion.

Yet it ought to be evident that when particles are vibrating with intense and almost unimaginable frequency or rapidity, and doing so as a unit-entity, the forces involved would be harder to change and harder to move than when the vibrations are weak, diffuse, and more or less dissipate; and it is precisely this compactness of vibrations and the closeness of their interaction which produce mass or amount of matter.

Thus if we compare various densities of chemical elements, we shall find, as instances, that platinum can be reckoned as 21.4, gold as 19.3, mercury as 13.6, lead as 11.3, copper as 8.9, iron as 7.8, the earth generally as 5.6, the diamond as 3.5, ordinary rock about 2.7, magnesium 1.7, the human body generally as 1.1, lithium as 0.6, air as 0.0013 — and here we have what we can call molecular densities if we wish; but when we come to the chemical attraction in these various substances, whether chemical elements or chemical compounds, we enter into another sphere of attributes and qualities having their own densities; yet the densities in either group of cases seem to be dependent in each instance upon the number and activities of the constituent parts of the units.

Really, I think that the querent has somewhat misunderstood my words as implying that I use the term 'dense' or 'density' somewhat arbitrarily and in a different sense from that ordinarily employed; and at the moment of this writing, I am not conscious of ever having done so.

MARIE CORELLI

Was Marie Corelli a real mystic?

I think she was. Some of her books are extremely interesting, and show an intuitive reception of gleams of light from the fountain of Truth, which, in her case, was from within her own Higher Self, touching, as it were, her literary brain. Yet, on the other hand, she was heavily laden by some of the things of this world, as for instance I understand she was of a very jealous temperament, jealous of other literary people, and apt to be critical even of her own friends. But, after all, that belongs to the artistic temperament almost always, and can be overlooked.

I think Marie Corelli did a good work as far as it went in raising many people to a realization of mysticism and magic who never would have been awakened, even in the slight degree in which she touched them, except through the medium of some pen like hers which was graphic, thought-arresting, and inflamed the imagination of this type of mind; and there are millions of them. She was an unconscious kind of Theosophist in half of herself.

On Foretelling the Future

J. B. Priestley says the Past, Present and Future are co-existent different vibrations existing at the same time in the same place, but our minds are capable of vibrating to only the Present because the Past has had some material effect on our mind and changed it, that is why we remember it. In other words, it has become part of us. The Future has not become part of us and so we cannot understand it except by noticing what the Past did to the Present, the Present did to the Future. He also says there is no Present really, but that it is just our perception of the unevolved in this plane (although it is evolved on another), the unevolved becoming the evolved.

Some of this seems curious to me. I can understand the clairvoyant going back into the past and seeing it as H. P. B. did, because it has happened and left a record. But how can the clairvoyant go into the future and see that? If one has a super mind one can foretell the future as long as it is the extension of the Present. I mean that one can deduce what will happen, if all the facts are known, just as a builder can foretell the future of a house he is building. But to see the future by this method would need a mind larger than all the libraries in the world and an exact machine to give all knowledge its true ratio of importance, and a knowledge of how much and how fast Karma was going to be unrolled. Algebraical equations with 4 roots are hard enough, but an equation with an infinite number of roots, combined in an infinite number of ways is much too hard for even the most advanced combination of Manas and Buddhi. So I still don't know how one can foresee the future.

The matter of 'seeing the future,' etc., seems awfully difficult to answer, and indeed it is in a way, and is downright difficult to one who has not had any training in Theosophy. But here is the answer:

In occult philosophy, the past, the present, and the future, blend together in eternity, or what is called the ETERNAL Now, for Eternity has neither past, present, nor future, it being an ETERNAL Now. Eternity, furthermore, is the fundamental — or as we might say, eternity and infinity are the two sides of the same ultimate Reality, the fundamental, the ALL.

What the spiritual Seer does is to rise from this plane on which past, present, and future seem so positive and real to us, into as it were the ranges of his own spiritual being which bathe so to speak in the Eternal Now; and in this way the past is unrolled before his eyes, and the present is seen to be but a continuation of it into what we call the future, and both are glimpsed as an eternal drama whose keynote is Now. Thus likewise should karman be viewed, the karmic past, the karmic present, the karmic future; and in this way we avoid falling into the error of fatalism on the one hand, and on the other hand into the equally great error of karmic indeterminance.

As an illustration, from another angle: an atom in my body contains electrons, any atom does. On these electrons let us say there are inhabitants, living their own tiny lives, but at an enormous rate of speed compared with our time. Thus a whole cosmic solar system so to speak, of atomic size, can come into being, live its innumerable aeons, and vanish many thousand times in one of our human seconds. In other words, one of our human seconds compared with electronic time, is almost 'eternally' long.

Now, imagine an inhabitant on such an electron, living at its tremendous rate of speed which to us humans would seem incomparably quicker than a lightning flash. Yet to the electronic inhabitant, long years would be going by. To him there would be a future which we, with our slower time, would not appreciate except as a now. Thus the electronic inhabitant, because of his intense tempo, immense speed, would be undergoing his past, present, and future; whereas we, with our far more majestic time, with its slow rhythmic pulses, would scarcely realize it except by intellectual thought. To us it would be just simply now.

In exactly the same way, the gods, whose time-tempo is incomparably stately and to us humans what we would call slow, look upon *our* past, present, and future, which to us seem so real, as scarcely differentiated, because our time by comparison with theirs is so rapid. We have next week, next year, a billion years from now, but these are our tiny little human years. To one of the higher gods, the entire manvantara of our solar system would be scarcely a billionth part of that one god's seconds in that god's time. So in our solar system we would be looking forward into millions of years ahead, and looking back into millions of years of the past; whereas the god's consciousness would scarcely be aware of the entire life-period of the solar system as other than a tiny fraction of an instant.

Do you see now how it is possible to read the future? The Seer, the spiritual Seer, not the pretentious and half-baked clairvoyant, but the spiritual Seer, simply raises his consciousness into another tempo, into another higher plane, in which past, present, and future are visible to its vision as a Now. This of course requires initiatory training. But every adept is trained, depending upon his grade in the hierarchy, trained in some degree at least.

Now another thing: never forget that free will exists for every monad great or small in infinity. So that the tiny electronic inhabitant, just like the human on our big globe: each one has his own portion, so to speak, of free will, that is if we can divide free will up into portions that way! Really, free will is the amount of spiritual vitality and intellect that the evolving individual has been able to grasp through inner growth. Thus free will can be greatly increased, but it exists even in the tiniest atom, although of course on the scale of those spheres. Therefore, no matter what the time-ratio is, no matter whether one can foresee the future in large or in small, the entity having his portion of free will can always change his future course by that free will, which does not mean acting contrary to the future, because this would be impossible, but modifying his own conduct with regard to the future, so that he can do, or refrain from doing, in proportion as his free will is strong or weak.

MYSTERY OF THE GROWING PLANT

What is there in the consciousness of a plant that gives it the impulse to grow towards the light and succeed, no matter what obstacles impede its progress?

The consciousness of a plant, and indeed that of a beast, or even of a man — and we may add, the almost latent consciousness of the mineral kingdom — is the spiritual, combining with the astral, fluid in the constitution of a plant, let us say, which possesses the undying instinct or hunger to move forwards and upwards; and it is this instinct for growth, or seeking the Light as we say, which is the pushing cause or the great urge behind all evolution to better and higher things.

Thus the plant-seed, if it happens to be caught in some awkward place where the light is difficult to obtain, will as it grows, because of this monadic fluid urging it to grow and reach upwards towards what it wants, twist and turn around a stone or up through pavement, until it pushes its first tiny green blade to the light. It is really a most beautiful thing to think of and to watch, and has been a puzzle for science for two hundred years or more.

Theosophy supplies the answer, as I have tried to state it. I have seen a stone pavement broken or burst by some tender little plant, which by its monadic instinct knew the light was on the other side of the stone or the asphalt above it; and instead of growing and growing and growing under the asphalt or stone until it came to the edge, and then poking its way into the light, it just pushes with its tender little blade-points between the particles of the pavement, and breaks them apart little by little, until finally, like the chick leaving the egg, pecking through the shell, it pokes its nose into the light of the world above. It is the monadic fluid, or vital-astral fluid — the same thing in its lower form — which is instinct with intuitive consciousness, which drives or impels the plant to do exactly the right thing to reach the light.

INDIVIDUALITY AND PERSONALITY

Does Theosophy teach that we always retain our individuality in all states of consciousness?

Yes it does indeed, provided that we use 'individuality' in the technical Theosophical sense. Remember that the individuality is a very different thing from the personality. The individuality is the deathless part of us, the *individuum,* that which cannot be divided. Otherwise stated, it is the Monadic Essence, it is the inner God, the spark of divinity within us, that spark of the Cosmic Fire of consciousness-life-substance which is our inmost essence. This in its root is Âtman, the indivisible self, deathless, stainless, and in its own essence beginningless and endless; for it is of the very substance-consciousness of the Universe.

The personality is a vastly different thing; it is a reflexion merely of the individuality. The personality is like the moonshine, reflected light from the sun; and this personality is mortal always — and how fortunate it is that it is so! Fancy what it would be like, living in eternity in our present personalities: imperfect, undeveloped, feeble, inept, incapable of any great advancement, a poor understander, a very poor follower of noble things, incapable of receiving and retaining for any length of time the best that is in us.

Yet the personality is a wonderful instrument or vehicle through which the individuality works. I think we may say generally that the individuality is the spirit, and the personality is the mortal brain-mind of us; changing with each birth.

Thus it is clear why the individuality is the same, and that "we retain" it in all states of consciousness, for these various states of consciousness, in all their manifold and often bewildering phases and shifting qualities and attributes, when traced to their ultimate or original source, are light-stuff from the Âtman. Consciousness contains many mysteries; and the real part of us is conscious even in those phases of consciousness wherein the personality is unconscious — a curious play upon words, yet containing a profound truth, and pointing to the same thought contained in the Sanskrit aphorism: *Âtmânam âtmanâ paśya,* "Know the self by the Self."

IMMORTALITY AND GOOD AND EVIL

I have been reading the record of H. P. B.'s Inner Group in this month's FORUM *(January, 1941), and in an "Editor's Note" the statement is made that only by becoming actively good or evil can one achieve immortality. The ordinary folk, neither very good or evil, cease to be. Now, if I read this aright, it seems very terrible, and although a return to this troublous world does not seem enviable just now, one feels that surely those not wholly given up to evil have a better right to continue than the utterly evil.*

Also it does not seem consistent with the teaching that ALL *must eventually evolve to the highest.*

Perhaps I am not clear in my reasoning, for I am still very much a beginner in Theosophical thought. I read and re-read the articles in the FORUM, *and often find that after many studies light dawns. But I do find this latest problem beyond me.*

I am not at all astonished that the questioner was puzzled at the language used in the article in *Leaves of Theosophical History* as quoting from H. P. B.'s Inner Group, and the reason is that the teaching as here imbodied is given patterned after the peculiar language of the French Qabbalist Éliphas Lévi, who is notorious for extreme statements on the one hand (for that was his psychology), and on the other hand for the singularity of his paradoxes. Yet because he was intuitive in some respects, H. P. B. often quoted him either verbatim or in substance.

Take careful note of the following facts: The *Monads* whether of gods or of men or of beasts or of plants or of stones or of elementals, are immortal, for they are spiritual consciousness-centers. *But* the references in the passage that bothered the questioner, do not point to the monads, but to the various souls of the different hierarchies of lives or different kingdoms of lives, which either must rise up into immortality and 'god' by joining with the spirit within them, or in other words with the spiritual side of the monad; or attain immortality in what is called "evil," by descending and becoming unified with what we Theosophists call absolute matter. In this way, philosophically speaking, there is immortality; and this is the important word here, *self-conscious* immortality either with the divine or with the absolutely material: absolute Spirit on the one hand, or absolute Matter on the other hand — so far as our own universe is concerned, that is.

We human beings, although immortal in our monads, cannot be called immortal in our souls, because our consciousness is interrupted by death. And here is the point to remember: A person is not immortal if there ensue long lapses of his consciousness, although he is immortal in the other sense of never-ending inner or monadic consciousness. Thus we human beings are immortal in our monads, conditionally immortal in our souls, and mortal in our bodies, because these last change and our stream of consciousness is interrupted by death. The soul, if worthy of it, has its dreamy blissful state in the devachan, and then is reimbodied; but this is obviously not immortality of the *self-conscious soul,* because this consciousness changes. Immortality means an unchanging consciousness without modifications or variations, an uninterrupted continuance of a stream of thought, so to speak.

Now, if this stream of thought or of consciousness is interrupted by death, we cannot call it immortal. We must call it mortal, even though that stream of thought, because based in the monad, takes up its continuance when reimbodiment occurs. The difficulty lies in the odd way of using the word 'immortal' in the sense employed by Éliphas Lévi and H. P. B. in this extreme thought quoted.

Thus the gods are immortal from the beginning of a manvantara to its ending, comprising billions of years; but we human beings, and monads less evolved than the gods, have many interruptions from the beginning of a manvantara to its end; and we cannot thus be called immortal, because of these interruptions. Nevertheless we *are* immortal in our spiritual monads; and when we as humans or souls shall have become allied with our spiritual monads, and become Buddhas or Bodhisattvas or Christs, then we shall enter immortality in this peculiar sense of speaking.

The whole difficulty, therefore, is in understanding the peculiar technical sense in which the word 'Immortal' is used in this extract. Hence Theosophists often speak of the soul as being mortal, conditionally so, or as being immortal, conditionally so, as H. P. B. does in *The Key to Theosophy.* The soul becomes immortal when it unites with the Buddha or Bodhisattva or Christ within itself, its "Father in Heaven," or in other words when the soul unites with the Monad. Then it enjoys the immortality of the monad, uninterrupted consciousness.

CENTERS OF ANCIENT MYSTERY-TEACHINGS

Could you name for us the centers where Mystery-Schools existed in ancient times?

The mistake of all scholars and mystics is to put too much emphasis upon *places* as Mystery-Schools. And this is why comparatively little is

said about localities and places of Mystery-Schools in occult literature —
ours, for instance.

From time immemorial there have been Schools of the Mysteries, some
more or less publicly known like those of Eleusis and Samothrace in Greece,
others thought to exist, whispered about, but not known to the multitude.
These Schools of the Mysteries were formed always of two aspects, the
exoteric and the esoteric. Those schools which emphasized more strongly
the exoteric aspect — which was a noble work in its way because it attracted the attention of the populace and raised their eyes to higher things
— were such places as the Greek Eleusis and Samothrace, Abydos and
Thebes in Egypt, Ephesus in Asia Minor.

Eleusis and Samothrace were almost wholly devoted to the Mysteries,
and hence they are so often spoken of, and have become wrongly looked
upon as the type of Mystery-Schools elsewhere in the world. This is not
so. Most of these Mystery-Schools were attached as secret bodies to the
main temples of different countries. In other words, every *great* temple
had its private or secret Mystery-School which was unknown to the multitude or partially known. And this applies to all ancient countries. This
does not mean that every ancient temple had a Mystery-School, for that
is not true. It was only the main centers of religious teaching that were
the places where the secret Mystery-Schools existed — not always, but
usually so. Now this it seems to me is quite clear, and I hope you will
understand it.

Sometimes the Mystery-Schools, as above said, were attached to the
greatest of the temples; but the greater Schools of the Mysteries were those
which paid no attention to buildings of any kind, mainly for the reason
that buildings would at once attract attention and draw public notice,
which is the very thing that these more secret, more esoteric Schools tried
to avoid. Thus sometimes, when the temples were mere seats of exoteric
ritual, the Mystery-Schools were held apart in secret, conducting their
gatherings, meetings, initiations, initiatory rites, usually in caves carefully
prepared and hid from common knowledge, occasionally even under the
open sky as the Druids did among the oaks in their semi-primeval forests
in Britain and in Brittany; and even in a few cases having no permanent
or set location; but the Initiates receiving word where to meet from time
to time, and to carry on their initiatory functions.

The location of these places was most carefully hid from everyone's
knowledge, except that of the Initiates. Thus as regards Druidism and Mithraism and Judaism, as instances, the secret Mystery-Schools were often
carried on in these underground or subterranean chambers; or even as in
the case of the former two, in the midst of a forest — such, for instance, as

Stonehenge in England, Carnac in Brittany, various places for Mithraism in the Roman Empire, and various places in Judaea, etc.

In India, certain ones of the great cave-temples like Karli, and one or two mentioned by H. P. B., were Mystery-Centers. There were equivalent ones in Ceylon and the south of India.

Memphis, Abydos, Thebes, Abu-Simbel, and Karnak in Egypt, were Mystery-Centers. Sippar in Assyria, Ecbatana in Medea, Babylon and Ur and Lagash were also others. But it would be a mistake to say that all the different countries which had places of exoteric worship were all likewise centers of esoteric initiations, for they were not.

A LINE OF ZOROASTERS

There are several references to a series of Zoroasters, some of the statements giving thirteen as the correct number, others twelve or fourteen. Could you tell us how many Zoroasters there really were?

The number of Zoroasters who have appeared from time to time is confusing, so long as we consider, and wrongly consider, these Zoroasters to be reimbodiments of one single ego, instead of different egos imbodying what we may interpret from the occult records as the 'Zoroaster-spirit.' The truth of the matter is that in the scheme and terminology of Zoroastrianism, every Root-Race and sub-race, and minor race of the latter, has its own Zoroaster or Zoroasters. The term Zoroaster means in Zoroastrianism, very much what the term Buddha does in Buddhism, or Avatâra does in Brâhmanism. Thus there were great Zoroasters, and less Zoroasters — the qualificatory adjective depending upon the work done by each Zoroaster, and the sphere of things. Hence we can speak of the Zoroasters as being thirteen in number from one standpoint, or fourteen from another; or like the Manus in Brâhmanism, or like the Buddhas in Buddhism, we can multiply each of these by seven again, or even fourteen if we take in every little branchlet race with its guiding Zoroaster-spirit.

MYSTERY-SCHOOLS OF TODAY

Is it true that there are Mystery-Schools similar to those of the Ancients functioning today? — and if so, where are they, and why are they not better known?

People like concrete facts, but there is just a danger in giving concrete facts. Dynamite is a concrete fact, whereas we can *talk* about explosions with safety.

If I were to tell openly where some of the Mystery-Schools are situated, these places would be pestered and overrun, not so much now, because it might take years for people to grow to believe, but in future time. For example, the Mystery-Centers today in Tibet are largely held in secret places in the mountains, but there is a Mystery-School right in Shigatse, and I don't care to specify the place, for obvious reasons!

Just as in the past, the same general system of both exoteric and esoteric aspects of teaching the Occultism of the ages, in other words, the *same system of Mystery-Schools, exists even today*. Only today, the exoteric form has been largely replaced by the different activities of the Theosophical Movement which itself is exoteric as a Movement.

The esoteric groups of Mystery-Schools are perhaps more numerous today than they have been for thousands of years, but they are more secretly conducted and more carefully hid.

You ask where these secret centers exist. My answer is, generally speaking, one in every great country; although as a matter of fact, 'great' refers not to frontiers or the rolling leagues of land, but to influence. Thus a little country like the Netherlands might be the center of a secret Mystery-School whose ramifications and influence would extend over half of Europe — 'great' in the sense of being at peace and quiet, etc. Yet as a matter of fact, every single National unit of the globe, has its own secret spiritual protectors, who as a body form a true esoteric center. We can call these the Occult Guardians of a people. Thus Britain has hers, Germany has hers, Russia has hers, likewise so with Switzerland, France, Italy, Spain, Portugal, China, India, Japan, the United States, Mexico, Canada, Brazil, etc., etc., etc.

There is still a third aspect of this question which is much more complicated than the man in the street might think. There are actually groups whose sole business is forming occult centers of Initiation, preparation of students for esoteric work in the world, and for the safeguarding of priceless treasures, the heirlooms of the human race, treasures both intellectual and material. The chief of such groups lives in what Theosophists call Śambhala. It is the center of the Occult Brotherhood of Tibet, called of Tibet merely because that happens to be at the present time the land chosen by them as the most easily guarded. There is another branch brotherhood, affiliated with the Chief Brotherhood of Tibet in Syria, still another one in Egypt, still another one in South America. There is one in Mexico and there is one in the United States. There is likewise one in Europe.

All these smaller groups are affiliates or subordinate to the mother-group of the Occult Hierarchy in Śambhala. Please understand that Śambhala is just the old Sanskrit name given to this occult center from almost immemorial time. The word Śambhala itself has no great occult significance, I mean in the numerological sense or anything like that. It might just as readily have been called the Brahma Vidyâ Âśrama, or by some similar name, but the ancients called it Śambhala, and we merely perpetuate the same old name.

Do not confuse these occult centers just last spoken of with the National Guardians previously mentioned. These National Guardians never interfere in politics. One might almost say that their attempt is to undo the evil wrought by national and international political combines and activities. The National Guardians supervise the spiritual and intellectual welfare of the people over whom they watch, as far as karman and the natural intuitive faculties of the various peoples allow it to be done, but they never interfere in politics. They never make wars or revolutions or anything of that kind. Their work is purely spiritual, moral, intellectual, and wholly benevolent, and indeed universal, and is a silent guide to the intuitive minds of the different races. All these National Guardians are as it were envoys or deputies of one or other of the occult centers mentioned above.

How Old is the Aryan Race?

In your article on 'The Cradleland of Our Race,' in THE THEOSOPHICAL FORUM, *June, 1937* [see p. 16 this volume], *the birth of the Aryan stock from Atlantean tribes is given as 7 to 8 million years ago (p. 410). On page 413, it is stated twice that it is 4 or 5 million years since the original germinal condition of the Fifth Root-Race, though as a race "sui generis" it is about 1 million years old. What puzzles me is the difference between the 7 or 8 million and the 4 or 5 million years as the age of what I supposed was the same Race. Does the larger number refer to that hint in* THE SECRET DOCTRINE *that the Aryans could trace their descent back to Lemuria-Atlantis?*

In dealing with time-periods in a general article it naturally is difficult to find English words to give the exact picture the writer desires to paint. Hence, on reading your note I see how my words could have been misunderstood; yet I do think a careful reading of the article in *The Forum* compared with the diagram I gave in *Fundamentals* on page 251, of how a race is born from, or originates in, the middle period of the parent race, will show what I had in mind. I will now try to explain.

Every Race, Root-Race I mean, great stock-Race, takes its origin, its beginnings, its genesis, i.e. its birth as a differentiated, that is different, stock from its parent at about the middle point of that parent's age or time-period. This we can properly call the birth of the new race, likening it to the birth of a child. This in the case of the Aryan Race was between four and five million years ago. The Atlantean Root-Race has lasted altogether from its birth to its present time some eight million years, that is from its germinal period to its now dying out scattered remnants of savages. So we can truly say the Atlantean Race, including its germinal period all down the ages to its now scattered savage remnants, is about eight million years old; but our own Aryan Race, so called, is only four million plus years old from its birth, born at the half-period of the Atlantean Race, say four or five million years ago.

On the other hand, when we consider that a Race before it is born, i.e. before it becomes a distinctly differentiated Race from its parents, must have had its germinal growth, slowly through the ages differentiating from its parent, we see that we can trace the germinal period of a Race, such as our Aryan Race, back almost to the beginnings of the Atlantean Race. So that our own Aryan Race from its germ-period to the present day is about seven million years old.

Of course, the characteristics of a Race in its germ-period are so closely alike to its parent-stock, that in the case you submit, the germ-period of the Aryans really showed them as scarcely differentiated from the Atlanteans. Yet these germs grew through the ages, and after three million years or so, at about the middle period of Atlantis, became the distinctly differentiated Aryan Race.

Thus take the case of a human being: the average human being is born as a baby, not in the infancy of its parents, but when its parents have attained let us say their majority, roughly at about middle age or somewhat before. Yet the germ of a child when it exists in its parent's body can be said to be so like the parent's body, even the parent's body in its early youth, that it is scarcely differentiated from the parent. This analogy is a feeble one, but it will express what I am trying to say with regard to the Races. This is what I had in mind when writing the article.

To recapitulate: (a) our Aryan Race from its germinal beginnings in early Atlantis is about seven million years old, although this is not a proper way to count it. It is merely rounding out the picture. These germs in Atlantis slowly through the ages of Atlantean heyday became more and more differentiated into a Race apart, and this occurred at about the middle period of Atlantis, and this was the real birth or beginning in that sense of the Aryan Race.

(b) Yet so slowly does nature work in these things, that our own Aryan Race was quite Atlanteanesque, so to speak, until about 1,000,000 years ago when it very definitely in all respects shook off the Atlantean characteristics, and became a true Race *sui generis*. Our own Aryan Race is now in its kali-yuga, beginning it, and the new Sixth Root-Race is already around us in millions of scattered individuals, beginning feebly to differentiate into the Sixth Root-Race qualities; and in some three hundred thousand years from now, while we Aryans are ending our kali-yuga, the Sixth Root-Race will be said to be definitely born as the Sixth Root-Race, but will remain Aryanesque for millions of years yet, until our own Aryan Race is represented only by degenerate remnants; at which time the new Sixth Root-Race will be becoming typically a race *sui generis* itself.

Consciousness After Death

I have heard that after-death consciousness in the Kâma-loka is really only a dream-consciousness, however vivid. Is it, then, ever possible to be conscious, while in the Kâma-loka, of what takes place on earth?

The matter of the human soul being conscious after death of what passes on earth, or among truly loved friends, is very far from being the simple thing that the spiritists imagine. They do not know the teaching of the god-wisdom, and it is quite natural for them to think that the human consciousness should go on uninterrupted after death with perhaps a slight unconsciousness at the moment of death itself. They utterly fail to take into account the frightful, perfectly ghastly, torture that in nearly every case possible, such consciousness after death would mean, could the dead look back upon earth and see what is happening to the ones left behind, and feel the utter inability to help; see disease, misery, wickedness perhaps, crime perhaps, sin, misfortune, as well as the good things.

Nature is infinitely more just and kind than that. And this is the reason why for all normal human beings, that is those neither very high nor very low, in other words, neither initiates, nor great sorcerers, unconsciousness supervenes at death, and the kâma-loka is what I have often described it to be.

But, here is an interesting point. It has been said regarding the kâma-loka and the devachan that the more spiritual the man or woman who dies, the less is the kâma-lokic experience. The soul of such a noble spiritual character shoots through the kâma-loka like a meteor, and unconscious of it, and therefore unconscious of things on earth. So you see that when we rise above the average of good men and women and begin to enter the class of somewhat nobler souls we have the characters that make for no post-mortem consciousness whatsoever, no consciousness of the kâma-loka horrors or dreads or fears, but immediate unconsciousness awakening into a very blissful devachan after the second death.

Now then, going still higher, when we have reached the grade of the initiates: they by this time have been taught to remain conscious not only in sleep, but after death also. But they do this self-consciously, and the after-death state in their cases has no terrors or horrors for them, except perhaps the disgust that they feel for astral cesspools.

Of course, in the case of sorcerers or extremely malignant and evil characters, they have a long kâma-lokic experience, very intense, and just because their consciousness is still so earthly, they can even by magnetic sympathy in many cases come to see as it were, or to feel as it were, as in a sort of day-dream what is passing on earth, not every detail but, depending upon the individual, a more or less clear 'getting it.'

The Occult Doctrine Concerning the Ego

On page 402 of June, 1938, Forum it is implied that in the Christian sense the soul is static throughout eternity in unchanging essential characteristics (?) and it is alleged that our theology makes no distinction between "Immortal" (not dying) and "immutable" (not changing). This is not so; and it is scarcely fair to imply that present-day theologians could be so stupid. Last century there may have been unthinking people who vaguely half supposed that immortal life was a condition without progress or evolution. To argue seriously against such an absurd conception as existing in our own time is surely flogging a dead horse?

The actual difference between the theosophical and the Christian view of immortality in progress is rather that the latter tends to conceive of that unending evolution as proceeding in a straight line steadily upwards — while the former probably would envisage it as undulatory or evolution in successive waves?

Some additional exposition as to the writer's views on the distinction to be made between 'immortal' and 'immutable' would add to the value of that excellent and illuminating article.

This is both interesting and suggestive, and I welcome the opportunity to elucidate the subtil point in Buddhist philosophy I was expounding in the article referred to for I have found that it is precisely this point which the Christian mind is totally ignorant of or completely misunderstands.

It is to be regretted that in this matter of the Christian conception of an enduring and unchanging egoity of the soul, our correspondent, in common with most Christians, still persists — however evolved their ideas may be as compared with the Christian ideas of olden times — still persists, I say, in looking upon the ego as essentially unchanging in its individuality or egoity. Now this is precisely the subtil point mentioned above, and it is what I was alluding to when I spoke of "the imperishable, immortal soul in the Christian sense, static through eternity in unchanging essential characteristics." For this certainly is just what Christianity claims for the soul, to wit, that its individuality is imperishable; and this is just the point at issue. Individuality must evolve as everything else does, otherwise it can never pass from the less to the greater. The occult doctrine claims that this individuality, or its egoity, in other words the ego, at one time-period in eternity must enlarge into something incomparably and vastly grander, thus changing even the characteristics of its egoity, otherwise it will remain always relatively the same limited egoity or individuality.

I am well aware that modern-day Christian speculation, theological or other, is quite likely to admit that the soul in the Christian sense enlarges its views, enhances its conceptions of life and of the eternal verities. But this is beside the present argument. The occult doctrine states that it is the ego, the individuality itself, which passes from personal egoity in its lower stages to an enlarging individual egoity in its higher stages, still enlarging into an impersonal individuality in still higher stages, and so forth, virtually *ad infinitum*. It is obvious, then, to any philosophical mind that this constant changing of individuality not only implies but shows that the ego of the early stages is not the ego of the intermediate stages; and again, that the ego of the intermediate stages changes over into the enlarged ego of the more advanced stages, etc. In other words the occult doctrine postulates and proves, logically and of course philosophically, that the ego not merely experiences an enlarging of conceptions, but itself changes and therefore is not an eternally perduring, unchanging individual entity. Here is just the subtil point which virtually all Christian writers known to me either cannot understand or wilfully misunderstand.

To recapitulate: Admitted that modern Christians allow that the soul in their sense undergoes enlarging views, widening conceptions, deepening of consciousness, etc., etc., which is what the above writer seems to claim, and which is the typically modern Christian view, I believe; yet this is precisely the point which the occult doctrine says is utterly insufficient, for it is not merely a changing of attributes and functions of the egoity which the occult doctrine postulates, but that the egoity or individuality itself is constantly changing, evolving always into something greater, the thread of individuality continuing but becoming always something different because grander.

As an illustration: the just-born child is not a fully 'egofied' entity which merely enlarges its views and gains experiences as it grows through youth to manhood; but it is the actual change of the baby into the youth, and the youth into the adult which takes place. The Theosophist says that this is due to the ever-enlarging increments of spiritual individuality which incarnate *pari passu* with the growing child, the growing youth. But we add that even this individuality itself on the spiritual planes passes over during cosmic ages into larger things. If not, then we must state that the individuality or ego of the billion years in the past was exactly in the state or condition of consciousness *in essentia* that it will be in ten billions of years from now, the only difference being that its experiences have grown, and that its outlook is larger; and this conception the occult doctrine rejects as totally insufficient.

The Christian postulates a created soul — at least this is orthodox Christian theology — which *in its essence* is created an individuality, an ego, different from all other egos, and that this individualized egoity persists unchanging through eternity *as* that ego. This is what the occult doctrine denies. First it denies the soul's 'creation,' and second, it states that every ego *in its essence* is a spark or Ray from Divinity itself, but that its egoity is as changing on its own planes, i.e., as much subject to evolving growth, only through immense periods of time, as are even the different physical bodies or reincarnations in and through which the evolving ego itself manifests from life to life. Thus, just as the Caius or Marcus of old Rome may be reborn John Smith or William Brown, two different bodies and two different lower personalities, both due to past karman or actions, to past destiny in other words, so does the ego itself, the spiritual ray from the divine, have its individuality colored because of changing consciousness in evolution through long periods of time; which actually means that the *young* ego, i.e., when it first appears from the bosom of the Divine in a great cosmic manvantara, is one thing, but that the essence of it will reappear at the end of that cosmic time-period as the same divine spark, but with an entirely modified or sublimated egoic individuality. In fact we can logically call it a different individuality, but the product of the same divine essence. Thus we say one's egoship itself changes character as the cosmic ages roll by, each such change however being like a pearl on the divine thread-self or Sûtrâtman.

The immense reach of this occult conception is at once seen when we reflect how it changes our outlook as regards ourselves and the universe around us. We are not unchanging individual egos, for ever separate in eternity from each other because of individually differing egoities, but are individually one divine essence, otherwise Rays from the Cosmic Source, and thus there is a consciousness in all of us which is one and identic, the highest part of us. To this divine source we are journeying back, each evolving ego carrying with itself its accumulated wisdom and experiences; thus in due course, when the time shall arrive, being able to remember all its immense and intricate past and yet evolving continuously forth this utter oneness in essence with all other egos.

It should be now clear that the subtil point of this argument is one of the highest importance, for we are not, as the Christians say, merely brothers in the spirit, and sons of Almighty God, but actually are brothers in manifestation, and *identities* in our highest.

The Buddhists say therefore very truly that the soul as an imperishable, unchanging individuality in its egoity is a mere dream, for even the souls change in their egoity, rising from lower to higher things. And yet, wonderful paradox because wonderful truth, the thread of point-consciousness which we call the Monad endures through all these changes carrying with it as treasured experience all the different souls or egos through which it has passed as phases in its aeons-long evolutionary journey.

In a few words: Christian theory, whether ancient or modern, postulates an imperishable, albeit perhaps learning, personal ego, which lasts unchanging in its ego-personality for ever; whereas the Esoteric Philosophy rejects this as being both unphilosophical and unscientific, and declares the for ever enduring but evolving spiritual *individuality* manifesting at periodical intervals in and through egoized personalities.

I have repeated myself here deliberately endeavoring to state the occult view-point in somewhat varied language.

Finally, if it is true, as the writer above seems to imply, that Christian conceptions of the human soul are so changing as to become more and more like unto the archaic idea of the Occult Philosophy, this is indeed good news, and is to be welcomed as an immense advance over mediaeval theologic dreamings.

THE STATUS OF THE MAHÂBHÂRATA AND THE RÂMÂYANA

I am taking up the study of the Indian epics, the MAHÂBHÂRATA *and the* RÂMÂYANA, *with my class, and would like to be able to tell them more about the correspondences of many of the characters with the various Cosmic Planes and Principles. It seems evident, for example, that the five Pândava princes in the* MAHÂBHÂRATA *have a special symbology, and also, in the* RÂMÂYANA, *Râma and Sîtâ and their friends and enemies. Could you throw more light on the subject?*

Answering your question about the relative places of the five Pândava princes, supposed to have correspondences with the Cosmic Planes, Elements, etc.: If I were you I would not bother my head about any such thing. Let us look at the situation exactly as it is. The *Râmâyana* and the *Mahâbhârata* are the two great epic poems of India, just as the *Iliad* and the *Odyssey* were and still are the two great epic poems of Greece, or the Greater and the Less *Edda* we may call the two great epic poems of Scandinavia; and there are similar epics, one or two or three, belonging to other countries.

Now then, let us turn to and keep in mind the Indian epics only. These are not wholly and solely mystical or occult works. Let us keep that idea perfectly clear. No more so than is the Jewish Bible, no more so than are the *Iliad* and the *Odyssey,* etc. The *Mahâbhârata* and the *Râmâyana* are fundamentally ancient Indian history and legend, with all the mists and glamor of antiquity veiling them, and they contain in addition a great many beautiful, truly mystical and occult, teachings; and a few really splendid minor episodes, like the *Bhagavad-Gîtâ,* and the *Anugîtâ,* which have been interspersed in the epic-story, for this is according to Hindû tastes.

Thus, really, the *Râmâyana,* for instance, is essentially the struggle of Râma against his enemies, mostly of the south, in Lankâ, the Râkshasas, etc., which is but a modern Aryanized legendary version of the history of the struggle of the early Fifth Race in its Indian branch with the Aryanized Atlanteans of Lankâ, an island-continent now sunken except its northern headland, which is Ceylon.

Similarly, the *Mahâbhârata,* as I remember it, is a legendary epic telling in poetic, and occasionally almost fairy-tale, style, the struggles of early Aryan settlements in India, Aryans themselves fighting amongst each other, and also fighting against the aboriginal, so called, inhabitants of the great peninsula.

Now, there you have in a thumb-nail sketch just what the *Mahâbhârata* and *Râmâyana* are, and actually also just what the *Iliad* and the *Odyssey* are when applied to Greek legendary story or history. These great epics are part history, part legend, and part religious instruction. When I say religious, I mean philosophical, and mystical, and occult, also.

Now it is quite possible for a clever writer to extract from so generally glamorous and mystical a work as the *Mahâbhârata* or *Râmâyana,* correspondences between the five Pândava princes on the one hand, or between Râma and Sîtâ on the one hand, and something or somebody else on the other hand, correspondences perhaps with Cosmic Planes or Principles. In the early days of the T. S. this was a favorite pastime or relaxation of Theosophical writers. This finding of correspondences, however, could be applied with good reason to these episodes taken from the *Mahâbhârata* like the *Bhagavad-Gîtâ,* or the *Anugîtâ,* because these episodes are not so much the historical part, or the legendary part, but are deliberately written, semi-occult, religio-philosophical treatises, interspersed here and there in the legendary, historical material, because this way of doing things is beloved of the Hindû mind.

If I were you I would not bother my head about these things, and I would tell your class the plain reason why. It is something like trying to do the same thing with the Hebrew Testament, or the Christian New Testament. One who is clever in finding, or thinking he finds, occult correspondences, can find lots of correspondences, real or imaginary, between the patriarchs, for instance, of the Old Testament, and the Planes or Principles of Nature, or between Jesus and his disciples and the Planes or Principles of Nature. But such correspondences, while having some reason, are always shaky, and are pleasant rather as a pastime than actual, solid esoteric study.

Therefore I repeat, if I were you I would not bother my head about any such correspondences between the five Pândava princes and something in Nature; and you can get a picture of what I am here writing, and get this picture clear-cut in your mind, and then when you are asked questions from people who do not know what the *Mahâbhârata* and *Râmâyana* are, you can just explain it to them, pointing out that not any one in any country of these great epics, whether of Asia or ancient Europe, or ancient America, is a thoroughly, or typically, exclusively occult treatise on esoteric correspondences, etc. But all of them are legendary history based on facts now lost in the night of time, but seen through the distorting glass of legend by much later writers who are correct in their facts, but like all legendary writers deliberately embroider their theme, and introduce perfectly sound, religious teaching, as in the *Bhagavad-Gîtâ,* and the *Anugîtâ,* in the Hindû epic.

The Meaning of Aum

Will you explain the meaning of the passage in The Voice of the Silence *referring to Kala-Hansa:*

The syllable A is considered to be its (the bird Hansa's) right wing, U, its left, M, its tail, and the Ardha-Mâtrâ (half metre) is said to be its head.

It is the Ardha-Mâtrâ (half metre) which puzzles me.

Here again you have picked out one of the less important things, which I dare say you realize yourself. Just as in all religions there is always a certain class who are seeing wonderful mystic meaning in this or that or some minor detail, which may be quite interesting and important in a small way, but it does not rank among the fundamental, or topnotch, or through-and-through important, things — such is the case with the simply reams of stuff that have been written not only by Hindûs through centuries, but even by Europeans, about the so-called sacred syllable Om or Aum. It is simply amazing how this one word has exercised the ingenuity and mystical feelings of literally centuries and centuries of generations of Hindûs belonging to almost all Schools.

The word is a sacred name on account of its vibrational quality, and used to be used in ceremonial magic, pronounced aloud, although in most secret privacy. And from this one fact, connected with which is the reverence that used to be paid to the Hebrew and Christian AMEN, arose all this vast literature of guessing and mystical and semi-mystical writing.

Now all this talk that H. P. B. has in *The Secret Doctrine, The Voice of the Silence,* and elsewhere, is merely a kind of appeal to those interested in this kind of thing, in order to attract them to her really deep teachings. That is why she made so much of them.

However, now, here comes the point: Kala-Hansa, of course, is the Bird of Time, which means the bird of cycles, and the bird stands as a symbol for the Reincarnating Ego taking its flight across time and space, mostly time. The same can be applied to the Universes and the Cosmic Logos which in the Universe is, so to speak, the Reimbodying Ego.

Now then, of course today Hindûs consider this word so sacred, whether OM or AUM, that they themselves rarely or never pronounce it above a whisper, and mostly merely pronounce it in the head as it were, without voicing it. So much for that point.

Thus AUM stands for the Kala-Hansa; and from this mystical thought, the mystical saying runs that A stands for one wing, the U stands for the other wing, and the M stands for its tail, and the Ardha-Mâtrâ, or short half-syllable, stands for its head. The Ardha-Mâtrâ really here does not mean a syllable, or a half-syllable rather, but that connexion between the sounds A U, and again between U M, which gives inner direction and one-pointedness to the whole pronunciation of the word, and for that reason is called its head, the head of a bird being the first part of it, and guiding its flight. The bird takes its flight on its wings, which support it. The tail serves as a guide to the direction, and the head leads the way.

Now the mystics say in connexion with this word that it is the symbol, the Ardha-Mâtrâ, of the consciousness guiding the pronunciation; or, changing the figure of speech, the Ardha-Mâtrâ or half-syllable is the consciousness guiding the karmic forward progress of the mystic flight of the Ego or Bird, as it is the consciousness which gives the tone to the pronunciation of the syllable. Thus a singer singing a song not merely changes from note to note, but it is just in that change between any two notes that there is a kind of consciousness-sound wherein the singer's ability to make an impression, what might be called his vitality, or his individuality, expresses itself. It is called a half-syllable because it is so short. And yet as it is the point where the consciousness enters in, shifting over from note to note, and therefore guiding the sound, it is called the head of the bird.

You will see that out of such a little thing has grown all this big literature about the Hindû sacred word.

THE TERM PÂRAMITÂ

Will you kindly point out the derivation of the word PÂRAMITÂ?

This is a Sanskrit word, and is compound, formed of *pâram,* which means 'the other shore,' in the technical sense of this word, in the beautiful Buddhist way of speaking, which means the other shore, or over the river of life, instead of *this* shore which is the material existence where sorrow and pain and all the rest of it exist. Thus 'the other shore' means attaining perfect enlightenment because one's consciousness has passed over all the illusions of the material world to the other shore of spiritual glory and peace and freedom and wisdom and love.

The other part of the compound *pâramitâ* is *itâ,* which comes from a Sanskrit verb meaning 'to go,' and is the past participle of this verb; and hence in English can be translated 'gone': go, gone; and *ita* is this Sanskrit past participle, meaning 'gone.' Then this past participle is turned into a noun, and this makes it *itâ;* and hence, as a noun, the meaning is, by paraphrasing it, 'successful going,' or 'successful reaching.'

Thus the whole compound means 'the successful reaching of the other shore.'

Please note also — and this will make the matter a little clearer to you — *pâramita* means 'one who has successfully reached the other shore,' whereas, as said above, *pâramitâ* is the compound noun describing this, and therefore is to be translated as 'the successful reaching of the other shore.'

WAS CHRISTIANITY RESPONSIBLE FOR THE DARK AGES?

Some people say, I fear after but a superficial study of the matter, that Christianity is responsible for the Dark Ages in Europe which so quickly followed the establishment of Christianity as a State religion. They also quote H. P. Blavatsky to this effect. Is this the recognised Theosophical viewpoint?

The statement that came from H. P. B. I think was that the downward cycle to which the questioner refers began some five hundred years before the Christian era, and that is true. But you must not suppose from this that it was Christianity, or the beginning of the Christian era, that was solely responsible for the Dark Ages then to come, for this is unjust, it is untrue. It is true, however — and I trust any Christian friends will forgive me for this plain speaking — that had Christianity remained utter true to the teachings of its grand Master, the work that Christianity set out to do would have been far better done, and the Dark Ages might have never come upon the West as actually took place.

The truth was this: that a descending cycle began some few hundred years before what is now called the beginning of the Christian era. It was a cycle going downward, what Plato would have called a beginning of a Cycle of Spiritual Barrenness: and the Christian movement, then a Theosophical movement of its time in the countries around the Mediterranean, was begun in an effort to stem the horrors that were bound to come, to throw a new wave of spirituality into the thought-life of men in the Occident. The Orient needed it not, but the Occident did. And for hundreds of years it did act as a brake, a brake on the charge of human life which was running downhill. And in ways it did good. But oh, how more blessed might have been the results if their great Master's life and teachings had been the example of his followers as their conduct in their own lives. It was a spiritual movement started in order to help mankind on a cycle running downwards before it began to reascend.

It is quite wrong and unjust, nevertheless, as some people have done, namely men whose hearts have been hurt by what they have seen of the wrong-doings of the Christian Church in the past — it has been unjust to that Church and Christianity *as Christianity* to blame it wholly for the Dark Ages. There were great and good men among the primitive Christians and they labored nobly. The pity of it is there were not more who labored to lift men during that cycle which a few of them at least knew was a cycle running downwards.

We Theosophists today have a similar work to do but on differing lines: a cycle beginning its rise commenced some time before H. P. B. came to the Western world; and a rising cycle — very slow now, but it will be constantly rising for a while — has set in. And the dangers here in their way are just as serious, perhaps more subtil, difficult to deal with, than are the dangers afflicting men or menacing men when the cycle runs downward. Perhaps the greatest danger facing us today in this era of universal change and overturnings generally due to cosmic causes, is the increasing outbreak of psychic eruptions from the astral light, something foretold by the Masters, about which H. P. B. warned us. We have just to look around the world to see, seeing to understand.

For my part, I would we had the backing of a great enlightened Christian organization, filled with the spirit of their Avatâra-Master, which with our own organization could see and understand the dangers that menace men. With its power and wealth, and presumably accepted order and perhaps interior discipline, if it could only be fired unto a new vision of the spirit of their Master Jesus, then these Christians of the type of their Master would be working with us hand in hand, for our movements really would be one. But where, alas, alas, may we Theosophists find such a devoted organization of what I may call primitive Christians, infilled with the spirit of their great Master?

THE TEN AVATÂRAS OF VISHNU

I have been puzzling over a list of the ten avatâras of Vishnu, as given in the Brâhmanical scriptures, and wondering if there is not some connexion between them and the scientific conception of evolution. Could you throw any light on this? The list follows: 1. Matsya, the Fish; 2. Kûrma, the Tortoise; 3. Varâha, the Boar; 4. Narasimha, the Man-lion; 5. Vâmana, the Dwarf; 6. Paraśu-Râma, Râma with the Ax; 7. Râma, hero of the RÂMÂ-YANA; *8. Krishna, the spiritual instructor of Arjuna; 9. Buddha; 10. Kalki, the White Horse.*

This line of avatâric descents really is in the evolutionary line of progressive growth, even as European science teaches it. You have, first, the Fish, the Reptile, the Mammal, the beginnings of the humanity, young Humanity, as such more or less developed but unspiritual; then Râma of the Moon, Chandra, showing the beginnings of the workings of mind, and then Krishna; the avatâric initiate Gautama the Buddha, and finally the Kalki-Avatâra, the summit or highest of all. I might add that all these names do not imply and were never intended to imply that Brâhmanical esotericism taught the descent of divinities into the respective animate beings named here. These names of different animals and men are technical, and like all zoologic mythology were chosen because of certain attributes that these various animate beings have.

Now, these avatâric descents do not appertain solely to a race or a root-race, nor to a globe, nor to a chain, nor to a solar system alone. But because Nature repeats herself by analogy, for the simple reason that the little must have in it and reproduce whatever its parent the whole contains, therefore the same line of enlarging understanding, of evolutionary development, takes place in all the spheres *mutatis mutandis*. So that these avatâric descents we can ascribe or allocate to the solar system, to the planetary chain as a whole, to a round, to a globe, to a root-race, to a sub-race therein.

It is very interesting too, that although this line of ten items, ten avatâric descents, is typically Hindû, nevertheless the same scheme, suggesting growth in knowledge and wisdom and power, with all consequent spiritual and other attributes and faculties attending thereupon, were and still are found in systems of religio-philosophical and mystical thought other than the Hindû, as for instance, in Mithraism. The Mithraists had seven degrees — actually ten or twelve — seven degrees of advancing knowledge and growth in understanding. We would say seven esoteric degrees in the esoteric cycle, beginning with the lowest and rising through various degrees to the highest therein. Thus, for instance, they taught that the neophyte began his course of experience, and he was given a name, the name of a bird as I recollect. I do not remember them all in the Mithraic system, but the first grade was called *Corax,* the crow or the raven, and the neophyte who successfully passed that grade was called technically a crow. It did not mean that he was a crow. It was a technical word (the raven in Mithraic mythology was the servant of the Sun) marking his stage of evolutionary growth, development. Just as in the avatâric list the evolutionary growth is indicated from the less to the greater, from the fish through the reptile, through the mammal, headed by man, etc., etc.

The second grade in the hierarchy of the Mithraists was *Cryphius,* Occult, higher than the crow. The third grade was that of the soldier. The fourth grade was that of the lion; and so forth up to the highest, which was *Pater,* the Father or hierophant. These were technical terms marking the advancing degrees of initiation. And to show a still greater similarity to this scheme, the Mithraists said that these same seven or ten grades of growth or advancement mark the stages of the after-death journey of the excarnate being through the planets — their ladder of life, each one a stage.

Somewhat the same thing was found in Christianity. Christian neophytes were called fishes, so that they even said of themselves: "We are little fishes. Our great Fish is our Master Jesus." Why did they choose such a curious and unpleasant little animal to designate themselves by? For certain reasons of their own which we can easily imagine. Fishes could swim in water, and are perpetually hungry, and are going through the water, which is the astral light, signifying the material world and its temptations, and all that kind of thing; hungering for light all the time. If you catch the thought, you will see the reason why the earliest Christians called themselves little fishes.

I might add that in connexion with the highest of these avatâric grades, that of the Kalki Avatâra, marked by the white horse, riding the white horse: the horse is a symbol of the Sun; the bull or cow is a symbol of the moon; and you may remember how in Egypt and Persia, India, Babylonia, and other places, these animals were used as symbolic suggestions. Pictures of Egyptian buildings, temples, shrines, and those of other peoples, show the sacred cow, the sacred bull, the sacred horse, and so forth. As the horse stood for the sun, so the tenth Avatâra here would be an Avatâra of Vishnu or Mahâ-Vishnu, of the Sun.

What do we learn from this? This scheme, in addition to being the names given by human beings to the Avatâras, from the first to the tenth, represents likewise the technical names given to neophytes in esoteric schools. The lowest chela was called a fish, just as in Mithraism he was called by the name of a bird. The chela who had taken the second degree successfully was called a tortoise. When he took the third successfully, he was called a boar; and the highest of all was called an incarnation of the Sun, a Son of the Sun technically, called a white horse, or a brilliant horse, a dazzling horse.

You know, we can glean something else from this line of avatâric descents. If you examine this carefully, you will see in time, that these different items in the ascending list from one to ten represent the ten sub-races in any one root-race, commonly enumerated as seven. Actually there are twelve.

Is Hypnotic Practice Ever Justifiable?

After having unconditionally condemned some 90% of all hypnotic phenomena and practices, is there any justification whatever in at least some of it, primarily in therapeutics? Such things as local anesthesia by hypnotism, prevention of birth-pains by the same means, seeming cure of small psychological defects and bad habits. This is at present done on a rather large scale, and it seems to be divided in two main categories: (a) under hypnosis and (b) without hypnotic sleep and solely by mental suggestion. My question does not refer to magnetization which, of course, can be of great help when done by clean-minded unselfish people.

Hypnotic practice is almost always bad, even though, somewhat like blood-transfusion, there are rare successes occasionally. It is just like playing with some dangerous explosive. It is fundamentally and generally bad because it weakens the will of the subject instead of evoking the will from within outwards into action thus building up a structure of inner life and power. Every repetition of hypnosis renders the subject still more flabby, still more negative, still weaker, and subjects the subject more and more to leaning on the outer instead of evoking inner powers.

Now of course like everything else, it is conceivable as a theory that an Adept, a Mahâtman for instance, knowing nature's laws and all the tricks and oddities and peculiarities of human psychology and the astral body, could as an abstract theory use hypnosis in certain minor cases beneficially. But this is merely a theory, and I can assure you that no Mahâtman or Adept ever would do such a thing, because the fundamental idea is wrong.

They want to bring out or develop the will-power and inner vital strength of men, and hypnosis sends these last fine things to sleep, weakens them, emasculates the inner powers of reserve.

Still as a mere academic theory, by an Adept hypnotism could be used safely.

Now of course in some local things, like stroking with the hand on an affected part of the body to relieve pain such as a headache, this is really not so much hypnotic sleep in minor degree as a kind of mesmerism or animal magnetization, soothing the nerves but not weakening the will, the healthy body quieting, soothing the tangled and angry nerves of the invalid. And this is not bad if no attempt is made, as just said, to affect the will of the subject or his body as a whole, if it is purely local; because in the first place it is not hypnotism purely speaking, as this word is popularly understood, and in the second place it is purely local and the benefits are derived from the clean, strong magnetism of the operator. It is in fact animal magnetism in these last cases; and if the animal magnetism is healthy and clean, probably no harm is done and the patient can receive temporary relief, although it is not permanent because the cause is not eliminated.

I will say in this connexion that even auto-hypnosis or self-hypnosis, where the subject hypnotizes himself or herself by various means known for ages past, such as staring at a spot or a bright light or a piece of crystal or glass, or even looking at the tip of the nose concentratedly, or at the navel: all those things which are so well known are emphatically not good because they mean using the will by the subject himself to send his higher will upwards and out of the picture, and induce in the lower part of the constitution a false tranquillity or quiet by what is almost mechanical means. In other words the nerves, instead of being roused into clean wholesome healthy activity upon which the inner will can work, are put to sleep, hypnotized (which means sending to sleep), and the brain and nervous system sink below the threshold of ordinary consciousness into the vibrational rates of the glass, or other object stared at. Quiet is induced, but it is the quiet of death, of the mineral kingdom.

Therefore while self-hypnosis is not as bad as hypnosis by others, it again is emphatically not good and is not used by the true Adepts, only by magicians and Shamans and medicine men of barbarous tribes. It is this power exactly which gives the steady unwinking eye of the snake its hypnotic power over a bird or a rabbit or a mouse, popularly called fascination. The glittering eye of the human hypnotizer starts hypnotism off with the same process. It is all unfortunate and if not exactly bad in its better side, is certainly not good.

Therefore all these things should be avoided. They are unwholesome.

They lower the vibrational level down into the lower kingdom instead of raising the vibrational rate of consciousness upwards into the higher psychical, intellectual and spiritual realms.

VIBRATION, COHESION, AND ATTRACTION

In THE THEOSOPHICAL FORUM, *January, 1936, in the last paragraph on pages 35 and 36 the statement is made as follows:*

. . . it is perfectly true that the more rapid the vibration, the greater the frequency of vibration a color has, the closer to matter it is; because what we call matter, physical matter, is intensity of vibration, of force. . . . The greater the frequency of vibration, the more condensed the substance is.

What we cannot understand is that by analogy the molecular vibration of matter as exemplified in ice, water and steam seems to us to be exactly opposed to the above statement. An explanation would surely be appreciated.

An interesting question, this, and shows the result of study and conscientious thought. It is likewise a good illustration of the working of mâyâ, in its philosophical sense, in our minds. There is, however, no contradiction, and the querents would easily understand the situation, I believe, if they will remember that in what I wrote in the passage quoted from me, I was referring to the sphere of the atoms, to the vibration-frequencies in the atomic sphere, and including obviously what modern science calls those infinitesimal bodies dubbed electrons. The querents apparently have forgotten this, and find their difficulty, such as it is, in the realms of *molecular cohesion* — in other words, in the realm of molecules; whereas, as said, I was speaking of *chemical attraction,* the world of the atoms.

Furthermore, my reference was specifically to the different phases of light which we humans call colors; although of course the principle which I pointed to is universally applicable. In the first place, the difference between ice, water and steam is the difference between a solid, a fluid and a gas, which latter has been torn from the body of the fluid, water, by the intrusion of an 'outside' force — heat in this case. Obviously, by heating a body, solid or fluid, we can vaporize it if the heat be sufficient, and thus the freed molecules of water are in a state of temporary and rapid molecular vibration; but these molecules are nevertheless of the same substance as the solid, or the fluid, from which they have been torn as particles of vapor or gas. The analogy drawn by the querents is not a perfect one.

Consider a moment: the particles or molecules of water-gas or water-vapor called steam are in a state of relatively high individual movement, as compared with the body of water from which the steam or particles of water have been drawn or torn. Extract the heat, in other words chill the gas or vapor called steam, and we have the molecules of water again coalescing to become drops, which unite and become a body of water again. In the case of steam, we have broken the molecular cohesion of the water-particles, and thus have freed them and have made them into vapor or gas by the application to the water of an 'outside' energy or force, to wit, heat. But the molecules of water-vapor bombarding each other, let us say in a container, as steam or water-gas, and doing so at what seems to us a high rate of motion or vibration, are nevertheless moving with extreme slowness as individual molecules when we compare them with the almost incomprehensible vibration-frequencies of the electrons in an atom, which scientists now tell us are in movement around the atomic nucleus or atomic core at an almost incomprehensible rate of speed, some quadrillions of revolutions per human second.

Take the case of ice: the electronic vibration-frequencies in this apparently inert, relatively rigid body, are tremendously greater than the individual movements of the particles or molecules of water-vapor or gas which we call steam; in the former case, that of the atoms and electrons, we are dealing with vibration-frequencies which we call wave-lengths held in unity by chemical attraction; in the case of the latter, we are dealing with relatively much slower movements of water-particles freed as individuals by the application of an outside force, to wit, heat.

The point to remember is what I tried to indicate in the extract quoted from me, to wit, that the higher the rate of electronic or atomic vibration, i.e., the higher the vibration-frequencies of and in the atoms, the smaller the light-waves, and consequently the greater is the condensation or condensing of the particles involved, thus producing matter whose density is the greater the higher the vibration-frequencies are. This should be clear, especially when one remembers that the high rate of the atomic and electronic vibration-frequencies remain the same in the steam as they are in the ice-water, or likewise in the solid ice.

The querents, as said, have made a mistake in analogy, for they have tried to contrast *molecular cohesion* with *chemical attraction;* and although both chemical attraction and molecular cohesion are manifestations of electro-magnetic energy, they are not the same kinds or productions thereof, and just here is where the alleged analogy falls.

All this should be clear enough, and if the querents will ponder over the facts hereinbefore stated they should easily see that they are trying to compare two different kinds of things, and to draw an analogy therefrom. They should compare chemical attraction with chemical attraction, or molecular cohesion with molecular cohesion, if they want to have a perfect analogy.

Iron can be vaporized into gas; but the electrons and the atoms, whether in the solid iron or in the iron-gas, have the same vibration-frequencies in both cases; what I have done is merely to affect or modify the cohesion of the iron molecules by the introduction of an 'outside' element, heat.

PLATO ON REINCARNATION

Do you know of a clear-cut statement by Plato that would show that he accepted Reincarnation? I am wading through some of his books now, but have not found anything very direct yet.

There is not a single thing that Plato wrote saying: "I accept the doctrine of Reimbodiment," but there are a number of passages in his dialogs which cannot mean anything else except such a belief. But we must remember that in those days in Greece and throughout the entire Greek world the full teaching of Reincarnation was given out solely in the Mysteries.

On the other hand, the Pythagoreans did teach the doctrine of what was called Metempsychosis, at the back of which is Reincarnation; but it meant a good deal more than that. All the ancient world believed in Reimbodiment, but in different manners and in different ways and under different forms of expression; but to say boldly and baldly that Pythagoras or Plato or any other great philosopher of the Greek world "taught Reincarnation," coming from the mouth of a Theosophist, means today to the 'man in the street' that such a philosopher taught Reincarnation as the Theosophist teaches it openly and more or less distinctly; and this is not the fact.

Many are the Greek allusions to it. Empedocles, for instance, says in substance in one of his fragments still remaining: "I was once a bush; I was once a boy; I was once a maid; I was once a fish in the glittering sea." That is not our doctrine of Reincarnation as taught today; and yet it is our doctrine if you understand the meaning behind this.

We have to be careful; we cannot afford to be slipshod as some Theosophists have been in the past in boldly making the statement that all the ancient world "taught Reincarnation," which means to the public that it taught Reincarnation as presented today by Theosophists; and any scholar could challenge such a statement. The ancient Initiates knew the doctrine, knew what all these different statements meant; and if our modern Theosophists understood Reincarnation better they would understand that the ancient philosopher taught absolute truth, taught different aspects of the general doctrine of Reimbodiment; but the modern, clear-cut, very definite teaching of the reimbodiment of the Reincarnating Ego is inadequate to express it in its fulness.

All the ancient world taught Reimbodiment; and that is one of the reasons why in my lectures and in my books I keep harping upon the difference between Reincarnation, Rebirth, Transmigration, Metempsychosis, and Metensomatosis, as being all different views or aspects of the one general doctrine of Reimbodiment. It is not just a matter of words. I am trying to bring order into the situation, to get accuracy; and the scholars of the future will appreciate it. It is just like the doctrine concerning the Absolute or the proper spelling of Karman: we need to have accuracy and definiteness and precision.

COMPLICATE NATURE OF MAN

According to Theosophical doctrines, man is a septenary being, in addition to his physical body having six other principles as a part of his constitution. (a) Is it true then, that in addition to his present physical body manifesting on this our material earth, he would also simultaneously be manifesting on six other material globes or planets in an appropriate physical body or vehicle, all seven physical vehicles on the seven material globes each having its own six other principles functioning in their respective spheres, contributing each and all to the Monadic center? (b) If this is so, would all seven physical vehicles die and reincarnate again at the same time, or each at a different time, depending upon the karmic energies of each vehicle?

The foregoing question does not lack profound interest; and by the changing of two words — which words because they are esoteric cannot here be stated — the question would deal with a typically esoteric matter, connected with man's septenary constitution. However, and answering with as much brevity as possible in view of the complex factors involved, and having in mind the intuitive thought behind the question, I would reply briefly to the questioner's query (a): No, if by the word 'material' is meant physical bodies on other physical planets — Globes D of their respective chains — of our Solar System.

The fact is that man in his septenary constitution has one 'material' or rather 'physical' body only; and as he is now manifesting on our own Planetary Chain, and on Globe D thereof in the Fourth Round, this his physical body is the physical body that we all know — yours, mine, any other man's or woman's physical body on this Earth.

Yet there is an intuition in this question which is struggling to find utterance, or rather to find phrasing in which it may clothe itself; and I believe that future study will prove to this querent the accuracy of this observation of mine.

Now, the querent's intuition points directly to the fact of man's composite nature, which is divisible after different manners; for instance, our usual exoteric manner which H. P. B. gave to us, and there is none better for its own purposes; then there is another manner which has been more favored by the Vedânta and the Târaka-Râja-Yoga, to which H. P. B. likewise approvingly alludes in her *The Secret Doctrine,* Vol. I, page 157, and which refers more particularly to the different monads forming man's composite constitution. When we remember that these different monads are, each one of them, a growing and evolving entity, each one at some date in the distant future to be an individual of septenary character, we see not only the intuition in the querent's question, but also the profound truth of the famous old statement found in all mystical literature that man is a microcosm or small copy of the Macrocosm or Great Original; and, on exactly similar lines of analogy, every one of the monads in man is an as yet imperfectly evolved microcosm of the complete man as we recognise him.

With regard to the latter question, the querent's (b), it is seen from the foregoing part of my answer that there is not more than one physical body at any one time for man, and that this physical body is now found on our Globe D, Earth; and hence, the answer to this question (b) again is No. Yet just here I must enter a *caveat,* and point out that the same intuition before noticed is here again struggling to express itself, and it does seem to me as if this questioner had an inkling of a certain esoteric and very difficult teaching concerning the Outer Rounds. Be this as it may, my answer stands correct, that man's septenary constitution at any one time works through one physical body only, and that in the present phase of human evolution this physical body is the one in which we, as individuals, are incarnated on this Earth.

MEAT-EATING VERSUS VEGETARIANISM

There are differences of opinion in our Lodge on the subject of eating meat. Some of the members teach that we are doing the animals a great service by killing and eating them, thus raising them to higher states and helping them to evolve. They even go so far as to state that if we did not kill the animals and eat them, their evolution would immediately come to a stop. They point to the civilization of India: how it has degenerated, and then quote a phrase from THE MAHATMA LETTERS about a bird eating a butterfly, the butterfly becoming the bird.

Others hold that there are other ways of helping the animals: for example, loving them, as a mother with her helpless babe loves and cherishes it not because of the amount of mind it manifests, but because of its need and helplessness. They say that meat-eating involves disregard for the suffering of countless innocent animals, so tenderly referred to by Master

K. H. as these "infant entities." They also point out that the animals have the use of our human life-atoms after our physical death.

These differences of opinion sometimes give rise to a painful degree of disharmony in our Lodge-meetings. If we could only have some teaching that would reconcile these conflicting views!

This is indeed a question which comes popping up constantly in our Theosophical life, and pretty much everywhere. We have hundreds and hundreds of vegetarians in the T. S., although we have perhaps an even larger number of members in the T. S. who feel that they need a little meat, but who probably in their hearts wish it were not so, for no Theosophist likes even to think of some creature giving up its life in order to feed other beings.

So difficult is this question to handle without deeply wounding the feelings of thousands of Theosophists, that we have always taken the attitude that it is our duty to be just to others, and not to criticize others for differing from us. Actually, I am sure, if there has been anywhere such criticism, it is because of the deep moral sense that all our members have, whether they eat meat or not, concerning this and other questions. The meat-eaters do not like to feel that their brothers, the non-meat-eaters, are speaking unkindly of them, or are charging them with being cruel, etc., and on the other hand, our vegetarian members very naturally resent the imputation that some meat-eating members make that the vegetarians are narrow-minded and one-sided in their views.

With my sympathies on both sides, because I see the good in both sides (I mean the good in the human beings on both sides), and also seeing how both sides are so very earnest, I long ago came to the conclusion whenever my advice is asked in such a matter, to say frankly that no Theosophist has a right to criticize another Theosophist. Thus a Theosophist who eats meat has no right to criticize a brother-Theosophist who is a vegetarian; and of course vice-versa; the vegetarians should not sneer at the meat-eater, nor make the meat-eater feel that he is gross and untheosophical. In other words, live and let live in this thing.

Abstractly, of course, I think it probably true to say that every Theosophist living wishes that the habit of meat-eating had never become established, and realizes that not to eat meat of course is more beautiful than to eat meat. But on the other hand, it is unfortunately true that among Occidentals whose ancestors for several thousands of years have gorged themselves with meat, the bodies of most Occidentals really feel that they need meat in order to retain what they call their "fitness."

But I see hope in this matter, for the vegetarian movement is growing all over the world, not very fast perhaps, but nevertheless growing; and more and more people every year are eating less and less meat, and finding combinations of vegetable foods that seem to supply all the needs of the body.

But these matters must be handled not roughly, nor in a revolutionary way, trying to overthrow things in a single day; any such movement should come in slowly.

I myself find that my body really needs a little meat or fowl or fish, but I do not eat much, and as the years go by I am eating less and less of it. There was a time for many years when I was a most rigid vegetarian; years and years, I say, a vegetarian; so I know both sides of the matter, and have sympathies on both sides.

Therefore I suggest that all the members of our Lodges do their best to avoid this topic, at least in their lodge-meetings of every kind. I do not ask anyone to give up his convictions or her convictions because that would be untheosophical. But just try to avoid discussing this subject.

Every Theosophist by nature and training and study is compassionate and desires to become more and more so every year. But no Theosophist likes to be insulted, or to have his habits criticized. So the best way is to follow the beautiful Theosophical rules of not judging others, and in such matters as this to avoid by mutual consent any further discussion of it, at least in lodge-meetings.

I have the deepest sympathy with the kindliness and spirit of compassion that Theosophical vegetarians have; but I also understand the other point of view of those Theosophists who feel the need, at least at present, of eating a little meat; and I never condemn, nor do I judge. If anybody asks me about vegetarianism, I always commend it, say it is fine; and then I add: "Some day I hope that meat-eating will have been outgrown by the race as I think certainly it will be in future time."

Now as to the other matter involved in your question: that of the effect upon the beasts themselves: I fear that even some of our own dear F. T. S. make a complete mistake when they allege that if we humans eat flesh of animals, the evolution of these animals is quickened. There is such a teaching as this in the world, but I can tell you the idea is absolutely wrong. The confusion here is between the souls of the beasts we kill for food, and whose evolution is certainly not helped by such killing; and the life-atoms merely of the bodies of such beasts. Thus, to say that the beasts, that is to say the beast-souls, are quickened in their evolution if we eat their bodies, is to say something absolutely wrong. It is, however, true that the life-atoms in the beasts' bodies can be raised somewhat by entering into the bodies of humans. But this mere fact, which H. P. B. taught as long ago as 1879, should not be used as an argument for meat-eating, because it is forgetting the other fact: that the beast, that is the soul of the beast, does lose its body when its body is killed, and therefore loses time; and its evolution, instead of being quickened, is actually somewhat retarded because it loses time; and this despite the fact that the beasts, when they die, incarnate very, very quickly. They still lose a little time, which is something.

Try to get this clear, then. It is not true that the evolution of the beasts is hastened when we kill them and use their bodies for food. But it is true that the life-atoms of these dead beast-bodies are helped a little bit when taken into the human body. But the help they get is so slight that it would be monstrous to argue that we should kill the beasts so that we could help the life-atoms of their bodies by eating their bodies.

How about the souls of the beasts that have to die when they give up their bodies? This is awfully hard on the souls of these poor beasts. I honestly do not think any one of our Theosophists could have been very serious in using the above argument about helping the animal evolution by killing them. Such a belief I am sure is from thoughtlessness and from a wrong understanding of the teaching, as, for instance, given in *The Mahatma Letters to A. P. Sinnett* in one or two places.

And as a last word, let us drop any more discussion, at least in lodge-meetings, on this matter of vegetarianism or meat-eating. We have so much Theosophical work to do, the world is so harassed and anxious, it needs our Theosophical light so badly. The aching hearts and minds hungry for truth in their millions all around us, should make us energetic and active in our lodge-work, and in extending its influence, so that we can give out Wisdom to others, and give to them the help that we have received. Really we have no time for quarrels in a lodge. I think it is almost criminal to allow such disagreements to continue and to make the lodge-members feel that their lodge-room is no longer a Theosophical home for them where they all can meet in brotherly love and mutual helpfulness. *This last is what a lodge-room must be.*

The Monad and the Monadic Essence

What is the relation between the Monadic Essence and the principles which H. P. B. mentions: Âtma-Buddhi?

Âtman and Buddhi together form what we Theosophists call the Monad. When the Mânasic fruitage of past lives is 'added' to it, then we have what is called the Reincarnating Ego. Âtman means 'self'; and, as a spark comes from a fire, so likewise is the Âtman which inspirits a man, a spark from the Fire of Universal Consciousness — the Paramâtman or Brahmâtman to use the Sanskrit terms; and that Essence which works within the Monad, i.e., Âtma-Buddhi, is the Monadic Essence, the heart of the Monad.

To put the matter in other words: Âtman is the Self; but even though it belongs to the divine part of the constitution of a human being, nevertheless because this human entity is a manifested entity — however great the manifestation is — the Âtman is, as it were, limited and therefore is not absolute infinity.   But that Essence which is in Âtman and which is the essential being of the Âtman, is the kosmic Paramâtman.   The Monadic Essence is, as it were, a divine Atom or divine particle of the Paramâtman. Therefore the Monadic Essence is the heart of Âtman, the core of it.

TYPES OF DEVACHAN

In THE KEY TO THEOSOPHY *H. P. B. says that after death the Methodist will be a Methodist, the Mohammedan a Mohammedan, at least for some time, in a perfect fool's Paradise of each man's creation and making. Will this be in Kâma-loka or Devachan?   I say the latter, as there is no consciousness in the Kâma-loka, and H. P. B. herself has described Devachan as a fool's Paradise.*   THE MAHATMA LETTERS *(page 103) speaks of "the pleasures realized by a Red Indian in his 'happy hunting grounds' in that Land of Dreams."*

The answer to this question is in general a Yes, an affirmative.   H. P. B. certainly meant mainly the devachan, since it is a mere reflexion of the spiritual vision, imperfect and poor as it is, of the man who has just died: whatever that man was in a spiritual way he will continue to be in the devachan afterwards.   Thus the imperfect vision, for instance, of a Methodist or a Roman Catholic or a Mohammedan — imperfect when compared with that of a Buddha since it is a lack of *complete* inner vision, inner spiritual growth — will continue in the devachan in a sublimated sort of way in the "fool's Paradise," so that the Methodist will be a Methodist, but an improved Methodist, the Roman Catholic ditto, the Mohammedan ditto, and so forth.   So much for this part of the question.

Yet it is obvious that the kâma-loka, being the stage preceding the devachan, will not change the character of the man who has just died; and if he has died filled with the thoughts of Mohammedanism, or of Methodism, or of the Baptist, or of the Roman Catholic, he will still be this or that in the quasi-consciousness of the kâma-loka.   So we can say he will still remain a Methodist, or a Roman Catholic, or a Mohammedan, through the purging process of the kâma-loka; and then the finest part of the man will enter the devachan, the "fool's Paradise," in which he will still have his dreams of a glorified Methodism or Roman Catholicism or Mohammedanism, or

Judaism, or whatever his quasi-spiritual thoughts on earth were. So there is a certain truth, when this is understood, in the other statement also, that even in the kâma-loka the man's character is not changed.

I might add that of course an ego is not cleared of *all impurities* thus becoming perfect before entering the devachan, as he would then be of the status of a Buddha. Nor do I mean that it is necessarily an "impurity to be cleared away" to be a Methodist or any other religionist. Of course when a man becomes through evolution so spiritually evolved that he is a Bodhisattva on earth, or a Buddha, then he will just pass through the kâma-loka and devachanic states almost unconsciously, for the man is above them, and he enters a lower or higher Nirvâna according to his development. And Nirvâna means a vision of Reality.

CAN WE HELP THE KÂMA-LOKIC ENTITY?

Is it possible for the living to give help to the human kâma-lokic entity in its struggle to free itself at the time of the second death? Would a living person be likely to feel the influence from that struggle on the part of one who in life had been closely connected with him, especially on inner lines?

Nature is too merciful to allow but the merest fragments of psychic or emotional contact between the living and those in kâma-loka. If it were otherwise, our lives would be a hell.

The entities in kâma-loka as a rule are semi-conscious or unconscious. It is only the very evil sorcerers, black magicians, or the grossest kind of beings while in body, who have a consciousness which we would call awake-consciousness when they reach the kâma-loka. Consequently, all the kâma-lokic processes, except in the cases of the few mentioned above, take place automatically and as it were unconsciously or as in a dream, perhaps a nightmare, perhaps perfect unconsciousness in the case of the average person; but a real hell of feeling in the cases of the sorcerer and the tremendously heavily gross person. But, after all, these last are few.

It is of course true that a spiritual love on the part of the survivors can reach even to the devachan after the kâma-loka is ended; yes, and even as it were help the interim Bardo-period in the kâma-loka. But it must be a spiritual love, and the effect itself is to bring an atmosphere of more peace to the kâma-rûpas in kâma-loka; and the same thing after those in kâma-loka have shaken off the kâma-rûpa and have entered the devachan state. Yes, a spiritual love, not an emotional one, does help the entities in kâma-loka to a certain degree, especially if those entities are nice clean decent average people, and are not sorcerers or gross materialists.

The main point to remember is that those in kâma-loka should be left absolutely alone. Nature is infinitely the kindliest. The kâma-loka experiences for average people are dreamlike or even pure unconsciousness. They are just as it were in unconscious sleep; and any attempt to touch them, even with emotional love or emotional thought, can at times, if the thought and magnetic impulse is strong enough, give them a fictitious temporary awakening, and then they feel unhappy, for they are half awake and surrounded by atmospheres they do not understand, and they feel as if they were in a bad dream.

So it is much better to leave the kâma-loka entities strictly alone, even if they are our dearest friends. Of course a gentle warm current of impersonal friendship does no harm, and as explained above, may even do a little good in helping to purify the atmosphere around the kâma-lokîs, if I may invent a term.

Cataclysms as Ways of Establishing Balance

In The Secret Doctrine, *Volume II, at the end of the first part, H. P. Blavatsky gives us a description of the terrible catastrophes which will take place during the transition-period from the Fifth to the Sixth Root-Races. It seems to me that Nature works in a rather hard way. Is it not possible for the great spiritual Leaders of evolution on this planet — if not to prevent — at any rate to mitigate the effects of these terrible disasters, during which millions of human beings and animals perish? Is this due not only to cosmic but also to individual karman?*

Yes, to both, to both kinds of karman; and also to racial karman, and planetary karman. The questioner is a highly intelligent man, but there lurks throughout his question the old feeling that 'Nature is not just as I think she ought to be.' Presumably the idea is that if someone else had had the shaping or founding of natural law, of natural being, it would have been more shapely and kindly done. I wonder! Nature's heart is compassion absolute, because that compassion is absolute harmony. Nature moves on a cosmic scale, and in comparison therewith our ordinary brain-minds are microcosmic, with small reaches of understanding of the great cosmic issues involved, and, so far as the racial karman is concerned, of any Root-Race or Sub-Race, with small understanding of her sweeping away in catastrophic or cataclysmic activities millions of animals and millions of men.

How about the millions of men and millions of animals that die daily, and, yea, that are sometimes, perhaps not in their millions, but in their hundreds and thousands, killed, murdered, wantonly slaughtered? All these things, all these catastrophes and cataclysms, are one of Nature's ways of re-establishing balance, equilibrium; just as disease in a human body is a purgation, a purging the system of poison. Just so, Nature's ways in its own purgations are these cataclysms and catastrophes.

The so-called 'Leaders of evolution,' of which this querent writes, do indeed strive continuously through the ages to mitigate the sorrow and pain, to stem the heavy hand of destiny, if it is possible, or at least as much as it is possible to stem the tide of intellectual and psychical disintegration. But they never work contrary to Nature's laws. They cannot. They are in very truth the servants of the Law, and therein lies their enormous power.

Cataclysms and catastrophes are occurring constantly. How about this horrible war? How many millions have perished so far from direct or indirect causes? Look at the beasts who die daily in almost countless numbers all over the earth — some of them wantonly slain; others slain by accident.

The world is full of misery and pain brought about by ignorance and by distorted mental views and by unbridled passion; and the time finally comes when these accumulate so greatly that Nature can tolerate no more; and then the crash comes. Is it not so all through natural being? A human body will stand so much abuse, so much strain, and then it gives way. Nature acts likewise on the greater scales. All of it is karmic. Yet the entities which are swept off the face of the earth, so to speak, which pass out, within an hour, or a day, or a week, or a month, or a thousand years, or ten thousand years, learn by it — learn the karmic lessons.

Then pause and look at the other side of the picture. Look at the beauty, look at the sublimity, of the Sons of Light who work through the ages and whose strong hands hold back the accumulated karman from its crushing humanity at one blow; they form the 'Guardian Wall' around humanity. Consider that carefully.

Consider the light side of Nature as well as its automatic retributive or so-called dark side. Nature is divided into two parts, into two phases, so to say, and these two phases or parts are filled on the one hand with the Sons of Light, and on the other hand with the Brothers of the Shadow: one is the realms of spirit, and the other is the realms of matter.

KARMAN AND IDIOCY

Would it be possible for an average man to be 'punished' by an incarnation as a complete idiot, and in the following life to take up afresh from the status he had before the 'idiotic' life?

In THE ESOTERIC TRADITION (p. 974) a footnote states that there may be cases of a lesion or injury, before birth or after, which may cause this

state of idiocy. Even in this case the condition must be the result of kar-
man, or it could not have happened? One would think that if a man is his
karman such an entity must have had an attraction downwards, from which
he will have to work upwards again, or go still farther down and become
a lost soul. Is it possible for one who had been very cruel to an idiot to
be punished by experiencing that condition himself? Hardly, I imagine,
as his intermediate nature being absent, no impression could be made on
it, and that life would be punishment pure and simple, and not a lesson
learned.

Certainly the result of karman in all cases. Furthermore, while it is
abstractly possible for a thoroughly normal human being to have to undergo
an unpaid karmic debt such as idiocy in the next following life, it is so
extremely unlikely that the degree of improbability almost reaches certainty.

The reasoning is this: that karman is not haphazard on the one hand,
nor are its parts divorced from the general karmic frame or set-up; so that
an idiotic incarnation almost certainly is preceded by shadows casting their
images before, a general weakness of character, a more or less obvious degeneration, producing finally its culmination in the idiotic state. But of
course, while this is logically the rule, and is clearly seen to be such by any
thinking person, I would not go so far as to say that a thoroughly normal
person could not possibly have a karman, as yet unworked-out from some
distant life, which would produce relative simple-mindedness or idiocy. It
is possible, but so extremely unlikely that it is almost a certainty that
normality is not followed by abnormality. The whole situation depends
on the fact that a man *is* his karman, as the questioner states.

As regards the latter part of the question: If I understand the question
correctly I would answer in this wise: We must remember that karman is
not just brute mechanics. The moral principles back of karman are essentially spiritual. Keeping this in mind we can see how karman might work
in the case of one who is cruel to animals, who are relatively mindless when
compared with men (which does not mean that they have no mind, however), or in the case of a man who is cruel to an idiot because he despises
the poor idiot's lack of mind. We can see that with the spiritual and moral
causes of karman back of and working in the constitution of the cruel
individual, this very cruelty will *slowly* close the gates of intellectual and
spiritual inspiration in that cruel man; so that little by little the very fact
of his having lack of sympathy for the beasts or for the idiot, will tend to
make the cruel man himself slowly through incarnations become less and
less "minded" as it were, having less and less of the seeing, penetrating
mânasic faculty. Thus in a sense a man is punished by the way he injures

or is cruel to others. But these things do not come suddenly. They are a process of degeneration. Cruelty continued through a life, or two or three, is a degenerative process, a breaking down of the moral fiber, and of spiritual and intellectual insight. And what does this mean but a slow and gradual loss of the mind through indulging in persistent cruelty?

So reasoning thus, we can say that after a long time — two, four, six lives, heaven knows how many — one who despises another for being an idiot, or who is cruel to the relatively mindless beasts, slowly brings about incipient idiocy in himself; and we are thus punished by the backwash of the very energies we originally set in motion. This is what is meant by the saying that the man who takes up the sword will perish by the sword. The man who is cruel will perish by his own cruelty, and others will be cruel to him. The learning of the lesson takes place during the process. Of course it is obvious that a complete idiot cannot learn lessons as a man endowed with mind can. But the process of approaching idiocy enables the soul to gather the lessons of suffering and repentance, which may even save the man from final idiocy, if he is sufficiently evolved to take warning in time. Then if he changes his cruelty to kindliness and gentleness, and opens the channels above once more, his sufferings and the danger he sees ahead of him, will have been his karmic retribution, what the questioner calls the "punishment," and he may suffer horribly during this process, bringing about a moral and intellectual regeneration.

Pygmies, Todas, Eskimos, Negroes

Of what Race are the pygmies — the 'dwarfed-races of the Poles'? The Secret Doctrine *says:*

The Third 'Race' *"having fallen down in godliness, they mixed with animal races, and intermarried among giants and pygmies* (the dwarfed-races of the Poles)." — Vol. II, p. 331.

Have not the pygmies higher Manas?

What a most marvelously confused question — confusion worse confounded! 'Pygmies,' in this questioner's mind, seem to be the pygmies of the earth of the present day; and these pygmies of the earth of the present day are simply the degenerate representatives of what were even in Atlantean days degenerate race-stocks. But the pygmies that the extract from *The Secret Doctrine* here refers to, were pygmies some twenty or twenty-five feet tall, and were the latest representatives of the degenerate humanity of the last part of the Third Root-Race. They were called 'pygmies' because they had decreased so in size as compared with their ancestors; and they lived in the northern parts of the earth.

Even the Atlanteans when they were no longer in their primal period but verging well towards the middle of their Race, were twenty-five or more feet tall — twenty-five of our feet tall and perhaps taller. The humanity of the Third Root-Race were titans in size, even larger.

Of course the pygmies have a higher Manas, even the Pygmies of Africa today. This question is an excellent illustration of an intuitive mind taking words too literally. As said, 'the dwarfed races of the Poles' were the degenerate relics, the remnants, of the Third Root-Race, having then become Atlantean. Every Root-Race has its degenerates, its inferior races so-called; and this word 'inferior' must not be used absolutely, but only in a relative sense. Every race also has its higher sub-races. Every Root-Race has its savages and its highly civilized nations and peoples, that is to say, every Root-Race after the middle point of the Third Root-Race.

The pygmies of Africa today, for instance, and the pygmy-tribes of people you will find elsewhere today on the face of the earth, are merely degenerate representatives of what even in Atlantean times were degenerate stocks.

Are the Eskimos descendants of the pygmy-races who mixed with the Third Race?

The Eskimos are the descendants of northern Atlantean peoples, descendants of some of the very latest of those northern Atlantean stocks which had become stranded or isolated in the far north just as the Pygmies became stranded in Africa. The Eskimos do not go back so far as the Pygmy-race spoken of in the extract from *The Secret Doctrine*, above, except in the general sense that every human race is the child of the preceding Root-Race. If the Eskimos were the descendants of the Third Root-Race, then we are also. But what we now call the Eskimos are the dying-out remnants of certain minor tribelets of Atlantean date which even then had become worn out.

But this is not the case with all the savages or barbarians on the earth today. There are some savage or barbarian tribes which are being held and guarded as the seeds — the seed-humanity — of aeons to come. And I can give you one instance in point which may interest you. It is the Toda-people in India, concerning whom H. P. B. wrote her series of articles entitled, 'A Strange Tribe of the Nilghiris.'

The Negroes are going to play a prominent rôle on the face of the earth before their time comes to pass away; but then they will no longer be what we now call Negroes. If we proud Occidentals could see ourselves as we were four or five million years ago, we would not pleasantly acknowledge our own ancestors. And I can tell you that if the Atlanteans could see us — we humans of our present Fifth Root-Race as we are — they would think that we were perfect monsters: puny, tiny Lilliputians, with neither strong intellectual power nor physical strength, afflicted with diseases both hereditary and other; incapable of controlling ourselves either in love or in hate.

This is the picture that we would present to them. And we of the Fifth Race look back upon our ancestors of Atlantean days as monsters of iniquity, black with sin — and so they were. We at least have advanced in spirituality. We have gained something, and it is an enormous gain. And if you could see the Sixth Root-Race to succeed us, you would probably say: "What extraordinary and unpleasant-looking creatures!" This is a fact.

We have not developed the proper faculties of proportion yet to enable us to appreciate the beauty of the Sixth Root-Race to come; and even in the Fifth we hardly know what real beauty is. Even in our art, beauty is in discussion as concerns its nature.

How would you like to be hairless, with two backbones, one eye, and no teeth? How would you like to shed your skin and the nails of fingers and toes yearly: to cast your skin as a serpent today does in its own times? How would you like to be no longer either a man or a woman, but a sexless 'thing,' as you would probably say today in scorn? Indeed if our modern scientists could catch one of these beings of the coming Sixth Root-Race, they would put him in a glass case, and exhibit him over the civilized world today as a monster, a teratological curiosity. The splendid spiritual and other faculties which such a Sixth Root-Race being would manifest would be utterly misunderstood.

ORIGIN OF THE SÛRYA-SIDDHÂNTA

In FUNDAMENTALS OF THE ESOTERIC PHILOSOPHY *it is said that the* SÛRYA-SIDDHÂNTA *claims an age of "somewhat more than two million years, according to popular interpretation." — p. 119. Does it antedate the* RIG-VEDA, *and is anything definite known about its origin?*

Nothing whatsoever that is definite, or accepted as definite by Occidental scholars, is known of the age of the *Sûrya-Siddhânta* except its own internal testimony or statements; and this internal testimony modern European Orientalists regularly reject as being what they call interpolations at a later date. There is absolutely no proof of this supposition. There is no reason to doubt the original authenticity of these statements in the *Sûrya-Siddhânta;* but European Orientalists will not admit that it is possible, in view of modern European evolutionary theories of the age of man, for civilization to have produced a book like the *Sûrya-Siddhânta* two million years ago or more, they simply deny it off-hand; all of which is high-handed, arbitrary, unreasonable, unsupported by a shred of evidence, and some day will be simply laughed at as an example of what is now called Occidental nineteenth and twentieth century 'criticism.'

The *Sûrya-Siddhânta* states in its picturesque and metaphoric way, that it was dictated by the Sun himself, through a projected solar representative, to the great Sage Asuramaya, whom H. P. B. mentions in *The Secret Doctrine,* just at the end of the Satya-Age of our present Mahâ-Yuga of which we are now in the Kali-Yuga part. Asuramaya received the dictation around the opening of the Tretâ-Age, which is just at the end of the Satya-Age, and wrote it down; and this is the Introduction to the *Sûrya-Siddhânta.* It claims thus to have been written before the beginning of the Tretâ-Age, which, counting backwards from our time, since we are at the beginning of Kali, is a period which covers the Dwâpara which we have ended, and the Tretâ-Age which preceded the Dwâpara, to wit, 864,000 years, plus 1,296,000, which make something more than two million years.

The *Sûrya-Siddhânta* is one of the best known astronomical works of ancient India, and shows really marvelous mathematical skill and ability, and comes very close to, and in some cases to virtual identity with, the modern time-periods of astronomy that our most skilled western mathematicians and astronomers have found. In some cases there are differences, probably due to changes of various kinds. It also deals with other things, such as yugas or time-periods in their various lengths, divisions of time itself into infinitesimal quantities, and general astronomical subjects, including not only the time-periods of the Sun, Moon, and planets, but also dealing with eclipses, seasons of the year, etc., etc. It has been translated into English by a man called Burgess, whose translation was revised later by the famous Professor Whitney of Yale.

As to the question whether it antedates the Vedas, here there are no data whatsoever except internal data. My own opinion is that it does, for the following general reasons: The *Rig-Veda* which is the main Veda, and from which the others really were derived, seems to have been throughout past ages the chief religious and mystical book or scripture of the earliest Aryans who are now called the Aryan Hindûs; and hence probably is not much older than the Aryan Race itself as a distinct race, let us say about a million years. It shows many signs of a primitive type of people, but yet contains, when you know how to read it, a vast fund of esoteric suggestion, and by all classes of Hindûs is looked upon as their most sacred book. Everything ultimately is referred to the Vedas for proof, that is, whenever arguments arise. If it is in the Veda, so to speak, argument drops, opposition ceases.

Now the *Sûrya-Siddhânta*, having been delivered to Asuramaya according to its own statements two million years ago, is evidently, if I am correct in my former assumption, about twice as old as the Veda; and thus the *Sûrya-Siddhânta* was a late Atlantean work, evidently the product of skilled Atlantean astronomers in the days when Atlantis was perishing. H. P. B. speaks of Asuramaya as having been one of the famous ancient astronomers and scientists of Atlantis, in its last days of course. This would mean that the *Sûrya-Siddhânta* was composed about two million years ago, when presumably Asuramaya lived, and when the Aryan Race in its first beginnings was 1,728,000 years old; but this refers to the date of the Aryan Race in its infancy before it became a race apart and *sui generis*. In its infancy it really was practically a part of the Atlantean civilization. Our own Aryan Race has been a true Aryan Race or a race *sui generis* for only about a million years from our present time.

It must always be remembered that Root-Races, and indeed all subordinate races, over-lap each other greatly, and in *Fundamentals of the Esoteric Philosophy* there is given a graphic diagram of the manner in which each race springs from or is born at about the middle point of the preceding race. Thus each new race for several millions of years is in its embryonic or infantile stage, and slowly grows into prominence as the preceding race slowly descends into obscurity.

Thus it was that Asuramaya, the Atlantean astronomer and scientist, could with almost equal right be considered as appertaining to the first beginnings of the Aryan Race. But it is better to call him Atlantean, because the Aryan Race in those days were not the 'top dogs' to use our modern phraseology, but were somewhat like the backward and barbarian races today, with the single exception that our backward and barbarian races today are degenerate remnants of former great civilizations. The Negroes today would correspond in their unevolved state somewhat to what the Aryan Race was in its infantile condition.

LOOKING WITHIN

You continually advise us to look within. In what way does Theosophical 'looking within' compare with the psychologists' introspection?

It seems to me that the psychologists have seized a part of a truth; but the teaching of Theosophic introspection goes far beyond that. Too often the introspection, if I may use this word, of modern psychology is a pondering and a brooding upon the vagrant and flitting thoughts of the lower brain-mind, upon one's wishes and hopes and petty loves and hates — a morbid self-examination of the lower parts and faculties of us; and I think that it is very unwholesome. There is altogether too much of that.

What we need to do is to *free* ourselves from the lower part of us, to lift our eyes to the spiritual Olympus, to rise out of the murk and the mire and the mud and the dirt, to strike the shackles from our limbs and to wing our ways into the inner states of the spirit. Does modern psychology tell us that we must devote ourselves to the inspirations of almighty wisdom, and of impersonal spiritual love? Never! It does not know enough; but it thinks it knows quite enough to teach what are in many cases downright perversions of reality. Some aspects of modern psychology will tell us that if a naughty child does certain naughty things, it is because of an unexpressed sex-complex. I think that the instilling of ideas like this into the mind of any innocent child is a moral crime, because it is a suggesting to a child to do what perhaps never occurred to it to do. It is monstrous.

But teach a child to be self-forgetful, to introspect in the higher way, to examine its motives, to look carefully into its yearnings and to rule them, and you will help it and guide its feet. This is the psychology of the archaic school, which is ours, which is Theosophy. Psychology really means what the word itself actually says: the study of the *soul* of man, instead of the study, as it is in modern psychological schools, mostly patterned after the doctrines of Freud of Vienna, a study of the physiological-mental reactions of the body.

Children are responsive to thoughts put into their minds, and the only right way of bringing up a child is to surround it with the thoughts and influences, and if you can the environment, of harmony and beauty and peace and love, teaching it lessons of kindliness and self-forgetfulness, instead of teaching it to concentrate all its thoughts upon the beastly impulses of the animal man.

DID JESUS SUFFER?

When Jesus suffered, does it mean that he had violated some fundamental law?

No, I would not say that. You have touched upon a very esoteric topic of thought. If you only knew what we Theosophists have to say about the Avatâra Jesus and his life and teaching, you would not have thought it necessary to ask me this question. In the first place — and I hope that I will not tread upon any sensitive corns here — we Theosophists don't believe that Jesus suffered in the manner that the legend relates. The story of Jesus as told in the Christian Gospels is a mystery-tale, a tale setting forth certain experiences in the initiation-chambers, with Jesus as the type-figure around which the mystic lessons were woven.

Let me try to illustrate what I mean. One of the grades of initiation was called Theopathy, from two Greek words *theos,* 'god,' and *pathein* 'to sorrow,' 'to suffer.' It means the 'suffering' or 'bearing' of a god — not that it is a god which suffers, but an entity which suffers the entrance into himself of a divine influence. He supports the god in his being, he becomes the vehicle of the god and carries the god, resigns his own individual identity or character for the time being in order to become a manifestation, an Avatâra so to say, of the god. He suffers the god to work through him. Thus did Jesus.

It is our teaching, furthermore, that Jesus called the Christ never was crucified, never suffered on the Cross, in the manner outlined in the legend. The entire story of Jesus as we have it in the Christian New Testament is a story of the Mysteries. An initiation-mythos was written around the exquisite figure of a great Sage and Seer called Jesus, the Avatâra. Around the individuality of that great and noble Sage and Seer was woven a series of tales and legends portraying in mystical, and as it were, esoteric and secret, form, a part of what takes place in the initiation-chambers.

The Purânas and the Great Epics of India

I have been trying to place the Purânas in relation to other Sanskrit literature. Some modern writers say they are of much later date than the Vedas and the Upanishads, yet their name means 'ancient.' How do they fit in with the Vedas, Upanishads, Vedânta, etc.? In other words, are they an entirely separate set of works, as would seem to be the case; and if so, were they contemporaneous with, or earlier or later than, for instance, the Vedas?

The Purânas are much later than the Vedas, if we consider them as composed, or works complete, in literary form — whether written down or repeated from memory as exact traditions; and everyone has noted the phenomenal memory-capacity of the Hindûs. They are called 'Purânas,' a word which means 'ancient,' because they actually are archaic legends, stories, traditions, containing a vast amount of truth both exoteric and esoteric, which for ages and ages throughout the early part of the Aryan Race were passed from generation to generation as legends, historic stories, quasi-mythical tales, etc., etc. Yet their transmission has been phenomenally accurate. Thus in their origins as legends, it is probably quite correct in point of truth and fact to say that they are as old as the composed *Rig-Veda* and possibly even older, going back to Atlantean times as legends of gods and heroes and men. But as composed works, bearing different names such as the *Vishnu-Purâna* and the *Linga-Purâna,* and the *Skanda-Purâna,* etc., etc., they are probably of later date than the *Ṛig-Veda,* but still immensely older than the date which European Orientalists always try to give to them. They are probably several hundreds of thousands of years old, even in their present fully composed literary shape, which does not mean in their written shape. But I mean as fully composed literary treatises, originally handed down through the brain and phenomenal memories of the Hindûs from guru to pupil, and thus through the ages.

They are much older than the Vedânta, even as composed works, although it is to be remembered that the Vedânta as a system of thought and apart from its formulations into a philosophic system is — I mean the philosophical principles of the Vedânta are — probably as old as anything on earth, running far back into the glory of the best part of Atlantis — and by best here I mean the spiritual part, such as it was; for the Vedânta, which means 'The End of the Vedas,' in the sense of 'the complete meaning of the Vedas,' contains philosophical principles which are identical with the Esoteric Philosophy. As a formulated system, however, the Vedânta is usually reckoned as dating from Śankarâchârya, who lived some hundreds of years, say five hundred more or less, before the Christian Era.

The epic works of India, like the *Mahâbhârata* and the *Râmâyana* the Hindûs call the *Itihâsa* — a Sanskrit word meaning 'thus indeed it happened,' which shows that the Hindûs look upon these books, and always have looked upon them, as historical works, somewhat as the Greeks did Homer's *Iliad* and *Odyssey*. These epic works are historically of far later date than the *Sûrya-Siddhânta,* or the legends of the Purânas, i.e., the Purânas in their earliest shape or form, and probably later than the *Ṛig-Veda,* because they represent in their legendary quasi-historical manner, various episodes of epic character in the history of the Aryan Hindû Race, which really describe in brief form their struggles as the new Aryan Race against the declining power of the Atlantean peoples. So great was the scorn of the early Aryans for the degenerate Atlantean sorcerers, that they describe them under such terms as Râkshasas, or Yakshas, etc., which some modern European Orientalists who do not understand the situation, call imps, or goblins or evil spirits; the Atlanteans were all these indeed in one sense, because they were degenerate sorcerers, but they were nevertheless human beings, and not unincarnate nature-spirits.

Summarizing briefly, I would actually go so far — although I admit that it would be downright difficult to adduce what European scholars would call literary proof — I would go so far as to say that the Purânas, as their name 'ancients' shows, are among the most hoary relics of an archaic and now forgotten antiquity, which the conservative genius of the Hindû people has managed to transmit through the ages to our own days;

and I mean the Purânas not as they at present exist as more or less shapely and complete literary works, but in their original condition as bodies or collections of legendary and mythical and indeed historic tales and stories handed down from generation to generation through the ages, until different Schools of thought, represented by different men working upon this vast body of legendary material, collected and segregated it into the different Purânas with the definite and distinct names that exist today; and among all which there are such immense similarities as well as curious differences. But even this 'composition' or collection and segregation of the Purânas into distinct treatises is itself extremely ancient, probably running back some hundreds of thousands of years. Such at least is my own considered opinion, after some forty years spent in study of this and kindred subjects.

The great difficulty that European Oriental scholars have to fight against, which is indeed a most pathetic stumbling-block of their own manufacture which they persist in throwing before their own feet, is their subservience to the mistaken modern scientific evolutionary ideas, that the human race is only a few hundred thousand years old or a million or two years at most, and that it has slowly arisen during this ludicrously short period from a beastly or quasi-beastly condition, to its present state of *homo sapiens*. Knowing nothing of universal history except scraps, and having their historical horizons usually limited by the cases of Greece and Rome, Egypt, and Persia, etc., they have no conceptions of civilizations following each other in periodic times, and only vague ideas of continents sinking under, while other continents are rising above, the waters of the changing oceans. Thus these European scholars wilfully telescope everything into the few hundreds of thousands of years that they admit as existing between man's origin and the present day; and into this bed of Procrustes they force with equal wilfulness everything to fit, and when it does not fit, or adjustments cannot be made, the constant answer to inquisitive questions is, 'myths,' 'superstitious man in his infancy,' etc., etc. But anthropology, ethnology, and archaeology, have made giant strides since the day when H. P. B. wrote; and today the representatives of these and of other sciences are not so cock-sure as they formerly were, and doubts are beginning to creep in all along the line. Consequently the wholly false and easy 'set-up' imagined by European scholars of H. P. B.'s day, of early mankind being fascinated by natural phenomena such as sunlight and storms and wind and the thunderbolt, etc., etc., and their wonderment making them sing mystical and religious hymns which later became the *Rig-Veda,* and that as time went on poets and historians arose and astrologers and quasi-astronomers, and myth-makers who gave birth to all the later literature — all this easy poppycock 'set-up' is crumbling to pieces;

and our modern scholars are far more modest and therefore more truly scholarly than were their predecessors of fifty or one hundred years ago. Now they are beginning to admit the possibility, and even in some cases the probability, that the human race in its various branches over the earth, is far older than has been supposed, and may possibly even have brought civilizations into birth, of which all that remains now is but a memory and the legends of the peoples of the earth.

The Separation of the Sexes

Please may I know what is really meant by the teaching about the separation of the sexes in an early Root-Race. Is this connected in any way with the idea of 'twin-souls'?

As regards this question concerning the separation of human individuals into distinct sexes which took place more or less during the Third Root-Race: this separation of each individual was brought about by the natural course of early human evolution, and is founded on the dual nature of mind, of the mânasic part in us. When mind entered into the previously 'mindless' race, the dual character of mind immediately made itself felt throughout all the lower quaternary, and when I say 'immediately,' I mean dating from that time. Thus it was that the androgynous race of the time slowly drew apart into the separate individuals as they now exist, into man and woman in other words; and the animals and indeed some of the plants likewise followed suit because of the strong psychic impression made by the human race on the astral mold of our world.

Thus this separation was a purely natural affair, based fundamentally on what you can call the positive and negative sides of mind; or you can otherwise phrase it as being based on the bi-polar character of the manas within us. Thus sex is really very little higher than the lower parts of the manas, and consequently is not a spiritual thing at all, a mere passing phase in evolution. As the human race evolves and rises out of the lower mind into the higher, sex will disappear.

In connexion with this, let me utter a word of warning: the idea of some rather sensuous people that the higher nature of human evolution is to be achieved by 'the union of twin souls' is altogether wrong. The secret lies in the individual himself or herself, for in each individual there are the two poles. Thus it comes about that a human individual for two or three or more incarnations is a man or a woman; and as karman makes for adjustment in these things and prevents extremes, slowly such an individual begins to lean or have a bias towards the other half of mankind, as I have often explained, and when that reaches a certain point, then the man's incarnations become feminine, and the woman's incarnations, as above explained, become masculine. Thus it is that our destiny swings us from incarnations as a man to incarnations as a woman, then back to a man, then back to a woman; and this will last until sex disappears slowly and inevitably.

The twin-soul idea is a very dangerous one, and in fact fundamentally all wrong. What we must strive to do is to rise above sex in both thought and feeling, directing our efforts towards the spiritual within us, in which there is neither sex nor any of its attributes.

QABBALISTIC AND THEOSOPHIC PRINCIPLES

I notice in Chapter Two of FUNDAMENTALS OF THE ESOTERIC PHILO-SOPHY, *that man is divided into four parts: (a) Neshâmâh, (b) Rûahh, (c) Nephesh, and (d) Gûph. Over all these four principles, there is the Ineffable, the Boundless called 'Êin Sôph. Would the author of* FUNDA-MENTALS *kindly give me his opinion about the correspondences or the differences between these four principles and the Qabbalistic triad consisting of the three highest Sephîrôth: (a) Kether (the Crown), (b) Hhochmâh (Wisdom), and (c) Bînâh (Intellect) — all emanations of 'Êin Sôph, the Boundless.*

This thoughtful question contains profound suggestions; and the mere fact that the questioner seeks for correspondences or differences between the Qabbalistic Quaternary as given in *Fundamentals,* and the Qabbalistic highest Cosmic Triad of Sephîrôth, shows that he himself has actually answered his own question, but probably is not fully aware of it.

The four human principles as given by me in *Fundamentals,* are reflexions or 'projections,' as it were, of all the nine Sephîrôth of the Qabbalistic Cosmic Tree of Life; and the differences in manner of enumerating or of expressing the Cosmic Principles and the human principles depend upon the fact that the human principles are reflexions or 'projections' as above said, of the Cosmic Sephîrôth. The three highest Sephîrôth, as given, and properly given, in the question, are the originals or correspondences of what in man in the Theosophical philosophy are called Âtman, Buddhi, Manas; Kether corresponds to Âtman, Hhochmâh corresponds to Buddhi, and Bînâh corresponds to Manas.

In another sense, Neshâmâh corresponds to the Divine Monad, Âtma-Buddhi; Rûahh corresponds to the Spiritual Monad, Buddhi-Manas; and Nephesh corresponds to the Human-Astral Monad, or Kâma-Manas-Prâna. Gûph is in either case, whether cosmic or human, the mere vehicle of all the other higher principles, and in the case of man corresponds to the physical-astral body.

All the Cosmic Sephîrôth are born from the bosom of 'Êin Sûph, or the
Boundless, and hang as it were like a pendant therefrom; very much as the
three highest principles in man, Âtman, Buddhi, Manas, are born from the
bosom of the Boundless, and are eternally therein, hanging like a pendant
therefrom; the lower four principles of man hanging like a second pendant
from these higher, just as the lower six Sephîrôth hang as a pendant from
the three highest Sephîrôth.

We thus see that the correspondences are very close, when properly
understood, as I have endeavored briefly to outline them in the preceding
paragraphs.

ANDROGYNOUS AND HERMAPHRODITE

My study of THE SECRET DOCTRINE *and other of H. P. Blavatsky's
writings leads me to infer that her use of the words 'androgynous' and
'hermaphrodite' has reference more to the duality of spirit and matter in the
universe, rather than to a duality of sexes, masculine and feminine. Is this
right?*

Yes, quite right. Used by Theosophy, and as a rule by H. P. B., the
word 'androgynous' does not mean 'double-sexed,' except when very distinctly imbodied beings are referred to. When it is used of entities of
spirit, things obviously, entities obviously, which have no sex — for sex is
but a passing phase of our earth evolution, for us and the beasts and the
plants — it is used only to signify what in philosophy is called duality,
the dual characteristic of manifested nature. This is sometimes called the
positive and negative, sometimes the feminine and masculine, these latter
two words being borrowed from human life, not meaning that one side of
the universe is actually male and the other actually female, which would
be utterly ludicrous, but merely meaning that at a certain point, at manifestation in fact, duality supervenes. That is all it means.

Of course when we refer to imbodied beings, then it is perfectly proper
to speak of mankind as androgynous, double-sexed, of which the as yet
vestigial organs remaining in the physical frame are remnants out of that
hoary past. So *androgynous,* when used of the Universe, signifies only the
duality of spirit and matter, consciousness and vehicle, spirit and substance
— using any pairs of words you like. And this androgynous or dual character of all the manifested worlds began indeed with Cosmic Buddhi or
Mahâ-Buddhi; but actually only began to show itself on the plane where
Fohat especially works, which is the plane of Cosmic Kâma. Above that
the two rays from the one ascend to reunite; and you have an example in
yourselves: the individual ego, or the individual spirit, during its imbodiments breaks up into the septenary constitution, one side of which you may

call spirit, and the other side, the vehicular; one side consciousness and the other side vehicle; one side you may call will and the other side consciousness. It does not matter what you call them: duality is there.

But duality springs forth from the Âtman, the fundamental basic egoity or Monad in the human being, and the human being simply copies in his constitution and structure what the universe is. According to the axiom of Hermes: "As it is above, so is it here below." Study here below what you see, thereby gaining a key to knowing the Divine. The Divine reflects itself in its distant offsprings in its distant vehicles — the imbodied Universe as in man. The Âtman reflects itself in the man feebly because of our imperfectly evolved vehicles; and evolution consists not in a growth of these spiritual realities to something greater, so much as a perfecting of the vehicles, such as mind, through which the divine ray passes so that they may continuously grow, as evolution proceeds in its refining and unfolding powers — so that the divine ray may ever shine forth in larger and greater splendor. That is what all evolution means: from within outwards. Just as the seed brings forth the plant, the plant the bud, the bud the flower, and the flower the seed: the seed, the plant, the bud, the flower, the seed, the plant, the bud, the flower. Nature repeats herself ceaselessly. She reimbodies, reimbodies, reimbodies.

THE TEMPTATION OF JESUS

I thought that it was only before we had entirely learnt something that we had to struggle with ourselves about it, but that when we, in previous lives, had quite overcome some special temptation, this temptation never occurred to us again, and we did not even get the idea of its possibility. I thought this was the way by which we have to win the different virtues one by one. Will you please explain why Christ should have felt any temptation to be relieved from his great task. Why should he have said, "Remove this cup from me," and have to pray in anguish in order to be victorious over temptation? I think that he should by then have got over this stage.

This question takes it for granted that the legend told of Jesus in the New Testament of the Christians is an actual history. It is *not;* the 'Gospel' story is merely an idealized fiction, written by Christian mystics in imitation of esoteric mysteries of the 'Pagans,' showing the initiation trials and tests of the candidate for initiation; and it is not very well done, there being much error and many mistakes in the 'Gospels.'

A man called Jesus — the Hebrew name being Jeshua or Joshua — really lived, who was a great and good man; also an initiate into the secret doctrine of his period; and around him, after his death grew up many legends and tales, which were woven in later days — say a century after his death — into the so-called 'Gospels.'

Yes, the questioner is right in saying that once we have fully conquered a temptation, we are safe from future attacks of it, but only provided we are *watchful and on guard eternally*.

The Destiny of the Animal Kingdom

Re the animal kingdom: Many species are dying out today. Some day — the life-wave having moved on to Globe E — Globe D will have merely śishtas left on it. Will there be any animals in the Fifth Round? Many students are mixed up on this; so am I. If there will be animals in the Fifth Round, will that mean the animal kingdom as we know it today (but more highly developed), or only some of the highest species?

When a life-wave, any life-wave: human, animal, vegetable, mineral, elemental, or dhyân-chohanic: moves from our Globe D on to Globe E, it leaves śishtas behind on this Globe D. What are these śishtas? They are waiting for the same life-wave which will have passed through the globes on the ascending arc, to come down the globes on the descending arc in Round Five; and when they reach Globe D, our earth, these śishtas will begin to increase in number because of the incoming monads from the life-wave, and the same life-wave — in the case of your question the animal life-wave with its subordinate life-waves or orders and varieties and genera, etc. — will begin to tend to expand. Consequently there will be animals in the next round.

But here is a very interesting point: the animals will tend steadily to pass into nirvânic rest, I mean their monads will from now to the end of our chain-manvantara. Every round will show fewer animals, the reason being that as time goes on and as the steps up the ascending arc are passed one by one, fewer and fewer animals will be able to make the grade upwards. The calls of matter will be too strong. Thus at the end of the Fifth Round on Globe D, the śishtas of such animal life-waves will be much fewer than in the preceding round on this globe, because the monads will be entering their Nirvâna for the reasons above stated. Otherwise stated, the individuals of those animal life-waves will have largely died out from this plane because the monads will have gone into Nirvâna; and during the Sixth Round the animals, although much more progressed than now they are, will be extremely few; and before the Sixth Round is ended will have died out entirely, with the exception of the anthropoid apes and possibly some of the higher monkeys. The anthropoid apes will have become then no longer anthropoid apes really, although their more evolved bodies will still continue, but they will be very, very low humans in quasi-anthropoid bodies, nevertheless humans of low grade. During the Seventh Round even these will have disappeared, but their monads during the next chain manvantara will be low humans in appropriate bodies then.

Thus generally speaking, animal monads tend more and more on the upward arc to go into Nirvâna. Their bodies, there being no monads to incarnate, will tend to die out.

The cause of this is that the door into the human kingdom, (which means the attaining of self-consciousness), closed in the middle of the Fourth Round; and the animals now are just hanging on as it were because of the impetus or momentum they got in coming down the descending arc. This momentum has carried them up to the present,will carry them onward even into the Fifth Round where, as stated before, they will mostly die out because they cannot climb higher. The spiritual self-conscious nature has not evolved forth from their monads; and consequently there is no sufficient attraction upwards in them, and thus they fall back behind the procession, and die out.

In other words the animals will no longer reproduce themselves. The monads of many animals have already entered their Nirvâna even during this Fourth Round — the grossest of their kind. Some of them, those which still remain, persist mainly by the momentum spoken of and because of dawning mind in them which still keeps them here.

BUDDHISM AND THEOSOPHY

Could you give a little explanation of the difference between Theosophy and Buddhism as it is generally taught today amongst the masses?

That is a good question, and one I like, because if I were not a Theosophist, I most emphatically would have accepted the doctrines of the Lord Gautama, the Buddha, as the most humane, the most philosophic, the most generous, the most princely, not only in their attitude towards men, but in the effect they produce upon men.

The difference is that between the mother and a very lovely daughter. The sublime mother is Theosophy, the lovely daughter is Buddhism. I would say that even as Buddhism is practised today, some 2500 years after the passing of its great Founder, even today it is the most theosophical of all the religions existent, the most generous, the most tender in its understanding of human problems; and in its dealing with them, without a vestige of anything that is harsh, unkind, or colored by hatred in any form. It has no doctrine of arbitrary punishment. Its doctrine of retribution based on cosmic law or karman, is retribution infinitely just. The evil that ye do will live after you, and ye yourselves the doers of it will meet it one day, and until ye undo the evil that ye have wrought it will abide — wonderfully logical, satisfying, and comforting.

Just see how this takes hold of the human heart. The true Buddhist says of his injurer: "He has injured me terribly. I pity him. I desire no revenge. That would be but adding my might to the evil that is wrought, for some day the evil that he wrought upon me will fall, helpless man, upon him, and in addition he will have the evil that that evil-doing wrought in his own character. A double evil. I, his victim in this life, will receive recompense, double the recompense of the wrong, the injury, done unto me, because I shall have retributive compensation for the wrong, and because I do not in my turn hit back at my injurer, I have the increments of strength of character thus growing out of the injury wrought upon me, which is a double good to myself, who have suffered. I have the recompense in my own soul, that I know how to be patient and strike not, hit not back."

Divinity breathes through that. It is the very heart of pity, of compassion. And that is pure Theosophy. In other words, Buddhism is but a lovely daughter of a still more lovely mother. Christianity is its daughter, Brâhmanism is its daughter, Taoism, all the religions of India, Persia, China, Egypt, of ancient Europe, and of the Americas. They all sprang from this one source, our God-Wisdom, as we call it, kept in the Guardianship of the Mahâtmans, greatly evolved men. But I think that Buddhism is the loveliest of the daughters, because the truest. Fidelity has crowned her. Justice has followed her footsteps.

How May One Find His Guru?

Mr. Judge says in LETTERS THAT HAVE HELPED ME: *"Each man who determines in himself that he will enter the Path, has a Guru." Will you please tell me what Guru this is and how one may find that Guru?*

It is quite true that any man who determines in himself that he will enter the Path has a Guru, as Judge said. However, this Guru may be either one or both of two things: first, his own Higher Self, than which there is no loftier Guru for a man on earth; and second, also one of the Teachers who because of spiritual and psychological sympathy inborn or inherent, is the natural Teacher for such aspirant; and this is the fact whether the aspirant knows anything about it or not. Some day when the aspirant has grown to the stature enabling him to receive open instruction, this will happen, but it *may* be ages before this direct instruction is received consciously. But the fact remains that every human being is as it were by Nature's occult sympathy allied to some greater Teacher; and he must be ready for the time when he may be put in direct touch either with his own Higher Self, or with the outer Teacher or Guru who will help him to come in touch with his own Higher Self. But remember that the inner man, the spiritual man, the Higher Self, is the loftiest Teacher that a man can have.

Do We Ever Incarnate as Beasts?

In view of the teaching of Theosophy: "Once a man always a man," what would be the explanation of some of the Oriental teachings that speak of a man's coming back to earth as a tiger or an elephant, etc. — and also of the many traditions in western countries of a beast being possessed by a human spirit?

No human being ever incarnates as a beast. Let that fact stand as unequivocal and without exception. And this is for the reason that there is absolutely a mental-psychical barrier preventing a human mind from entering a beast psycho-vital apparatus. Of course, this could be done by an act of magic, by some Black Magician, and hence have arisen the stories of werewolves, lycanthropy, and so forth. But this act of black magic simply proves the general and invariable law: that no human being ever can, in the course of nature, incarnate as a beast.

On the other hand, when a sorcerer, or a man of continuously evil life, through many, many incarnations on a steady downward grade, grows less and less human until the rupture with the spiritual and human monad takes place, in which case there is no longer a man, but merely the lower quaternary with somewhat faint impressions or psychical shadowings of humanity in it — when this takes place, I say, the entity is no longer a human ego, but as it were an abandoned lower quaternary or human machine, virtually a human shell, which already is so degenerated that it is practically on the level of beasthood. But the humanity, the ego, the human being, of it has long since fled.

Such an abandoned vehicle is attracted to beast-bodies and even to plant-bodies, by the natural attraction of likes, at a still lower degree of descent and dissolution of the lower quaternary. Yet this is not, please note, the incarnation of a human being, because such a degenerated, disintegrated, semi-annihilated human quaternary is no longer really human. An analogy is a human body enlivened by a human soul forming a man. When the body is laid aside at death, the man is gone, but there is the form of the man, the life-atoms of the man which disintegrate and pursue their way. The body is given to the dust, and many of the life-atoms even of such a true man which belonged to the body, incarnate in beasts because again of natural attraction of like to like, of animal to animal, as has already been explained. I hope this is clear.

Be it noted, however, that such cases of degenerate human quaternaries, while fairly numerous in actual fact, are nevertheless actually quite rare or infrequent when compared with the immense number of beings forming humanity.

CYCLES IN CHINA

In THE OCEAN OF THEOSOPHY *I came across this statement in chapter xiv, p. 124: "The Chinese always were a nation of astronomers, and have recorded observations reaching far back of the Christian era, but as they belong to an old race which is doomed to extinction — strange as the assertion may appear — their conclusions will not be correct for the Aryan races." Somewhere I believe you have said that China was on the upward trend of the present cycle. We have searched for the reference but have not been able to find it. What is the truth of this matter? Mr. Judge may have written in a wider sense than you, who may have had in mind a small, specific cycle.*

The questioner's understanding of my meaning is quite correct. Here we have a case where brief statements, each one correct, refer to different things; and readers who are too quick in perusal and not thoughtful enough, immediately say: Oh, a contradiction. There is none! The facts are as follows:

The Chinese, that is the pure Chinese or those nearly pure in race, are the degenerate descendants even today of the Seventh Sub-Race of the Atlantean Root-Race. Consequently, when we take in the immense periods of geologic time, they have nearly reached their end; and speaking in immense time periods are soon "doomed to extinction"; but, speaking in terms of smaller time-periods such as we humans easily can grasp, that is to say of several thousands of years, which are small geologically, the Chinese still have a brilliant future before them, and are now on the upward rise. There will be Chinese for thousands of years yet, although steadily mixing and showing a tendency to die out as pure Chinese.

Thus Judge is right because he was referring to long geologic periods so to speak. I was right because when I spoke, I was referring to the shorter time-periods of some thousands of years, or a good many hundreds of years. Actually the Chinese today are striving to come to the fore again as a national unit, and they will do so, and very soon, perhaps within a hundred years, and have a relatively brief period of power and glory, and then they will go down again; perhaps later rise to another still shorter period, and then go down again; and keep doing this until finally they vanish as a racial unit. Thus we can say with Judge that they are "doomed to extinction," for the reasons above given; and we can say with equal truth that they are rising on an ascending small cycle. What happens with the Chinese happens, or will happen, with all other racial units. Each has its turn; each has its beginning, its growth, its culmination in power and splendor, its senescence and decay, and its vanishing.

SPIRITUALISM

Please say how these two quotations can be harmonized: ". . . the wave of spiritualistic phenomena . . . has been aided by the Nirmânakâyas." (Last para., chap. xi, ECHOES FROM THE ORIENT) and ". . . the most insane and fatal of superstitions — Spiritualism." (THE MAHATMA LETTERS TO A. P. SINNETT, p. 284.)

This certainly does look like a contradiction, but it is instead a paradox, and can be easily reconciled. I speak from recollection, as I have not the book at the moment before me, but as I recall the passage in Mr. Judge's *Echoes from the Orient,* when the entire context is taken into careful consideration, he himself reconciles the paradox. This reconciliation lies in remembering two things, first that Spiritualism as it is commonly understood is a "superstition" and a very "fatal" one, that is as it is understood by spiritists generally, who look upon human beings after death as being merely a prolongation or continuation of the ordinary human earth-men in a purely mythical Summerland, where they appear to be living in a kind of inane and idiotic atmosphere of self-satisfaction. In fact, it is nothing but a dream-situation, and takes no account of the septenary constitution of man, nor the different parts of this constitution, and the destinies which these various parts respectively undergo after death.

It is the old folly of the everlasting personal, unchanging ego, which the Christians have adopted in another form; and the spiritists do not realize the truth. Hence, spiritism as understood is actually a truly "fatal superstition."

On the other hand, in a world which was typically materialistic when H. P. B. came to do her work in the West, which generally, excepting good Church people, had no belief whatsoever in the survival of anything in man, which looked upon man as being little more than a body, and his mind and emotions and ethical sense a kind of ethereal effluvium of the purely material forces working in the human brain — to such a world, I say, the teachings of the spiritists, which taught that there was something more in man than a mere physical body, even if it was only a kind of prolongation of the ego in a dreamland, was an idea which represented something higher than the grossly materialistic views of the scientists, and the equally materialistic views of the church people.

It was this touch of not exactly spirituality, but of looking to something higher than the material body, which was the part of spiritualism fostered by the Nirmânakâyas as instilling in the mind of the materialistic West that man was something more than the physical body, which as this West then thought as represented by its science, was the be-all and end-all of man.

Now the spiritistic phenomena which were utterly unexplainable by the materialistic science of the day, did instil thoughts of something more being in man than merely his body, unknown forces of a psychic and mental kind, which were, however, falsely called "spiritual"; and the foregoing is just the reason also why H. P. B., when she first began her public work, began to work among the spiritists, because they were trying to free themselves, however erroneously, from the dominant materialistic thought, teaching, tendencies, and soul-destroying hopelessness of the time. It was in this minor manner that the Nirmânakâyas did, as it were, aid and support the spiritistic phenomena in so far as these latter were genuine and not faked.

Thus you see, the two quotations are not contradictions, but together form a paradox, and are easily explained in the above manner.

To summarize: Spiritism itself in the light of true knowledge is a "fatal superstition"; but yet the spiritistic phenomena when genuine and not faked are true, and taught and even yet do teach the materialists that man has forces in him and faculties and attributes which the materialists cannot explain by referring everything to man's physical vehicle. Hence these genuine phenomena were supported and even aided at the time, although now no longer aided, by the Nirmânakâyas.

EUTHANASIA

What light do the Theosophical teachings throw on the question of Euthanasia?

Euthanasia, a Greek word meaning 'easy death.' I take it, from trying to probe into the thought of the unknown querent, that he or she is referring to modern propositions painlessly to kill certain ones of the human race whom certain others judge to be quite ready to pass out?

Do you need to ask me a question like that? Do you honestly think that any human being is wise enough, profound enough in insight, to see beyond and within and above the tortured body? Why, the majority of the proponents of this system of doing away with the suffering of loved ones do not even recognise that there is anything beyond the tortured body. Their hearts are wrung and in turn tortured with the suffering they see.

It is often compassion that gains adherents for this theory. But I am not one of them. Modern medical science is amply able to still the pains. As long as there is life, that unfortunately afflicted, karmically unfortunately afflicted, soul is learning. How could we stop the abuses that almost invariably would arise should the practice of Euthanasia become legalized in any civilized country? Think of the doors it opens to criminal practices of many kinds under the hypocritical guise of compassionate action! Euthanasia is far too dangerous. Think about it. No safeguard sufficiently strong could be thrown around the beds of our helpless and trusting loved ones, should such a proposition become a law. I am against it ethically, spiritually, because of the compassion in my heart. I would never dare to take the life of a fellow human being, even under the guise of pity!

Do We Evolve in Eternity

One of the basic ideas underlying the Theosophical Teachings is that we are eternally evolving in Eternity. Now this does not seem to be a logical statement. Surely Eternity implies a static conception of everything in it. One can evolve in time only — one cannot evolve in Eternity as Eternity implies an absence of time, and if there is no time, what can the individual evolve in? Is it logical to assume that we are evolving from infinity to infinity in Eternity? It seems to me that if an entity is a dynamical evolving thing, then it must have a static background to evolve against. On the other hand, if it is a static thing, it must have a dynamic background to be static against. Surely the very word evolution means growth IN TIME. Then if that growth is in Time, it cannot be in Eternity. Then if it is not in Eternity, it must have had a beginning and it must be working to an end?

A thoughtful man and a deep question. He is right in his remarks about evolution being a finite process, which nevertheless takes place within the bosom of endless Duration, or what Westerners call Eternity; and there does seem a logical quirk here, but it is a seeming one and not a real one, for the following general reasons: All evolution takes place in periodic, repetitive world-periods, called manvantaras, separated, each one from its successor, by equally long world-periods of rest, called pralayas. Now, these periods of manvantara and pralaya succeed each other in serial order throughout eternity, that is throughout endless Duration, for it is impossible to imagine a beginning of them, or impossible to imagine that they ever can cease. If we can so imagine, then we should ask ourselves: How is it that they are now?   Eternity is not an actor.   It cannot produce things, for eternity can produce only eternals; and no such manvantara or pralaya, however vast its time-period, is anything more than a wink of the eye in endless Duration.

Now, this line of reasoning shows us that precisely because these periodic intervals exist, and we cannot ever show that they at any time did not exist, nor can we at any time show that in the future they shall ever cease to exist, we are logically driven to infer that they must have been continuing thus throughout eternity.   But the evolving *beings,* what we call the monads, are each one of them rooted in eternity so to speak; i.e., the very essence, the highest, loftiest, divinest essence or substance of each such monad, is eternity, infinity, itself.   Thus it is only the outward aspects, the garments or veils or what the Hindû mystic calls the 'dreaming' of Brahman, which evolve in the serially succeeding manvantaras and pralayas. Thus it is that the *process* of evolution is finite, because it deals with finite and evolving beings and things.   Yet the heart or essence or inmost of the inmost of these beings is utter divinity, is eternity, is infinity; and the Hindûs express this beautiful phrase, and so do we Theosophists, by the Sanskrit words: Tat twam asi — THAT thou art!

THEOSOPHISTS' ATTITUDE TOWARDS MILITARY FORCE

What is the general attitude of Theosophists towards an armed force, military or naval?

Emphatically, as the Theosophist's first thought, being a lover of his fellow-men, he is opposed to war, and violence of any kind, with all his heart.   But we are sane people, and I do not think any sane individual today would go so far as to say that the armed forces of the United States are out for ruthless violence or for slaughter.   To me they are like a national police; and they do a policeman's work in the world, something very fine indeed; and the ideal armed forces of any country stand for the same thing. If we did not have police patrolling our streets, see what would happen to us, to our lives, to those we love, and to our property!

Now if force is misused, that we condemn emphatically; but we do not condemn — as sane, honest, earnest people who love our fellows — the proper application of strength where strength only will bring about peace and order, and when used honestly for the protection of the weak and helpless.   The armed forces of a country certainly can be misused and abused, and that is a crime; and it has happened again and again and again in the history of the world.   But we must not condemn the armed forces of our country, of any country, which in theory, and usually in practice, stand for the preservation of order, the upholding of right and law, and the assuring of honest and peaceable men and women that their daily pursuits are safeguarded and protected.

Militarism is one thing; that is the abuse. The preservation of law and order by even armed strength if need be is not abuse. A lunatic hastening to set fire to a building, or to do some foul crime — should he be allowed to do it merely because he is human and because we love our fellow-men? What sane man would say that? He must be prevented even by strength and controlled force if it has to be called forth. But that is not ruthless use of strength; it is decent use of strength.

A Theosophist stands for love, brotherly love; but love is sometimes strong, it is never weak and feeble. It upholds right, protects the weak, insists upon justice, will even raise its strong arm to bring these about if there be no other way. In the latter case, pitiful perhaps — but we have to face facts.

Some day the human race will outgrow the need of armed police forces for its protection, will outgrow the need of surgery, will outgrow the need of remedies for human disease and other ills. But as long as we human beings, with our millions in the prisons showing conditions as now they are, cannot control ourselves, wreaking violence upon others if we have the chance, or perhaps because we are at times too weak to hold ourselves in against temptation and evil-doing, society has to be protected, and it is proper. We grieve over it, but we are sane people and recognise facts as they are.

REAL MEANING OF PANTHEISM

Are Theosophists Pantheists?

No, and yet, in a deeper sense, yes. We do not accept Pantheism as it is taught in the West, taught, I mean, not as something to be believed in, but mistaught and misrepresented as something philosophically wrong coming down to us from the ancients — all which supposition is false and arbitrary. The West's ideas of Pantheism were born in the West, and it is just these last ideas that we repudiate. The Occident says that Pantheism means that every stock and stone, every plant and flower, every sun or bit of physical material, is "God." That is the Pantheism as misunderstood in the West. We do not accept it. It is not the Pantheism of the archaic Orient nor of the archaic ages in any part of the world. The Occidental we must call material Pantheism.

The other, true spiritual Pantheism, we do accept in common with the universal consensus of mankind: that whatever is high or low is of divine origin and returns ultimately to divinity, that all springs forth from utterly incomprehensible, nameless MYSTERY, inconceivable by man, and therefore inexpressible in human language. Yet of IT, man has inextinguishable intuitions, for out of it he comes, in it he lives for ay, unto it he returns, and it is his own inmost — the source of All, beyond even the All, and encompassing the All! and hence the ancient Vedic Sages simply called it THAT.

Now, as THAT is utterly boundless everywhere, limitless, frontierless, both in space and in duration, and it is the source of all intelligence and love, of all power and form, of everything, they call this doctrine Pan-theism, all-divine, all from the divinity. So that the true Pantheism does not say that every stock and stone, or flower or bit of wood, every globe and comet or sun and beast and tree, or reptile and insect, is "God"; but that the divine, the utterly divine, the super-divine, Para-parabrahman, THAT, is the utterly incomprehensible Source and encompassing Life of All. From it all comes; even the globe and the sun and the star come forth in hierarchies containing other hierarchies, themselves contained by others vaster still. Hence all is divine *in essence,* though naturally not in form; so that the stone or the globe or the beast or the wood or the flower or the sun or the planet, or what not, is not God, but is a tiny particle, so to speak, in the veil or garment of the Incomprehensible. Just as when I lay my hand upon a man I touch not the man. I touch but a portion of his physical expression. The real man is invisible, within-above, and his highest is incomprehensible, sublime. That is the Pantheism of which the West has no cognisance; so that when you read of Pantheism in western books, you must not misunderstand them to mean true Pantheism, but what they misconstrue true Pantheism to be.

JESUS AND BUDDHA

In your Society, whom do you consider the greater Master, Jesus Christ or Gautama-Buddha?

Our Society has a platform which is broad and free, and grants liberty of conscience to all its Sections, which are practically autonomous under our Constitution. Hence it is a matter of very small importance whether one Theosophist thinks that Jesus Christ is the greatest Master, and whether some other Theosophist thinks that Gautama-Buddha, or some other Teacher of men, is the greatest Master. To me, such a question is of minor interest, because the thing of great importance is the sublime Message of Theosophy which it is our duty, as genuine Theosophists, to give to the world, and it is not at all our private opinions or feelings about the Great Ones which should govern our official viewpoint or conduct.

To us, Jesus, the Avatâra, of Palestine, was one of the great Theosophical Masters, as was also, of course, Gautama the Buddha, and as were others of the spiritual and intellectual Titans of history; and personally it is a matter of small importance to me which one of the world's Great Teachers different men may think to be the greatest. To me the most important thing of all is to bring to suffering mankind and to our dark world the life-giving, light-giving, healing spirit of Theosophy, the sublime Wisdom of the gods.

Ever-Moving Infinite Life

The First Fundamental Proposition, so The Secret Doctrine *tells us, is that there is "An Omnipresent, Eternal, Boundless, and* Immutable Principle*." In the same connexion we read that "This Infinite and Eternal Cause . . . is the rootless root of 'all that was, is, or ever shall be.' " If this "immutable principle," itself rootless, is the root of all that is, i.e., the root of the mutable and ceaselessly changing existences on all planes of manifestation, then it would seem that it must bear within its bosom the seeds of mutability, and therefore not be "immutable." Please unravel this, to me, seeming paradox.*

It is a question which has been a perennial puzzle of Occidental philosophy and religion, and, indeed, needlessly so.

In the first place, when H. P. B. wrote *The Secret Doctrine,* she had to use words. She had to use words which would be understood. The consequence was that, using understandable words for untrained minds, she clothed Infinitude with a label, with labels. But Infinitude is without qualities, without attributes, without definable terms, of any kind that the most spiritual human imagination can place there, and nobody knew this better than H. P. B. herself. Any such attempt to define is a limitation. Defining means drawing a boundary. That is impossible with Infinity. The word itself means Boundless. Nevertheless, she had to use words to give an adumbration of her thought, for her thought was to teach Christians and Christianly-reared Theosophists that the Boundless is no Creator, is not a Demiurge, is not a motive Cause, does not move, whether in parts or in wholes, to produce creations. So she said 'immutable.' Yet, this Immutable is simply the ever-moving infinite Life, always in movement: Life itself, infinite, boundless, beginningless, endless, without terms, which cannot be defined within limits or compass of any human adjective or human noun. We can simply say that it is the infinite Life for ever, from eternity unto eternity, in unceasing movement; and this Motion is itself. I hope this gives some light on the matter.

This Life is to our human understanding composed of incomputable hierarchies of droplets of Spirit so to speak, as the vast ocean is composed of droplets of water, one and yet many — always one, never moving as a complete ocean, but eternally in motion throughout all its parts, in motions, and in movements. While one part is calm, another part moves. The part that was calm begins to move, but the part which was in movement ceases its motions and becomes calm. These are the universes which appear and again disappear into its boundless bosom: Itself, fruits of its bosom; self, selves, of Itself; and thus throughout eternity on all planes.

Occidentals cannot understand that Infinity to our conception, to our understanding, does not, cannot, ever move infinitely as an infinite unit or One, for this would make it no longer infinity, but a One. Infinity is expressed by the zero-symbol containing all Ones. In other words, it is not an infinite creator. If it were, it would produce an infinite creation. H. P. B. was trying to show that the Parabrahman of the occult philosophy is no creative god, active, moving, mutable. Christian theology is filled with contradictions because Christian theology has attempted to define, and therefore to delimit, to encompass, the limitless, that which is frontierless, "without body, parts and passions" as they say — and yet a Creator! Contradictory.

Take anything in the infinite womb of the cosmic Life: you, me, a sun, a planet, on whatever plane, superdivine, divine, spiritual, intellectual, astral, physical, or beneath the physical. Any entity anywhere, any monad anywhere, which is an offspring, a child, of the cosmic Life for ever within it, cannot ever move out of it, is always there from eternity unto eternity; and yet that monad is unceasingly in movement because its heart of the heart, the core of the core of the heart of the heart of the core of the core of it, is Infinitude.

Thus it is that the universes appear and disappear like the "sparks of eternity." In their exterior forms of manifestation, they are mâyâvi, illusions; but the heart of each, the essence of each, is the Cosmic Life in all its unending realms and reaches. And therefore the heart of each is Infinitude: the heart of me, the heart of you, the core of me, the core of you, is the root of me, the root of you, reaching endlessly into the infinite Cosmic Life.

Now that infinite Cosmic Life never moves *as an individual* to produce; yet as an infinitude of monads, as the ocean is an infinitude of droplets of water — its very essence is production. Electricity, for instance, to take a very homely simile or analogy, is universal, is cosmic. Considered as an endless essence it is immutable, but in infinite parts or portions of itself is in unceasing activity. Life is infinite, and yet the infinite Life is builded up, so to say, at least we humans so understand it, of infinite lives, each such life a monad, the heart of which being the whole cosmic life, but being as a monad a droplet therein. Thus the Cosmic Life is immutable because *it is no individual;* it does not act or move or function *as an individual,* which means a monad. It is the encompassing life of all monads, their mother, eternity, Boundless, out of which all comes, back into which all sinks when its course is run, to reappear again for another manvantaric rise to greater heights of glory, then sinking again to its rest; as we men die, only to be reborn.

Thus there is no contradiction; but the two statements complement each other, explain each other. The "Immutability" spoken of is such only to our very limited human understanding, much as the ephemeral life and tiny mind of a gnat would look upon the moving of the sun in heaven as no moving at all, but as being immutability and motionless. So we men, being unable to encompass within the ranges of our feeble understanding or even of our intuition the first and last and greatest function of Infinitude, which is infinite MOTION itself, speak of it as being "immutability." On the other hand, to call it "mutable" would be equally false, because "mutable" is a merely human adjective descriptive of certain human and other natural phases of manifested life.

Lao-Tse Legend

Lao-Tse is given 81 years for intra-uterine growth in one article in your magazine and 72 in another: Which is the more correct, and what is the occult significance of these legends? 9 × 9 = 81. 9 × 8 = 72. His last avatâric appearance is stated to have been his ninth.

Seventy-two and eighty-one are both very mystical numbers in ancient reckonings. Thus 72 is 6 × 6 × 2, otherwise 6 × 12. Or again, it may be looked upon as 60 + 12, which is 5 × 12 plus the basic 12 again. And 5 × 72 comes to 360, which is 3 × 10 × 12. Many other similar figures could be got, all of them having an astronomical and occult basis. Thus again with 81; it is 3 × 3 × 3 × 3, or 3 to the 4th power; or again, it is 9 × 9 — nine universally being considered the number of change, and 9 itself is 6 + 3 or 6 + 6/2. Or again, 81 is 3 × 27, one of the lunar numbers; and 81 is 72 + 9, 72 itself being 8 × 9. We thus see a constant recurrence and involving of the famous old root-numbers, 1, 2, 3, 4, 5, 6, 9, 10, 12, and their multiples. What does the Hebrew Bible say of a man's being three score years and 10, equaling 70, a round way of speaking of 72? The heart-beats of the average human being, whether standing or lying, change from about 60 a minute to 72.

Answering the above question: call it 72 if you like. The above-mentioned long period of intra-uterine growth was the archaic, mystic way of saying the number of years he was carried in the womb of his mystic Mother: Trial, Experience, learning as a chela, before he was finally "born again," or what the Indians call a *dwija*, "twice born." That is all it means. It does not mean as a physical embryo that his mother carried him for 72 years. That is ridiculous, and is an excellent example of how the Ancients cloaked esoteric facts in ordinary day-to-day events, often exaggerating these events so tremendously as almost to shout from the house-tops that they were but cloaks, metaphors, allegories. On this exact line of argument, the ancient stories about Virgin-births, Saviors born of Virgins, have the identic explanation. The Saviors are the great adepts born of the divine Sophia or Wisdom, or of the Spirit as it is sometimes called.

THE ANCIENT PÂLI LANGUAGE

What can you tell me of the Pâli language?

Pâli really is a Prâkrit-language of ancient India, and was undoubtedly the cultured form of that language spoken over a probably large part of India at the time when the Buddha lived. Pâli itself had its less cultured forms which were spoken by the masses, the uneducated, just as we have the same thing in certain European countries today, or in Japan, or in China. There is the language of the literary classes, and the popular slangy language of the masses. Connected with Pâli linguistically, was Sanskrit, which was really the sacred language of the Brâhmanas and held more or less private or secret by them. The Sanskrit even in those ancient times was the vehicle for the archaic Wisdom-teachings of the Aryan peoples of India, such as the Vedas, and the Purânas, and the Upanishads, and the great Epics, the *Râmâyana* and the *Mahâbhârata*. But Pâli was one of several other languages of culture in ancient India, all which were of so-called Prâkrit character, although very little is known about these other literary languages. Pâli has survived to the present time because for some curious reason it became the linguistic vehicle in which were enshrined the teachings of Buddhism, i.e., of Southern Buddhism, much as Latin has survived because enshrining the teachings of early medieval Christianity. Just as there were in ancient Italy many other Italic tongues, each one having its literary or cultured form, and likewise its popular idiom, so it was in ancient India.

Pâli is not a 'washed-out Sanskrit.' Sanskrit was rather a mystery-language which was 'composed' or 'builded up' to perfection by initiates of the Sanctuaries; and because it was thus constructed into an almost perfect expression of human thought, at least for that day, it was called *saṃskṛita* (संस्कृत), which means 'composed,' 'constructed.' Thus Pâli is not a true child of Sanskrit, but is and was the literary form of one of the ancient languages of India popularly spoken over an apparently wide stretch of the Indian Peninsula, and which has survived for the reasons above stated.

Buddhism, Brâhmanism and the Adwaita-Vedânta

Why after the death of the Buddha did Buddhism very largely leave India and take root and thrive in neighboring countries? Could Śankarâchârya be called a Buddhist?

As regards Buddhism: this noble religious philosophy had wide vogue and spread over almost the whole of India, and it was in its heyday in the times of Chandragupta and Aśoka, two great Buddhist monarchs who were mainly instrumental also in encouraging Buddhist missionaries and supporting them, i.e., those who carried Buddhism into Northern Asia and into the lands to the east and south of India. This was during the heyday of Buddhism in India. Brâhmanism of course, with various other Indian systems, survived through those hundreds of years of Buddhist glory in India mainly because Buddhism is essentially tolerant and mild. But little by little, after the passing of the Buddhist heyday in India, Brâhmanism again got the upper hand, and this for various reasons, one reason being a partial decay of the original Buddhist spirit of enthusiasm in the Buddhists themselves; partly also because Brâhmanism is a form of high religious and philosophical thinking which is native and therefore sympathetic to Indian thought; and partly because, as H. P. B. and myself have pointed out, Buddhism originally was really a sort of Brâhmanism of the Sanctuaries which the Buddha communicated to everyone who could and would take it, and thus, being extremely recondite in its deeper aspects, made less appeal to the masses on the whole than did the cultus and ceremonials, the pageantry and forms, and the mythological literature, of Brâhmanism. Thus, little by little Buddhism faded out from India, but increased *pari passu* in China, in Tibet, and in all the countries to the north of India, as well as in Siam and Burma and Ceylon and Java, the countries south and east of India, thus in time forming the two great Buddhist philosophical and geographical divisions which exist in the present day.

The Buddhism of the North was, from its first inception, highly mystical, philosophic, and typically esoteric in type. The Buddhism of the South was, from its beginning, highly philosophical but less mystical in presentation and far more pragmatical in spirit than the Buddhism of the North. Now, the real teaching of the Buddha in most of its branches can

be gained, at least exoterically, by welding together both the Mahâyâna
of the North and the Hînayâna of the South.

It is natural that European Orientalists, like the late Professor Rhys
Davids, should ascribe reasons for the downfall of Buddhism in India which
seem to these European Orientalists as being sensible and probable causes;
and they are not to be harshly criticized for this supposition, because they
have no other means of judging why Buddhism finally failed in India. But
the real truth was that Buddhism, coming from the inner Sanctuaries of
Brâhmanism itself, and being as it were an esoteric side of Brâhmanism in
those days, swept the land like a spiritual fire as long as the Buddha and
his arhats and his immediate disciples were there to guide it; but the later
Indian Buddhists lost this spiritual fervor of enthusiasm and clarity of insight and gradually sank back into Brâhmanism in its various forms.
There, then, is the whole thing in a nutshell.

Finally, there is a very important although typically occult and esoteric reason for the passing of original Buddhism out of the Indian Peninsula, and it lay in a situation which is extremely difficult adequately to
describe, and yet was the main contributing cause of the Buddhist decline
there. The facts are as follows: In his immense love and pity for mankind, and in his desire to bring certain fundamental secret teachings of the
Sanctuaries to the attention of the multitudes for their spiritual succor and
intellectual and moral health, Gautama the Lord Buddha made on the
whole in so doing an almost perfect presentation of the philosophic and
ethical side of the Ancient Wisdom-Religion; but, shortly before his Nirvâna, he realized that there had been an insufficiently adequate elaboration
of the mystical and religious aspects or portions of the Wisdom-teachings,
except in so far as the Buddha's immediate circle and his arhats were concerned. In order, therefore, to correct this insufficiency, Gautama the
Buddha some fifty or more years after his passing, brought about the birth
and being of the Avatâra, the great Śankarâchârya, the Buddha himself
supplying the psychological apparatus of this great Hindû Teacher of the
Adwaita-Vedânta. Thus it was that, although born in the South of India,
and some fifty or more years later than the passing of the Buddha, Śankarâchârya was, so to speak, a 'reappearance' as Śankarâchârya, of the human part of Buddha Gautama. The Theosophical reader will understand
at once what is here meant when he recollects the Theosophical teaching
of the doctrine of the Avatâras. As Śankarâchârya grew to manhood and
began to do his work, his teaching, which almost from his own day and up
to the present time has been called the Adwaita-Vedânta, or non-dualistic
Vedânta, spread like wild-fire over the Indian Peninsula; and this really
great Teacher drew into the circle of his Doctrine the larger part of the

most intuitive and philosophical minds in India of all ages since his day, so that even in our own times, the Adwaita-Vedânta is perhaps the most popular and most widely accepted form of philosophic and mystical Brâhmanism known.

Indeed, so closely akin and so similar in philosophical and mystical teaching and outlook are the Adwaita-Vedânta of Sankarâchârya with the Mahâyâna-doctrines of Northern Buddhism, that the bigoted critics of both describe the Adwaita-Vedânta as a "masked or disguised Buddhism," and similarly describe the Northern mystical Buddhism as a "masked or disguised Adwaita-Vedânta." The criticism is absolutely true in fact, because the Adwaita-Vedânta and the esoteric Buddhism of Gautama were virtually identic. Thus it was that the Avatâra Sankarâchârya, the 're-appearance,' as above said, of the 'human part' of the Buddha-Gautama, was perhaps more instrumental than any other single cause in bringing about the fading out of the philosophical and ethical Buddhism of the beginnings — a strange paradox which gives us food for deep thought.

It is also true that the mystical Mahâyâna-Buddhism of the North was on the whole a truer presentation of the complete doctrines of the Buddha as he taught them to his arhats than was the more formally philosophical presentation of original Buddhism as we find it even yet imbodied in the doctrines of the Southern School, called the Hînayâna.

Hence, if the student will combine the Adwaita-Vedânta of Sankarâchârya with the magnificent mystical and occult philosophy and sublime ethic of early Buddhism, the latter now mostly imbodied in the Mahâyâna, he will have not only the original Doctrine of the Buddha-Gautama as the latter taught it to his arhats and his immediate pupils, but will likewise see the identity of such unification of the two with the archaic Esoteric and Occult Wisdom of the ages, today called Theosophy.

STATUS OF MAHOMET

I have been greatly interested in your statements about Mahomet, but cannot quite reconcile them with a passage occurring in THE OCEAN OF THEOSOPHY. *W. Q. Judge speaks of Mahomet as a lesser Avatâra. The passage I am referring to is to be found in chapter xiv, German edition, page 164, line 16. Retranslated into English it reads: "Mahomet was a lesser Avatâra for the special part of a race, and belonged to the civil, military and religious class."*

What W. Q. Judge says of Muhhammed as a 'minor Avatâra' is quite correct, but a strong emphasis should be laid upon the word 'minor,' the truth being that Muhhammed can be called an Avatâra, but only by a great extension of the meaning of the word 'Avatâra.' Muhhammed did a certain racial work under the influence of a Ray from the Planetary Spirit, but was not conscious of his mission in this sense of the word, and was, in fact, but very little higher than any other noteworthy man who is made an instrument of karmic activity. In this sense only was Muhhammed a minor Avatâra, and he did indeed, as Judge says, belong to the 'civil, military, and religious' type.

EVIL, THE CONFLICT OF WILLS

What is your opinion as to the origin of evil? There is no doubt that we are part and parcel of the Universe; but when we come to think that the scheme of creation is based on universal slaughter, and pain and anguish, I as a man who believes that our lives should be a peaceful transition from youth to old age, and that our life should be a period of enjoyment and happiness — I just cannot understand it. This terrible intelligence, this wonderful power, this horrible force, that governs the Universe, whatever it may be — to me it is diabolic. It fashions the tiger, it gives the unfortunate animals no opportunity to get away from the danger that surrounds them. What gives the poison to the snake, the fangs to the tiger, the idea that men should fight each other and slay each other, if it is not that we are nothing but a conflicting hierarchy of conflicting ideals, destined some day to rise out from this cosmic turmoil, and to enjoy celestial bliss?

What you have pointed out is of course something that occurs to every student of life and of the things around us. I remember that when I was a boy, this very question was the first one of a serious character that occurred to me, and it was only when my eyes were opened that I learned that happiness without contrast cannot exist; that there is no peace which has not been earned. How many times have I not as a child, as a young man, said to myself: They talk about Almighty God, a merciful Father, and yet the Universe is filled with strife and pain! Evil sometimes prevails over good, at least temporarily; what a monster God must be, the Maker of it all, to have made things thus!

Your thoughts are very natural indeed and have my deepest sympathy; but we must accept things as they are, and the explanation of the problem is this: that no 'God' is the maker or creator of the iniquities of which you speak. Beside the poison is its antidote; beside disorder is order; dishonor proves honor; darkness could not exist except for light. We cannot at once change our portion of the material universe with all its evil phases; but these are only events in the marching army of beings passing forwards and upwards through space-time. It is out of suffering that we learn; and thank the immortal gods that the universe is so constituted that we can learn. Fancy a universe so constituted that there was nothing in it but peace and happiness, and dull, inactive sloth lasting unto eternity! It would be a hell. There is something within me which yearns to bring light to those who have it not; there is something within me which yearns to give the compassionate hand; there is something within me which is more precious than my own being, which makes me yearn to help my fellows. Fancy what it would be if I were deprived of this exquisite joy of doing my bit to raise the world's burden.

We cannot make the Universe different from what it is, and it is what it is because of karman — the intricate and intertwined karman of uncounted multitudes of beings learning through growth and suffering and pain to take part in the Cosmic Labor guided by Compassion, infinite Sympathy, and Love for all that is, to join the hosts of the bright gods. The horrors that the questioner speaks of most certainly exist; but ineffable beauties exist also. Why not likewise speak of the beauties in nature? Why not speak of its orderliness, its law, peace, growth, and the expansion of consciousness that all beings undergo throughout the cycling periods of time? Why not speak of the beauty of natural being as well as of its horrors? Disease exists indeed, but so does health. Crime exists, but so do men who are no criminals. Horrors exist, but so likewise are they counterbalanced by the beauties, and by the symmetrical, shapely, and holy things in life that are an eternal joy.

The Universe is as it is; and these horrors I now will explain, giving you the Theosophic teaching of the origin of evil. Briefly, then, all these things exist in and from evolving creatures, imperfect entities, innumerable multitudes of them, all learning through suffering and sorrow and pain to become orderly, to be loving, to be compassionate, to be peaceful, to be inwardly and outwardly beautiful — in the original sense of the word beauty.

All this reminds me of the old Christian idea of Heaven. I remember what my dear father, who was a clergyman, taught me about Heaven: If I were a very good little boy, when I died I would surely go to Heaven and sit on the right hand of God and sing songs eternally. That course of life did not appeal to me at all. It did not answer anything in my own being; and when I grew older and heard the arguments that were given to men, and likewise the philosophical ideas current among men concerning so-called immortality I rejected the immortality as presented, because this immortality was merely a speculative immortality of the personal man with all his imperfections, manifold and sometimes monstrous; and I could not stand the thought that if that doctrine were true, I was destined to pass eternal aeons without end as an imperfect entity; no matter how much I might change, I was supposed to be always the same egoic being. No, I wanted to grow in a different manner; I wanted to become greater, and to give vent and expression to the locked-up spiritual and intellectual and other powers within me. I discovered that there is no immortality for the personal man, because if there were, then the personal man *must* remain relatively unchanged. If he changed in the remotest way, he was then no longer the same — and the supposed immortality vanishes. Instead of immortality of the personal man, we Theosophists say that there is eternal, endless evolution, endless growth, endless expansion of faculty, of power, always bringing out more and more what is locked up within, passing from the low and evil regions of the Universe up into the higher; and when there, turning and extending a compassionate hand in help to those in the lower darkness. I learned the great and profound truth that even the ego changes, that even the spirit evolves to vaster things, so that the immortality of the ego, or what is called the personal man, was but the vain dream of an obscured imagination.

Evil certainly exists in the world, but it arises out of the fact that the world is filled full with imperfect beings and entities — just as there are likewise innumerable hierarchies of relatively perfected and godlike beings. Because the former are imperfect, they act in consequence in distorted and what we men call evil ways. This produces the disharmony, the preying of entity upon entity, and the consequent suffering and pain. Follow out this profound teaching. As just stated, above these multitudes struggling in the lower realms, there are the great regions of the gods. It is quite possible that they may have their problems too, and personally I think they have; but they are regions which to us human beings are incomparably light, holy, majestic, and our inner spiritual and intellectual natures are native there. From there, come into our minds and our hearts our noblest impulses to do deeds of good; our noblest intellectual aspirations are born in these inner divine and spiritual realms. In fact, our spirit is native there.

CHILDREN'S INVISIBLE COMPANIONS

What is the explanation of the 'invisible companion' which some children speak of constantly as almost part of themselves?

An interesting question, and one which likewise shows how greatly we adults have lost the intuitive recognition of spiritual companionship that children — unless spoiled by over-fond and over-doting parents — still retain.

It would be quite a mistake, I believe, to suppose that these dear little ones are self-consciously aware, as adults might be, of any invisible companion; what they have is a distinct 'feeling,' or inner conscious cognisance, of the spiritual presence of the inner Self, to which 'presence' a child will often give a name, and of which, taking individual children as instances, they are the human radiance.

Only recently, comparatively speaking, out of the devachanic condition in which this spiritual presence was a living reality, although not there and then understood as something separate — for indeed it is not — the Ray reaching incarnation and imbodying itself, in the manner which I have endeavored to describe in my *The Esoteric Tradition* and elsewhere, still retains the intuition of the spiritual presence of the inner Self; and the child's mind, instinctively feeling this presence, but not having the developed brain-mind as yet to argue about it or analyse it, recognises the fact, and talks of what we adults call, or might call, 'an invisible companion,' or by some such similar phrase.

As a matter of fact, highly developed human beings who are likewise esoterically trained, are self-consciously aware of this spiritual companionship, so much so that Adepts and Initiates know the fact in its proper relations, and speak of this inner Self working through them by various terms, such as 'Father-Flame,' 'Father in Heaven,' 'Father-Fire,' etc., etc. In other words, the adept knows and recognises his inner Self as the 'invisible companion,' and puts himself under its steady and unfailing guidance and inspiration. Little children, still fresh from the spiritual realms, likewise, as said above, feel the fact, though not with the self-conscious analysis of the Adept; but they recognise it unconsciously, so to speak, as a 'feeling'; and the unspoiled child will frequently be so impressed with this invisible companionship that it will speak of it to others.

In the case of the Adept-soul, the invisible companion is precisely what was meant by the Avatâra-Jesus when referring to his 'Father in Heaven.'

CYCLES WITHIN CYCLES

What is the manner in which the great Cycles in the evolution of a Root-Race are repeated on a smaller scale in the development of the various sub-divisions of it? Do they not overlap each other to a considerable extent?

You are asking what may seem to you to be a very simple question, but you yourself will see, after a moment's reflexion, that it is an extremely involved one, because your question calls for an entire elucidation or explaining of the intricacies of Nature's cyclical workings, and how the large includes the small. This is a tremendous order! It would take a volume just to answer your one question, which is a question which has occurred to many, and precisely because it is so involved is one reason why it has always been side-stepped from H. P. B.'s time to our own. It would take literally hundreds of pages to give a complete exposition, and days and days of hard work in dictation.

However, there are always general rules, and until the gods give me a year or two of more time, I am afraid you will have to be satisfied. The general rule is — and it is a wonderful key — that the small repeats the great, that little yugas not only are included in the greater yugas, but repeat them on their own little scales. Example: The present Fifth Root-Race, considered as a whole, and including all its minor sub-races, whether great or small, is now in its Kali-Yuga, which began something over five thousand years ago, at the death of Krishna, and will last into the future for about 427,000 years. Keep in mind that this is the Kali-Yuga of the entire Root-Race, the great Kali-Yuga.

Now, then, all the minor cycles or yugas of this Fifth Root-Race will, some of them, be rising, and some of them be falling, and inter-working with each other, and yet will all be subject to the great Kali-Yuga of the Root-Race, which has just begun. Thus, a minor yuga or race may be in its youth, and rising to its flowering, but yet, because it is included in the great descending Kali-Yuga, will, although having a sharp rise, be nevertheless subject to the general decline of the great Kali-Yuga.

Next, every minor cycle, great or small, included in the Root-Race, in its turn is septenary, and therefore has its own little kali-yuga, and its numerical relations are about the same. Just as the great Kali-Yuga is 432 thousand years long, so a little kali-yuga may be perhaps only 432 years long, or possibly 4,320, or possibly even 43,200. The Hindû or Aryan Race which was one of the very first sub-races of our own Fifth Race, is now in its own racial kali-yuga, in addition to belonging to the Fifth Root-Race, and therefore of course belonging to the great Kali-Yuga of the Root-Race. But it is striving to rise into flowering again, and will do so in the future.

In the small scale, Spain is in its short kali-yuga, as also Portugal. Italy has just ended a short kali-yuga and is striving to rise again.

Unfortunately, our Fifth Root-Race being a very materialistic one, i.e., being heavily sunken in matter due to our Fourth Round, these rises are mostly along the lines of materialisms. Furthermore, our own European general stock of Races, which we may call the European sub-race or family-race perhaps, has been steadily rising since the downfall of the Roman Empire, and will continue to rise, with various smaller shocks and falls and risings again, for some six or seven or possibly eight thousand years more. And then there will be a rapid descent until their kali-yuga is reached, a small kali-yuga, when there will be a great European catastrophe of Nature.

This will be some sixteen or eighteen thousand years from now, possibly fifteen or possibly seventeen thousand years. I have never had time to get any really exact figures. But you can say 'about' 16,000 years hence. This period will see the submersion of the British Isles. Most of France will be under the water, also Holland, some of Spain, a good deal of Italy, and other places. Of course all this won't take place in a night. There will be premonitory signs, such as slow sinkings of the coast, and great earthquakes, etc.

RATIONALE OF PRECIPITATION OF THE MASTERS' LETTERS AND THE HARE BROTHERS' ATTACK ON H. P. B.

I have been reading a book only recently issued, WHO WROTE THE MAHATMA LETTERS? *by the brothers H. E. Hare and W. L. Hare. The general line of criticism adopted by the authors appears to me most unfair, and yet I myself have often been puzzled in regard to the fact that certain of these Letters contain expressions similar to H. P. B.'s own expressions. I know of course from what I have read regarding* THE MAHATMA LETTERS *that some of them were transmitted by H. P. B. Would it be possible for an explanation to be given of this?*

All the various idiosyncrasies of speech and of mannerism, all the various Gallicisms on the other hand, and the various imperfections of punctuation, orthography, grammar, and what not, to which the critical Hares point triumphantly as largely originating in H. P. B.'s mind — all these were well understood since H. P. B.'s days as being due to the mental and psychical idiosyncrasies of the amanuenses or chelas, i.e., disciples, through whom most of the Letters of the Mahâtmans came.

What else could we expect? A ray of sunlight streaming through stained glass will chequer the wall or the floor upon which the ray falls with the colors of the glass through which it passes; nevertheless the original ray is there.

Let the following facts be understood, as they have been for some forty years or more by thoughtful Theosophists: (a) The Masters themselves on only the very rarest of occasions wrote with their own hands any letters whatsoever, and consequently those that they did so write, if indeed any, can probably be counted on the fingers of one hand; consequently these letters are the fewest of all; (b) almost equally rare, but more numerous than those classified under (a) are what have been popularly called "precipitations," or communications which were "dropped" or found in unexpected places by the recipients thereof; and consequently these are relatively very few likewise; and (c) the great majority of all the letters received from the Masters by individuals in those early days came through different amanuenses or transmitting chelas (disciples), among the number of whom we know perfectly well are to be counted H. P. B. herself, Damodar, Bavaji, Bhavani-Rao in one or two cases, and one or two others, probably not excepting the well known and erudite Hindû Theosophist and scholar Subba-Rao.

Now, the important point to be noticed in this connexion is that all these transmissions of intelligence, in other words all these different letters or communications, including the various notes, chits, etc., etc., passed through the medium of the transmitting minds of the chelas who received them and passed them on to their different destinations, and often by the very prosaic and ordinary means of the postal system.

The Messrs. Hare are extraordinarily behind the times in not being aware of the fact that the many experiments of what it is now popular to call telepathy or thought-transference or mind-reading, conducted by earnest men of unquestionable ability and reputation, have established the fact that such telepathic transmission of intelligence is not only possible but actually of more frequent occurrence than most human beings realize; but in the early days of the Theosophical Society, in the heyday of the materialism of Haeckel and Huxley and Tyndall and Moleschott, and all the other bigwigs of the time, even so common a fact as telaesthesia, or telepathy, or thought-transference or mind-reading, was not only not accepted, but even ridiculed — and this against the common testimony and common experience of mankind for ages; for it is one of the most ordinary facts of human life to experience the wordless or unspoken transmission of human thought.

Now then, such transmission of intelligence from Master to pupil or chela, is more or less precisely what today is called thought-transference or telepathy or mind-reading, if you wish, only in vastly more perfect form because the transmitter is a mahâtmic intelligence, and the receiving mind of the chela is a highly trained one; and, indeed, telepathy or thought-transference, etc., are merely minor instances of the general rule. The experiments conducted during the last forty or fifty years in mind-reading or thought-transference have shown clearly that it is *ideas* which are transmitted and received, but which are almost always distorted or twisted by the untrained mind of the receiver or recipient, and almost invariably more or less colored by the mind or psychological apparatus of the recipient; so that while the essential idea is often received, it is frequently distorted or deformed.

Precisely the same thing, but with less degree of distortion or deformation, must by the nature of the case take place when the transmitting chela receives the essential ideas more or less clearly, and occasionally and sometimes even often in the very language of the transmitter's mind and thought; but coming through the psychological apparatus of the chela, the original ideas are more or less subject to be given forth with marks or with the mental clothing of the chela himself. Thus it would actually have been amazing if there had not been Gallicisms in H. P. B.'s transmission of the essential original idea which was received clearly; but coming through H. P. B.'s mind, with her excellent knowledge of French and her acquaintance with Americanisms, it was almost certain that the message would be transmitted more or less, now and then, here and there, with a French turn of phrase, or with an American spelling to which H. P. B.'s mind had been accustomed.

Similarly so with messages received through and passed on by other chelas — each one gave his own particular "atmosphere" or included more or less of his or her own mental characteristics to the message as handed on; yet the original idea, the essential thought, the fundamental language and intelligent conception, were always there, and this fact accounts for the grandeur and profundity found in such transmitted messages.

This leads us directly to the second of our points, which the critical Hares utterly ignore. This second point is the matter of the characteristic individuality in literary form or matter commonly called literary style. It is extraordinary that not a word in direct or specific allusion is made by the two authors of this book to the immense differences in the *literary styles* of M. on the one hand, and K. H. on the other hand, and neither of these two in literary style or in literary quality is at all comparable with H. P. B.'s own style when she wrote directly from her own mind. The stamp of literary style alone is so well recognised by every competent scholar and student as to be one of the very best means of judging the authenticity of documents, that the omission by the Hare brothers of any allusion to these immense differences in style, constitutes a defect of the gravest character in their attempted criticism. The style of M. for instance, is outstanding for its directness, its abrupt masculinity, its pungency in aphorism, etc.; whereas the style of K. H., though equally profound in thought with M.'s, is markedly different: flowing in character, smooth and easy in narrative, often semi-humorous in relation, and what has been neatly called "gentle" as compared with what has likewise been called the "rough" style of Master M.

H. P. B. when writing alone never wrote anything which in profundity could compare with the literary material of the two Masters, nor with its strength, however fine and really wonderful her own writings were; and her style is enormously different from theirs, although possessing undoubted charm and attractiveness of its own. One has but to compare the literary style and atmosphere of the two volumes, (a) *The Mahatma Letters to A. P. Sinnett*, with (b) *The Letters of H. P. Blavatsky to A. P. Sinnett*, to see how forcefully telling this argument of literary style and atmosphere is.

I turn with a final word again to the matter of the messages received from the Masters through their chelas. As stated above, I have called this relatively perfect telepathy or thought-transference or mind-reading — call it by what name you will. It is most important to keep this in mind, because if it be kept in mind, then if the critic be likewise honest, he will see the absurdity as well as the futility of hammering, as upon something new, upon what has been known to Theosophists for the last forty or fifty years, and what has been at the same time proved to be a fact by the independent researches of scientific and other men — thought-transference — which produced the Mahâtma Letters as written documents. The trained mind and will of the Master directed his thought, consisting of clear-cut, sharply defined ideas, to the mind and into it of the receiving but trained amanuensis, who received the *ideas* more or less clearly in accordance with his training or development, and transmitted those ideas as faithfully as he or she was able to; but passing through the amanuensis' mind, the transmitted intelligence was bound to be colored by the mental characteristics of the mediator — the disciple's mind — through which it passed. Hence the presence of Gallicisms when H. P. B. was the transmitting chela, and of an occasional Americanism; and similarly so, *mutatis mutandis,* when chelas other than H. P. B. were the transmitting mediators.

OBSCURITY OF TEACHERS' LIVES

Why is it so difficult for us to get authentic records of the lives of the great Teachers and Philosophers of the world? There always seems to be so much obscurity and uncertainty about them.

Let me ask whether the very obscurity that surrounds the life and work of these men such as Cagliostro, Apollonius of Tyana, Saint-Germain, and Jesus, of whom no authentic records whatsoever exist, does not itself prove, in view of the tremendous interest, fascination, that their lives have aroused, that they were men beyond the ordinary? They come, no one knows whence. They live and do their work, no one knows how. They succeed, and they disappear from among men, and no one knows when or where they die. The same can be said of all four men I have mentioned.

What, after all, is of value in the lives of such great men? The place of their birth or the place of their passing? The record of their lives such as we have it? What makes the story of Jesus so dear to the human heart?

It is not the fact that he is supposed to have been born and to have lived in one place, and supposed to have died elsewhere. It is not even the so-called historic record of his life as we have it — in a most unhistoric way! embroidered with legend — but what he taught, what he did, the life of the man as it appears, as it has made its appeal to human hearts.

Personally I think that there is something intentional in all this. You know, among the early Christians there was a sect who were called by their opponents the Docetists, in other words 'believers in appearances,' who taught that it really was not the authentic Jesus who died on the Cross as one crucified, but an appearance. 'Heretics' the orthodox called them. Yet I wonder!

Of course it would be perfectly lovely to know all about Saint-Germain and Cagliostro and Jesus and Apollonius of Tyana, but the trouble is that the records are not there. That is the point. I do not mean to say that it is wrong to want to know these personal things, but they do not exist on record; they have been hid or withdrawn. Consequently they cannot be found; and any history purporting to be a record of their lives in my judgment is largely fabrication.

INACTION IN DEEDS OF MERCY

To what extent should help and healing be rendered another suffering soul without interfering with the necessary experience of that soul? — the one who receives help?

It seems to me that your question takes it for granted that it is wrong to come to the aid of one who needs help because he is undergoing a karmic experience which he has brought upon himself, and therefore is learning a lesson that is needed! Now that idea of inaction in deeds of mercy is a false idea. In following a line of thought like that we become hard-hearted. We say, or we would say: "What does it matter to me? He is simply learning the experiences that he has brought upon himself. Let him learn them, and the sooner he has learned the lesson the better for him." Ah! but that is not the real teaching. The teaching is love and compassion, that it is our bounden duty to help each other, and that you cannot grow or evolve yourself without exercising the powers of love and compassion and wisdom that you have innate within you. Hatred gives them no exercise. Indifference gives them no exercise.

We never *interfere* with the karman of another when we help him. Never! We are simply making good karman for ourselves; and furthermore when we help a man it is obviously his karman to be helped by us. Actions in deeds of mercy do not change Nature's majestic forces of readjustment, because these forces are fundamentally based on harmony and sympathy, which are the very elements of what manifests in man as brotherly love. If you help your brother, it is obviously his karman to have you help him. If the opportunity is offered to you, it is your karman and also his karman that the help is proffered and given and received.

Remember that whatever is, is karman. Whatever is, is karmic consequences. It is one of the links in the chain of causation, that brought the timely help and the supporting hand. In either case, the man who refrains from giving help, or the man who rushes to aid, is acting karmically; and the one who refrains, brings upon himself the consequences of his selfish evil-doing; for inaction in a deed of mercy becomes an action in a deadly sin, because mercy is ethical, it is equitable, it is harmonious, it restores equilibrium, it makes for peace. Injustice and cruelty are inharmonious. They make for disharmony. New and bad karman is thereby made. Remember the law: Inaction in a deed of mercy becomes an action in a deadly sin.

Sympathy Through Suffering

To the ordinary man in the street it sometimes seems strange that man should have to go through all the sorrow he has in order to reach perfection, and that it should have to last such a long time. I should like an answer from you so that I may pass it on.

Why is it that sorrow and suffering are in the world, and that they are so enduring? My answer may seem a little hard, but some things in life at first blush do seem a bit hard; yet when understood we find the 'hardness' is merely the strong hand of the law guiding our footsteps. Here is the explanation: All growth is attended with growing pains; a change of condition is a change of state and of consciousness, and human nature in its weaker parts, such as we human beings possess, is so constituted that it rebels at changes; it likes to remain in the old ruts, to run along the familiar lines which humanity has followed for so many ages. But sorrow, pain, suffering, even sickness, are among our best friends.

Now this seems like a hard saying, a dark saying; but how true it is! Consult your own lives. What is it that has put steel into your characters? What is it that has opened your hearts to compassion, rendered perhaps hard and unkind by prosperity and slothful ease? It is the jars and the knocks of misfortune. It is sorrow that teaches us fellow-feeling, sympathy, pity, compassion, that teaches us to help others, so that we now understand their tribulations, so that we now understand after we ourselves have suffered and sorrowed, what they are going through. It is sorrow and pain and suffering that refine us. We are like the ore cast into the molten furnace, into the melting heat; and sorrow and pain purify us so that we come out bright and glittering gold.

Be not afraid of sorrow; be not afraid of trial. They are our best friends; and see what a manly doctrine this is. It is a doctrine of compassion; it is broad-minded, it is human, it is humane, it is sympathetic, it is full of wisdom and quiet peace. The heart which has never been wrung with sorrow has no fellow-feeling for others. The mind which has never been tormented with sorrow and doubt has a veil before it. Sorrow and doubt awaken us, quicken our intellects, open our hearts, and expand our consciousness; and it is sorrow, suffering, sickness, pain, which are among the gentle agents, the merciful ministers, of the evolutionary process. The man whose heart has never been wrung with sorrow cannot understand the sorrows of others. The man who has never sorrowed, knows no greatness. He is great neither in heart nor in mind. Greatness, ethical majesty, spiritual and intellectual power, spring forth from trial.

Index

INDEX

MEMORANDUM

THE following is the list of articles in this present volume not edited by the author, most of them having been transcribed from shorthand notes after his death in September, 1942.

From TRANSACTIONS OF THE HEADQUARTERS LODGE

The Root-Race and its Sub-Divisions
The Life-Period of a Planetary Chain
How the Human Soul Returns to Earth
Remnants of Neolithic and Paleolithic Ages
The Sevenfold Seven Principles
Monkeys, Apes and Early Man
Evolution into the Human Kingdom — III

From STUDIES IN "THE MAHATMA LETTERS"

Devachan and the Seven Principles
What are the Śishtas?
Differences in the Second Round
Last Moments Before and After Death
Light From the East
The Nature of the Buddhic Principle
Tsong-Kha-Pa and Planetary Spirits
Manvantaras, Kalpas, etc.
Hints on the History of the Root-Races
Processes After Death